THE CULTURE OF CITIES

BOOKS BY LEWIS MUMFORD

THE CULTURE
OF CITIES

LEWIS MUMFORD

A HARVEST/HBJ BOOK
HARCOURT BRACE JOVANOVICH
NEW YORK AND LONDON

Copyright 1938 by Harcourt Brace Jovanovich, Inc.
© *1966, 1970 by Lewis Mumford*

Hardbound   ISBN 0-15-123255-5
Paperbound   ISBN 0-15-623301-0

PRINTED IN THE UNITED STATES OF AMERICA

def

As far back as 1915, under the stimulus of Patrick Geddes, I began to collect the materials that have gone into this book. Like my hitherto published papers and books on architecture, community planning, housing, and regional development, the present study rests primarily on first-hand surveys, conducted in many different regions: beginning with a close study of my own city and region—New York and its immediate hinterland. It both attempts to explore in a more unified way a field hitherto worked on divergent lines by specialists, and to establish, for the purpose of communal action, the basic principles upon which our human environment—buildings, neighborhoods, cities, regions—may be renovated. Certain aspects of life, those ordinarily treated under the head of ethics, religion, and education, remain to be dealt with at another time. Even at the risk of an occasional repetition of thought, I have had to parallel in this volume parts of Technics and Civilization; but it should be plain that the two works, while independent, are complementary: each seeks to explore what the modern world may hold for mankind once men of good will have learned to subdue the barbarous mechanisms and the mechanized barbarisms that now threaten the very existence of civilization. 　　　　　　　　　　　　　　　　*L. M.*

PREFACE TO THE
1970 EDITION

When 'The Culture of Cities' appeared a generation ago, the literature of cities was still extremely meager. Despite the work of Marcel Poëte and Pierre Lavedan, the urban historians, Max Weber, the sociologist, and my own master, Patrick Geddes, most of the current thinking about cities proceeded without sufficient insight into their nature, their function, their purpose, their historic role, or their potential future. The brief Introduction that opened 'The Culture of Cities' put the whole process of urban development in a fresh perspective; and the chapters that followed were so far in advance of current thinking that I have no hesitation in reprinting them without altering a word —though further observation and experience have called for various minor revisions I have made in later works.

From the outset, 'The Culture of Cities' was widely hailed as an outstanding interpretation and a worthy successor to its earlier companion volume, 'Technics and Civilization.' But despite a certain measure of popular success, the book exerted little influence in the United States. To many urban planners, administrators, and academic specialists, its constructive proposals seemed too remote from 'practical' financial and political requirements to be acceptable; and even some of my onetime co-workers and friends regarded my picture of the increasing demoralization and disintegration of Megalopolis as farfetched and unduly pessimistic.

But elsewhere in the world, as it turned out, 'The Culture of Cities' proved to be a timely and encouraging contribution; and during the next two decades, while hope was still "too like despair for prudence to smother," it exerted a marked influence. The very parts of the book that offended the American specialists in planning and housing made sense to the peoples of Britain and the occupied countries of Europe, whose cities, from Warsaw to London, were being reduced to rubble. They had no difficulty in envisaging Necropolis, the City of the Dead: it was already there. They knew all too well that something had gone wrong with civilization itself: the mounting disasters from 1914 on had prepared their minds for the constructive changes that would be necessary to rebuild their world on a sounder human foundation.

In some countries, notably Britain, 'The Culture of Cities' served as a guidebook to reconstruction and renewal. Despite its high price, the first English edition sold out promptly; and half a generation ago, in a poll of municipal officials in Britain, it was still chosen, almost unanimously, as the one book essential for a planner's education. Not the least service performed by this work was to re-enforce the policy for handling urban growth, not by endless suburban extensions, or heavier internal congestion, but by building New Towns: the method advocated and demonstrated by Sir Ebenezer Howard and his associates in the successful building of two garden cities. These proposals, for long dismissed as 'romantic' or 'old-fashioned'—and even now strangely denounced by Jane Jacobs as an effort to destroy the city— were, so far from being backward, half a century ahead of their time, for Howard's 'Garden Cities of Tomorrow' had been published in 1898.

If 'The Culture of Cities' encouraged and stimulated many people in Britain, it had an even more extraordinary, if more limited, effect upon the younger planners of the continent. (The one exception here was France, whose leading urban propagandist, Le Corbusier, had set the fashion for those extravagant high-rise structures that have conformed so admirably to the bureaucratic and technocratic—above all, financial—requirement of the dominant pecuniary-power economy.) Though only a few copies of the American or English editions had trickled into the occupied countries before 1939, they had an effect out of all proportion to their numbers. Summarized in translations, the book, I am happy to report, was used in underground schools of planning in Poland, the Netherlands, and even in Greece. The one copy available in Poland, Matthew Nowicki told me, was actually taken by a prisoner to Auschwitz, and miraculously survived, like its possessor, to return to Warsaw. Similarly, in Finland, a copy of the Swedish edition—brought back, I believe by Alvar Aalto—was presented to the Prime Minister as offering valuable proposals for Finland's housing and planning after the war.

But soon after the war ended, in the letdown that too often follows an all-out collective effort, the tide turned against such a radical approach to urban and regional rehabilitation. Though the ideas put forward in 'The Culture of Cities' continued to have an indirect effect upon the design of the British New Towns from 1947 onward, and had a direct effect upon the rebuilding of Coventry, not least its Shopping Center, more fashionable thought, extrapolating past tendencies, turned toward further metropolitan concentration, with high-rise building for residences as well as offices, with ruthless, socially destructive modes of 'urban renewal,' with the reckless dispersal of population by means of multi-laned expressways that daily poured pollution-laden streams of traffic into the city, turning even the proud boulevards of Paris into mere parking lots. In short, Le Corbusier's bureaucratic concept of the modern metropolis—artfully disguised as *'la ville radieuse'*—temporarily won out.

As a result, by the mid-nineteen-fifties, a professor of urban planning did not hesitate to dismiss 'The Culture of Cities' as a 'Museum Piece.' In 'The Urban Prospect' I have paid my respects to the reigning authorities in urban planning, the technocrats and bureaucrats, the statisticians and mathematical modellers who turned their backs upon the ecological and cultural realities of the city in the hope of transferring all its essential activities to the computer; and I will not trouble to repeat those disrespectful compliments. Enough to say that I only wish I had written more such 'Museum Pieces'; for the very parts of 'The Culture of Cities' that were rejected as obsolete or irrelevant—the chapters on megalopolitan disintegration, on The Politics of Regional Development, and on the Social Basis of the New Urban Order, like my earlier descriptions of environmental pollution—were precisely those that had grown immensely in significance. At least the younger generation has now caught up with me.

Meanwhile, my own thinking did not halt at the point I had reached in 1938. As a professor of City and Regional Planning at the University of Pennsylvania during the nineteen-fifties, I found it necessary to cover the entire span of urban history; and I accordingly expanded the historic chapters of 'The Culture of Cities' into the wider panorama of 'The City in History': a book whose measure has still to be taken. In conceiving that new work, I intended to follow it with an equally exhaustive account of the contemporary urban prospects: a generous expansion of the second half of the present volume. But since there is no immediate likelihood of my completing such a book, there is all the more reason for bringing out the present volume in its original form; for it is in these final chapters that the ecological foundations for a balanced urban environment were laid down. For those who wish to pursue this line of thinking further, I would suggest the final chapters of 'The Pentagon of Power' (1971).

LEWIS MUMFORD

Spring 1970

CONTENTS

CONTENTS

ILLUSTRATIONS

NOTE: *Illustrations and captions are an integral part of the book: but designed to be consulted separately without breaking the flow of the text. References to them in the index are denoted by the plate number, enclosed in brackets.*

THE CULTURE OF CITIES

INTRODUCTION

The city, as one finds it in history, is the point of maximum concentration for the power and culture of a community. It is the place where the diffused rays of many separate beams of life fall into focus, with gains in both social effectiveness and significance. The city is the form and symbol of an integrated social relationship: it is the seat of the temple, the market, the hall of justice, the academy of learning. Here in the city the goods of civilization are multiplied and manifolded; here is where human experience is transformed into viable signs, symbols, patterns of conduct, systems of order. Here is where the issues of civilization are focused: here, too, ritual passes on occasion into the active drama of a fully differentiated and self-conscious society.

Cities are a product of the earth. They reflect the peasant's cunning in dominating the earth; technically they but carry further his skill in turning the soil to productive uses, in enfolding his cattle for safety, in regulating the waters that moisten his fields, in providing storage bins and barns for his crops. Cities are emblems of that settled life which began with permanent agriculture: a life conducted with the aid of permanent shelters, permanent utilities like orchards, vineyards, and irrigation works, and permanent buildings for protection and storage.

Every phase of life in the countryside contributes to the existence of cities. What the shepherd, the woodman, and the miner know, becomes transformed and "etherealized" through the city into durable elements in the human heritage: the textiles and butter of one, the moats and dams and wooden pipes and lathes of another, the metals and jewels of the third, are finally converted into instruments of urban living: underpinning the city's economic existence, contributing art and wisdom to its daily routine. Within the city the essence of each type of soil and labor and economic goal is concentrated: thus arise greater possibilities for interchange and for new combinations not given in the isolation of their original habitats.

Cities are a product of time. They are the molds in which men's lifetimes have cooled and congealed, giving lasting shape, by way of art, to moments that would otherwise vanish with the living and leave no means of renewal or wider participation behind them. In the city, time becomes visible: buildings and monuments and public ways, more open than the written record, more subject to the gaze of many men than the scattered artifacts of the countryside, leave an imprint upon the minds even of the ignorant or the indifferent. Through the material fact of preservation, time challenges time, time clashes with time: habits and values carry over beyond the living group, streaking with different strata of time the character of any single generation. Layer upon layer, past times preserve themselves in the city until life itself is finally threatened with suffocation: then, in sheer defense, modern man invents the museum.

By the diversity of its time-structures, the city in part escapes the tyranny of a single present, and the monotony of a future that consists in repeating only a single beat heard in the past. Through its complex orchestration of time and space, no less than through the social division of labor, life in the city takes on the character of a symphony: specialized human aptitudes, specialized instruments, give rise to sonorous results which, neither in volume nor in quality, could be achieved by any single piece.

Cities arise out of man's social needs and multiply both their modes and their methods of expression. In the city remote forces and influences intermingle with the local: their conflicts are no less significant than their harmonies. And here, through the concentration of the means of intercourse in the market and the meeting place, alternative modes of living present themselves: the deeply rutted ways of the village cease to be coercive and the ancestral goals cease to be all-sufficient: strange men and women, strange interests, and stranger gods loosen the traditional ties of blood and neighborhood. A sailing ship, a caravan, stopping at the city, may bring a new dye for wool, a new glaze for the potter's dish, a new system of signs for long distance communication, or a new thought about human destiny.

In the urban milieu, mechanical shocks produce social results; and social needs may take shape in contrivances and inventions which will lead industries and governments into new channels of experiment. Now the need for a common fortified spot for shelter against predatory attack draws the inhabitants of the indigenous village into a hillside fortification: through the compulsive mingling for defense, the possibilities for more regular intercourse and wider co-operation arise. That fact helps transform the nest of villages into a unified city, with its higher ceiling of achievement and its wider horizons. Now the collective sharing of experience, and the stimulus of rational criticism, turn the rites of the village festival into the more powerful imaginative forms of the tragic drama: experience is deepened, as well as more widely circulated, through this process. Or again, on another plane, the goldsmith's passive repository for valuables becomes, through the pressure of urban needs and the opportunities of the market, the dynamic agent of capitalism, the bank, lending money as well as keeping it, putting capital into circulation, finally dominating the processes of trade and production.

The city is a fact in nature, like a cave, a run of mackerel or an ant-heap. But it is also a conscious work of art, and it holds within its communal framework many simpler and more personal forms of art. Mind *takes form* in the city; and in turn, urban forms condition mind. For space, no less than time, is artfully reorganized in cities: in boundary lines and silhouettes, in the fixing of horizontal planes and vertical peaks, in utilizing or denying the natural site, the city records the attitude of a culture and an epoch to the fundamental facts of its existence. The dome and the spire, the open avenue and the closed court, tell the story, not merely of different physical accommodations, but of essentially different conceptions of man's destiny. The city is both a physical utility for collective living and a symbol of those collective purposes and unanimities that arise under such favoring circumstance. With language itself, it remains man's greatest work of art.

Through its concrete, visible command over space the city lends itself, not only to the practical offices of production, but to the daily communion of its citizens: this constant effect of the city, as a collective work of art, was expressed in a classic manner by Thomas Mann in his address to his fellow-townsmen of Lübeck on the celebration of the anniversary of Lübeck's foundation. When the city ceases to be a symbol of art and order, it acts in a negative fashion: it expresses and helps to make more universal the fact of disintegration. In the close quarters of the city, perversities and evils spread more quickly; and in the stones of the city, these anti-social facts become embedded: it is not the triumphs of urban living that awaken the prophetic wrath of a Jeremiah, a Savonarola, a Rousseau, or a Ruskin.

What transforms the passive agricultural regime of the village into the active institutions of the city? The difference is not merely one of magnitude, density of population, or economic resources. For the active agent is any factor that extends the area of local intercourse, that engenders the need for combination and co-operation, communication and communion; and that so creates a common underlying pattern of conduct, and a common set of physical structures, for the different family and occupational groups that constitute a city. These opportunities and activities superimpose upon primary groups, based upon traditional acceptances and daily face-to-face contact, the more active associations, the more specialized functions, and the more purposive interests of secondary groups: in the latter the purpose is not given, but chosen: the membership and the activities are selective: the group itself becomes specialized and differentiated.

Historically, the increase of population, through the change from hunting to agriculture, may have abetted this change; the widening of trade routes and the diversification of occupations likewise helped. But the nature of the city is not to be found simply in its economic base: the city is primarily a social emergent. The mark of the city is its purposive social complexity. It represents the maximum possibility of humanizing the natural environment and of naturalizing the human heritage: it gives a cultural shape to the first, and it externalizes, in permanent collective forms, the second.

"The central and significant fact about the city," as Geddes and Branford pointed out, "is that the city . . . functions as the specialized organ of social transmission. It accumulates and embodies the heritage of a region, and combines in some measure and kind with the cultural heritage of larger units, national, racial, religious, human. On one side is the individuality of the city—the sign manual of its regional life and record. On the other are the marks of the civilization, in which each particular city is a constituent element."

Today a great many things stand in the way of grasping the rôle of the city and of transforming this basic means of communal existence. During the last few centuries the strenuous mechanical organization of industry, and the setting up of tyrannous political states, have blinded most men to the importance of facts that do not easily fit into the general pattern of mechanical conquest, capitalistic forms of exploitation, and power politics. Habitually, people treat the realities of personality and association and city as abstractions, while they treat confused pragmatic abstractions such as money, credit, political sovereignty, as if they were concrete realities that had an existence independent of human conventions.

Looking back over the course of Western Civilization since the fifteenth century, it is fairly plain that mechanical integration and social disruption have gone on side by side. Our capacity for effective physical organization has enormously increased; but our ability to create a harmonious counterpoise to these external linkages by means of co-operative and civic associations on both a regional and a world-wide basis, like the Christian Church in the Middle Ages, has not kept pace with these mechanical triumphs. By one of those mischievous turns, from which history is rarely free, it was precisely during this period of flowing physical energies, social disintegration, and bewildered political experiment that the populations of the world as a whole began mightily to increase, and the cities of the Western World began to grow at an inordinate rate. Forms of social life that the wisest no longer understood, the more ignorant were prepared to build. Or rather: the ignorant were completely unprepared, but that did not prevent the building.

The result was not a temporary confusion and an occasional lapse in efficiency. What followed was a crystallization of chaos: disorder hardened uncouthly in metropolitan slum and industrial factory districts; and the exodus into the dormitory suburbs and factory spores that surrounded the growing cities merely widened the area of social derangement. The mechanized physical shell took precedence in every growing town over the civic nucleus: men became dissociated as citizens in the very process of coming together in imposing economic organizations. Even industry, which was supposedly served by this planless building and random physical organization, lost seriously in efficiency: it failed to produce a new urban form that served directly its complicated processes. As for the growing urban populations, they lacked the most elementary facilities for urban living, even sunlight and fresh air, to say nothing of the means to a more vivid social life. The new cities grew up without the benefit of coherent social knowledge or orderly social effort: they lacked the useful urban folkways of the Middle Ages or the confident esthetic command of the Baroque period: indeed, a seventeenth century Dutch peasant, in his little village, knew more about the art of living in communities than a nineteenth century municipal councilor in London or Berlin. Statesmen who did not hesitate to weld together a diversity of regional interests into national states, or who wove together an empire that girdled the planet, failed to produce even a rough draft of a decent neighborhood.

In every department, form disintegrated: except in its heritage from the past, the city vanished as an embodiment of collective art and technics. And where, as in North America, the loss was not alleviated by the continued presence of great monuments from the past and persistent habits of social living, the result was a raw, dissolute environment, and a narrow, constricted, and baffled social life. Even in Germany and the Low Countries, where the traditions of urban life had lingered on from the Middle Ages, the most colossal blunders were committed in the most ordinary tasks of urban planning and building. As the pace of urbanization increased, the circle of devastation widened.

Today we face not only the original social disruption. We likewise face the accumulated physical and social results of that disruption: ravaged landscapes, disorderly urban districts, pockets of disease, patches of blight, mile upon mile of standardized slums, worming into the outlying areas of big cities, and fusing with their ineffectual suburbs. In short: a general miscarriage and defeat of civilized effort. So far have our achievements fallen short of our needs that even a hundred years of persistent reform in England, the first country to suffer heavily from disurbanization, have only in the last decade begun to leave an imprint. True: here and there patches of good building and coherent social form exist: new nodes of integration can be detected, and since 1920 these patches have been spreading. But the main results of more than a century of misbuilding and malformation, dissociation and disorganization still hold. Whether the observer focuses his gaze on the physical structure of communal living or upon the social processes that must be embodied and expressed, the report remains the same.

Today we begin to see that the improvement of cities is no matter for small one-sided reforms: the task of city design involves the vaster task of rebuilding our civilization. We must alter the parasitic and predatory modes of life that now play so large a part, and we must create region by region, continent by continent, an effective symbiosis, or co-operative living together. The problem is to co-ordinate, on the basis of more essential human values than the will-to-power and the will-to-profits, a host of social functions and processes that we have hitherto misused in the building of cities and polities, or of which we have never rationally taken advantage.

Unfortunately, the fashionable political philosophies of the past century are of but small help in defining this new task: they dealt with legal abstractions, like Individual and State, with cultural abstractions, like Humanity, the Nation, the Folk, or with bare economic abstractions like the Capitalist Class or the Proletariat—while life as it was lived in the concrete, in regions and cities and villages, in wheatland and cornland and vineland, in the mine, the quarry, the fishery, was conceived as but a shadow of the prevailing myths and arrogant fantasies of the ruling classes—or the often no less shadowy fantasies of those who challenged them.

Here and there one notes, of course, valiant exceptions both in theory and in action. Le Play and Reclus in France, W. H. Riehl in Germany, Kropotkin in Russia, Howard in England, Grundtvig in Denmark, Geddes in Scotland, began half a century ago to lay the ideological basis for a new order. The insights of these men may prove as important for the new biotechnic regime, based on the deliberate culture of life, as the formulations of Leonardo, Galileo,

Newton, and Descartes were for the more limited mechanical order upon which the past triumphs of our machine civilization were founded. In the piecemeal improvement of cities, the work of sanitarians like Chadwick and Richardson, community designers like Olmsted, far-seeing architects, like Parker and Wright, laid the concrete basis for a collective environment in which the needs of reproduction and nurture and psychological development and the social processes themselves would be adequately served.

Now the dominant urban environment of the past century has been mainly a narrow by-product of the machine ideology. And the greater part of it has already been made obsolete by the rapid advance of the biological arts and sciences, and by the steady penetration of sociological thought into every department. We have now reached a point where these fresh accumulations of historical insight and scientific knowledge are ready to flow over into social life, to mold anew the forms of cities, to assist in the transformation of both the instruments and the goals of our civilization. Profound changes, which will affect the distribution and increase of population, the efficiency of industry, and the quality of Western Culture, have already become visible. To form an accurate estimate of these new potentialities and to suggest their direction into channels of human welfare, is one of the major offices of the contemporary student of cities. Ultimately, such studies, forecasts, and imaginative projects must bear directly upon the life of every human being in our civilization.

What is the city? How has it functioned in the Western World since the tenth century, when the renewal of cities began, and in particular, what changes have come about in its physical and social composition during the last century? What factors have conditioned the size of cities, the extent of their growth, the type of order manifested in street plan and in building, their manner of nucleation, the composition of their economic and social classes, their physical manner of existence and their cultural style? By what political processes of federation or amalgamation, co-operative union or centralization, have cities existed; and what new units of administration does the present age suggest? Have we yet found an adequate urban form to harness all the complex technical and social forces in our civilization; and if a new order is discernible, what are its main outlines?

What are the relations between city and region? And what steps are necessary in order to redefine and reconstruct the region itself, as a collective human habitation? What, in short, are the possibilities for creating form and order and design in our present civilization?

These are some of the questions I shall pose in the following study. Wherever possible, I shall utilize for answer concrete contemporary examples: a procedure that is all the easier because the germs and embryonic forms of the new order are by now, for the greater part, in existence. But where this is impossible, I shall seek to uncover the essential principle upon whose basis a viable answer or solution may be predicted.

Today our world faces a crisis: a crisis which, if its consequences are as grave as now seems, may not fully be resolved for another century. If the destructive forces in civilization gain ascendancy, our new urban culture will be stricken in every part. Our cities, blasted and deserted, will be cemeteries for the dead: cold lairs given over to less destructive beasts than man. But we may avert that fate: perhaps only in facing such a desperate challenge can the necessary creative forces be effectually welded together. Instead of clinging to the sardonic funeral towers of metropolitan finance, ours to march out to newly plowed fields, to create fresh patterns of political action, to alter for human purposes the perverse mechanisms of our economic regime, to conceive and to germinate fresh forms of human culture.

Instead of accepting the stale cult of death that the fascists have erected, as the proper crown for the servility and the brutality that are the pillars of their states, we must erect a cult of life: life in action, as the farmer or the mechanic knows it: life in expression, as the artist knows it: life as the lover feels it and the parent practices it: life as it is known to men of good will who meditate in the cloister, experiment in the laboratory, or plan intelligently in the factory or the government office.

Nothing is permanent: certainly not the frozen images of barbarous power with which fascism now confronts us. Those images may easily be smashed by an external shock, cracked as ignominiously as fallen Dagon, the massive idol of the heathen: or they may be melted, eventually, by the internal warmth of normal men and women. Nothing endures except life: the capacity for birth, growth, and daily renewal. As life becomes insurgent once more in our civilization, conquering the reckless thrust of barbarism, the culture of cities will be both instrument and goal.

CHAPTER I.　PROTECTION AND THE MEDIEVAL TOWN

1: Stripping Off the Medieval Myth

Before one approaches the medieval town one must strip off the false wrappings in which successive generations have swathed this portion of the European past. The Middle Ages were defamed during the early Renascence for vices that actually belonged to their defamers: history offers many instances of the "transferred reproach." Thus the earlier inhabitants of historic cities were vilified for demolishing precious Roman monuments that were not in fact destroyed until the very period that professed to value them, the age of the new humanists.

Let us depart, to begin with, from the notion that the period from the tenth to the sixteenth century was a compound of ignorance, filth, brutality, and superstition; for such a description does not altogether fit the life of Europe as a whole even during the worst parts of the Dark Ages, which still felt the civilizing influences of Celtic monasticism and the resolute order and economy of Charles the Great. This view of the Middle Ages is partly a product of the eighteenth century "Gothic Romances," with their lurid pictures of torture chambers, cobwebs, mystery, and madness. No doubt such elements existed; but they no more characterized the civilization as a whole than the existence of armed gangsters and organized rackets and fascist pirates entirely characterizes our present civilization. One must not magnify the black spots in the past nor minimize those in our own day.

One must of course equally set aside the charming tapestry of the Middle Ages, composed by Pugin, Ruskin, Morris, and similar writers: they often treated intentions as if they were facts and ideals as if they were realizations. Above all, this version forgets that if the Middle Ages were governed by bold warriors and patient craftsmen, it was likewise a period of embryonic capitalist enterprise and audacious technical improvements: eager merchants, adventurous entrepreneurs, canny inventors: a period that invented the mechanical clock, made radical improvements in mining, sailing, and military attack, and learned to cast iron and manufacture glass spectacles and utilize physical energy on a scale never before achieved by any other civilization.

Our Middle Ages is far richer in detail than the earlier versions; and as respects the management of industry and the building of cities one finds even more to commend than did the most ardent early advocates of Catholic piety. There is a social kinship between our own age and the age of the guilds that parallels the relation I pointed out in Technics and Civilization between the eotechnic and the neotechnic complexes. And in the domain of cities, we have tardily begun to realize that our hard-earned discoveries in the art of laying out towns, especially in the *hygienic* laying out of towns, merely recapitulate, in terms of our own social needs, the commonplaces of sound medieval practice. Does this seem topsy-turvy? On the contrary: it was the myth that was baseless.

2: The Need for Protection

Between the date that symbolizes the fall of Rome and the eleventh century, when the cities of the West awakened to a new life, lies a period that is hard to describe but important to understand. It was out of the incurable misery and terror of this age that certain special attitudes toward life grew up which powerfully affected the development of all the dominant social institutions of the West—particularly the city. Five centuries of violence, paralysis, and uncertainty had created in the European heart a profound desire for security. When every chance might prove a mischance, when every moment might be one's last moment, the need for protection rose above every other concern, and to find a safe haven was about the most one asked from life.

In Italy and France the old ways, it is true, had never entirely disappeared: hence the pagan undercurrents in that life: hence the

twelfth century Renascence, so much more vital, both as continuation and as rebirth, than that which was to follow. But a disorganization and diminishment of the forces of civilization did characterize this period: the worst effects became visible only around the
ninth century. Slavery, which had taken root in Roman agriculture,
was introduced on a wide scale by the conquering barbarians; and
the population, never far from famine, actually decreased. Military
terrorism and its parasitic economy led to a devolution of the city:
people left these stony wastes because they were driven to accept life
at a subsistence level. Even when they remained in the neighborhood
of an old city, like Mainz or Trier, it was no longer a meaningful
part of their active life: only the shell remained. Its stones served as
caves in the rock might have served—bare hiding places for those
fleeing from the wrath to come.

If the Saracen encirclement of the Mediterranean hastened the
passage from the uniform organization on the old imperial lines to a
feudal economy of local production, barter, and consumption, under
special local customs and local laws, the final blow was given at the
other end of Europe by the invasions of the Norsemen in the ninth
century. The final blow—and the first move toward recovery. These
Norse raids were conducted in small boats that pierced the heart of
the countryside between Brittany and the Elbe: no district was immune to their sacking, burning, slaying. The terror of these visitations must have created a new community of interest between the
feudal lord and his dependents; but it also showed the technical inferiority of the local war-band in opposing attacks carried on by
more audacious, perhaps more highly specialized, opponents.

Sheer necessity led to the rediscovery of an important fact. In the
crude state of Western military technics in the ninth century, the
strength and security of a fortified stronghold, perched on some impregnable rock, could be secured even for the relatively helpless
people of the lowlands provided they built a wooden palisade or a
stone wall around their village. Such a wall, particularly when surrounded by a moat, kept the attacker out, and made his weapons
ineffective. In terror of the invaders, the inhabitants of Mainz, for
example, restored at last their dilapidated Roman wall. Under com-
missions from the German emperor, Henry I, walls were built even

around monasteries and nunneries to guard them from attack. And in Italy, too, walls were built again at the end of the ninth century in order to repel the Hungarians and other invaders.

This discovery, fortunately, proved to be double-edged. If the wall could protect the town from outside invasions more successfully than the feudal war-band, could it not also protect the community from the invasions and usurpations of these greedy and arrogant "protectors"? By means of the wall, any village could become another stronghold: people would flock to that island of peace, as originally they had submitted in desperation to the feudal gang-leaders or had given up the hopes of domesticity to find protection in a monastery or a nunnery. Life in the open country, even under the shadow of a castle, ceased to be as attractive as life behind the urban wall. Stockades, such as one still sees in Lucas Cranach's woodcut of the siege of Wolfenbüttel in 1542, were a cheap price to pay for such collective security of life and property, such regularity in trade and work, such peace in thought and worship.

Note the sequence. First the cowering countryside, with its local production and mainly local barter: social life gathered in little villages or in "suburbs," as the agricultural settlements that nestled under the castle's walls were called. Then a deliberate physical reconstruction of the environment: the wall: protection made permanent and regular. In this security from outside raids and impositions, local craftsmen and peasants and fishermen, under privileges wrung from their local lord, came together for a regular weekly or fortnightly market: presently they sought permanent quarters for themselves in a spot that combined so many advantages in living. It is significant to note that, as Hegel points out, the *new* quarter of Regensburg, in the eleventh century—as distinguished from the royal and the clerical quarters—is that of the merchants. As social life became more solid and compact, this industrial and merchants' quarter, the suburb, became the town center; and the seats of feudal and ecclesiastical power tended to become more suburban.

This urban movement was a chequered one. It marched under various banners, issued out of different circumstances, and produced diverse results. Sometimes urbanization was deliberately promoted by the feudal lords; often it was opposed by them, particularly by the princes of the Church, above all, when the rights of political and economic independence were claimed by the new townsmen. In some countries, as in England and France, municipal freedom was promoted by a temporary coalition with the central power, as a means of weakening the feudal nobles who challenged the king's dominion. But, opposed or helped, the population flowed into these protected centers, built and rebuilt them, and in a few centuries created perhaps the highest type of urban civilization that had been known in Europe since the fifth century in Greece.

3: The "Increase of Population and Wealth"

The revival of trade is often taken, even by eminent scholars like Pirenne, as the direct cause of the city-building and civilizing activities that took place in the eleventh century. But the fact is that this urban renascence and its characteristic agents date from the previous century: their locus is not the isolated market, but the monastery.

Up to the time of the Norse invasions, the monasteries had served as a secure haven amid all the stormy uncertainties of life. In fact, the monastery had during this period performed the functions of the city in transmitting, if not greatly enlarging, the social heritage. Thanks to the knowledge the Benedictines preserved, sometimes even of Roman agricultural practice, it was many levels above the state of the surrounding countryside. Here the arts of building flourished and the technics of glass manufacture and decoration were carried on; above all, it was here that the written record was preserved and manifolded. In facing the new conditions of life in the ninth century, the monasteries were not in the least backward. The nunnery of Gernrode in Germany was called Kloster und Burg; and this meant something more than that the place was fortified.

A regular market worked to the advantage of the feudal lord or monastic proprietor. Considerably before the grand revival of trade in the eleventh century one finds under Otto II (973-983) that permission was given to the Widow Imma, who was founding a cloister in Kärnten, to provide a market and a mint and to draw taxes therefrom: typical characteristics of the new urban foundations. In the time of Otto, according to Hegel, most of the market privileges were granted to religious proprietors rather than to temporal lords. These markets, under the supervision of the monastery, were probably older than the walls which later provided security of a more material order; for as early as 833 Lewis the Pious in Germany gave a monastery permission to erect a mint for a market that was already in existence. The market peace, symbolized by the market cross that stood in the market-place, could not be broken without suffering heavy penalties. Finally, under this royal aegis, a special market law, applying to fairs and markets, with a special court having jurisdiction over traders, came into existence. The various forms of security offered by religion, by jurisprudence, and by standard economic practice entered into the foundation of medieval towns.

The revival of trade in the eleventh century, then, was not the critical fact that laid the foundation of the new medieval type of city: many actual foundations antedated that fact. Commercial zeal was rather a symptom of a far more inclusive revival that was taking place in Western Civilization; not least, it was a mark of the new sense of security that the walled town itself had most potently helped to bring into existence. If trade is one symptom, the political unification of Normandy, Flanders, Aquitaine, and Brandenburg is another; and the land reclamations and forest clearance of the monastic orders, such as the Cistercians (founded in 1098), is a third. The confusion scholars have fallen into here derives partly from the fact that they read present motives back into past situations, and partly because they have not distinguished carefully between local, regional, and international markets. Local merchants, as distinguished from craftsmen who sell their own goods, could have played only an insignificant part in the eleventh century revival.

In general, the early trade revival on semi-capitalistic lines was confined to the luxury wares that entered into international commerce. This was incapable of fostering the growth of towns until the towns themselves had come into existence. Moreover, the special international market was the Great Fair, held usually once a year: there merchants from all parts of Europe would come together. But this type of merchant, with his caravan and his armed guards and his special treaties for political protection moved from place to place: he was a glorified peddler, more like the Yankee merchant captain of the early nineteenth century than like an urban business man. To fancy that these wandering international traders were responsible for the original growth of the medieval town is to put the cart before the horse.

It was rather a revival of the protected towns that helped the reopening of the regional and international trade routes, and led to the inter-European circulation of surplus commodities, particularly those of little bulk, wine from the Rhine, spices and silks from the East, armor from Lombardy, woolen goods from Flanders, leather from Pomerania, across the footways and waterways of Europe. Cities formed stepping stones in this march of goods: from Byzantium to Venice, from Venice to Augsburg, from Augsburg over the Rhine—and so, too, from Baltic cities, down to the Mediterranean.

The great fairs of the Middle Ages no doubt laid the foundation for the international capitalism of the sixteenth century, localized earlier in Florence and Augsburg, and later in Antwerp and Amsterdam, before it finally crossed in the eighteenth century to London. No less than the Crusades, the Fairs furthered the interchange of regional modes and patterns of life. But if the cultural importance of international trade was high, its economic importance—particularly as a source of urban growth—has been grossly exaggerated for the early Middle Ages. The fact is that even at a later period than the eleventh century the merchants with their retainers accounted, according to von Below, for only a small part of the town's population: far smaller than today. For the *producers* in the early medieval town composed about four-fifths of the inhabitants, as compared with two-fifths in the modern city.

Once the food supply was enlarged, once urban settlements became secure, commerce did serve as a powerful stimulus to growth: above all because it was necessary to pay for luxuries in money. As the demand for finery grew, and as more money was needed for the equipment of the feudal soldiery, the feudal lords had a special incentive to transform their holdings into urban areas which brought in a large return in cash rent. Urban rents may not have exclusively provided the funds for capitalist enterprise, but capitalist enterprise certainly stimulated the desire for urban rents. This gave the feudal landlord an ambivalent attitude toward the city. As power ceased to

[TOP] Verona: colonized by the Romans in 89 B.C.; leading city in the Lombard League in the twelfth century. Embanked rivers were no less important than hillside sites or the more elaborate canals, moats, and walls that surrounded other medieval cities for protection. Note the Campanile standing in isolation among the lower buildings. The erection of these bell-towers in the thirteenth century helped synchronize the activities of the townsmen and peasants within earshot of the new tower clocks. (*Photograph: Ewing Galloway*)

[MIDDLE LEFT] Dinkelsbühl. Blocked vista and irregular, upward pointing silhouette: gabled roof, tower, and spire worked in esthetic harmony. The tracery of ironwork in the standard and shield of the foreground was a fine feature of civic art, especially notable in South Germany. Arms, symbols, emblems, denoting the status and function of a class or an occupation were commonplaces in civic ritual, a connecting link between costume and architecture. Signs and signboards, with symbols and images rather than words and numbers, occupied an important place in the streets through the eighteenth century, when Watteau did not disdain to paint them. The harness maker's horse and the cigar stores Indian remained in American towns and villages through the whole nineteenth century. The transformation of the medieval sign into the blatant advertisement of the nineteenth century hoarding marks the degradation of civic art as effectually as the similar change from the modest uniform tombstone slab to the ostentatious competition of monument and mausoleum in the nineteenth century cemetery. (*Photograph: Ewing Galloway*)

[MIDDLE RIGHT] Rothenburg-an-der-Tauber: another typical profile, irregular but harmonious, following the contour of the land, with the more significant buildings thrusting against the sky. Organic planning and building, not for show but for defense, civic association, the expression of common values. This contemporary photograph closely coincides, in the various types of building and their arrangement, with many woodcuts in the Nürnberg Chronicle. (*Photograph: Ewing Galloway*)

[BOTTOM] Segovia. The hill-site as a means of defense: likewise the domination of the gigantic cathedral over the lesser buildings of the secular life. The bounding wall of the old city is still visible in the foreground; and as in Verona, the buildings show the typical low-pitched Mediterranean roof; but the principle of social organization and visual composition nevertheless closely resembles that of the northern cities: the same irregular silhouette, the same variety within a common pattern, the same crescendo movement in vertical space—contrasting with the horizontal movement of baroque planning—from the secular to the sacred, from the individual to the collective: counterpart of the hierarchical order of Heaven. (*Photograph: Ewing Galloway*)

[TOP LEFT] The great Marienkirche (Lady Church) above the supporting roof-tops of the burgher city. While the chaster Cathedral was the home of the clericals, the Marienkirche was built by the bourgeoisie, an emblem of their riches and power in the days when leadership in the Hanseatic League belonged to Lübeck. Religious art was one of the great export products of this city; hence one local museum contains chiefly replicas of the indigenous altar pieces and carvings.

[TOP RIGHT] Surviving fragment of the town wall and the gate that opens to the Landstrasse, banked with ancient linden trees, which leads to the fishing village and summer resort of Travemünde. (See Buddenbrooks by Thomas Mann.) The beauty of the surviving gates repeats the salute of the Seven Towers as one approaches Lübeck across the flat surrounding landscape.

[MIDDLE] Town Hall and Market Square, with the Marienkirche on the left. While the buildings of the foreground, right, belong to later periods, the town hall and church are survivals of the great period of Backstein Gothik. The touch of Venice in the design of the Town Hall may well not be an accident in a town once justly famous for its St Mark's Bread, or marzipan.

[MIDDLE INSERT] Typical late medieval burgher houses: office and temporary warehouse as well as residence. Garden spaces in rear, which belonged to the more modest houses of the thirteenth century, have been overbuilt: sometimes with summer wings whose windows opened more directly on the garden. Kitchen and offices on lower two floors: parlors on upper floors, often with a glass-enclosed chamber separating the elders from the young folks at dances and parties. Spacious quarters but bad ventilation; big windows but no direct contact with the sun: physiologically, a lowering of the cruder but more healthy early standards of accommodation. Note formal resemblance between these dwellings and the warehouses: partly due to lack of differentiation, partly because they belong organically to the same order. (*Photograph: Catherine Bauer*)

[BOTTOM LEFT] Heilige Geist Hospital: a medieval foundation for the aged: still in use as the old men and women sunning themselves in front prove. Each pensioner has a cubicle within the great nave. The design is closer to that of a late medieval hospital for the diseased than is the more domestic sort of foundation for the aged still found in England and the Low Countries.

[BOTTOM RIGHT] Salt warehouses along the Trave: highly important in the days when salt fish for the fast days of the Church played a unique part in international trade: indeed, the migration of the herring from the Baltic to the North Sea in the early fifteenth century was a decisive factor in the decay of the Hansa towns and the rise of Amsterdam and Norwich. Rivertowns like Rouen and Lübeck were in the early centuries in a better position for navigation and defense than towns nearer the open ocean. (*Photograph: Catherine Bauer*) be represented in his mind in purely military terms, he was tempted to part with a modicum of control over his individual tenants and dependents in order to have their responsible collective contribution in the form of cash payments: demands the land-bound serf could not meet. This was an important secondary stimulus to the building of towns.

Capitalism itself, however, was a disruptive rather than an integrating force in the internal life of the medieval city. It supplanted the old protective economy, based on status, mollified by religious precept, by a trading economy based on individual enterprise and the lust for gain: the economic history of the town is largely a story of the transformation of a group of protected producers living in a state of relative equality, into a small group of privileged merchants for whom the rest of the population ultimately toils. This change was already over the horizon when Chaucer wrote his wistful economium on the Former Age, when "ther lay no profit, ther was no richesse." By providing a nest in which the cuckoo bird of capitalism could lay her eggs, the walled town made it possible for her own offspring to be crowded out by the boisterous newcomer it harbored.

Beneath the revival of industry that took place between the eleventh and the thirteenth century was a fact of more fundamental economic importance: the immense extension of arable land and the application to the land of more adequate methods of husbandry. Wooded areas in Germany, a wilderness in the ninth century, gave way to plowland; the Low Countries, which had supported only a handful of dejected fishermen, were taken over and transformed into one of the richest productive soils in Europe. As early as 1150 the first polders, land reclaimed from marsh or sea by means of dykes were created in Flanders. (Agricultural irrigation was practiced in Milan as early as 1179.) The breeding of horses, the invention of an improved harness and the use of the iron horseshoe, the spread of querns, water mills, and windmills—these improvements endowed the new communities with relatively vast sources of power. This not merely transformed mining and metallurgy: it removed the need for servile labor and added to the surplus of human energies that had always existed in the more favored regions.

In the course of three centuries the Europe we know today was opened or re-opened for settlement: a feat exactly comparable to the opening up of the American continent between the seventeenth and the twentieth century. Indeed, one may regard the American conquest as a continuation of the original process on a new soil, for the colonization of New England, at all events, was on medieval urban lines, as that of Virginia and South Carolina was on the typical feudal pattern.

This vast extension of the agricultural base and this enormous increase in power in turn made possible the increase of population. According to Boissonade, the region between the Rhine and the Moselle increased its population tenfold between the tenth and the thirteenth century. The English counties, which had numbered 1,200,000 souls in 1086 reached a total of 2,355,000 toward 1340. The birthrate was perhaps higher; the number of people who survived was certainly greater; and this fact was not confined to the newly exploited territories of the North. Italy had made such progress in its agricultural economy as to number at least ten million souls in the fourteenth century. Better established and more favorably situated with respect to the higher civilizations of the East, Italy was the leader in both the material and the spiritual revival. In the thirteenth century Venice was a magnificently organized municipality; and Venice and Milan each then had probably over 100,000 people.

The Germanic cities, with perhaps the exception of the old Roman bordertown of Wien, averaged a much lower population; but there was no lack of energy in the German colonization movement, or in the process of urbanization. For in the course of four centuries 2500 cities were founded; and the municipal framework then laid out lasted substantially until the nineteenth century: the very outlines of municipal territory often remained, though in the meanwhile the town had filled them up. During the peak years of the movement not merely did the number of cities multiply, but the rate of urban population growth, as far as it can be estimated, was roughly comparable to that recorded in the nineteenth century. At the end of the twelfth century, for example, Paris had about 100,000 inhabitants; and at the end of the thirteenth century something like 240,000. In 1280 Florence had 45,000 inhabitants, and in 1339 around 90,000.

Trade, industrial production, mechanization, organization—all these facts helped expand the life of the cities. But they do not account for the feeding of the hungry mouths. People do not live on coins, even if the local mint has the exclusive privilege of coining them; nor do they live on air, even though "city air makes people free" as the saying went. The thriving life of these towns had its origin in the agricultural improvement of the countryside: an improvement that was spotty, and vitiated ultimately by the reckless deforestation that accompanied it, but sufficient to create unheard-of stores of energy: even the dismal colonization lands in Pomerania could send their honey and wax and hides back to the more industrial towns of the West. This agricultural improvement was duly transported into the city in the gardens, the cultivated spaces, and the common fields within the city itself. For except for a few congested centers, the town of the Middle Ages was not merely *in* the country but *of* the country: food was grown within the walls, as well as on the terraces, or in the orchards and fields, outside.

4: Lordly Scadders and Medieval New Edens

If the new methods of military protection accounted for the popularity of cities as places for residence and productive work, a special set of economic motives nevertheless existed which accounts for the headway this movement made. The liberation of towns was a step toward the efficient ordering of economic life: the replacement of barter by money, and of life-service by urban piecework or seasonal hire: in short, the transition, to use Maine's old distinction, from status to contract. The eighteenth century myth of the social contract was a rationalization of the political basis of the medieval town, whose survival in Geneva Rousseau knew. For the corporate town was in fact based upon a social contract between the landed proprietor and the settlers or inhabitants.

The cities movement, from the tenth century on, is a tale of old urban settlements becoming more or less self-governing cities, and of new settlements being made under the auspices of the feudal lord, endowed with privileges and rights that served to attract permanent groups of craftsmen and traders. The city charter was a social contract; the free city had legal as well as military security, and to live in the corporate town for a year and a day removed the obligations of serfdom. Hence the medieval city became a selective environment, gathering to itself the more skilled, the more adventurous, the more upstanding—probably therefore the more intelligent—part of the rural population.

Political interest in this period usually centers on the struggle for power between the urban bourgeoisie and its overlords. This tends to neglect the part that feudalism itself had in encouraging the growth of cities. Many of the conflicts in the old centers came from attempts to drive a hard bargain with the new citizens, rather than from absolute resistance to granting any privileges whatever. For towns were founded on a great scale throughout Europe, particularly on the borderlands, by the great proprietors: even in the old centers the habit of bequeathing land to a church or a monastery put the Church in control of large areas of urban land. Many of the new towns were frontier posts, as in Gascony and Wales; and they resembled such later foundations in America in that they served as a means of making a fresh start.

On the political side, I shall quote Tout, whose study of medieval town planning was a landmark in English in this field. "The political necessity for town making arose earlier than the economic need. In the humble beginnings of the new towns of the Middle Ages, military considerations are always paramount. A strong ruler conquered a district adjacent to his old dominions, or wished to defend his frontier against a neighboring enemy. He built rude fortresses, and encouraged his subjects to live in them, so that they might undertake the responsibility of their permanent defense." But since the serf, after all, had a permanent claim to the land he was tied to, it needed some extra bait to move him two or three hundred miles away: for the first time he had bargaining power, and the proprietor was forced to meet the demands of the new settler half-way.

By fighting, by bargaining, by outright purchase, or by some combination of these means, the towns won the right to hold a regular market, the right to be subject to a special market law, the right to coin money and establish weights and measures, the right of the citizens to be tried in their local courts and to bear arms in their own defense. All of these rights might or might not lead to complete local self-government, as in the great Hansa towns; but at all events it endowed the local community with many of the marks of what is now called in pious legal phrase a sovereign state. In general, member-ship in the urban community, even in such an insignificant little town as Lorris in France (which got no general right of self-government), meant freedom from forced payments and from military service, as well as freedom to sell one's possessions and go elsewhere. Citizen-ship gave its possessor mobility of person: indispensable for the rise of a trading class.

When a feudal lord desired to equip an army, join the Crusades, or indulge the new luxuries that seeped into Europe after the Cru-sades, he had only one economic source of wealth: his land. Under feudal custom he might not usually alienate the land or sell it off; but by dividing it up, by encouraging the growth of towns and found-ing new centers, he could increase his annual rents. Even though, with the customary long leases, rents might rise slowly for the original proprietor, his heirs would nevertheless in the course of time claim the unearned increment of the city's growth and pros-perity. The same desire for "ready money" eventually took hold of the religious orders which, by gift and inheritance, steadily came into possession of ever larger urban domains. One must not forget that even in London down to the twentieth century a few feudal pro-prietors, the Duke of Bedford, the Duke of Westminster, and the Crown, had title to the most heavily exploited areas. In Germanic law land was placed in a special category that set it apart from build-ings or personal property.

Almost as important as the actual rent in cities were special sources of urban income in which the proprietor of the land had a share: tolls at the bridges and the local market, customs imports and fines from courts, all of which multiplied as the town itself increased in population. Originally, in a pioneer town, it might be necessary to remit taxes to the newcomer provided he built a house: tax exemp-tion to promote housing is a very old dodge. But later, such entice-ments could be omitted: houses might be at a premium. As with all speculative enterprises, some towns might more than justify the land-lord's hopes; and others, like many of the fortified towns (bastides) in Southern France, might remain economically as well as socially

torpid. But town building itself was one of the major industrial enterprises of the early Middle Ages. Villages that succeeded in achieving the necessary privileges might hope to have their urban status
confirmed by productive enterprise, trade, and cultural wealth.

Now we can understand feudalism's ambivalent attitude toward
this movement. The free city was a new source of wealth, but the
challenging self-confidence and independence of the people who ral-
lied to the Commune was a threat to the entire feudal scheme. The
town concentrated man-power and economic power and the weapons
of defense; but it drained off man-power from the countryside, leaving a greater share of the oafs and dullards behind: eventually the
urban need for labor power would undermine the institution of serfdom. In Italy, the opportunities for civil life attracted the nobles to
the town; in the countries of Northern Europe, this class usually held
aloof, clinging to the boar hunt and the "brittling of the deer," the
open air life, and the smoky manorial hall, remaining themselves
more akin to the peasants they oppressed than to the townsmen they
freed. As urban occupations step by step drove out the rural ones that
had at first been pursued in the city with almost equal vigor, the antagonism widened between town and country. The city was an exclusive society; and every townsman was, in relation to the country-
folk, something of a snob, with such snobbery as only the upstart and
the *nouveau riche* can achieve. This fact was eventually to contribute
toward the undoing of urban freedom and self-government.

5: Domination of the Church

The ideas and institutions of medieval civilization concern us here
only as they affected the structure of cities and the development of
the organs of their cultural life. But unless one understands these
ideas, the purely physical shell must remain blank.

In Western Europe, after the fall of the Roman Empire, the one
powerful and universal institution was the Church. Membership in
that association was a constant source of life and well-being; and to
be cut off from its communion was so great a punishment that, until
the sixteenth century, even kings trembled before it. The fundamental political divisions of society, surviving all other ties and allegiances, were the parish and the diocese; the most universal form

of taxation was the tithe, which went to the support of the great estab-lishment of Rome. No small part of the economic life was devoted to the glorification of God, the support of the clergy and of those who waited on the clergy, and to the construction and maintenance of ecclesiastical buildings—cathedrals, churches, monasteries, hos-pitals, schools. By itself, the local church would often be a "museum of Christian faith," as well as a house of worship: the presence of a saintly hermit walled up in his cell near its doors, or even the bones and relics of such a saint, would be an attraction to the pious. Churches and monasteries that possessed such relics became the goal of a pilgrimage: the bones of Thomas à Becket at Canterbury, the Chalice Well at Glastonbury, where Joseph of Arimathea was sup-posed to have dropped the Holy Grail—these things drew men to cities no less than the possibility of trade.

In the early Middle Ages, even business and religion were in or-ganic relationship: so much so that business would copy the institu-tions of religion in the organization of its trading posts: the Hansa settlements were plainly fashioned on monastic lines, and exacted the same sort of narrow devotion. But at the end of the Middle Ages—and this is one of the signs of the end—even pious matters have a worldly tinge: one seeks security, no longer in the depths of the Church, but in a shrewd loan, backed by a note, and ultimately vouched for by the armed might of the state. "Faith" gives way to "credit."

Perhaps the most important civic effect of this other-worldly re-ligion, with its enfolding protection, its abstentions, its withdrawals, was that it universalized the cloister. Medieval culture, constantly "in retreat," had its *claustrum*, where the inner life could flourish. One withdrew at night: one withdrew on Sundays and on fast days: so long as the medieval complex was intact, a constant stream of disillusioned worldly men turned from the market place and the battlefield to seek the quiet contemplative round of the monastery. The ineffectiveness and costliness of artificial forms of illumination even prolonged the withdrawal of the night: and winter served, so to say, as the cloistered period of the year. This universal concentration on the inner life had its compensatory effect on the imagination: the vulgar daylight perceptions were illumined by the impassioned hal

lucinations and visions of dream: the figures of the inner eye were
as real as those that fell peripherally on the retina. And though protestantism in the sixteenth century brought in a distrust of the wanton
eye, it preserved for private use the habits of the cloister: prayer
and inner communion.

Today, as we shall see later, our architecture has passed from the
cave to the garden, from the monument to the dwelling house. But
in throwing open our buildings to the daylight and the outdoors, we
will forget, at our peril, the co-ordinate need for quiet, for darkness,
for inner privacy, for retreat. The cloister in both its public and
private form is a constant element in the life of men in cities. Without formal opportunities for isolation and contemplation, opportunities that require enclosed space, free from prying eyes and extraneous stimuli and secular interruptions, even the most externalized and
extraverted life must eventually suffer. The home without such cells
is but a barracks: the city that does not possess them is but a camp.
In the medieval city the spirit had organized shelters and accepted
forms of escape from worldly importunity. Today, the degradation
of the inner life is symbolized by the fact that the only place sacred
from interruption is the private toilet.

6: The Service of the Guild

The unattached person during the Middle Ages was one either
condemned to exile or doomed to death: if alive, he immediately
sought to attach himself, at least to a band of robbers. To exist, one
had to belong to an association: a household, a manor, a monastery,
a guild; there was no security except in association, and no freedom
that did not recognize the obligations of a corporate life. One lived
and died in the style of one's class and corporation.

Outside the Church, the most universal representative of corporate
life was the guild. When one first encounters the guild in England
in Anglo-Saxon times, it is primarily a religious fraternity under
the patronage of a saint, meeting for brotherly comfort and cheer,
insuring its members against the dire accidents of life and providing
a decent burial. It had features not unlike those of the later English
friendly society, or the Society of Freemasons, Elks, or Odd Fellows.
The guild never lost this religious color: it was a brotherhood

adapted to specific economic tasks but not wholly engrossed in them: the brothers ate and drank together on regular occasions: they formulated regulations for the conduct of their craft: they planned and paid for and enacted their parts in their mystery plays, for the edification of their fellow-townsmen: and they built chapels, endowed chantries, and founded schools.

Such unions and brotherhoods had existed among the urban craftsmen of the Roman empire; they lingered on in Byzantium; and though the connection remains obscure, perhaps the memory of them, like the memory of a far remoter event, Alexander's spectacular conquests, remained alive in popular myth, if not practice, during the Dark Ages. In Germany, among the first guilds of which there are records, apart from burial associations, are those of the weavers of Mainz in 1099, and the fishermen of Worms in 1106. If the growth of the merchant guild in general anticipated by half a century or so the growth of the craft guilds, it must be remembered that, except in international trade, the line between craftsmen and merchants was not closely drawn till the fourteenth century in the northern part of Europe. So that, during this period, craftsmen were, according to Gross, admitted to the merchant guilds and probably constituted the majority of the members.

The merchant guild was a general body, organizing and controlling the economic life of the town as a whole: regulating conditions of sale, protecting the consumer from extortion and the honest craftsman from unfair competition, protecting the traders of the town from the disorganization of their market by outside influences. The craft guild, on the other hand, was an association of masters working up their products and banded together to regulate production and establish standards of workmanship. In time, each of these institutions found its physical expression in the city: at first in modest houses or rented rooms, later in special guild halls and market halls that sometimes vied in magnificence with the town hall or the Cathedral. Ashley notes that the cost of these buildings was "one of the circumstances which led to and seemed to justify the demand for heavy entrance fees": this in turn led to the restriction of membership to the more wealthy members of the community. Not the first or last time in which the pomp of a great architectural shell has destroyed the creature who burdened himself with its creation.

Note the difference between the medieval community and that of the modern city. In industry, since the eighteenth century, it is the organization of the economic process that has taken definite corporate form in the factory, the business corporation, the chain store. Political associations, such as the Chamber of Commerce, the Manufacturer's Association, and the Trade Union for long had no integral part in the economic organization: they sprang up at the edges, included only a part of the population concerned, appeared belatedly; and in no case, not even that of the trade union, did they cover any large part of the cultural life of their members. In the medieval town, the actual organization of industry was simple: the primary fact was association. It was in fulfillment of its social purposes that the Guild became a health and old-age insurance society, a dramatic society, an educational society.

Once the economic motive isolated itself and became the all-engrossing end of the guild's activities, the institution decayed: a patriciate of wealthy masters rose within it to hand on their privileges to their sons and to work together to the exclusion and disadvantage of the poorer craftsmen and the growing proletariat. By the time the religious dissensions of the sixteenth century broke up the religious brotherhood itself, its co-operative economic nature had already been seriously undermined. The fat people were battening upon the lean people. In fact, the guild rises and falls with the medieval city: the guilds are the city in its economic aspect, and the city is the guilds in their social and political aspect.

The center of the municipality's activities was the town hall. In the beginning, according to Dehio, the town hall was a free-standing building in the market-place, usually of two stories, containing two halls, that on the lower floor being originally used for the finer wares that needed protection from the weather, not afforded by the booths that lined the market-place itself. The upper room would be used for the meeting of the mayor and the council, for the administration of justice, for the reception of ambassadors, and for periodic feasts and drinking bouts. The remains of the latter, incidentally, linger on in modern London, along with the ghost of the old Livery Companies, in the famous feast at the Guildhall that follows the annual election of the new Lord Mayor, and the Lord Mayor's parade.

In the town hall, too, toward the close of the Middle Ages, the leading families, drawn chiefly from the wealthier circle of the wholesale merchants, might—to the envy of the rest of the population—hold their dances and routs. It became, in fact, a sort of collective palace for the patriciate: hence it was often called a "theatrum" or playhouse. Here marriages would be celebrated with due pomp: a provision that has survived, with genuflections toward democracy, down to the present day: note the acknowledgment of the older order in the two special marriage chambers, first and second class, in the new Hilversum Town Hall in Holland. Thomas Mann, in Buddenbrooks, has given us a last faltering glimpse of that old life.

By membership in the municipality one escaped feudal dues: one assumed burgher responsibilities. Not merely was military service imposed on males who were not officers of the church, but the police force of the town was selected by rotation from among the burghers: the duty of watch and ward. In modern times, we have such service only for war or some sudden disaster: but in the medieval city it struck much closer home, and it is a serious question whether the leaving of such functions of protection to the care of a professional police has not weakened the sense of civic responsibility and done away with an effective means of education. To patrol one's city at night: to know its dark alleys under the moon, or with no light at all except one's lantern, to enjoy the companionship of the watch— was this not an early practical example of William James's Moral Equivalent of War: more useful, more humane, than any national scheme of military training? In assuming the policeman's duty of regulating traffic at crossings during the hours when children are going to and from school, the American school child is perhaps recovering some of that sense of responsibility which disappeared in the eighteenth century with the final collapse of the medieval municipality.

Here, as in most other departments, there existed great differences between the conditions in the eleventh century, still bare and constricted and precarious, and those in the sixteenth century, when wealth had poured into the city and heaped up. At the beginning the

Civic responsibility and interrelatedness)

city was striving as a social unit to establish its existence: the very insecurity promoted neighborly effort and even solidarity between the various ranks and occupations. They needed each other, and voluntary groups of neighbors formed, as Schevill has emphasized, very much as they would form today under pressure in a small New England village. When the privileges had been won, and when great disparities in riches appeared between the "successful" and the "unsuccessful," when wealth as well as station was inherited, then the walls between the classes became more important than the protective barrier that had once made the city one.

At the close of the Middle Ages wealthy individuals began to endow schools, build asylums for the aged and the orphaned, taking over functions once performed by the guild, precisely as the new despots were taking over for the country as a whole the political privileges of the free cities. But when one attempts to generalize the period as a whole, one may still echo Gross, deeply though he was imbued with a Victorian distrust of the closed corporation and the protective policies of the guild "Exclusive of the inhabitants of the privileged *sokes*, the . . . population was more homogeneous than that of towns existing at present; there were in the former fewer class distinctions, more equality of wealth, and more harmony of interests than in the latter." These are the words of one who was no admirer of the medieval economic system: they therefore carry double weight.

The social activities of the town shrank as the new capitalistic economy grew up. Outside the Church, only one institution survived from the old guilds and even increased its power and influence: perhaps the most important single institution in the medieval town. With an instinctive recognition of its importance, the name of this institution was originally the common term for all guilds in the twelfth century: universitas. Like other forms of craft guild, the aim of the university was to prepare for the practice of a vocation and to regulate the conditions under which its members performed their work. Each of the great schools that originally formed the university, jurisprudence, medicine, and theology, was professional in character: the general humanistic education that began to come in with the Renascence college, particularly in England, was an upper class graft on the original tree.

Beginning with Bologna in 1100, Paris in 1150, Cambridge in 1229, and Salamanca in 1243, the university lay down the basis of a co-operative organization of knowledge on an inter-regional basis: scholars flocked to these centers from every part of Europe, and in turn, the masters studied and taught at distant centers. The combination of scientific knowledge, political knowledge, and sacred knowledge, which the university offered in its faculties, had no exact parallel in any other culture. The germs of the university doubtless were latent in the Library-School at Alexandria or in the lecture system of the Roman municipalities: but in the university the organization of knowledge was elevated into an enduring system, which did not depend for its continuance upon any single group of texts: the system of knowledge was more important than the thing known. In the university the functions of storage, dissemination, and creative addition were adequately performed. As the cloister of the monastery might be termed a passive university, so the university might be called an active cloister: it made explicit, concrete, and systematic one of the enduring functions of the city: withdrawal from immediate practical responsibility and the critical reappraisal and renewal of the cultural heritage.

Here was a social invention of the first order: for this alone the medieval corporation would be important. And the very independence of the university from the standards of the market and the city, fostered the special sort of authority it exercised: the authority of verifiable truth, ratified by the methods of philosophic dialectic, factual scholarship, and scientific method, as these have been developed from period to period. The vices of such an organization may be many; and its services during the intervening centuries have not been of uniform value, for the university shares to this day the exclusiveness and the professional conservatism of the guild system, and it has sometimes put a brake upon discovery and creation, so that the major contributions to knowledge have often been made outside its walls. Nevertheless, the enlargement and transmission of the social heritage would have been inconceivable, during the last three centuries, without the agency of the university. As the Church ceased to be the repository of modern values, the university gradually took over the office. The university has become for the modern city what the Cathedral was for the predominantly religious culture of the Middle Ages.

7: Medieval Domesticity

In most aspects of medieval life, the closed corporation prevailed: even the city originally was so restricted. But compared to modern life, the medieval urban family was no private unit: it included, as part of the normal household, not only relatives by blood but a group of industrial workers as well as domestics whose relationship was that of secondary members of the family. Young men from the upper classes got their knowledge of the world by serving as attendants in a noble family; while apprentices and journeymen lived as members of the master craftsman's family. If marriage was perhaps deferred longer for men than today, the advantages of home life were not entirely lacking, even for the bachelor.

The workshop was a family: likewise the merchant's counting house. The members ate together at the same table, worked in the same rooms, slept in the same dormitory, joined in the family prayers, participated in the common amusements. Chastity and virginity were the ideal states; but even the prostitutes formed guilds, and in Hamburg, Wien, and Augsburg, for example, the brothels were under municipal protection. When one remembers that syphilis did not make its definite appearance, at least in malignant form, until the late fifteenth century, even prostitution constituted a smaller threat to domestic health and well-being than it did in the following centuries.

The intimate union of domesticity and labor, surviving now in the city only in petty shops or in the household of an artist, dictated the major arrangements within the dwelling house itself. Naturally, between the rude huts and stone enclosures of the tenth and eleventh centuries, and the elaborate merchant houses that were built from the thirteenth to the sixteenth century there was a difference as great as that between the seventeenth century dwelling and a New York apartment house today. Let us attempt, nevertheless, to single out the common factors in this development.

[TOP LEFT] Sixteenth century market-place: Antwerp. Primitive use of light for civic celebration. Contrast the occasional extravagances and festivities of the medieval order, to celebrate the arrival of an emperor, the birthday of a saint, the victory of an army, with the permanent order of illumination used in Broadway or Piccadilly Circus. Note the size and scale of the Town Hall, symbol of the relative importance of civic authority in the towns of the lowlands: the Cloth Hall at Ypres shows the equivalent might and majesty of the textile guilds. Where feudal or royal power dominated, as in Edinburgh or Durham, the castle would bulk largest. In London, however, with its small guildhall and big Tower the symbolism is not quite so accurate.

[TOP RIGHT] Children at play in the open spaces of a Dutch city: rolling hoops, whipping tops, walking on stilts, flying kites. The wiping out of the playfields and archery butts of the medieval order was one of the prime sins of overcrowding in the big capitals and other overcrowded towns. The paling fence in the background is a reminder of the frequent use of wood even in the Low Countries, where most of it was imported from the Baltic forests.

[MIDDLE] Tournament in München, with the Cathedral on the left. The survival of feudal practices in the medieval town: due partly to the usually continued maintenance of the castle by the lord and his retainers. Such spectacles, in contrast with the guilds' plays and pageants, were primarily aristocratic. The market-place had many uses: it served as agora, acropolis, theater and stadium all in one. The print is dated 1568.

[BOTTOM] Florence. Holy procession, winding about the streets and market places, finally to enter the Cathedral for the culminating ceremony. The slow irregular order of the procession contrasts with the brisk mechanical order of the march: the difference between them is that between two civilizations, and this fact is recorded in the whole design of the city. In the medieval city, of the less geometric type of plan, the tortuous and the unexpected, infinite variety without spatial progression, are characteristics of design. In the later baroque city visual axes and straight lines are urban counterparts of mechanical movement toward a fixed goal: the street to the right of the Campanile shows the new mutation. In the present procession note the relative absence of lookers-on: ritual, like drama in the medieval city, is arranged for participants, who both see and do.

[UPPER LEFT] Fuggerei in Augsburg: sixteenth century housing foundation for the deserving poor: often built by the richer guilds, in this case the gift of an individual capitalist, Jacob Fugger. The houses are two rooms deep, well-lighted, built in parallel rows: an early example of Zeilenbau. The Fuggerei forms a unified neighborhood unit with a handsome little chapel of its own. Water is still piped only to the fountains. Housing standards here compare favorably with those of present day in all but the best workers' housing.

[UPPER RIGHT] High Street in Stamford, Lincolnshire: good vernacular tradition of sixteenth and seventeenth century: strong, clean, light and spacious: the wide windows across the whole front are typical of this period: see the Antwerp market-place on Plate 3.

[MIDDLE LEFT] Magdalen College, Oxford: built 1474-81. Open type of planning around quadrangle, as in many monasteries, housing foundations, and as in the various Inns of Court in London. Such islands, enclosed by walls and buildings, sometimes entered by a court from the street, expressed that need for solitude, protection, sanctuary, which was a formative factor in medieval culture: a type of order that was foreign to the unbalanced extraverted life of the Renascence. But in organic adaptation to modern needs, a not dissimilar type of planning, with each function rationally ordered in appropriate zones surrounded by open spaces, has come in with the twentieth century: see Plates 27 to 32.

[MIDDLE RIGHT] Market-place in Bremen: late sixteenth century buildings still excellently preserved. The temporary structures of the periodic market had its equivalent in the temporary structures used for tournaments, plays, festivals. Contrary to the usual idée fixe of the Middle Ages, the early part of this period was more fluid and mobile than the present age, with its vast mass of fixed utilities, frozen as capital investments.

[BOTTOM LEFT] The Shambles in York: row of shops with overhanging fronts. The open shop front demanded protection against the inclement weather: hence the narrow street, the deliberately broken pattern of streets—to break the force of the wind—and even perhaps the overhangs, which served partly as protective arcade where complete arcades were not provided.

[BOTTOM MIDDLE] Medieval town garden. The checkerboard layout was typical of medieval garden plans: they contradict the notion of medieval order as necessarily capricious or irregular. Bathing pools were not uncommon and gardens within the walls were universal: see Plate 15.

[BOTTOM RIGHT] Spire of the Cathedral at Ulm. Though not erected till the nineteenth century the design of this lofty structure was made when the rest of the Cathedral was built: its final embodiment marks that essential continuity with their medieval past, so characteristic of German cities.

Houses were usually built in rows around the perimeter of their rear gardens: sometimes in large blocks they formed inner courts, with a private green, reached through a single gateway on the street. Free-standing houses, unduly exposed to the elements, wasteful of the land on each side, were relatively scarce: even farmhouses would form part of a solid block that included the stables, barns, granaries. The materials for the houses came out of the local soil and they varied with the region: now wattle and daub, now stone or brick. Their type depended upon economic factors, and the wider use of half timber and stucco after the fourteenth century arose partly out of the need for building cheap houses for the rising proletariat. The earliest houses would have small window openings, with shutters to keep out the weather; the later, permanent windows of oiled cloth or paper. In the fifteenth century glass, hitherto used mainly for public buildings, became more frequent: at first only in the upper part of the window. The glass would be heavy, irregular, feebly transparent; and the leads that held it would further reduce the amount of light. By the sixteenth century, however, glass had become cheap and fashionable. The popular saying in England about Hardwick Hall—"more glass than wall"—was equally true of the burgher houses. In North Germany and England a broad bank of window would extend across the whole house at each story, front and rear, thus making up in effect for the tendency to deepen the house. The effort of governments in the eighteenth century to raise revenue by means of window taxes partly arrested this popular development: an atrocious stupidity. Result: the sixteenth century house is often closer to modern requirements for light and air than the common run of Victorian mansions.

Heating arrangements steadily improved. This fact, plus the increased use of distilled liquors, as fortification against inclement weather, partly accounts for the outburst of human energy in the North: winter gradually ceased to be a period of stupefied hibernation. The open hearth in the middle of the floor, scarcely as effective as the arrangements in an Indian tepee, gave way to the fireplace and the chimney. Fireproofing went along with this development; for originally, lacking proper materials, the poorer burghers were tempted to experiment with wooden chimneys: an unduly optimistic practice repeated in the early settlement of New England. In 1276 Lübeck passed an ordinance enforcing the use of fireproof roofing and the fireproof party wall; and in London, after the severe fire of 1189, special privileges were given to people building in stone and tile; while in 1212 thatched roofs were ordered to be whitewashed, the better to resist fire.

As for the plan of the house, it varied with the region and the century; yet certain features remained common. Viollet-le-Duc has shown us the ground plan of a French house, with a shop on the ground floor connected by an open gallery with the kitchen in the rear. The two formed a court, where the well occupied a corner. There was a chimney in the kitchen and in the living room or *grande salle* above the shop: from the latter there is access to the dormitories above. Heyne's plan of an old house in Nürnberg is not essentially different; but, as in the surviving houses from the seventeenth century, there are more interior rooms, a kitchen and a smaller room on the ground floor, a heatable room above the kitchen, and a number of chambers, with a toilet on the second floor directly above that on the first.

The only form of modern hallway was the open gallery: this was a common feature in houses not built around a closed court. It survived in the design of inns, where a means of circulation was specially necessary, and the internal hall, because of the absence of artificial light, was not an attractive solution. The main outlines of this type of house lasted right down through the seventeenth century, even later. But as one went downward in the economic scale, arrangements would be less differentiated and the space more constricted: the one room apartment, still common among the poor in many countries, possibly had its origin in the more industrialized cities of the late Middle Ages.

The fact that the burgher house served as workshop, store, and counting house prevented any zoning between these functions. The competition for space between the domestic and the working quarters, as business grew and the scale of production expanded, was also perhaps responsible for encroachment over the original back gardens by sheds, storage bins, and special workshops. Mass production and the concentration of looms in great sheds was known in

Flanders in the fourteenth century, and operations like fulling, mill-ing, glassmaking, and iron-making required a more isolated type of workshop: in these industries came the earliest break between living and working. But at first the family pattern dominated industry, just as it dominated the organization of the Benedictine monastery. Sur-vivals of this regime lingered on in every European city: the habit of "living in" long retained by London drapers, with the men and the women divided into dormitories, was a typical holdover from the Middle Ages.

In the disposition and specialization of rooms in the Middle Ages the ways of the aristocracy filtered down but slowly to the rest of the population. Comforts that were enjoyed by lords and ladies alone in the thirteenth century did not become popular customs until the seventeenth or even the nineteenth century. The first radical change, which was to destroy the form of the medieval dwelling house, was the development of a sense of privacy. This meant, in effect, with-drawal at will from the common life and the common interests of one's associates. Privacy in sleep: privacy in eating: privacy in religious and social ritual: finally privacy in thought. In 1362 Langland, in Piers Plowman, chided the tendency of the Lord and Lady to withdraw from the common hall for private meals and for private entertainment. He must have foreseen the end of that re-ciprocal social relation between the stationary upper and lower ranks of the feudal regime: a relation that had mitigated its oppressions. The desire for privacy marked the beginning of that new alignment of classes which was to usher in the merciless class-competition and individual self-assertion of a later day. In the castles of the period one notes the existence, not merely of a private bedroom for the noble owners: one also notes the private toilet, perched over the moat: the first hint of the twentieth century arrangement for a private toilet. (Monasteries, however, had long had collective latrines in separate buildings.)

The separation of the kitchen from the dining room is not char-acteristic, probably, of the majority of the population in any country today. It had taken place in the monastery because of the scale of the preparations, and it was copied eventually in the manorial hall and the fine town house. But the common quarters offered this incentive to social living: they alone were usually heated. That the medieval house was cold in winter perhaps accounts for the development of inner rooms, insulated from the outer walls by air. Yet the cold could not have been unendurable, or else people in the Middle Ages would have worn nightdresses, instead of "going to their naked bed," as numberless illustrations depict them. Privacy in bed came first in Italy, among the upper classes; but the desire for it developed slowly; even in the seventeenth century maidservants often slept in trundle beds at the foot of that of their master and mistress.

Until the curtained bed was invented, sexual intercourse must have taken place for the most part under cover, and whether the bed was curtained or not, in darkness. Privacy in bed preceded the private bedroom; for even in seventeenth century engravings of upper middle class life, and in France, a country of refinement, the bed still often occupies part of the living room. Under these circumstances, the erotic ritual must have been short and almost secretive, with little preliminary stirring through eye or voice or free movement: it had its intense seasons, especially spring; but the late medieval astrological calendars, which depict this awakening, show the lovers having intercourse in the open with their clothes on. In short, erotic passion was more attractive in the garden and the wood, despite stubble or prickly stems or insects, than it was in the house, on a mattress whose stale straw or down was never quite free from musty dampness. For lovers in the medieval house the winter months must have been a large wet blanket. An endless succession of pregnancies punctuated the married lives of all but barren women, and brought many of them to early graves. No wonder virginity figured as the ideal state.

To sum up the medieval dwelling house, one may say that it was characterized by lack of differentiated space and differentiated function. In the cities, however, this lack of internal differentiation was offset by a completer development of domestic functions in public institutions. Though the house might lack a private bake-oven, there was a public one in the baker's or the cook-shop. Though it might lack a private bathroom, there was a municipal bath-house. Though it might lack facilities for isolating and nursing a diseased member, there were numerous public hospitals. And though lovers might lack a private bedroom, they could "lie between the acres of the rye," just outside the city's walls. Plainly, the medieval house had scarcely an inkling of the two important domestic requirements of the present day: privacy and comfort. And the tendency in the late Middle Ages to deepen the house, chiefly under pressure of rising ground rents, progressively deprived those who worked most steadily indoors, the mother, the domestics, the children, of the necessary air and light which dwellers in much cruder country hovels could have. Mark this paradox of "prosperity." As long as conditions were rude—when people lived in the open, pissed freely in the garden or the street, bought and sold outdoors, opened their shutters and let in full sunlight—the defects of the house were far less serious than they were under a more refined regime.

It was no lack of care and concern for children that made the infant mortality records so black, so far as we may estimate them: the cradle, the hobby horse, and even the toddler, for the child who had not yet learned to walk, are depicted in sixteenth century prints: these cherubs were treated with love. But the domestic environment became increasingly defective; and such diseases as are spread through either contact or respiration must have had a maximum opportunity for sweeping through the family in the late medieval house. The urban dwelling was indeed perhaps the weakest link in medieval sanitary arrangements; for in other respects, the standards were far more adequate than most Victorian commentators—and those who blindly repeat their mistakes—believed.

8: Hygiene and Sanitation

What gave the early medieval town a sound basis for health was the fact that, though surrounded with a wall, it was still part of the open country. Until the fourteenth century, these two types of environment were scarcely differentiated. The village had not been devoted purely to agriculture since handicraft, at the time of the English Domesday Book, had flourished there; nor were the towns, for centuries to come, wholly industrial: a good part of the population had private gardens and practiced rural occupations, just as they did in the typical small American town up to about 1870. At harvest time, the population of the town would swarm out into the country, as the slum dwellers of the East End still migrate to Kent for the hop-picking. One has only to read the household recipes of the Goodman of Paris, who was of the well-to-do merchant order, to see how the more prosperous burghers kept a leg firmly planted in each world. Near the city, the fowler and the rabbit hunter could go after game. Fitz-Stephens noted that the citizens of London had the right of hunting in Middlesex, Herefordshire, the Chiltern Hundreds, and part of Kent. And in the streams by the city, fishing was diligently pursued: not merely on the coast but inland. Augsburg, for example, was noted for its trout; until 1643 many of the city officials took their pay in trout.

This strong rural influence can be marked on the early city plans; all but a handful of medieval towns were closer to what we should now call a village or a small country town than a city: "greatness" did not mean a big population or a spreading territory. In the original towns, with the exception of a few that kept to original Roman foundations or were constricted by topographical obstacles, ample gardens spread in the rear of the houses. The size of the medieval houseblock was not standardized; but in general a hundred-foot depth was common and a fifty-foot width was not unusual. Since it was customary to build row houses, for cheapness, for compactness, and above all, perhaps, for maximum protection against cold, this would mean that in some cities houses originally would show their long side to the street, as they still do at Grantham, for example, in England: a type of planning that did not come back till the development of modern workers' housing estates in England. Gardens and orchards, sometimes fields and pastures, existed within the city, as well as in the "suburb" outside: endless illustrations and plans as late as the seventeenth century prove how universal these open spaces were. Goethe describes such a fine rear-garden, so favorable to a genial family life, in his Dichtung und Wahrheit. Medieval people were used to outdoor living: they had shooting grounds and bowling grounds and tossed the ball and kicked the football and ran races and practiced archery. When the open spaces filled up, Botero notes, Francis I provided a meadow near the river for the scholars of the University of Paris. The spirit of this hearty informal play is carried on, even today, in the merriest of all urban parks, the Jardin du Luxembourg.

In sum: as far as usable open spaces go, the medieval city had at its foundation and through most of its existence a far higher standard for the mass of the population than *any later form of town*, down to the first romantic suburbs of the nineteenth century.

To form a notion of medieval standards of open space in building one must turn to such surviving semi-public buildings as the Inns of Court in London, the colleges at Oxford or Cambridge, or to the Homes for the Aged, such as one still finds in Holland. One must not look at the narrow streets between the houses without remembering the open green, or the neatly chequered gardens, that usually stretched behind. I lay emphasis on the rural character of the medieval town for two reasons: first, because a false notion about its dinginess and overcrowding has grown up, which has no foundation at all in most cities except the notorious fact of *post*-medieval overcrowding; and second, because the existence of these open spaces shows that sanitary arrangements were not necessarily as offensive as they have been pictured, nor vile smells as uniformly ubiquitous. How the original open spaces got built over one may learn in a typical instance from Stow. The Parish church of St. Mary Bow needed room in the churchyard for the burial of the dead, but was by the middle of the fifteenth century hemmed in with houses. John Rotham, in his will, gave a certain garden in Hosier's Lane to be a churchyard. After a hundred years the overcrowded capital could not even afford open spaces for the dead: so this plot was built on. Garden: graveyard: houseplot: finally, in the seventeenth century, the back-garden might be built over, too—and the resultant insanitary mass would then be regarded by the hopeful nineteenth century investigator as "typical medieval" overcrowding.

Up to a generation ago American country towns existed in which neither the streets nor the privies were much more advanced, technically, than they were in the early Middle Ages. But they were neither as foul nor as dangerous to health as might be fancied, just because of the openness of their layout. The point is that crude sanitation is not necessarily bad sanitation: indeed, a medieval farmhouse, in which the common dung pile served as domestic privy, was not as inimical to health, probably, as the pre-Pasteur town of the nineteenth century, blessed with refined water closets—and a water supply drawn from the same river into which the sewage of the town above was emptied. There is no proof that visitations of the plague were much worse in the medieval town than in the American or European town of the first half of the nineteenth century; nor is there sufficient proof that poor sanitary arrangements alone were responsible for the origin or the virulence of medieval epidemics. Consider the death rate from influenza in 1918 in countries entirely outside the war-zone, or from poliomyelitis in its recurrent waves today. If the medieval expectation of life was low, a defective diet, especially a defective winter diet, must perhaps take as large a share of the blame as the defective disposal of fecal matter.

As the cities increased in size and density of population, their rural base was undermined and new sanitary difficulties arose out of the very fact of density. Not alone the density of the living but the congestion of the dead, who were buried for convenience and piety, not outside the city's walls, but in the vaults or graveyards of the parish churches. By the seventeenth century the overcrowded conditions here constituted a serious sanitary menace, through seepage into the water supply; and in a few cosmopolitan centers, like Paris or London, this may have been true at an earlier date. But in the twelfth and thirteenth centuries, these breeding places for disease were no more congested than the city itself. And as early as the sixteenth century special provisions were made toward sanitary control and decency in the matter of excrement: thus Stow mentions an ordinance which commands that "no man shall bury any dung or goung within the liberties of the city" nor "carry any ordure till after nine-o'clock in the night," that is, after bedtime.

On these matters, as Professor Thorndike points out, evidence favorable to many medieval cities is indisputable. He quotes Bruni's eulogy of Florence in which Bruni remarks that "some towns are so dirty that whatever filth is made during the night is placed in the morning before men's eyes to be trodden underfoot, 'than which it is impossible to imagine anything fouler. For even if there are thousands there, inexhaustible wealth, infinite multitude of people, yet will I condemn so foul a city and never think much of it.'" Similarly, Leland, a later observer, in his journeys about England makes special mention of the dirt whenever he comes across it: it is rare enough to deserve comment. As long as the open spaces and gardens remained, as long as the countryside was easily accessible to the dung-farmer, the normal smells of the medieval town were not more offensive than those of the farmyard; nor were the evils overwhelming.

What applies to human excreta applies also to garbage. Leftovers were eaten by the dogs, the chickens, and the pigs, which acted as general town scavengers. The ban on pigs and the general introduction of paving comes in about the same time: by the sixteenth century, in well-managed towns that had made provisions for street cleaning, there was also a ban upon keeping pigs in any part of the town, even in the gardens behind the houses. But in the early days the pig was an active member of the local Board of Health. Like a great many medieval institutions the pig lingered on in more backward centers till the middle of the nineteenth century: in Manchester, for example, and in New York, the great world emporium.

Non-edible waste was doubtless harder to dispose of: ashes, tannery offal, the scourings of wool: but certainly there was less of it than in the modern city: tins, iron, broken glass and paper did not form such gigantic heaps. Here again, a few overgrown centers doubtless polluted their streams even in the Middle Ages; but big towns like Paris and London were quite exceptional places; and in the run of medieval towns the damage was insignificant. In the main, the waste materials were organic ones, which decomposed and mingled with the earth; and in these flimsy nests of buildings, particularly in the earlier centuries, there would be outbreaks of fire, famous in the annals of almost every town, which subjected whole streets and quarters to the most powerful of germicidal agents. It was the plating of the medieval town in imperishable materials and the heaping up of the living in smaller quarters, with more meager open spaces, that created the filthy conditions that met the eye in the seventeenth and eighteenth centuries. The worst conditions prevailed when the city had lost its natural rural base, and had not yet created an adequate mechanical substitute.

Two other matters closely connected with hygiene remain to be discussed: the bath and the drinking water supply. Even as early as the thirteenth century the private bath made its appearance: sometimes with a dressing room, as we learn from a sixteenth century Nürnberg merchant's household book. In 1417, indeed, hot baths in private houses were specially authorized by the City of London. If anything were needed to establish the medieval attitude toward cleanliness the ritual of the public bath should be sufficient. Bathhouses were characteristic institutions in every city, and they could be found in every quarter: complaint was even made by Guarinonius that children and young girls from ten to eighteen years of age ran shamelessly naked through the streets to the bathing establishment. Bathing was a family enjoyment. These bath-houses would sometimes be run by private individuals; more usually, perhaps, by the municipality. In Riga as early as the thirteenth century bath-houses are mentioned, according to von Below; in the fourteenth century there were 7 such houses in Würzburg; and at the end of the Middle Ages there were 11 in Ulm, 12 in Nürnberg, 15 in Frankfurt-am-Main, 17 in Augsburg, and 29 in Wien. Frankfurt had 29 bath-house keepers as early as 1387. So widespread was bathing in the Middle Ages that the bath even spread as a custom back into the country districts, whose inhabitants had been reproached by the writers of the early Fabliaux as filthy swine. What is essentially the medieval bath lingers in the Russian or Finnish village today.

Bathing in the open, in a pool in the garden or by a stream in the summer time of course remained in practice. Public baths however were for sweating and steaming and thorough cleanliness: it was customary to take such a purging of the epidermis at least every fortnight. In time, the bath-house came to serve again as it had in Roman times; it was a place where people met for sociability, as Dürer plainly shows in one of his prints, a place where people gossiped and ate food, as well as attended to the more serious business of being cupped for pains or inflammatory conditions. As family life in the late medieval town deteriorated, the bath-houses became the resort of loose women, looking for game, and of lecherous men, looking for sensual gratification: so that the medieval word for bath-house, namely, stew, comes down to us in English as a synonym for brothel: indeed, it is so used as early as Piers Plowman.

The provision of drinking water was also a collective function of the town. First the guarding of a brook or spring: the provision of a fountain in the public square and of other fountains in the local quarters: sometimes within the block, sometimes on the street. As numbers increased, it was necessary to find new sources and distribute old ones over a wider territory. In 1236 a patent for a leaden conduit to convey water from Tyborne Brook to the City of London was granted; pipes were laid in Zittau in 1374; and in Breslau in 1479 water was pumped from the river and conducted by pipes through the city—probably such wooden pipes as are illustrated in Bauer's De Re Metallica, and were used, on Manhattan Island for example, down to the nineteenth century. As late as the fifteenth century the provision of water conduits in London was a matter for private philanthropy, like hospitals or almshouses.

The author of the Maison Rustique warns his readers against the use of lead pipes: the dangers of lead poisoning had presumably been noted. As with baths, the piping of water to fountains, whence it was distributed by hand to the houses, was not as convenient as the private water supply that began to trickle in, all too literally, in the seventeenth century. But to offset this, it satisfied two important functions that tended to disappear with the reign of greater mechanical efficiency—art, in the shape of the handsome fountains that decorated the squares and public places of the medieval city, and sociability, the occasion for meeting and gossiping as people waited their turn around the village pump. The pump, no less than the tap-room, served as local newspaper for the quarter.

The diffused local water supply of the medieval town was, finally, a source of strength in defense. When, in the seventeenth century, the growing cities were forced to seek outside their fortifications for water, they put themselves at the mercy of an army that could command the open country. But in the big cities, the population grew more rapidly than the technical means and the capital necessary to capture sufficient water for its inhabitants: this partly accounts for the loss of cleanly habits and for the water famines that overtook the seventeenth century capitals, and made the later development of the industrial town so vile.

In its remedial measures for health, the medieval town was far in advance of its contemptuous Victorian successor. The holy orders founded hospitals in almost every town: there would be at least two in most German towns, one for lepers and one for other types of disease, according to Heil; while in "big" cities, such as Breslau, with its 30,000 population in the fifteenth century, there would be as many as fifteen, or one for every two thousand inhabitants. Plainly cases that in more recent times would have been treated at home must at this earlier period have had systematic hospital care: a fact which mitigated the lack of domestic facilities.

Municipal physicians made their appearance in the fourteenth century: in Konstanz as early as 1312. In Venice a permanent health magistracy was created in 1485, to which in 1556 inspection and enforcement machinery were added which long served as a model to the rest of Europe. Contagious diseases, incidentally, were usually isolated outside city walls: the value of isolation wards, with separate toilets, had long been established by the better-equipped monasteries. The establishment of quarantine, for people passing in and out of cities from foreign parts, was one of the major innovations of medieval medicine. Much as travelers hated it, it was based on sound empiric observation, and the gradual eradication of leprosy in Europe, thanks to the same policy of isolation, was nothing less than a triumph.

In the main, then, the medieval town was not merely a vital social environment: it was likewise adequate, at least to a greater degree than one would gather from its decayed remains, on the biological side. There were smoky rooms to endure; but there was also perfume in the garden behind the burgher's house: the fragrant flowers and the savory herbs were widely cultivated. There was the smell of the barnyard in the street, diminishing in the sixteenth century, except for the growing presence of horses: but there would also be the odor of flowering orchards in the spring, or the scent of the new mown hay, floating across the fields in early summer. Though cockneys may wrinkle their noses at this combination of odors, no lover of the country will be put off by the smell of horse-dung or cow-dung, even though mingled occasionally with that of human excrement: is the reek of gasoline exhaust, the sour smell of a subway crowd, the pervasive odor of a garbage dump, or the chlorinated rankness of a public lavatory more gratifying? Even in the matter of smells, sweet-ness is not entirely on the side of the modern city.

As for the eye and ear, there is no doubt where the balance of ad-vantage goes: the majority of medieval towns were infinitely superior to those erected during the last century. One awoke in the medieval town to the crowing of the cock, the chirping of birds nesting under the eaves, or to the tolling of the hours in the monastery on the out-skirts, perhaps to the chime of bells in the new bell-tower. Song rose easily on the lips, from the plain chant of the monks to the refrains of the ballad singer in the market place, or that of the apprentice and the house-maid at work. As late as the seventeenth century, the ability to hold a part in a domestic choral song was rated by Pepys as an indispensable quality in a new maid. There were work songs, distinct for each craft, often composed to the rhythmic tapping or hammering of the craftsman himself. Fitz-Stephens reported in the twelfth century that the sound of the water mill was a pleasant one amid the green fields of London. At night there would be complete silence, but for the stirring of animals and the calling of the hours by the town watch. Deep sleep was possible in the medieval town, untainted by either human or mechanical noises.

If the ear was stirred, the eye was even more deeply delighted. The craftsman who had walked through the fields and woods on holiday, came back to his stone-carving or his wood-working with a rich harvest of impressions to be transferred to his work. The build-ings, so far from being "quaint," were as bright and clean as a medieval illumination, often covered with whitewash, so that all the colors of the image makers in paint or glass or polychromed wood would dance on the walls, even as the shadows quivered like sprays of lilac on the façades of the more richly carved buildings. (Patina and picturesqueness were the results of time's oxidation: not original attributes of the architecture.) Common men thought and felt in images, far more than in the verbal abstractions used by scholars: esthetic discipline might lack a name, but its fruit were everywhere visible. Did not the citizens of Florence vote as to the type of column that was to be used on the Cathedral? Image makers carved statues, painted triptychs, decorated the walls of the cathe-dral, the guild hall, the town hall, the burgher's house: color and design were everywhere the normal accompaniment of the practical daily tasks. There was visual excitement in the array of goods in the open market: velvets and brocades, copper and shining steel, tooled leather and brilliant glass, to say nothing of foods arranged in their panniers under the open sky. Wander around the survivals of these medieval markets today. Whether they be as drab as the Jews' Market in Whitechapel, or as spacious as that on the Plain Palais at Geneva, they still have some of the excitement of their medieval prototypes.

This daily education of the senses is the elemental groundwork of all higher forms of education: when it exists in daily life, a community may spare itself the burden of arranging courses in art appreciation. Where such an environment is lacking, even the purely rational and signific processes are half-starved: verbal mastery cannot make up for sensory malnutrition. If this is a key, as Mme. Montessori discovered, to the first stages of a child's education, it continues to be true even at a later period: the city has a more constant effect than the formal school. Life flourishes in this dilation of the senses: without it, the beat of the pulse is slower, the tone of the muscles is lower, the posture lacks confidence, the finer discriminations of eye and touch are lacking, perhaps the will-to-live itself is defeated. To starve the eye, the ear, the skin, is just as much to court death as to withhold food from the stomach. Though diet was often meager in the Middle Ages, though the religious often imposed abstentions upon themselves in fasts and penances, even the most ascetic could not wholly close his eye to beauty: the town itself was an omnipresent work of art; and the very clothes of its citizens on festival days were like a flower garden in bloom.

9: Principles of Medieval Town Planning

The layout of the medieval town followed the same general patterns as the village. There were street villages and street towns: there were crossroads villages and crossroads towns; there were circular villages and circular towns; and finally, there were irregularly accreted villages and towns of the same apparently aimless and accidental pattern.

The common mistake of supposing that the last type is typically medieval rests upon a misreading of the facts; while the correspond-ing belief, uttered by Spengler, that the rectangular city pattern is purely a product of the final stage of the hardening of culture into civilization, or a special example of soulless mechanization par-ticularly marked by the appearance of the American city, is even more willfully fallacious.

At the very beginning of the Middle Ages one discovers the reg-ular, geometrical type of plan, with the rectangle as the basis of subdivision: even the monastery of St. Gall in the ninth century ex-hibited in its ground plan and disposition of buildings the use of straight lines and right angles. This order preceded both military colonization and the development of capitalistic forms of regularity. In general, one may say that a geometric layout is more character-istic of freshly founded towns, and that the irregular layouts, with blocks of different dimensions, with varied perimeters, were a prod-uct of slower growth and less systematic settlement. But the distinc-tion does not always hold.

Sometimes the use of the rectangular block unit is coupled with a rectangular outline for the city as a whole: see Montpazier in South-ern France. Sometimes this pattern exists within a circular bound-ing wall; and sometimes, as in Montségur, a rectangular unit is in-telligently modified so as to adapt it to the contours and natural boundaries of the site. Rectangular platting has been subject to a vast amount of superficial interpretation, particularly by writers who fail to note that the pattern may in fact be as rural in origin as the windings of the most capricious cowpath. In all probability, the layout of fields in rectangular strips or plots is a product of plow culture on land of low relief: indeed the Etruscan priest used to define the boundaries of the rectangular Etruscan town by means of a plow. Or still earlier, the rectangular town may have grown out of the use of piles and long horizontal wooden beams in lake villages.

Confusion has arisen here because of a failure to grasp the dif-ference, familiar to students of biology, between homologous and analogous forms. A similar form does not necessarily have a similar significance in a different culture; and so, too, similar functions may have quite different forms. Thus the rectangle meant one thing to an Etruscan priest, another to Hippodamus, the planner of the Piraeus, a third to the Roman legionary, spading up his camp for the night, and a fourth to the City Plan Commissioners of New York in 1811. To the first, the rectangle might symbolize cosmic law: to the last it simply meant the maximum possibilities for real estate speculation.

There is indeed a certain ground for thinking of medieval plans as more irregular than most modern plans: this was because uneven sites were more frequently utilized, since they had advantages in fortification and defense. Medieval builders had no *a priori* love for symmetry as such: it was simpler to follow nature's contours than to attempt to grade them down or even them up. Internal traffic for wheeled vehicles made no demands for regular streets; as long as water came from wells and springs, a steep rocky site might be as satisfactory as a low-lying one. (Note how the drumlins of Boston were occupied and platted long before the Back Bay Fens were drained and captured for residence.) Indeed, it is by its persistent power of adaptation to site and to practical needs that the medieval town presented such multiform examples of individuality: the planner made use of the irregular, the accidental, the unexpected; and by the same token, he was not averse to symmetry and regularity when, as in the frontier towns, the plan could be laid out in a single step on fresh land. Many of the surviving irregularities on medieval plans are due to streams that have been covered over, trees that have been cut down, old balks that once defined rural fields.

Whether adaptive or geometrical, of slow growth or quick development, on an old Roman foundation, like Köln or on an entirely new site like Lübeck or Salisbury, the determining elements in the medieval town are the bounding wall, and the central open space where the principal church is usually located, and where the town hall, the guild hall, the market and the inns, finally cluster. The wall, with its outside moat, both defines and symbolizes the town: it made it an island. To retreat, to wall off a secure place, to interpose armor between the naked flesh and the sword, or a dogma between doubt and the harsh facts of life—all these actions were conceived and performed in the same style. This was not a world of wide horizons, shadowy borderlands, clouds and mist, uncharted seas and giddy distances. It was a world of sharp definitions: what could not be paced and measured, defined and classified, immediately dropped into the realm of the mythological. Walls of custom bounded the economic classes and kept them in their place: virtue was white: vice was black. To be unclassed, unbounded, was essentially to be defenseless. Philosophical nominalism, which challenged the objective reality of classes, was as destructive to the medieval conception of the world as cannonballs proved to be to the old palisades and walls of the city: no wonder the Church bristled at the heresy.

Though the wall existed for military defense and the main ways of the city were usually planned to facilitate rallying to the main gates, the psychological import of the wall must not be forgotten. One was either in or out of the city; one belonged or one did not belong. When the town gates were locked at sundown, and the portcullis was drawn, the city was insulated from the outside world. As in a ship, the wall helped create a feeling of unity between the inhabitants: in a siege or a famine the morality of the shipwreck— share-and-share-alike—developed easily. But the wall also served to build up a fatal sense of insularity: all the more because of the absence of roads and quick means of communication between cities.

Usually near the center of the city, both for practical reasons of assembly and for symbolic reasons, was the principal church or cathedral: here the main routes might converge, although they rarely crossed or attempted to form a continuous route: the market place was not a device for attracting or pumping out fast-moving traffic. In the shadow of the church, sometimes hugging its walls for protection, the regular market takes place: this square forms an agora and an acropolis in one. Sometimes the chief buildings in the market place form conspicuous islands, with access on all sides; sometimes they are directly attached to the neighboring houses: but it is highly unusual to find them surrounded on four sides by a wide open plaza, as the "improvers" of the nineteenth century transformed them.

The central position of the church or cathedral is the key to the layout of the medieval city: within its narrow area its towers, or the shadows they throw, are visible from every point, and the difference in size between its towering walls and the little houses that huddle at the base is a symbol of the relation between sacred and profane affairs. When one finds the market square spreading beside the Cathedral one must not be tempted to assign to these institutions the same values they have today: it was the first that was occasional, and the second whose services were regular. The market place grows up by the church because it is there that the citizens most frequently assemble. It was in the church, in the early days, that the city's treasury was stored; and it was in the church, sometimes behind the High Altar, that deeds were deposited for safekeeping; because of its central location, in quarter or city, the arms might even be kept in the church. In fact, one must think of the early church as what one would now call in America a community center building: not too holy to serve as a dining hall for great public festivals.

The scale of the market place is not directly determined by either the height of the main buildings or the size of the city: it is rather adapted to marketing and public ceremony, for it is on the porch of the cathedral that the miracle plays were enacted: it was within the square that the guilds set up their stages for the performance of their mystery plays; it was here that great tourneys would be held. It was not merely acropolis but amphitheater. Often one market place will open into another subordinate square, connected by a narrow passage: Parma is an example. Except in the church, where grandeur and height were important symbolic attributes, the medieval planner tended to keep to human dimensions. Almshouses would be founded for seven or ten men; and instead of building one large hospital, it was commoner to provide a small one for every two or three thousand people: similarly Coulton reckons that there was one parish church for every hundred families. In London in the twelfth century, according to Fitz-Stephens, there were 13 conventual and 126 smaller churches. The habit of erecting such buildings continued long after the social need had exhausted itself: note the church-building that went on in the City of London under Wren. This decentralization of the essential social functions of the city not merely prevented overcrowding and needless circulation: it kept the whole town in scale. Here the physical form confirmed the social fact, and the social fact gave significance to the physical form. The loss of this fine sense of scale, which one notes in the over-sized burgher houses of the

North, or the crazy towered urban fortresses in Italy, was symptomatic of social pathology.

The street occupied in medieval city planning a quite different
place than in an age of locomotion. Except in the country, we inevitably think of houses being built along a line of predetermined
streets. But on the less regular medieval sites it would be the other
way about: groups of trades or groups of institutional buildings
would form self-contained quarters or "islands." Within these "islands," and often outside, as part of the connecting urban tissue,
the streets were essentially footways: marks of the daily comings
and goings of the inhabitants. "Islands" formed by the castle, the
monasteries, or the specialized industrial section of the technically
more advanced towns were characteristic features: they had their
counterpart in the little internal "islands" one encounters in the
Northern countries in the housing foundations for the aged or the
poor. The Fuggerei in Augsburg is the most handsomely built survival of this mode, although the Dutch and English foundations of
the same period surpass it in spaciousness.

In the early medieval city, the street was a line of communication
rather than a means of transportation: the unpaved streets were more
like the courtyard of a farm. The streets were sometimes narrow and
the turns and closures frequent: there was a difference in breadth
between the main streets and the subordinate ones. When the street
was narrow and twisting, or when it came to a dead end, the plan
broke the force of the winter's wind and reduced the area of the
mud: the overhang of the houses not merely gave extra space to
the inhabitants above but furnished a partly covered way to the
pedestrian. Sometimes the building was constructed to form an
arcaded walk, as in the street leading up to das Goldene Dachl in
Innsbruck: protection against summer sun or winter sleet. One must
not forget how important this physical protection against the weather
was: for the stalls and booths of the handicraftsmen and merchants
were not generally put behind glass until the seventeenth century:
the greater part of the citizen's active life was spent outdoors. The
closed narrow street and the exposed shop were complementary: not
till glass closed the second could new conceptions of town planning
open up the first.

Some three centuries before wheeled vehicles became common the street lost its rural underfooting. Paving for the pedestrian came in as early as 1184 in Paris, 1235 in Florence, and 1310 in Lübeck; while by the end of the fourteenth century, even in England, Langland could use the figure "as common as the pavement to every man that walketh." Often these early efforts applied only to a single important street; and the movement spread so slowly that it did not reach Landshut in Bavaria till 1494, although that other great technical innovation, window-glass, was used by South Bavarian farmers, according to Heyne, in the thirteenth century. The provision and care of paving reminds one of another feature about the management of the medieval town: for here again it was association that was put on a public basis, while physical organization was, more often than not, on a private basis. Certainly this applies to paving, lighting, and the piped water supply. By the sixteenth century the first two were usually mandatory; but they were carried out by the private householder for his particular private property. The cleaning of streets likewise for long remained a private concern: a custom that lingered through the nineteenth century in London in the institution of the crossing sweeper. (Medieval practice still applies to the building and maintenance of sidewalks.) Under the paving act that prevailed in Northampton in 1431, the municipal authorities had the power to order the owners of the property to have and keep in repair the street in front of their houses and adjoining their property; but "no property owner was compelled to extend the pavement into the street above 30 feet, so it became the duty of the town to pave the market and similar wide places."

As the physical utilities of the town became more complicated, the need for more detailed municipal regulations and for more zealous and far-sighted municipal enterprise became greater. The growth of population gradually centered political attention more and more upon the mechanical means of existence, and the institutions bound up with common interests and feelings, with the common ideology, became more feeble, if they did not disappear. This change was closely associated with those larger transformations that marked the growth of a technical and capitalistic culture. Finally, in the nineteenth century, the physical organs and activities became the main determinants of plan, and the social life of the city was squeezed, as it were, into the accidental apertures left open by railroad extension and real estate speculation.

10: Control of Growth and Expansion

How did the medieval town grow? To what extent did it grow? These questions bring us face to face with important aspects of both the polity and the culture, as well as the physical necessities, of medieval life.

As long as the simple wooden palisade or masonry wall sufficed for military protection, the wall was no real obstacle to town extension. Technically, it was a simple matter to tear down the wall and extend the city's boundaries once the inner spaces had been filled up. Florence, for example, enlarged her wall circuit for the second time in 1172, and not more than a century later built a third circuit that enclosed a still greater area. This was common practice in the growing towns up to the sixteenth century. But even at its widest, no medieval town usually extended more than half a mile from its center. The "historic mile" of Edinburgh stretched between the extreme limits of castle-top and the Holyrood Abbey on the outskirts.

The limitations on the medieval town's growth were rather of a different nature: limitations of water supply and local produce: limitations by municipal ordinance and by guild regulations which prevented the uncontrolled settlement of outsiders: limitations of transport and communications which were overcome only in the advanced eotechnic cities that had waterways instead of roadways for traffic, such as Venice. For practical reasons alone, the limitations on horizontal expansion were speedily reached. In the early centuries of city development, between the eleventh and the fourteenth, as in the seventeenth in New England, the surplus population was cared for by building new cities, sometimes close by, but nevertheless an independent and self-sufficient unit. The medieval city did not break through its walls and stretch over the countryside in an amorphous blob.

Contrary to the common impression, however, medieval urbanism was far from static. Not merely were thousands of new urban foundations made during the early Middle Ages; but settled towns that found themselves physically hampered or inconveniently located moved to other sites: Lübeck changed its site in order to better the means of trade and defense, and Old Sarum was abandoned and Salisbury created with a ready expenditure of energy for which there are few modern parallels outside devastated areas. How far the actual layout was the work of an official city architect it is difficult to determine. But toward the end of the Middle Ages the municipal buildings would be designed by such an official; and by that time the city architect was often a man in the top rank of his profession, like Elias Holl in Augsburg. Order in private building, too, came through his supervision.

But population growth was not governed by the covetousness of the real estate speculator: even colonization towns did not increase indefinitely in population. The general pattern of town growth was that of small cities, distributed widely over the landscape: Reclus, indeed, discovered that the villages and towns of France could be plotted with amazing regularity on the pattern of a day's walk back and forth between them. This urban pattern corresponded to the economic one: facilities for shipping food were extremely limited —Francis Bacon died as a result of making one of the first experiments with cold storage—and power, whether obtained through wind mills or water mills or sailing ships, was similarly distributed. While internally, the importance of the Church and its accessory institutions limited the growth of the town almost as much as the provisional definition of the wall itself: its buildings served as cohesive nucleus.

At all events, the facts are plain. The typical medieval town ranged in size from three or four hundred, which was frequently the size of a fully privileged municipality in Germany, to forty thousand, which was the size of London in the fourteenth century: the hundred thousand achieved earlier by Paris and Venice was highly exceptional. Toward the close of the period, Nürnberg, a thriving place, had in 1450 about twenty thousand inhabitants, while Basel had around eight thousand. Even on the fine soils of the lowlands, supported by the technically advanced and capitalistically exploited textile industries, the same thing holds: in 1412 Ypres had only 10,736 inhabitants, and Louvain and Brussels, in the middle of the same century, had between 25,000 and 40,000. As for Germany, town life was concentrated in some 150 large cities, of which the largest did not have more than 35,000 inhabitants. All these statistics, it is true, date from the century after the Black Death, which in some provinces carried off half the population; but even if one doubles the figures the towns themselves, in terms of modern population massings, were numerically small. In Italy alone, partly because of the early rise of capitalism there, do these figures have to be increased. The phenomena of overcrowding and overbuilding—as well as indefinite suburban expansion—did not come in until the capacity for building *new* cities had, for reasons to be discussed in the next chapter, greatly diminished.

11: The Stage and the Drama

Every culture has its characteristic drama. It chooses from the sum total of human possibilities certain acts and interests, certain processes and values, and endows them with special significance: provides them with a setting: organizes rites and ceremonies: excludes from the circle of dramatic response a thousand other daily acts which, though they remain part of the "real" world, are not active agents in the drama itself. The stage on which this drama is enacted, with the most skilled actors and a full supporting company and specially designed scenery, is the city: it is here that it reaches its highest pitch of intensity.

Between the underlying facts of life and the drama of a culture there is something of the same relation that exists between daily events and the dreamwork of a sleeper, who transposes and magnifies certain fragments of actuality in relation to the trends and conflicts in his inner life. Actual life provides the material for both dream and culture: but both are warped by the pressure of fear, power, ancient traumas, or newly awakened desires. The practical, day-to-day occupations tell much about a culture; but until one has located and envisaged its essential drama, it is impossible to affix to the actors and the scenery the values that they actually had for their participants and spectators. In one culture a rose is purely a botanical species: in another, it has greater significance as an allegorical symbol of passion.

What was the essential drama of the medieval culture? It took place within the Church; it concerned the passage of sinning man through an evil and painful world, from which he might emerge through repentance into heaven, or sink through hardness of heart or confirmed mischief into hell. The earth itself was but a mean stopping place, a wayside tavern of ill fame, on the way to these other worlds. But nothing that concerned this drama was mean: on the contrary, the Church, founded through an act of God, brought into the world constant reminders of the grace and beauty that was to come: though art and music might tempt men from a higher life, they also indicated its possibility, indeed its immanence. Life was a succession of significant episodes in man's pilgrimage to heaven: for each great moment the Church had its sacrament or its celebration. Beneath the active drama was the constant chant of prayer: in solitude or in company, men communed with God and praised him. It was in such moments, only in such moments, that one truly lived.

Whatever else the medieval city was, in its busy turbulent life, it was above all things a stage for the ceremonies of the Church. Just as in an industrial age, the imagination soars to its highest level in a railroad station or bridge, in medieval culture practical achievement reached its peak in the service of a great symbol. Men who had little to eat gave part of that little to say prayers and masses, light candles, and build a mighty fabric, in which legend, allegory, and knowledge crystallized in nave and altar, screen and wall-painting. On isolated occasions of great religious exaltation, such as Henry Adams described in Mt. Saint Michel and Chartres, they might even carry the very stones that were needed to the site, rich and poor alike. The sin of pride might enter into the building of such monuments: Eugene O'Neill did well to interpret Marco Polo as a medieval Babbitt, and there was more than a touch of vainglory in the famous announcement of the burghers of Florence when they laid their plans for their Cathedral. But pride was not pettiness: luxury and art were not sordid concessions to an otherwise foreign culture. The Duomo in Florence *is* a great building; and it was in the construction of such buildings that the ordinary energies of the medieval community were lifted to a higher potential.

No sedentary student, viewing this architecture in pictures, no superficial observer, taking up a position and attempting to plot out axes and formal relationship, is in a state to penetrate this urban setting even in its purely esthetic aspect. For the key to the visible city lies in the procession, above all, in the great religious procession that winds about the streets and places before it finally debouches into the church or the cathedral for the great ceremony itself. Here is no static architecture. The masses suddenly expand and vanish, as one appoaches them or draws away: a dozen paces may alter the relation of the foreground and background, or the lower and upper range of the line of vision. The silhouettes of the buildings, with their steep gables, their sharp roof lines, their pinnacles, their towers, ripple and flow, break and solidify, rise and fall, with no less vitality than the structures themselves. As in a fine piece of sculpture, the silhouettes are often inexhaustible in their variety: the outlines vary no less constantly than the relations of the planes.

Within the general medieval pattern, deep changes in feeling took place. Radically different life experiences separate the confident sobriety of the great Romanesque buildings, as solid as a fortress, from the humanism of the magnificent Lady Churches that defied the dogma of the wall with the heresy of the fragile window and the flying buttress; or again, from the sickly, over-ripe estheticism of the fifteenth century, which embroidered its buildings because it lacked the patience and the honesty and the courage to put its soul into the weaving of the fabric. But through all these changes, the setting itself possessed vitality: it incorporated these successive moments of the spirit without losing form. The towers of the churches raised the eyes to heaven: their masses rose, in hierarchic rank, over all the lesser symbols of earthly wealth and power: through their stained glass windows the light burst in aureoles of splendid color. From almost any part of the city, the admonitory fingers of the spires, archangelic swords, tipped with gold, were visible: if hidden for a moment, they would suddenly appear as the roofs parted, with the force of a blast of trumpets.

The lines of the subordinate buildings did not necessarily run upward: horizontal banks of windows are common in the houses and horizontal string courses often separate the parts of a church tower, in England no less than in Italy. In the Palace of the Doges in Venice, begun in 1422, there is already, perhaps, a touch of bureaucratic discipline. But the movement of the eye is up and down, if only because the blocked vista is a characteristic of medieval planning and design. The eye blocked, it moves upward. The body blocked in movement, it changes its position and goes on in another direction. So one walked about the streets: so one joined in a guild pageant, or in a religious procession, turning and winding till one reached the portals of the church. Let us look at a medieval procession through the eyes of a late contemporary who left behind a precious picture of the occasion. The time is early sixteenth century: the place is Antwerp: the witness is Albrecht Dürer.

"On Sunday after Our Dear Lady's Assumption, I saw the Great Procession from the Church of Our Lady at Antwerp, when the whole town of every craft and rank was assembled, each dressed in his best according to his rank. And all ranks and guilds had their signs, by which they might be known. In the intervals, great costly pole-candles were borne, and three long old Frankish trumpets of silver. There were also in the German fashion many pipers and drummers. All the instruments were loudly and noisily blown and beaten.

"I saw the Procession pass along the street, the people being arranged in rows, each man some distance from his neighbor, but the rows close behind the other. There were the Goldsmiths, the Painters, the Masons, the Broderers, the Sculptors, the Joiners, the Carpenters, the Sailors, the Fishermen, the Butchers, the Leatherers, the Clothmakers, the Bakers, the Tailors, the Cordwainers—indeed, workmen of all kinds, and many craftsmen and dealers who work for their livelihood. Likewise the shopkeepers and merchants and their assistants of all kinds were there. After these came the shooters with guns, bows, and crossbows, and the horsemen and foot-soldiers also. Then followed the watch of the Lord Magistrates. Then came a fine troop all in red, nobly and splendidly clad. Before them, however, went all the religious orders and the members of some foundations, very devoutly, all in their different robes.

"A very large company of widows also took part in the procession. They support themselves with their own hands and observe a special rule. They were all dressed from head to foot in white linen garments made expressly for the occasion, very sorrowful to see. Among them I saw some very stately persons. Last of all came the Chapter of Our Lady's Church, with all their clergy, scholars, and treasurers. Twenty persons bore the image of the Virgin Mary with the Lord Jesus, adorned in the costliest manner, to the honor of the Lord God.

"In this procession very many delightful things were shown, most splendidly got up. Wagons were drawn along with masques upon ships and other structures. Behind them came the Company of the Prophets in their order, and scenes from the New Testament, such as the Annunciation, the Three Holy Kings riding on great camels, and on other rare beasts, very well arranged. . . . From the beginning to end, the Procession lasted more than two hours before it was gone past our house."

Note the vast number of people arrayed in this procession. As in the church itself, the spectators were also communicants and participants: they engaged in the spectacle, watching it from within, not from without: or rather, feeling it from within, acting in unison, not dismembered beings, reduced to a single specialized rôle. Prayer, mass, pageant, life-ceremony, baptism, marriage, or funeral—the city itself was stage for these separate scenes of the drama, and the citizen himself was actor. Once the unity of this social order was broken, everything about it was set in confusion: the great Church itself became a sect, and the city became a battleground for conflicting cultures, dissonant ways of life.

12: What Overthrew the Medieval City?

As the nineteenth century idea of unceasing change and progress raises for us today the problem of stabilization and equilibrium, so the medieval idea of protection raised, from the fourteenth century onward, the problem of how life and growth and movement were to take place in a world governed by the ideas of safety and salvation. Must the armor be removed? Must the wall be torn down? Or did this civilization have the capacity to arrive, without disintegration, at a wider synthesis?

About the ensuing facts, there is little occasion for dispute. After the sixteenth century, the medieval city tended to become a mere shell: the better the shell was preserved, the less life was left in it. Its creative day was over. That is the history of Carcassonne, Bruges, Chipping Camden, or Braunschweig. Where the external form was rapidly altered by pressure of population and new measures of economic enterprise, the inner spirit was transformed, too. In the first series of examples the body retained its shape because the new currents of life had drifted elsewhere. But the old shape did not express the new life: so the city became in effect a museum of the past, and its inhabitants, if not curators, had only a mean restricted part to play in the new culture. Such puddles of medieval life, sometimes dried up, sometimes rank with decay, are still scattered over Europe.

The protected economy of the medieval city was capable of being maintained by one fact alone: the superiority of the city over the barbarous, insecure life of the open country. So great were its advantages in the way of training men for orderly economic effort, fostering skill by every variety of emulation and gain, that industry for long was not tempted to seek the low wages of the country, or accept the low standards and the clumsy technical equipment of the rural craftsman. Municipal restrictions might be onerous to the more speculative enterprisers; but they were easier to endure than feudal restrictions, and since they rested on rational common consent, they were less capricious. Even the nobility appreciated these urban advantages: life and the goods of life at least had the spice of variety in the city.

By the sixteenth century the disparity between city and country, politically speaking, had been partly removed. Improvements in transport by water had lessened the distance between city and countryside; and since feudal dues had been converted into money payments in many regions, people could remain in the open country or go back and forth without falling into the status of serfs or liegemen. One evidence of this equalization is the number of dialogues gentlemen wrote in the sixteenth century weighing the advantages of the two environments: the two modes were at last near enough to be compared.

This new parity was abetted by the fact that security was gradually being established in the open country through the rise of a central authority in the newly consolidated states. When the kings put down the warring nobles, industry could prosper outside organized municipalities: protected by the symbolic might of the law, industry might spring up in a non-enfranchised village, beyond the pale of any older municipal government. Merchants with capital enough to purchase raw materials and the instruments of production—knitting machines for instance—could farm their work out in the countryside, paying subsistence wages instead of town rates, escaping regulations as to employment made by the guilds, cutting under the urban standard of living, and in general playing the devil with the regulated market. Under this regime, infant labor came in.

Moreover, toward the close of the Middle Ages the mining industries and the glass industries played a far larger part than they had played at the beginning. These industries, in the nature of the case, were usually placed outside the limits of the earlier settlements; and from the first they had taken on most of the features of later capitalistic industry, for the same reasons that were decisive later: the machinery of production was too expensive to be purchased by a single man or worked by a family unit; and the methods themselves required the hiring and organization of whole gangs who were usually employed as wage laborers, and who could be hired only by an employer with enough capital to tide them over between the season of production and the moment when sales were finally made. Proportionately, a larger part of the industrial population came to get its livelihood outside the incorporated municipalities: even if these industries gave rise to urban settlements, they remained competitors with the guild-protected centers.

The old monopolies had been achieved by the co-operative action of the burghers for the benefit of the town. From the sixteenth century on the new monopolies issued in England and France were not town monopolies but trade monopolies: they worked for the benefit of the privileged individuals who controlled the trade, no matter where they were scattered. For these producing monopolies, the whole country was a province; and their promoters, like Sir Richard Maunsell, the English glass manufacturer, were either drawn from the nobility or speedily elevated to it. Big industry, investment banking, and wholesale trade were not on a single town basis. Even within the incorporated municipalities the old guilds and corporations crumbled, first in Italy, then elsewhere, before the attack of financially more powerful groups that often usurped the very function of town government through their ability to hire mercenaries.

The growing importance of international commerce from the fifteenth century on took advantage of weaknesses that were inherent in the craft guild and the walled town. The first weakness is that they were both on a purely local basis: to exercise monopolistic control within their walls it was essential that they should be able to govern the realm outside, too: this meant harmony with the countryside plus a federal union of cities. Now and then the guilds of one town might help those of another, as the guilds in the neighborhood of Colmar supported the Colmar guild of bakers on a ten year strike. But on the whole, the guild was able to exercise its authority only over those who actually came to practice within the walls of the town. Once the lanes of travel opened and the countryside became safe, the towns were helpless.

As an organization of crafts, the guild had one further weakness: it was incapable of meeting the new situation that had sprung up in industry—as incapable as the craft unions of the American Federation of Labor were of organizing the motor industry. Jurisdictional disputes between the crafts took place: this divided their energy and caused them to fight against their own fellows instead of against the big merchants who were becoming more powerful and more bent on exploiting both the little masters and the proletariat. As the guilds grew more exclusive, the excluded turned to the non-protected industries. In addition, many new types of worker, unskilled, but of increasing weight in the new industrial routine, dockers, porters, navvies, were not brought into the guild organization. This growing class helped depress the standard of living and began to constitute that casual labor reserve upon which capitalistic industry was to cast its own characteristic form of organization.

Still another factor was the extension of the class war. The medieval system, based on a hierarchy of social rank, of course knew no economic equality: there were vast gaps between rich and poor, master and beggar. But in the earlier part of the period, when urban land was fairly evenly divided and the means of production were largely individual tools, the mobility of the skilled journeymen partly insured him against victimization. In those days there was far less of a spread between upper and lower ranks: they had a common city, a common culture, a common religious faith.

In the textile industry of Flanders and Northern Italy, the characteristic breach between workers and masters appeared as early as the thirteenth century: the newly introduced spinning wheel and draw-loom exercised an influence comparable to that of the spinning jenny and the power loom five centuries later. In Köln the weavers temporarily succeeded in overthrowing the patriciate in 1370-71. But the odds were against the guilds; their victories were brief. While they operated on a local basis, their opponents, through family marriages and alliances and international contacts, were united on a European basis. Hence the ruling classes could bring many forms of pressure and authority to bear at a single point.

Apart from the weaknesses of the guilds, the defect of the medieval urban policy was that it had never—outside certain regions in Italy —embraced a sufficient area of countryside. It was an island in a hostile sea. Ecologically speaking, the city and countryside are a single unit; if one can do without the other, it is the country, not the city, the farmer, not the burgher. The triumphs of art and invention in the city had made it doubly contemptuous of its rural neighbors; the countryman was treated as a dependent, or what was worse, a foreigner. Cities attempted to solve the problem of a common union by forcing their peasant neighbors into a state of subjection. In Italy they denied the peasants the privileges of citizenship; and in Germany the Bannmeilenrecht compelled the nearby peasants to supply the city with both food and the necessities of industry. Instead of creating allies in the open country, who could have helped strike at the roots of feudal power, they created a sullen wall of enemies.

The power of the feudal aristocracies and the princely dynasties, though challenged, was never successfully displaced over any considerable period by any combination of cities in Europe. When the cities joined the king, in order to lessen the impositions of the nobles or ecclesiastics, they succeeded only in displacing a local tyrant by a more ubiquitous one: presently they found themselves the subjects of the state they had helped create. The essential difficulty was that the political unit, the economic unit, and the religious unit were not in symmetrical relationship, and were not unified in any common frame-work other than the dynastic state. Power, privilege, ancient custom had made the political map of Europe a crazy quilt of conflicting jurisdictions and disparate allegiances and meaningless particu-larisms.

Various attempts at confederation were made, indeed, between re-lated cities. In addition to the enterprising and relatively enduring union of Hansa cities, there was a League of Swabian Cities in 1376 and a Rhenish League in 1381, while England had the Union of Cinque Ports. In Italy, during the same century, Lombardy, the Romagna, Tuscany, Umbria, and the Marches were partitioned be-tween 80 city states, or, as Toynbee puts it, in one half of Italy in A.D. 1300 there were more self-governing states than could be counted in the whole world in 1933. The unifications that took place during the next two centuries reduced these Italian self-governing municipalities to ten political units: but that change was accom-panied by a loss of freedom, autonomy, and power.

It was in Switzerland and Holland that the problem of the federal unification of the corporate towns and the countryside was actually solved without undermining the political integrity of the urban unit; and it is to the Swiss and Dutch cities that one must turn for perhaps the most successful examples of the transition from the medieval to the modern order. That the Swiss achieved unity without despotism or submission to the arbitrary forms of centralized authority shows that the feat was technically possible: moreover, it gives color to the notion that it was humanly practicable on a wide European basis, since the three language groups in Switzerland, with their mountain barriers to transportation and intercourse, gave the country almost as many obstacles to unity as the most diverse territories of Europe as a whole. The proof was genuine, but the example was not infectious: actual life in other regions took a different political course.

Now territorial unification and internal peace and freedom of movement were all highly necessary conditions for the new system of capitalistic industry. Centralized power developed in states like England and France, with at least the passive connivance of the underlying corporations and communities, because of the tangible benefits that flowed from the establishment of the king's peace, the king's justice, the king's protection that insured travel on the king's highway. From the standpoint of trade, transportation, and travel, conditions had actually been worsening since the twelfth century. Along the Rhine, for example, there had been only nineteen toll stations toward the end of that century: in the thirteenth twenty-five more were added, and in the fourteenth another twenty: so that by the *end* of the Middle Ages the total was something over sixty: the stoppages and the burdensome fees might occur as often as every six miles.

Road tolls, bridge tolls, river tolls, town tolls—these economic exactions had been multiplying precisely at the moment when the routes of trade were lengthening and when the constant flow of goods was becoming more important to a stable economic market. In addition, the lack of uniform coinage, combined with the dubious inflationary policies of this or that needy ruler or town, offered another handicap to commerce. Except in the provinces mentioned, the cities of Europe were too insular, too parochial-minded, too jealous of their special privileges to solve the problems by common measures. External conformity, enforced by the military power of the state, stepped in to perform the task where co-operative methods were not tried, or were given but a partial grudging trial and had failed. And inept self-government, leading to bankruptcy, often provided an opportunity for the central authority to step in and set matters straight—at the sacrifice of urban liberties, as in France.

We who live in a world consumed by a similar folly, now embracing the planet rather than the continent of Europe, can without any sense of ironic superiority understand this fatal impasse. The medieval corporations, plainly, sought to solve within the walls of the town problems that could be solved only by breaking down the walls and deliberately pooling their sovereignty and their control in a wider unity. Every aspect of European life was involved in this re-orientation: it was not simply a question, as Dante thought, of putting a Pope or an Emperor at the head of the temporal realm. Forerunner in so many political departments of the National State, the medieval town proved the impossibility of meeting the situation by purely local adjustments. The island-states of today are cracking into chaos for similar reasons—still pursuing the same obstinate methods, still aiming at a delusive autarchy.

Only one institution was perhaps capable of transcending this narrow parochialism and these futile monopolistic efforts: that was the universal Church. But the diminishing universalism of the Church itself was organically a phase of the disease that undermined medieval culture: another negative sign of the new capitalistic organization of society, which was creating a new spiritual power, physical science, a new order of dedicated men, the bureaucrats and commercial enterprisers, and a new hierarchy of values, based on the supremacy of the physical world and material goods. From the thirteenth century on the Church, if it did not lose immediately in spiritual authority, had gained in worldly estate—and that is one of the surest ways of undermining spiritual authority. Poor people resented the rich ecclesiastics: there was often more ascetic renunciation in the counting house than in the monastery.

Had the Church remained economically disinterested, it could perhaps have joined forces with the cities and provided a framework for their union. But though the Dominican and Franciscan orders arose in the thirteenth century and quickly made their way, preaching and building, into the city, the Church itself remained rooted in the feudal mold of the past. When it transcended that mold it was to succumb to the very forces and the very ways of life that its essential teachings condemned. By the sixteenth century, the authority of the Church was seriously undermined from within. Corruption had become a constant stench in Rome, and the very blessing of the Church, the indulgence, was farmed out on a share basis to the leading investment banker of the time, Jacob Fugger.

If the international religious order was incapable of preserving the medieval regime by renewal from within, protestantism, which rested on a national basis and issued in a state-supported Church, was even less capable of serving the needs of cities. The protestant doctrine of justification by Faith and the doctrine of Divine Election came in with credit finance and the rise of the self-perpetuating urban patriciate: the visibly elect, the manipulators of intangible values. With the coming of protestantism the old fellowship in the city weakened: cleavages in matters of faith increased the forces of eco·

nomic disruption and further destroyed the possibilities of creating a united front. The validity of the universal Church was denied; the reality of the group was denied; only the individual counted on earth as in heaven: nominalism or social atomism. This common débâcle was summed up in the caustic lines of Robert Crowley, writing in the sixteenth century:

> *And this is a city*
> *In name but in deed*
> *It is a pack of people*
> *That seek after meed [gain].*
> *For officers and all*
> *Do seek their own gain*
> *But for the wealth of the Commons*
> *Not one taketh pain.*
> *And hell without order*
> *I may it well call*
> *Where every man is for himself*
> *And no man for all.*

What Langland had predicted in the fourteenth century in his long harangue on the wiles and perversities of Lady Meed had in two centuries finally come to pass throughout European society. The city had almost ceased to be a common enterprise for the common good; and neither the local authority of the municipal corporation, nor the universal authority of the Church, was sufficient to direct for the benefit of the commonwealth the new forces that were making headway throughout European civilization.

There is little more to be said about the medieval city. Its economic and its social basis had disintegrated, and its organic pattern of life had been broken up. Slowly, the form itself became dilapidated, and even when it continued to stand, its walls enclosed a hollow shell, harboring institutions that were also hollow shells. It is only, as it were, by holding the shell quietly to one's ear, as with a sea-shell, that one can catch in the ensuing pause the dim roar of the old life that was once lived, with dramatic conviction and solemn purpose, within its walls.

monastery and the new country house in his description of the Abbey of Thelema. These are significant symbols. No verbal generalization, still less such pat terms as "Renascence" or "Baroque" or "Neoclassic," can do justice to all the varieties and gradations of form that mark the transition period. No two cities exhibit quite the same combination of architectural characteristics.

The fact is that only a handful of people in any age are its true contemporaries. Only sluggishly do the mass of people respond to the currents that are sweeping through the ruling classes or the intellectual élite; if this is mainly true even today, it was more so before universal literacy had quickened the pace of communication. What historians are tempted to characterize as the traits of an age indicates quite as much about their own standpoint and frame of reference as it does about the objective facts. For the purpose of clarity one should perhaps adopt for sociology a parallel set of terms to the Mendelian classification of biological traits into dominants and recessives; and one should add two other useful categories: survivals and mutations. In Rome before Constantine the Christian Church was a mutation: within the city one would scarcely be aware of its presence: living in crypts and catacombs on the outskirts, it hid even its physical presence. In the medieval city the Church was a dominant: no part of life could fail to record its existence and its influence. In the great seventeenth century capitals, the Church had become a recessive: still an imposing visible presence, but no longer a unifying and dynamic social force. In the metropolis today the Church is a survival: its power rests upon numbers, wealth, *material* organization, not upon its capacity to give its stamp to the daily activities of men: it claims much, but except by repetition and rote, it contributes little to the active spiritual life of the city.

What "characterizes" an age? Mainly, the dominants and recessives, for they bear the active inheritance of the past and they focus the successful forces of the present. But the survivals often occupy a larger part of the visible scene than either the dominants or the recessives: they modify these new elements, sometimes they retard their introduction, sometimes they achieve fresh power by submitting themselves to the process of renovation. Survivals of ancient, pre-Christian religions, belief in sympathetic magic, belief in wizardry, still linger in various strata of the modern mind, immune to the germicidal action of positive science: they are, in effect, an automatic provision against a too narrow basis of continuity in the social heritage. Was it not partly through the stimulus of magical dream books, like that of Artemidorus Daldianus, that Dr. Sigmund Freud made his profound psychological discoveries on the function of dreams? As for the fresh mutations, often isolated, feeble, struggling for bare existence, they usually can have but little contemporary effect: their influence may be as limited as was Leonardo's astonishing technical perspective and inventive ingenuity in the fifteenth century—thinking that would have been magnified many diameters had it appeared in the more genial milieu of the early nineteenth century.

Between the fifteenth and the eighteenth century a new complex of cultural traits took shape in Europe. Both the form and the contents of urban life were in consequence transformed. The new pattern of existence sprang out of a new economy, that of mercantilist capitalism, a new political framework, that of a centralized despotism or oligarchy, usually focused in a national state, and a new ideological form, that of mechanism, whose lines were first laid down in the monastery and the army. But until the seventeenth century all these changes were sporadic and tentative: they were restricted to a minor· ity: they were effective only in patches: they were in an embryonic state, receiving nourishment from an older society, from which they were soon to emerge with a lusty squawk.

In order to understand the discipline and order of the post-medieval city, one must penetrate more fully into the disintegration of the medieval synthesis. And here after one has made due allowance for the choices of men and for the immanent development of institutions, one must perhaps give greatest weight to an overpowering accident: the devastation caused by the Black Death in the fourteenth century. For the real Renascence in European life, the great age of city building and intellectual triumph, had begun two centuries before that event, and had achieved its symbolic apotheosis in the work of an Aquinas, an Albertus Magnus, a Dante, a Giotto.

The so-called Renascence that followed in the fifteenth century was rather in the nature of an illusory belief on the part of its contemporaries: they mistook the brilliant spray of the falling rocket for the energy that had originally lifted it into the air. Thorndike has indeed properly raised the question as to whether there was not a general falling off in civilization and scientific productiveness after the twelfth and thirteenth centuries. He cites the contrast in Petrarch's mind between the happy, confident days of his youth, "when there was no need to close the town gates after dark or keep the walls in repair," when Petrarch was able to wander alone at night in the mountains near Avignon, and the conditions in his old age, when this once-peaceful landscape had become infested with robbers and wolves.

Meanwhile, the plague had intervened: a breach in continuity, a lowering of vitality had followed, like that which comes after an exhausting war. Social disorders resulted: the spread of war and military despotisms, the suppression of academic freedom at the universities, and the studied subordination of the spiritual powers in the interest of temporal authority: a parallel to what is going on in Germany, Italy, and various other parts of Europe again today. The transformation of the universities from international associations of scholars to nationalistic organizations, servile to the new rulers, impervious to "dangerous thoughts" went on steadily.

Within a few centuries, every department of social life showed signs of profound debility or decay. In the fifteenth century, according to von Below, there was the beginning of organized gambling in houses provided by the municipality. And the same tendencies appeared in the Church; not merely the buying of offices and the sale of blessings, but the general recrudescence of superstition. Belief in witchcraft, rejected by St. Boniface in the eighth century and treated as a crime by the laws of Charlemagne, was given the final sanction of the Church in 1484. And it was in the seventeenth century, marked by the appearance of Galileo and Newton and the exact methods of physical science, that the persecution of witches became popular. Indeed, some of the most vicious offenders in this respect were the new scientists and scientific philosophers themselves: people like Glanvill who in almost the same breath were predicting the triumph of science and the complete transformation of the physical world by technics.

From medieval universality to baroque uniformity: from medieval localism to baroque centralism: from the absolutism of God and the Catholic Church to the absolutism of the temporal sovereign and the National State—there is a passage of four or five centuries between these phenomena. Let us not obscure the essential nature of this change by referring solely to its esthetic accompaniments: the unearthing and measurement of classic monuments, the discovery of Plato and Vitruvius, the worship of the Five Orders in architecture. These facts give only a superficial clue to what was happening. The underlying tendencies of the new order did not become visible until every aspect of life had departed from the medieval whole and re-united under a new sign. This did not occur until the seventeenth century. It was then that the intuitions of precursors like Alberti were finally expressed in the baroque style of life, the baroque plan, the baroque garden, and the baroque city.

Because all these tendencies were finally brought to a head in the baroque city, I have chosen to use this term—originally contemptuous —as one of social description, not of limited architectural reference. The concept of the baroque, as it shaped itself in the seventeenth century, is particularly useful because it holds in itself the two contradictory elements of the age. First: the mathematical and mercantile and methodical side, expressed to perfection in its rigorous street plans, its formal city layouts, and in its geometrically ordered landscape designs. And at the same time, in the painting and sculpture of the period, it embraces the sensuous, rebellious, anti-classical, anti-mechanical side, expressed in its clothes and its sexual life and its religious fanaticism and its crazy statecraft. Between the sixteenth and the nineteenth century these two elements existed together: sometimes acting separately, sometimes held in tension within a larger whole.

In this respect, one may regard the early Renascence forms, in their purity, as proto-baroque, and the neo-classic forms, from Versailles to St. Petersburg, as "late" baroque: while even the careless uncontrolled romanticism of the gothic revivalists might be considered, paradoxically, as a phase of baroque caprice. None of this makes sense if one thinks of the baroque as a single moment in the development of architectural style. But the widening of the term has gone on steadily during the last generation; and a certain original vagueness and contradictoriness in the epithet adds sanction to this special use. In terms of the city, the renascence forms are the mutation, baroque forms are the dominants, and neo-classic forms are the survivals in this complex cultural transformation.

2: Territory and City

From the beginning of the Middle Ages two powers had been jockeying for leadership in Western Europe: one was royal, the other municipal. Even in the great days of the Free Cities there were parts of Europe where the royal power had consolidated more swiftly and had kept the cities themselves in a state of feudal vassalage: England, Aquitaine, Sicily, Austria. Where royal and imperial power was weakest, as in Northern Italy, the city achieved its fullest independence as a political entity. But even where it was strong, as in Aragon, royal power was far from absolute: witness the oath sworn by the subjects of the King of Aragon: "We, who are as good as you, swear to you, who are not better than we, to accept you as our king and sovereign lord, provided that you observe all our liberties and laws; but if not, then not."

The consolidation of dispersed feudal estates and the creation of continuous fields of political administration within a clearly defined frame was important for the welfare of the communities concerned. The real question was whether this consolidation was to be undertaken on behalf of a small privileged class, or whether it was to be achieved through a free union of cities and regions. Unfortunately the cities themselves, as we have seen, were not immune to the temptations of a predatory and parasitic life, made possible by the command of military weapons: they undertook exploitation by force both in home territories and in more distant imperialistic ventures: alternately repeating the political mistakes of the Spartans and the Athenians.

The more powerful cities often sought to conquer their weaker neighbors, if for no better purpose than to suppress a rival market: and in times of war, from the end of the twelfth century on, they would in Italy transfer a great measure of executive power to a special officer, the Podesta, who in the emergency was released from the bondage of law.

In short, to achieve despotic power over their neighbors, the cities consented to the loss of their own internal freedom: what is more, they lost the moral case against other forms of despotism. As I have already pointed out, the only part of Europe where the civic corporations and the territorial state were unified without loss of civic liberty was the Swiss Cantonal Confederation.

In the early Middle Ages, the great feudal lords had succeeded in feeding their retainers, collecting their rents, and securing a modicum of peace and order in their domains only by being in continual movement from one estate to another. The court was a mobile camp: vigilance and movement were the price of power. This held for kings as well as lesser nobles. The royal ministers, the royal judges, the whole apparatus of government and fiscal control, was essentially a mobile one: authority was maintained by personal supervision. During the fourteenth century in the great monarchies of England and France, this process came to an actual halt. The records of the courts, the rolls, the registers, the archives, the correspondence, not to mention the officials themselves, had become too numerous and bulky to move. As population and territory increased in size, direct personal supervision became impossible: impersonal administration and delegated authority became necessary.

Though the popular movement for parliamentary control did not maintain itself very successfully except in England, the modern state began to shape itself in the fourteenth century. Its marks are a permanent bureaucracy, permanent courts of justice, permanent archives and records, and permanent buildings, more or less centrally located, for conducting the official business. The process was well described by Tout. "By Henry II's reign," Tout observes, "the English king had centralized so much authority under his immediate jurisdiction that all men of substance had frequent occasion to seek justice or to request favors at court." This movement, or rather, this *settlement,* took place first in financial administration, which had its special seat at Westminster: it was gradually extended to all the other offices of State. And the process itself was a reciprocal one: the centralization of authority necessitated the creation of the capital city, while the capital city, commanding the main routes of trade and military movement, was a powerful contribution to the unification of the state.

Mark that the capital city had a social as well as a political rôle to play. In the capital, provincial habits, customs, and dialects were melted down and recast in the image of the royal court: the so-called national image, national by prescription rather than in origin. Centuries were needed to effect a unification even in such extra-personal activities as the regulation of weights and measures: it was not until 1665 that Colbert proposed to "bring the whole of his majesty's kingdom within the same statutes and within the same system of weights and measures." Even security of life and property did not follow very swiftly in every corner of the new national realm: as late as 1553 in the Guides des Chemins de France there were notations in the open spaces between towns of "brigandage" or "Dangerous Forest."

The consolidation of power in the political capital was accompanied by a loss of power and initiative in the local centers: national prestige meant the death of local municipal freedom. The national territory itself became the connecting link between diverse groups, corporations, cities: the nation was an all-embracing society one entered at birth. The new theorists of law, as Gierke pointed out, were driven to deny that local communities and corporate bodies had an existence of their own: the family was the sole group, outside the state, whose existence was looked upon as self-validated, the only group that did not need the gracious permission of the sovereign to exercise its natural functions.

Once political power had been thus consolidated, economic privileges were obtained by individuals, not from the city, but from the prince; and they could be exercised, as a rule, anywhere in the realm. After the sixteenth century, accordingly, the cities that increased most rapidly in population and area and wealth were those that harbored a royal court: the fountainhead of economic power. About a dozen towns quickly reached a size not attained in the Middle Ages even by a bare handful: presently London had 250,000 inhabitants, Naples 240,000, Milan over 200,000, Palermo and Rome, 100,000, Lisbon, port of a great monarchy, over 100,000; similarly

Seville, Antwerp, and Amsterdam; while Paris in 1594 had 180,000.

As the great states of the modern world took shape, the capitals continued to monopolize population. In the eighteenth century the cities with over 200,000 included Moscow, Wien, St. Petersburg, and Palermo, while already in the 100,000 class were Warsaw, Berlin, and Copenhagen. Toward the end of the eighteenth century Naples had 433,930 inhabitants, Paris around 670,000, and London over 800,000; while the trading cities like Bristol and Norwich, or the industrial cities like Leeds, Manchester, Iserlohn and Paderborn for the most part remained small in size: that is, with less than fifty thousand inhabitants. The trading town of Hamburg and the industrial town of Lyons, both with secure medieval foundations and a continuing economic life, are the main exceptions; for they both had over 100,000 inhabitants at the beginning of the nineteenth century; but up to then they did not represent the dominant forms of political and financial power.

In contrast to the medieval regime, power and population were no longer disconnected, scattered, decentralized. Only in the Germanic countries did the older type of municipal economy effectively linger on; and the growth of Brandenburg-Prussia in the seventeenth century changed the shape of things even there. The state grew at the expense of the component parts: the capital city grew out of all proportion to the provincial cities, and in no small measure at their expense. Though natural capitals were usually situated at points of special advantage for trade and military defense—these being elements that entered originally into their selection—the baroque rulers brought all the powers of the state to bear to confirm these advantages. Where a natural center was lacking, they imitated at a distance Peter the Great's colossal willfulness in the founding of St. Petersburg.

In short, the multiplication of cities ceased; city building was no longer, for a rising class of small craftsmen and merchants, a means of achieving freedom and security. It was rather a means of consolidating political power in a single center directly under the royal eye and preventing such a challenge to the central authority from arising elsewhere, in scattered centers, more difficult to control. The age of free cities, with their widely diffused culture and their rela-

tively democratic modes of association, gave way to the age of absolute cities: a few centers that grew inordinately, leaving other towns
either to accept stagnation or to stultify themselves in hopeless gestures of imitation.

Law, order, uniformity—all these are special products of the
baroque capital: but the law exists to confirm the status and secure
the position of the privileged classes, the order is a mechanical order,
based not upon blood or neighborhood or kindred purposes and affections but upon subjection to the ruling prince; and as for the uniformity—it is the uniformity of the bureaucrat, with his pigeonholes, his
dossiers, his red tape, his numerous devices for regulating and systematizing the collection of taxes. The external means of enforcing
this pattern of life lies in the army; its economic arm is mercantile
capitalist policy; and its most typical institutions are the standing
army, the bourse, the bureaucracy, and the court. There is an underlying harmony that pervades all these institutions: between them
they create a new form for social life—the baroque city.

3: Instruments of Coercion

In the growth of the modern state, capitalism and technics and
warfare play a decisive part; but it is impossible to assign a prior
rôle to one or the other. Each developed through internal causes and
in response to a common milieu; and the state developed along with
them.

How did the modern doctrines of absolute political power arise?
Why did the political despot emerge so easily out of the concentra-
tions of economic capital and political authority that took place in
the fourteenth century Italian city, with more than one guild, more
than one family, contending for the position? How did the fashion
of despotism, creating big despots like the Tudors and midget despots
like the minor rulers of German states, spread over Europe—despots
who have their counterparts, sometimes their origins, in the new business men and financiers? There is another name for this growing
belief in absolute power: one might call it the illusion of gunpowder.

The old saw that gunpowder brought about the ruin of feudalism
is far from being true. Although feudal independence could not resist the centralization of power in national monarchies, gunpowder

had the effect of giving the feudal aristocrats a new lease on life, rescuing them from the pressure of the walled towns; for gunpowder increased the range, power, and mobility of the professional soldiers —and arms was the age-old profession of the feudal leader. In a very real sense, however, the introduction of gunpowder early in the fourteenth century—that century which undermined so many medieval institutions—sounded the death knell of the free cities.

Up to this time security had rested mainly on a very simple technical device: the moat and the wall: sufficient defense against raiding warriors who carried no heavy instruments of assault. A well-fortified city was virtually impregnable: even as late as Macchiavelli's day he remarked that the "cities of Germany . . . are fortified in such a manner that . . . to reduce them would be tedious and difficult, for they all have the necessary moats and bastions, sufficient artillery, and always keep in the public storehouses food and drink and fuel for one year."

Down to the fifteenth century, defense had the upper hand over assault. Alberti's advanced treatise on city planning, published posthumously, did not reckon with cannon, and the new art of fortification played but a minor rôle. Indeed, artillery was so imperfect and was used with so little skill at first that, as Guicciardini remarks, the besieging of towns was slow and uncertain; and until the French invasion of Italy under Charles VIII, with an unprecedented number of troops, 60,000, and with iron cannonballs instead of stone, all moving at a hitherto unheard-of speed—until this happened cities were on equal terms, or rather more than equal terms, with the attacking parties. Thereafter, conditions were reversed: while a non-explosive stone or iron ball, which the defender's cannon could employ, did but little harm when dropped among companies of men, it could do great damage when used in assault for breaking open a wall or dropping through a roof. The new artillery of the late fifteenth century made cities vulnerable.

In the attempt to equalize military conditions, the towns from this point on were compelled to abandon their old system of simple walls, defended for the most part by a citizen soldiery. They were forced to hire soldiers, so that they might sally forth and engage the enemy in open battle; and after the successful defense of Milan by Prospero

Colonna in 1521 they were forced to adopt the new methods of fortification that had been worked out there by the Italian military engineers. These new fortifications were far more elaborate than the old walls: they had outworks, salients, bastions, in starlike formations which permitted both the artillery and the armed infantry to rake the ranks of the attacking forces, from whatever side they might approach. By bringing the muskets of the defenders to the outmost positions they could theoretically put the city itself, whose circumference would be many hundred yards behind, beyond the reach of the enemy's most powerful gun. For two centuries these ingenious defenses seemed to promise security: but like so many other forms of military protection, they cast a dreadful social burden upon the protected population, and were ultimately responsible, in many cities, for those vile conditions for which the medieval town has been so often reproached.

Instead of the simple masonry wall, which an ordinary house mason might plan or build, it was necessary now to create a complicated system of defense that called for great engineering knowledge and a vast expenditure of money. These fortifications, difficult to build, were even more difficult to alter except at a prohibitive cost. The old walls could be extended to include a suburb: they did not handicap natural growth and adaptation. But the new fortifications prevented lateral expansion. In the sixteenth and seventeenth century cities, fortification must have had the same effect upon finances that the building of subways so often has had on the modern metropolis: they put an intolerable burden on the municipality and exposed it to the exorbitant aid of the financier.

Even under a centralized regime, as in France, the inhabitants of Metz offered their services gratis, so that they might accomplish at an expenditure of 25,000 livres work that would otherwise have cost 50,000: a voluntary effort to escape heavy financial impositions. Despite the frequent use of forced labor in France, the social cost was no slight one. Unproductive capital expenditures, diverting energy from the production of consumable goods, drain a people's resources even when the cost is not expressed in terms of money. Perhaps one of the great advantages of the English towns after the sixteenth century, which aided England in the race for commercial supremacy, was that they alone were free from this tax on their resources.

No less disastrous than the financial costs of construction were the direct results upon the population itself. While the old-fashioned city was divided into blocks and squares and then surrounded by a wall, the newly fortified city was planned as fortification, and the city was fitted into this straight-jacket. Whether old or new, its opportunities for expansion were over. New growth could take place only vertically; and no prudent burgher would build his house outside the walls in a possible no man's land. Administrators like Richelieu indeed ordered every building razed in the territory surrounding a fortified town: the city lay, as Paris did until but the other day, in the midst of a waste of non-building land, subject to artillery fire.

Not alone did the new fortifications remove the suburbs and gardens and orchards too far from the city to be reached conveniently except by the wealthier classes who could afford horses: open spaces within were rapidly built over as population was driven from the outlying land by fear and disaster, or by pressure of enclosure and land-monopoly. This new congestion led to the destruction of medieval standards of building space even in some of the cities that kept their medieval form and had preserved them longest. Overcrowding had in fact begun in the capital cities even before the seventeenth century: Stow notes in London that stone buildings were being replaced by wooden-framed ones to save space taken up by the heavier stone walls, and four and five story buildings were taking the place of two story ones. (The change from masonry to steel cage construction took place in the late nineteenth century American city for the same reason.) But in the seventeenth century these practices became universal: the systematic building of high tenements began—five or six stories high in old Geneva or in Paris, sometimes ten or twelve in Edinburgh.

This pressure of competition for space forced up land values in the political capitals. High land values, as in Berlin from the time of Frederick the Great on, hardened into a bad pattern for housing: overcrowding of the land, absence of play areas for children, lack of light, air, interior accommodation: high rents. Slum housing for a large part of the population, not simply for beggars, thieves, casual laborers and other outcasts, became the characteristic mode of the growing seventeenth century city. The existence of those slums defiled the high esthetic principles of the architects and builders in the same way that the frequent use of the corridors in Versailles as common urinals defiled the exorbitant esthetic pretensions of that court.

By the sixteenth century the practices of the Italian engineers dominated city building. Dürer's treatise on urban fortification gives only scant attention to the city proper; and in most of the other books and plans on the subject the city is treated as a mere appendage to the military form: it is, so to say, the "unoccupied" space that is left. Leonardo da Vinci, like Palladio, dealt in his notebooks with the city proper, suggested the separation of pedestrian ways from heavy traffic arteries, and went so far as to urge upon the Duke of Milan the standardized mass production of workers' houses. But despite these pregnant suggestions, his contributions to the art of city building remain poor and meager compared with his extraordinary zeal in improving the art of fortification and assault. It is easy to see where both opportunity and creative energy lay.

Eventually the new movement reached its summit in the types of fortification devised in the seventeenth century under the great engineer, Vauban—a method so complete that it required a new arm of the army, also systematized by Vauban, the miners and sappers, to overthrow it. Although the art of fortification had entailed endless sacrifices, it collapsed soon after it had evolved this final form. The new spy glass improved the fire of artillery; and the increased mobility of supplies, through canals and roads and the organization of a responsible commissariat, gave an impetus to the mobile army: meanwhile the territorial state itself had become the "City" that was to be defended.

4: War as City-Builder

The intensive development of the art of fortification shifted the emphasis in building from architecture to engineering, from esthetic design to material calculations of weight, number, and position: prelude to the wider technics of the machine. But especially it altered the urban picture from the short-range world of the medieval city, with its walking distances, its closed vistas, its patchwork space, to

the long-range world of baroque politics, with its long-distance gun-
fire and its wheeled vehicles and its increasing desire to conquer
space and make itself felt at a distance.

A good part of the new tactics of life sprang from an impulse toward destruction: long-range destruction. Christian piety and capitalist cupidity combined to thrust the new conquistadors across the
seas to plunder India, Mexico, and Peru; while the new type of
fortification, the new type of army, the new type of industrial workshop, best exemplified in the vast arsenals and arms factories, con-
spired to upset the relatively co-operative ways of the protected
town. Protection gave way to ruthless exploitation: instead of security, men sought adventurous expansion and conquest. And the proletariat at home was subject to a form of government no less ruthless
and autocratic than that which ground the barbaric civilizations of
North and South America into pulp.

War hastened all these transformations; it set the pace for every
other institution. The new standing armies, vast and powerful and
awe-inspiring in peace time no less than in war, transformed war
itself from a spasmodic to a continuous activity. The need for more
costly sinews of war put the cities into the hands of usurious
oligarchies that financed the ruler's mischievous policies, lived sumptuously on the profits and loot, and sought to entrench their positions
by backing the ensuing despotism. In an economic crisis the guns
of the hired solidiery could be turned, at the first signs of revolt,
upon the miserable subjects. (The English escaped the baroque
pattern earlier than other countries by turning tables on their Stuart
despot.)

In the Middle Ages the soldier had been forced to share his power
with the craftsman, the merchant, the priest: now, in the politics of
the absolute states, all law had in effect become martial law. Whoever could finance the army and the arsenal was capable of becoming master of the city. Shooting simplified the art of government: it
was a quick way of ending an embarrassing argument. Instead of
accepting the ordinary accommodations that ensure the healthy expression of diversities of temperament and interest and belief, the
ruling classes could dispense with such give-and-take methods: their
vocabulary recognized only "take." The gun, the cannon, the stand·

ing army helped produce a race of rulers who recognized no other law than that of their own will and caprice—that fine race of des-pots, sometimes imbecile, sometimes talented, who elevated the suspicions and delusions of the paranoid state into a political ritual. Their totalitarian imitators today, with no smaller delusions but with greater capacities for destruction, now threaten the very existence of world civilization.

The transformation of the art of war gave the baroque rulers a powerful advantage over the real corporations and groups that con-stitute a community. It did more than any other single force to alter the constitution of the city. Power became synonymous with numbers. "The greatness of a city," Botero observed, "is said to be, not the largeness of the site or the circuit of the walls, but the multitude and number of inhabitants and their power." The army, recruited for permanent warfare, became a new factor in the state and in the life of the capital city. In Paris and Berlin, and other lesser centers, these standing armies created a demand for special forms of housing, since soldiers could not be permanently quartered on the population without provoking a sense of grievance: witness the result of such an attempt in the British colonies of North America. The army barracks have almost the same place in the baroque order that the monastery had in the medieval one; and the Parade Grounds—the new Champ de Mars in Paris, for instance—were as conspicuous in the new cities as Mars himself was in Renascence painting. Turning out the guard, drilling, parading, became one of the great mass spectacles for the increasingly servile populace: the blare of the bugle, the tattoo of the drum, were as characteristic a sound for this new phase of urban life as the tolling of the bells had been for the medieval town. The laying out of great *Viae Triumphales*, avenues where a victorious army could march with the maximum effect upon the spectator, was an inevitable step in the replanning of the new capi-tals: notably in Paris and Berlin.

Along with the barracks and drill grounds, which occupy such large sites in the big capitals, go the arsenals. In the sixteenth cen-tury an extraordinary number of such buildings were erected. By 1540 Francis I had erected eleven arsenals and magazines: this went on, at a keener or slower pace, in all the other capitals. Soldiers, as Sombart has pointed out, are pure consumers, even as in action they are negative producers. Their demand for dwelling quarters was accompanied by a demand for provisions and drink and clothes on a similar scale. Hence the ranks of public houses and the army of tailors around the barracks quarters; indeed, a second standing army of shopkeepers, tailors, publicans, and whores springs up—the more miserable members of which owe their plight, perhaps, to the effect of the never-ending succession of military conflicts that agitated Europe and reached a climax in the eighteenth century. (See Sorokin's able statistical summary.)

Do not underestimate the presence of a garrison as a city-building agent. In 1740 the military population of Berlin numbered 21,309 out of a total of about 90,000 people: almost a quarter. The presence of this mass of mechanized and obedience-conditioned human beings necessarily touched every other aspect of life. The army supplied the model in its discipline for other forms of political coercion: people got into the habit of accepting the aggressive bark of the drill sergeant and the arrogant brutal manners of the upper classes: they were copied by the new industrialists, who governed their factories like absolute despots. Hutton in his history of Birmingham relates how the lord of the manor in "1728 . . . seized a public building called the Leather-Hall and converted it to his private uses. . . . The constable summoned the inhabitants to vindicate their rights, but none appearing, the Lord smiled at their supineness and kept the property." Beneath the superficial polish of baroque upper class manners there is the constant threat of an ugly, coercive discipline. These two qualities thread through every aspect of its life, even its luxury and folly.

5: The Ideology of Power

The two arms of this new system are the army and the bureaucracy: they are the temporal and spiritual support of a centralized despotism. Both agents owed no small part of their influence to a larger and more pervasive power, that of capitalist industry and finance. One must remember, with Max Weber, that the rational administration of taxation was an accomplishment of the Italian cities in the period *after* the loss of their freedom. The new Italian oli-

garchy was the first political power to order its finances in accordance with the principles of mercantile bookkeeping—and presently
the fine Italian hand of the tax-expert and financial administrator
could be observed in every European capital.

The change from a life economy to a money economy greatly
widened the resources of the state. The monopoly of rent, the booty
from piracy and brigandage, the loot of conquest, the monopoly
of special privileges in production and sale through patents granted
by the state, the application of this last system to technical inventions
—all these resources swelled the coffers of the sovereign. To increase
the boundaries of the state was to increase the taxable population: to
increase the population of the capital city was to increase the rent of
land. Both forms of increase could be translated ultimately into
terms of money pouring into the central exchequer. Not merely did
the royal governments become capitalistic in their workings, founding industries of their own, in arms, porcelain, tapestry: but they
sought, under the notion of a "favorable balance of trade," to create
a system of exploitation in which every sovereign state would receive
more in exchange, in measure of gold, than what it had given.

Capitalism in its turn became militaristic: it relied on the arms
of the state when it could no longer bargain to advantage without
them: the foundations of later colonial exploitation and imperialism.
Above all, the development of capitalism brought into every department secular habits of thought and matter-of-fact methods of appraisal: this was the warp, exact, orderly, superficially efficient, upon
which the complicated and effulgent patterns of baroque life were
worked out. The new merchant and banking classes emphasized
method, order, routine, power, mobility, all the habits that tended to
increase effective practical command. Jacob Fugger the Elder even
had a specially designed traveling set made for himself, containing
a compact, efficiently organized dining service: nothing was left to
chance. The uniformity of the die that stamped the coin at the
National Mint became a symbol of these emergent qualities in the
new order. Interests that were later sublimated and widened in physical science first disclosed themselves in the counting house: the
merchant's emphasis upon mathematics and literacy—both so necessary to long-distance trade through paid agents acting on written

instructions—became the fundamental ingredient in the new education of the grammar schools. It was not by accident that Newton, the physicist, became master of the mint, or that the merchants of London helped found the Royal Society and conducted experiments in physics. These mechanical disciplines were in effect interchangeable.

Behind the immediate interests of the new capitalism, with its abstract love of money and power, a change in the entire conceptual framework took place. And first: a new conception of space. It was one of the great triumphs of the baroque mind to organize space, make it continuous, reduce it to measure and order, to extend the limits of magnitude, embracing the extremely distant and the extremely minute; finally, to associate space with motion.

These changes were first formulated by the painters and architects, beginning with Alberti, Brunelleschi, and Uccello. While the Flemish realists, working in the medium of the advanced spinning industries, had accurate perceptions of space, it remained for the Italians of the fifteenth century to organize space on mathematical lines, within two planes, the foreground-frame, and that of the horizon line. They not merely correlated distance with intensity of color and quality of light, but with the movement of bodies through the projected third dimension. This putting together of hitherto unrelated lines and solids within the rectangular baroque frame—as distinguished from the often irregular boundaries of a medieval painting—was contemporary with the political consolidation of territory into the coherent frame of the state. But the development of the straight line and the uniform building line, as a means of expressing uniform motion, took place at least a century before the building of actual façades on visually limitless avenues.

Similarly, the study of perspective demolished the bounding wall, lengthened the distance toward the horizon, and centered attention on the receding planes, long before the wall was abolished as a feature of town planning. This was an esthetic preface to the grand avenues of baroque design, which at most have an obelisk, an arch, or a single building to terminate the converging rays of the cornice lines and the pavement edges. The long approach and the vista into space—those typical marks of the baroque plan—were first discovered by the painter. The act of passage is more important than the object reached: there is keener interest in the foreground of the Farnese Palace than in the gawky façade that caps the hill. The new Renascence window is definitely a picture frame, and the Renascence painting is an imaginary window which, in the city, makes one forget the dull courtyard that an actual opening would reveal.

If the earlier painters demonstrated Cartesian mathematics before Descartes, on their system of co-ordinates, the general sense of time likewise became more mathematical. From the sixteenth century on the domestic clock was widespread in upper-class households. But whereas baroque space invited movement, travel, conquest by speed —witness the early sail wagons and velocipedes—baroque time lacked dimensions: it was a moment-to-moment continuum. Time expressed itself, not as cumulative and continuous, but as disjunctive: it ceased to be life-time. The social mode of baroque time is fashion, which changes every year; and in the world of fashion a new sin was invented—that of being out of date. Its practical instrument was the newspaper, which deals with scattered, logically incoherent "events" from day to day: no underlying connection except contemporaneity. If in spatial forms repeating patterns take on a new meaning—columns on the façades of buildings, ranks of men on parade—in time the emphasis rests on novelty. As for the archaeological cult of the past, it was plainly not a recovery of history but a denial of history. Real history cannot be recovered.

The abstractions of money, spatial perspective, and mechanical time provided the enclosing frame of the new life. Experience was progressively reduced to just those elements that were capable of being split off from the whole and measured separately: conventional counters took the place of organisms. What was real was that part of experience which left no murky residues; and anything that could not be expressed in terms of visual sensations and mechanical order was not worth expressing. In art, perspective and anatomy; in morals, the systematic casuistry of the Jesuits; in architecture, the fixed proportions of the Five Orders, and in city building, the elaborate geometrical plan. These are the new forms.

Do not misunderstand me. The age of abstract analysis was an age of brilliant intellectual clarification. The new system of dealing with mathematically analyzable fragments instead of with wholes gave the first intelligible collective means of approaching such wholes: as useful an instrument of order as double-entry bookkeeping in commerce. In the natural sciences, the method of abstraction led to the discovery of units that could be investigated completely *just because* they were dismembered and fragmentary. The gain in the power of systematic thought and in the accurate prediction of physical events was to justify itself in the nineteenth century in a series of mighty advances in technics.

But in society the habit of thinking in terms of abstractions worked out disastrously. The new order established in the physical sciences was far too limited to describe or interpret social facts, and until the nineteenth century even the legitimate development of statistical analysis played little part in sociological thought. Real men and women, real corporations and cities, were treated in law and government as if they were imaginary bodies; whilst presumptuous fictions, like Divine Right, Absolute Rule, the State, Sovereignty, were treated as if they were realities. Freed from his sense of dependence upon corporation and neighborhood, the "emancipated individual" was dissociated and delocalized: an atom of power, ruthlessly seeking whatever power can command. With the quest for financial and political power, the notion of limits disappeared—limits on numbers, limits on wealth, limits on population growth, limits on urban expansion: on the contrary, quantitative expansion became predominant. The merchant cannot be too rich; the state cannot possess too much territory; the city cannot become too big.

Botero, contemporary with this development, noted its implications. "The founders of cities," he said, "considering that laws and civil discipline could not be easily conserved and kept where a mighty multitude of people swarmed (for multitudes do breed and bring confusion) they limited the number of citizens beyond which they supposed the form and order of government they sought to hold within their cities could not else be maintained. But the Romans, supposing power (without which, a city cannot long be maintained) consisteth for the most part in the multitude of people, endeavored all the ways and means they might to make their country great."

In the desire for more subjects—that is, for more cannon-fodder, more milch-cows for taxation and rent—the desires of the Prince coincided with those of the capitalists who were looking for larger and more concentrated markets. Power politics and power economics reinforced each other. Cities grew: rents rose: taxes increased. None of these results was accidental.

6: Movement and the Avenue

Since I am dealing with an age of abstractions, I purpose to follow its style. I shall treat of the part before I discuss the whole. First the avenue: then the separate institutions and buildings: only after that the city, as an esthetic if not a complete social unit.

The avenue is the most important symbol and the main fact about the baroque city. Not always was it possible to design a whole new city in the baroque mode; but in the layout of half a dozen new avenues, or in a new quarter, its character could be re-defined. In the linear evolution of the city plan, the movement of wheeled vehicles played a critical part; and the general geometrizing of space, so characteristic of the period, would have been altogether functionless had it not facilitated the movement of traffic and transport, at the same time that it served as an expression of the dominant sense of life. It was during the sixteenth century that carts and wagons came into more general use within cities. This was partly the result of technical improvements that replaced the old-fashioned solid wheel with one built of separate parts, hub, rim, spoke, and added a fifth wheel, to facilitate turning.

The introduction of wheeled vehicles was resisted, precisely as that of the railroad was resisted three centuries later. Plainly the streets of the medieval city were not adapted either in size or in articulation to such traffic. In England, Thomas tells us, vigorous protests were made, and it was asserted that if brewer's carts were permitted in the streets the pavement could not be maintained; while in France, parliament begged the king in 1563 to prohibit vehicles from the streets of Paris—and the same impulse even showed itself once more in the eighteenth century. Nevertheless, the new spirit in society was on the side of rapid transportation. The hastening of movement and the conquest of space, the feverish desire to "get somewhere," were manifestations of the pervasive will-to-power.

"The world," as Stow remarked when the fashion was taking hold in London, "runs on wheels." Mass, velocity, and time were categories of social effort before Newton's law was formulated.

Movement in a straight line along an avenue was not merely an economy but a special pleasure: it brought into the city the stimulus and exhilaration of swift motion, which hitherto only the horseman had known galloping over the fields or through the hunting forest. It was possible to increase this pleasure esthetically by the regular setting of buildings, with regular façades and even cornices, whose horizontal lines tended toward the same vanishing point as that toward which the carriage itself was rolling. In walking, the eye courts variety, but above this gait, movement demands repetition of the units that are to be seen: it is only so that the individual part, as it flashes by, can be recovered and pieced together. What would be monotony for a fixed position or even in a procession, becomes a necessary counterpoise to the pace of fast-moving horses.

In emphasizing the demands of wheeled traffic, which became urgent in the seventeenth century, I do not wish to neglect a characteristic need that disclosed itself at an even earlier period: the need of avenues for military movement. Alberti, who is in every sense the chief theoretical exponent of the baroque city, distinguished between main and subordinate streets. The first he called—and the name is important—*viae militares*, or military streets: he required that these should be straight. Anyone who has ever led a company of men through an irregularly planned city knows the difficulty of conducting them in martial order through its windings and twistings, particularly when the streets themselves are ungraded: inevitably, the individual falls out of alignment and the ranks present a disorderly appearance. To achieve the maximum effect on parade, the maximum appearance of order and power, it is necessary to provide a body of soldiers either with an open square or a long unbroken avenue.

The new town planners had the needs of the army constantly in mind: Palladio seconded Alberti. In addition to observing that the ways will be short and convenient if planned in a straight line, and so large that horses and coaches be no hindrance to each other when they meet, Palladio says that "the ways will be more convenient if they are made everywhere equal; that is to say, that there be no place in them where armies may not easily march." This uniform over-sized street, which was to become such a blight in the development of neighborhoods in new cities, and which was to add so greatly to the expenses, had purely a military basis.

Palladio's further definition of the military avenue is equally significant: he distinguished them from the non-military kind by pointing out that they pass through the midst of the city and lead from one city to another, and that they "serve for the common use of all passengers for carriages to drive or armies to march." Accordingly Palladio dealt with the military streets alone because non-military streets ought to be regulated according to the same principle as military ways, and the more alike they are the *"more commendable they will be."* In view of the importance of the army to the ruling classes, it is no wonder that military traffic was the determining factor in the new city plan, from the first mutation in Alberti to the final survival in the laying down of Haussmann's boulevards in Paris.

The esthetic effect of the regular ranks and the straight line of soldiers is increased by the regularity of the avenue: the unswerving line of march greatly contributes to the display of power, and a regiment moving thus gives the impression that it would break through a solid wall without losing a beat. That, of course, is exactly the belief that the soldier and the Prince desire to inculcate in the populace: it helps keep them in order without coming to an actual trial of strength, which always carries the bare possibility that the army might be worsted. Moreover, on irregular streets, poorly paved, with plenty of loose cobblestones and places of concealment, the spontaneous formations of untrained people have an advantage over a drilled soldiery: soldiers cannot fire around corners, nor can they protect themselves from bricks heaved from chimney tops immediately overhead: they need space to manoeuvre in. Were not the ancient medieval streets of Paris one of the last refuges of urban liberties? No wonder that Napoleon III sanctioned the breaking through of narrow streets and cul-de-sacs and the razing of whole quarters to provide wide boulevards: this was the best possible protection against assault from within. To rule merely by coercion, without affectionate consent, one must have the appropriate urban background.

In the new city, or in the formal additions made to old centers, the building forms a setting for the avenue, and the avenue is essentially a parade ground: a place where spectators may gather, on the sidewalks or in the windows, to review the evolutions and exercises and triumphal marches of the army—and be duly awed and intimidated. The buildings stand on each side, stiff and uniform, like soldiers at attention: the uniformed soldiers march down the avenue, erect, formalized, repetitive: a classic building in motion. The spectator remains fixed: life marches before him, without his leave, without his assistance: he may use his eyes, but if he wishes to open his mouth or leave his place, he had better ask for permission first.

In the medieval town the upper classes and the lower classes had jostled together on the street, in the market-place, as they did in the cathedral: the rich might ride on horseback, but they must wait for the poor man with his bundle or the blind beggar groping with his stick to get out of the way. Now, with the development of the wide avenue, the dissociation of the upper and the lower classes achieves form in the city itself. The rich drive: the poor walk. The rich roll along the axis of the grand avenue: the poor are off-center, in the gutter: and eventually a special strip is provided for the ordinary pedestrian, the sidewalk. The rich stare, the poor gape: insolence battens on servility. The daily parade of the powerful becomes one of the principal dramas of the baroque city: a vicarious life of dash and glitter and expense is thus offered to the butcher's boy with a basket on his head, to the retired merchant out for a stroll, to the fashionable housewife, shopping for bargains and novelties, to the idle mob of hangers-on in all degrees of shabby gentility and downright misery—corresponding to the clients of imperial Rome.

"Mind the carriages!" cried Mercier in his eighteenth century Tableau de Paris. "Here comes the black-coated physician in his chariot, the dancing master in his *cabriolet*, the fencing master in his *diable*—and the Prince behind six horses at the gallop as if he were in the open country. . . . The threatening wheels of the overbearing rich drive as rapidly as ever over stones stained with the blood of their unhappy victims." Do not fancy the danger was exaggerated: in France the stage-coach, introduced in the seventeenth century, killed more people annually than the railroad that followed

it. This increase in the tempo of life, this rapid motion, these superficial excitements and dangers, were the psychological sweetening of
the bitter pill of autocratic political discipline. In the baroque city
one might say, "The carriages move swiftly," just as people say in
present-day fascist Italy, "The trains run on time."

There was only one desirable station in this despotism; it was that
of the rich. It was for them that the avenue was made and the pavement smoothed out and springs and cushions added to the wheeled
vehicle: it was to protect them that the soldiers marched. To keep a
horse and carriage was an indispensable mark of commercial and
social success; to keep a whole stable was a sign of affluence. In the
eighteenth century the stables and mews crept into the less savory
quarters of the capitals, behind the wide avenues and the sumptuous
squares, carrying there the faint healthy smell of straw and manure.
If the fowls no longer cackled at dawn, the restless stomp of a high-
bred horse might be heard at night from rear windows: the man on
horseback had taken possession of the city.

7: The Shopping Parade

The military parade had its feminine counterpart in the capital:
the shopping parade. The ritual of conspicuous waste took up an
ever larger share of the time and effort of living: competitive spending affected every class; for "the same flourishing pride has dictated
new methods of living to the people, and while the poorest citizens
strive to live like the rich, the rich like the gentry, the gentry like
the nobility, and the nobility strive to outshine one another, no wonder that all the sumptuary trades increase." In the baroque period
the medieval sumptuary laws, governing the dress and expenditure
of each class according to tradition, began to fall into disrepute, even
when they were not actually lifted from the statute books. Luxury,
instead of distinguishing special public festivals and celebrations,
became a daily commodity. Competitive luxury. To spend *more* was
more important than to spend *enough*.

The old open market, while it did not disappear from the cities
of the Western World, henceforth restricted itself largely to provisions: it was only in the poorer quarters, like the Jews' market in
Whitechapel, that one could still pick up a dress, a pair of trousers,

or a stove from an open cart; though in Paris, more tenacious of medieval habits than would appear on the surface, the nineteenth century department stores were compelled to open up street-stands, at least in the lower middle class neighborhoods. Market squares where people gathered no longer had a place in the new urban lay-out: the circles and stars of the new plans, with their jam of wheeled traffic, had no place for chaffering or cheapening.

The open air shop, the outlet for the workroom in the rear, tended to disappear, too: the new type of shop took shape behind glass win-dows, greatly enlarged to cover the whole front and serve as a center of display. No effort was spared to decorate the interior smartly, particularly in the more modish commodities. To fit up a pastry-cook's shop with plate glass windows and pier glasses and glass lan-terns and twenty-five sconces for candles and six large silver salvers, and to paint the ceiling and carve the columns and gild the lanterns took a pretty sum. It is a modern custom, observes Daniel Defoe in The Compleat English Tradesman, to "have tradesmen lay out two-thirds of their fortune in fitting up their shops. . . . 'Tis a small matter to lay out two or three, nay five hundred pounds."

The display market for goods already made, rather than produced on the order system, had already come into existence: from the seven-teenth century on, it gradually encroached into one line after another, hastening the tempo of sale and placing a premium upon the visual enticement of the buyer. The special market day lingered on in rural neighborhoods; but in the commercial town every day tended to be market day. Buying and selling became not merely an incidental traffic in the conveyance of goods from producer to consumer: it became one of the principal preoccupations of all classes. "Market-ing" rested on the basis of domestic needs: "shopping" was a less urgent, a more frivolous, occupation. Shopping furnished excite-ment: it afforded a special occasion for the lady of the house to dress up, to sally forth, to exhibit her own person.

"I have heard," said Defoe, still obviously shocked by the prac-tice, "that some ladies, and these, too, persons of good note, have taken their coaches and spent a whole afternoon in Ludgate Street or Covent Garden, only to divert themselves in going from one mercer's shop to another, to look upon their fine silks and to rattle

Baroque order was heralded by a series of great mathematical and mechanical conquests: the conquest of space through the use of the magnetic compass at sea, the rediscovery of the Greek conception of the earth as sphere, the projection of accurate maps through the use of co-ordinates for latitude and longitude, the development of trigonometry, the invention of the telescope with its lengthening of visual distance, and the discovery of the mechanical laws of perspective. Mechanization of time: mechanization of space: mechanization of power.

[TOP] New market-place: transitional between the medieval market and the avenue market and open circle of later planning. Uniform roof line: symmetrical placement of buildings, duplication of churches and towers on each side of the avenue of approach: a perfect example of the order theoretically laid down by Alberti and, later, Palladio.

[FIRST LEFT] Regimentation of space extended even to park design after Le Nôtre: the sacrifice of the autonomy of living forms to visual order: Procrustes at play. The public use of open spaces for promenade was possible in the medieval city only on the walls. This new vehicle of recreation and ceremony is a courtly product. Contrast it with the romantic Victorian park, refuge of the solitary individual, spoiled even by signs of human occupation. The two poles are the parade ground and the wild forest. Fill in the parade ground with uniform rows of trees in military formation and you have the formal park: thin out the forest irregularly and you have the romantic park. The nineteenth century endeavored to combine philanthropy (crowds) with naturalism (privacy). Today we must plan the entire region with special zones and structures appropriately set off to fulfill each personal and communal function.

[FIRST RIGHT] Renascence ceiling: same order of design as the new city plan, with a central open circle, converging lines for traffic, and irregular house-blocks: see Plate 8.

[SECOND] Early royal art gallery for easel-paintings: removable art, no longer designed for a specific social context.

[BOTTOM LEFT] Counterbalancing of the mechanical by the sensuous: politeness, graceful movement, artful relaxation: the claim of Venus against Mars. See Sombart's Luxus und Kapitalismus.

[BOTTOM RIGHT] Baroque bedroom. The same artist, in this series of prints on the five senses, has depicted the bed also in the dining room. Privacy and specialized functions came in slowly. Closed doors and open fires in the bedroom yielded new erotic variations: including the visual pleasure of nakedness.

[TOP] Tuileries esplanade: swift movement, with the aid of horsepower, was one of the privileges of the rich and great: cavalcades dash along the straight avenues between Versailles and Paris. Note the six-horse coach, as well as the mounted men. "Four companies of the French Guard and two of the Swiss Guard parade every day in the court of the minister between the two railings, and when the king issues forth in his carriage to go to Paris or Fontainebleau the spectacle is magnificent." (Taine.) Public coaches, proposed by Pascal, were introduced in Paris in the mid-seventeenth century, and in 1650 Nicolas Sauvage at the Hotel de Fiacre in the Rue St Martin first offered wagons and horses for hire: beginnings of modern urban transportation. But streets long remained badly paved; good roads awaited Telford and Macadam; hence water transportation kept its importance. As late as 1803 London had 3000 wherries on the water, as against 1000 hackney coaches and 400 sedan chairs.

[MIDDLE LEFT] Ball, Versailles: diffusion of eroticism in luxury, and sustenance of the will-to-power in a success outwardly spectacular and imposing. *Courtliness:* slow gestures and dignified movements: emphasis of separation from the spontaneity and uncouthness of the "lower classes." *Courtesy:* the mollification of privilege: imagination and reciprocity in the smaller acts of life. *Courtship:* the labyrinthine approach to sexual union: the difference between a hunter's approach to an animal and the butcher's.

[MIDDLE RIGHT] Teatro San Carlo at Naples: model of many of the great theaters and opera houses that followed. The theater dominated this period: architecture became scene painting. Upper class life was an effort to put on a good show: the elect had speaking parts. From the sixteenth century on theater buildings were erected in Italy: one of the first was the Teatro Olimpico at Vicenza, designed by Palladio and erected by Scamozzi in 1584. The transplantation of the theater from the Church to the Court, and the settlement of the wandering players' troupes in a permanent abode, were characteristic urban developments: even the popular theater in England was under the patronage of the nobility.

[BOTTOM] Ranelagh Gardens, London. One of a series of popular pleasure resorts that lasted as such into the nineteenth century. After temporary banishment they reappeared in the newer guise of the later nineteenth century amusement park, itself partly an outgrowth of the International Fairs. In the earliest type, court forms predominated: see the description of Sir Roger de Coverley's visit to Vauxhall Gardens in the Spectator Papers. The specialized pleasure resort is the urban form of this baroque mutation: Bath, Baden-Baden, Monte Carlo, Saratoga.

and banter the shopkeepers, having not so much as the least occasion, much less intention, to buy anything."

As the permanent market took form both producer and consumer
tended to become more anonymous: it was the middleman who made
a name for himself by anticipating the idiosyncrasies of the buyer
or by manipulating his taste and judgment. To avoid striking in the
dark, a new patron and purchaser assumed control of the market:
Dame Fashion. Again I must quote the invaluable Defoe: "Every
tailor invents fashions, the mercer studies new patterns, the weavers
weave them into beautiful and gay figures, and stores himself with
a vast variety to allure the fancy; the coachmaker contrives new
machines, chairs, Berlins, flies, etc., all to prompt the whimsies and
unaccountable pride of the gentry. . . . The upholder [upholsterer]
does the like in furniture, till he draws the gay ladies to such an
excess of Folly that they must have their houses new furnished every
year; everything that has been longer than a year must be called old,
and to have their fine lodgings seen by a person of any figure above
twice over, looks ordinary and mean."

Money was supreme: the customs of the market were not confined
to the shops. Vicomte d'Avenel, whose history of property gives invaluable documentation of goods and prices, has put the matter well.
"It was in the past, under the ancient regime, from the end of the
Middle Ages to the Revolution, when force did not exercise a great
place and when public opinion counted for little, that money ruled
in France. Almost everything could be bought, power and honors,
civil and military employment, and the nobility itself, whose titles
were inseparable from the ground upon which they rested. It was
necessary to be rich to become somebody, and if the favor of a prince
occasionally distinguished a poor man, it would at the same stroke
make him rich, since riches were the ordinary consequence of
power."

Life, even aristocratic life, expressed itself most easily in terms of
trade and money. In a moral homily of the sixteenth century on
serving men, note the figure of the very opening passage: "In this
Bourse or Exchange of Human Affairs, which consisteth (as it were)
altogether in merchandise, buying and selling, it is very meet that
there should be all manner conditions and callings . . . summoned

on forfeiture of ten pounds on Issues to appear, with money and ware always ready, to maintain the mundane market." Life was like that. By hook or crook, by trade or theft or public corruption or financial enterprise, one got hold of money: "rapine, avarice, expense" made life "mean handiwork of craftsman, cook, or groom." Wordsworth's sonnet was a compact indictment.

In the great capital cities, too large for people to know their neighbors, the standards of the market came generally to prevail. People sought by overt display to make a decisive impression as to their station in life, their taste, their prosperity: every individual, every class, put on a front. Fashion is, so to say, the uniform of the day, and well-to-do people wore this uniform in the home or the street with the same discipline as the soldier on his military parade. Venice had set the pace in dictating personal fashions, thanks to the charm of her courtesans; Paris took up these duties in the seventeenth century; and thereafter each national capital served as pattern for the rest of the country. Part of the economic use of the capital city, from the standpoint of the great factors and importers, *was to discredit local goods, which varied in pattern, in color, in stuff, in texture, in decoration, in accordance with local tradition, and give circulation to those in use at the capital. Slippery metropolitan styles undermined the sobrieties of craftsmanship, even as they annulled the traditional preferences, or idiosyncrasies, of maker and customer.*

Some hint of this state had already become plain in the sixteenth century; for Stow is at pains to "answer the accusation of those men, which charge *London* with the loss and decay of many (or most) of the ancient cities, corporate towns, and markets within this realm. . . . As for retailers thereof, and handicraftsmen, it is no marvel if they abandon country towns and resort to London; for not only the court, which is nowadays much greater and more gallant than in former times . . . but also by occasion thereof the gentlemen of all shires do fly and flock to the city, the younger sort of them to see and show vanity, and the elder to save the cost and charge of hospitality and house-keeping." Fashion competition, which was the life of baroque trade (and remains its chief bequest to later capitalism), was also largely the death of the customary in-

dustries of the provincial towns. Eventually they were forced to produce for the anonymous distant market or lose their industries entirely. The effect of this is observable in our irregional system of
production and distribution down to the present day. Economists
often tend to confuse it with the natural effects of regional specialization.

In this economy, the centralization of the baroque capital, which
involved costly wastes in transport, became a special virtue. "The
magnitude of the city of London adds very considerably to the Inland
Trade, for as the City is the center of our trade, so all the manufactures are brought hither, and hence circulated again to all the country. . . ." "How many thousands," Defoe exclaims again in another
place, "I might say how many hundreds of thousands of men and
horses are employed in the carrying and re-carrying to and from
London the growth of England and the importations of foreign countries; and how many of these would stand still and want business
. . . if this great city was divided into fifteen cities . . . and they
were situated in so many different places remote from one another,
where the countryside within 20 or 30 miles round would be sufficient for them and able to supply them, and where every port would
import its own goods from abroad."

This last passage is a succinct explanation of the difference between the medieval urban economy and the baroque state economy:
no better could be offered. But in terms of social energetics and cultural life, what Defoe took for a eulogy is actually a damning indictment.

The military capital as an agent for enforcing uniformity and
standardization, in the annual uniforms of fashion no less than in
the uniforms of the soldiery, was a necessary contribution to the
mechanical standardization that made possible the further mechanization of the whole process of production. And just as in the regular
façade of the new palaces at St. Petersburg one sees, beneath the
ornament, the bare skeleton of the paleotechnic factory, so, in the
formal elegances of the baroque city plan, one already sees the
dreary mechanical subdivision of the industrial town. Note that the
critical changes took place first in the form of play, show, luxury:
this was the specific baroque contribution.

One last remote outcome of the tendencies I have been discussing must be noted: the evolution of the fashion parade into a specialized type of city. While spas and watering places where people went for reasons of health had never fallen out of existence, in the eighteenth century these old resorts took on new life as people began to flock to them for a new reason: fashionable display. The parade (Corso) became not merely the core but the very reason for existence of a new kind of city: Bath, Margate, Brighton, Ostend, later Baden-Baden, Carlsbad, Travemunde, the Riviera, Saratoga Springs. Here were places where people of fashion met: met in order to exhibit themselves at the proper season, sometimes under the pretext of seeking health, but also to enjoy life, untainted by any visible connection with trade and industry, occupations that were already filling the capital with obnoxious sights, sounds, and smells. Here all the typical baroque pleasures were available: particularly gambling, dress, flirtation, music, sometimes the theater. These new cities were in effect minor courts, ruled by a self-elected prince, specialist in dress and manners, despot of fashion—the dandy. A whole town would grow up around this parade, eventually, and business would crowd in again once more and take precedence over courtliness; so that Atlantic City, for example, a typical latter-day vulgarization of the baroque mode of life, is in detail an extension of Broadway, Fifth Avenue, Market Street, no more restful than the first, scarcely more maritime in character than the last.

8: The New Divinity

The breakup of the medieval church set free the "ions" that were re-polarized in the baroque city. One may seize the process in a concrete figure, if one considers how each element in the old structure was appropriated by a special institution, sect, or group. Follow the dismemberment: the protestants captured the preacher's rostrum and made it the core of their new chapels, where no graven image competed with the speaker's face, and no rich ceremonial distracted attention from his urgent voice. The aristocracy commanded the painter and the architect: art was carried away to special halls and galleries, and to make the process easier, the new easel picture took the place of the wall fresco. Angels and saints became Bacchuses

and Graces: first secular faces of popes, courtiers, business men sur·
round the Holy Image: finally they displace it. The choir, which once
chanted hymns to God, was removed to the concert hall or to a bal-
cony of the ballroom: the religious festival became the court
masque, to celebrate a mundane birthday or a wedding; while the
drama, leaving the porches of the church, where the clergy and
guildsmen had once enacted their mysteries and moralities, was
turned over to professional actors under the patronage of the nobility: their first raffish quarters are on the outskirts of the city.
The chapter-house, with its complement of at least formally celibate
clergy, became the aristocratic men's club of the nineteenth century:
exclusive, monastic, even if ostentatiously sybaritic: the Carlton, the
Reform, and their imitators.

Finally the nave, the bare assembly place, became the bourse. Do
not fancy that the latter is a wild imaginary parallel: in the seventeenth century the brokers plied their trade in the nave of St. Paul's,
and the money changers all but drove the representatives of Christ
from the temple—till at last the stench became too great for even a
venal church to endure. Wren's unused plan for the reconstruction
of London after the fire handsomely recognized this new order of
life. He did not give the dominating site to St. Paul's: he planned the
new avenues so as to give this honor to the Royal Stock Exchange.

This analytical decomposition of the church gave each institution
a special opportunity to flourish in its own right. On the positive side,
this was another witness to the visual clarification and the intelligent
specialization of functions that characterized baroque order. All these
institutions had become detached from the church because fresh life
and growth were stifled there: there would have been no Shakespeare
if the Church had kept control of the drama, and no great Rembrandt
portraits if he had continued to paint the staple group portraits of
the complacent worthies of the Guild. But these various fragments of
art and culture were dispersed with respect to the population as a
whole: dispersed and put out of their reach. It was only in the court
of the Prince that the parts were united again to form a new whole
for the exclusive benefit of those who wielded power.

We have seen what became of the medieval cathedral. But what
became of its God? Here the transformation can be recorded only

in terms of blasphemy. The absolute ruler by divine right usurped the place of the Deity and claimed his honors; he might even call himself Le Roi Soleil, superstitiously arrogating to himself the myth of a Pharaoh or an Alexander. In the new cult, the part of the Virgin Mary, most powerful intercessor at the throne of heaven, was taken by the king's mistress. The powers and principalities of the new Heaven, indispensable to its regimen, were the courtiers who crowded around the throne of the Monarch and proclaimed his glory. The parallel was not absent from even pious minds in the seventeenth century. "Whoever," said La Bruyère, "considers that the king's countenance is the courtier's supreme felicity, that he passes his life looking at it and within sight of it, will comprehend to some extent how to see God constitutes the glory and the happiness of the saints."

Learned flunkies wrote treatises to prove the despot's direct connection with heaven, to uphold his omnipotence, to admonish obedience to his divine commands. When their rationalizations fell short of his own exorbitant claims he might even, like James I of England, take a hand in writing the necessary eulogium himself. "The prince," according to Castiglione, who wrote the classic treatise on the Courtier, "ought to be very generous and splendid, and give to all men without reserve, because God, as the saying runs, is the treasurer of generous princes." Fortune's cornucopia must indeed be inexhaustible at the rate it was drained at court: Avenel reports that one of the great ballets at Versailles, in which one hundred and fifty people took part, came to a hundred thousand francs.

This demand for unlimited funds infected every rank in society; and it was the key to the economic policies of the absolute state. When taxation did not supply sufficient means for the prince and his favorites, he resorted to pillage: distant kingdoms in the case of Philip of Spain, or nearer monasteries for Henry VIII: when these did not suffice, he robbed the poor man of his pennies in order to bestow gold on those already rich. Hence the whole policy of licenses and patents: one needed a special permission, to be obtained at a price, even to build a house.

The growth of a bureaucracy to superintend these exactions and further the distribution of privilege added to the burden on the community: the Circumlocution Office was a convenient means of taking care of retainers and their younger sons: from St. Petersburg to Whitehall it was an inevitable appanage of upper class society. "Never was bureaucracy carried to such a point of exaggeration, extravagance, and tiresomeness," wrote Mercier. "Never did business so drag since the creation of this army of clerks who are in business what footmen are in service. References, regulations, registrations, formalities of all kinds have multiplied with such profusion and so little discernment."

It finally came down to this: a whole country was run for the benefit of a few dozen families, or a few hundred, who owned a good share of the land—almost half in France in the eighteenth century— and who battened on the unearned increments from industry, trade, and urban rents.

9: Position of the Palace

City building, in the formal sense, was an embodiment of the prevalent drama and thema that shaped itself in the court: it was, in effect, a collective embellishment of the life and gestures of the palace. The palace faced two ways. From the urban side came rent, tribute, taxes, control of the army and control of the organs of the state; from the countryside came the well-built, well-exercised, well-fed, well-sexed men and women who formed the body of the court and who received honors, emoluments, and the perquisites the king magnanimously bestowed. Power and pleasure, a dry abstract order and an effulgent sensuality, were the two poles of this life. Mars and Venus were the presiding deities, until Vulcan finally cast his cunning iron net of utilitarianism over their concupiscent forms.

The court was a world in itself; but a world in which all the harsh realities of life were shown in a diminishing glass, and all its frivolities magnified. Pleasure was a duty, idleness a service, and honest work the lowest form of degradation. To become real in the baroque court, it was necessary that an object or a function should bear the marks of exquisite uselessness. The most powerful waterwheels of the seventeenth century and the great hydraulic pumps that counted among its chief technical advances were used merely to work the fountains in the Gardens of Versailles. Fischer von Erlach's steam pump, the first used in Austria, was not applied to a mine but in the gardens of the Belvedere Palace in Wien; and that significant agent of production, the automatic power-machine, achieved its first great success applied to buttons (the stamping machine), to ribbons (the narrow automatic loom), and to army uniforms (the first sewing machine).

The ritual of the court was an attempt to confirm the make-believe of absolute power by a special drama. I know no better picture of the environment, no more fulsome demonstration of its narcotic illusions, than the panegyric uttered by Nicholas Breton:

"Oh, the gallant life of the Court, where so many are the choices of contentment, as if on earth it were the Paradise of the World: the majesty of the sovereign, the wisdom of the Council, the honour of the Lords, the beauty of the Ladies, the care of the officers, the courtesy of the gentlemen, the divine services of the morning and evening, the witty, learned, noble, and pleasant discourses all day, the variety of wits and the depth of judgements, the dainty fare, sweetly dressed and neatly served, the delicate wines and rare fruits, with excellent music and adorable voices, masques, and plays, dancing and riding; diversity of games, delightful to the gamester's purposes; and riddles, questions, and answers; poems, histories, and strange inventions of wit, to startle the brain of good understanding; rich apparel, precious jewels, fine proportions, and high spirits, princely coaches, stately horses, royal buildings and rare architecture, sweet creatures and civil pleasure; and in the course of love such carriage of content as sets the spirit in the lap of pleasure, that if I should talk of the praise of it all day, I should be short of the worth of it at night."

One need not underscore the counter-accents of actuality: the lees in the wine, the inane conversation that passed for wit, the unwanted babies that got past the barriers of the fashionable contraceptives known from the sixteenth century on to the upper classes of France and Italy. There was still enough plausibility in the picture even when the sour notes were accounted for. The motto written over the door of Rabelais' Abbey of Thelema was: Do as You Please. Over the palace gates there was an extra proviso: As Long as It Pleases the Prince. One must however add one fact that is too often left out of the conception of this ceremonious and sensuous baroque life. Its ritual was so tedious that it veritably bored people to distraction. The daily routine of Prince and courtier was comparable to that of a Ford worker in an assembly plant: every detail of it laid out and fixed, as much for the sovereign as for his entourage. From the moment the Prince's eyes opened to the last moment when his mistress left his bedchamber, he was, so to say, on the assembly line.

Perhaps this pervasive tedium accounts not only for the effortful frivolity, but for the element of sheer vagrant mischief, like the outbreak of schoolboys who have been kept under too strict confinement, in baroque state policy. Much of the intricate plotting and counterplotting was the work of bored virtuosos of diplomacy who liked nothing better than to prolong the game itself. Surely the eternal standing, waiting, bowing, scraping—of which Taine has given an unforgettable picture in his description of the ancient regime—must have run against the grain of well-fed men and women. Small wonder that spectacular amusements played such a large part in their lives.

Unfortunately, the very distractions of the court became duties. The performance of leisure imposed new sacrifices. The dinner party, the ball, the formal visit, as worked out by the aristocracy and by those who, after the seventeenth century, aped them, gave satisfaction only to those for whom form is more important than content. No small part of the life described in Vanity Fair and The Red and the Black, at one end of the nineteenth century, and by Proust at the other end, consisted of visiting and "paying court": formalities. Proust noted that it was at the time of Louis XIV that a serious change had come about in the life of the aristocracy, which had once had active responsibilities, grave duties, serious interests: the only questions treated with moral earnestness were those which concerned manners. As in so many other departments of life the baroque court here anticipated the ritual and the psychal reaction of the twentieth century metropolis. A similar grind: a similar boredom: a similar attempt to take refuge in "distractions" from the tyrannical oppression that had become a routine and from the routine that had become an overwhelming oppression.

10: Influence of the Palace on the City

One detects the influence of the baroque court upon the city in nearly every aspect of its life—it is even the parent of many of the new institutions that were later claimed by democracy for its own. There is no parallel type of intercourse between the castle and the market-place in the medieval city; if anything, the influence moved in the reverse direction: the feudal aristocracy became urbane.

Thanks to aristocratic patronage, the theater took its modern form in London, Paris, and the minor cities: the special hall in which the audience is seated according to rank and ability to pay, and in which, from their fixed positions, they become the passive spectators of a drama which is seen, as it were, through the transparent show-window, revealed by an opened curtain. Thanks to the princely desire to bring home loot from foreign conquests and to acquire by purchase or patronage what could not be obtained by arms, the great collections of art that form the Vatican Museum, the Louvre, and the National Gallery were first started. And at the very moment that music was being driven out of the home—as the result no doubt of the growing distance in education, manners, and taste between the master of the house and his menials—it achieved an independent existence in the baroque orchestra: therewith the concert hall makes its appearance.

One by one these new institutions mark their existence on the new city plan. Now a national theater in Naples, now a concert hall in Wien, now a museum and gallery in London. Sometimes they come under private auspices: sometimes with royal or municipal support; but always in the image originally stamped by the court. Perhaps the first baroque feature to be opened to the public and duly incorporated in the city was the park: the new equivalent of the smaller pleasure grounds and playing fields of the medieval city. The broad landscape park, preserved in the heart of the city, remains perhaps the greatest single contribution that the baroque period of city building made to modern urban existence. But even here the spirit of the age asserted itself. When the Crown planned Regent's Park in London the park itself was appreciated as a device for increasing the ground values of the neighboring properties held by the Crown.

It was on the side of pleasure and recreation that the influence of the court was most potent. The pleasure garden, such as Ranelagh Gardens in London in the seventeenth century, and Vauxhall and Cremorne Gardens in the eighteenth, was an attempt to supply the pleasures of the palace to the commonalty at a reasonable price per head: the French equivalent was the Bal Masque and the German parallel the more domestic and *ordentlich* Beer Garden. These pleasure gardens were popular in the baroque period, and remained so in New York, which took them over, down to the Civil War. They consisted in a large central building where dances and routs could be held, and where great feasts could be given; and of gardens and woods where people might roam on a fine night, eating, drinking, flirting, love-making, watching fireworks or lantern displays. Swings and roundabouts made their appearance here; likewise, at the beginning of the nineteenth century, the aristocratic love of speed came out in the more popular promenade aérienne, or chute-the-chutes. In time, the older elegant features of baroque taste disappeared; beginning first, perhaps, in the great international fairs more rowdy forms of amusement, more dangerous distractions—like the Ferris Wheel —came to the front: only the tawdry glitter remained in a Coney Island. But the point of origin is as plain as the downward path.

If the pleasure garden grew on one stem of baroque life, the museum—originally the very consummation of the acquisitive life— grew on the other stem. At first the museum proceeded from the motive of scientific curiosity, as in Aristotle's collections; and after the Alexandrian age of learning the "museum" was reduced to the collections of saints' relics—a bone, a tooth, a phial of blood—in the medieval churches. But museum collections in the modern sense began with the collections of coins and inscriptions that took form as early as the fifteenth century in Italy: these anticipated by a few years the natural history collections of a von Netteshyn, a Paracelsus or an Agricola. Indeed, the writings of the latter were instrumental in causing the Elector Augustus of Saxony to form the collections that have since developed into the museums of Dresden.

In every part of Europe this random search for curiosities and wonders and specimens took place: a primitive "collection economy" of the mind. Acquisition for acquisition's sake was the very spirit of the age: the curiosity parade of the museum was a sort of learned counterpart to the shopping parade: in its earliest form, it was mainly another example of vain display. In the transformation of these cabinets of curiosities, these cabinets of coins, these cabinets of etchings into independent public edifices, the court and the aristocracy played a leading part. But the opening of the British Museum in 1759, after Sir Hans Sloane's bequest was a landmark in *popular* culture; for when display ceased to be merely a private gratification of the possessor it had the possibility of becoming a means of public education.

Half-way between pleasure and curiosity stands one last bequest of the court: the zoological garden. The keeping of wild animals, especially the more exotic ones from foreign parts, was an attribute of kings even in the Middle Ages: they would sometimes be used in processions, like the animals in the traveling circus of the nineteenth century. The extension of these collections of living animals, the provision of permanent quarters and exhibition grounds for them, took place as part of the same movement of an acquisitive and scientific culture as created the museum. Like the museum, they furnished a suitable destination for the explorer's and hunter's trophies. Here was a fresh contribution to the city: a symbol of that feral state which man too easily forfeits when he seeks the comforting presence of his own kind in the city. The playful antics of the monkey, the imperturbability of the hippopotamus, the gay sleek motions of the sea-lions—all these things, if they did not bring the citizen in touch with nature, at least had a relaxing effect upon overstretched urban ego: they gave a common pleasure to the adult and the child. Even such moth-eaten baroque relics as the dancing bear or the organ grinder's monkey often served as the one touch of animal gaiety between the drab walls of the nineteenth century street. Is it by accident that these vestigial emblems of court life were usually presided over by an Italian?

11: Bedroom and Salon

If the influence of the court was effective in the city at large, it was no less so in the household: at all events, in the houses of the middle classes and their economic superiors. Here the habits of the court, both for good and bad, prevailed. For bad in that a new domestic despotism grew up, which had its source in the vast number of disfranchised people who crowded into the capitals to sell their services for a pittance. The good side was the esthetic improvement in manners, perhaps not altogether unaffected by the increased knowledge of the bland and perfect forms of Chinese civilization; and above all, the spread of privacy within the home: a fact which gave rise to a new code of sexual manners, embroidering the preliminaries of sexual intercourse, and tending to lengthen the period of amatory youth for both sexes. The very word courtship, for that preliminary play which includes the display of wit and charm as well as physical passion, shows how much our erotic life owes to the practice of the court: it is a late sixteenth century coinage.

The change in the constitution of the household manifested itself in various ways. First, by the gradual divorce of the home, henceforth a place for eating, for entertaining, and in a secondary way for rearing children, from the workplace. The three functions of producing, selling, and consuming were now separated in three different institutions, three different sets of buildings, three distinct parts of the city. Transportation to and from the place of work was first of all a privilege of the rich merchants in the big cities: it was only in the nineteenth century that it filtered down to the other classes in the city, and, instead of being a privilege, became a grievous burden. As the result of the household's becoming exclusively a consumer's organization, the housewife lost her touch with the affairs of the outside world: she became either a specialist in domesticity or a specialist in sex, something of a drudge, something of a courtesan, more often perhaps a little of both. Therewith the "private house" comes into existence: *private from business*. And every part came increasingly to share this privacy.

This growth of domesticity partly signified the weakening of public interest among the middle class citizens, especially among the excluded religious sects. Among the middle classes, there was a natural tendency to substitute private life for public affairs. Deprived of his liberties, unable often even to vote for his municipal officers or take part in the official business of his town unless appointed by the Prince, it was natural that the citizen's interest should shift, or become more restricted. If he were a member of a banned religious sect, as many among the merchant classes were, the incentive was even greater. To use a Victorian catchword: the middle classes began to keep themselves *to* themselves.

To make up for lack of effective domestic work, a new type of housework was invented that took up the slack and enriched the ritual of conspicuous consumption. I mean the care of furniture. The fixtures of the medieval household were equipment: chairs to sit on, beds to sleep in: icons to pray before: so much and no more. Furniture is really a re-invention of the baroque period: for by furniture one means useless or super-refined equipment, delicate vases to dust, inlays and precious woods to polish, metal work to keep shiny, curtains to be shaken and cleaned, bric-a-brac and curios to be washed. Display outstripped use; and the care of furniture commanded time that once went to the weaving of tapestries, the embroidery of garments, the making of useful household preserves, perfumes, and simples. These new burdens were inflicted upon house· wives and domestics at the very moment that the form of the house itself had changed, multiplying the number of private chambers to be supplied with wood, coal, water, and raising the height of dwellings from two flights of stairs to five, one below ground.

Up to the seventeenth century, at least in the North, building and heating had hardly advanced far enough to permit the arrangement of a series of private rooms in the dwelling. But now a separation of functions took place within the house as well as within the city as a whole. Space became specialized, room by room. In England, following the pattern of the great houses, the kitchen was broken off from the scullery, where the dirty work was done; and the various social functions of the kitchen were taken over by the living room and the parlor. The dining room was separated from the bedroom; and though in the seventeenth century a lady's bedroom still served as a reception room for her guests, whether or not the bed stood in an alcove, in the eighteenth a special room for meeting and conver· sation, the drawing room, the salon, came into existence. And the rooms no longer opened into each other: they were grouped along the corridor, like houses on a street. The need for privacy produced this special organ for public circulation.

[TOP] Courtyard of the Royal Exchange, London. The rise of the international Bourse in the sixteenth century signalized the change from a goods economy to a money economy, in which trading took place without actual sight of or contact with the goods that were bought and exchanged. The newspaper, beginning with such international reports as those sent back to the House of Fugger, was a necessary accompaniment of this new institution: for international prices were affected by wars, temporary monopolies, gluts, and shortages; and those who got the first news of these events could profit by them. A good part of every metropolitan newspaper is still devoted to financial items.

[MIDDLE LEFT] Interior of Bank of England. Transformation of the goldsmith's depositary into the modern bank is such a complex social phenomenon that the process of banking is still overlaid with magical prescriptions that have nothing to do with the essential relationships. Ideally, the bank is a responsible agency for allocating the collective potential energies of a community into a multitude of nicely inter-related channels where the conversion into kinetic energy and human productivity may take place with a minimum loss. But the conception of banking as a private function of speculators and profiteers has overlaid the necessity of creating responsible publicly controlled bodies performing such collective services. Speculation and abstemiousness, luxurious display and miserly hoarding, economic service and capitalist incantation went hand in hand: an ambivalence reflected in the architecture of the city.

[MIDDLE RIGHT] An early Parisian department store: display shopping and ready-made goods for sale. The Female Tatler (London, 1709) observed that "the shops are perfect guilded theaters." With the increasing size of the city and the increasing distance of the hinterland from which it draws goods, the middleman enters the scene as a go-between for the buyer and seller: carting, water-transportation, warehousing, jobbing, credit purchase all become specialized institutions with specialized buildings. The convenience of having wide assortments of goods available at any time is immense: hence buying and selling become daily occupations: urban hand-to-mouth living, as contrasted with the countryman's long-range seasonal foresight. But the price paid for this convenience is also huge: sometimes destitution for the producer, sometimes bankruptcy for the middleman: eventually higher prices for the consumer.

[BOTTOM] The shopping promenade, with the wide, glass-enclosed shop front, with its goods attractively on display, but protected against the sun and rain. The combination of shopping with wheeled traffic, the tendency to transform every avenue into a shopping avenue, instead of concentrating purchase in market squares, is a characteristic bequest of the mercantile city: an element of de-building and disorganization. It introduced confusion into the domestic quarters and, as the streets lengthened, uselessly multiplied the amount of competitive commercial space, without regard to service or even to profit.

[TOP LEFT] Place de la Concorde, facing the Madeleine through the Rue Royale. A place dedicated solely to wheeled traffic and vistas: but a barrier to safe pedestrian movement, and without a concourse of vehicles, a little empty. The agoraphobia of the Middle Ages here gives way to a claustrophobia, characteristic bequest of a period of restless movement and exploration: the feeling is purer in such later plans as this than in earlier places like the Place des Victoires, which still record the drag of surviving medieval forms. (*Photograph: Ewing Galloway*)

[TOP RIGHT] Arc de Triomphe: the baroque avenue in action: a theater for marching men and spectators. The Place de l'Etoile with its radiating avenues is an admirable emplacement for artillery to command the approach of threatening mobs—and was so intended. Compare this two-dimensional circle, with its formal movement of traffic, with the clover-leaf pattern of the modern motor roads, designed functionally for the movement of cross-traffic in various directions, without friction or stoppages, by means of viaduct and underpass. (*Photograph: Ewing Galloway*)

[MIDDLE LEFT] Rue de Rivoli: partly built under Napoleon I and extended by Haussmann under Napoleon III. Effective city planning, because the street and the arcaded buildings that line one side were conceived as a unit; a contrast to the notion of arbitrarily laying out blocks and quarters for unknown (therefore speculative) purposes. (*Photograph: Ewing Galloway*)

[MIDDLE RIGHT] Diagonal avenues, lined with trees. Here the irregular block shapes are fairly well-managed; but the determination of their size, contour, and orientation by the external needs of traffic is foreign to the functional method of laying out residential neighborhoods. Throughout the Renascence, straightness was a laudatory description of a street or avenue: straightness and breadth. To the street as the theater of swift traffic many other essential urban needs were sacrificed from the seventeenth century on: the curved street, the dead-end, the cul-de-sac, were reviled as old-fashioned or obstructive. The tree-lined boulevard was the highest expression of baroque street planning: forerunner, in the Avenue du Bois de Boulogne, of the universal parkway. (*Photograph: Ewing Galloway*)

[BOTTOM LEFT] Place Royale, now Place des Vosges: built in 1605. With the Place Vendôme the masterpiece of early formal planning: even though the elevation is marred by the awkward Mansard roofs.

[BOTTOM RIGHT] Middle class street in Zürich: typical baroque survival in modest scale, characteristic of a wide variety of cities from Boston and Baltimore to Geneva and München. Order, decency, good manners. Drab and depressing in the old Brownstone section of New York or the duller parts of South Kensington and Pimlico, but usually a happy contrast to the romantic suburb.

Privacy was the new luxury of the well-to-do; only gradually did the servants and the shopkeepers' assistants and the industrial workers have a trace of it. Even in the fine houses of the nineteenth century, the domestics often slept in the kitchen or in a bunk adjacent to it, or in dormitories. Now, privacy had been reserved, in the medieval period, for solitaries, for holy persons who sought refuge from the sins and distractions of the outside world: only lords and ladies might dream of it otherwise. In the seventeenth century it went with the satisfaction of the individual ego. The lady's chamber became a boudoir, literally a sulking place; the gentleman had his office or his library, equally inviolate; and in Paris he might even have his own bedroom, too. For the first time not merely a curtain but a door separated each individual member of the household from every other member.

Privacy, mirrors, heated rooms: these things transformed full-blown love-making from a seasonal to a year-round occupation: another example of baroque regularity. In the heated room, the body need not cower under a blanket: visual erethism added to the effect of tactile stimuli: the pleasure of the naked body, symbolized by Titian and Rubens and Fragonard, was part of that dilation of the senses which accompanied the more generous dietary, the freer use of wines and strong liquors, the more extravagant dresses and perfumes of the period. Flirtation and courtship created those movements of suspense and uncertainty, of blandishment and withdrawal, that serve as safeguards against satiety: a counterpoise to the regimentation of habit. These lusty men and women were never so much at home as when they were in bed. Ladies received callers in bed; statesmen dictated their correspondence in bed; an undercurrent of erotic interest thus permeated the household, sometimes bawdy, sometimes brutal, sometimes romantic, sometimes tender—every shade from the bedroom of Juliet to that in which Joseph Andrews almost lost his virtue. The private needs of the bedroom even penetrated the garden: the summer house, the temple of love, or the more aristocratic maze, composed of high box hedges: places remote from the prying eyes and admonitory footsteps of even the servants.

Meanwhile other technical changes haltingly entered the dwelling house. The invention of the water-closet by Sir John Harrington in

1596 made an important sanitary improvement in the house; but the fashion did not spread fast; for even the interior dry privy was introduced into France in the eighteenth century as an English novelty; while the Palace of Versailles, built regardless of expense, did not have even the conveniences of a medieval castle: portable commodes on wheels were used. Before the invention of the trap and the ventilating stack for the water-closet, the backing up of sewer gas into the dwelling house almost counterbalanced the advantages of the new improvement: witness the British concern during the nineteenth century with "bad drains." With the eotechnic device of the water-closet came another practice directly derived from the Chinese: the use of toilet paper: more important for domestic hygiene than the wallpaper that came in more or less simultaneously.

With all its luxurious display, the baroque city will not bear close inspection in the matter of hygienic and sanitary standards: the typical medieval town was more salubrious. Much though the body was now celebrated in poesy and painting, or systematically investigated in physiology, the people of the period neglected to clean it as thoroughly as the preceding culture had done. Perhaps because of the dangers of syphilis, the medieval bath had begun to fall out of use in the sixteenth century: even among the Jews, who might have been expected in their ghettos to preserve medieval habits so thoroughly in harmony with Mosaic sanitation, the ritual bath that used to take place in the Synagogue—the Mikveh—was given up during the Renascence. The new Baptists might insist upon total immersion; but one experience seems to have lasted them a lifetime.

Perhaps the rising price of hot water had something to do with this lapse, among the common people at least: it would follow upon the scarcity of wood fuel in the immediate neighborhood of the bigger cities. But the fact itself is beyond doubt. In 1387 there were 29 bathmen in Frankfort; in 1530, none. In the seventeenth century, after a breach, the bath was re-introduced as a foreign importation, a luxury, a means of renovating the body after a debauch: the so-called Turkish or Russian bath. But almost immediately these baths became pleasure haunts and houses of assignation: bagnio again meant brothel. Dirt diseases, such as smallpox, flourished in this period; and with the crowding up of the cities the volume of water that had been sufficient when the mains were installed in the sixteenth century proved altogether inadequate. Since these mains were often neither renewed nor extended, the inhabitants of the town would have a much smaller quantity of water per capita in the eighteenth century than they had had two or three centuries before. When the bathroom finally made its way into the house in the nineteenth century, to the chants of mechanical progress that then arose, only a belated antiquary might possibly recognize that Johann Andreae had assigned such a room *to each three room apartment* in his ideal city, Christianopolis, and that such rooms had been common, in the better burgher houses in Germany, in the Middle Ages.

12: The Muddle of Speculative Overcrowding

When one speaks of the new standard of domesticity, one refers only to the middle and upper class dwellings. Even here the new comforts, the new luxury of privacy, the new sensuous ornateness, came in but slowly. The change was marked more rapidly in decoration, from wooden ceilings to plaster ceilings, from paneled walls to papered walls, from heavy overwrought oak furniture to the more delicate mahoganies and maples, from gothic motifs to classic motifs, than in the more essential parts of the structure. The change of scale, the new sense of spaciousness, the raising of the ceiling in northern climates—a deliberate innovation by Vanbrugh—gradually produced an internal order that corresponded to the new baroque avenues outside.

But this expansion of upper class quarters was at the expense of lower class dwellings: if one opened up, the other became more constricted. Overcrowding and land speculation were the canker worms that ate into the heart of the lovely baroque flower: with them goes that rise of land values which was to solidify the consequent physical depression and give it a permanent form. Some of the baroque princes themselves were not unaware of the dangers of overcrowding; for the movement had begun in the capital cities as early as the fifteenth century: in Piers Plowman one finds the observation that if landlords sold honestly they would not build so high; and Robert Crowley wrote a vigorous poem about the rent raisers.

The stoppage of building congestion in the city, however, would have been possible only if the forces that were thrusting people into the city had been controlled at the source: if rural economic conditions had been improved, if provincial industry had been placed on a parity with that in the capital, if new cities had been founded and old ones put in repair and extended, if the upper classes had been deprived of their monopoly of land and other privileges, and if taxation had been adjusted so as to lop off the unearned increment from congestion. Unfortunately, the expropriation of the peasant and the depression of the urban worker went hand in hand. Competition for space by poor unprotected immigrants had the same effect on seventeenth century Paris as on eighteenth century Manchester, and nineteenth century Liverpool and New York: the ground rents rose and the living quarters worsened. A hectare of land in Paris was in the thirteenth century worth 2600 francs, according to Avenel: in the twentieth century a hectare in the same district was worth 1,297,000 francs. Who benefited by this rise? Not the occupants. Whose incomes kept pace with it? Not those of the workers.

"The worker of the Middle Ages, who had an annual income of a thousand francs, could pay without difficulty for a little house from one hundred to two hundred francs a year: his situation became still better when rents went immensely lower in the fifteenth century by reason of the abundance of empty dwellings, while wages had gone up 1200 francs. But at the moment when the journeyman did not, from 1550 to the end of the eighteenth century, earn any more than 675 francs per year, and when the poorest Parisian houses rented for 350 francs, one perceives why it was necessary for him to give up living under a separate roof." With appropriate variations this condition held throughout Europe. From the standpoint of the working classes, the period after the middle of the sixteenth century was one of increasing exploitation, and with regard to their quarters, one of increasing dilapidation and constriction.

The contrast between the new residence quarters of the rich and the decaying medieval quarters, now overbuilt and crowded, or the even more wretched new accommodations, was marked in every city where the two were placed side by side: Paris, London, Edinburgh, Berlin. To understand this servility and depression, one must realize that before the humanitarian conscience of the nineteenth century had begun to alter social attitudes, destitution had been accepted as the normal lot in life for a considerable part of the population. In the seventeenth and eighteenth centuries, it has been estimated that as much as a quarter of the urban population consisted of casuals and beggars. In a memorandum dated 1684 the Chief of Police in Paris referred to the "frightful misery that afflicts the greater part of the population of this great city." Between forty and sixty-five thousand were reduced to outright beggary.

The groundwork of a large servile proletariat was a necessary feature of the blaze and pomp of baroque life. For just as even kings were reduced to using plaster and gilt for ornament when the supply of marble and more costly decoration came too high, so gentlemen who wished to have a great retinue in attendance were forced to draw upon the poor and the starving, since for all their boast of riches, they did not have enough money to pay their menials in competition with a healthy labor market. Without a surplus of casuals, there would have been a general scarcity, and service would not have been so cheap. Lackeys and flunkeys and domestic servants of all kinds, if not uprooted from the country, were drawn from the horde of people that had swarmed into the metropolis. Some of them rose into service, where they were provided with a uniform, a more or less sufficient supply of food, occasional opportunities for pilfering, and security of employment during good behavior. In these respects, army service and domestic service had many points in common. The rest begged and cadged and seized odd jobs, they sank further into thieving, pimping, pickpocketing and prostitution, and they ended up in the gutters of Gin Lane or the gallows of Tyburn. I have taken these examples from London: Wien, Madrid, Naples or Berlin would have served equally well.

Given this large proletariat at the mercy of the market, there went on a steady downward movement in housing accommodations for the mass of people, who could no longer afford a cottage of their own or had a chance to board in the house of their master, but rented a shakedown where they could. Overbuilding of land and over-occupation of houses caused grievous sanitary difficulties in London, for example, as early as the sixteenth century. For about fifty years, from 1582 to 1632, there were frequent references to those evils and half-hearted attempts to correct them. After this upper class greed and lower class necessity largely took their course.

The Lords of the Council in 1583 found that overcrowded buildings had greatly increased the danger of pestilence and riot. Attention was drawn to the congestion that resulted from dividing up single houses meant to house a single family: a practice that was to become almost universal in every growing town during the next three centuries. In 1593 an act of Parliament observed that "great mischiefs daily grow and increase by reason of pestering the houses with diverse families, harboring of inmates, and converting great houses into several tenements, and exacting the erecting of new buildings in London and Westminster."

Almost needless to say, these proclamations and edicts went for nothing: the poultices soothed the doctor's conscience; they could not cure the patient's ache. In so far as the efforts to prohibit building were successful, without removing the causes of congestion, they only intensified the existing evils. But ground rents went up as living conditions went down: public vices could be capitalized as private benefits. The Old Soldiers' Homes, which the military capitals began to boast in the seventeenth century, might be palatial, like that Wren created in Chelsea: the new workers' homes were designedly hovels.

The transformation of the older houses into clotted tenements, where a whole family could be cooped into a single room, was not sufficient to accommodate the increased population. New quarters must be built which would accept these depressed conditions as a standard. According to Roger North's autobiography, speculative building began on a large scale in London with Dr. Barbone's ventures, after the Great Fire of 1666. The decrease in housing quarters then gave him a favorable opportunity. "He was the inventor of this new method of building by casting of ground into streets and small houses, and selling the ground to workmen by so much per front foot, and what he could not sell, built himself. This had made ground rents high for the sake of mortgaging, and others, following his steps, have refined and improved upon it, and made a superfoetation of houses round London."

For the rotten perfection of this system we may thank the seventeenth century; but it awaited the introduction of the steam engine and the large scale factory for this method of building to become standardized practice more or less throughout the Western World; often in worse forms, rarely in better ones. As land values rose, building heights rose, too, in cities where land monopoly or topographic obstacles lessened the amount of available building space. The more congested the land, the higher the income; the higher the income, the higher the capitalizable value of the land. London was saved from the worst results of this vicious circle by the fact that so much of the land was in feudal holdings on long-term leases; but when Frederick the Great departed from Germanic custom and put the land on a Roman basis, with the same status as the structure, he opened the way for that untrammeled realty speculation which corrupted the planning and block-layout of Berlin down to the formation of the German republic in 1918.

In short, congestion brought financial reward: slum properties often earned much higher returns than investments in more respectable parts of the town. The transformation of the poverty of the East End into the riches of the West End was the supreme magic of baroque finance: wealth out of illth. It played a major part in that over-expansion and over-concentration which, by the time of Cobbett, had made his epithet, The Wen, an accurate description of every capital city.

13: The Baroque Plan

Except for overseas colonization, the chief new cities built from the sixteenth to the nineteenth century were the "Residenzstädte," places selected for the permanent home of the Prince and his court. Mannheim, Karlsruhe, and Potsdam belong to this group. The town extensions that took place on the new lines were usually done in capital cities, like Naples or München, or in towns like Edinburgh and Nancy where the new bourgeoisie had achieved almost aristocratic pretensions. The new plan distinguished itself from the older medieval accretions by the use of straight lines, regular block units, and as far as possible uniform dimensions; and the new order is symbolized in the roundpoint with its radiating streets and avenues, cutting impartially through old tangles or new gridirons.

The prototype of the asterisk type of avenue plan was, as one would expect from a hunting aristocracy, the royal hunting park itself. Here the long lanes, cut through the trees, enabled the hunters to rally at a central point and go galloping off in every direction. Hunting, and the breakneck riding that accompanies it, remains to this day the privileged sport of the aristocracy in every country. The central meeting point, the roundpoint or *place* of the new plan, was originally the seat of the hunting lodge. When the plan for Versailles was laid down, the palace itself was set on the site of the old hunting lodge where Louis XIV had first wooed his mistress, Madame de la Vallière. The palace at Karlsruhe was likewise on the site of a hunting lodge. But in the plan, this meeting place had a different context: the palace gathered to itself the new avenues of the city as the ruler himself gathered together the political power that had once been dispersed among a multitude of groups and corporations. All the main avenues would lead to the palace. And when one raised one's eyes in the street, the palace, as often as not, would close the vista.

In France, this type of plan was extremely popular: in fact, it left its marks in the suburban districts of Garches and Meudon. But it was imitated over as wide an area as Western Civilization itself—places as far apart as Samarkand and Washington. The plan of Samarkand, as it stood at the end of the nineteenth century, was indeed classic in every respect. There was a citadel, and to the east the old city spread out. Raying out from the citadel were the streets and boulevards of the new town, moving westward. Is it by accident that these boulevards terminated, north and south, in a barracks and a military hospital?

For the asterisk plan there was however another parallel point of origin. In the early starlike schemes of fortification, the city proper became a regular polygon, usually eight-sided; and the main streets were either divided in the form of a cross, or placed so as to converge in the center from each of the angles of the octagon. When the fortification lost its efficacy, the main effect of this pattern was to make the city, or the quarter, a sector of the original spiderweb, with the other avenues radiating out into the park or the open country.

The scheme of central places, dominated by monuments, flanked symmetrically by public buildings, and avenues spreading out from this center, profoundly altered every dimension of planning. For the avenue now became definitely the horizontal frame of the terminal buildings: though these edifices might be capped by a dome, the main effect of the planning was to increase the importance of the regulating horizontal lines. Not merely did the domes of the central buildings seem to float: the principal buildings themselves, when set apart by broad avenues, likewise floated in space: if the medieval town was conducive to claustrophobia, the absolute city had just the other effect—that of promoting agoraphobia. The repetitive motifs, the use of a small stock of classic forms, only added to the sense of visual emptiness in the new street pictures. Only by tying the park and the alley of trees very close to the urban street picture could a certain bleakness in the architecture be avoided: the Avenue de l'Observatoire and the Champs Elysées have a warm quality that was not altogether forgotten in the nineteenth century Parisian boulevard.

But, as I have hinted before, the city was sacrificed to the avenue in the new plan. The uniform avenue brought traffic and confusion into parts of the city that had been quiet and self-contained, and it tended to stretch the market out along the lines of traffic, instead of providing local points of neighborhood concentration. Moreover, the avenue determined the size and the shape of the block; and the needs of domesticity were consistently subordinated to the ostentatious demands of wheeled traffic.

It is possible to represent the new method of platting and laying out towns by a geometrical symbol: a circle like Freudenstadt, an octagon, like Villa Nuova, a partial star like Karlsruhe or Mannheim. What does this mean? It means that the abstract figure determines the social contents: the institutions of the community no longer generate the plan and modify it in accordance with the special needs of living. If the topography is irregular, the land must be evened out, at whatever absurd cost in materials and manpower, merely in order to make the plan work. So difficult, however, is this that most baroque city building took place on level sites. Not alone did this add to the expense of city development: but the increase of wheeled vehicles also added expense by entailing the use of a heavier type of paving: the widening and lengthening of these avenues further multiplied the costs.

Now, the function of geometry in planning is to clarify and guide. Like every other type of useful abstraction, it must be conditioned by facts and give way to facts when the latter point to some aspect of life that has escaped the formula. Up to a point, the mathematical approach of the absolutist planner had a value in normalizing the procedure of laying out quarters, blocks, and individual plots. In a period where changes were rapid and where custom could no longer be sufficient guide, such an approach might be helpful, at least expedient. Unfortunately, baroque planners were too confident about the type of order they imposed: they had no place even in their three-dimensional planning for the factor of time, and, in turn, they gave themselves no time to study the topographic peculiarities of the place. Having gone to the monuments of Greece and Rome for their original inspiration, these classically trained minds had no sense of time as a process of development. All those changes and adaptations that are inevitable with further growth, they left out of their purview: hence their plans were too symmetrical, their order too exclusive and rigid, to allow as a rule for the needs of further generations. A baroque plan was a geometric achievement: it must be laid out and built up at a stroke: if possible under the guidance of an architectural despot. Since to alter this type of plan, to introduce fresh elements, is to spoil its symmetry, even the superficial esthetic contents of the plan could be preserved only by severe administrative regulations. Where these were maintained, as in Paris, order might be preserved on the surface for many generations.

As long as a single proprietor or builder carried out the planning and building of a new quarter within a limited time it might have great consistency and elegance: witness Bath, Nancy, Potsdam. But when the plan existed only in patches, as in London, or when the execution of a good part of it was left for future action, as in Washington, the result might be a disorder that could hardly be distinguished from what would have existed without the plan: witness the sordid slum that is still Pennsylvania Avenue. While these new planners devoted themselves most zealously to the creation of settings for public buildings, our present age finds most to admire in the more intimate marks of formal design: the Place des Vosges (originally the Place Royale) in Paris, 1612; the Place Vendôme, 1708; the parts of Nancy built between 1705 and 1763, the parts of Bath built between 1763 and 1767, the squares of eighteenth century Blooms-bury and Mayfair, or those of nineteenth century Belgravia.

Here was the new order at its best. Its ingredients were exceed-ingly simple, and owed very little to the spurious cult of the past. A common square, oval, or circle, with a railed park in the center whose trees and shrubberies formed a green enclosure for the ap-proaching street. Common building materials throughout: brick, stucco, or stone bound in the same color the whole façade. A common roof-line with a point of accent, in the form of a pediment, at the point required in the design, not by the demand of some individual wishing to be more conspicuous than his neighbors. These qualities of design were based upon a common financial standing, a common social status, and a common standard of taste.

But one must not look too closely, even in upper class quarters, behind the handsome classic front. Observe the backs of the fine houses in Charlotte Square, Edinburgh: they are barracks. Follow the alleys that lead off the grand avenues: you will find a slum.

Definitely, such order was class planning: it symbolized the com-mon front of the possessing classes. This point was admirably illus-trated in a sixteenth century dialogue between a countryman and a city man. The former extols the advantages of the country and the sociable life he enjoyed there with his honest neighbors—"graziers, butchers, farmers, drovers, carpenters, carvers, taylors, and such like men, very good and honest companions." His opponent answers: "And so I think, but not for you, being a gentleman." "What," ex-claims the countryman, "would you have me live alone and solitary. That were worse than to be dead." To which the gentleman of the town replies: "Nay, neither, for if you did for the most live in court and city among the better sort, you would ever find company there, *fit for your estate and condition.*"

14: Architectural Forms

Between the sixteenth and the nineteenth centuries there are three formal styles: each bears the marks of a special phase in social and economic development. They succeed each other and intermingle, these new modes of building: hints of the last stage were already present in the sixteenth century.

The first phase is that which is usually tagged as early Renascence. The serene eye-opening of the fifteenth century: the unearthing of statues and monuments, in a state of mingled ecstasy and awe: the quest leading to the horizon and the arched sky above it. The symbol of this first stage is the round arch: every object, from a lady's mirror to a new monument will bear this sign. While the new standardization may be expressed in repeating patterns of column and window, the new regularity and uniformity is only carried on at first for a short distance in the street picture. One may discover a Renascence square, a street, a place: but one looks in vain for a Renascence avenue or a Renascence city: so far they existed only in the mind.

Then the pace of life quickened and the turbulent forces of religious criticism and economic adventure and mechanical invention set up new pressures and counter pressures. The invention of printing gave to the processes of standardization the authority of the printed word and the mechanically copied drawing and plan: book knowledge assumed greater authority than craft-experience, and literacy presently became an indispensable mark of good building. To know the classic forms described in the newly printed work of Vitruvius, to keep in touch with the printed prescriptions of an Alberti, a Vignola, a Palladio, became more important than to understand the needs and the processes of life of one's contemporaries. The courts encouraged this cult and the more practical groups in the city were powerless to oppose it: only the homes of the people and their workshops continued to be built, for the greater part, in the vernacular manner. At the same time other elements of standardization appeared besides the printed word: uniformed armies, uniform codes and laws, uniform coinages. As if in contradiction, a new lawlessness appeared, too: in religion the authority of the individual conscience, against the institutions of the Church; in government, the will of the prince, against local laws and hitherto inviolable customs; in private life, an unbridled sensuality that, for the upper classes, recognized no limits to eating, drinking, and sexual intercourse except animal exhaustion. The machine and the sensual life,

reformation and license, fanaticism and frivolity, equally characterized the new order that became uppermost in the seventeenth century.

On one hand, a more pedantic study of the Five Orders and a more
faithful effort to geometrize life: the street vista was lengthened
and the house type standardized on the façade. On the other hand,
more defiant caprice in dealing with this mass of organized pedantry:
the classic forms were used merely as the skeleton for more voluptu-
ous corporeal members: the columns of the churches writhed like
the body of an African dancer, and the interiors of the churches
might be transformed into ballrooms by the mere expedient of removing the altar. The broken pediment and the spiral symbolize this
new phase. Ornament became more profuse and the interiors were
strewn with life and the representations of life: sea shells of glitter-
ing gold and cornucopias and garlands of flowers and flying cherubs
and the warm fragrant bodies of men and women in love, as conceived by a Fragonard, a Watteau, a Greuze. The strong solemn reds
and blues of the old rose windows of the cathedrals became the
frivolous blues and pinks and whites of the new baroque interior:
in the rococo churches, heaven became visible in gilt and plaster: a
materialization of the vulgar dream of St. John of Patmos.

In one sense, this second phase of the Renascence represented a
falling away from the limpid purity of the early moment: just as
current spasms of religiosity were but a tawdry substitute for the
integral faith of the twelfth century church. This fact gave to the
first use of the word baroque, as Croce has properly contended, the
derogatory meaning of something bombastic and weakly florid. But
this new architecture symbolized the growing divisions and contradictions in the whole life of European culture. If it pushed the abstractions of mechanism too far in one direction, in its one-sided
craving for power, it pushed the anti-mechanical animus too far in
another. Often the same building or the same street picture would
express both elements. Perhaps the sorriest symbol of all is the type
of steeple that became common in the seventeenth century: this old
medieval symbol that had pointed to heaven came back in a sort of
caricature: height was achieved by superimposing one set of columns
above another, till the thin pedantic mass was crowned by a minia-
ture temple of love.

But the most representative symbol of baroque design in both its weakest and its most creative phase is the seventeenth century formal garden or park. This is a formal composition in space, in which the natural growths and efflorescences become merely subordinate patterns in a geometrical design: mere carpet and wall paper, artfully pieced together out of nature's foreign materials. The clipped alley, in which the trees are turned into a smooth green wall: the clipped hedge: the deformation of life in the interests of an external pattern of order—here was something at once magnificent and preposterous, as if Procrustes had been given the inspiration of Raphael.

Finally, the awakening moment of the early Renascence and the tormented conscience of the Reformation and Counter-Reformation, was replaced by the frigid correctness of old age. With the seventeenth century came the age of academies, and formal correctness took precedence over the inner content and the irresistible creativeness of a living art. The codification of architectural design was a natural effort to preserve a common front at a moment when the real interests and activities of people were becoming more divided, more disparate, more filled with internal contradictions. The publication of the Architectura by De Vriese in 1557 was a prelude to a movement that was to dominate architecture in the eighteenth century and issue forth into crazy copybook simulacra in the nineteenth. Under this precedent, measurement and imitation take the place of intelligent design.

Beginning early in the Prado and in Versailles, this phase of architecture creeps like a numbing frost over the more vital forms, either withering them into black shrunken stems, or casting its own cold glaze over the once-animated form. This phase achieved most authority and, architecturally speaking, counts for least: ultimately it produced, at many removes, those monuments, too dead even to be incorrect, that crowned the new civic centers in the United States after 1900: the corpse-like classicism of the New York Public Library, the Lincoln Memorial, the Supreme Court Building, or the new government office buildings in the Washington Triangle.

This final frigidity was pre-figured in many early Renascence discussions and projects; but it took a couple of centuries before social regimentation had removed the last touches of vitality. It is associated with the lifeless plans, in which convenience is sacrificed to axial grouping, in which abstract symmetry dictates the shape and arrangement of rooms and the pattern of the windows, in which—in the city—churches may be built on each side of a plaza merely in order to achieve visual balance. Later this type of planning became commonplace: witness the planning of governmental Berlin in the eighteenth century.

The last phase of the baroque is an age of paper patterns, paper plans, paper constitutions: even warfare was taken over by the academy and conducted according to accepted rules of strategy. Although Ruskin's reasons were often bad, and his failure to perceive the creative moments in the new architecture was unfortunate, his instincts about the Renascence and classic modes of building were, on the whole, correct. There was something sinister in this new order: if it sacrificed the craft autonomy of the worker to the vanity of the architect, it equally sacrificed the uses of life to the formalities of plan and elevation.

The seventeenth century feeling for outward unity was perhaps best summed up by Descartes, who is one of the most representative thinkers of the period, not least because he was a soldier as well as a mathematical philosopher. "It is observable," said Descartes, "that the buildings which a single architect has planned and executed are generally more elegant and more commodious than those which several have attempted to improve. . . . Thus, also, those ancient cities which from being at first only villages have become, in the course of time, large towns, are usually but ill laid out compared with the regularly constructed towns which a professional architect has freely planned on an open plain; so that although the several buildings of the former may often equal or surpass in beauty those of the latter, yet when one observes their indiscriminate juxtaposition, there a large and here a small, and the consequent crookedness and irregularity of the streets, one is disposed to allege that chance, rather than any human will guided by reason, must have led to such an arrangement. And if we consider that nevertheless there have been at all times certain officers whose duty was to see that private buildings contributed to public ornament, the difficulty of reaching high perfection with but the materials of others to operate on will be readily acknowledged."

There could be no sharper contrast between the two orders of thinking, the organic and the mechanical, than here: the first springs out of the total situation, the other simplifies the facts of life for the sake of an artful system of concepts, more dear to the mind than life itself. One works co-operatively with "the materials of others," perhaps guiding them, but first acknowledging their existence and understanding their purpose: the other, that of the baroque despot, insisting upon *his* law, *his* order, *his* society, is imposed by a single mind working under his command. For those on the inside of baroque life, the courtier and the financier, this formal order was in effect organic: it represented the values they had created for themselves as a class. For those outside, it was a denial of reality and a form of oppression.

To understand the final limitations of the baroque plan, one must ask what provisions were made for the civic nucleus? In the neighborhood, none: the local market and the school are not given special positions and sites on the plan: nor does the local park within the big square serve even as a minor playground except for the children of those who have legal access to the square. But in the city as a whole, there is a civic nucleus, in subordinate relation to the Prince's palace; and the theory of this nucleus was admirably set forth by Palladio. "To return to the principal squares, to those that ought to be joined the Prince's palace, or that for the meeting of the states, as the country is either a monarchy or a republic. The exchequer or the public treasury, where the money and treasure of the public is lodged, ought to join them likewise, as well as prisons. These latter were anciently of three sorts; one for such as were debauched or immodest . . . and which we now assign to fools or mad-folks; another was for Debtors . . . and the third was for traitors or wicked persons."

The palace: the exchequer: the prison: the mad-house—what four buildings could more completely sum up the new order, or symbolize the features of its political life? It was by combinations of one or another of these institutions that the baroque community was built; and it was on variants of one or another of their plans and forms that the streets and town-planning extensions and new cities of the period were built.

Truth is that something vital had been forgotten in the culture of the baroque gentleman; and it was naturally missing from the cities he conceived and executed. What was this element—religion? Not in externals, for in sheer mass of building the Church continued to occupy an undiminished place in the city. What was lacking in this scheme was suitable provision for work. No interest in labor as such: hence no suitable provision for the workplaces of industry, or even for the counting houses of the merchant, on the city plan. Special industrial buildings were indeed beginning to dot the eotechnic city: the dwelling house, even with the aid of sheds, could not assimilate the processes of big industry. Brewers, founders, dyers, fullers, tanners, weavers with establishments that brought together a hundred looms or more—all these crafts demanded a special place in the city. As for watermills and windmills, they had become essential to the industrial existence of the town after the twelfth century: their masses formed an ever more obtrusive part of the new street picture and the new skyline. Docks and storage sheds were hardly less important.

What part did architectural theory or urban design have in the evolution of these structures? Practically none: they were not covered in the formal plan or the cult of the Five Orders. Evelyn, who did so much to promote reforestation, was in advance of his culture in this department: he proposed to remove every industry requiring large fires from the heart of London to the district between Greenwich and Woolwich, and prevent similar buildings from being erected near the city in future. Tallow melting and butchering and soap-boiling were not to be carried on within the city, either: co-ordinately he suggested laying all the lower grounds on the outskirts into fields, separated by thick plantations of fragrant shrubs, to improve the air of the city. But these were the suggestions of an extremely able and far-sighted man: one may examine a score of ideal baroque city plans without finding that the planner had the faintest notion of the part played by industry in cities. The most characteristic mark of baroque planning was the effort to keep industry out of sight: zoning

for the eye. Ledoux's early nineteenth century attempt to monu-
mentalize industrial buildings was a belated exception.

Occasionally, the engineer would attempt to apply to his industrial
buildings the same formula he employed on public monuments:
Smeaton's lighthouses and Rennie's Waterloo Bridge are examples.
But such tags of ornament could not conceal the fact that the principle for an effective synthesis was lacking. Hence the most gracious
forms of baroque planning took place in those parts of the environment where these contradictions and incompatibilities did not wreck
the surface order: above all in the country house and the great country estate. Outside the court, the *life* of this period expressed itself,
as *dis*-order: muddy boots of reality walking over the elegant carpets.

15: What Saved the Olympians

For the mass of people in the baroque city, the result of its political absolutism, its mercantile enterprise, and its ruthless system of
taxation was deterioration of environment and a depression of the
standard of life. But the Olympians themselves were saved: so long
as they spent part of the time on their grand estates in the country,
and so long as the city itself was not invaded too heavily by machine
industry, with its dirt and its congestion of neighboring quarters,
their environment was a salubrious one. They had order, and they
had space: they alone. Just as capitalistic enterprise itself was partly
a protest against the stale privilege and staler routine of the guilds;
so the cult of luxury was a protest against making a special virtue
of poverty and abstention: miserliness and middle-class thrift.

So, too, the open order of baroque planning was an effort to
counteract, not the original defects of the medieval city, but the defects that had accreted with time, through an accumulation of vested
interests and the failure to replan drastically when occasion demanded: still more perhaps, the niggardly overbuilding of open
spaces practiced after the sixteenth century by the new urban bourgeoisie. Even the classic order of architecture can be explained
partly as an attempt to wipe off the meaningless dribble of ornament
that characterized the flamboyant gothic of the fifteenth century.
The esthetic purity of the baroque plan was forced; its type of order
was limited: but it marked, within its limits, an attempt to make a

[TOP] Royal Crescent at Bath: one of the culminating points of eighteenth century upper class planning. Formal order and coherence of a palatial sort, achieved by the collective pooling of resources by the individual occupants, by the unified control of the land, and by a comprehensive design executed by a single mind that controls and orders all the elements: possible only when there is a consensus in society: a common point of view and common values. The relation of buildings and open spaces here shows a closer kinship to modern esthetic and social conceptions than does the more typical urban plan of Covent Garden, below. Here is standardization and uniformity, of the strictest sort, without the usual connotations of dreariness. (*Photograph: Aerofilms*)

[FIRST LEFT] Street view of another circle at Bath: the architectural form is nearer the quiet eighteenth century English vernacular than to the somewhat more pretentious classic façades of the Royal Crescent. The crowded servants' quarters under the roof remind one, however, of the class exploitation and servility that accompanied this regime. (*Photograph: Carl Feiss*)

[SECOND LEFT] The class front in the new town of Edinburgh: like Karlsruhe, Nancy, and Bath one of the great examples of coherent upper class town planning made possible by unified ownership of large parcels of land and centralized, co-ordinated design and building: conditions which disappeared in the nineteenth century, only to be recovered in the publicly aided housing projects of today. Later exigencies broke the roof line and spoiled the esthetic effect of this example: the irregularity, so inevitable in medieval façades, is mere disorder in the baroque street picture.

[BOTTOM LEFT] Rear of a handsome façade in Edinburgh: barracks architecture, facing a catwalk: typical indifference to rear views characteristic of scene painting. An architecture of fronts. Beautiful silks: costly perfumes: dirty bodies. Elegance and smallpox. Out of sight, out of mind. Modern functional planning distinguishes itself from this purely visual conception of the plan by dealing honestly and competently with every side, abolishing the gross distinction between front and rear, seen and obscene, and creating structures that are harmonious in every dimension: planning for the human organism as a whole.

[MIDDLE RIGHT] Arcade in Covent Garden: the Renascence theme in its purity. (*From London; the Unique City, by S. E. Rasmussen: New York, 1937. By permission of the Macmillan Company, Publishers.*)

[BOTTOM RIGHT] Plan of Covent Garden in the eighteenth century: except for the axial approach of Russell Street, the disposition and scale of this square is closer to late medieval Italian than to more absolutist concepts of baroque order. But note overcrowding of the surrounding blocks and courts: notably the airless buildings bounded by Maiden Lane and Half Moon Streets. Broad Court, lower right, is a typical late medieval form.

The mastery of water and soil, the building up of polderland by means of dykes and canals, the utilization of windmills for keeping the land below sea level from flooding, the multiplication of windmills as prime movers, gave the Netherlands their pre-eminence in the seventeenth century: mastery of the practical life in every aspect of agriculture and industry. Their continued eminence in horticulture, their fine craftsmanship in wood and pottery, the complete electrification of railroads and farmhouses no less than cities, has again given these communities a leadership, rivaled only by the Scandinavian countries, in the essential arts of modern civilization. Though the bigger Dutch cities suffered the characteristic paleotechnic blight—so badly that special probationary quarters are sometimes used when removing Dutch slum dwellers to improved dwellings—they retained an architectural and civic tradition capable of renewal. Hence the essential continuity between the Amsterdam of the seventeenth century (*top and middle left*) and a modern housing development like that of Oud in Rotterdam (*top right*), to take the least traditional modern work as a test. Note again the kinship between modern housing and the early seventeenth century Home for the Aged at The Hague with its spacious windows (*third right*). The air view of Naarden (*bottom*) shows the late medieval city in a state of marvelous preservation. The outlines of the fortifications admirably illustrate the baroque military engineer's art; the conversion of these bastions and salients into parks is a classic example of swords unexpectedly beaten into plowshares, to the great hygienic advantage of the town. But see how the Dutch highway engineers, with an indifference to beauty and efficiency still too common in their profession, have stupidly pushed the main motor road into the center of Naarden, instead of by-passing it. The generous open spaces behind the houses accentuate the comeliness of detail, as well as that which characterizes the whole. An excellent urban environment, almost a garden city, greenbelt and all. The Wieringermeer village (*second right*) in the Zuyder Zee development is another example of continuity: but with that tendency to overaccent the traditional that the historical-minded townsman often too readily shows when dealing with the peasant or farmer: a habit of mind that overlooks the fact that the latter is often as eager to exchange his traditional dwelling for a better modern one as he is to exchange the pump for running water, or horsepower for electricity if he can get it: a fact particularly notable in Holland.

fresh start and to think out the necessities of life as they appeared to a contemporary. In its clarity and precision there was something vital: an urgent challenge to the complacent Struldbrugs of the medieval order.

But what saved the Olympians was not their faked classical gestures or their despotic order: what saved them was their new sense of space, and their deliberate effort to bring the country back for their personal use into the town. With the garden and the park, with the morning canter on horseback, with their fencing and dueling, with their visits and their courtship in spacious rooms, with their dances and their theaters, they developed a routine of life that kept their youth, at least, at a high level of biological well-being: their bodies responded to command. Apart from their necessity for turning the performance of leisure into a work routine, they had created in their urban quarters a balanced environment for life. They had what the Germans call Lebensraum, living space, or what one might dub colloquially "space to turn around in." Hence in a period when the landed aristocracy was forced to meet the competition of a new race of industrialists and financiers the aristocracy created for themselves a city in which they could propagate their customs and their biological issue by reason of their all-round fitness. Life for people in other quarters of the city, for the puritan who frowned on the drama and the dance, for the businessman who was suspicious of frivolity and idleness, for the drudge tied to some minute mechanical occupation, was at lower key than in the quarters of the Olympians.

This effort to span life in all its dimensions, this delight in sensuous extravagance, in the body's appetites, in all that the ear, the eye, and the touch could make their own, was an essentially different attitude from that which had governed the Middle Ages. If it had developed first in the cinquecento artists and scholars and courtiers, it had now at last by the eighteenth century created its form in the city. These things were to have revolutionary implications. After the French Revolution, the city began one by one to absorb the institutions of the court and the aristocracy: the common man began to feel, in the words of an old American popular song, "What's good enough for Rockie is good enough for me." The successful industrialist first imitated the aristocracy: then whole bodies of people began to demand similar privileges for the city at large. What is called the rise of democracy is, as far as the city is concerned, the diffusion of baroque privilege: so that by the twentieth century even the most reluctant of upper class housing reformers might admit that the poor were entitled to the privilege of privacy. But by this time the possibilities of modern life could no longer be effectively conceived in terms of the baroque environment.

16: Fulfillment and Renewal

The best examples of a culture are not always the most characteristic ones; for what is most typical is what is most time-bound and limited. Dekker and Chapman are characteristic of Elizabethan London, while Shakespeare, though he shared this milieu, transcended it at a hundred points. This is likewise true of the culture of cities. In the sixteenth and seventeenth centuries certain fresh city forms came into existence; they were characteristic of neither medieval nor baroque civilization. And these types, which are not "transitional" since they led only in their own direction, have more significance for us today than do the classic specimens of the period.

If one takes Amsterdam as the most important example of a city that effected the transition without losing form, that is not to disparage the vitality of other Dutch cities. It is rather to show, by taking the hardest example, that the rapid commercial expansion and the physical growth of the post-medieval city need not have raised insuperable obstacles to order. Throughout its main period of expansion, Amsterdam did not lose its unity; and though its medieval quarter finally decayed, the city as a whole did not deteriorate, except for a brief period in the nineteenth century.

The original form of Amsterdam was an irregular one. With great foresight the planners of the sixteenth century laid out in advance a series of canals and long, shallow building blocks that rounded out the shape of the city and provided effective water connection with the harbor. They created a unified organism, not an abstract geometrical figure. In the new large-windowed houses the builders produced a domestic form that remained stable until the growth of the nineteenth century proletariat turned the speculative builder to the laying out of hideous tenements. The combination of tree-lined water courses and unified block fronts had an irresistible charm: all the more because in Holland the canal brings the country into the heart of the city, in canal boats laden with vegetables and flowers. The pretentious water courses before Nymphenburg or Versailles are, by comparison, empty settings for a mere costume play: historical but inane.

The technical development of the Dutch city was based on the marvelous control of water, not merely for communication and transport but for the sculpture of the landscape, established by the Dutch engineers. Their influence, like that of the advanced horticulturists with their glass houses, was felt throughout Europe: the Dutch farm and the Dutch garden became patterns for a progressive balanced agriculture. And this command of water was felt within the city as well as on the polders: it gave the Dutch town not merely a clean façade and a frame of verdure but a super-clean interior, such as could be established, with the aid of sand or holystone and sea water, on the most shipshape of vessels. The big windows of the seventeenth century small house in Holland, repeated today alike in the architecture of the radical Oud and that of the conservative Granpré-Molière, brought into the house an amount of sunlight and fresh air that corresponded to that which Johann Andreae pictured in his Utopia. Hooch's paintings preserve the very color and light in these dwellings. In general, the layout and amenities of the Dutch brick cottage of this period were not merely in advance of its contemporary upper class housing: they are still above the level that has so far been reached by a good share of modern housing.

No less outside the baroque frame was another phenomenon of the seventeenth century: the New England village. The center of the village was an open common, dominated by the meeting house and the town hall. These three institutions served as a rallying point for the community, the common for military drill as well as for the pasturing of cattle. Around the central area were set the separate houses, sometimes a single line on a block, with deep rear gardens, large enough for a small orchard as well as a vegetable plot. Tall elm trees on each side of the road furnished shade from the torrid summer sun and partial windbreaks against the winter wind—a perfect unison of man and nature. At a time when the medieval city was being encysted, when people swarmed behind massive fortifications, here in America a more open type was being kept in existence, surrounded, like so many early medieval towns, by a simple wooden stockade.

In the seventeenth century the great capitals had begun to absorb population with no effort at limitation. But the New England town during this period ceased to grow beyond the possibility of socializing and assimilating its members: when near crowding, a new congregation would move off under a special pastor, erect a new meeting house, form a new village, lay out fresh fields. Hiving off to new centers discouraged congestion in the old ones; and the further act of dividing the land among the members of the community in terms of family need, as well as wealth and rank, gave a rough equality to the members, or at least guaranteed them a basic minimum of existence. Each family had its rights in the common lands; each family had fields on the outskirts as well as gardens near their homes; each male had the duty of participating in the political affairs of the town through the town-meeting. A democratic polity—and the most healthy and comely of urban environments: a typical contrast to the despotic order of the dominant baroque city. To describe it is almost to define everything that the absolute order was not.

While the cities of Europe were decaying or being transformed into a more mechanical pattern, the countryside was undergoing improvement and rejuvenation. The finest stone villages in the Cotswolds in England—Burford and Bybury for example—date in their final stone form from the period that must otherwise be described as one of decay. The gradual disappearance of the three-field system and the unification of scattered strips into larger parcels created the more unified landscape of post-medieval Europe, with its broad division of fields, sometimes with definite boundary marks and hedges, sometimes in the older open forms, as in some parts of Bavaria and Switzerland. The wild forest became the park: the feudal village, stimulated by the fresh infusion of hand-industry escaping from the closely regulated towns, got almost its first opportunity to command goods from the outside world. So the grace and solidity that were departing from the medieval town took up residence in the new villages; and it is from these surviving villages in England, Holland, France, and Germany today that one can get one's best notions of the layout of the older towns, now hopelessly confused in their formations with the debris of half a dozen different cultural epochs.

These practical common-sense advances in city development were burked by the prevailing ideology; for "progressive" ideas gave authority and economic power to the big city. The ruin of the balanced region, with a multitude of small cities and villages connected by a network of canals and roads, and amply supplied with water and wind power, has been little noted in political history. I have pointed out in Technics and Civilization how the earlier invention of a more efficient prime mover, Fourneyron's water turbine and the turbine windmill, might perhaps have provided the coal mine and the iron mine with serious technical competitors, based on a further development of eotechnic methods. With the co-ordinate development of science, this might easily have led directly into the present neotechnic phase of industry. While it is useless to linger over these vanished possibilities, one would be blind to ignore the fact that they once existed. For no one can know this period and its urban culture who is not conscious of the strange eddies and countercurrents that ruffle the stream of actual events.

Today one looks with a fresh eye on these mutations: the Dutch city and the seventeenth century New England village. As in the penetrating psychology of a Spinoza or a Rembrandt we find a spirit more akin to our own than in the sharp mechanical analysis of a Descartes or the more typical portraiture of court painters like Van Dyck, so in these urban forms we find an early experimental anticipation of patterns for a living environment, like those we must eventually create, in terms of our own culture, for a whole civilization. For the Dutch town architects and the preachers and governors of New England, had a far more significant understanding of the life of men in cities than did the baroque princes: their synthesis was a more inclusive one, and in terms of real life, it is Louis XIV and Le Nôtre whom we must now consider the provincials. Versailles was essentially a spoiled child's toy, precisely as what Spengler worshipfully calls high dynastic politics was, realistically considered, only child's play: adult infantilism disguised as national statesmanship and architectural magnificence. The planners who have reclaimed the Zuyder Zee, the architects who have built a multitude of wellknit modern communities over the face of that great garden which is Holland, follow a sturdier tradition.

CHAPTER III.

THE INSENSATE INDUSTRIAL TOWN

1: The Displacement of Population

The despotic impulse has been scarcely less tenacious in its hold upon society than the medieval ideology. Armies, governments, capitalistic enterprises, still show the characteristic animus and form of this order. Is it strange that governmental planning was usually conceived in the baroque image throughout the world? It was the characteristic style of bureaucrats: true pigeonhole architecture. And certain typically baroque institutions, like the hotel, which had its origin in Rome in the sixteenth century, did not achieve complete form until the nineteenth.

If in Paris or in Wien the style still retained a little of its old vitality—as in Garnier's Opera House, for example, or in the more chaste Renascence arcades of the Rue de Rivoli—that was only because so little had changed in these cities in the underlying social and economic relationships. Despite its many functional weaknesses, the baroque in its classic mode was destined to remain during the nineteenth century the image of order. Almost all the city planning or building that was esthetically worth attention before the middle of the nineteenth century was along classic lines: the work of Schinkel in Berlin, of the brothers Adam in London and Edinburgh, or that of L'Enfant, Bulfinch, Jefferson, Ramée, and Latrobe in America.

Meanwhile the solidarity of the upper classes was visibly breaking down; the court was becoming supernumerary. In every quarter, the principles of aristocratic education and culture were being displaced by a single-minded devotion to pecuniary success. The new industrialists and bankers, intent on making money and extending their powers through their canny initiatives, had no use for habits of life that did not give them a direct edge over their competitors. Uncouth people, rich speculators who had made a lucky gamble, ruthless factory organizers who had pushed their way to the top, ambitious men, avaricious men, the Napoleons of the factory and the counting house, people as innocent of the principles of humane self-control as a diapered baby, pushed themselves into the established ranks.

The baroque dream of power and luxury had at least human outlets, human goals: the tangible pleasures of the hunt, the dinner table, the bed were constantly in view. The new dream of human destiny, as the utilitarians projected it, had little place for even sensual delights: it rested on a doctrine of productive avarice and physiological denial; and it took the form of a wholesale disparagement of the needs of life.

Yet the triumph of the iron discipline of the machine was not complete. The repressive regimentation that entered the new factories was counterbalanced by the tremendous release from restrictive regulations of all kinds that attended the free movements of peoples over the face of the earth. Within the state there were similar contradictions. The French Revolution looked like a triumph of popular democracy over aristocratic privilege: at least a victory of the middle classes. But it was this revolution that created that hitherto unheard-of engine of destruction, the National Army, and introduced recruitment by popular conscription: it gave the rulers of the state a power that the most absolute princes had rarely dared to exercise.

The cities of the nineteenth century embodied with utmost fidelity all the confusions and contradictions of the period of transition. Those centers in which the new energies and the new discipline of society were most completely focused showed the greatest departures from the best norms: between 1820 and 1900 the chaos of the great cities is like that of a battlefield, proportionate to the very extent of their equipment and the strength of the forces employed. In the new provinces of city building, one must now keep one's eyes on the bankers and the industrialists and the mechanical inventors. They were responsible for most of what was good and almost all that was bad. In their own image, they created a new type of city: that which Dickens, in Hard Times, called Coketown. In a greater or less degree,

every city in the Western World was stamped with the characteristics
of Coketown.

The political base of this new type of urban aggregation rested on
three main pillars: the abolition of the guilds and the creation of a
state of permanent insecurity for the working classes: the establishment of the open market for labor and for the sale of goods: the
maintenance of foreign dependencies as source of raw materials,
necessary to the new industries, and as a ready market to absorb
the surplus of mechanized industry. Its economic foundations were
the exploitation of the coal mine, the vastly increased production of
iron, and the use of a steady, reliable—if highly inefficient—source
of mechanical power: the steam engine.

Actually, these technical advances depended socially upon the invention of new forms of corporate organization and administration.
The joint stock company, the limited liability investment, the delega-
tion of administrative authority under divided ownership, and control of the process by budget and audit were all matters of co-operative political technique whose success was not due to the genius of
any particular individual or group of individuals. This holds true,
too, of the mechanical organization of factories, which greatly augmented the efficiency of production. But the basis of this system, in
the ideology of the time, was thought to be the atomic individual: to
guard his property, to protect his rights, to ensure his freedom of
choice and freedom of enterprise, was the whole duty of government.

This myth of the untrammeled individual was in fact the democ-
ratization of the baroque conception of the despotic Prince: now
every enterprising man sought to be a despot in his own right: emotional despots like the romantic poets: practical despots like the
businessmen. Adam Smith indeed had a comprehensive theory of
political society: he had a correct conception of the economic basis
of the city and valid insight into the non-profit-making economic
functions. But his interest gave way, in practice, to the aggressive
desire to increase the wealth of individuals: that was the be-all and
the end-all of the new Malthusian struggle for existence.

Perhaps the most gigantic fact in the whole urban transition was
the displacement of population that took place over the whole planet.
For this movement and resettlement was accompanied by another

fact of colossal import: the astounding rise in the rate of population increase.

In 1800 England had a population of a little over nine million, Germany had some twenty-four million, France about twenty-seven million, and the United States not much over five million. By 1930, their population in round numbers had risen to respectively forty-five million, sixty-six million, forty-two million, and one hundred twenty-three million. This increase affected industrially backward countries like Russia, with a predominantly rural population and a high rate of births and deaths, quite as much as it affected progressive countries that were predominantly mechanized and de-ruralized. The general increase in numbers was accompanied by a drawing of the surplus into cities, and an immense magnification of the bigger centers. Urbanization increased in almost direct proportion to industrialization: in England and in New England it finally came about that almost eighty per cent of the entire population was living in centers with more than twenty-five hundred population.

Into the newly opened lands of the planet, originally peopled by military camps, trading posts, religious missions, small agricultural settlements, there came an inundation of immigrants from countries suffering from political oppression and economic poverty. This movement of people, this colonization of territory, had two forms: land pioneering and industry pioneering. The first filled the sparsely occupied regions of America, Africa, Australia, of Siberia and, later, Manchuria: the second brought the overplus into the new industrial villages and towns. In most cases, these types came in successive waves.

During the eighteenth and nineteenth centuries, the people of Western Europe re-initiated a process that had gone on in the tenth and eleventh centuries. They opened up millions of acres of new land, whose surplus of furs, hides, timber, metals and cereals they could send back to Europe. In the New World, in particular, the suppressed land hunger of the European, whose land had been carefully controlled by the feudal landlord or the Crown, who felt more and more constricted as the local population rose above its medieval level—this suppressed land hunger led irresistibly to colonization.

Impoverished, sometimes starving men, were willing to forego all the advantages of a socialized and settled life in order to have the elementary privilege of having enough food to eat and enough land to produce most of it. Sometimes they never actually reached their goal, but rotted away in the big seaports into which they were dumped, without the means of going further. But the goal itself was plain. Land meant security. Land meant power and independence. Land might even mean individual riches, when sufficient settlers crowded together to form cities. Lured by these possibilities thousands of families began to explore new geographic provinces, test new soils and new modes of agriculture, acquire new habits of working and living.

This land migration in turn helped to bring to the European system of agriculture the resources of hitherto untapped parts of the world: particularly a whole series of new energy crops, maize and potato—and that instrument of relaxation and social ceremony, the tobacco plant. Moreover the thrusting open of tropical and subtropical lands added a further energy crop now supplied to Europe for the first time on a grand scale—cane-sugar. A surplus of grain had already made possible the distillation of liquors in the seventeenth and eighteenth centuries: whiskey, cognac, and the poor man's drink, gin, supplemented the imperfect fireplaces and stoves with an internal application of warmth: potent if treacherous aids in facing all manner of rough weather. And with the cultivation of the wheatlands of the New World, wheaten flour began to come again into common use, instead of the barley and oaten flour which had, in so many parts of Europe, become the staple ingredient for bread.

Plainly this enormous increase in the food supply was what made possible the increase of population. And the external colonization in new rural territories thus helped to create that surplus of men and women and children which went toward the internal colonization of the new industrial towns and commercial emporia. Villages expanded into towns; towns became metropolises. The number of urban centers multiplied; the number of cities with populations above five hundred thousand increased, too. Extraordinary changes of scale took place in the masses of buildings and the areas they covered:

vast structures were erected almost overnight. Men built in haste, and had hardly time to repent of their mistakes before they tore down their original structures and built again, just as heedlessly. The newcomers, babies or immigrants, could not wait for new quarters: they crowded into whatever was offered. It was a period of vast urban improvisation: makeshift piled upon makeshift.

Mark that the rapid growth of cities was no mere New World phenomenon. Indeed, the rate of city growth was swifter in Germany after 1870, when the paleotechnic revolution was in full swing there, than in new countries like the United States: this despite the fact that the United States was steadily receiving immigrants. Though the nineteenth century was the first to rival the early Middle Ages in large-scale land colonization and settlement, the premises upon which these enterprises were conducted were far more primitive than those of the eleventh century. Colonization by communities, except in the case of little idealistic groups, the most successful of which were the Mormons, was no longer the rule. Every man was for himself; and the Devil, if he did not take the hindmost, at least reserved for himself the privilege of building the cities.

A blight that had its origin in England's dark Satanic mills, as William Blake called them, laid its diseased fingers on the new cities and stultified the further development of the old ones. Here was a chance to build on a firm foundation and make a fresh start: such a chance as democracy had claimed for itself in political government. Almost everywhere that chance was fumbled. In an age of rapid technical progress the city, as a *social* unit, lay outside the circle of invention. Except for utilities such as gas mains, water pipes, and sanitary equipment, often belatedly introduced, often slipshod and inadequate, the industrial city could claim no important improvements over the seventeenth century town. Indeed, the most wealthy and "progressive" metropolises often denied themselves elementary necessities of life like light and air that even backward villages still possessed. Until 1838 neither Manchester nor Birmingham even functioned politically as incorporated boroughs: they were man-heaps, machine-warrens, not organs of human association.

2: Mechanization and *Abbau*

Before we inquire how this vast flood of people found urban accommodation, let us examine the assumptions and attitudes that people brought to the new task of city building.

The leading philosophy of life was the offspring of two entirely dissimilar types of experience. One was the rigorous concept of mathematical order derived from the study of the motions of the heavenly bodies: the highest pattern of mechanical regularity. The other was the physical process of breaking up, pulverizing, calcining, smelting, which the alchemists, working with the mechanically advanced mine workers of the late Middle Ages, had turned from a mere mechanical process into the routine of scientific investigation. As formulated by the new philosophers of nature, neither this mathematical order nor the systematic analysis of matter had any place for organisms or societies: neither institutional patterns nor esthetic patterns derived from the external analysis of the "physical world." The machine alone could embody this order.

Art, religion, personal culture, the building of cities, all felt the results of this systematic indifference to organic events and organic patterns. So far as these disciplines remained true to themselves, they tended to lose an essential connection with the social complex; whilst people who were in harmony with that complex, who expressed it, who profited by it, forfeited some of the attributes of men. In this new environment, only machines could be quite at home; for they express order, purpose, regularity, without the mechanically irrelevant need for love, or sympathy, or beauty.

So immersed are we, even at this late date, in the surviving medium of paleotechnic beliefs that we are not sufficiently conscious of their profound abnormality. Few of us correctly evaluate the destructive imagery that the mine carried into every department of activity, sanctioning the anti-vital and the anti-organic. Before the nineteenth century the mine had, quantitatively speaking, only a subordinate part in man's industrial life. By the middle of the century it had come to underlie every part of it. And the spread of mining was accompanied by a general loss of form throughout society: a degradation of the landscape and a no less palpable disordering of the communal environment.

Agriculture creates a balance between wild nature and man's social needs. It restores deliberately what man subtracts from the earth; while the plowed field, the trim orchard, the serried vineyard, the vegetables, the grains, the flowers, are all examples of disciplined purpose, orderly growth, and beautiful form. The process of mining, on the other hand, is destructive: the immediate product of the mine is disorganized and inorganic; and what is once taken out of the quarry or the pithead cannot be replaced. Add to this the fact that continued occupation in agriculture brings cumulative improvements to the landscape and a finer adaptation of it to human needs; while mines as a rule pass quickly from riches to exhaustion, from exhaustion to desertion, within at most a few generations: they are the very image of human discontinuity, here today and gone tomorrow, now feverish with gain, now drained and exhausted.

From the eighteen-thirties on, the environment of the mine, once restricted to the original site, was universalized by the railroad. Wherever the iron rails went, the mine and its debris went with them. Whereas the canals of the eotechnic phase, with their locks and bridges and toll-houses, with their trim banks and their gliding barges, had brought a new element of beauty into the rural landscape, the railroads of the paleotechnic phase made huge gashes: the cuts and embankments for the greater part long remained unplanted, and the wound in the earth was unhealed. The rushing locomotives brought noise, smoke, grit, into the hearts of the towns: more than one superb urban site, like Prince's Gardens in Edinburgh, was desecrated by the invasion of the railroad. And the factories that grew up alongside the railroad sidings mirrored the slatternly environment of the railroad itself. If it was in the mining town that the characteristic process of *Abbau*—mining or un-building—was seen at its purest, it was by means of the railroad that this process was extended by the third quarter of the nineteenth century to almost every industrial community.

The process of un-building, as Wheeler pointed out, is not unknown in the world of organisms. In un-building, a more advanced form of life loses its complex character; there is an evolution downward, toward simpler and less finely integrated organisms. "There is," observed Wheeler, "an evolution by atrophy as well as by increasing complication, and both processes may be going on simultaneously and at varying rates in the same organism." This held precisely true of paleotechnic society: it showed itself clearly in the organization of urban communities. A process of up-building, with increasing differentiation, integration, and social accommodation of the individual parts in relation to the whole was going on: an articulation within an ever-widening environment was taking place within the factory, and indeed within the entire economic order. Food-chains and production-chains of an extremely complicated nature were being formed throughout the planet: ice traveled from Boston to Calcutta and tea journeyed from China to Ireland, whilst machinery from Birmingham and Manchester found its way to the remotest corners of the earth. A universal postal service, fast locomotion, and almost instantaneous communication by telegraph and cable synchronized the activities of vast masses of men who had hitherto lacked the most rudimentary facilities for co-ordinating their tasks.

But at the same time, an *Abbau*, or un-building, was taking place, often at quite as rapid a rate, in other parts of the environment: forests were slaughtered, soils were mined, whole animal species, such as the beaver, the bison, the wild pigeon, were practically wiped out, while the sperm whales and right whales were seriously decimated. Therewith the natural balance of organisms within their ecological regions was upset, and a lower and simpler biological order—sometimes marked by the complete extermination of the prevalent forms of life—followed the Western man's ruthless exploitation of nature for the sake of his temporary and petty profit-economy.

Above all, this un-building took place in the urban environment. The loss of form and the loss of effective social institutions for transmitting and enlarging the social heritage can indeed be seen at their worst in the mining towns that sprang up during this period: the oil towns, the coal towns, the gold towns, the copper towns, the diamond towns, that began their existence in a "rush," like the tropismic flight of moths toward strong light, and that collapsed, again and again, into empty hulks, or continued in existence as production centers without evolving for themselves any of the other attributes that make life in close communities valuable to man. To this day, these towns remain, despite precious efforts at philanthropy, among the darkest and most benighted parts of the world; their inhabitants, often cut off from physical contact with the rest of the world because of their mountainous terrain, cut off likewise by poverty and cramped desires, are even in free countries the most feudally organized part of the population: here the company town, with its mean power of exploitation and tyranny, has flourished.

Physically, life is at a minimum in these mining areas; and socially, outside the fellowship of work, in an occupation still so dangerous that it calls for heroic efforts and no less heroic sacrifices for one's comrades, these towns are even more destitute. The mining spore, the factory spore, the undifferentiated industrial district— these are the lowest contemporary forms of even semi-permanent organized life. Towns that have been formed by the physical expansion and coalescence of these spores remain, for the most part, areas of barbarism. Exceptions exist: the physical rehabilitation of the Ruhr district and its comprehensive planning as a region for living as well as working, presents a civilized contrast to the usual blight and affliction; but it happens that this Rhineland is one of the oldest continuously occupied industrial centers in the world: its culture dates back to Roman days.

As long as the idolum of the machine remained uppermost, the two processes of up-building and un-building went on together. The *Abbau* reached its lowest point in England around 1840; and at a somewhat later date in other countries. I shall confine most of my observations to England. Here the non-city achieved its classic form; and it was here that the most decisive reactions against un-building first took place.

3: The Postulates of Utilitarianism

In so far as there was any conscious political regulation of the growth and development of cities during the paleotechnic period it was done in accord with the postulates of utilitarianism. The most fundamental of these postulates was a notion that the utilitarians had taken over, in apparent innocence, from the theologians: the notion that a divine providence ruled over economic activity and ensured, so long as man did not presumptuously interfere, the maximum good through the dispersed and unregulated efforts of every individual. Another way of putting it is that they regarded industry as an internally self-regulating system that achieved a harmonious balance through the individual pursuit of pecuniary gain. The non-theological name for this pre-ordained harmony was laissez-faire. The protestant's right of private judgment became the systematic calculus of society.

The historic justification for laissez-faire needs no demonstration now: it was an attempt to break through the network of stale privileges and franchises and trade regulations that the absolute state had imposed upon the decayed economic fabric and dwindling social morality of the medieval town. The new enterprisers had good reason to distrust the public spirit of a venal court or the social efficiency of the Circumlocution Offices of the growing taxation-bureaucracy. Hence the utilitarians sought to reduce governmental functions to a minimum: they wished to have a free hand in making investments, in building up industries, in buying land, in hiring workers. Unfortunately, the pre-ordained harmony of the economic order turned out to be a superstition: the scramble for power remained a scramble, and individual competition for ever-greater profits led the more successful to the practice of monopoly.

In practice, the political equality that was slowly introduced into the Western polities from 1789 onward, and the freedom of initiative that was demanded by the industrialists were contradictory claims. To achieve political equality and personal freedom, strong economic limitations were necessary. In countries where the experiment at equality was made without attempting to rectify annually the effects of the law of rent, the result was a stultification of the original purpose. In the United States, for example, the free bestowal of land upon settlers in 160 acre tracts under the Homestead Law did not lay the basis of a free polity: within a generation the unequal properties of the soil, the unequal talents of the users, had resulted in gross social inequalities. Without systematically removing the fundamental disparities that grew out of the private monopoly of land, the inheritance of large fortunes, the monopoly of patents, the only effect of laissez-faire was to supplement the old privileged class with a new one.

The freedom demanded by the utilitarians was in reality freedom for unrestricted profits and unlimited aggrandizement. Profits and rents were to be limited only by what the traffic would bear: decent customary rents, and a just price, were out of the question. Wages, too, were limited in their downward leveling only by the endurance of the poor: theoretically they should drop to the lowest amount of food and shelter necessary to return the laborer to his job. The ruling classes wished to preserve individual initiative and freedom of contract (that is, social helplessness) for the workers: their right to accept starvation wages was held sacred. They themselves, however, maintained an almost unbroken class front on any issue that concerned their pocketbooks as a class; and they never scrupled to act collectively when it was a question of beating down the working classes.

This theological belief in pre-ordained harmony had, however, an important result upon the organization of the paleotechnic town. It created the natural expectation that the whole enterprise should be conducted by private individuals, with a minimum amount of interference on the part of local or national governments. The location of factories, the building of quarters for the workers, even the supply of water and the collection of garbage, should be done exclusively by private enterprise seeking for private profit. Free competition was supposed to choose the correct location, provide the correct time-sequence in development, and create out of a thousand unco-ordinated efforts a coherent social pattern.

Laissez-faire, even more than absolutism, destroyed the notion of a co-operative polity and a common plan: did not the utilitarian expect the *effects* of plan to appear from the unrestricted operation of random private interests? By giving rein to chaos, reason and order were to emerge: indeed rational planning, by preventing automatic adjustments, could only interfere with the higher workings of a divine economic providence. The test of social success was not the consequences to society in good homes and healthy lives and a friendly environment: the sole test was the pecuniary reward that flowed to the enterpriser. If his rewards shrank, the enterprise was "unwise" and its automatic cessation must follow, by bankruptcy if not by choice: if they increased, the enterprise was blessed, and would expand. We shall presently follow the results of this mystical doctrine as it worked out in the housing of the town laborer.

The main point to note now is that these doctrines undermined such municipal authority as had survived, and they discredited the city itself as anything more than a "fortuitous concourse of atoms" —as the physics of the time described the universe—held together temporarily by motives of self-seeking and private profit. Even in the eighteenth century, before either the French Revolution or the paleotechnic revolution had been consummated, it had become the fashion to discredit municipal authorities and to sneer at local interests. In the newly organized states, even those based on republican principles, only matters of national moment, organized by political parties, counted in men's hopes or dreams.

The time of the Enlightenment, as W. H. Riehl sharply said, was a period when people yearned for humanity and had no heart for their own people; when they philosophized about the state and forgot the community. "No period was more impoverished than the eighteenth century in the development of a common community spirit; the medieval community was dissolved and the modern was not yet ready. . . . In the satirical literature of the time, whoever wanted to portray a blockhead represented him as a Burgomaster, and if he wished to describe a meeting of Jackasses, he described a meeting of Town Councillors."

This contempt for the civic business of the local community, this scorn for the old agents of the common weal, this childish belief in the industrialist as the divinely appointed agent of a Higher Power, prepared the way for the complete un-building of the city. The brakes of tradition and custom were lifted from the exploitation of land; there was no limit to congestion, no limit to rent-raising: there was no standard of order or decency or beauty to dictate the division and layout and building up of urban structures. Only one controlling agent remained: profit.

Urban growth had indeed begun, from industrial and commercial causes, even before the paleotechnic revolution was well started. In 1685 Manchester had about six thousand people; in 1760 between thirty and forty-five thousand. Birmingham had four thousand at the first date and almost thirty thousand in 1760. But once the concentration of factories abetted the growth of towns, the increase in numbers became overwhelming. Since the increase produced extraordinary opportunities for profit making, there was nothing in the current traditions of society to curb this growth; or rather, there was everything to promote it. Wherever the land could be broken up into individual parcels, and exploited by competing individuals, wherever, that is, the population could increase freely, the lid was off. Every norm was disregarded: every limitation pushed aside. "The roof was the limit," and business succeeded in raising the roof.

Note one more point. In their relation to the land, the new industrial interests were two-faced. Historically the new oligarchy of big enterprisers, bankers, and industrialists were in opposition to those whose wealth rested mainly on the soil. But despite loud professions of laissez-faire, the new industrial interests sought their own special kinds of monopoly, through patents, trade marks, special subsidies, tariffs, and exclusive rights of exploitation in colonial markets: above all, they needed the privilege of calling upon the soldiery of the state to defend their property and their persons in case of an uprising on the part of the workers—an event they actively dreaded with a fear that grew out of their own capacity for terrorism and injustice, rather than an objective appraisal of the workers' talents for revenge. Even the great philosopher of this regime, Herbert Spencer, whose theoretic individualism had so far advanced toward anarchy that he tended to reject public enterprise even in street paving or sewage disposal, nevertheless firmly upheld the function of the state as policeman.

By allowing the landlord to exploit urban land monopoly the industrialist not merely assented to a sort of equilibrium of privilege: he also favored himself as a potential owner of land, and logically carried out, not his fictitious doctrine of "free enterprise," but his actual policy of a limited monopoly framed so as to favor the more aggressive members of his own class. Hence the weakness of Henry George's effort in Progress and Poverty (1879) to dissociate business enterprise from landlordism. In a society where pecuniary values were uppermost and where no social motives were permitted to stand in the way of financial aggrandizement, such distinctions could gain no hold upon the industrial interests. The displacement of privilege in land could only come through the initiative of the community as a whole, with an enlightened and militant working class as the spearhead. In this respect, Thomas Spence was a greater realist than a Henry George or a Theodor Hertzka.

4: The Technics of Agglomeration

In the first stage of the factory system in England, water power was all-important: hence the woolen industry tended to spread through the valleys of Yorkshire, where such power was abundant. Even in the Manchester region the cotton manufacturers were often attracted at first to the open country by cheap land for their huge plants, a docile working population, and easy access to power: so, too, in New England.

It took the better part of a century before all the agents of agglomeration were developed in equal degree: before the advantages offered industry in the towns counterbalanced the lure of independent organization in separate factory villages, sufficient to make the former the prevailing mode. Once these agents played into each other's hands, the attractive power of the city became irresistible; and the cities came to absorb an ever larger share of the natural increase in population.

By the end of the eighteenth century most of the necessary conditions were satisfied in London, Paris, and Berlin: hence the ability to pile people into these throbbing centers was limited now only by the human tolerance for an obnoxious environment. Unfortunately, on this score, human beings show qualities that remarkably resemble those of the pig: give swine a clean sty on hard ground with plenty of sunlight, and they will keep it remarkably clean: put them in the midst of muck and putrescence underground, and they will accommodate themselves to these conditions. When starvation and homelessness are the alternatives, there is apparently no horror to which defeated men and women will not adapt themselves and endure.

Apart from the incentive of profit, industry itself, from the beginning of the nineteenth century onward, became an active factor in urban agglomeration. Eotechnic industry had, in the nature of things, been decentralized: wind power and water power caused its spread along the coast lines and rapid-flowing rivers; the unit of production was necessarily limited in size, and only in a minor degree was there any advantage in the concentration of a *single* industry or plant. Despite occasional large munitions factories and textile plants, the small workshop was the typical unit.

The use of Watt's steam engine as a prime mover in the seventeen-eighties changed all this. Steam worked most efficiently in big concentrated units, with the parts of the plant no more than a quarter of a mile from the power-center: every spinning machine or loom had to tap power from the belts and shafts worked by the central steam engine. The more units within a given area, the more efficient was the source of power: hence the tendency toward giantism in textile factories, which covered a large area and were usually five stories high. Big factories, such as those developed in Manchester from the eighteen-twenties onward—repeated in New Bedford and Fall River—could utilize the latest instruments of power production, whereas the smaller factories were at a technical disadvantage. A single factory might employ two hundred and fifty hands. A dozen such factories, with all the accessory instruments and services, were already the nucleus of a considerable town.

In their attempts to produce machined goods at low prices for consumption in the world market, the manufacturers cut costs at every point in order to increase profits. The most obvious place to begin this paring was in the wages of the workers. In the eighteenth century, as Robert Owen noted, even the most enlightened manufacturers made unsparing use of child labor and pauper labor: but when the ages of child workers were legally regulated and the supply diminished, it became necessary to tap other sources. To have the necessary surplus of workers, to meet the extra demands in the busy seasons, it was important for industry to settle near a great center of population, for in a country village the support of the idle might fall directly upon the manufacturer himself. It was the fluctuating rhythm of the market, its spurts and cessations, that made the large urban center so important to industry. For it was on an underlayer of irregular labor, fitfully employed, insufficiently paid, that the new capitalists managed to depress wages and meet any sudden demand in production. Size, in other words, took the place of an efficiently organized labor market. Topographical agglomeration was a substitute for a well-timed and nicely regulated mode of production.

If the steam factory, producing for the world market, was the first factor that tended to increase the area of urban congestion, the new railroad transportation system, after 1830, greatly abetted it. Power was concentrated on the coal fields. Where coal could be mined or stored or obtained by cheap means of transportation, industry could produce regularly throughout the year without stoppages through seasonal failure of power. In a business system based upon time-contracts and time-payments, this regularity was highly important. Coal and iron exercised a gravitational pull on many subsidiary and accessory industries: first by means of the canal, and after 1830, through the new railroads. A direct connection with the mining areas was a prime condition of urban concentration: to this day the chief commodity carried by railroads is coal for heat and power.

The dirt roads, the sail-power, the horse-power of the eotechnic transportation system had favored a dispersal of population: within the region, there were many points of equal advantage. But the relative weakness of the steam locomotive, which could not easily climb a grade steeper than two feet in a hundred, tended to concentrate the new industrial centers on the coalbeds and in the connecting valleys: the Lille district in France, the Merseburg and Ruhr districts in Germany, the Black Country of England, the Allegheny-Great Lakes region and the Eastern Coastal Plain region in the United States.

Port cities, because of their overseas connections, played an equal part in this assemblage. They became the termini or junction towns of the main lines, and they served likewise, by this fact, to concentrate more narrowly the routes of ocean travel, so that a few great ports, like Liverpool, London, New York, Antwerp, and Hamburg gathered to themselves a disproportionate share of traffic and burdened themselves with an extra source of population congestion. With the steady increase in the size and draft of ships, these disparities grew: smaller ports lost their trade to the big ports where the channels were deep, the railroad connections many, and where the concentration of commercial enterprise made it possible to make the necessary investments in dredges, docks, cranes, warehouses and similar facilities. (Liverpool's exceptionally far-sighted public provision of docks, markets, and warehouses in the eighteenth century gave it a unique place.) In short: numbers begot numbers; and concentration, once well started, tended to pile up in ever-increasing ratios, claiming increase by inertia where it could no longer promise more effective economic performance. Industry prospered in the big metropolises into which raw materials, unemployed workers, and unemployed capital were automatically drifting: both technics and capitalism during the nineteenth century promoted urban congestion.

Population growth, then, during the paleotechnic regime, showed two characteristic patterns: a general massing on the coal areas, where the new heavy industries, iron and coal mining, smelting, cutlery, hardware production, glass manufacture, and machine building flourished. And in addition a partly derivative thickening of population along the new railroad lines, with a definite clotting in the new industrial centers along the great trunk lines and a further massing in the greater junction towns and export terminals. Along with this went a thinning out of population and a running down of activities in the back country: the falling off of local mines, quarries, and furnaces, and the diminishing use of highways, canals, small factories, local mills.

Most of the great political and commercial capitals of the baroque period, at least in the Northern countries, shared in this growth. Not merely did they usually occupy geographically strategic positions: they had special resources of exploitation through their intimacy with the agents of political power and through the central banks and bourses that controlled the flow of investments. Moreover, they had the further advantage of having gathered, for centuries, a vast reserve of miserable people at the margin of subsistence: what was euphemistically called the Labor Supply. The fact that almost every great capital became *ipso facto* a great industrial center served to give a further push to the policy of urban aggrandizement and congestion.

5: Factory and Slum

The two main elements in the new urban complex were the factory and the slum. By themselves they constituted what was called the town: a word that describes merely the fact that more than twenty-five hundred people are gathered in an area that can be designated for postal communication with a proper name. Such urban masses could and did expand a hundred times without acquiring more than a shadow of the institutions that characterize a city in the sociological sense—that is, a place in which the social heritage is concentrated, and in which the possibilities of continuous social intercourse and interaction raise to a higher potential the activities of men.

The factory became the nucleus of the new urban organism. Every other detail of life was subordinate to it. Even the utilities, such as the water supply and the minimum of governmental buildings that were necessary to a town's existence often, if they had not been built by an earlier generation, entered belatedly: an afterthought. It was not merely art and religion that were treated by the utilitarian as mere embellishments: intelligent political administration was in the same category.

The factory usually claimed the best sites: mainly, in the cotton industry, the chemical industries, and the iron industries, the sites near a waterfront; for large quantities of water were needed now in the processes of production, supplying the steam boilers, cooling hot surfaces, making the necessary chemical solutions and dyes. Above all, the river or canal had still another important function: it was the cheapest and most convenient dumping ground for all soluble or semi-soluble forms of waste. The transformation of the rivers into open sewers was a characteristic feat of the paleotechnic economy. Result: poisoning of the aquatic life: destruction of food: befouling of water so it was unfit to bathe in.

For generations, the members of every "progressive" urban community were forced to pay for the sordid convenience of the manufacturer, who often, it happened, consigned precious by-products to the river, for lack of the scientific knowledge or the empirical skill to use them. If the river was a liquid dumpheap, great mounds of

ashes, slag, rubbish, rusty iron, and even garbage blocked the horizon
with their vision of misplaced and unusable matter. The rapidity of
production was in part matched by the rapidity of consumption, and
before a conservative policy of scrap utilization became profitable,
the formless or deteriorated end-products were cast back over the
surface of the landscape. One might almost measure the "prosperity"
of the paleotechnic community by the size of its scrapheaps and junk-
piles.

The testimony that substantiates this picture is voluminous; indeed, it is still open for inspection in the older industrial cities of
the Western World, despite herculean efforts to cleanse the environment. Let me however quote from an early observer, Hugh Miller,
the author of Old Red Sandstone: a man thoroughly in harmony with
his age, but not insensitive to the actual qualities of the new environment. He is speaking of Manchester in 1862. "Nothing seems more
characteristic of the great manufacturing city, though disagreeably
so, than the river Irwell, which runs through the place. . . . The
hapless river—a pretty enough stream a few miles up, with trees
overhanging its banks and fringes of green sedge set thick along its
edges—loses caste as it gets among the mills and print works. There
are myriads of dirty things given it to wash, and while wagonloads
of poisons from dye houses and bleachyards throw into it to carry
away, steam boilers discharge into it their seething contents, and
drains and sewers their fetid impurities; till at length it rolls on—
here between tall dingy walls, there under precipices of red sandstone—considerably less a river than a flood of liquid manure."

Note the environmental effect of the *massing* of industries that the
new regime tended to make universal. A single factory chimney, a
single blast furnace, a single dye works may easily have its effluvia
absorbed by the surrounding landscape: twenty of them in a narrow
area effectively pollute the air or water beyond remedy. So that the
unavoidably dirty industries became through urban concentration far
more formidable than they were when they had existed on a smaller
scale and were more widely dispersed about the countryside. At the
same time clean industries, such as the making of blankets, which
still goes on at Witney in England, with bleaching and shrinking
conducted out in the open air of a charming countryside, became

impossible under the old rural methods in the new centers: chlorine took the place of sunlight, and for the healthful outdoor work that often accompanied the older processes of manufacture, with changes of scene as well as process to renew the spirit of the worker, came the dull drudgery of work within a dirty building hemmed in by other dirty buildings. Such losses cannot be measured in pecuniary terms; and we have no calculus for figuring out how much the gains in production must be offset by the palpable sacrifice of life and a living environment.

While factories were usually set near the rivers, or the railroad lines that paralleled the rivers (except where a level terrain invited diffusion), no authority was exercised to concentrate factories in a particular area, to segregate the more noxious or noisy industries that should be placed far from human habitations, or to zone for purely domestic purposes the appropriate adjacent areas. Factories were permitted to exist wherever the owner happened to have bought enough land to build on: "free competition" alone determined location, without thought of the possibility of functional planning; and the jumbling together of industrial, commercial, and domestic functions went on steadily in industrial cities.

In areas with a rough topography, such as the valleys of the Allegheny plateau, a certain amount of natural zoning might take place, since only the river bottoms would afford enough space for a big mill to spread. Otherwise living quarters were often placed within the leftover spaces between the factories and sheds and the railroad yards. To pay attention to such matters as dirt, noise, vibration, was accounted an effeminate delicacy. Workers' houses, often those of the middle classes too, would be built smack up against a steel works, a dye plant, a gas works, or a railroad cutting. They would be built often enough on land filled in with ashes and broken glass and rubbish, where even the grass could not take root; they might be on the edge of a dump or a vast permanent pile of coal and slag: day in and day out the stench of the refuse, the murky outpouring of chimneys, the noise of hammering or of whirring machinery, accompanied household routine.

So widespread was this deterioration of environment, so hardened have people in big cities become to it in the course of a century, that even the richer classes, who can presumably afford the best, to this day often indifferently embrace the worst. By continued extensions over their backyards, some of the finest houses off Fifth Avenue are built almost back-to-back: dark, dingy quarters, fit for disciples of Midas. One of the most fashionable residence districts in New York is situated plump between a huge gas works and an electric power station; the South Side of Chicago, once lined with sumptuous mansions, is close to the sickening effluvia of the monster-stockyards; while potentially the finest residential quarters in London, Westminster and Chelsea Reach, are befouled by the factories that have long been permitted to occupy the Lambeth and Battersea shores. Small wonder the rich have failed to understand the housing problem: they never discovered their own.

As for housing itself, the alternatives were simple. In the industrial towns that grew up on older foundations, the workers were first accommodated by turning old one-family houses into rent barracks. In these made-over houses, each separate room now would enclose a whole family: from Dublin and Glasgow to Bombay, the standard of one room per family long held. Bed overcrowding, with three to eight people of different ages sleeping on the same pallet, often aggravated room overcrowding in such human sties. This type of overcrowding, as we have seen, had been going on in the big capitals since the sixteenth century; and by the beginning of the nineteenth, according to Dr. Willan, who wrote a book then on the diseases of London, it had produced an incredible state of physical defilement among the poor. The other type of dwelling offered to the working class was, essentially, a standardization of these degraded conditions; but it had this further defect—the plans of the new houses and the materials of construction usually had none of the original decency of the older burgher houses: they were jerry-built from the ground up.

In both the old and the new quarters a pitch of foulness and filth was reached that the lowest serf's cottage scarcely achieved in medieval Europe. It is almost impossible to enumerate objectively the bare details of this housing without being suspected of perverse exaggeration. But those who speak glibly of urban improvements during this period, or of the alleged rise in the standards of living, fight shy of the actual facts: they generously impute to the town as a whole benefits which only the more favored middle class minority enjoyed; and they read into the original conditions those improvements which three generations of active legislation and massive sanitary engineering have finally brought about.

In England, to begin with, thousands of the new worker's dwellings, in towns like Birmingham and Bradford, were built back to back. (They still exist.) Two rooms out of four on each floor therefore had no direct daylight or ventilation. There were no open spaces except the bare passages between these doubled rows. While in the sixteenth century it was an offense in many English towns to throw rubbish into the streets, in these early paleotechnic towns this was the regular method of disposal. The rubbish remained there, no matter how vile and filthy, "until the accumulation induced someone to carry it away for manure." Of the latter, there was naturally no lack in the crowded new quarters of the town. The privies, foul beyond description, were usually in the cellars; it was a common practice to have pigsties under the houses, too, and pigs roamed the streets once more, as they had not done for centuries in the larger towns. There was even a dire lack of toilets: the Report on the State of Large Towns and Populous Districts (1845) states that "in one part of Manchester in 1843-44 the wants of upward 7000 inhabitants were supplied by 33 necessaries only—that is, one toilet to every 212 people."

Even at such a low level of design, even with such foul accompaniments, not enough houses were built in many cities; and then far worse conditions prevailed. Cellars were used as dwelling places. In Liverpool, one-sixth of the population lived in "underground cellars," and most of the other port cities were not far behind: London and New York were close rivals to Liverpool: *even in the present decade there were 20,000 basement dwellings in London medically marked as unfit for human occupation.* This dirt and congestion, bad in themselves, brought other pests: the rats that carried bubonic plague, the bedbugs that infested the beds and tormented sleep, the lice that spread typhus, the flies that visited impartially the cellar privy and the infant's milk. Moreover the combination of dark rooms and dank walls formed an almost ideal breeding medium for bacteria, especially since the overcrowded rooms afforded the maximum possibilities of transmission through breath and touch.

If the absence of plumbing and municipal sanitation created frightful stenches in these new urban quarters, and if the spread of exposed excrement, together with seepage into local wells, meant a corresponding spread of typhoid, the lack of water was even more sinister. It removed the very possibility of domestic cleanliness or personal hygiene. Even in the big capital cities, where some of the old municipal traditions still lingered, no adequate provision for water was made in the new areas. In 1809, when London's population was about a million, water was available over the greater part of the city only in the basements of houses. In some quarters, water could be turned on for only three days in a week. And though iron pipes made their appearance in 1746, they were not extensively used until a special act in England in 1817 required that all new mains be built of iron after ten years.

In the new industrial towns, the most elementary traditions of municipal service were absent. Whole quarters were sometimes without water even from local wells. On occasion, the poor would go from house to house in the middle class sections, begging for water as they might beg for bread during a famine. With this lack of water for drinking and washing, it is no wonder that the filth accumulated. Open drains represented, despite their foulness, comparative municipal affluence. And if families were thus treated, one need scarcely turn to the documents to find out how the single workers fared: the flotsam and jetsam of casual labor. Deserted houses of uncertain title were used as lodging houses, fifteen or twenty people in a single room. In Manchester, according to the police statistics of 1841, there were some 109 lodging houses where people of both sexes slept indiscriminately; and there were 91 mendicant lodging houses. "Playfair told the Health of Towns Commission in 1842 that in all Lancashire there was only one town, Preston, with a public park, and only one, Liverpool, with public baths."

This depression of living quarters was well-nigh universal among the workers in the new industrial towns, once the paleotechnic regime was fully established. Local conditions sometimes permitted an escape from the extremes of foulness I have been describing: the housing of the millworkers at Manchester, New Hampshire, were for example of a better order; and in the more rural industrial towns of America, particularly in the Middle West, there was at least a little free elbow room and garden space for the workers. But wherever one looks, the improvement was but one of degree: the *type* had definitely changed for the worse.

Not merely were the new cities as a whole bleak and ugly, environments hostile to human life even at its most elementary physiological level, but the standardized overcrowding of the poor was repeated in middle class dwellings and in the barracks of the soldiers, classes which were not being directly exploited for the sake of profit. Mrs. Peel cites a sumptuous mid-Victorian mansion in which the kitchen, pantry, servant's hall, housekeeper's room, butler's and footmen's bedrooms were all placed in the cellar: two rooms in front and two rooms in the rear looked onto a deep back basement: all the others were "lighted" and "ventilated" by panes of glass high up in the ceiling. Corresponding forms of degraded housing were worked out in Berlin, Wien, New York, and Paris during the middle of the nineteenth century. The new apartment houses of the middle classes backed upon deep, airless courts that had all the characteristics of cellars even when they were technically above ground.

To judge by popular oratory, these defects were narrow in range, and, in any event, have been wiped out during the past century through the onward march of science and humanitarian legislation. Unfortunately, popular orators—and even historians and economists who supposedly deal with the same set of facts—have not formed the habit of making firsthand surveys of the environment: hence they ignore the fact that great clots of typically paleotechnic housing exist in only slightly modified form throughout the Western World today: even back-to-back houses and cellar-lodgings. These clots not merely include most of the worker's dwellings built before 1900; they include a great part of what has been done since, though they show improvements in sanitation. The surviving mass of housing that was built between 1830 and 1910 does not represent *even the hygienic standards of its own day;* and it is far below a standard framed in terms of present-day knowledge of sanitation, hygiene, and child care—to say nothing of domestic felicity.

"Slum, semi-slum, and super-slum—to this has come the evolution of cities." These mordant words of Patrick Geddes apply inexorably to the new environment. Even the most revolutionary of contemporary critics lacked genuine standards of building and living: they had no notion how far the environment of the upper classes themselves had become impoverished. Thus Friedrich Engels not merely opposed all "palliative" measures to provide better housing for the working classes: he seems to have held the innocent notion that the problem would be solved eventually for the proletariat by a revolutionary seizure of the commodious quarters occupied by the bourgeoisie. This notion, quantitatively considered, was fatuously optimistic; socially speaking, it merely urged as a revolutionary measure a process that had gone on in the older towns as the richer classes moved out of their original quarters and divided them up for working class occupation. But above all the suggestion was extremely naïve because it did not perceive that the standards embodied in the more pretentious residences were *below* those which were desirable for human life. In other words, even this revolutionary critic was apparently unaware of the fact that the upper class quarters were, more often than not, intolerable super-slums. The necessity for increasing the amount of housing, for expanding the space, for multiplying the equipment, for providing communal facilities, was far more revolutionary in its demands than any trifling expropriation of the quarters occupied by the rich would be. The former notion was merely an impotent gesture of revenge: the latter demanded a revolutionary reconstruction of the entire social environment—such a reconstruction as we are on the brink of today.

6: Houses of Ill-Fame

Let us look more closely at these new houses of the working classes. Each country, each region, had its own special pattern: tall tenements in Glasgow, Edinburgh, Paris, Berlin, Hamburg, or two story buildings, with four, five, sometimes six rooms in London, Brooklyn, Philadelphia, Chicago: vast wooden firetraps called three-deckers in New England, or narrow brick row houses, still clinging to an older Georgian row pattern, in Baltimore. But they are united by certain common characteristics. Block after block repeats the same formation: there are the same dreary streets, the same bleak alleys, the same absence of open spaces for children's play and gardens; the same lack of coherence and individuality to the local neighborhood. The windows are usually narrow; the interior light insufficient; no effort is made to orient the street pattern with respect to sunlight and winds. The painful grayish cleanliness of the more respectable quarters, where the better-paid artisans or clerks live, perhaps in a row, perhaps semi-detached, with a soiled pocket-handkerchief of grass before their houses, or a tree in the narrow courtyard in the rear— this respectability is almost as depressing as the outright slatternliness of the poorer quarters: more so indeed, because the latter often at least have a touch of color and life, a Punch-and-Judy show in the street, the chatter of the market stalls, the noisy camaraderie of the public house or bistro; in short, the more public and friendly life that is lived on the poorer streets.

The age of invention and mass production scarcely touched the worker's house or its utilities. Iron piping came in; likewise the improved water closet; eventually the gas light and the gas stove, the stationary bathtub with attached water pipes and fixed outlets; a collective water system with running water available for every house, and a collective sewage system. All these improvements slowly became available to the middle and upper economic groups after 1830; within a generation of their introduction they indeed became middle class necessities. But at no point during the paleotechnic phase were these improvements made available to the mass of the population. The problem for the builder was to achieve a modicum of decency *without* these new expensive utilities. This problem remained soluble only in terms of a primitive rural environment. Thus the original division of Muncie, Indiana, the Middletown of Robert Lynd's survey, had houses eight to a block, each on a lot sixty-two and a half feet wide and a hundred and twenty-five feet deep. This certainly provided better conditions for the poorer workers than what followed when rising land values crowded the houses and narrowed the garden space and the play space, and one out of four houses still lacked running water. In general, the congestion of the industrial town increased the difficulties in the way of good housing, and added to the cost of overcoming these difficulties.

As for the furnishing of the interiors, Gaskell's picture of the housing of the working classes in England strikes the lowest level; but the sordor continued, despite minor improvements, in the century that followed. The effects of pecuniary poverty were in fact aggravated by a general falling off in taste, which accentuated the impoverishment of the environment, by offering to the poor barbarous wall paper, meretricious bric-a-brac and framed oleograph pictures, and furniture derived from the worst examples of stuffy middle class taste: the dregs of the dregs.

In China a friend of mine reports seeing a miner, bent with toil, tenderly fondling a stalk of delphinium as he walked along the road; but in the Western World, down to the twentieth century, when the allotment garden began to have its civilizing effect, the same instinct for fresh vital form was destined to feed on the deliberate monstrosities that the manufacturer offered to the working classes under the guise of fashion and art. Even religious relics, in Catholic communities, reached an esthetic level so low as almost to be a profanation. In time, the taste for ugliness became ingrained: the worker was not willing to move from his older quarters unless he could carry a little of its familiar filth, confusion, noise, and overcrowding with him. Every move toward a better environment encountered that resistance: a real obstacle to decentralization.

A few such houses, a few such lapses into ugliness, would have been a blot; but perhaps every period could show a certain number of houses of this description. Now, however, whole quarters and cities, acres, square miles, provinces, were filled with such dwellings, which mocked every boast of material success that the "Century of Progress" uttered. In these new warrens, a race of defectives was created. Poverty and the environment of poverty produced organic modifications: rickets in children, due to the absence of sunlight, malformations of the bony structure and organs, defective functioning of the endocrines, through a vile diet; skin diseases for lack of the elementary hygiene of water; smallpox, typhoid, scarlet fever, septic sore throat, through dirt and excrement; tuberculosis, encouraged by a combination of bad diet, lack of sunshine, and room overcrowding, to say nothing of the occupational diseases, also partly environmental. Presently the recruiting sergeant was not able to use the children of this regime even as cannon-fodder: the medical discovery of England's mistreatment of her workers, during the Boer War and the World War, did perhaps as much as any one other factor to promote better housing.

The crude results of all these conditions may be followed in the mortality tables for adults, in the disease rates for urban workers compared with agricultural workers, in the expectations of life enjoyed by the various occupational classes. Above all, perhaps, the most sensitive barometer of the fitness of the social environment for human life is the infant mortality tables.

Wherever the comparison was made between country and city, between middle class quarters and poor quarters, between a low density district and a high density district, the higher rate usually fell in the latter class. Had other factors remained the same, urbanization by itself would have been sufficient to lop off part of the potential gains in vitality. Farm laborers, though they remained throughout the nineteenth century a depressed class in England, showed a much longer expectation of life than the higher grades of town mechanics, even after municipal sanitation and medical care had been introduced. Indeed, it was only by a continual influx of new life from the country that the paleotechnic city could survive at all: the new towns were established in the mass by immigrants. In 1851, out of 3,336,000 people of twenty years and upward, inhabiting London and 61 other English and Welsh towns, only 1,337,000 had been born in the town of their residence.

As for the infant mortality rate, the record is even more disgraceful. In New York City, for example, the mortality rate for infants in 1810 was between 120 and 145 per thousand live births; it rose to 180 per thousand by 1850, 220 in 1860, and 240 in 1870. This was accompanied by a steady depression in living conditions: for after 1835 the overcrowding was standardized in the newly built tenement houses. These recent calculations corroborate what is known about the infant mortality rate in England during the same period: there the rise took place after 1820 and fell most heavily on the towns. There are doubtless other factors responsible for these retrograde tendencies; but the new towns, as an expression of the entire social complex, conditioning hygiene, diet, working conditions, wages, child care, education, had an important part to play in the result.

There has been much unwarranted congratulation over improve- ments in urban health under industrialism because those who be- lieved that progress automatically occurred in every department of life during the nineteenth century refused to face the harsh facts. They did not let themselves make comparative studies between town and country, between the mechanized and the unmechanized; and they assisted further in creating confusion by using crude mortality tables, not corrected according to age and sex groups, and not there- fore allowing for the heavier distribution of adults in the cities and the larger incidence of children and old people in the countryside. These statistics made town mortality rates look more favorable than they really were on close actuarial analysis. To this day scarcely the beginnings have been made toward a satisfactory analysis of births and deaths, health and disease, in relation to environment. By lumping urban and rural rates together in a "national" figure the relatively poorer showings of the "prosperous" industrialized and urbanized areas have been concealed.

Similar misleading analyses continue to be made, even today. Thus Mabel Buer has attempted to vindicate the industrial revolu- tion from the charge of creating urban blight by making a study of the changes in the death rate that took place *before* 1815—that is, before the overcrowding and bad sanitation and general urbanization of the population had produced their characteristic devitalizing re- sults. There is no need to cast doubt upon this earlier improvement any more than one need forget the steady *general* drop in the death rate throughout the nineteenth century. But it fails to wipe out the equally indisputable fact of later deterioration.

Instead of giving credit for the early advance to the industrial revolution, one should give due credit to quite another department— the increase of the food supply, which provided a better diet and helped raise resistance to disease. Still another factor may have had a part: the wider use of soap made possible through the increased amount of available fats. The use of soap in personal hygiene may have extended from the washing of the nipples of the nursing mother to the child in her care: finally it passed by example from the femi-

nine to the masculine half of society. This increased use of soap is
not easily measurable in trade schedules; for soap was originally a
commercial monopoly, and as such, a luxury article: ordinary soap
was produced and consumed within the household. The spread of the
soap-and-water habit might well account for the lowering of infant
mortality rates before the nineteenth century; even as the dearth of
water and soap might account in part for the deplorable infant death
rates of the paleotechnic town.

Mark this: hygienic poverty was widespread. Lack of sunlight,
lack of pure water, lack of untainted air, lack of a mixed diet—these
lacks were so common that they amounted to a chronic starvation
among the greater part of the population. Even the more prosperous
classes succumbed; sometimes prided themselves on their vital deficiencies. Herbert Spencer, who was a nonconformist even to his own
creed of utilitarianism, was forced to preach the gospel of play and
physical relaxation to his contemporaries; and in his Essays on Education he went so far as to make a special plea to parents to permit
their children to *eat fruit*. The mischief was universal. Only those
relics of an older culture, the country clergyman, the landed aristo-
crat, the artist, had enough sense to flee the paleotechnic environment, as the ladies and gentlemen of Boccaccio's Decameron fled
from the plague in Florence. Doing so, they had their reward: not
riches perhaps, but length of days. Do you doubt it? Consult the
life insurance tables.

7: Resistance to Barbarism

That people remained in any degree human in this depauperate and
devitalized environment was a triumph. That the working classes
could raise families and keep their children from utter physical and
moral debasement was a tribute to their heroic fiber. On a moral
level, the standard of the paleotechnic town often remained high. If
Catholicism, Baptism, Wesleyanism, perhaps made the worker oblivious to his actual environment, too patient toward oppression, too
content with his mean station in life, they nevertheless prevented him
from sinking spiritually to the level of his physical surroundings.

It is partly to this poor remnant of the old Temple City, embodied
now in sheet-iron chapels and tawdry red-brick churches, designed

in debased gothic—it is to this fragment that one must attribute some of the saving grace that kept it from outright barbarism. From the older gospel of Christianity, but still more from the new social gospel first preached as a political doctrine during the French Revolution and later elaborated as an economic creed in socialism, came important compensations. The first was a survival; the second a mutation. In the slums and working class quarters a new hope was born. From the depths of the proletariat came the dream of a more friendly social order and a more humane way of life than a mechanistic capitalism had made possible.

Out of the friendly societies, a surviving bequest of the guilds, the new trade unions began to spring up. Around the table of a public house, that vestigial club of the workingman, a more purposive sociability was born. Here plans were made for banding against the employers; here projects for universalizing the ballot, for raising wages and shortening hours, for regulating the general conditions of industry and eventually taking command of the state were first hazily argued and inchoately formed. In some half-used building, a bare room, like that of a dissenter's chapel, would become the meeting place for those who were struggling for some modicum of economic security: trade union headquarters. The bleak walls, lighted by a bluish gas flame, the room itself reached by a rickety flight of stairs and a dusty passage, did not provoke a feeling of confidence and power. Two generations must pass before the Maison du Peuple in Brussels and other cities would serve as social centers for the working classes. Still: the early unionists did not make the mistake of confusing a beautiful building with a strong union: the spirit was firm though the shell was weak.

Similarly, a group of Rochdale weavers pooled their pennies to purchase tea outside the retail system: thus they founded the cooperative movement without a modicum of help from the classes above: an attempt to eliminate the sacred motive of private profit. This movement, in less than a century, came to rival in power and size and capital—as it was to surpass immensely in moral significance—the greatest capitalistic corporations of the world: clear proof of the absurdity of the contention that without opportunities for unlimited profits and unlimited individual aggrandizement the talent and skill necessary to run great collective enterprises cannot be summoned forth.

Rochdale weavers: Lancashire cotton spinners, who, though starving thereby, stuck to the anti-slavery cause; resolute trade unionists: decent workers in every paleotechnic town throughout the Western World—their sturdy examples modify one part of our just indictment of the environment. All the outer evils remained real: the brutality, the exploitation, the befoulment and the depression. These things were persistently inimical to life at its best, cramping it, frittering away its energies, robbing it of gaiety and sweetness. But despite these grave handicaps, the spirit of the working classes, who suffered most acutely, was not overwhelmed: again and again these heroic men and women displaced circumstances and rose superior to the motives that governed their rulers, even as they rose superior to the stultifying environment that capitalism had provided for men and masters alike. Perhaps as compensation, the most debased urban environments sometimes stimulated the most valiant efforts at change. Were not the miners, more than once, the leaders in revolutionary unionism—and in Europe did they not provide out of their own membership great choral societies?

In fact, the slum offered the worker compensations that the new villa quarter did not possess. There is snobbery in the grand salon of the ocean steamer, but not in the storm-tossed lifeboat. When people are shorn of all expectation of worldly goods and worldly success, they find their neighbors: reduced to a bare crust, Lazarus finds it easier to share the scrap with his neighbor than Dives does the surplusage of his banquet. The Circe of capitalism might transform the workers' dwellings into pigsties; she could not metamorphose all their inhabitants into swine. Thrust into this cruel environment, the workers of Europe, after enduring much, threw off their passive rôle: they took the first steps forward toward a new order of co-operative endeavor, out of which the city, as a conserver of the human heritage, could again arise. It needed, perhaps, this last exasperated contact with the paleotechnic hell to give mankind, in desperate revulsion, a fresh vision of heaven. At all events the vision slowly took form.

8: The Minimum of Life

From the standpoint of theoretic capitalist economics there was no housing problem in the paleotechnic town. Even the meanest paid worker could be housed at a profit, in strict accordance with his income, provided no outside standards based on health and safety were introduced to mar the free play of economic forces. If the result was a slum, that fact was a justification of the slum, not a condemnation of the profit system.

Unfortunately, this method of housing was not a permanently satisfactory one. Sooner or later, the question of standards upset the pure equation of supply and demand. Diseases could not be segregated: the laundress or the milkman might introduce typhoid fever into the most exclusive quarters of the city. Sheer self-protection demanded that the upper classes should concern themselves with the housing of the poor. So the first public attacks on the evils of housing came from the heads of the health departments in London and New York. The health officers pointed out that poverty, malnutrition, and bad housing were correlates of crime and disease.

By the middle of the nineteenth century, the housing problem was discovered, if not rigorously defined. In the industrial towns there was usually a chronic shortage of living quarters for the lower paid workers; and the quality of the accommodations offered was below the minimum current standards.

The attempt to remedy this situation took various forms. Philanthropists like the American merchant, Peabody, and Prince Albert, formed in London philanthropic associations to promote better housing for the poor and during the next half century they built an experimental series of working-class homes. This example was followed in other metropolises. Beginning in 1851 in England, through the initiative of Lord Shaftesbury, an attempt was made to establish minimum standards of sanitation: the decent repair of workers' houses and the provision of a minimum of paving, water, open spaces, and sewer drainage in the new quarters, was ultimately enforced by law. Private initiative, like that of Ruskin's disciple, Octavia Hill, working strictly within the lines of capitalism, attempted to show that with the proper upkeep and supervision of slum quarters, the conditions of backward properties could be improved to the common advantage of owner and renter. As early as 1851 the Netherlands permitted communes to expropriate land for housing purposes; and in 1873 the city of Amsterdam provided sites and furnished funds to an association formed to construct sanitary dwellings for workingmen. Finally, beginning in Belgium in the eighties, an effort was made to supply money at lower rates of interest to special societies dedicated to the provision of good workers' dwellings.

All these experimental initiatives had a certain educational value; they proved that something better could be done. Unfortunately, neither the second nor the third built new quarters; while in England local authorities were very reluctant to make use of their new powers to declare insanitary buildings vacant, or tear them down. As for the Model Housing Associations, their propaganda was better than their performance.

In England, for example, the Metropolitan Association for Improving the Dwellings of the Industrial Poor—a title that says much— was founded in 1842. By 1851 they had succeeded in building a model tenement, which won a prize in the Crystal Palace Exposition. When compared with the quarters that had been built for workers up to this time, these dwellings were palatial. Judged by reasonable human standards, they were extremely cramped. Worst of all: the improvements embodied in these model dwellings, privacy, sanitary devices, and water, added to the cost of the structure.

Here at the beginning the reformers knocked their heads against an inexorable fact: a fact that still makes adequate housing within the framework of unregulated private capitalism all but impossible. James Hole, a contemporary writer on housing, recognized the crux of the difficulty when he wrote that the worker "cannot have wide streets and proper conveniences for his house without paying for these advantages, and the cost has been frequently brought forward as an objection to such improvements; and, in fact, to all proposals for raising the standard of workingmen's dwellings, either by legal restriction or by the building of better houses when undertaken as a measure of philanthropic enterprise." Those reasons and those objections still linger on today.

The point cannot be gainsaid. Higher standards *do* mean higher costs. There were only two ways of meeting these increased costs: one was to raise the wage level for the lower income groups; the other was to provide a public subsidy out of taxes to make up for the difference between what the worker's family can afford, and what he must pay in order to have better accommodations in new quarters. Thus the two family houses built by this London association cost about 450 pounds; and the rent of from three shillings sixpence per week to four shillings was at the time within the reach only of regularly employed skilled artisans: it did not touch the problem of housing the great mass of underpaid workers. In order to offset these costs, the reformers—wishing to do something—were forced to whittle down the necessary improvements.

From the beginning, the usual panaceas were offered: above all, that which has been resurrected again today, namely, mass production and mechanization of the process of building. In designing the Langbourn buildings for Mr. Alderman Waterlow the architect had the joinery made to uniform size and pattern and attempted to effect a saving through building the walls of artificial stone, consisting of clinkers and Portland cement. Had the method effected any real economies, the example might have spread; *but even in the relatively simple dwellings of the early Victorian period, without the mechanized utilities of our present age, the advantages of such economies in the shell of the fabric were unexpectedly small.*

Result: model tenements were forced to lower earlier standards of good housing. It was only by comparison with contemporary slums that they could be thought of as improvements. In London, after 1850, model dwellings were six story tenements, as contrasted with the usual two and three story buildings in the older quarters of the East End: models of congestion. In establishing these new barracks for the poor, the reformers sought to conserve their properties by an extra-legal series of regulations: regulations that were posted on the walls, enforced by inspection, re-enforced by the penalty of expulsion.

In other words, they suppressed some of the worst features of capitalistic housing by methods which, if applied to the old quarters, would often have made them more agreeable for human habitation than what the reformers themselves could show. By such prudent management these model structures sometimes accumulated a surplus profit, above the six per cent to which they restricted themselves. But even with speculative profits eliminated, the provision of new sanitary facilities and conveniences resulted in higher rents. Hence these model quarters were usually occupied by classes economically above the level of those for whom the dwellings were originally intended.

The net result of model tenement building and remedial legislation aiming at higher standards, was to give the sanction of law, philanthropy, and municipal effort to a low grade urban environment. Doolittle, Bernard Shaw's Dustman in Pygmalion, might well prefer the unsupervised licentiousness of his original slum to the sordid respectability of the new quarters. Such minimum standards, finally, had the effect sometimes of calling the attention of builders and land exploiters to possibilities they had guilelessly passed by: the new minima upset the more generous provisions that often continued to prevail through local custom. Schumacher points out that this took place in Germany; and there is little doubt that it was also a consequence of "housing reform"—particularly after New York City's model law—in America.

Perhaps here we have a key to the essential human achievement of the new urban culture: it worked out a minimum of life. There have been periods in the past that exhibited greater animal ferocity, gashing or burning the flesh of people who had sinned against the prevailing moral code or theological beliefs. But the nineteenth century, smugly conscious of its new humanitarian principles, converted such outright brutalities into a slow quiet process of attrition and inanition. A minimum of schooling: a minimum of rest: a minimum of cleanliness: a minimum of shelter. A gray pall of negative virtue hung over the urban improvements of the period, and its highest boast was the expansion of these minimum conditions and these negative gains.

The quintessence of this minimum life was achieved in the prison. Indeed, one might without much exaggeration say that housing reform was preceded by prison reform, as John Howard preceded Shaftesbury; and the prisons embodied most of the negative improvements that were introduced for the benefit of free citizens of the noncriminal classes, in the factories and tenements. The factory maintained the coercion of the prison: the enforced silence, the repetitive routine, the lockstep, the constant surveillance of the foreman or jailer: often enough a formidable prison wall would be around the structure, too; and the new housing quarters, with their closely calculated number of cubic feet of air and square feet of window space, cut off from sight of grass and flowers by the dusty paved courts and the dustier streets, could not have been more adequately designed if the sole object of the building were punishment.

The speculative spread of the industrial town meant the growth and spread of a dreary prison environment. The reward an honest man got for a faithful day's labor was not measurably different from that which a more erring member of society got as punishment: indeed, the "freedom" of the first was another name for anxiety and insecurity and fearful humiliation. A minimum of life: malnutrition at every level. When, according to Olmsted, the teachers in the Ragged Schools of New York took their pupils for a holiday in the country they "found it quite impossible to prevail upon them to refrain from completely ravishing the private gardens of the benevolent gentlemen who have offered them entertainment." Was it a wonder? The children were starved. Indeed, half the anti-social symptoms that broke out in the new towns, the brawls, the pervasive drunkenness, the love of violence, were not special signs of inner depravity: they were blind reactions to the environment: a step higher, perhaps, than complete submission to its degradation.

9: Paleotechnic Drama

In the routine of Coketown's life, what respite existed from the monotony of subdivided occupations: from the warped, one-sided attempt to drive human energies into a single channel: mechanical production: financial gain? After his weekly spree in the tavern or the brothel, the worker returned to the factory or the mine more cheated, more defeated, more empty of life, than ever. Dickens reduced the facts of paleotechnic life to the simple terms of a school-boy's primer; but his observation holds a great measure of truth: Dombey loses his wife, Gradgrind betrays his son and daughter, because these hard utilitarian rationalists overlooked the need for spontaneous joy and human understanding.

Nevertheless, one or two elements of drama still remained in the industrial town. The main drama revolved around the factory: its actors were the masters and the leaders of labor, and the workmen themselves took part, now as actors, now as passive chorus. It was in the lockout and the strike, those double-edged weapons, each of which cuts sharply into the hand that wields it, that the inert weight of impersonal forces and passive adjustments suddenly became lightened by a deed. The drama was a grim one, and, in the picket line, or by the factory gate, the action might become deadly: while behind the scenes, in the silent heroism of the workers' homes, there was often sacrifice on the level of high tragedy. The stakes might seem sordid, at best trivial: half an hour less of work, a few shillings more per week, the restoration of a dismissed comrade, the willingness to meet and bargain: but for the workers those little matters meant life and death. And this was the major tragedy: the workers' utmost success still meant only such life as might exist within the paleotechnic prison. Without the possibility of the strike, however, the filth, the monotony, the starvation, the anxiety, would have been unbearable: and the strike alone brought the possibility—and therewith the necessity—of a comradeship that could break through the mechanical partitions of the factory. An alternative to Mr. Stiggins' Grand Junction Ebenezer Temperance Association.

With the polis itself gone in the industrial non-city, politics became supreme. The ghost of the old civic unity now spread over national and imperial territory by the device of representative government and universal suffrage: the lure of the ballot led men to concentrate their political interests upon abstract issues, and parliaments attempted to solve by purely legal formulae matters that demanded concrete experiment and the co-operation of engineers, architects, administrators, artists. Most successful in fostering the political drama, then, were such issues of war and peace as lent themselves to the machinations of the politician: a good war, in Afghanistan or the Soudan, might save a bad peace. Thumb through the old files of the Illustrated London News. In the most turbulent years you will look in vain for scenes of strikes and demonstrations: instead, you will be filled with images of the far-flung British armies and the exotic places in which they conducted their missionary and military operations.

The ancient medieval civic pomp, which had lingered in Leeds, for example, till the middle of the eighteenth century, according to the Webbs, disappeared: by the middle of the nineteenth century the pageantry of the Lord Mayor's parade in London had become so dull and threadbare that it prompted the ridicule of Mr. Punch. But in the bleak industrial towns *national* politics became drama, battle, sport: its orators were the chief actors, its protagonists were the greatest prize-fighters, its parliamentary leaders were the leading generals, and its election bouts, with their speeches and their torch-light parades and their hysterical mass enthusiasms, were the principal occasions for emotional release: more universal even than the revival meeting. Politics in fact in the industrial city took the place that the motion pictures and the football and cricket matches do under a later regime. In every such center the political auditorium became the chief civic institution: Exeter Hall, Albert Hall, Madison Square Garden, the endless Mechanics' Halls. Sonorous oratory served the double function of stimulant and anesthetic: exciting the populace and making it oblivious to its actual environment. In the ranks of the Trade Union movement itself mere political windbags rose to leadership: men who commanded crowds in order to sate their narcissism: copious in emotion, diffident, fumbling in action. Such actors threw in the shade the type of personality whose grasp of the practical life and whose administrative skill would have equipped him to run the industry on behalf of the workers: the latter kind of organizer either remained frustrate, or deserted to the capitalist camp, where his talents were more readily recognized and given freer play. This migration of the proletarian élite into the commercial or political bureaucracy was a weakness that only the co-operative movement, apparently, knew how to cope with.

The final word on this systematized exploitation of wind and verbiage was written, not by Lenin or Mussolini, but by William Morris in News from Nowhere. In his Utopia the only use he could find for the old Houses of Parliament at Westminster was as a storage place for dung. Genuine democracy needed more persistent organs of association, and more specialized competence, than the talkers whose wiles governed political parties could muster. Even today those organs, that competence, have still to be locked together in an effective reciprocal arrangement, in which the principle of rational criticism and consent will be combined with the acceptance of the authority that science and functional ability must in the nature of things wield.

10: The Non-Plan of the Non-City

The standardization of the factory-slum was the chief urban achievement of the nineteenth century. Wherever the steam engine, the factory, and the railroad went, an impoverished environment usually went with them. To make this development easier, it was necessary to have an appropriate type of urban layout. Fortunately the mechanical city plan had been invented before the machine-conditioned town itself had come into existence.

If the layout of the town has no relation to social activities and needs other than those of the surveyor, the real-estate speculator, and the jerry-builder, the simplest means of organizing it topographically is by means of rectangular blocks: blocks of identical size, separated by streets and avenues of standard widths. This plan offers the engineer none of those special problems that irregular parcels with curved boundary lines present. An office boy can figure out the number of square feet involved in a street opening, or in a sale; and a lawyer's clerk can write a description of the necessary deed of sale, merely by copying a standard document. With a T-square and a triangle, finally, the municipal engineer, without the slightest training as either an architect or a sociologist, could "plan" a metropolis. The neatness of the mechanical drawing, as in the plan of 1811 for New York, would obscure the extent of the eventual civic folly.

This rectangular type of plan is often referred to as a particularly American contribution to city planning; but like so many "American" innovations, it had its origin in the Old World; and if it is more conspicuous in American cities, this is merely because other types of planning were, after the nineteenth century, less influential. From the seventeenth century on the extension of old towns, Stuttgart and Berlin, for example, took place by the addition of regular rectan-

gular blocks. Such a mechanical extension could proceed into an indefinite future, toward an ever-receding horizon; and once the boundaries of walls and fortifications were let down, either figuratively or
by actual demolition, cities began to grow by a process of indefinite
accretion. The essential urban unit was no longer the quarter: it was
the block, projected as a function of a traffic artery.

From the standpoint of the new real-estate speculators, this type
of plan was perfect. Each lot, being of uniform shape, became a unit,
like a coin, capable of ready appraisal and exchange. Such block
platting provided the maximum number of valuable corner lots, with
double exposures; and it permitted "plans" to be made for unlimited
future development without foresight or responsibility. Being conceived as a purely physical agglomeration of buildings, the town
planned on rectangular lines could sprawl in any direction, limited
only by gross physical obstacles and the means of transportation.
Every street might be a traffic street; every section might be a business section. Indeed, to permit the progressive intensification of land
use, with a corresponding rise in rent and realty values, was the
prime virtue, from the capitalist standpoint, of this inorganic type
of plan. So deeply ingrained has this point of view become that in
the zoning plans made by allegedly competent authorities in the
United States, something like sixteen per cent of the urban area has
usually been allotted to industry, although the needs of actual business, as Bartholomew shows, are amply covered by an average use
of under five per cent.

Even from the most limited physical point of view, most of these
rectangular plans were highly inefficient. By usually failing to dis-
criminate sufficiently in the first instance between traffic arteries and
residential streets, the first were not made wide enough and the
second were usually too wide, thus throwing the cost of excessive
paving and over-lengthy utilities lines upon residential districts that
could ill afford them. (The refined meanness of the English by-law
street was an exception; but even here, as Unwin was brilliantly to
demonstrate in Nothing Gained by Overcrowding, money was thrown
into excessive street acreage that could have been spent to better
purpose on internal parks and play areas.) By paying no attention
to topography the municipal engineer opened the way for fat pieces

of "honest" municipal jobbery in the grading and filling of streets. On steep hilly sites, like that of San Francisco, the rectangular plan, by failing to respect the contour levels of the hillside, placed a constant tax on the time and energy of its inhabitants, and inflicted on them and their heirs a daily economic loss, measurable in tons of coal and gallons of gasoline wasted, to say nothing of undoing the major esthetic possibilities of a hill-site that is intelligently platted.

Although the absence of the short-cuts provided on the diagonal baroque plan has also been held a point against the checkerboard plan, one must admit that the wasteful and unusable plots formed by diagonal avenues at their point of concentration probably even up accounts. What was more serious, in causing waste and confusion, was the platting of checkerboards within the highway net created by old roads: the irregular direction of the latter would often create a crazy pattern of streets which the municipal engineer never brought together: Brooklyn offers many examples. The indifference to geographic contours, in the application of the formal gridiron to the land-surface, was nothing short of sublime: the engineer's streets often swept through swamps, embraced dump-heaps, accepted piles of slag and waste, climbed cliffs, and ended up a quarter of a mile beyond the low water mark of the waterfront.

In the layout no thought was given either to the direction of the prevailing winds, the placing of industrial districts, the salubrity of the underlying foundations, or any of the other vital factors involved in the proper utilization of a site. Hence there was no functional differentiation on the plan between the industrial, the commercial, the civic, and the residential quarters. In a street map, all these parts looked alike, although their requirements for traffic alone, no less than for efficient work, were different. *This means that in reality no section was suitably planned for its specific function.* As a result, industry and business were encouraged—until zoning ordinances were tardily introduced at a much later stage of development—to spread everywhere. External regularity: internal disruption.

Since the main purpose of the inorganic gridiron plan was speculation and sale, it succeeded admirably on its own premises. The first step in the development of the town or the new quarter was the platting of the streets: the next step was the division of the blocks into building lots and their early sale in individual parcels to the private owner or builder. Once the land had been hopelessly broken up into separate lots under separate ownership, it was practically impossible to make a socially co-ordinated development for a single block, to say nothing of a whole quarter. When land was needed for any public purpose, the buying out of the owners became one of the great handicaps to good public management: a process that lent itself in many cities, not only to tedious delays, but to various forms of blackmail and graft. (The Lex Adickes, which permitted the assemblage of parcels and the pro-rata distribution on a better plan to the individual owners, did not come in, even in Germany, until 1902, And the much earlier principle of excess condemnation which permits the municipality to condemn more land for a public purpose than it actually needs, in order to have control over the surrounding development, likewise was used with great diffidence.)

As for an expression of the permanent social functions of the city in the new type of plan, it was utterly lacking. Although civic centers might sometimes be provided in new towns, as they were in the early nineteenth century in the plans for Cincinnati, St. Louis, and Chicago, by the time the gambling fever had risen these municipal sites would be sold to pay for their street extension and street paving. When the need arose for sites for city halls and law courts and municipal administration buildings, for schools and universities and parks and playgrounds, the appropriate parcels of land would have been already in individual ownership, sometimes already built upon. Even if these tracts could then be purchased, the cost of assemblage or condemnation, the cost of demolition, the cost of the original and now useless structures, all raised the total cost; while the size and shape of the new parcel and the disposition of the surrounding streets might be altogether inappropriate to its functional use. It is only when special sites are located and delimited before building has taken place, as in the medieval bastides, that the rectangular plan affords a possibility for intelligent social adaptation. This implies a degree of civic co-ordination that the municipal engineer cannot, by himself, practice.

The reckless extension of the paleotechnic town was accompanied by the progressive destruction of open spaces; and as the periphery widened, the open country became ever more remote from the center. The filling up of small brooks and streams, the covering over of the canals, the building up of vacant lots, demanded that equivalent spaces be restored for the use of growing children within the city. But the very growth of the city increased land values; so that plots that could easily have been afforded for playgrounds and playing fields, if planned for the original development, rose so high in price that their acquisition became excessively costly, if not prohibitive. No serious public recognition of even the need for public playgrounds came, however, until after 1870, and the movement itself did not begin to make headway until the twentieth century. Hence a peculiar function of the paleotechnic street: it was forced to take the place of the back-garden of the medieval town or the open place of the baroque order. Thus this paved area, adapted primarily to wheeled traffic, became also park, promenade, and playground: a grim park, a dusty promenade, a dangerous playground.

Even where overcrowding of the land did not exist—for example in many of the towns of Midland America—the broad street was taken as a peculiar symbol of progress; so that it was laid out with an amplitude that bore no functional relation to its present or potential use. The value of such street planning was largely decorative: it was a symbol of *possible* traffic, *possible* commercial opportunity, *possible* conversion into more intensive uses: it thus provided an extra excuse for the fantastic land values that were sometimes optimistically tagged onto the abutting properties. The surviving civic traditions of New England were not better shown than in the fact that towns like Pittsfield and New Bedford, though submitting to industrialization, kept conservatively to narrow streets—thirty to sixty feet in width—and thereby eased the burden of taxes on the adjacent houses and gardens. They thus kept some of the advantages that a new generation of planners was to re-discover in the platting of the modern industrial garden village at the end of the nineteenth century.

All over the Western World during the nineteenth century new cities were founded and old ones extended themselves along the lines I have just described. The first sign of a boom would be the extension of skeleton streets, consisting of curbstones, and standpipes for the water system. The multiplication of these streets unnecessarily widened the city and added to the amount of expensive pavement, expensive sewers and water mains, permitted growth to take place in the most costly fashion possible, by scattered individual houses, instead of by compact settlements, and increased the unnecessary burden of man-hours spent in transportation. The better all these facilities were from the technical standpoint, the worse they often proved in terms of social values: money was being spent prematurely, sometimes spent on the wrong functions, usually in the wrong order.

The pecuniary values derived from urban growth were roughly in proportion to the size of the city, the importance of its commercial life, and the density of its population. Did not the financiers and industrialists who governed the nineteenth century towns regard growth as the very essence of civic success? Each new city made a chart of its increase in population and predicted its future as a great metropolis of its region. At the beginning of its growth, the citizens of Toledo, Ohio, proved statistically to their own satisfaction that by the end of the nineteenth century it would be greater than Chicago or New York. This belief in unlimited growth was pervasive. People gambled on such growth, and then tried to put a bottom under their hopes by deliberately attracting business and industry and population away from competing towns: sometimes by gifts of land, even factory buildings, without ever demanding that the manufacturers who settled in the town guarantee a wage level high enough to keep the new workers from being a public liability. New York, indeed, not only built the Erie Canal to ensure her connection with the hinterland but managed later, through securing differential freight rates worked out at the expense of other towns, to maintain her monopoly of the oceanic and continental traffic routes.

The rectangular street and block system, projectable indefinitely toward the horizon, was the universal expression of capitalistic fantasies. The abstract street-net, with its lots selling and renting by the front-foot, became the dominant expression of the city. The hope for a steady rise in the unearned increment was at its lowest in the meaner factory towns: it achieved its maximum of feverish excitement in the great commercial and political centers. So far from expressing utilitarian interests (other than profit) these plans carried the system of absolutist abstractions even farther away from reality. Paleotechnic planning had the mechanical regularity of the baroque without its coherence: the despotic restrictions without the esthetic mastery and the visual compensations. Even when a great piece of planning was undertaken, as in the conversion of the old wall around Köln into a boulevard, the bordering houses would, stylistically speaking, present a picture of dull esthetic caprice: so-called individuality.

The ultimate unit in this rectangular street platting, the atom of mechanical design, was the individual rectangular plot into which each block was divided. Rarely, in big cities, was the width of this plot greater than twenty feet; often, as in parts of Baltimore, it was only fifteen or twelve: but the depth might be a hundred or a hundred and twenty-five feet. As long as row houses were two rooms deep, this platting was tolerable; but as soon as the need for more dwelling space grew, the natural line of expansion was not laterally, to embrace a second costly plot, but backward, to eat up the backyard areas and to increase thereby the sunless interior space. Bad enough for individual houses: worse when the same system of lot-units constricted the building of multiple-family houses or office buildings.

The desire to utilize every square foot of rentable space possessed the owner, even when he was building for his own use, and not for sheer pecuniary exploitation; and in its search for profits it often over-reached itself, for an overcrowded plan does not necessarily bring the maximum financial return. Cumbrous, uneconomic plans, with a maximum amount of wasteful corridor space and dark ill-ventilated rooms, characterized the two-family houses, the three deckers, the higher tenements. And the habit of letting the shape of the individual lot determine the plan and layout of the house dominated the imagination of the architect: he lost the ability to design freely in more comprehensive units, built for common living and not for individual division, individual ownership, individual sale. The individual rectangular lot was his sole determinant. It needed the social criticism of the present generation, backed by detailed cost analysis, to compel the architect to think in terms of light, insolation, open space, communal grouping; and even today, so deeply embedded is the pecuniary order of thinking, it is hard for the architect fully to embrace his freedom.

In short: as practical urban design, the dominant method of planning was simply a bad dream. Millions of people are still living in the midst of blighted areas, destitute of civic comeliness, paying bitter tribute day by day to the collective hallucinations that governed the layout of the paleotechnic town.

11: A Close-up of Coketown

One may grant that at the tempo at which industrialism was introduced into the Western World, the problem of building adequate cities was almost insoluble. The premises which made these operations possible also limited their human success. How build a coherent city out of the efforts of a thousand competing individualists who knew no law but their own sweet will? How integrate new mechanical functions in a new type of plan that could be laid out and speedily developed—if the very essence of such integration depended upon the firm control of public authorities who often did not exist, or who, when they did exist, exercised no powers except those specifically granted by the state, which put individual property rights at the top. How provide a multitude of new utilities and services for workers who could not afford to rent any but the most destitute types of shelter? How create a good physical plan for social functions that themselves remained abortive? It was small wonder that almost the only examples of good planning were on traditional lines: planning flourished better in historic cities, under the guidance of a surviving baroque bureaucracy (as in Paris and München) than in those newer centers where a fresh start could, theoretically, have been made.

Cities that still contained vital residues of medieval tradition, like Ulm, sometimes managed, through the slow tempo of their growth and a bold policy of large-scale municipal land ownership, to effect the transition with relatively little loss. Where industry came in explosively, however, as in Nürnberg, the results were as vile as in towns that had no historic shell whatever. And in the New World, towns were built as late as 1906 (Gary, Indiana) with no regard for any physical features except the location of the industrial plant. The very century that boasted its mechanical conquests and its scientific prescience left its social processes to chance, as if the scientific habit of mind had exhausted itself upon machines, and was not capable of advancing further. The torrent of energy that was tapped from the coal beds ran downhill with the least possible improvement of the environment: the mill-villages, the factory agglomerations, were socially more crude than the feudal villages of the Middle Ages.

The new urban emergent, the coal-agglomeration, which Patrick Geddes called the conurbation, was neither isolated in the country nor attached to a historic core. It spread in a mass of relatively even density over scores and sometimes hundreds of square miles. There were no real centers in this urban massing: no institutions capable of uniting its members into an active city life. Only the sects, the fragments, the social debris of old institutions remained, left like the flotsam of a great river after the flood has receded: a no-man's land of social life. These new cities not merely failed for the most part to produce art, science, or culture: they failed at first even to import them from older centers. When a surplus was locally created, it was promptly drained off elsewhere: the rentiers and financiers employed it upon personal luxuries, or upon philanthropies, like that of Carnegie's Music Hall in New York, which often benefited the capital cities long before any similar bequests were made to the region from which the riches were originally drawn.

Approach more closely the paleotechnic town: examine it with eye, ear, nose, skin. The ordinary observer, because of the growing contrast with the emerging neotechnic environment, can at last see what only poets like Hugo or Ruskin or Morris saw a hundred years ago: a reality which the philistines, tangled in their utilitarian web of dreams, alternately denied as a sentimental exaggeration or greeted with enthusiasm as an indisputable mark of "progress."

Night spread over the coal-town: its prevailing color was black. Black clouds of smoke rolled out of the factory chimneys, and the railroad yards, which often cut clean into the town, mangling the very organism, spread soot and cinders everywhere. The invention of artificial illuminating gas was an indispensable aid to this spread: Murdock's invention dates back to the end of the eighteenth century, and during the next generation its use widened, first in factories, then in homes, first in big cities, later in small centers; for without its aid work would frequently have been stopped by smoke and fog. The manufacture of illuminating gas within the confines of the towns became a characteristic new feature: the huge gas tanks reared their bulk over the urban landscape, great structures, on the scale of a cathedral: indeed, their tracery of iron, against an occasional clear lemon-green sky at sunrise, was one of the most pleasant esthetic elements in the new order.

Such structures were not necessarily evil; indeed, with sufficient care in their segregation they might have been handsome. What was atrocious was the fact that, like every other building in the new towns, they were dumped almost at random; the leakage of escaping gas scented the so-called gas-house districts, and not surprisingly these districts frequently became among the most degraded sections of the city. Towering above the town, polluting its air, the gas tanks symbolized the dominance of "practical" interests over life-needs.

Night had already come into the pottery districts in the eighteenth century through the use of cheap salt glazes; now it closed in everywhere, in Sheffield and Birmingham, in Pittsburgh and Lille. In this new environment black clothes were only a protective coloration, not a form of mourning; the black stovepipe hat was almost a functional design. The oil and smudge of soft coal spat everywhere; even those who washed their hands left a rim of undissolved grease around the side of the washbowl. Add to these constant smudges on flesh and clothing the finely divided particles of iron from the grinding and sharpening operations, the unused chlorine from the soda works, the clouds of acrid dust from the cement plant, the various by-products of other chemical industries: these things smarted the eyes, rasped the throat and lungs, lowered the general tone, even when they did not produce on contact any definite disease. As for the reek of coal itself, it is perhaps not a disagreeable one: man with his long savage past has become fond of musty odors: so perhaps its chief misdemeanor was that it supplanted, and made people insensitive to, other smells.

Under such conditions, one must have all one's senses blunted in order to be happy; and first of all, one must lose one's taste. This loss of taste had an effect upon diet: even well-to-do people began to eat canned goods and stale foods, when fresh ones were available, because they could no longer tell the difference. The loss of elementary taste-discrimination extended to other departments than food: color-discrimination became feeble, too: the darker tones, the soberer colors, the dingier mixtures, were preferred to pure bright colors, and both the Pre-Raphaelites and the Impressionist painters were reviled by the bourgeoisie because their pure colors were thought "unnatural" and "inartistic." If an occasional touch of bright color was left, it was only in the signs on the hoardings—for Coleman's mustard or Reckitt's blue—paper surfaces that remained cheerful because they frequently had to be changed.

Dark, colorless, acrid, evil-smelling, this new environment was. All these qualities lowered human efficiency and required extra compensation in washing and bathing and sanitation—or at the last extreme, in medical treatment. The cash expenditure on cleaning alone was no small expenditure in the paleotechnic town, at least after the need for cleanliness itself was acknowledged. Take one item alone from a typical paleotechnic survival: Pittsburgh today. Its smoke pollution began early, for a print in 1849 shows it in full blast. Today the annual cost of keeping Pittsburgh cleaned has been estimated at $1,500,000 for extra laundry work, $750,000 for extra general cleaning, and $60,000 for extra curtain cleaning. This estimate, some $2,310,000 per year, does not include losses due to the corrosion of buildings or the increased costs of painting woodwork, nor yet the extra costs of lighting during periods of smog. So much for pecuniary losses. But what of the incalculable losses through disease, through ill-health, through all the forms of psychological deterioration from apathy to outright neurosis? The fact that such losses do not lend themselves to objective measurement does not make them non-existent.

Indifference to these forms of devitalization during the paleotechnic period rested mainly on invincible ignorance. In Technics and Civilization I quoted the indignation and surprise of a leading apologist for this civilization, Ure, over the testimony offered by the acute physicians called before Sadler's Factory Investigation Committee. These physicians referred to the experiments made by Dr.

Edwards of Paris upon the growth of tadpoles, proving that sunlight was essential to their development. From this they concluded—we now know with complete justification—that it was equally necessary to the growth of children. Ure's proud answer was that the gas lighting of factories was a sufficient substitute for the sun. So contemptuous were these utilitarians of nature and well-tried human custom that they brought up more than one generation upon a devitalized diet, based purely on the consumption of calories. That diet has been modified during the last twenty years by a fresh budget of scientific knowledge. Unfortunately, the paleotechnic environment is less amenable to correction; and it still casts its blight over tens of millions of people.

Next to dirt, the new towns boasted another distinction, equally appalling to the senses. The baneful effects of this blight have been recognized only in recent years, thanks to advances in technics not unconnected with that typical neotechnic invention, the telephone. I refer to noise. Let me quote an ear-witness account of Birmingham in the middle of the nineteenth century.

"In no town in the world are the mechanical arts more noisy: hammerings incessantly on the anvil; there is an unending clang of engines; flame rustles, water hisses, steam roars, and from time to time, hoarse and hollow, rises the thunder of the proofing house [where firearms are tested]. The people live in an atmosphere vibrating with clamor; and it would seem as if their amusement had caught the general tone, and become noisy, like their inventions." The indifference to clang and racket was typical. Did not the manufacturers of England keep Watt from reducing the noise made by his reciprocating engine because they wanted auricular evidence of its power?

Today, numerous experiments have established the fact that noise can produce profound physiological changes: music can keep down the bacteria count in milk; and by the same token definite ailments, like stomach ulcers, seem to be aggravated by the strain of living, say, within sound of an elevated railroad. The diminishment of working efficiency through noise has likewise been clearly established. Unfortunately, the paleotechnic environment seemed specially designed to create a maximum amount of noise: the early hoot of the factory whistle, the shriek of the locomotive, the clank and urge of the old-fashioned steam engine, the wheeze and screech of the shafts and belting, the click and whirr of the loom, the pounding of the drop hammer, the mutter and snuffle of the conveyor, the shouts of the workers who worked and lived amid this varied clamor—all these sounds abetted the general assault on the senses.

When reckoning up the vital efficiency of the country as compared with the city, or the medieval town as opposed to the paleotechnic town, one must not forget this important factor in health. Nor have recent improvements in certain departments, the use of rubber heels and rubber tires, for instance, lessened the strength of the indictment. The noise of the gasoline driven motor cars and trucks in a busy city, as they start up, change gears, acquire speed, is a sign of their deplorable technical immaturity. Had the energy that has been put into styling hoods gone into the design of a silent engine, the neotechnic city would not be as backward as its paleotechnic predecessor in the matter of noise.

Recent experiments with sound in Chicago show that if one grades noise by percentages up to 100 per cent which is the sound— like an artillery cannonade—that would drive one mad if continued over an extended period, the countryside has only from eight to ten per cent noise, the suburbs fifteen, the residential districts of the city twenty-five per cent, commercial districts thirty per cent and industrial districts thirty-five. These broad lines would doubtless hold almost anywhere during the last century and a half, though perhaps the upper limits were higher. One must remember, too, that the paleotechnic towns made no effort to separate factories from workers' homes; so that in many towns noise was omnipresent, in the day and often in the night.

Considering this new urban area on its lowest physical terms, without reference to its social facilities or its culture, it is plain that never before in recorded history had such vast masses of people lived in such a savagely deteriorated environment. The galley slaves of the Orient, the wretched prisoners in the Athenian silver mines, the depressed proletariat in the insulae of Rome—these classes had known, no doubt, a similar foulness; but never was human blight so widespread; never before had it so universally been accepted as normal —normal and inevitable. The point becomes all the more appalling

[TOP] Coketown, alias Smokeover, alias Mechanicsville, alias Manchester, Leeds, Birmingham, Merseburg, Essen, Elberfeld, Lille, Roubaix, Newark, Pittsburgh, or Youngstown. Here, Preston: a cotton town in England. The factory units in the center, and the gas tanks on the right pre-empt the space: by the inefficient utilization of coal in the steam engine and domestic earth, the smoke of the chimneys covers the landscape, blotting out the sun, rasping the lungs. Rows of workers' houses crowd close under the shadows of the factories and scatter into the distance: no zoning, no open spaces except the railroad yards in the distance or the mean streets, with their meanly standardized and wretchedly planned dwellings: no parks, no gardens, no playgrounds. The poor mechanical order of foreground violated, even on its own terms, by the disorder of the background. (*Photograph: Ewing Galloway, Aerofilms*)

[MIDDLE LEFT] Railroad yards and steel plants in Cleveland, Ohio. The railroad and the industrial plant controlled paleotechnic urban development, even the surface order of rectangular planning was frequently disrupted by their superior claims. Smoke pollution was constant; noise and dirt ubiquitous. The railroad, so far from being used to zone heavy industries in the open country, away from the areas of residence, brought them into the heart of the town, until land values rose high enough to compel a partial removal of ironworks and chemical plants to the outskirts. Paleotechnic filth, disorder, and poverty remain as a widespread survival in towns, big and little, throughout the world: witness Boston and Washington no less than Chicago and Detroit. (*Photograph: Ewing Galloway*)

[MIDDLE RIGHT] Steel and armaments: the big Krupp works at Essen. In the foreground, close to the mills, are the workers' houses. Contrast this formation with that of the neotechnic order shown on Plate 29. While armament manufacture, like mining, often provided the worst conditions of housing to begin with, the example of Godin at Guise and Krupp at Essen showed the possibility of a different order of domestic building under industrialism.

[BOTTOM] Another type of paleotechnic disorder: Hanley, a pottery town, which came to life in the eighteenth century with the introduction of the Chinese technique of making porcelain and the rise of great industrial fabricators and designers, above all Wedgwood. One of the Five Towns so lovingly described by Arnold Bennett, himself a product of them, in An Old Wives' Tale and Clayhanger. Pottery kilns placed next to dwellings, as if there were no difference between a furnace, a kiln, and a domestic workshop. The mass production of pottery for eating vessels and wash-bowls, toilet bowls, and urinals was a genuine triumph of the paleotechnic period: but as with so many of its short-sighted achievements, the means often defied and partly annulled the end. (*Photograph: Ewing Galloway*)

[TOP LEFT] Manchester Cotton Factory: a great working unit formed about the steam engine and its connected shafting. In such factories the typical paleotechnic inventions were quickly introduced, such as gas-lighting to overcome inadequate interior lighting even by day, and elevators, more than a generation before their use in office buildings or residences. Schinkel, viewing these factories, felt that they were prophetic of the new architecture: not observing that the architecture was already in existence in the superior vernacular forms that prevailed in England between 1780 and 1830.

[TOP RIGHT] London market: continuation of the busy huckstering of the medieval town. Like the Halles in Paris, this building shows current technical innovations: slender iron posts, sheet iron and glass roof. Growth and concentration of the food market was an inevitable accompaniment of paleotechnic city agglomeration: but only a few cities, like Baltimore, continued the tradition of the large, centralized neighborhood market. (See Zola's Le Ventre de Paris.)

[SECOND LEFT] Celebration of the opening of a railroad in the forties. Section by section the railroad extended its environment from mountain top to port, quickening the tempo of life, binding together distant communities, widening the market, and developing trunk lines and express routes at the expense of older forms of transportation. Its main freight was and still is coal.

[THIRD LEFT] Rally of the striking Gas Workers' Union in the eighteen-eighties: a typical act of the supreme paleotechnic drama—the struggle between the haves and the have-nots for money and power and security. So great was the terror of the working classes on the part of their exploiters that, as the Hammonds document, army barracks were deliberately scattered over the industrial towns in England: an army of occupation. Similar building of militia armories, in heavily defensive buildings, took place in the United States after the seventies.

[SECOND RIGHT] London slum, drawn from life by Gustave Doré for Harper's Weekly. A hell of depression and misery and hopeless degradation. Foul odors, vermin, vile food, drunkenness and promiscuity were the chief by-products of its depauperate and crowded existence: crime and disease were but the inevitable psychological and physiological responses.

[BOTTOM] Peace meeting in Exeter Hall. Sweetness, light, pious hopes, and unrelieved futility: the impossibility of a doctrine of Peace and Progress based upon the struggle for existence, bitter economic competition, and the survival of the fittest—i.e., the more rapacious and brutal types. Oratory largely took the place of the more personal drama of the theater during the Victorian period: issues, questions, problems, matters to be talked about, debated, framed in resolutions, and voted on occupied attention: a habit that placed a premium upon the eloquent verbalists and flouted the different procedures of the artist, scientist, and engineer, with their technique of planning and design and experiment.

when one realizes, not only the absolute unfitness of this environment for human life, but its extraordinary quantitative multiplication. In 1850 there were but six towns with over one hundred thousand population in the United States, and but five in Germany. By 1900 there were thirty-six such places in the United States and thirty-three in Germany.

12: The Old Curiosity Shop

We have followed in detail the process of decomposition and unbuilding in the new industrial and commercial city: we have watched a bleak ideology and a coarse practical routine deface the landscape, undermine the body, desiccate the spirit. If our gaze has been narrowed to the factory and the slum, it is because they were the new dominants, and because quantitatively they occupied so large a space.

The survivals of the past, including many useful ones, capable of being re-conditioned for life at a higher level than the buildings that replaced them, were swept away in almost every growing city during the nineteenth century in a fever and a fury of demolition. Old open spaces were built over, and old buildings were hastily destroyed: trim medieval market-places became dusty plazas, and quiet, well-insulated residential quarters became opened up to traffic, through the systematic widening and straightening of old streets. A factory, a new block of offices, a railroad yard, had the right of way over the finest monuments of the past. One cannot object to such replacement when the new is in any sense the equivalent of the old. But in many cases the new building was a tawdry makeshift, thrusting its way into the picture, not because it better expressed the vital social needs of the new day, but because it offered some callous philistine the opportunity for speculative gain.

The same disintegration took place in every other part of the city's culture: it is effectively symbolized in the new architectural forms.

There was, indeed, a moment in the development of form when in England it seemed as if a new synthesis might be created. Between 1780 and 1830, owing to the strong vernacular impulses that persisted, it seemed as if the false alternatives of classicism and romanticism would be thrown off. Middle class houses were built in this period that might—had they become universal forms—have met halfway the best of Manchester's factories. Schinkel, when he visited Manchester, had an intuition that in these new buildings the source of a new form could be found: had he looked at the squares and row houses of Bloomsbury he would have found their direct equivalent. And the design that accompanied Robert Owen's proposed factory colony even suggested how these simple, common-sense forms might have been worked out in terms of workers' housing: his plan is still sounder than a great many more elaborate housing developments that have been put up in England during the last generation.

In all these various initiatives there was an early anticipation of an effective synthesis of modern materials, modern methods of construction, and modern needs: symbols of positive science and co-operative effort. Soane in England showed it in some of his work; so did Schinkel in Berlin; but the proof of its soundness is that the same spirit appeared, perhaps even more clearly, in the work of anonymous builders and designers, in bold and beautiful forms. This mutation—although real—was swamped in the proliferation of fashionable architectural weeds: noxious weeds like the filthy factory slums, sentimental weeds like the cottages and churches of the gothic revival, weeds transported from arid areas, like the brittle classic structures that became schools, banks, court houses, government offices. By the middle of the nineteenth century the mutations were so far lost that when Philip Webb designed the Red House for William Morris, he went back to the vernacular form of the late seventeenth century, romanticized further by ogive patterns in the brickwork: a type of house with relatively small windows—instead of beginning at the point where the best domestic building of a generation earlier had left off.

Not merely was there a break in form. The movement toward synthesis was further handicapped by the earlier disruption of symbols. Almost all the leading architects in Europe, from Wren onward, exhibited this disruption. Who would guess that the Schinkel who projected the clean design for a department store in Berlin also designed extremely romantic gothic churches, while he dreamed in his paintings of buildings even more deeply saturated with wild mysticism and mysterious gloom? Such a gap between building and faery, between architecture as the flesh and bones of civilization and architecture as stylistic fancy dress, had been opened up indeed by the architects of the Renascence. But they at least had the justification of believing for the moment that their fancy dress was reality: they read the old texts: they aped the old gestures: they looked upon themselves as continuators of a more noble manner of life, once lived by the Greeks and the Romans. In this respect, most of the new classicists, the new medievalists, the eclectics, were humbugs: they made no attempt to reduce the distance between their background and their life. Though the medievalists might affect piety and preach a return to the Middle Ages, their efforts were as half-hearted and their buildings were as sterile as the Renascence forms they derided.

In short, the gothic revival, from first to last, from Horace Walpole to Pugin, from Scott to Ralph Adams Cram, remained the work of a sect. Even when it sought to embrace every element in civilization, its premises were antagonistic to that mission: it rejected the best along with the worst. As in religion, the architectural sects multiplied throughout the nineteenth century: so that, by the middle of the period, the hope for a common form based upon the prevalence of some narrow set of historic types was doubly lost. Though once Ruskin foolishly suggested that salvation lay in going back to a single style, that of the thirteenth century in Lombardy, his own historic interpetations proved, if they proved anything, that this was as impossible as the suggestion that the novels of Dickens and Reade should be cast in the mold of The Divine Comedy or The Song of Roland.

The age demanded new forms, for new functions had come into life, and a multitude of new associations and organizations, a new kind of civic ritual, had grown up in the city—along with a new attitude toward the universe and a new feeling for nature. None of these demands could be framed or satisfied in the old forms: none of these new feelings could be symbolized in a Roman column or in a gothic vault. When the architects of the period resurrected old symbols, they felt the plutonian touch of this new society: in spirit, if not in material, they turned to iron. Only in their plans—as Dr. Behrendt has shown in relation to Persius—did they advance to contemporary ground. Byzantine cottages and Swiss chalets, Italian villas and Moorish palaces, began to fill the Victorian landscape in the villa quarters around the British and the American cities. Germany, more insulated before 1870, attempted with sentimental clumsiness to recapture architectural "Bilder aus der deutschen Vergangenheit."

By the third quarter of the nineteenth century, the disruption had become complete. A single avenue might contain, as the result of a decade's building, souvenirs from cultures millennia apart and from regions at the remotest ends of the earth, now modified with cast-iron ornament or "original" embellishments, now copied with photographic lifelessness. Under this impulse every city, in proportion to the available wealth and historical scholarship, tended to become an Old Curiosity Shop: a junkheap of discarded styles, cut off completely from the culture that had given them a rational meaning.

What was the result of this cultural rag-picking? Variety? No: the solidification of chaos: an order no less mechanical in its unexpected façades and its reproductive ornament than the meanest byelaw street of identical houses. Every avenue was designed in accordance with the most inexorable of laws—the law of chance. The street picture lost all consistence: it was a jumble of competing styles, carried out in no common material, ordered to no common visual end. The ground plan might be that of a rectangular plot in a rectangular block; but even that fact did not make for order, since a large building might be placed alongside a shabby cramped building, and a church might be dwarfed by a nearby warehouse. The actual design of the façade and the evolution of the interior as often as not denied the limited surface order. Individualistic style competition—mistakenly looked upon as a sign of a quite different state, individuality—took the place of that collective mastery of form which characterizes a vital culture.

Meanwhile, the only contemporary style that manifested vitality, that of the mechanical age itself, was carefully kept out of the architect's training. Even the engineer, seeking confirmation from the esthete, bashfully hid his clean forms under melancholy iron foliage. And as if the architectural picture itself was not sufficiently chaotic, a crisscross of telegraph wires, trolley poles, railroad bridges, elevated structures, and competitive advertisements completed the visual disorder.

This collapse of form was of course as visible in the interiors of buildings as on the streets. Within the home it was associated with the proliferation of ugly sub-baroque decoration and with the cult of comfort. Shall we say that this hard-bitten age sacrificed all the older esthetic pleasures of ear and eye to the pleasures of tactile relaxation? Instead of beauty, a new quality was demanded—comfort. Ottomans, ranged with pillows, to meet each cushion of flesh with a softer cushion of horse-hair or down: super-upholstered chairs, stuffed and over-stuffed. There is some reason to think that the Victorian middle classes, who could afford warm bedrooms, nevertheless made love by preference beneath blankets, under cover of darkness: thus reducing sexual intercourse to purely tactile terms.

Bare was a term of reproach in Victorian decoration. One of Conan Doyle's early characters almost goes insane because placed in a bare, white-washed room, and Tolstoy was regarded as a saint by his disciples because his bedroom was in the Victorian sense "unfurnished." Just as nakedness of the body caused a flutter of shocked reproof, even when exhibited in statues, so naked architectural forms not merely seemed "harsh": they seemed indecent. The change took place early: note the "carpenter-gothic" details with which even the excellent Downing improved the severe and excellent farmhouse architecture of the early nineteenth century. And as the outer environment in the paleotechnic town became more bleak, the domestic interiors filled up and spilled over with ornament: every square foot of the wall must be covered with pictures, bad reproductions, if not originals: every square foot of floor must be covered with carpets, which caught and held the dust and prolonged the menial duties of those who were supposed to keep them clean: every shelf must be crowded with vases, knick-knacks, souvenirs, shells from the seashore, minerals from distant mountains, sandalwood boxes from India, lacquered trays from China, cloisonné from Japan. Double and triple layers of hangings obscured the light and filtered out a little dirt from the street, but in turn became dirty: table covers, with tassels or embroidery, and covers upon the table covers, and doilies upon those, formed another rampart of decoration. Wax flowers under glass cases, or a left-over ormolu clock: dried flowers in the fireplace in summer: immortelles in a wreath around the portrait of a deceased member of the family—dust and desiccation, fancywork and ornament: in short, the art of the what-not.

In this pursuit of interior decoration the middle class dwelling, like the city outside, became an old curiosity shop; and though up to the eighties the Victorians often avoided historicism, and made their furniture in shapes whose incredible ugliness was the product of an active, if appalling, imagination, after this a reviving cult of the antique completed the parallel. As for the worker's dwellings, imitating all these fashions in the only forms open to the worker's purse, they were little better than a rubbish heap. But no matter how sordid the room, it would not be bare: I have lived in a Bloomsbury lodging house in which every vase on the mantel-shelf was broken, and had thus lost the only value it ever possessed esthetically: that of being whole. The cult of the formless, it would seem, could go no further than it did in decoration. It prevailed over the whole period that began around 1830; its worst inroads were marked by the atrocities duly celebrated in the Great Exhibition of 1851 in London, and of 1876 in Philadelphia; and it did not receive its first sharp check until the eighties, when the esthetic movement took shape under Whistler, William Morris and their varied collaborators. Comfort was associated with ugly superfluity: misplaced art: purposeless manufacture: decorative dirt.

And as form broke up, formlessness itself was theoretically systematized: the age made a virtue of necessity. For the spirit of romanticism, as it took shape in the eighteenth century ruin and the informal landscape, or in the nineteenth century Jardin Anglais, was essentially a denial of the importance of form: more than that, it was a justification of the processes of decomposition. Shrinking from the problem of orderly collective control, people overvalued the wild, the irregular, the unrestricted—forgetting the fact that the wilderness itself could not continue to exist, on the edge of the paleotechnic environment, without eventually invoking bold administrative supervision by the community over the land and the land-uses. For nature to be untouched and unspoiled, men must collectively determine the appropriate means of exploitation and refrain from opening up to competitive ownership that which should be sequestered for the large common good.

"Beauty alone," observed Sir Uvedale Price, one of the chief exponents of romantic design, "has hitherto been aimed at." Beauty, in the romantic mind, meant a certain utilitarian order and purposefulness: the new planners set their minds in another direction and sought to preserve—and if necessary to introduce—the rough, the unexpected, the decayed, the disorganized, the dilapidated. They preferred deformed trees to those that were well-grown, rocky landscapes to lush, nourishing meadows, and the more scraggly conifers to rounded symmetrical trees like the horse-chestnut and the maple. What they sought was not a livable landscape but a picturesque landscape. And the same animus that they displayed toward nature had a part in their conception of architecture: hence their fake abbeys, their newly built ruins, such as the crazy castle of Pichelsberg near Potsdam, done in the English fashion.

In a sense, this worship of national history recognized something that the classic architects with their static forms tended to overlook— the dynamic quality of time, the effect of duration upon form. But unfortunately the romantics centered their interest in the last process in the cycle of growth—the stage of decay and death. They should have been primitives and have begun, so to say, with a live baby: but in fact they were decadents and began with a corpse.

In fine, this cult of the picturesque was a disguised form of laissez-faire—applied wholesale to the environment. The accidental, the unforeseen, and the perverse became new values. Whatever could not be reduced to an orderly pattern, whatever denied man's collective control and defied his organization and avoided the human measure, was exalted.

While this cult had its origin in the landscape painting of the seventeenth century, as the very word picturesque indicates, it was carried to a logical conclusion in the paintings of Turner, the contemporary of Watt and Bentham and Stephenson. For Turner pushed the belief in formlessness, symbolically, to its final state: all the solid realities of the earth, buildings, trees, men, were dissolved in his atmospheric effects of mist and cloud. Given a sufficiently heavy blanket of fog, the new industrial environment itself became, as it were, disembodied. Turner seized that fact and turned it to creative uses. Behind the curtain of atmospheric effects, architecture disappeared: a castle on a bold headland became an amiable blur; so did a factory or a railroad viaduct by a foul river. The general effect was to make man's most strenuous efforts at disciplined expression seem unimportant or insignificant. To be successful, from this point of view, buildings must fall into ruin, and orderly plans must miscarry.

In this manner, romanticism was anti-communal and anti-architectural, for all its tendency to exalt the institutional order of the Middle Ages. Lawlessness was the only rule it recognized and the wilderness was its only proper home. As a counterpoise to a sessile routine and a humdrum institutional life, there was a need, no doubt, for this new expression of the spirit. But applied to urban buildings, such an animus turned the city into a mechanical jungle, which was in fact the urban counterpart of the landscape park, as developed theoretically in the writings of a Repton, a Gilpin, a Price, a Downing—little though these romantics might have been prepared to recognize their saturnine urban offspring. The unexpected, the disorderly, the dilapidated, prevailed to such an extent in the cities of the nineteenth century, both new and old, that the very precision and articulateness of a good mechanical order, which at very least one might reasonably have expected to emerge in the new civilization, were lost. As an expression of a machine culture, or as an environment planned intelligently for mechanized production, the new cities were defective. Much of the "new" architecture of the last twenty years, with its one-sided glorification of the factory as a *standard* of form, must be recognized as an extremely belated attempt to build the utilitarian city.

13: The Triumph of Iron

There was however one department of building that occasionally showed something better than picturesque sprawl or dead standardized ugliness: that which was based upon the use of iron. Here, if anywhere, the paleotechnic period excelled; and here it found its first approach to a coherent form, in the planning and building of its great iron structures.

Inevitably, when the utilitarians thought of forms for their new industrial fabrics, they thought either of converting iron into natural materials, or natural materials into iron. The first impulse was silly: the imitations in cheap woods and metals of the grain of a fine natural wood was a typical triumph of cheap romantic decoration, like the translation of stucco into marble in the baroque period: Schinkel actually brought this perversity back to Germany from England. But the other impulse was honest enough, given the new necessities of life and the new powers of the machine. In discussing the architecture of the new Smithsonian Institution, Robert Dale Owen predicted that the time would come when iron would be commonly used in all sorts of buildings. Long before, Faustus Verantius in the sixteenth century had suggested that iron might be used for walls and for the roofs of big buildings, like churches.

At last these predictions and hopes were fulfilled. Toward the end of the eighteenth century the first iron bridge in the Western World —China had long known them—was built over the Severn. And early in the nineteenth century iron was used to frame the roof of the Central Markets in Paris; for iron's great quality in spanning space, its strength in cross section both under compression and tension, gave it a special place in such structures. The first original step in the application of iron to building, however, came toward the end of the eighteenth century in England: the erection of glass and iron conservatories. Such hot-houses were an eotechnic invention: Albertus Magnus, who had a reputation in the thirteenth century for being a magician, showed flowers growing in mid-winter to one of his visitors—presumably in a glass hot-house. And these conservatories, either as an annex to the house or a special feature of the garden, had become common in the great country houses of France and England.

This effort finally crystallized—and the symbolism is appropriate in every respect—in the design of the Crystal Palace in London by Joseph Paxton, the engineer, who had achieved his reputation as a builder of hot-houses. The great Crystal Palace in Hyde Park sheltered the Industrial Exhibition of 1851, the first such exhibition to be conducted on an international scale. Both as a technical feat and as an imaginative application of modern design to modern materials, the Crystal Palace was perhaps the foremost contribution to building that had been made since the development of the ogive and the flying buttress. For the heavy forms of masonry it substituted the relative lightness of the iron skeleton; for the solid masses and enclosures of the old-fashioned supporting walls, the new design substituted open space bounded by mere filaments of glass. What was spacious became more spacious by interposing only the lines of construction between the eye and the landscape or sky without.

In the thirteenth century cathedrals, in the sixteenth century mansions and town houses, in the early nineteenth century dwellings in England, people had not been afraid of such broad surfaces of glass. Now, however, they cowered a little before the possibilities that their mechanical triumphs had opened up to them. When the time came to translate Paxton's daring initiatives into other buildings in the city, the result was a disappointment. James Buckingham, most energetic of Victorian utopian writers, might imagine a new city whose avenues would be covered by iron and glass arcades: such arcades might even be built here and there as an annex to the shopping parade, from Naples to Westminster. But there was no real congruence between this imaginative architectural form and the new environment.

Need I stress the reason? Glass is of all possible building materials the one that most requires a clean atmosphere. Its smooth surface does not absorb dirt and grime, but permits it visibly to accumulate, and in the act of accumulation it loses its own best qualities. Glass could be at its best in the eotechnic Dutch town, woven around canals, with plenty of water and little smoke: but in the paleotechnic town it was in downright contradiction to the rest of the environment: however cheap its original cost, the upkeep in cleaning was prohibitive. Even the brightest of iron and glass department stores, such as the Bon Marché in Paris, speedily looked a little dingy.

Ironically enough, the Victorian blindness to the visible environment exhibited its opacities most profoundly in the use of glass. For the only type of building in which Paxton's construction was repeatedly used was the dirtiest spot in town; the railroad station: the last place where glass could be used with profit. Most of the train-halls of the new stations were great sheds of glass and iron. From the St. Pancras Station in London, built as early as 1866, to the later

stations like that at Frankfort-am-Main or Hamburg, these structures were often, in the abstract, very handsome—especially those
built after the great Hall of Machines in the Paris Exposition of
1889 had achieved something like a perfect engineering and architectural solution of the problem of spanning the space.

But the actual effect of the glass sheds was to keep the smoke and
effluvia of the locomotives from being dissipated at once into the
surrounding air: hence they produced the maximum concentration
of choking gases and dust, to welcome the stranger or speed the
parting guest. Meanwhile the glass covering became almost as
opaque to the sun's rays as it would have been if solid iron or brick
had been used instead. In short, the misuse was ludicrous. Small
wonder that these new types of construction awaited for fuller use
the technological improvements that produced the neotechnic phase:
electricity, the distillation of coal, smokeless cities.

The cheapening of steel through the utilization of the Bessemer
process nevertheless had a direct effect upon architecture. Form
coalesced swiftly in the decade of the eighties, particularly in the
hands of the bold architects who dominated the scene in Chicago.
As a result of competition for central sites within a limited building
area in American cities—a competition originally intensified by the
inadequacy of surface transportation and the lack of instantaneous
oral communication over a distance—the architects of the United
States, uncontrolled by Old World building heights and municipal
regulations, had from the eighteen-sixties onward been pushing up
the height of masonry constructions at the instance of the ground
landlord. In order to go higher, the supporting wall had to be thick-
ened inordinately at the base; and this took away rentable space. A
new material, a different method, were needed.

In the eighteen-forties a New York engineer, James Bogardus, had
introduced iron members as supporting columns and had greatly
opened the face of commercial buildings. Now iron was added for the
horizontal beams; and since iron rapidly loses strength under heat,
the metal members were surrounded by a fire-resistant material.
When these various parts were articulated together, as was first done
theoretically by Leroy Buffington and practically by Major Jenney
in Chicago, first in the Home Insurance Building (1885) and com-

pletely in the Leiter Building (1889), an entirely new type of construction appeared: the iron cage and the curtain wall. This translated into colossal paleotechnic forms the vernacular frame and
clapboard construction of the old American farmhouse. The outer
wall became a mere boundary of the interior space, as in the Crystal
Palace itself; instead of the building's being a shell, it became essentially a skeleton—a skeleton with internal organs for equalizing the
temperature and for circulation, with a tough external skin.

This invention greatly simplified difficult constructions; and the
more positive architectural talents of the time, like Louis Sullivan,
were quick to take advantage of it and to further its logical development. Unfortunately, like so many Janus-headed inventions, it was
the antisocial features of this new method that were exploited. The
system of construction was used to squeeze the last drop of rent out
of a site by overcrowding the land; putting a thousand people on a
spot that had hitherto accommodated but a hundred. Result: intensified land speculation, site-crowding, increased traffic congestion—
frequently lack of daylight and decent working space within the new
buildings. Likewise a constant tendency to pyramid land values and
structures, recapitalizing the original values on the basis of prospec-
tive congestion, and using the advance in values as an excuse for
perpetrating further congestion. Finally, an urban form, towering
against the skies, in which the actual living demands of men and
women were subordinated at every step to pecuniary considerations.

From a purely esthetic standpoint, the early Chicago skyscraper
was a triumph. Essentially it has been unsurpassed by later designs:
it must be put alongside the early Manchester cotton mills, the
Crystal Palace, the Brooklyn Bridge, and its immediate contemporary, the Eiffel Tower. *These were expressions of the power and
order that were inherent in the new mechanical complex.* They were
structures purposefully designed to assist the organization of productive machinery, to exhibit goods to large crowds in a well-venti-
lated building, to enable traffic to pass over a wide body of water,
or to serve as a signpost of technological achievement itself: rational
means toward rational ends. Such triumphs had little effect upon
the ordering of the rest of the environment. In this utilitarian age,
the truly mechanical remained an exception; and half-baked com-

promises in form, the not-yet mechanical, the sentimentalized mechanical, the less-than-adequate mechanical, continued to prevail.

Yet all these forms had a preparatory meaning: a meaning that was to come forth once more with the opening of the neotechnic phase in industry. The Crystal Palace prepared the way for the synthetic materials and the clean surfaces used in neotechnic urban architecture: the Eiffel Tower prepared the way for the electric power pole and the radio transmission tower: the skyscrapers made possible, through their experimental organization, a new type of building with flexible interiors, adjustable from generation to generation to new demands of life. While from the tops of tall steel towers, almost as high as the Eiffel Tower itself, the populace became aware—as from the Ferris wheel and chute-the-chutes of the amusement park—of the new angle of vision of the approaching airplane, soaring and diving through space. Within the common industrial scheme, a new order, an appropriate form, was slowly coalescing at last.

14: Far from the Madding Crowd

Those who valued paleotechnic civilization were inclined to be contemptuous of the countryside; whereas those who were sensitive to rural sights and sounds and who enjoyed rural occupations, fled, when they could, from the blackened walls of Coketown.

Throughout this period the impulse to escape, although it could not cure the diseases of industrialism, took special forms that momentarily counteracted the compulsions of the day's routine and its defilements. For the belligerent, there was war and piracy, for the ambitious, there was colonization in new lands, for the powerful, the planning of parks and landscapes, for the reflective, rambling, musing, botanizing in rural retreats. For the rising middle classes of the nineteenth century the romantic retreat took the form of building villas and suburbs, where the spreading agglomeration of Coketown could be temporarily kept at bay. In the city, Mars and Vulcan had become friends. Venus, neglected, sought the consolations of domesticity in a distant suburb.

The impulse toward suburban living perhaps came directly from the more temporary escape of the watering place or the summer resort. Mr. Van Wyck Brooks has pointed out that in the discovery of almost every important summer resort in America, artists and writers, people who gauged life by other standards than the pragmatic one, were mainly responsible: sensitive to the environment, they served like the hazel wand to indicate the places where the springs of life were still flowing. Unfortunately, the effect of these recreation centers was too limited: even the chosen few who visited them returned eventually to the city to dissipate their vigor and lust of life in its smoky streets. Some more permanent form for the exodus was needed: the answer was the middle class romantic suburb.

In embryo, the modern suburb already existed in the sixteenth century: quite different in function and purpose from the so-called suburb around the medieval town, which often served rather for summer residence and recreation. There is an allusion to the new type in The English Courtier. "The manner of most gentlemen and noblemen also is to house themselves (if they possibly may) in the suburbs of the city, because most commonly, the air there being somewhat at large, the place is healthy, and through the distance from the body of the town, the noise is not much; and so consequently quiet. Also for commodity we find many lodgings, both spacious and roomethy, with gardens and orchards very delectable. So with good government we have as little cause to fear infection there as in the very country; our water is excellent and much better than you have any, on ground and fields most pleasant."

That briefly sums up most of the advantages of the new suburb: pure air and water, quiet, space, rural beauty. As the crowding became more universal during the next three centuries, the demand to get away became more imperious: if one did not leave on one's own initiative the doctor's orders would prescribe it. Soame Jenyns remarked in 1795 that tradesmen's wives who felt suffocated by the smoke of London must have their villas at Clapham; and though this tendency developed more slowly in the pure industrial city, which often knew no alternative possibility, it characterized most of the mixed towns with their infiltration of a rural aristocracy and leisured people. At first, the possibilities of suburban living were limited to those who could afford a horse and carriage of their own, or who could make the daily journey to town by public coach. But by the eighteen-twenties in London—later of course elsewhere—a

[TOP] Tenements in Farringdon Road, London: characteristic of model housing for the working classes in the big cities, whether undertaken on old slum properties or in new areas. An effort to circumvent high land values by overcrowding the land, instead of reducing the living place per family as in less-organized slums. The economies in building cost, sometimes put forward in support of high buildings for urban housing, are offset by higher costs of upkeep when paid specialized services supplant self-service.

[SECOND RIGHT] One of the model houses for the working classes exhibited in the Great Exhibition of 1851. Four flats in a unit equipped with an external stairs. Each had a lobby, a living room with a heating cupboard (150 square feet); scullery with sink, rack, dustshaft, ventilator, meatsafe, coalbin; three bedrooms with external ventilation (one of 150 square feet and two of 50 square feet), and a water closet flushed from a cistern. Hollow brick construction. In terms of mid-nineteenth century standards a superior type: but also an expensive one: which accounts for the relative lack of emulation. Hence the usual alternative was the drab ill-designed "model tenements." The White buildings in Brooklyn were a notable exception before the present generation: though cramped internally they had a *Laubengang* arrangement of apartments and were ranged on the perimeter of a good-sized court.

[THIRD RIGHT] Collins plant at Collinsville, Conn. Axes and edged tools: founded 1828. Early industrialists prided themselves on the superior advantage of such plants located in the countryside; apologists for the factory system alleged that most of the evils imputed to the system were due to urban overcrowding. Industrial villages like Collinsville were typical of New England before 1875, and extended through Ohio into Wisconsin. American factory towns like Syracuse, Rochester, Grand Rapids, to say nothing of Muncie, Indiana (see the Lynds' Middletown) often preserved the cottage system of housing and tree-lined streets: sometimes even the garden plots and the opportunities for hunting and fishing of the simpler agricultural town. But social life in such factory centers remained destitute: often the physical environment, as in the chain of brass towns in the valleys around Waterbury, would be miserably deteriorated.

[BOTTOM] Proposed model industrial village. Here church and school are duly provided for; but the only available open spaces within the neighborhood are the streets: a backward step from the Fuggerei three centuries before.

[LEFT] Portion of Central Park, New York, designed by Olmsted and Vaux: consummate example of romantic planning: deliberate separation of pedestrian paths, carriage drives, and crosstown traffic thoroughfares: a mutation that anticipated the organization of the modern city. By placing houses on these winding roads and paths, set behind a front garden, one arrives (with a few minor changes) at the plan of the romantic nineteenth century suburb or town-extension.

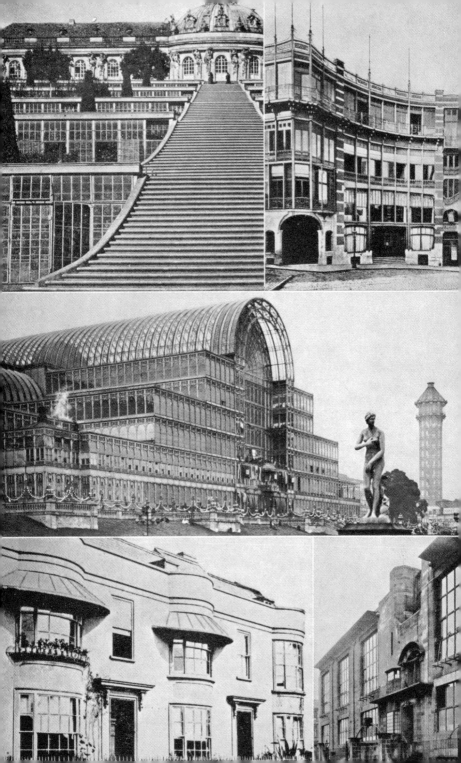

[TOP LEFT] Rear of the palace at Potsdam. Utilization of glass in hot-houses and shelters was first a royal luxury: it here creates a structure close to the modern factory in lightness and openness and flexibility of internal space. The spread of the hot-house to horticulture is reinforced by the spread of hot-house principles to other types of building. While the hot-house is a primitive form for using solar light and heat, technically more adroit forms for heating and power production are obviously on their way: forms that will demand that unobstructed spread to the sun which characterizes a well-designed and well-oriented modern community—in contrast to the costly artificial horrors of so-called super-cities, as projected by paleotechnic and megalopolitan architects and planners.

[TOP RIGHT] Maison du Peuple in Brussels: the more democratic equivalent of the Settlement House. Designed by Horta: able example of L'Art Nouveau, with a grasp of functional relationships and expression, to say nothing of technical delicacy, sometimes lacking in the more formal cubistic designs that followed. Hull House (1892) and the Whitechapel Art Gallery (1899) show a similar vigor of expression: they were the mutations in the megalopolitan scheme that were to have deep significance for modern types of community design and organization.

[MIDDLE] Crystal Palace: the design of a hot-house builder, Joseph Paxton. This glass and iron structure heralded an epoch. (*Photograph: Ewing Galloway*)

[BOTTOM LEFT] Domestic use of glass in large windows characterized vernacular building from the sixteenth century on. Particularly in England between 1780 and 1830 the row house demonstrated a freedom and a clean adroitness that links it with contemporary building—plain walls, large windows, rational plans and elevations: houses in which domestic ease and comfort were not sacrificed to show. Mirrors and glass walls altered the character of both house and occupants.

[BOTTOM RIGHT] Glasgow Art School (1898) designed by the Scotch architect, Mackintosh. It points to the continued relation between the painter's studio of the nineteenth century and the new expressions of life in architecture. The painters of the nineteenth century led the exodus away from the town into a more vital environment: Fontainebleau, Barbizon, Arles, Worpswede. Their residences and working quarters, with their wide studio windows, brought light and sun into the heart of the living room; while the palettes and forms of the impressionists reinforced the hygienists' demands for light, air, sunlight, nakedness.

new environment was taking shape on the outskirts: Barnes, St. John's Wood, Hampstead, later Bedford Park.

At first the street pattern of these new villa districts remained regular. The houses, even if externally given over to neo-gothic caprice were the usual spacious houses with regular, often square ground plans and high-ceilinged rooms: pseudo-Greek temples with an altar in every room but no god. Following romantic principles, house and plot pattern and garden changed: the street avoided straight lines, even when no curves were given by nature; when the cult of naturalism finally invaded German town planning toward the end of the nineteenth century contour levels of even the minor sort were treated as definitive guiding lines for the sake of the irregularity they produced: an exaggerated rebuke to the engineer's habit of forgetting them completely.

But after allowance is made for these lapses, the fact remains that the suburb served as an experimental seedbed for the new domestic architecture. It was in the suburban house that Richardson made his decisive advance toward a new architecture, and after him, Frank Lloyd Wright; it was in the suburb that Sitte effectively applied his post-baroque doctrines of the discontinuous street, and thus made one of the first systematic efforts to insulate the new domestic quarters from through-traffic. By economizing on paving, curbing, wide road-ways, and similar extravagant utilities, the suburb often created a far better residential scheme than the city: the money thus saved could go directly into trees, gardens, open spaces. Simple natural forms were less expensive than mechanical substitutes: no small discovery in an age that believed that iron piping was cheaper than privet hedges, or paper flowers, made in sweatshops, more commendable than those grown in the earth.

But the very popularity of this move to escape partly robbed it of its success. Land values went up on the outskirts of every town, sometimes in sound agricultural territory, in expectation of suburban developments. By the time the impulse reached the lower middle classes and the manual workers, the form of the suburb had changed, too, into a derisive caricature: rows of cramped cottages, with a grass rug in the front, a minor drying green and catwalk in the rear—half an hour or more away from the place of work. Even for the well-to-do the growth of a suburban neighborhood usually meant a progressive intensification of use: a change in site values: eventually a further change in use toward completer coverage of the land. As the city crept nearer the suburb, its purity and solitude vanished, along with its ample gardens: finally it would be swallowed up, as Chelsea and Hammersmith and Hampstead, suburbs all, were swallowed up, in the growth of London.

Two points should be noted about this new type of community. First it was a segregated community, not merely set apart topographically from the central areas of a city: but its occupants were laterally segregated from other economic classes. Except for a small detail of tradesmen and handymen, the suburb was a one-class community: it boasted, in fact, of its "exclusiveness"—which means, sociologically speaking, of the fact that it was not and could not become a city. Further, suburban living encouraged a complete segregation of consumption from production: there was no visible connecting link, except the iron rails that led to the city, between the barbarous industries that manufactured the goods and the romantic suburban homes, remote from the grime and the sweat, where these things were consumed.

In the industrial town, poor men demonstrated: beggars held out their hands in the street: the eye, if it were not carefully averted, would behold a slum, or at least a slum-child, on a five minute walk in any direction. In the suburb, the illusion of an innocent world could be preserved, without encountering these inconvenient reminders of social brutality. Here domesticity could flourish, forgetful of the exploitation upon which so much of it was based. Here individuality could prosper, oblivious to the pervasive regimentation beyond its curving roadways and naturalistic gardens.

In short, the romantic suburb was a collective attempt to live a private life: an effort to make the apparatus of Coketown tolerable to the possessing classes by enabling them to profit by its goods and avoid its evils, to have the best of both worlds. Women and children first is a sound motto; and the instincts that prompted this exodus by the middle classes were sound; life was actually in danger in the new factory slum, and the merest counsel of prudence was to flee—flee with all one's goods, as Lot and his household had fled before the sultry hell of Sodom and Gomorrah. But unfortunately this sound motto did not apply to the women and children of the working classes, despite many pious hopes vouchsafed in the middle of the nineteenth century that cheap fares and special workers' trains would at once solve the housing problem of the poor and permit everyone to spend part of his day in a rural environment.

In a sense, the suburb was woman's special contribution to the new urban complex: for the suburb alone met the needs of child-bearing and child-rearing. Untainted by thoughts of child labor, foul air, prostitution, the home achieved a new spaciousness: the long Victorian novel and the strong Victorian parent were both largely by-products of the suburban fireside. As the sense of privacy increased, the suburbanites copied the romantic Byrons and Lamartines. They made a virtue of idiosyncrasy. If a private retreat, why not a private religion, why not a private architecture? Dickens caricatured these private crotchets in his picture of the Old 'Un, Mr. Wemmick's father, in Great Expectations: with his castellated house and his moat and drawbridge and sunset salute. But it was impossible really to caricature an impulse that had, from the beginning, a constant air of unreality.

The desire for privacy, for exclusiveness, for an environment of snobbish isolation—these things are drawn from the same root. The fact was that the collective economic methods of paleotechnic civilization and the common social life did not bear looking at. The individuality of the suburban cottage, now expressing itself in painful excrescences of "original" ornament, or again in no less painful imitation of historic styles—this "individuality" was in effect a confession that the proud philistines of the period had neither the intellectual penetration to analyze their condition nor the courage and the imagination to transform it. The suburb was a pharisaic way of passing by on the other side: leaving the civic organism itself in the gutter.

So much for the weakness of this movement. One must realize nonetheless that like so many other impulses of romanticism it was a healthy reaction, to be condemned, not for what it did, but for what it omitted to do. After all the suburb was a first semi-collective attempt to create for the middle classes, if not for the whole community, a biological environment on an urban basis. That was a rational purpose. These new houses were more spacious as a rule and more open to the sun than the dingy rows that lined the streets of the town; and this new setting, with its trees and lawns and gardens, was more sweet to the eye and ear and nose than were the city's pavements. In these open spaces, with their nearby fields and streams, children could play and gambol again, as even the children of the wealthiest had but little chance to do in the big centers. In the suburb there was space for gardening and caring for children: for playing at lawn tennis, croquet, or at bowls: puttering around the carpenter's workbench. In short, the suburb was nearer to providing a balanced round of activities—outside daily work—than the paleotechnic city. If not as healthy as the countryside proper, the suburb would still be healthier than the congested city, once its water supply and its sewage disposal were taken in hand.

In creating a better biological environment, however, the builders of the suburb failed to take account of the need for a more adequate social environment. On the contrary, the suburb usually fell off from even the low standards of Coketown: it started a de-politizing process that has been steadily spreading as the suburb itself has been spreading throughout our civilization. The suburb was a "Teilstadt," a specialized urban fragment: just as much so as the meanest coal town, iron town, cotton town. Hence it lacked the necessary elements for extensive social co-operation, for creative intercourse, for an expansion of the social heritage as a whole. Consuming much, it produced little, created less. The stimulus of variety, the shock and jostle and challenge of different groups, were largely absent from its life. For the inhabitants of the suburb lived divided lives. Their purses were in the central city; their domestic affections were concentrated one or two hours away, in the villa. Neither side of their lives could be wholly active, wholly efficient. The necessary routine, with its daily shuttling between home and workplace, between nest and market, undermined life at both extremes. *Spatial concentration has an essential part to play in psychological focus—and that above all was lacking in this new regime.*

Hence a final paradox: the most lasting benefits in the suburban pattern of development came from a handful of industrialists who

worked within the heart of the paleotechnic scheme and who—sometimes quite literally—stuck to their guns. Godin at Guise, Krupp at
Essen, Salt at Saltaire, Cadbury at Bourneville, Lever at Port Sunlight, all heralded at the beginning of the nineteenth century by the
hardheaded fanaticism of Robert Owen—these men made a sound
contribution to urban life. They accepted the vital principles of
romanticism, the delight in nature, the concern for children, the
interest in healthy rural sports, as a basis for a new type of community development. But they did not forget the factory: they united
the domestic and the industrial scheme in the same general frame.
In this handful of exemplary developments, the foundation for a
new attack upon the problems of housing and city development were
finally laid: they paved the way for the new biotechnic conception
of a balanced urban environment—what was first called the Garden
City.

15: The Woodlanders

If the so-called working class suburb was merely a peripheral
slum or semi-slum rather than a central one, a new element nevertheless entered the city, at about the same time, which improved the
environment. The new landscape park. In a sense, this was merely a
remodeling of the baroque park which, as a setting for the royal
palace, had remained in the capital cities of Europe. Under pressure
of democratic and humanitarian demands, these parks had been
thrown open to the inhabitants. But in the nineteenth century the
nature of the park was altered: its mission was, as Olmsted said
of Central Park, to provide for the masses of the city a brief equivalent of a visit to the countryside. The designers recognized the need
of the saving opposite within the city. This was the more positive
side of romantic disorder.

In what form do these new pastoral spaces first appear? To achieve
peace and quiet, to insulate oneself from the noisy lanes of traffic,
one must—do not laugh!—visit the dead. Mount Auburn Cemetery
in Boston was one of the first of the new landscaped areas, spread
out in ample acres, which was designed to resuscitate the living as
well as solemnly to enfold the deceased. In this crazy utilitarian
world, it was the dear departed who enjoyed most fully a good en-

vironment; while the dark caves of houses were more like catacombs than homes for the living. Life came back to the town by way of the graveyard; just as in more than one city the removal of tombstones served to turn the churchyard into a necessary breathing space for congested quarters. This is not the first time in recorded history, from the days of the Egyptian tomb-builders onward, when the dead were abundantly supplied with the necessaries of life that were denied to the quick.

In the main, the great capitals, still under the sway of baroque standards, still profiting by the regular seasonal migration of the county families, were more receptive to the idea of the landscape park than were the purely industrial towns. London and New York responded to the idea sooner than Pittsburgh and Leeds. In the capitals, indeed, there was this further stimulus: the avenues were becoming too congested for the fashionable display of equipages, which were an important part of the surviving baroque ritual, and the country had become too inaccessible to aristocratic horseback riders. It was necessary to set aside special areas where the merchant princes and their wives could drive. To achieve their own special privileges, they had to secure municipal support for such open greens.

The leaders in this whole movement to re-ruralize the town were the Americans Downing and Olmsted: the latter one of the vital artists of the nineteenth century. He took the capricious naturalism of the earlier lovers of dead trees and broken branches, and the meaningless irregularities of the Jardin Anglais, and created new harmonies, based upon a closer study of the lay of the land and of native plant formations. He was not afraid to use the commonest wild flowers and native shrubs in his planting; and he followed the contour lines in the laying out of paths and roads. These naturalistic plans accordingly saved expense on grading, filling, and vain architectural embellishment; and his native plants had a better chance of surviving without excessive labor than had the exotics of an earlier school of design. But his plans were animated by technical intelligence and civic foresight. He was the first planner to see the necessity—in his extremely original design for Central Park—of deliberately separating pedestrian traffic from wheeled traffic by creating underpasses and overpasses that permitted them to operate as sepa-

rate systems. This bold scheme anticipated by more than two generations the rational layout of the modern town, as first comprehensively
set down by Messrs. Henry Wright and Clarence Stein at Radburn,
New Jersey: a major contribution.

By 1870 Olmsted had carried his thinking about parks beyond his
original conception of the big landscape park, lying in the midst of
the growing city. He saw that even better tracts of land might be
destroyed on the outskirts, and that by the time the urban mass had
reached these outlying areas they might be just as badly needed.
Hence he outlined the conception of the complete *park system*. This
system began with the individual square for local promenade and
meeting, and the individual playground for active recreation. Such
grounds were connected up by strips of roadway, greensward, and
rows of trees, called parkways: elongated versions of the strip common of New England—already embodied in the Avenue des Champs
Elysées. Accordingly, by increasing passages of open space, it led
into such neighboring wild landscapes—like that of the Palisades in
New York or Middlesex Fells in Boston—as might and should be
preserved. Olmsted's disciple, Charles Eliot, Jr., saw the further
necessity of using the riverside and sea-coast areas, no less than the
pastoral or mountain landscape so dear to the older romantic planner; and had Eliot's timely warning been carried into political action,
by creating permanent park strips and footpaths along the beaches
and promontories of Massachusetts and Maine, that splendid coast
would not have been turned into the dissolute landscape-slum so much
of it has now become.

This conception of a *continuous* environment of public greens and
open spaces as an essential element in urban planning—and not an
afterthought or a mere embellishment—was an important contribution to sound contemporary city design: in a more systematic and
highly developed form it must still govern every rational conspectus
of the new city. Neither the medieval town nor the baroque town had
such continuous areas: indeed, the notion of the country and the
city as being continuously inter-related and inter-penetrating was
foreign to the earlier conception of urban organization.

Unfortunately, the attempt to thrust park areas into a paleotechnic
street-net met with countless obstructions. Though experience proved

again and again that, even upon purely commercial terms, these new open areas paid for themselves by raising the land values along adjacent properties, the commercial interests tended nevertheless jealously to oppose the removal from speculative action of such large tracts of land. Meanwhile, the premature platting of streets and the speculation in building lots, which went on in every growing center, made it difficult to get hold of the necessary land. The failure to make the park system central to planning resulted in a certain belatedness in every program for parks and playgrounds: by the time the need had become pressing enough to demand action, the price tended to be prohibitive. Smaller towns here had an advantage over bigger ones, though too frequently they failed to seize it.

Still, the landscape park and the park system were real social mutations in urban form: perhaps the only ones of importance, outside the plan of the romantic suburb, that the period could point to. In Europe, by a happy sort of revenge, the old baroque fortifications, which had done so much to cause congestion, were torn down and replaced by parks: these formed the lovely rings and starlike green salients around a Bremen, a Lübeck, a Wien, a Cracow, a Köln. The immediate platting of big landscape parks helped break up the clotted urban massing of the great metropolis and softened the rigors of life for its inhabitants: and the best of these parks, such as Prospect Park in Brooklyn, count among the proudest works of art of this century. Eventually, the idea and the example touched even the sordid milieu of the pure industrial towns, creating a guilty conscience, if not a fresh will-to-order. By 1890 the typical paleotect had begun to lose a little of his pride and self-confidence in the insensate environment he had helped create.

16: Reaction

One may well close this picture of paleotechnic urban form with a quotation from John Storer, in his essay on Our Cities, published in 1870. "It may be doubted whether, among the arts yet to be discovered, or at least perfected, among the almost uninvestigated sciences to be shaped into form, worked out in theory, and harder still, in practice by the strong men of the future, should not be included the art and science of city life. . . . To mould the vast con-

geries of life massed around a given center, say ten miles around
Charing Cross, for instance, into a systematic organism, so as to give
the most good possible to every one of the vast human family therein
contained, is a matter difficult of achievement, and one admitting
a vast improvement over all former precedents."

The statement was admirable. And after fully canvassing the defects of the paleotechnic town, one must balance up accounts by admitting that nothing one can say today is more rigorous or more penetrating than the criticisms of a sanitarian like Chadwick or Richardson or Simon, of a political reformer like Shaftesbury or Buckingham or Bellamy, of a prophet like Ruskin or Morris, of a creative
geotect like Olmsted. For the first people to discover what was wrong
with these vast, inconsequential urban clottings, and the first to take
vigorous steps to rectify the manifold evils, were the more intelligent,
public-spirited members of this society. They attended to first things
first. It was the leader of Victorian estheticism, John Ruskin, who
begged the industrial leaders not to worry about art until they had
provided for the inhabitants of their towns clean air and pure water
and easy access to the country. "When you know how to build cities,
and how to rule them," he observed in Munera Pulveris, "you will
be able to breathe in their streets, and the 'excursion' will be the
afternoon's walk or game in the fields round them."

And even on the social side of existence, the towns had begun
during the early part of the nineteenth century to make a great contribution. For this century, which is so often falsely called the age of
individualism, in reflection of the callous public morals of the rich,
was in essence an age full of associational experiments: closer to the
spirit of Fourier than its smug leaders imagined. If the physical
organization of the new urban areas was entirely inadequate, one
must remember, nevertheless, that within the interstices of these
towns, new organs for social co-operation and social thought were
defining themselves: the trade union, the scientific society, the consumers' co-operative society, the public library: means whereby the
military-capitalistic regime could be eventually transformed into a
social commonwealth.

CHAPTER IV.

RISE AND FALL OF MEGALOPOLIS

1: The New Coalition

The story of every city can be read through a succession of deposits: the sedimentary strata of history. While certain forms and phases of development are successive in time, they become, through the very agency of the civic process, cumulative in space. The point of maximum accumulation, the focus of past achievements and present activities, is the metropolis. The emergence of the big city from the multitude of regional cities that characterized the Middle Ages is so obvious a fact that certain economic historians have described the change as that from a town economy to a metropolitan economy. The characterization is mainly sound, but is the fact a permanent one? Will life continue to ebb out of the villages and country towns and regional centers? Will urban life come to mean the further concentration of power in a few metropolises whose ramifying suburban dormitories will finally swallow the rural hinterland?

Many analyses of contemporary city growth have taken this development to be a final one. Vast plans have been drawn up in various metropolises for continuing this process, and for absorbing a greater population: even in countries whose rate of population increase has been steadily diminishing, the continuance of metropolitan aggrandizement has been taken for granted. Unhappily for these hopes and plans even the blind drift of contemporary forces does not promise a continuance of this process: it is self-limiting. Meanwhile the disabilities and burdens of metropolitan development have been heaping up. Already, one can detect a new economic and social pattern: a step beyond the metropolitan economy.

So far from representing adequately the forces of modern civilization, the metropolis is one of the biggest obstacles to their fruitful human use. In what ways is this true? How has it come about? And what alternatives lie before us? Those questions I purpose to answer.

Thorstein Veblen made us familiar with the conflict that is latent between mechanical enterprise and commercial enterprise: between the old-fashioned industrialist, whose fun was in the day's work, and whose pecuniary gains were testimonials of success after the event, and the new kind of financier, growing out of the banker and speculator, for whom pecuniary gain was the be-all and end-all of existence. Up to a point this distinction is a genuine one. It is reflected in the environments they have helped to create. One may distinguish roughly between producing cities and consuming cities: between the Five Towns, Pittsburgh, Lyons, Turin, Essen, on one hand, and London, New York, Paris, Berlin, Rome, and their subsidiary pleasure resorts, on the other.

During the paleotechnic period, when great fortunes were being made in steel and coal and oil and machinery, money would be amassed in the back country, at the expense of local resources and the local population, and then spent, if not completely dispersed, in cities far remote. The very means of luxurious expenditure were often wanting in the industrial towns. Beginning in the third quarter of the nineteenth century, the center of gravity shifted from the producing towns to the capital cities: free competition, which was the dominant catchword of the early nineteenth century, if never the universal practice, gave way to the effort to achieve practical monopoly or quasi-monopoly.

This movement broke down the partition between the various classes in society that had hitherto been relatively isolated. A coalition of land, industry, finance, and officialdom was formed in almost every country in order to effect the maximum amount of pecuniary exploitation. The agents of power, the aristocracy, the political bureaucracy, and the army began to direct "national interests" toward the service of the industrialist: they sought raw materials and markets capable of absorbing his excess production: hence the partition of Africa, Asia, and similar "backward" sections of the world. The industrialist, in turn, abandoning his naïve belief in laissez-faire and free enterprise, came to rely upon his imperialistic allies to help stabilize industry and to give it monopoly advantages: hence protective tariffs, subsidies, export subventions.

This coalition of economic interests was in good part responsible for the continuous increase of population in the great capitals during the nineteenth century, and for the building up of new metropolitan centers. The overgrown city, instead of appearing as an isolated phenomenon, an emblem of purely political concentration, became the dominant type: Coketown, the pure industrial city, was the recessive form after 1890.

Even in the most secluded provincial town, the pattern of institutional life was a metropolitan one: the shibboleths of power-politics, the orgiastic urges of nationalism, the acceptance of both the commercial and the cultural trade-marks of the metropolis became well-nigh universal. England, whose utilitarians had turned the green country of Shakespeare into the Black Country of Dickens, proceeded during the nineteenth century to paint the rest of the map red. In successive waves of belligerent exploitation, other countries followed suit. The colors of life, ebbing from the insensate milieu of the industrial town, flowed back into the metropolis in the gay uniforms of the Guards and Cuirassiers.

The basis for metropolitan agglomeration lay in the tremendous increase of population that took place during the nineteenth century. Peoples of European stock multiplied from about two hundred million during the Napoleonic Wars to about six hundred million at the outbreak of the World War. This stock, which accounted for only about one-sixth of the population of the earth in Malthus' day, rose to about a third of it in a little over a century. In 1800 not a city in the Western World had over a million in population: London, the biggest, had only 959,310, while Paris had a little more than half a million, and Wien about half of that. By 1850 London had over two millions and Paris over a million inhabitants: they were still without serious rivals. But by 1900 eleven metropolises with more than a million inhabitants had come into existence, including Berlin, Chicago, New York, Philadelphia, Moscow, St. Petersburg, Wien, Tokyo, and Calcutta. Thirty years later, as a result of this feverish concentration of capital and the military and mechanical means of exploitation, there were twenty-seven cities with more than a million population, headed by New York and grading down to Birmingham, including metropolises on every continent, even Australia. The rise of cities with a population of over a hundred thousand was equally marked: likewise the spread of vast suburban rings around the central districts of all these cities. Nearly one-half of the population of the United States at the time of the 1930 census lived within a radius of from twenty to fifty miles of cities with over a hundred thousand inhabitants. The mere alteration of scale and extent resulted in qualitative changes in these centers.

2: The Tentacular Bureaucracy

What forces furthered this process of urban agglomeration? What made the metropolis the image of social hope and economic enterprise, even for those parts of the world whose dear ways of life were sapped and undermined by the extension of "la ville tentaculaire"?

The means of agglomeration were the continental railroad lines and the worldwide lanes of ocean commerce: means which brought an endless flow of raw materials and foods into the metropolis: all roads led to the capital. But the civic force was the centralization of the organs of administration in the great capitals, and the growing dependence of every type of enterprise, political, educational, economic, upon the process of administration itself.

Once the means of instantaneous communication were available, there was a fresh incentive to concentrate the organs of administration: production could be controlled, the shipment of goods routed, orders given and canceled, credits extended and the exchanges of goods and drafts cleared, on a single spot. Remote control, first embodied in the separation of staff and line in the army, spread to business operations. With the manufacture of the typewriter in the seventies, and the coincident spread of high speed stenography, more and more business could be conducted on paper. Mechanical means of communication: mechanical means of making and manifolding the permanent record: mechanical systems of audit and control—all these devices aided the rise of a vast commercial bureaucracy, capable of selling in ever remoter territories.

The word bureaucracy had indeed become a discouraging by-word for inefficiency by the middle of the nineteenth century: Dickens needed no special powers of invention to create Sir Tite Barnacle and the Circumlocution Office. Everyone experienced, throughout the financial and political world, the difficulty of getting things done by direct action. The simplest civil act required legal sanctions, documents, verifications. From the searching of a deed up to the establishment of civil rights in marriage, no one could move without the aid of special functionaries. Lawyers, who knew the prescribed forms and technicalities, formed a large part of the growing professional population: their services were needed in the observance, and even more in the tactful breach, of the law.

In all this development, the political bureaucracy served as a special target for chronic disparagement: it was supposed to have a monopoly of roundabout methods and a finicking attention to form. But the businessman's self-righteous indignation about the monstrous growth of political bureaucracy was extremely humorless. Such an attitude overlooked the fact that the *greatest development of bureaucracy during the last century took place within the realm of business itself:* this development put to shame the punier additions to the governmental bureaucracy. Plainly, no great corporate enterprise with a worldwide network of agents, correspondents, market outlets, factories, and investors could exist without relying upon the services of an army of patient clerkly routineers in the metropolis: stenographers, filing clerks, and bookkeepers, office managers, sales managers, and their varied assistants, right up to the fifth vice-president whose name or o.k. sets the final seal of responsibility upon an action. The housing of this bureaucracy in office buildings and tenements and residential suburbs constituted one of the major tasks of metropolitan expansion: their transportation back and forth to work, within a limited time-span, raised one of the difficult technical problems that confronted the city planner and the engineer.

Not merely did the bureaucracy itself require office space and living space: but the by-products of its routine came to occupy an increasing share of the new quarters: files, vaults, places for live storage and dead storage, parade grounds and cemeteries of documents, where the records of business were alphabetically kept, with an eye to the possibility of future exploitation, future reference, future lawsuits, future contracts. This age found its form in a new type of office building: a sort of human filing case, whose occupants spent their days in the circumspect care of paper: numbering, ticketing, assorting, routing, recording, manifolding, filing, to the end that the commodities and services thus controlled could be sold to the profit of the absentee owners of the corporation.

A new trinity dominated the metropolitan scene: finance, insurance, advertising. By means of these agents, the metropolis extended its rule over subordinate regions, both within its own political territory and in outlying domains: directly or indirectly, they expedited the flow of tribute back into the big centers. Economic enterprise, political power, social authority, once divided over the length and breadth of the land, now concentrated in the seven Romes. To obtain money, one must go to the metropolis: to exercise influence, one must achieve a prominent financial position in the metropolis. Here and there a lone wolf, like Henry Ford, would temporarily remain outside the system. But such isolation would be largely an illusion: mark how Ford himself, who once manufactured a car adapted to popular needs and rural life, finally succumbed to the lure of metropolitan style in the outer design of his car.

Monopoly capitalism: credit finance: pecuniary prestige—these are the three sides of the metropolitan pyramid. Whatever goes on in the big city ultimately traces back to one or another of these elements. The metropolis is the natural reservoir of capital under this economic phase; for its banks, its brokerage offices, its stock exchanges, serve as a collecting point for the savings of the surrounding country, and in the case of world capitals, for the surplus capital of foreign investors. Investors and manufacturers both gravitate to the metropolis: the more constant the need for credit capital, the more important for the borrower to be close to the big banks that can advance it.

The concentration of financial power in national or semi-national banks, like the Banks of England and France, or in the hands of politically irresponsible private bankers, like the Houses of Rothschild and Morgan, is a characteristic feature of this regime. As Balzac clearly saw at the very beginning of this concentration, the banker was supreme: directly or indirectly, he manipulated the puppets that appeared on the political stage: he contributed to the funds

of the political parties, and his sanction was as necessary to the success of a political policy or an industrial invention as his veto was
fatal.

But mortgages on metropolitan real estate, whose values are
"secured" by the continued prosperity and growth of the metropolis,
become a mainstay of savings banks and insurance companies. In
order to protect their investments, these institutions must combat any
attempt to lessen congestion; for this would also deflate the values
that are based on congestion. Note how the program for slum replacement and suburban re-settlement mapped out by the Roosevelt
administration in 1933 was undermined by the fact that the administration created at the same time another agency whose sole purpose
was to keep intact the existing structure of mortgages and interest
rates: a policy that made it impossible to scale down sufficiently the
grotesque burden of urban land values and urban debt.

In the medieval order, the fatalities and insecurities of life were
offset by the organization of guilds and friendly societies. In the
metropolitan regime, these services are performed by special financial corporations: insurance companies. Fire, flood, sickness, disa-
bility, accident, and death are all covered by one or another form
of insurance. In the calculations made to ascertain the rates of insurance, the first advances in statistical sociology took place; and in
intensive work toward health maintenance and disease prevention,
great organizations like the Metropolitan Life Insurance Company
have demonstrated the cash value of improvement in these departments by education and medical aid.

Unfortunately, within the current metropolitan scheme, insurance
is an attempt to achieve security by piling together at one point the
maximum number of risks. In the short run, the insurance company
may be solvent: in the long run, it becomes itself one of the elements
contributing to the bankruptcy of the regime as a whole. By their
control of vast capital resources, the insurance companies become the
effective landlords of distant farming lands, as well as of metropolitan real estate. Remote farms in Arkansas and Iowa, rubber
plantations in Brazil and power plants in Africa—these and a hundred other rural domains become directly tributary to the big city
through the agency of finance. So long as the productive mechanism

is in working order, the flow is continuous: but a drought, a dust-storm, an earthquake, a glut of commodities, or a war will seriously shake the fabric; and the existence of these implacable metropolitan claims may then stand in the way of rational political adjustment.

Hence the necessity for completing the process of metropolitan monopoly and concentrating the control even further. To prevent aggressive rivalry on the part of sub-metropolises and their provinces one final step is necessary: the effective monopoly of advertising, news, publicity, periodical literature. These four departments have diverse points of origin and represent various initial interests; but historically, they have been loosely tied together since the beginning, and within the metropolitan framework they finally coalesce. They work to a single end: to give the stamp of authenticity and value to the style of life that emanates from the metropolis. They establish the national brand: they attempt to control the national market: they create a picture of a unified, homogeneous, completely standardized population that bears, in fact, no relation to the actual regional sub-stratum—although in the course of time it partly succeeds in producing the thing it has imagined.

In all these efforts, the stage, the motion picture screen, the radio, no less than the newspaper and the printed book, concentrate upon fixing the national appetite upon just those products that the metropolis can sell at a profit. Similarly, they create an image of a valuable life that can be satisfied only by a ruthless concentration of human interest upon pecuniary standards and pecuniary results: the clothes of the metropolis, the jewels of the metropolis, the dull expensive life of Park Avenue and the Kurfürstendamm, Piccadilly and the Champs Elysées, become the goals of vulgar ambition.

Advertisement becomes the "spiritual power" of this new regime: ostentatiously or covertly, the greater part of the literature produced with the imprint of the metropolis is advertisement: an effort to establish the universal prestige of the metropolis, if not of this or that special product. Such methods, such standards, infect the older emblems of the spiritual power, the Church and the University: these institutions imitatively create huge ornate buildings, also in the spirit of advertisement, and are tempted grossly to copy the methods of the financier on whom they more and more rely. Example: the em-

ployment of commercial fund-raisers by various religious bodies
and institutions to acquire capital for buildings and other purposes.
Such a concordat between the ecclesiastical and the financial powers
has many parallels in the modern metropolis.

Where the organs of finance and publicity are concentrated, the
possessing classes are likewise brought together; for the ritual of
their life, as lived in public for the benefit of the illustrated newspapers and the newsreels, is an essential part of the pecuniary lure.
The concentration of the rich is a typical metropolitan phenomenon:
the wealth that they accumulate in the metropolis goes into private
foibles and public philanthropies, when it does not return to commerce in the form of further investments. The princely ritual of
conspicuous expenditure, no longer confined to the royal court,
gives rise to the special luxury industries of the metropolis: dress,
food, adornment. Because of the universal nature of metropolitan
standards, the exotic fashions of the rich are presently copied and
reproduced on a mass scale for the benefit of the entire populace. As for the more altruistic modes of expenditure, some, like
hospitals, are inherited from the past: some, like research foundations, are peculiar to the metropolitan economy itself: here, too,
the millionaire of the new regime takes the place of the absolute
prince.

In the second and third generations of money-making, philanthropy itself becomes a business of high repute. Just as about two
hundred corporations control about half the industrial capital in
America, so do a relatively small group from the financial classes
control the organs of culture in the metropolis and in a good part
of the outlying territories. When new lines of activity are to be promoted in the arts and sciences, it is inevitably to the swollen purses
of the metropolis that the promoters direct themselves: here, more
often than not, the new foundation settles. Thus a multitude of associations of national and international scope naturally have their
headquarters in New York, London, or Paris: charitable organizations, religious foundations, scientific and educational institutes.
Here patrons and clients come together: here competitive patronage
increases the opportunity for special interests to find support. A disproportionate share of power and influence and wealth has been

drained away from the hinterland: in order to recapture any of these things, it is necessary for the provincial to leave his home and fight for a place in the metropolis.

A third condition abets the agglomeration of population. Victor Branford suggested that the growth of imperial bureaucracies, coming as a result of political centralization in war, was the characteristic agent that transformed the industrial town or caused it to yield in power and influence and numbers to the metropolis. War is the forcing-house of bureaucracy: in America, the Civil War and the World War, in Europe, the Napoleonic Wars, the Franco-Prussian War, the Russo-Japanese War, and again the World War. The fact is that imperialism and financialism go hand in hand: exploitation, whether external or internal, requires protection: the protection of the flag, the protection of the military forces that march under the flag. As the population is heaped further into great centers, they must rely more fully upon distant sources of supply: to widen the base of supplies and to protect the "life-line" that connects the source with the voracious mouth of the imperial metropolis, become the functions of the army and the navy.

Whereas the agricultural base of the village is the local fields, and the base of the regional city is the local region, the base of the metropolis may be outside the political unit of which it is a member. In so far as it dominates those distant sources of goods and those distant markets, the growth of the capital can proceed indefinitely. Such an increase as London showed in a century, from one million to six million people, is unprecedented, so far as history offers any records for comparison; and it was dependent upon the worldwide transportation system and the worldwide system of capital investment and market-interchange that London had so vigorously helped to invent and knit together.

Beneath these tendencies toward centralization of power and agglomeration of people lies another economic fact. This is the increase of ground-rents that follows inevitably from such growth. In the metropolis the rent of land, no longer fixed by custom, no longer stabilized by slowness in change of use, rises by leaps and bounds. Parcels change rapidly from hand to hand, with successive increases in value, until they have "ripened" sufficiently to permit the fullest value to be plucked by the last owner who holds it just before its actual use. Under capitalism, the rise of land values attendant upon congestion is by itself sufficient motive for—and justification of—the whole process.

Do not fancy that this increase of values is incidental. On the contrary, strenuous efforts are made to ensure it. In Cobbett's day, he complained about the effect of the funding system upon the over-building of London: the gathering of rentiers into the capital was a powerful factor in its expansion. But there are other means of effecting this end: railroad systems are deliberately designed to compel passengers and goods to pass through the metropolis before going elsewhere: each great capital sits like a spider in the midst of its transportation web. In America, in addition, as Thompson points out, the rate structure is not based upon the actual cost of service: the charges are arbitrarily equalized in such a fashion as to give a sub-sidy to the big cities at the expense of the rival towns that are per-haps more conveniently located—even though the cost of handling freight in big cities is, by reason of their very congestion, dispro-portionately high.

By itself, the big city becomes the prestige symbol for the whole civilization. Life in all the subordinate regions is sacrificed to its temples of pleasure and towers of pecuniary aspiration, as life in the Valley of the Nile was sacrificed to the theocratic cult of the tomb-builders. So much for the economist's naïve myth that the gigantic metropolis is what it is merely because of its tangible eco-nomic benefits or the natural superiority of its geographic situa-tion.

3: Shapeless Giantism

Circle over London, Berlin, New York, or Chicago in an airplane, or view the cities schematically by means of an urban map and block-plan. What is the shape of the city and how does it define itself? As the eye stretches toward the hazy periphery one can pick out no defi-nite shape, except that formed by nature: a banked river or a lake-front: one beholds rather a shapeless mass, here bulging or ridged with buildings, there broken by a patch of green or the separate geometric shapes of a gas tank or a series of freight sheds. The growth of a great city is amoeboid: failing to divide its social chromosomes and split up into new cells, the big city continues to grow by breaking through the edges and accepting its sprawl and shapelessness as an inevitable by-product of its physical immensity.

Here the city has absorbed villages and little towns and reduced them to place names, like Manhattanville and Harlem in New York; there it has left the organs of local government and the vestiges of an independent civic life, as in Chelsea and Kensington in London; but it has nevertheless enveloped those urban areas in its physical organization. In this all-devouring growth, the outskirts during the last generation have grown faster than the center: in America, at twice the rate of the metropolis proper, and almost six times the rate of the non-metropolitan parts of the United States. Physically incoherent, socially disparate, these new metropolitan districts are at best statistical collections. Here and there in the mass one may partly trace the outline of a city: but the mass itself is not a city, in a functional sense, any more than the immediate countryside that surrounds it is a rural area.

What was purely a visual perspective in the baroque city becomes in the later metropolis a more pragmatic perspective of profits through urban extensions. In the upward extension of the city the same tendencies prevail: to increase urban heights and distances and numbers has now a direct financial motive.

Sometimes the shapelessness of the metropolitan aggregate is further expressed by the irregular blocks and the aimless inconsecutive streets, or the wild jumble of structures that have been superimposed on a regular pattern of streets: that is San Francisco, Chicago, Detroit, London. Sometimes there are large patches of orderly, consecutive growth: that is Paris, Berlin, Madrid, Buenos Aires. But the difference between one type of order and another is a difference in the *degree* of sprawl, confusion, de-building. As one moves out of the central district the vast enveloping aimlessness of this growth becomes overwhelming. No human eye can take in this metropolitan mass at a glance. No single gathering place except the totality of its streets can hold all its citizens. No human mind can comprehend more than a fragment of the complex and minutely specialized activi-

ties of its citizens. There is a special name for power when it is concentrated on such a scale: it is called impotence.

4: Means of Congestion

Contrary to popular belief the growth of great cities preceded the
decisive technical advances of the last two centuries. But the metropolitan phase became universal only when the technical means of
congestion had become adequate—and their use profitable to those
who manufactured or employed them. The modern metropolis, however, is an outstanding example of a peculiar cultural lag within the
realm of technics itself: namely, the continuation by advanced neotechnic means of the forms and ends of paleotechnic civilization. The
machines and utilities that will lend themselves to decentralization
in a life-centered order, here become a means either to increase the
congestion or afford some slight palliation: at a price.

The most characteristic technical achievements of the big city are
those that further congestion; and the first of these is the canaliza-
tion of water, its storage in vast reservoirs, its transmission through
vast mains, tubular rivers, from the open country to the heart of the
city. With reason New York prided itself on leading the way here:
the Croton system, opened in 1842, was both a handsome piece of
engineering and an intelligent means of combating some of the worst
effects of urban overcrowding. The provision of pure, municipally
supervised drinking water lowered the incidence of typhoid epidemics and helped offset the rising death rate in other departments:
accordingly, the seizure and purification of an abundance of water
has become a main line of municipal strategy. In closely settled
areas, or in areas of limited catchment, this brings the growing metropolis into conflict with other cities and other political divisions:
the fight between Arizona and California over the diversion of water
to Los Angeles became a bitter one: the very living of the farmers of
Arizona was threatened by the city's expansion.

Not merely does running water become a necessity of metropolitan life: the bathroom reappears with it. This improvement
comes to the mass of workers but slowly; but the facilities for cleanliness have now become accepted as a necessary part of the metropolitan standard of life: the bathtub becomes a permanent fixture,

[TOP LEFT] Grenoble. Natural circular plan. Irregular blocks dictated by topography and original circular wall.

[BOTTOM LEFT] Torino. Rigorous geometrical plan with blocks of almost uniform size. Varied size of squares and their placing indicates higher order of design than nineteenth century gridiron plans.

[MIDDLE LEFT] Delft. Irregular rectangular plan: natural adaptation to flat site, but with diagonal canal giving access to market square.

[TOP RIGHT] Nice. Acropolis type, like Athens, Geneva, Edinburgh. Fortified hill site and original settlement below: a true *Burg*. Typical Baroque town extension.

[BOTTOM RIGHT] Köln. Mixed type: regular Roman subdivision at center with irregular blocks of different sizes and shapes as later accretions.

Superficial observers often regard plans like those of Torino or the newer parts of Nice as the only authentic examples of urban order: while cities that have grown more slowly, with piecemeal changes and modifications, are looked upon as disorderly or even planless. But the more subtle organization of time and space, represented here by Grenoble and post-Roman Köln, has its own kind of order: the tactics of life, in all its manifestations, will include both types: the formal and the adaptive, the mechanical and the vital.

In the first type, the plan is preconceived on the lines of some regulating figure, like a circle or square, and the site and its structures are made to conform to the dominant idea. In the adaptive plan, the given conditions of soil and site are accepted and followed, with such reconstructions as convenience and necessity may dictate: the functions of life are not fitted into the mind's pattern but into nature's. The resulting order may be predominantly geometrical, as in Delft, or irregular, as in Grenoble. Note ample gardens within.

When the topographic outlines are bold and decisive, economy rests on willing conformity with the earth's contours. For lack of such acceptance, the "regular" plans of cities like San Francisco are not merely frightfully extravagant but badly adapted to meet the actual conditions imposed. Given the appropriate social conditions and the appropriate site, a formal plan may be genuinely organic: Wren's plan for London was a true expression of capitalism and mechanism, though it failed to reckon with survivals, and so came to nothing. The weakness of adaptive planning is that it sometimes gives more weight to the external factors of history and geography than they deserve: when the occasion arises, man can and should move mountains, cutting through natural obstacles opposing the inertia of tradition. Geometric planning tends to give too simple or arbitrary a form to complicated human functions: the procrustean fallacy: it boldly controls future needs without understanding them or being able to anticipate them. True organic planning embraces both elements, adaptation and formal order, timeliness and timelessness, functional adjustment and abstract clarity and coherence of design. Amsterdam is a classic example.

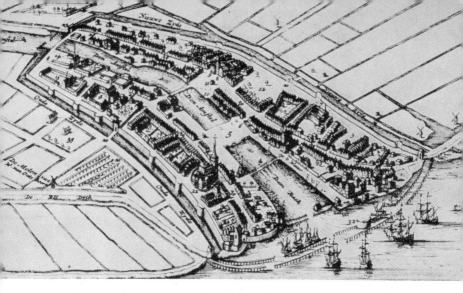

V: ELEMENTS OF PLAN [16 and 17] AMSTERDAM—ORGANIC PLANNING

[ABOVE] Stage One: The fishing and shipping town on the Amstel: a site not dissimilar to that of Geneva or Zürich. Banking and bridging of Amstel already begun. Harbor partly developed.

[BELOW] Stage Three: Development of large regular houseblocks on right of old city in adaptation to new facilities of water transportation: somewhat unfortunate continuation of field divisions and their orientation in smaller houseblocks.

[ABOVE] Stage Two: Utilization of original protective canal as a means of urban transportation: multiplication of water avenues of the city: increase of port facilities on new land to left.

[BELOW] Stage Four: Partial regularity of newer parts of city rounded out by what becomes a semi-circular web of canals. The resultant plan, though geometrical, is a magnificent adaptation to economic and social opportunities: what townplanner could have plotted this result at stage one?

E AFTEKENING VAN D'OUDE EN NIEUWE ... ROOJINGH DER STADT AMSTE

and presently the provision of hot water as well as cold water seems desirable. Such a level of bodily hygiene had never been reached before even among the upper classes: the pace of its introduction was undoubtedly quickened by the necessity for overcoming the disagreeable or dangerous effects of metropolitan living. As the installation of the bathroom becomes more elaborate, the cost of building per dwelling increases: hence an increasing constriction in room space sets in among the middle classes, who are the first to espouse frequent washing and bathing as necessities. A characteristic process: overt relief of the effects of congestion: *indirect increase of congestion itself.*

This flood of water cleanses the Augean metropolitan stable: so far well. For such cities as are exposed to military attack, however, it increases the precariousness of their existence in times of war. Not merely must the distant water supply be guarded against pollution; but the dams and pumping stations and viaducts must be guarded against bombing from the air. More than ever the water supply remains the key to permanent residence in cities; and since the very growth of the city blots out wells and defiles minor streams, there are no decentralized substitute sources worth speaking of. If the system as a whole does not work, the city will collapse. Should an enemy disorganize the water supply of the metropolis for as much as three days, the result would be a far more horrible loss of life than the worst conceivable vomit of poison gas from the skies.

The next important agent of congestion is the transportation system. In the early stages of metropolitan growth, this was met by the use of horse-drawn vehicles; and since the main metropolitan areas were laid out before 1900, it means that the entire street and avenue system had been designed for the use of carriages and wagons. As traffic increases, the elaboration of utilities follows: first macadam surfaces; later the wooden block; then asphalt. To keep these ways clean and clear, a public street-cleaning service must be supported: eventually, in the Northern cities, the cost of snow removal, in order to ensure regular transportation of goods and food, must be added, too.

An increase in transportation facilities, however, does not lessen congestion in the streets. Even with horse-drawn vehicles there were serious traffic difficulties in the first half of the nineteenth century: New York then experimented with creating a pedestrian's bridge over Broadway. Avenues must be widened: new avenues, more palatial in scale, must be broken through in order to make the necessary shortcuts and connections: sometimes solid blocks of buildings must be swept away. The extension of Seventh Avenue and the widening of Varick Street in New York cost over six million dollars a mile: the Wacker Drive in Chicago cost twenty-two million dollars a mile, while the double decking of Michigan Avenue cost sixteen million dollars a mile. These terrific costs put a serious curb on the wide reconstruction of the metropolis.

Where such improvements are financed, at least in part, by taxes and assessments against the properties benefited, they tend to produce a rise in rents, which in turn becomes capitalized in the form of higher land values. Result: more intensive uses, and in time the congestion thus produced results in a further traffic congestion that nullifies the improvement. No one has in fact suggested a means of providing these additional facilities for transportation without having precisely this effect upon taxes, upon land values, and upon occupancy. The burden of costs may be shifted; but the amount remains.

What holds of the street system holds even more of the mechanical transportation systems by subway and elevated railroad. Technically, these, too, are the pride and delight of the metropolis. With the coming of electric traction in the nineties large scale congestion became popular by multiplying tracks and trolleys on the surface of the town, and by building cuts and tunnels for sub-surface transportation. The architecture of the new stations, from the Paris Metro to Professor Grenander's handsome buildings in Berlin, or those of Adams, Holden and Pearson in London, are among the highest architectural achievements of the metropolis.

The result of all these assiduous attempts mechanically to mobilize and disperse, night and morning, the inhabitants of the metropolis is nevertheless plain: one and all, they have intensified the pattern of congestion. And the difference between the actual costs of transportation and the fares paid—about three cents in New York on every five cent fare—constitutes a public subsidy to the real estate speculator. Though such transportation systems open up new areas on the outskirts of the city, they but thicken the crowding at the center. Except for the Inner Circle Railway in London, metropolitan subway lines have been almost uniformly built so as to throw an *increasing* load of passengers into the central district. In the middle of the nineteen-twenties, as many as two million people came into Manhattan from the outlying boroughs and territories in a single day; and a good part of this traffic took place within the span of an hour and a half, morning and night.

Note the effect of all these new utilities as they cross and criss-cross, through and over and under the city. Beneath the visible city an invisible city grows apace: a buried city of water pipes and sewers and gas mains and electric cables and steam pipes and telephone wires and vast cellars where heat and electricity are produced for the buildings above: a city of ramifying subways and ominous tunnels in which the entire population spends no inconsiderable part of the day.

This underground city, growing step by step, followed the main outlines of the street-net on the surface. Because each property owner is a law unto himself, no attempt was made to work out a collective policy and a coherent plan which would enable this dual city growth to take place in an economic fashion. The necessary utility mains, which might have been carried through the cellars of buildings, are carried in the public territory occupied by the street: not merely is the cost of outside connections high, but no repair or change can be made in these utilities without periodically mangling the street and blocking the traffic.

Here is a paradox that runs through contemporary metropolitan civilization: the existence of a rational collective organization of the physical means of life without the necessary organs of collective asso‐ ciation and responsible social control. The result is that even in terms of purely mechanical efficiency the system is an extremely wasteful one.

In addition to these main public means of congestion, the metropo‐ lises of the Western World worked out a series of private means: vertical transportation by means of the elevator. Elevators were first used in this fashion in the early Manchester cotton factories; one of the first elevators to be run by steam power was that in the tower of the New York Crystal Palace in 1853, and shortly after the Civil War the first elevator was used in a New York apartment house. The example spread rapidly to the office building: it became the principal means, along with the steel-framed building, of increasing plot congestion. Until the first heights of building and setback ordinances were passed in New York in 1916, any individual owner was at liberty to overcrowd a site to a limit set only by the safety of the foundations and the superstructure. This vicious pattern has now become a symbol of material progress. For no reason at all, more than one recent housing project, in Rotterdam, in Paris, in Lyons, in Moscow, has copied these forms of metropolitan congestion. Even with the generous open spaces provided at Drancy, the achievement is as senseless as it is financially extravagant.

The result of such methods upon the transportation system was to increase the normal congestion by adding special pools and clots. The city plan worked out for New York in 1811, for example, was on the basis of four-story buildings. On those terms the street widths were adequate. In areas where buildings sixteen stories or more high came into existence, there was not enough land to provide sufficient streets alone, *without building sites*, on the previous scale. Fortunately for circulation, the *average* number of stories in New York remains today, despite skyscraper building, less than the number of Berlin or Paris.

The notion that vertical transportation relieves horizontal congestion is one of those desperate rationalizations that are sometimes put forward on behalf of a losing cause. Not merely does it promote an intensified use of the abutting streets and transportation lines: but it creates secondary forms of congestion within the building during the periods of maximum movement, at morning, noon, and night: hence further delays and stoppages.

5: The Costs of Costiveness

The facts of metropolitan congestion are undeniable. One reads them abstractly on the density maps and the transportation traffic maps: one participates in them in the clamor and the confusion of the streets: one encounters them in the constant stoppages of movement as one follows the traffic lights from one part of the city to the other; one becomes physically oppressed with the concrete fact of congestion in the crowded office elevator or in the even more tightly jammed subway train, rank with the odor of human bodies on a summer's evening. Congestion appears in the form of impeded movement and cramped space: lack of office room, lack of house-room: the universal presence of crowds. Such form as the metropolis achieves is crowd form: the procession on the Boardwalk at Coney Island, or the body of spectators in the boxing arena or the football stadium. To escape from these congested quarters requires skill and patience: *Watch your step! . . . What's your hurry?* Even the motor car, which originally carried with it the promise of swift movement and free command of space, becomes reduced, by the fact of congestion, to the limp of a faltering pedestrian. Confusion: constriction: costiveness—these are the typical by-products of metropolitan congestion. Those who seek to escape to larger quarters in the suburbs only serve to increase for those who remain the difficulty of getting beyond the spreading confines of the city.

Consider the costs of metropolitan congestion. We shall find that they are rising to a point that makes congestion financially unendurable, even if it were humanly tolerable.

The purely physical limits to metropolitan congestion are set mainly by three facts: the available amount of water, the point at which one metropolis begins to melt into a rival metropolis, and finally, the cost of mechanized transportation when the outskirts are too far from the center. But long before the first two points are reached, other serious handicaps enter.

First: the demand for water. As the metropolis absorbs more inhabitants, it must eat further back into its hinterland for water. In addition to the Croton system, New York was compelled to build the even grander Catskills system, tapping a source a hundred miles away. In less than twenty years, the need for a new source became evident: the city now reaches back for the waters of the Susquehanna River, claimed equally by the states of Pennsylvania and New Jersey. Each additional mile of tunnel and pipe, each additional reservoir, adds to the unit cost.

When the Regional Plan for New York made a study of the water system, it found that the cost of water during the decade of 1920 was between $35 and $65 per year per head. If the rate of growth then prevailing kept up, the cost by 1965 would reach $69 per inhabitant: in other words, a family of four would have, on a pro-rata basis, to pay $276 for water alone. This is almost as much as a good third of them can afford for the rent of their urban dwellings. The further increase of the use of water for industrial purposes, for bathing, and for air-conditioning will aggravate the need and raise the cost higher. Indeed, the latest toy of metropolitan engineering, air-conditioning, makes such huge demands for water that, if popularly adopted, it would almost be enough in itself to wreck municipal finances. Only its high upkeep per unit will forestall its collective collapse.

The cost of all the necessary transportation systems in a big city is equally massive: certain factors elude exact calculation. The initial capital cost, particularly for the underground systems, with their difficult tunneling and boring, is necessarily high: but this is only a part of the total expenses. Year by year one must add the cost of coal consumed in hauling around live human bodies: above all, one must add on the human cost, the physiological wear and tear, the psychological boredom and harassment and depression brought about by this daily shuttling between dormitory and workplace. Consider the number of man-hours reckoned in multiples of a million stupidly expended in the daily transportation of the human body: minutes and hours which, at the peak of traffic, cannot even be utilized in achieving the trivial anesthesia of the daily newspaper. Add to this the depression of the uncomfortable journey, the exposure to infectious diseases in the overcrowded car, the disturbance to the gastrointestinal functions caused by the strain and anxiety of having to reach the office or factory on time.

Emerson said that life was a matter of having good days; but it is a matter of having good minutes, too. Who shall say what compensations are not necessary to the metropolitan worker to make up for the strain and the depression of the twenty, forty, sixty minutes he spends each night and morning passing through these metropolitan man-sewers. A walk to work, as much as a mile each way, is at most seasons a tonic, particularly for the sedentary worker, who plays such a part even in the typical metropolitan industries: at the typewriter, the linotype machine, the sewing machine. In the subway, even more than in the water system and the sewage disposal system, one encounters a characteristic form of metropolitan waste: namely, *a vast expenditure of time, energy, money, human vitality upon an activity that has flatly no value in itself:* an activity whose main use is to uphold the crowd-prestige of the metropolis and increase the pecuniary values garnered by the ground landlords and the financiers.

The organized decentralization of industry and the building up of a series of sub-centers within what is now the metropolitan region would obviate a good part of metropolitan transportation. But this is impossible; for while congestion originally provided the excuse for the subway, the subway becomes the further excuse for congestion. An enlightened administrator like Mayor La Guardia may observe that he could do more effective improvement in a city with a million inhabitants than in one with five million; but that is not the metropolitan consensus. For congestion becomes frozen in the form of a price-pyramid: land rents and mortgages. Any attempt to reorganize the metropolis on rational lines threatens the stability of that pyramid: it would mean a collapse of values in the central area: a deflation of its putative claims on future wealth. For this reason almost every bank, every insurance company, every individual landowner, ultimately every savings bank depositor, has, as F. L. Ackerman has pointed out, a *stake in congestion.* The whole structure of our present pecuniary values and prestige values assumes the indefinite continuance of this metropolitan pattern.

All these hopes, however, are gigantic bubbles. During the last century, the costs of mechanical utilities necessary for a congested metropolitan existence have been steadily mounting. Hence, despite the fabulous riches that heap up in the metropolis, the municipality itself is constantly threatened with an expenditure out of all proportion to its income or its benefits. Failing to attack the problem of planning on the social and economic side, where alone effective control is possible, the metropolis fumbles with mechanical palliatives. The policy of living beyond its income, in the hope of making it up by further increases in population, which will bring in areas of taxation, is a chronic one in the metropolis: a habit imitated even by smaller cities with metropolitan pretensions. In America only an occasional city like Milwaukee is sufficiently free from these financial standards to show anything like solvency without piling up grievous social deficiencies. Actually, every new group of underpaid workers is a municipal liability: an extra tax on the budget.

And here finally is a new source of congestion. Each new utility requires a special corps of workers to build it and operate it, and a further increment of other workers to supply them with goods and services. Once the metropolis has reached a certain point of concentration, it tends to gather up population like a snowball rolling down hill: for the existence of an expanding market of consumers draws into the metropolitan area other industries, eager to take advantage of the concentrated market—and once again there is a demand for new transit routes, new municipal services, new housing. When the high costs of these municipal services no longer leave a profit for the enterpriser, the municipality itself assumes the burden: one might call this socialism by default. This change to collective ownership and the absence of profit does not improve the actual situation—in which vast sums of money are being expended to maintain a physical organization that should be decentralized and a structure of values that should be deflated.

And mark this: not merely does the cost of mechanical utilities rise directly with the size of the city: the cost of other municipal services rise, too. What is the social cost of robbery and other forms of crime? Robberies occur seven times as often in cities of over 250,000 population as in centers of 10,000: 189 people are known to the police per ten thousand in the bigger centers, as compared with 94 in smaller centers. This means more courts, more prisons, more policemen, more costly devices for maintaining what is hopefully called law and order.

Some of these costs of congestion must be borne directly by the citizens. Other costs are passed on in the form of higher prices for metropolitan products, even for products that are merely controlled financially by groups in the big center. But a large part of the burden is paid for in the form of deteriorated domestic quarters and poorer opportunities for living. The richest inhabitant of New York can afford a smaller patch of garden than the meanest inhabitant of many a country town: similarly the latter has often within sight and sound a refreshing environment that money cannot buy within the overgrown city. Sooner or later these costs and these deteriorations must be faced. When once such costly success is reduced to rational terms, the case for congestion is gone.

6: The Blighted Area

One must view the swift development of the metropolis from an ideal position in time and watch the transition that takes place over a period of a century. First the back gardens and the breathing spaces disappear, since the land is becoming too dear for such open areas: then the original residential areas are eaten into from within, as if by termites, as the original inhabitants move out and are replaced by lower economic strata: then these overcrowded quarters, serving as an area of transition between the commercial center and the better dormitory areas become in their disorder and their misery special breeding points for disease and crime: see the careful investigations of the Chicago sociologists. But every area in the metropolis tends to be a transitional area; and because of the very instability and uncertainty as to future uses, each area tends to go through a period in which the necessary repairs and renewals are not made. Since stability of uses and values means, from the commercial standpoint, a state little better than death, there is no motive in the existing economic regime sufficient to combat the habits that make for deterioration and blight.

The assumption upon which all this building is based is that population must continue to increase and values must vault skyward. The facts are that population may decrease, that values may go down, and that deterioration may be permanent. One can behold this contradiction at work in the zoning plans that have been popular in America during the last generation, following the example set by New York in 1916. Not merely do these zoning plans turn over to business and industrial uses from four to twenty times the area that could possibly be required at any future date, but they generously make provision for more intensive uses, when these are demanded by a sufficient number of owners, even though such uses would upset the general pattern that the city must rationally attempt to set up.

Moreover, none of these zoning ordinances suggest any practicable plan for deflating land values, thus permitting a change backward from a business to a residential use or from a tenement district to a park—although it is plain that sound adaptations to new needs must work both ways. The popular assumption is that values change in only one direction: upward.

But when blight sets in the opposite process happens. The inhabitants or the owners of buildings can no longer pay their share of municipal taxes; the street-cleaning department tends to overlook the more run-down neighborhoods, where the need for public hygiene is often worst, and even the fire inspectors and sanitary inspectors become lax: the repairs needed to keep blighted properties up to standard would do away with what little profits may remain in the investment, and so, by indifference or collusion or bribery, the city officials permit the blight to deepen. Roofs leak; plaster cracks on the walls; toilets fall into disrepair; pools of water gather in the cellar; the little patches of green, that once served as playgrounds, disappear, covered over with cinders, torn paper, discarded boxes, twisted bedsprings and broken iron. What may have been once a street of fine mansions—such as Euclid Avenue, Cleveland, or parts of the South Side in Chicago—is converted into low quarters, boarding houses and tenements, usually crowded, often filthy. The last stage is depopulation: deserted houses, in ruins: no rents: no taxes: a vast economic and civic liability.

The alternative to this form of progressive urban corrosion is the *standardization of blight.* The new-law tenement districts of the Bronx, the nearer one-family house districts of Queens, the sordid streets of Brixton or Clapham Junction, the tenements of Berlin and Hamburg and Paris built before the first World War—the difference between these structures and the blight that is produced by the piecemeal conversion of old structure is the difference between officially regulated prostitution, in segregated districts, and that which takes place at random. The most that is achieved in areas of regulated blight is an outward order and decency: but the content remains the same.

The fact is that these migrations of population and these alterations of use are inevitable consequences of metropolitan development under a capitalist system of production. For the rotten conditions near the center of the metropolis cause a flow into the outlying areas, to what seem by contrast better quarters. When these become built up, covered over, and run down, when their surrounding open spaces disappear by reason of the very movement they have attracted, those who can afford to jump once more beyond the pale of blight. But high land values tend to draw heavy industries that need more land to spread on toward the periphery of the metropolis: so the pressure at the center forms a new circle of blight; and rim developments are often as foul as those in the central area. Paris and London perhaps show these tendencies to a lesser degree than New York, Chicago and Philadelphia: but it is visible, through change of fashion or pressure of commercial competition, around the Place des Vosges or Berkeley Square.

Many observers of cities, as well as political administrators, tend to look upon the existence of blighted areas as an accidental fact in the modern city's development. On the contrary, the congestion of population at the center and the effort to compensate for instability by adding to the existing population, gives a large part of the building a purely transitory character: it is assumed that people will move in and out, that small businesses will eat into residential areas, that every residential street will be, potentially at least, a traffic and trading street, and that small stores and shops may, at some unpredictable point in space and time, be replaced by a department store or an office building. To plan a residential area so that it could only with great difficulty and wholesale changes be converted into any other kind of area is foreign to the metropolitan municipal engineer's mind. In this matter, a new order was instituted in London after 1910, in Amsterdam after 1920, and in other big cities at still later dates: but it has yet to become a dominant one, even in London, where re-building has been pushed most vigorously.

The blighted area may be defined as an area which is chronically unable to pay its share of the municipal services essential to its existence, and unable by reason of its economic status to pay for its own internal renovation and repair. All working class neighborhoods are by sheer poverty in a state of blight because, in the more outlying areas, the cost of the utilities that connect them with the center has risen steadily without any coeval rise in the income or economic privileges of the inhabitants; while in the center only intensive congestion of the foulest sort will "pay its way."

7: The Acceptance of Depletion

In the original urban formation, the central institutions of the city bear a direct relation to its whole population. Even when organized in quarters, with separate parish churches and subordinate markets, the central institutions are within walking distance. As the city increases in size, however, these central institutions occupy a relatively less important place in the active life of the citizens. (Observing this, the General Assembly of Massachusetts in the seventeenth century ordered that no one should live more than half a mile from his Common, lest he fail in his civic obligations.) In the metropolis, institutions that originally served 100,000 people fail to meet the needs of ten times that number. Even if the city only doubled in size, such institutes would fail merely by reason of internal congestion.

Now, the fact is that metropolitan expansion is accompanied by a permanent lag in building up the necessary communal institutions in the outlying sections: this, in fact, is one of the typical features of the sordid blighted areas: neglect by absence or by disuse. In such depressed quarters one may sometimes wander about for half a mile in any direction without finding a school, a public library, a playground, a firehouse, even a motion picture theater or a church: when one exists, it will be a makeshift.

In fact, just the opposite tendency exists: there is an increasing dearth of facilities. In other words, the Central District is the only part of the metropolis that really functions with anything like full efficiency, and it functions with respect to the needs of only a minority of the total population. Such an arrangement may satisfy the special interests of minorities: the music lover in the metropolis, for example, will have his desires sated in a fashion that the provincial center—*under a metropolitan economy*—can rarely afford. But as far as the diffusion of the highest metropolitan standards among every part of the population goes, the outcome is a mockery. The

cultural standard is little higher than the housing standard: slum-
level.

What is called the "growth" of the metropolis is in fact the constant recruitment of a proletariat, capable of accommodating itself
to an environment without adequate natural or cultural resources:
people who do without pure air, who do without sound sleep, who do
without a cheerful garden or playing space, who do without the very
sight of the sky and the sunlight, who do without free motion, spontaneous play, or a robust sexual life. The so-called blighted areas of
the metropolis are essentially *"do without"* areas. If you wish the
sight of urban beauty while living in these areas, you must ride in
a bus a couple of miles: if you wish a touch of nature, you must
travel in a crowded train to the outskirts of the city. Lacking the
means to get out, you succumb: chronic starvation produces lack of
appetite. Eventually, you may live and die without even recognizing
the loss.

The same rule—"growth by civic depletion"—holds true for the
provision of hospitals and playing fields and concert halls and colleges. These institutions often increase in size in order to measure up
to megalopolitan standards; but what is true for biological organisms
holds true, it would appear, for social bodies: effective growth requires cell-division, not merely a swelling of the original nucleus.
A parish church in a village of five hundred might hold a hundred
people, perhaps a crowded two hundred at one time. A hall that
holds three thousand people might be adequate for a town with fifty
thousand inhabitants; but it certainly cannot do justice to a city that
holds a dozen times that number. The streets alone can hold such
crowds: and unlike the medieval city, the metropolis is too huge to
give a direct sense of unity to those who gather on the streets for a
great celebration: no one can see or know what takes place in the
city at large without listening to the radio and consulting the newspaper.

Moreover, beyond a certain point, even mechanical devices demand
a limitation in size. With the use of loud speakers, the visible
presence of a speaker is futile in an arena so large that most of the
members of the audience are too far away to observe his expression
or even follow his gestures. One of the reasons that passive sports,

which put the emphasis upon the spectator, occupy such a large place in metropolitan routine is that the choice is one between vicarious exercise or none at all. Forty-five thousand people may attend a baseball game: but not even Chicago could boast the twenty-five hundred diamonds that would be necessary if each spectator claimed the right to play.

When institutions are planned rationally for convenience and for functional use, the metropolitan pattern does not suffice. To achieve a functional relationship, the unit has to be scaled to actual working capacity: reproduction rather than growth is what is required, while the effect of unified growth can be achieved through the orderly integration of the separate units. Where inorganic expansion of mechanical facilities takes place, a chronic deficiency results. The size of the building or the institution becomes a mere mask for this deficiency. Fifty thousand people gathered in a single place can do fewer things together than twenty-five groups of two thousand: their chief function is limited to *being* there and saying Hurrah! or Heil! at the right moment. That is why dictators love crowds and seek to provide bigger arenas and auditoriums for them: the bigger the crowd, the emptier their function.

Just as the great financial achievements of the metropolitan economy are based in part upon the monopoly of territories and raw materials, upon the exploitation of a growing urban proletariat, upon the transformation of the independent farmer into the tenant farmer, so its great achievements in urban growth are based upon the acceptance of blighted and sub-standard areas within the city: areas that are suburban, not because they are close to the countryside, but because they are below the current norms of civilization.

The very giantism of the metropolis leads to a depletion of its environment. On the surface, the massing of two or three million people within a relatively small central area should promote social intercourse; but except in the slums, where misery enforces a sort of neighborliness, there is a greater field for collective action in a village, for the ordinary man and woman, than there is in the most congested area. Complexity of organization does not necessarily mean richness and effectiveness of association: the mechanical principle of efficiency, which governs the first, as in a well-articulated factory, may actually obstruct the second: it is, in fact, where mechanical organization is *defective*, as in the queue waiting for a bus, that intercourse and association spontaneously awaken.

Beyond a certain point, density even obstructs association: if friendship requires a degree of isolated communion, so does neighborliness. There is less chance of knowing your neighbors on a block with a thousand people than on one that holds a hundred; for all association, even that in primary groups, has a selective aspect: it rests on the existence of recognizable faces and repeatable opportunities. Distance has an effect similar to density in breaking down associated life.

Neither the telephone nor the radio has diminished the importance of spatial nearness for all primary forms of intercourse. People who live in Oak Park and the South Side, in East Boston and Arlington, are nominally members of the same metropolitan complex: but for practical purposes they are sundered more effectively than if they were separated by three times these distances in the open country. Consider the difficulty of keeping the members of a trade union actively concerned in the affairs of their union, when, in order to attend to these affairs in the evening, they must either make the journey back again to the city from the dormitory where they live, at a great waste of time, sometimes with unendurable further fatigue, or they must remain in the center, at the cost of a meal which, even at its simplest, must be reckoned with seriously in a narrow budget. Small wonder that apathy sets in; or, to put it in its best light, that domesticity takes precedence over an effective political life.

At all events, in every metropolitan association, a social club, a museum, a trade union, a professional society, it is notorious that a small group tends to dominate its activities—usually composed of those who, either by topographical advantage, or by command of special means of transportation, are able to remain working at the center without undue sacrifice.

It is impossible here to go into all the perversions and miscarriages of civic functions because of the physical spread and the congestion and mis-planning of the mass city: hospitals placed on noisy dusty thoroughfares: overgrown schools so separated from the open country or even from parks that a bus-ride is necessary to introduce the pupils to the most rudimentary connections with living creatures and living plants: the emotional depression that follows the transition from a symphony concert to a crowded subway train: the discouragement to study when a student must travel an hour and a half each day on a subway train between his home and his high school.

The physical drain, the emotional defeat, of these cramped quarters, these dingy streets, the tear and noise of transit—these are but the most obvious results of megalopolitan growth: many of them cast a shadow upon the prosperous and the successful as well as upon the submerged members of the proletariat. For what the metropolis gives with one hand, it takes back with the other: one climbs its golden tree with such difficulty that, even if one succeeds in plucking the fruit, one can no longer enjoy it: the most successful of megalopolitans, wishing for life in his limbs, must take refuge in a country estate, or forego its advantages for Florida, Africa, the Riviera.

8: Defacement of Nature

Meanwhile, the urban agglomeration produces a similar depletion in the natural environment. Nature, except in a surviving landscape park, is scarcely to be found near the metropolis: if at all, one must look overhead, at the clouds, the sun, the moon, when they appear through the jutting towers and building blocks. The blare of light in the evening sky blots out half the stars overhead: the rush of sewage into the surrounding waters converts rivers into open sewers, drives away the more delicate feeders among the fish, and infects the bathers in the waters with typhoid: through the greater part of the nineteenth century typhoid was an endemic disease in big cities, brought in with the food supply, the shellfish, if not absorbed directly from the colon bacilli in the bathing or drinking water.

If the metropolis attempts to counteract these evils, it can do so only at a vast outlay: stations where the water is filtered and chlorinated, plants where the sewage is reduced and converted into fertilizer bring additional items of expense to the budget. If some isolated beauty in nature is preserved as a park, like the Bear Mountain Park, outside New York, it will be at a distance that requires half a morning to reach, even from the center of the city. When one arrives there one will find that a multitude of other people, equally eager to escape the metropolis, have by their presence created another metropolis—if not a wilderness-slum. One will see nature through the interstices of their bodies.

Indeed, the only successful metropolitan recreation grounds are those that accept the fact of overcrowding and give it appropriate form: a Wannseebad in Berlin, or a Jones Beach on Long Island: a vast stretch of waterfront domed by a vaster sky, well-organized, efficiently policed, with thousands of automobiles drawn up in ranks, giant pavilions, scores of assiduous life-guards on spidery towers, thousands of bathers basking in the sun and watching each other. A great mass spectacle: perhaps the nearest approach to genuine life, life esthetically intensified and ordered, that the metropolis offers.

As the pavement spreads, nature is pushed farther away: the whole routine divorces itself more completely from the soil, from the visible presence of life and growth and decay, birth and death: the slaughterhouse and the cemetery are equally remote, and their processes are equally hidden. The ecstatic greeting of life, the tragic celebration of death, linger on merely as mumbled forms in the surviving churches. The rhythm of the seasons disappears, or rather, it is no longer associated with natural events, except in print. Millions of people grow up in this metropolitan milieu who know no other environment than the city streets: people to whom the magic of life is represented, not by the miracles of birth and growth, but by placing a coin in a slot and drawing out a piece of candy or a prize. This divorce from nature has serious physiological dangers that the utmost scruples of medical care scarcely rectify. For all its boasted medical research, for all its real triumphs in lessening the incidence of disease and prolonging life, the city must bow to the countryside in the essentials of health: almost universally the expectation of life is greater in the latter, and the effect of deteriorative diseases is less.

But how find the country? The depletion of the metropolis does not stop at the legal boundaries of the metropolis: urban blight leads to rural blight. Since 1910 or thereabouts, the highways of motor traffic have begun to spread out from every metropolis in ever thickening and multiplying streams: these highways carry with them the environment of the metropolis: the paved highway, the filling station, the roadside slum, the ribbon development of houses, the roadhouse and cabaret. The farther and faster one travels, the more the life that accompanies one remains like that one has left behind. The same standardization of ugliness: the same mechanical substitutes: the same cockney indifference to nature: the same flippant attitude: the same celluloid pleasures and canned noise. A row of bungalows in the open country alongside an express highway is a metropolitan fact: so are the little heaps of week-end cabins by lake or stream or oceanside. Their density and concentration may not be greater than that of a rural village: but in their mode of life, their amusements, their frame of social reference, they are entirely metropolitan: hardly better or worse for being fifty miles away from the center.

Under this regime, every environment bears the same taint: its abiding picture of life is colored by the same newspapers, the same magazines, the same moving pictures, the same radio. Dependent upon the metropolitan markets for current cash, the outlying farming regions, mining centers, and industrial areas are all under the sway of metropolitan interests. What is not metropolitan is either the original bequest of nature, often neglected, misused, rundown, or a relic of an historical past when the community once showed an autonomous and autochthonous life. But the rural regions and the provincial towns taste only the metropolitan skimmed milk: the cream has been mechanically separated for the benefit of the big city. The provincial town now faces a poverty, or at least an impecuniousness, that is without the vicarious enjoyments of the metropolis, and without the residue of philanthropies, trusts, foundations, which provide the hospitals and libraries and institutions of learning in the big city: residual pledges of a better life.

The inhabitants of these rural areas, indeed, are taught to despise their local history, to avoid their local language and their regional accents, in favor of the colorless language of metropolitan journalism: their local cooking reflects the gastronomic subterfuges of the suburban woman's magazines; their songs and dances, if they survive, are elbowed off the dance floor: at best are given an audition at a metropolitan cabaret or radio station, where they are driven to

an early death by universal repetition. The whole moral of this
metropolitan regime is that one does not live, truly live, unless one
lives in the metropolis or copies closely, abjectly, its ways. Expensive ways: ways that may be turned into monetary profits for the
benefits of those who have a capital stake in the regime and who
live in the light of its reflected glory. This moral is implanted by
education, driven home by advertisement, spread by propaganda:
life means metropolitan life. Not merely is the exodus to the city
hastened, but the domination of the surviving countryside is assured:
the same hand, as it were, writes the songs and lays down the terms
for the mortgage.

In short: to scorn one's roots in one's own region and admiringly
to pluck the paper flowers manufactured and sold by the metropolis
becomes the whole duty of man. Though the physical radius of the
metropolis may be only twenty or thirty miles, its effective radius is
much greater: its blight is carried in the air, like the spores of a
mold. The outcome is a world whose immense potential variety, first
fully disclosed to man during the nineteenth century, has been sacrificed to a low metropolitan standardization. A rootless world, removed from the sources of life: a Plutonian world, in which living
forms become frozen into metal: cities expanding to no purpose,
cutting off the very trunk of their regional existence, defiling their
own nest, reaching into the sky after the moon: more paper profits,
more vicarious substitutes for life. Under this regime more and more
power gets into hands of fewer and fewer people, ever further and
further away from reality.

9: The Paper Dream City

When one examines the state of the metropolis one discovers a
curious hallucination: the notion that its size, power, mechanical
equipment and riches have effected a corresponding improvement
in the life of its inhabitants. What is the mechanism of this error?
We shall find it in the pseudo-environment of paper.

To believe that civilization has reached a culmination in the modern metropolis one must avert one's eyes from the concrete facts
of metropolitan routine. And that is precisely what the metropolitan
schools himself to do: he lives, not in the real world, but in a shadow

world projected around him at every moment by means of paper and celluloid: a world in which he is insulated by glass, rubber, cellophane, from the mortifications of living. When the metropolitan lives most keenly, he lives by means of paper. The classic caricature of this tendency was given by Samuel Butler. When he took his man, Alfred, a perfect cockney, to the peaks of the High Alps to show him the overpowering landscape, Alfred gave the scene a bored glance and said: "And now, if you please, Sir, I should like to lie down on the grass here and have a read of Tit-Bits."

The swish and crackle of paper is the underlying sound of the metropolis: more important to the inner content of its existence than the whining rhythm of its machines. What is visible and real in this world is only what has been transferred to paper. The essential gossip of the metropolis is no longer that of people meeting face to face on the crossroads, at the dinner table, in the market-place: a few dozen people writing in the newspapers, a dozen more broadcasting over the radio, provide the daily interpretation of movements and happenings. The principle of concentrated propaganda and irresponsible dictatorship is written over the popular intellectual activities of the metropolis: in its evaluations, no less than in its deliberate suppressions. It is a short step from a yellow journal proprietor, skillfully manufacturing the day's news, to a propaganda ministry in a war government or a fascist dictatorship. Was it not from the commercial advertisers that political governments perhaps learned not to argue about the merits of their actions, but to keep on asserting with forceful insolence whatever they wanted the public to believe?

All the major activities of the metropolis are directly connected with paper; and printing and packaging are among its principal industries. The activities pursued in the offices of the metropolis are directly connected with paper: the tabulating machines, the journals, the ledgers, the card-catalogs, the deeds, the contracts, the mortgages: so, too, the prospectus, the advertisement, the magazine, the newspaper. As early as the eighteenth century Mercier had observed this metropolitan form of the White Plague. Modern methods of manifolding have not lessened the disease: they have only changed easygoing slipshod ways, that often sufficed, for forms of exact record that are economically out of all proportion to the intrinsic importance of the matter recorded. What was a mere trickle in Mercier's day has now become a ravaging flood of paper.

As the day's routine proceeds the pile of paper mounts higher: the trashbaskets are filled and emptied and filled again. The ticker tape exudes its quotations of stocks and its reports of news; the students in the schools and universities fill their notebooks, digest and disgorge the contents of books, as the silkworm feeds on mulberry leaves and manufactures its cocoon, unraveling themselves on examination day. Buildings rise recklessly, often in disregard of ultimate profits, in order to provide an excuse for paper capitalizations and paper rents. In the theater, in literature, in music, in business, reputations are made—on paper. The scholar with his degrees and publications, the actress with her newspaper clippings, and the financier with his shares and voting proxies, measure their power and importance by the amount of paper they can command. No wonder the anarchists once invented the grim phrase: "Incinerate the documents!" That would ruin this whole world quicker than universal flood and earthquake.

The event in the newsreel, the drama on the motion picture screen, the disembodied speech of the radio announcer: this is the "eye of the world" and the "voice of experience" and the "march of time." The words and actions of men are more and more framed for their effect on paper: or they are posed, with a view to historical reproduction, in the photograph and the motion picture. That life is an occasion for living, and not a pretext for supplying items to newspapers or spectacles for crowds of otherwise vacant bystanders —these notions do not occur to the metropolitan mind. For the denizens of this world are at home only in the ghost city of paper: they live in a world of "knowledge about," as William James would have said, and they daily drift farther away from the healthy discipline of first-hand "acquaintance with."

Hence the importance of statistics. The principal achievements that quicken the metropolitan mind are quantitative ones: record-breaking in some fashion or another. Size competition is indeed the very mode of metropolitan expansion: a forty-story building is *ipso facto* a more important building than a two-story one, and a

university teaching ten thousand students is similarly more important than one teaching ten hundred. If these were not axioms in
the metropolitan mind it might be a prey to occasional doubts about
its own importance. To lop a quarter of a second off the running of
a mile, to sit on a flagpole three days longer than a rival, to graduate
so many hundred more bachelors of art a year, to build a building
ten stories higher than the nearest rival—these are typical metropolitan records—important only on paper. Metropolitans flout the
wise Biblical story of the king who insisted on counting his army.

This metropolitan world, then, is a world where flesh and blood
is less real than paper and ink and celluloid. It is a world where the
great masses of people, unable to have direct contact with more satis-
fying means of living, take life vicariously, as readers, spectators,
passive observers: a world where people watch shadow-heroes and
heroines in order to forget their own clumsiness or coldness in love,
where they behold brutal men crushing out life in a strike riot, a
wrestling ring or a military assault, while they lack the nerve even
to resist the petty tyranny of their immediate boss: where they
hysterically cheer the flag of their political state, and in their neighborhood, their trades union, their church, fail to perform the most
elementary duties of citizenship.

Living thus, year in and year out, at second hand, remote from
the nature that is outside them and no less remote from the nature
within, handicapped as lovers and as parents by the routine of the
metropolis and by the constant specter of insecurity and death that
hovers over its bold towers and shadowed streets—living thus the
mass of inhabitants remain in a state bordering on the pathological.
They become the victims of phantasms, fears, obsessions, which bind
them to ancestral patterns of behavior. At the very point where super-
mechanization takes hold of economic production and social intercourse, a treacherous superstition, a savage irrationality, reappear
in the metropolis. But these reversionary modes of behavior, though
they are speedily rationalized in pseudo-philosophies, do not remain
on paper: they seek an outlet. The sadistic gangster, the bestial
fascist, the homicidal vigilante, the law-offending policeman burst
volcanically through the crust of metropolitan life. They challenge
the dream city with an even lower order of "reality."

10: The Acquisitiveness of a Sick Metropolis

Over many precarious millenniums man's acquisitiveness has stood
him in good stead. Where nature's terms were hard the very restriction over the food supply and production placed a natural limit on
his tendency to gather and hoard: there was safety in nature's niggardliness. His habits were as innocent as the bee's or the squirrel's.

Capitalism made a special virtue of this tendency to store up food
and seed: only instead of vital goods, it substituted money, and so
far from hoarding money, like the miser, it sent it forth in order to
multiply itself in "gainful employment." Buying and selling ceased
to be agents of consumption: they were important as mechanisms of
profit. Consumption was confined, beyond the immediate wants of
the body, to those who commanded capital, acquired profits, and
were ready to consume with voracity. Once such attitudes became respectable, any scheme that kept human wants stationary or that encouraged a wantless life—the bias of a St. Francis or a Thoreau—
became a blasphemous rejection of the new gods. For a wantless
life means a marketless productive system: whereas stability in investment for profit demanded the concoction of fresh wants and the
continuous expansion of the market.

The expansion of the market has been one of the most characteristic attributes of the metropolitan regime: it is involved in the
whole scheme of substituting vicarious satisfactions for direct ones,
and money goods for life experiences. By the eighteenth century
the public markets and producers' shops of the medieval town were
being converted into specialized shops under continuous operation.
Even at this early date in Paris, in the reign of Louis XV, a banker
named Kromm founded a department store with some two or three
hundred employees. In 1844 a modern department store, the Ville
de France, opened in Paris with a hundred and fifty employees on
its staff.

If the vitality of an institution may be gauged by its architecture,
the department store was one of the most vital institutions in this
metropolitan regime. One of the first large buildings to employ iron
columns instead of a masonry wall was the A. T. Stewart department
store in New York; while Schinkel's design for a Berlin department

Political capitals: emblems of worldwide exploitation. Here political and financial power is concentrated: here the forces that parade as "national history"—a minor fragment of the total life of peoples and cities and regions—take shape. But the day of these dinosaur cities is over: their burdens outweigh their benefits. The orderly breakup of their unwieldy structures, and the reconstitution of their power and culture on a federal basis is one of the major tasks of urbanism.

[TOP] London, facing the Thames, with the relatively new Kingsway cutting through the partial order of Bloomsbury from Southampton Row, terminating in Bush House and the crescent of Aldwych. An imperial avenue, naturally lined with business offices of overseas corporations. Beautiful survivals of an older London however remain: the spacious quadrangles of the Temple by the Thames on the left, and the orderly building and gracious verdure of the Bloomsbury Squares of the foreground mingle with the irregular clottings of buildings in the uncontrolled spaces between. (*Photograph: Ewing Galloway, Aerofilms*)

[MIDDLE LEFT] Berlin: the formidable barracks city on the Spree: combination of Preussentum and Spekulantentum: also Junker arrogance and Slavonic servility. Imposing order in its public buildings and systematic foulness in its old rear court tenements. Its brief renascence as a more humane type of city coincided with the life-span of the German republic, with its temporary release from military preoccupations. The parks and housing communities created between 1920 and 1932, especially developments like Britz, Zehlendorf, and Siemensstadt, set a new standard in collective planning toward beauty and efficiency: a happy humane contrast with the grandiose triumphal ways and mass-squares planned by the later National Socialist regime. (*Photograph: Ewing Galloway*)

[MIDDLE RIGHT] Madrid: perched like a spider in the midst of a transportation web: originally a symbol of irregional unification, in defiance of the Basques, Catalans, Andalusians: transformed through the brutal Fascist uprising of 1936 into a symbol of Federal unity and democratic hope. The heroic resistance of Madrid's population to the systematic massacre of women and children conducted by the Fascists is a proof of those enduring human qualities that neither metropolitanism nor fascism can permanently wipe out: symbol of human vitality, human nobility, human sacrifice, capable of creating a new civilization. (*Photograph: Ewing Galloway*)

[BOTTOM] Rome: approach to St. Peter's seen from the Cathedral itself: pointing toward the Tiber, but suddenly cut short in its attempt to impose order by the historic tangle of buildings that blocks the connection. The memory of imperial destiny, the visible reminder of a splendid past—with a certain amnesia as to the causes of its downfall—recurs in the dreams of a Dante, a Rienzi, a Mussolini: it even seizes an alien race in the nineteenth century concept of the Pax Britannica. (*Photograph: Ewing Galloway*)

[TOP LEFT] Beginning of the typical metropolitan day: descent into Hades: in this instance the Paris Metro, with Art Nouveau decoration in iron that marks the neotechnic phase of subway building: the first underground being a coal-smudged inferno built in London in 1860. Underground quarters become part of the normal environment of the metropolis: repeated in effect even above ground. (*Photograph: Ewing Galloway*)

[SECOND LEFT] New York: Orpheus and Eurydice in the Kingdom of Pluto. The photograph is unavoidably idyllic: an actual subway crush effectually prevents the use of a camera. Rushing beneath geological strata, rivers, tall buildings, avenues, the fortunate travelers who have seats struggle to assimilate the day's dispersed events recorded in the newspaper. For those who stand, the subway becomes a cloister: a place of enforced inactivity and contemplation: if you will, a traveling prison. The acceptance of this environment, as a necessity of daily life, is perhaps no more singular than the acceptance of a day that includes no glimpse of the sun, no taste of the wind, no smell of earth or growing things, no free play of the muscles, no spontaneous pleasure not planned for a week in advance and recorded on a memorandum pad: in short, that day without an hour given to sauntering, which so amazed and horrified Henry Thoreau. Hence the need for synthetic stimuli. (*Photograph: Ewing Galloway*)

[MIDDLE RIGHT] London. Alternatives: a crowded bus, creeping through congested streets, spreading petrol fumes and the more deadly odorless carbon monoxide: or a railroad journey, over a longer distance, from a suburb, to the "City," over whose confusion hangs the dome of St. Paul's. (*Photograph: Ewing Galloway*)

[BOTTOM] Leipziger Strasse, Berlin: showing trolley cars and commercial buildings. The central district with its quick tempo, its strained concentration upon pecuniary affairs. Not as chaotic as an American metropolis, with its indiscriminate congestion: but scarcely less obsolete from the standpoint of working efficiency. (*Photograph: Ewing Galloway*)

[TOP RIGHT] Well-to-do suburb of London: Wimbledon. The development of a central district devoted to business, finance, and the accessory industries has its typical by-product: the dormitory suburb. The rapid growth of metropolitan districts in the twentieth century has been mainly a suburban growth: migration (encouraged by land speculators) to cheaper land, open spaces, temporarily more decent living conditions. In the obsolete mono-nucleated type of city this decentralization and dispersal of the main functions of urban living merely increases the extent of the waste and human wear-and-tear. In its ideal form, with large houses, spacious lawns and gardens, tree-bordered streets, the suburb is an upper class luxury. The great mass of the population, lured out to the periphery of the metropolis, get no closer to Wimbledon than the Long Island example shown on Plate 21: a mockery of the free standing house, the individual garden. (*Photograph: Aerofilms*) store in the eighteen-thirties, though never executed, was far ahead of the labored traditionalism of Messel's overpraised Wertheim store in Berlin. Finally, one of the best utilitarian buildings of the early twentieth century, a radical departure in design, was the Schlesinger and Meyer Building (now Carson, Pirie, and Scott) in Chicago.

Now, the department store is the spender's paradise. For a long while luxury spending, with its made-to-order goods, remained in small specialized shops: this holds even today on New Bond Street, the Rue de la Paix, and Madison Avenue. Below this level of expense, the department store has flourished; for it offers the buyer the greatest possible number of wares under one roof: it diversifies the temptations to buy at the same time as it concentrates the opportunity: sometimes it even adds to the normal routine of spending and sampling the vehement competition of the bargain counter. As the household industries disappeared from the metropolitan dwelling, and as household routines became more simplified, not less by the reduction of domestic space than by labor-saving devices, middle class mothers and daughters needed a fresh occupation. They found it in shopping: counter-shopping and window-shopping. On a Saturday night in an industrial town the flow of people through the main shopping street is the principal form of recreation and drama. The ultimate symbol of this acquisitive life was that final product of the metropolitan regime: the five-and-ten-cent store, which opened up this typical bourgeois excitement even to the very poor.

Each practical manifestation of a culture tends to leave a shadow-self in the mind: this may be the result of the economic institution itself, or it may issue out of the same cultural complex that created it. A whole series of such parallels exist in the spiritual life of the metropolis: one may accept them, without committing oneself to a purely materialist interpretation of culture. What is the big metropolitan university but a megalopolis of learning, a great cartel formed by the financial unification of a diversity of foundations and schools. With its jumble of buildings, its mechanical methods of intercourse, its mass production of students, its intellectual bookkeeping by points and credits, the overswollen university is the exact counterpart of the metropolitan life for which it prepares its students from all over the land. The universities of Chicago, Berlin, and

London have been built up during the last fifty years in the faithful
image of the city that surrounds them: the same technical adroitness,
the same aggressive emphasis on physical equipment, the same waste
of substance in material organization, and finally, the same innocence
of cultural values that are embodied, not in statistical achievements,
but in a mode of feeling, thinking, acting.

Similarly the department store, as Mr. Lee Simonson has pointed
out, has its exact counterpart in the big metropolitan museum. Culture and knowledge are regarded from this standpoint mainly as
a means of acquisitions and display. Historically the contents of the
art museum derive from the palace and the country house: displays
of loot that mark either ostentatious purchase or the military conquest
of foreign lands. (The form of the natural history museum is still
largely that of the trophy room of the country house, where the hunter
displays his horns, pelts, and skeletons.) In time, genuine esthetic and
scientific interests develop in these institutions; but the trustees of
the museums are more interested in abstract acquisition and honorific
display than in matters of truth, taste, and value. Physical size serves
again as a *substitute* for organization, as in the labor market: mechanical expansion is confused with significance.

No doubt the big museum may serve a rational function: but the
popular interest in it is a by-product of the search for pecuniary
profits that characterizes even the remoter provinces of this pecuniary
metropolitan culture. By the patronage of the museums, the ruling
metropolitan oligarchy of financiers and officeholders establish their
own claims to culture: more than that, they fix their own standards
of taste, morals, and learning as that of their civilization—thus
maintaining and stabilizing the favored pattern of acquisitive living.
Even when the patron is the municipality, the same ingrained habits
prevail: the worth of the museum will be gauged by the size of its
collections and the number of people who visit it. Consider the
monstrous installation of the Pergamon altar in Berlin: a vulgar
triumph.

Patrons and public alike, these *nouveaux riches* of the metropolis
are culture-shoppers. They tend to transform the chief institutions
of learning into vast department stores of the arts and sciences, where
everything is ticketed and labeled, where bargain attractions are

offered, where the turnover of goods is more important than the ultimate satisfactions of the purchaser. The growing bewilderment of the student and spectator, the patent sterility of his acquired knowledge and taste—none of these facts interferes with the tendency toward expansion. In the sciences, outside the museum, a systematic rationale has been laid down since the seventeenth century. But this fundamental order cannot be detected in the badly organized and feebly related collections of the great museums: on the contrary, the total impression is that of chaos, modified by good intentions and incidental patches of order. This chaos reflects accurately, not so much the state of science or historical research, as the disorganized contents of the metropolis itself.

Is there a single metropolitan museum of art or natural history in the world that could not profit enormously by being decentralized, with each unit reduced to a modicum of its present size, and completely reorganized? That the museum is a valuable type of cultural enterprise I have no doubt: in the final chapter of this book I shall, indeed, sketch out briefly its place in a genuine civic economy. But at present all its valid purposes are corrupted by the fact that its standards are, frankly, those of the department store: the lure of many unrelated articles and their random purchase, all under one roof. Around the art museum, an antique art market grows up, abetted by the instincts of the rich, for whom rarity has a market value apart from any other token of value: a rare wood carving is no less valuable than a rare postage stamp. When the supply of genuine antiques dwindles, copies are forged—or new reputations among modern artists are manufactured to take the place of the old. Sometimes the forgeries are consummately executed and deceive the experts who examine them: but their worth hangs, not on their esthetic merit, but on their genuineness: if that is demolished, they become worthless. To acquire goods without having contributed an iota of thought or energy to their production is the mark of metropolitan success. To acquire knowledge and taste without a single first-hand experience, such as that possessed by the artist and the craftsman and the woodsman and the hunter and the scientist is the mark of cultural acquisition as fostered, for the greater part, by the metropolitan museum.

Here, as elsewhere in the metropolis, there are counter-initiatives that throw a more favorable light over the picture, such as the redoubtable work done by the school extension department of the American Museum of Natural History in Manhattan, and similar attempts to decentralize and re-focus the museum's resources in other institutions. But the main outlines still hold. Aimless acquisition: reckless expansion: progressive disorganization—these are the dominating facts, and they bring their own nemesis.

11: Routine and Relaxation

Economically, the metropolis may be described as the urban embodiment of the international fair. Its routine is subordinate to the exhibition and sale of goods. But the fair has two sides: business and pleasure; and as business takes on a more abstract form, with greater stress on monetary manipulation, regularity, mechanism, mathematical discipline, the need for compensatory relief becomes greater. The traditional pleasures of the fair—jugglers, acrobats, gamblers, sideshows, sexual license of all sorts—cease to be sporadic: they too become part of the metropolitan routine. The metropolis itself may be described as a World's Fair in continuous operation.

Even in earlier days, fairs served in something the same fashion as national conventions and congresses do today: they provided suitable opportunities for relaxation from the strict observance of family ties, local customs, respectable ways. Indeed, the old St. James's Fair in London was closed by one of the most lascivious monarchs of England, Charles II, because of the excess of bawdy entertainment; while in great Nizhni Novgorod, at the end of the nineteenth century, the poorer prostitutes conducted their rites in public under the open sky: shouting their wares to the passer-by. In the metropolis the usual excess of unmarried males helps further to build up a whole fabric of institutions based upon the commercial exploitation of sexual interests: whore-houses, dance halls, burlesque shows and girl shows, houses of assignation and hotels that serve the casual couple.

These elements of the fair all become systematized, standardized, commercialized. Every step in relaxation from spontaneous horseplay to drunkenness, from flirtation with music to a sexual orgy, is conducted with a view toward producing a maximum profit for the enterpriser. Saturnalia charges what the traffic will bear. Bawdiness, no longer the goatlike outburst of animal spirits after the abstentions and rigors of the winter, becomes in itself a jaded, night-in-night-out part of metropolitan routine: it measures its titillations and charges accordingly. And since the overt code of Western society has no place for such compensatory outbursts or moral holidays, an additional air of furtiveness hangs over these enterprises, even when they have official sanction. Thus is formed a tie-up with the underworld of racketeers and criminals which introduces new elements of degradation into gambling and promiscuous sexual intercourse: connections between the "respectable classes" and the underworld, by way of pleasure, amusement, and sexual release, that tend to undermine the morale of the body politic.

With respect to these relaxations, the big city has the same advantage that international fairs once had: its very bigness makes it an admirable hiding place. Within its endless streets, the metropolis provides shelter from prying eyes: here the drunkenness that would be a public spectacle becomes a private foible: here the liaison that might disrupt a provincial family can be consummated with a minimum of exposure. A man and a woman incur less danger from gossip by going to bed together in a metropolitan hotel than they would if they merely dined together in the restaurant of a small provincial town.

Indeed, the advantages of the metropolis as a hiding place—an advantage that illicit lovers share with more violent breakers of law and convention—is not the least of its attractions to the visitors who swarm in from other parts of the country. If one has anything to conceal, the place to conceal it is among a million other people. The anonymity of the big city, its impersonality, is a positive encouragement to a-social or anti-social actions. Hence a professional form of surveillance, by an organized police, must take the place of neighborly scrutiny and pressure: a city of strangers lacks any other form of stabilizing check. The transformation of the town guard into the professional police, which first took place in Paris in the seventeenth century, marks one of the critical changes from a town econ-

omy to a metropolitan economy. There is perhaps a moral in the
fact that the Greek equivalent for policeman means citizen.

The a-social character of metropolitan routine can in fact be
partly deduced from the relative cost of police service in cities of
different size. In American cities with a million or more people,
the cost of police is sixty cents per inhabitant per year: in cities with
from three hundred to six hundred thousand it is forty cents; in
cities between one hundred and three hundred thousand, it is only
twenty cents, while cities with thirty thousand people or under pay
only ten cents. Doubtless the bigger cities get more in the way of
service: but they need it. In the United States, except in cases of
rape and manslaughter, the number of police cases per thousand
forms an ascending curve in direct relationship to the size of cities.

Among the specialized pleasures of the metropolis, those connected with nutrition or its surrogates play no small part: oral
erethism, stimulation through food and drink, has a place in metropolitan routine that was once reserved for special feasts and celebrations. The restaurants, the cafés, the saloons and pubs, are necessarily
ubiquitous; and their trade is intensified by the fact that the home
itself plays a smaller part in furnishing such stimuli. To speak of
the metropolis in the loftier economic ranks is to speak of the
Hermitage, the Adlon, Maxim's, the Ritz, the Colony Club: places
where the reputations built up in finance, law, or the theater are
put on parade. A certain psychological intensity goes into these expenditures on food and drink; for good eating and drinking are the
ultimate justifications of the metropolitan's day: stuffing, gourmand-
izing, sipping, he achieves a momentary euphoria that obscures the
eventual physiological derangement. Balzac's incarnation of the
antique collector and the gourmandizer in the single figure of
Cousin Pons was a master-stroke.

12. The Poison of Vicarious Vitality

In cheaper substitute forms, all these activities are pursued by
the masses; and they are enjoyed vicariously, at least, in the motion
pictures, the illustrated papers, the fashion advertisements. But the
crowds, as such, have their own forms of mass enjoyment: it is for
them that the lights twinkle on the avenues outside the theaters and

restaurants and cabarets they cannot afford to enter: it is to them that the advertiser appeals in a myriad of colored bulbs, tempting them to drink this whisky, ride in this motor car, or to renew their fading vitality with "pilules pinks pour personnes pâles."

By day, the crowd has its special parades: the passage of a potentate through the city: the carefully arranged reception to a general who has redeemed for civilization a barbarous country whose inhabitants cannot defend themselves with poison gas: the return of a girl who has swum the English Channel. And they greet these ambitious nonentities in the appropriate metropolitan fashion: not with flowers, as Lindbergh was greeted in still rural Mexico City, but by emptying on the head of the illustrious hero the contents of their waste-paper baskets, swirling festoons of ticker tape, or, when exhausted of the normal supply of paper, with ribbons of toilet paper: the ultimate mark of metropolitan approbation: Bravo!

The arrangement of such spectacles is an important contribution to metropolitan equilibrium, as the classes that rule the city almost instinctively understand: it is, so to say, the vulgarization of the prestige values of monopoly. Without such shows the bitter actualities of poverty and impotence might for the mass of metropolitans be almost unendurable: these spectacles help counteract the inferior sense of manliness and womanliness that develops under stress of mechanization, and they break down, likewise, through mass participation, that sense of loneliness which haunts the atomic individual in the big city. (See Jules Romains' keen depiction of The Lonely in Men of Good Will.)

Life comes back to the metropolis in the intercourse in spontaneous groups for which the great mass spectacles serve as occasion. Boxing matches, wrestling bouts, feats of dull endurance like bicycle races and dance marathons, spectacular exhibitions of derring-do like rodeos, or motor races and air races. All these exaggerations of strength, skill, daring, are necessary to stir the basic animal needs from their costive torpidity. Doing so, they promote at least the lowest form of sociality: the basic tie in this amorphous metropolitan body: gregariousness. What was once called the herd instinct is in fact the *residual* sociality of the metropolitan crowd. The stadium, where the great crowds assemble for these various spectacles, is, like the police force, one of the special stigmata of the metropolitan regime: here, if anywhere, is its essential drama: *spectacular* achievement and *spectacular* death.

In most of these performances an inverted sense of life is promoted through the presence of fear and the nearness to death. The maiming of the sacrificial victims is one of the high points in the spectacle, precisely as in the gladiatorial bouts of ancient Rome, or in the ritualistic murders of the Aztecs. Without death or the threat of death, the populace feels itself cheated: so that the more peaceful games, like baseball and horse-racing, must be spiced by gambling if they are to equal the excitement of a rodeo or a motor race. Not merely are those who actually see these morbid spectacles aware of them: by means of the newspaper, the radio, the newsreel, the most sadistic exhibitions are inflicted upon those who are humane enough still to loathe them with an honest human hate.

There is little doubt however as to the value of these spectacles from the standpoint of the exploiting groups: they tend to make people indifferent to the values of life. Satiated with milder forms of brutality, the spectator demands bloodier satisfactions. If games do not provide them sufficiently, he will manufacture occasions: note the zestful terrorism practiced by the bourgeoisie under the guise of restoring law and order in a labor conflict: note the prompt effort on the part of police to turn peaceful struggles for power into occasions for violence. The tameness of the metropolitan routine must have its compensatory mobilizations of ferocity.

Perhaps the best psychological interpretation of this regime has been given by John Ruskin: I must quote it in full, for the intervening years have only underlined and more fully substantiated his analysis of the metropolitan mind in Arrows of the Chace.

"What thought can enough comprehend the contrast between such [human] life, and that in streets where summer and winter are only alternations of heat and cold; where snow never fell white nor sunshine clear; where the ground is only a pavement and the sky no more than the glass roof of an arcade; where the utmost power of a storm is to choke the gutters and the finest magic of spring, to change mud into dust: where—chief and most fatal difference of state—there is no interest or occupation for any of the inhabitants but the routine of counter or desk within doors, and the effort to pass each other without collision outside; so that from morning to evening the only possible variation of the monotony of the hours, and lightening of the penalty of existence must be some kind of mischief, limited, unless by more than ordinary godsend of fatality, to the fall of a horse or the slitting of a pocket.

"I said that under these laws of inanition, the craving of the human heart for some kind of excitement could be supplied from *one* source only. It might have been thought by any other than a sternly tentative philosopher, that the denial of their natural food to human feelings would have provoked a reactionary desire for it; and that the dreariness of the street would have been gilded by dreams of pastoral felicity. Experience has shown the fact to be otherwise; the thoroughly trained Londoner can enjoy no other excitement than that to which he has been accustomed, but as for *that* in continually more ardent or more virulent concentration; and the ultimate power of fiction to entertain him is by varying to his fancy the modes, and defining for his dullness the horrors of death. In the single novel of Bleak House there are nine deaths . . . carefully wrought out or worked up to: one by assassination, Mr. Tulkinghorn; one by starvation with phthisis, Joe; one by chagrin, Richard; one by spontaneous combustion, Mr. Krock; one by sorrow, Lady Dedlock's lover; one by remorse, Lady Dedlock; one by insanity, Miss Flite; one by paralysis, Sir Leicester. It is the fact that all these deaths, but one, are of inoffensive, or at least, in the world's estimate, respectable persons; and that they are all grotesquely either violent or miserable, purporting thus to illustrate the modern theory that the appointed destiny of a large average of our population is to die like rats in a drain, either by trap or poison."

Have we not here a clue to that sadism of the imagination which still characterizes such a large part of the novels, the moving pictures, the dramas, the daily newspaper accounts of murder and violence? This sadism has helped harden the metropolitan world into a dull acceptance of the use of poison gas in civil riots or the massacre of unprotected citizens in time of war: fulsome totalitarian murder.

Let us sum up these diversions. To counteract an intolerable preoccupation with arithmetical abstractions and mechanical instru·ments, an almost equally abstract interest in the stomach and the sexual organs, divorced from their organic relations. To counteract boredom and isolation, mass spectacles: to make up for biological inferiority, a series of collective games and exhibitions, based on withering specializations of the body. In short, the metropolis is rank with forms of *negative vitality*. Nature and human nature, violated in this environment, come back in destructive forms: drugs, anodynes, aphrodisiacs, hypnotics, sedatives, are a necessary ac·companiment of this exacerbated state, strenuous efforts to recover the normal equilibrium of the healthy body and the healthy mind: salvation by aspirin. James Joyce, in Ulysses, projected this phan·tasmal state: he showed the mind of Leopold Bloom regurgitating the contents of the newspaper and the advertisement, living in a hell of unfulfilled desires, vague wishes, enfeebling anxieties, morbid compulsions, and dreary vacuities: a dissociated mind in a disinte·grated city: perhaps the *normal* mind of the world metropolis.

In this mangled state, the impulse to live departs from apparently healthy personalities, as it might depart from someone who had been crushed under the wheels of a locomotive. The impulse to die sup·plants it. And just as the will-to-live can triumph over all but catas·trophic accidents or derangements to the physical organism, so the will-to-die can eat cancerously into the personality, until the body itself, no matter how outwardly healthy, is tainted and finally is consumed by the malady.

Is it any wonder that Dr. Sigmund Freud found a death wish at the seat of human activity? The analysis does not lack justification, provided one remembers it is a historic phenomenon, time-condi·tioned, place-conditioned, culture-conditioned. The scene is Megalop·olis: in Freud's case, Wien; and the time is the period of imperial and financial collapse, in a structure already cracking before the first World War. At this particular moment, the death wish appears as a collective impulse: an effort to save life from further defeats, from more unbearable indignities, through suicide. Evil and sinister though this impulse may be, in terms of the life-values a genuine culture embodies, it is one degree better, perhaps, than extinction by slow paralysis.

13: A Brief Outline of Hell

Behold the present moment in Western Civilization. Examine the economic state of the metropolis during the last century and note how its infirmities have piled up.

The main economic problem for the metropolitan regime, even on its own premises, is to reduce its tendency to swing violently from prosperity to bankruptcy. To overcome this manic-depressive economic cycle without flattening out into a stable economic regime that would curb the further acquisition of wealth by the minority, presents, however, an inherent contradiction. For the metropolis is by its very nature in a state of permanent unbalance: its proletariat lacks good housing and an adequate diet, to say nothing of other opportunities, even during the most flatulent periods of prosperity. Hence its financiers and statesmen seek to prevent the pyramid of values from falling by broadening the base. American motor car manufacturers, choked at home, seek outlets in Europe: Japanese cotton mills seek buyers in India and Africa: surplus capital, unable to find investment markets at home or lured abroad by the less modest returns offered, exposes itself to forces beyond its control.

These new centers of economic gravity often fall within the base of another state or people. Conflicts result, sometimes with the states or peoples themselves. To command new areas for raw materials, to conquer new markets, to ensure the safety of new investment areas, to collect tribute from unsafe or irregular investments, to seize territory from weaker peoples, every state must devote itself to the expansion of its army and navy. Once the territory is partitioned, the states that were slow to join the scramble look enviously upon those in possession: they demand their share in the loot, their portion of the real or illusory benefits; and their threats constitute a further menace to this unstable order.

So far from improving conditions, imperialistic expansion only complicates the disorder: it increases the insecurity of the home areas, and it drains away economic vitality by concentrating production upon the materials of war and all its accessory equipment. To maintain the armed forces in a state of ready aggression, the proletariat must be further exploited and taxed: even the rich, to keep their wealth at all, must part with a share of it. The sense of insecurity thus produced tempts every class to keep its savings in a liquid form; and this in turn discourages long term investments at low interest rates, upon which improved production and far-sighted expenditures in consumptive equipment, such as housing and municipal utilities, depends.

Meanwhile, psychological tensions increase: belligerent impulses demand expression. The simple love of country and home and soil, a love that needs neither reasons nor justifications, is turned by the official apologists of the state into the demented cult of "patriotism": coercive group unanimity: blind support of the rulers of the state: maudlin national egoism: an imbecile willingness to commit collective atrocities for the sake of "national glory."

The buildings of the imperial metropolis serve as an appropriate background for these war-ceremonies and reinforce these pretensions. From Washington to Tokyo, from Berlin to Rome, the architecture of imperialism is a monotonous reflection of the military-bureaucratic mind. They exhibit the extravagance of the financial *arriviste*, without a touch of creative warmth: the dull façades of endless columns, the heavy armor of stone in which they are usually encrusted, their pompous emphasis of their historic predecessor, Rome, the solemn tomb-like quality of their offices and halls mark that failure in life-efficiency which is characteristic of this regime. And the quarters of the bureaucracy are planned with so little discretion that a few bombs strategically dropped from the air might paralyze the major government services for weeks at a time: except for the building of occasional vaults and underground chambers, this war-regime has not in the matter of planning and building and layout mastered the most elementary demands of war-protection.

But the growing war-bureaucracy presents an outward front of power: power as expressed in wide avenues, endless vistas of useless columns, and huge stadiums fit for martial exercises and games: the element of feeling, completely lacking in the stereotypes of architectural form, is provided by the crowds on the street: the children assembled for the singing of vainglorious national anthems, the crowds marching in parades, or the mob that assembles in the public square to behold, at a discreet distance, the leader of the state. This is the crowd whose simple hates, fueled by propaganda, transfers to foreign devils the unconscious hatred it dare not express for the classes that exploit it, or the unconscious contempt each member feels for his own thwarted self. Essential to this metropolitan regime are these passive atoms: metropolitan barbarians: a million cowards upon whose blank minds the leader writes: Bravery. A million scattered, bewildered individuals whom the rulers cajole, bully, and terrorize into a state of unity.

What follows? External conflicts pile upon internal contradictions. Psychologically, a violent paranoia, with pronounced delusions of grandeur, takes hold of the ruling classes: the alternative is something like collective dementia praecox: suspicion, hatred, isolation, desire to inflict destruction, appear in extreme forms. These psychological states are deliberately fostered by a positive cult of irrationality: intellectual disintegration is expressed in wishful systems of anthropology, sociology, and philosophy, which hold in contempt the most elementary obligations to respect fact or to establish new truths by the discipline of objective verification. The inactivity of despair alternates with national delusions of persecution, followed by attempts to inflict damage upon the putative persecutors. Read the tirades of hate that accompanied the first World War, from the *Hassgesang* of the Germans to the *Hang the Kaiser* campaign conducted by the righteous Lloyd George. Recall the extravagant hatreds expressed by the Italian fascists for the "sanctionist" powers: that is, for a major part of the civilized world. These exhibitions plainly belong to the domain of collective psychopathology.

Imperialism, pretending to conquer the wilderness and civilize the natives of backward areas of the planet, actually helps the wilderness creep in on civilization. It was so in the Roman era and it is so again today: only today the Romes have multiplied and the whole surface of the earth is now endangered. A regiment of eight-year-old children, learning the first formations of military drill, represents a lower state of savagery than that of the most ferocious cannibals: those who drill them are rejecting the birthright of civilization, and are thus more reprehensible than those who have never reached civilization. And truly it has been said: *one can not forgive them, for they know what they do,* even as they know what they do when they bomb defenseless cities and torpedo defenseless ships.

This systematic barbarism spreads like a cancer through the healthy tissue of urban life: the war capital, through its organs of indoctrination, makes every subordinate province war-minded. The actual conflict, when it finally takes place, is a mere bursting of a vast pus-bag of vulgar pretense and power. But the intervening period, although sometimes fantastically referred to as "peace," is equally a state of war: the passive war of war-propaganda, war-indoctrination, war-rehearsal: a preliminary maneuvering for position.

The metropolis, which is the focus of these war forces, thus comes to represent the maximum possible assault upon the processes of civilization. Observe one of the concrete results: periodic preparation for defense against an attack by air: the materialization of a skillfully evoked nightmare.

The sirens sound. School-children, factory hands, housewives, office workers, one and all don their gas masks. Whirring planes overhead lay down a blanket of protective smoke. Cellars open to receive their refugees. Red Cross stations to succor the stricken and the wounded are opened at improvised shelters: underground vaults yawn to receive the gold and securities of the banks: masked men in asbestos suits attempt to gather up the fallen incendiary bombs. Presently the anti-aircraft guns sputter. Fear vomits: poison crawls through the pores. Whether the attack is arranged or real, it produces similar psychological effects. Plainly, terrors more devastating and demoralizing than any known in the ancient jungle or cave have been re-introduced into modern urban existence. Panting, choking, spluttering, cringing, hating, the dweller in Megalopolis dies, by anticipation, a thousand deaths. Fear is thus fixed into routine: the constant anxiety over war produces by itself a collective psychosis comparable to that which active warfare might develop. Waves of fear and hatred rise in the metropolis and spread by means of the newspaper and the newsreel and the radio program to the most distant provinces.

Here is the final contradiction in metropolitan civilization. The city arose as a special kind of environment, favorable to co-operative

[TOP] Faery palaces and cloud-capped towers of Lower Manhattan, seen from Governors Island. Visually speaking, a miraculous mountain of buildings: the zenith of romantic architecture. To work in a skyscraper, even in the dingiest tower on an airless shaft, is a manifestation of metropolitan power, to have an office of one's own on an upper floor, blessed with sunlight and the view of the ferryboats gliding up and down the Harbor, is one of the highest emoluments of metropolitan success. (*Photograph: Ewing Galloway*)

[SECOND LEFT] The dream deepens; night falls. The great offices where a million people go through a million similar motions, day in and day out, adding, subtracting, multiplying, ticketing, labeling, checking, dictating and taking dictation, begging and borrowing, giving orders and carrying them out: high pressure bureaucracy. Great loft buildings where, to the whirr of machines, the latest fashion in women's clothes is speeded into production or the latest newspaper drops off the presses. Honeycombs of light, filled with temporarily neuter insects—in a hive that boasts ever fewer fertile queens. (*Photograph: Ewing Galloway*)

[SECOND RIGHT] The White Way: here the occasional blaze of the old-fashioned festival becomes the routine of commercial enticement: a stimulus for those seeking adventure and beauty, at so much per head, in the shops, cabarets, theaters, hotels. But these constant stimuli need constant stepping up of intensification: the alternative is satiety and boredom. Hence the demand for novelties. The need for irregular stimuli becomes the great problem of metropolitan culture in every phase: counterbalance to the compulsive automatisms and too-even regularities of metropolitan existence. The need is probably increased by the achievement of an artificial environment, with constant heating and air-conditioning and lighting: uniformities that raise physiological problems to organisms whose eyesight, muscle-tone, and nervous reactions demand a wider span of variation. Further physiological research may well upset many of the assumptions upon which metropolitan improvements in lighting and heating, for example, have been based—once variation is included in defining optimum conditions. (*Photograph: Ewing Galloway*)

[BOTTOM] The Sleeper Awakes: morning light. The dream city is still visible above the roofs of the tenements; but these massed dwellings show the power and glory of metropolitan life in true perspective: here are the homes of the sustaining proletariat, the local equivalent of the mean steel towns and oil towns, the depressed farming areas and manufacturing areas, through whose efforts the dividends are piled higher for the fractional portion of the entire population that effectively rules this metropolitan regime. (*Photograph: Ewing Galloway*)

[MIDDLE] Midtown District of New York: solidified chaos. Proof that under a financial economy the gestures of zoning, height-restriction, setbacks are futile: these skyscraper offices and factories have almost all been built since "restrictions" were placed upon overcrowding the land. Under the prevailing zoning ordinance, with no new building over 600 feet in height, the permitted capacity of the residential districts of New York, according to the New York City Housing Authority, would be approximately 77,000,000, while the commercial districts would provide for a working population of 344,000,000. Isolated skyscrapers, like the fine McGraw-Hill building (second skyscraper left-center) claim enough light and air for themselves, even if they rob their neighbors and help overcrowd local traffic; but even in Rockefeller Center the excessive land value frustrated, by its absurd demand for density, the first attempt at a rational plan. Subways, tunnels, double-decked streets, express highways, so far from relieving congestion, only intensify the economic need for it: hence the relief is but temporary, though the burden imposed is permanent. Warnings of complete traffic blockage and of the "menace of decentralization" are annually uttered by so-called traffic experts. But no real remedy exists that does not involve a deflation of values, a draining off of population, and a complete rebuilding of the entire metropolitan structure at a far lower density. (*Photograph: Ewing Galloway*)

[UPPER LEFT] Pattern of congestion in what is hopefully called a suburb: not the worst. The difference between this and other forms of metropolitan housing congestion requires micrometer measurements. (*Photograph: Ewing Galloway*)

[UPPER RIGHT] Self-defilement of the bourgeoisie: not a lower but an upper class slum immediately off the most expensive part of Fifth Avenue: characteristic of the reckless building over of back garden areas in both private houses and apartment houses. Dark, dismal, airless quarters: unfit for permanent habitation. Air conditioning is only a partial remedy for these subway dwellings: the lack of sunlight and a gracious environment—to say nothing of quarters fit for children—cannot be remedied without razing these super-slums. If this is what private initiative and ample means does for the rich, it is plain that they need public aid and more limited incomes.

[BOTTOM LEFT] Coney Island Beach on a summer day. The ritual is called recreation: prefaced and concluded usually by half an hour or more spent in a stifling subway. Pollution of beaches through sewage and garbage results in a closing off of bathing privileges or invokes the need for costly measures of relief: sewage and garbage disposal plants. (*Photograph: Ewing Galloway*)

[BOTTOM RIGHT] Grand Central Station, New York: an entrance to the city, partly put out of commission as a station by the overload of high buildings in its neighborhood. (*Photograph: Ewing Galloway*) association, favorable to nurture and education, because it was a *protected* environment. It was a collective utility that ensured order and regularity in the comings and goings of men, that diminished the force of nature's random onslaughts, and reduced the menace of wild animals and the more predatory tribes of men. Permanent settlement meant not only continuity but security. In the city, as in the agricultural villages, domestic functions and co-operative actions prevailed over the more predatory and destructive modes of life; man thus made himself the greatest of the domesticated animals.

A humane life, a civic life, is one that restricts the fear-producing elements and reduces fear to a prudent provision against the common mischances of existence. Only in a well-wrought domesticated environment, protected against disaster and the gnawing anticipations of disaster, can the higher activities for long flourish: solicitude for the young, tenderness for the aged, an underlying co-operation between rival groups and interests, prolonged and systematic thought directed toward truth, free expression in the arts, and creative release, under the discipline of humane standards, in the arts of living: in short, a mode of life in which man's biological and social needs are artfully wrought into a many-threaded and variegated cultural pattern.

Concentrated upon war, the metropolitan regime opposes these domestic and civic functions: it subordinates life to organized destruction, and it must therefore regiment, limit, and constrict every exhibition of real life and culture. Result: the paralysis of all the higher activities of society: truth shorn or defaced to fit the needs of propaganda: the organs of co-operation stiffened into a reflex system of obedience: the order of the drill sergeant and the bureaucrat. Such a regime may reach unheard-of heights in external coordination and discipline, and those who endure it may make superb soldiers and juicy cannonfodder; but it is for the same reason deeply antagonistic to every valuable manifestation of life.

Plainly, a civilization that terminates in a cult of barbarism has disintegrated as civilization; and the war-metropolis, as an expression of these institutions, is an anti-civilizing agent: a *non*-city. To assume that this process can go on indefinitely is to betray an ignorance of social facts: decay at last halts itself. While the tasks

of building, co-operation, and integration are never finished, un-
building may be completed in a few generations. The chief question
now before the Western World today is whether disintegration must
be complete before a fresh start is made.

14: Phenomena of the End

While the continuance of the metropolitan economy is curbed
by the destructive forces it piles up and releases, a more local set
of conditions operates with more direct impact upon metropolitan
expansion. In addition to its military vulnerability, the metropolis
is economically weakened by the fact of growth; and there comes at
long last a time when it cannot evade or pass on elsewhere the burden
of its own magnified expenses.

As long as the economic system works smoothly, the metropolis
may ignore the costs of congestion: when things begin to go ill, when
bankruptcy threatens, when inflation devaluates the claims of metropolitan creditors on the rest of the country, even the food supply
may be endangered. And how quickly the ornate central offices empty:
how inessential the giddy restaurants and the fifteen-room apartments
suddenly become! Even the museums may close their doors, as their
panicky patrons withdraw funds. Let the disorganization continue,
so that the metropolis can neither command the necessary force of
arms and law and common assent, nor furnish a modicum of goods
in return for the country's products, and the metropolis may be
starved out: the drift outward may begin. These are not hypothetical
alarms. Conditions in Central Europe and in Soviet Russia after
the first World War presented almost unbearable difficulties to the
harassed and starving metropolises, while out in the countryside, in
many regions, the peasant remained relatively secure and well-fed.

Even without the disorganization of war, similar circumstances,
of almost catastrophic dimensions, may arise: consider the state of
the big cities in the United States, between 1930 and 1935. The
National Resources Committee, in the 1937 report on Our Cities
makes this pertinent observation: "Insecurity of the urban worker,
his lack of reserve resources, and the impersonality and mobility of
urban life combine to make the problems of dependency more acute
and more widespread in cities than in rural areas. . . . One-fifth of

all the employable persons on relief in 1935 were located in the ten largest cities, and consisted mainly of unskilled workmen." Without the mobilization of national funds for public works projects and local relief, the demoralization of the great metropolises would have been appalling.

Apart from the latent hostility of the exploited countryside, nourishing grievances against the big city because of the low prices it gets in the market, and the high rate of interest it must pay on its loans, there are internal elements that place a limit to metropolitanism. The very cost of doing business in the big city is magnified by high land values, by expensive delays in transportation, by the high expense of storage: all these costs increase with congestion, and eventually they become prohibitive. The congestion of traffic alone in New York City during the nineteen-twenties was estimated by the Russell Sage Survey to involve a loss of $500,000 a day, or $150,-000,000 per year. And still it thickens: still it forms tedious snarls: finally the very *hope* of movement collapses.

In recreation, a different sort of inefficiency exists: instead of an overplus of physical equipment, there is a serious lack of sufficient space for play, and for lack of play areas, the toll of children killed or maimed on the streets rises. According to very conservative estimates, there should be a minimum of one acre of recreation space for every three hundred persons: many cities are able to afford more. Such a standard has been met in our generation in America by regional cities like Kansas City (400,000 inhabitants), Portland, Oregon (300,000), and Indianapolis (360,000): but in New York City there was but one acre of space to 1234 inhabitants.

Meanwhile, other expenses pile up: other breakdowns become chronic. The passenger transportation system, for example. The subways of great cities may serve as bomb-proof shelters during air raids; otherwise they are mainly obstacles to that conceivable decentralization of the metropolis which would reduce the burden of congestion by building up sub-centers of industry, business, and residence. As the lines extend, the costs increase: this means either higher fares for the worker, or higher taxes for the city as a whole.

Here, then, is the choice: a breakdown of functions through neglect, or a financial breakdown through the increased expense of adequate

service and repair. I have already cited the increased costs of police
service in the bigger cities. The same relationship holds for municipal
expenditures upon health: three times as much is spent per capita in
cities with over a million inhabitants as in cities with from thirty to
fifty thousand inhabitants: yet the *latter* present, on the whole, more
favorable vital statistics.

In short, one may say definitely that beyond a certain point, which
varies with regional conditions and culture, urban growth penalizes
itself. Too large a part of the capital outlays and annual income
of the city must be spent in devices for increasing congestion and
mechanically relieving its worst results.

The present economic scheme of the big city depends upon the
expectation of a stable income from an investment, public and private, that becomes ever more speculative, unstable, and insecure.
The growth of such a city means an increase of insecurity: to ensure
such growth, to subsidize it, to attempt to freeze this obsolete structure in the effort to maintain the financial values that have been
attached to it is to exhibit an ungovernable antagonism to prudence
and good sense. Metropolitan bankers, with their own narrow interests in view, may encourage such uneconomic folly: did they not in
the decade before the depression ingenuously overcalculate the
capacity of the metropolis to absorb new skyscrapers and hotels? But
a similar optimism as to the city's capacity to absorb tunnels, bridges,
double-decked streets, widened avenues, and underground transit systems is now unpardonable. That process cannot continue indefinitely.

There are perhaps parallels to all these weaknesses in many
smaller cities: but the reason should be plain: they, too, worked
under the canons of metropolitan finance and imitated the most
blatant defects of the metropolis. Note, for example, Cincinnati's
almost completed but never opened subway.

The cold facts upon which these conclusions are based are set
forth, with statistical substantiation, in a ten volume report: that
by the Russell Sage Foundation for the Regional Plan of New York.
The authority is unimpeachable: not least because the report naïvely
and wholeheartedly accepted the premises of metropolitan finance
and diligently endeavored to show on what terms the New York
agglomeration could be increased from a population of ten million

in 1930 to between twenty and twenty-nine million in 1965. What holds for New York holds with appropriate modifications for other metropolises and sub-metropolises. The end of their reckless expansion is near.

But there is one final limitation on metropolitan growth: more stringent than the rising cost of utilities or the unbearable municipal burden of blighted areas. I mean the cutting off of the supply of inhabitants at the source. In almost every country except Russia a tapering off process has begun for the population as a whole. Despite dictatorial threats, despite special rewards and bounties for large families, despite attempts to limit the supply of convenient contraceptives, the movement goes on. Hence the flood of people who imperiously demanded urban accommodation during the nineteenth century has spent its original force. Throughout the world, if this movement keeps up, the metropolitan economy will have to adjust itself to the fact of a relatively stable population and a relatively fixed market: an end to its hitherto boundless financial increments.

This movement toward the stabilization of numbers may, if intelligently directed, result in great human gains. It affords a breathing space for reorganization, and it will enable population to be planned and distributed in accordance with regional resources. But the finer this adjustment is, the less part can the metropolis play in it: for under conditions now prevailing, no big metropolis reproduces its own population through births: indeed, in the United States, only three cities with over a hundred thousand population have a reproductive index of over 1.0. *This fact alone reduces to complete nullity the notion that the metropolitan population pattern is a permanent one, or that it could, if dominant, maintain itself over any considerable period.* Without steady immigration, its population must sink. The biological norm of city growth, that is, the degree of concentration beyond which the community fails in reproducing the full quota of its members, is between twenty-five and fifty thousand. As we even out the economic and cultural differences between the rural and the urban environments, this tentatively fixes an upper limit for the size of the biotechnic city. With cities of such size forming the dominant element in the urban pattern, no country need utilize its hinterland as mere breeding ground.

No single element is perhaps sufficient to bring about an immediate breakdown in the metropolitan regime. But in actual life, these high costs, these economic disorganizations, these retrograde tendencies do not appear as isolated events: they come together and reinforce each other: abetted by a series of catastrophes, both immanent and imminent, they may easily mean the end of the entire civilization. Such a breakup has happened many times in history before. What we have been witnessing, during the last thousand years, is a cycle that societies in the past have never successfully smoothed out or short-circuited: a cycle from which even the most stable of civilizations—even that of the Chinese—has not been able completely to escape. Let us examine this movement: it may give us a clue as to the possibilities of achieving a comprehensive social and political reconstruction: a benign instead of a catastrophic outcome.

15: Cycle of Growth and Decay

During the last generation there have been numerous attempts to summarize the course of city development and to correlate this with the rise and fall of civilizations. One of the best-known of these interpretations is that of Oswald Spengler in the book euphemistically translated as The Decline of the West. He traced the development of the community from "culture" to "civilization": from its beginnings as the living expression of a people, harmoniously interacting upon a certain soil and swayed by a common feeling toward life and the earth and the universe, not yet formulated as philosophic vision, to the final stage, that which he called civilization, with its hard mechanistic organization of men and goods and ideas: rootless, spiritless, ultimately lifeless and hopeless: concentrated in a few world capitals that were no longer related to the land, where the malleable and changeable forms of earlier cultures were made over into dead stereotypes.

According to Spengler's early scheme, the process of mastery, which begins with agriculture, ends with a predominance of the machine: a contrivance in which there is for him something infernal, inimical to life. The business man and the engineer and the industrialist displace the artist and the peasant. But mechanism, tied to a ruthless scheme of exploitation, leads into savagery: Spengler acknowledged that fact and in his later formulations he even boasted of man's being a carnivore in order to justify the conclusion that the men of our time must heartily embrace savagery: submit to the lash of a Caesar and take part in his brutal machinations. There is of course a serious contradiction between Spengler's romantic belief in the predatory carnivore and the historic facts of rural domestication and urbane culture; but one may pardon Spengler's barbarous solecisms if only because he was one of the first in our generation to grasp the critical significance of the city in the development of culture.

A later interpretation of this cycle of development and deterioration is that of Arnold J. Toynbee, in his monumental survey, A Study of History. Toynbee's study is more profound than Spengler's, is based on a much richer grasp of historic facts, and does not neglect empirical evidence for the sake of preserving intact a literary figure. Unfortunately, Toynbee's theory of the development of civilization does not embrace the special function of the city, as both the instrument and the symbol of this process; and although he rediscovers the function of the cloister, in his conception of withdrawal-and-return as necessary for the process of renewal, he does not connect this with the process of urban development itself. Hence Toynbee is weak precisely at the point where Spengler is strongest: though his division of the component cultures into societies, and his schematic cycle of development rest on a closer reading of the historical evidence.

The most significant summary of all, from the point of view developed in this book, is likewise the earliest: that put forward by Patrick Geddes a generation ago in his outline of the six stages of city development, from polis to nekropolis. Like a true disciple, I have modified Geddes's scheme, something in the way that I modified his analysis of the paleotechnic and the neotechnic phases of the machine. Thus I propose to insert an earlier stage that he left out of the picture, and I have combined two of his later stages, those of Parasitopolis and Patholopolis into a single stage, since there is no observable time-interval between them. These modifications, made after his death, too late for his sanction, have the merit of placing the first three stages of the cycle on the rising curve, and the last three on the descending side; and this, I believe, is more in line with his essential views than his own original diagram.

First Stage: Eopolis. Rise of the village community. Development of permanent habitation and permanent external organs of association through the domestication of plants and the ensurance of a balanced food supply by the domestication of animals. Cultivation of the hard grains and legumes: also deliberate tree and vine culture: plentiful supply of proteins, vegetable fats, and fermented liquors. Surplus production in agriculture smooths over seasonal and cyclical irregularities and ensures an orderly routine of life: security and continuity. Permanent utilities for storage: translation of kinetic energy into potential energy (food storage) brings vast increase in power, economic and cultural.

Differentiation of the permanent dwelling house, and regular outlines of the village through systematic layout and orderly apportionment of land: pile villages, plains villages, etc. Important technical advances, especially in development of utensils and agricultural tools: basketwork, pottery, hoe, beginnings of systematic mining and tool-working: dawn of metallurgy. Fire as symbol of advance: hearth and altar. Oral transmission of tradition through occupational groups and through close companionship of senescents and youths. Association on basis of blood and neighborhood: predominance of primary groups. Culture continuous with life but limited by arbitrary restriction of experience (tabus), fear of departure from magical formulae, submissive respect for ancestral wisdom as transmitted by priesthood, and lack of stimulating intercourse with other cultures. First crude differentiation of villages on basis of topographic facts, local resources, indigenous occupations: mining villages, fishing villages, agricultural villages.

Arising probably in neolithic culture, the village remains the most enduring of collective forms. Its life underlies all subsequent transformations of civilization; and although villages that continue as such never climb more than part of the cycle upward and never participate except by adaptive infiltration in the advances made in the city, they likewise tend to escape the worst defects of decay. The agricultural village, not the market, is the prototype of the city: its utilities for protection, storage, and life-maintenance are the essential nucleus of the city: they become "etherealized" in culture-forms, at the same time as they are finally given concrete expression in the form of collective art: altar becomes temple: planting and harvest rituals become drama and theater, granary bin and cellar are village prototypes of library, archive, museum and vault. The village remains the essential root from which fresh urban shoots from time to time thrust upward: its form and content persist long after more differentiated urban types have flourished and disappeared. Hence the truth in the boast of the little village near Edinburgh:

> *Musselburgh was a borough when Edinburgh was none,*
> *And Musselburgh will be a borough when Edinburgh is gone.*

Second Stage: Polis. An association of villages or blood-groups having a common site that lends itself to defense against depredation: a common deity with a common shrine or temple, usually on or near the defensive site: a common meeting place where the special products and skills of the larger community may be interchanged in periodical markets. Rise in industrial productivity through the more systematic division of labor and the partial specialization of functions: development of trades and crafts: surplus of manufactured goods as well as surplus of food. Beginnings of mechanization: stamping, molding, casting, in the early river-civilizations, the watermill, the paved road, the general use of wheeled vehicles in Graeco-Roman civilization: special instruments of power and precision in addition to the above in modern civilization in its eotechnic phase.

Free energy: free time: release from incessant preoccupation with physical survival. Opportunity for further nurture of the family, for education, for the cultivation of the body in military and athletic exercise, for the discipline of the mind in contemplation and dialectics and science, and for the practice of the humane arts. Systematic medicine and health-culture. Further development of social division of labor through multiplication of purposive associations and organizations. Differentiation of theoretic from empiric knowledge: beginnings of mathematics, astronomy, philosophy: increased scope of a special class, immune to obligations of practical labor, devoted to preserving and extending the cultural heritage. Erection of special buildings that collectively embody new cultural and politi·

cal functions: temple, stadium, theater, guildhall, cathedral. Rise of the school, as the organ for systematically transmitting elements of social heritage to the young; and further differentiation of the cloister from the school: grove, shaded walk, porch, cloister, study, studio, laboratory. Civic unity and common vision of life symbolized in Temple or Cathedral. Increase of cultural storage by means of sculptured figures, painted images, monuments, books.

Preservation of rural occupations and rural customs, including the practice of piety toward ancestors and ancestral rites: the polis remains a collection of families; family organization tends to prevail in industry no less than in agriculture; and seasonal and other migrations between village and polis preserve and renew rural connections. Dependence upon the local region for water, building materials, food, and main industrial resources. Transformation of structures in impermanent materials into more durable ones: refinement of architectural detail: formal modifications of shrines and important buildings so as to reflect collective sentiments about life and the universe. Pervasiveness of esthetic and moral culture through all ranks of society: expression of a differentiated but still homogeneous way of life.

Third Stage: Metropolis. Within the region one city emerges from the less differentiated groups of villages and country towns. Taking advantage of a strategic location, a larger supply of potable water, a more defensible site, better land for agriculture, easier command of land routes or water routes, a safer harbor—usually with a number of these advantages coming together—one city succeeds in attracting larger numbers of inhabitants: it becomes the metropolis or "mother-city." In heaping up these advantages, the command of transportation routes probably marks the critical change: compare the Hittites with the Egyptians, or the land-locked Spartans with the adventurous, mobile, water-borne Athenians.

With a surplus of regional products, a specialized trade develops with other regions. This brings to the growing metropolis the necessary food supply, which can no longer be raised in the immediate vicinity, along with a host of stimulating goods from other regions: special fabrics, special forms, even esthetic patterns, unused by the traditional industries of the local region. Cross-fertilization of culture takes place: stimulus to fresh invention: stimulus to departures from routine. Long distance trading and long distance administration help further invention and create a necessity for abstract symbols: pictorial signs, numerical tables, alphabets. A foreign population of traders and students enters the metropolis: unabsorbed as citizens at first, since blood and neighborhood may still count, they bring the shock of fresh habits and ideas: challenges to old ways. Further specialization of economic and social functions: the specialized workshop: the specialized trading class: subdivisions of these. Large-scale development of library and university as storehouse and powerhouse of ideas. Development of more effective organs of centralized administration, apart from primitive courts and assemblies. Agriculture tends to be secondary to manufacture: manufacture in turn becomes an instrument of trade. Rivalry between patricians of the soil and new trades and industrialists of the metropolis: splitting off of landless workers, selling their labor, with no prospect of rise in economic rank. Also migration of an élite within the polity.

Religion, literature, the drama reach the stage of self-conscious criticism and expression: the systematic-rational grows at the expense of organic and instinctive modes of expression. Every part of the environment and the culture is deliberately remolded: written law supplements custom and common law, written language helps to shape the labile dialects of the surrounding regions and gives them a common medium of secondary intercourse: rational inquiry challenges customary acceptance. The representatives of religion, philosophy, and science, no longer united as a single priestly hierarchy, pursue separate paths: the gap between sacred knowledge and secular knowledge, between empiricism and theory, between deed and idea, tends to widen; but out of these oppositions and likenesses, out of these hostilities and wider friendships, new syntheses come forth. A similar refocusing takes place in every other department of life: emancipation from fixed patterns and stereotyped routine. Fusion of the instinctive, the imaginative, and the rational in great philosophies and works of art: maximum release of cultural energy: Platonic Athens: Dantean Florence: Shakespearean London: Emersonian Boston.

Signs of weakness appear beneath the surface. Increasing failure to absorb and integrate disparate cultural elements: beginnings of an individualism that tends to disrupt old social bonds without creating new order on a higher plane. Professionalizing of war, already differentiated as a culture-trait, acquires new energy through increasing technical equipment, and new impetus from economic rivalry. Opening up of a grave breach between the owners of the machinery of production and the workers, whether slave or free: beginning of the class struggle in active form. Fixation on pecuniary symbols of gain, as the growing class of merchants and bankers begin to exercise greater influence.

Fourth Stage: Megalopolis. Beginning of the decline. The city under the influence of a capitalistic mythos concentrates upon bigness and power. The owners of the instruments of production and distribution subordinate every other fact in life to the achievement of riches and the display of wealth. Physical conquest by military means: financial domination by trade and legal processes: loans, mortgages, speculative enterprises. The agricultural base extends: the lines of supply become more tenuous: the impulse to aggressive enterprise and enterprising aggression grows as the lust for power diminishes the attraction of all other attributes of life: as the moral sense becomes more callous and the will-to-culture increasingly impotent. Standardization, largely in pecuniary terms, of the cultural products themselves in art, literature, architecture, and language. Mechanical reproduction takes the place of original art: bigness takes the place of form: voluminousness takes the place of significance. Triumph of mechanism in every department: passivity: manual helplessness: bureaucratism: failure of direct action.

Megalopolis ushers in an age of cultural aggrandizement: scholarship and science by tabulation: sterile research: elaborate fact-finding apparatus and refined technic with no reference to rational intellectual purpose or ultimate possibilities of social use: Alexandrianism. Belief in abstract quantity in every department of life: the biggest monuments, the highest buildings, the most expensive materials, the largest food supply, the greatest number of worshipers, the biggest population. Education becomes quantitative: domination of the cram-machine and the encyclopedia, and domination of megalopolis as concrete encyclopedia: all-containing. Knowledge divorced

from life: industry divorced from life-utility: life itself compart-
mentalized, dis-specialized, finally disorganized and enfeebled. Representatives: Alexandria, third century B.C.; Rome, second century
A.D.; Byzantium, tenth century; Paris, eighteenth century; New York,
early twentieth century.

Over-investment in the material apparatus of bigness. Diversion of
energy from the biological and social ends of life to the preparatory
physical means. Outright exploitation of the proletariat and increasing conflict between organized workers and the master classes. Occasional attempts at insurance by philanthropy on the part of the
possessing classes: justice in homeopathic doses. Occasional outbursts of savage repression on the part of frightened bourgeoisie, em-
ploying basest elements in the city. As conflict intensifies rise of a
coalition between landed oligarchy, trained in combat, and a megalopolitan rabble of speculators, enterprisers, and financiers who furnish the sinews of war and profit by all the occasions for class-sup-
pression, price-lifting, and looting that it gives. The city as a means
of association, as a haven of culture, becomes a means of dissociation and a growing threat to real culture. Smaller cities are drawn
into the megalopolitan network: they practice imitatively the megalopolitan vices, and even sink to lower levels because of lack of higher
institutions of learning and culture that still persist in bigger centers.
The threat of widespread barbarism arises. Now follow, with cumulative force and increasing volume, the remaining downward movements of the cycle.

Fifth Stage: Tyrannopolis. Extensions of parasitism throughout
the economic and social scene: the function of spending paralyzes all
the higher activities of culture and no act of culture can be justified
that does not involve display and expense. Politics becomes competition for the exploitation of the municipal and state exchequer by
this or that class or group. Extirpation of organs of communal and
civic life other than "state." Caesarism. Development of predatory
means as a substitute for trade and give-and-take: naked exploitation
of colonies and hinterland: intensification of the cycles of commercial
depression, following overexpansion of industry and dubious speculative enterprise, heightened by wars and war-preparations. Failure
of the economic and political rulers to maintain the bare decencies

of administration: place-hunting, privilege-seeking, bonus-collecting, favor-currying, nepotism, grafting, tribute-exacting become rife both in government *and* business. Widespread moral apathy and failure of civic responsibility: each group, each individual, takes what it can get away with. Widening of the gap between producing classes and spending classes. Multiplication of a *Lumpenproletariat* demanding its share of bread and shows. Overstress of mass-sports. Parasitic love of sinecures in every department of life. Demand for "protection money" made by armed thugs and debased soldiery: organized looting, organized blackmail are "normal" accompaniments of business and municipal enterprise. Domination of respectable people who behave like criminals and of criminals whose activities do not debar them from respectability.

Imperialistic wars, internal and external, result in starvation, epidemics of disease, demoralization of life: uncertainty hangs over every prospect of the future: armed protection increases all the hazards of life. Municipal and state bankruptcy. Drain of local taxes to service increasing load of local debt. Necessity to appeal to the state for further aid in periods of economic disorganization: loss of autonomy. Drain of national taxes to support the growing military establishment of the state. This burden penalizes the remnants of honest industry and agriculture, and further disrupts the supply of elementary material goods. Decrease in agricultural production by soil-mining and erosion, through falling off in acreage, through the withholding of crops from the city by resentful husbandmen. Decline in rate of population-increase through birth control, abortion, mass slaughter, and suicide: eventual absolute decline in numbers. General loss of nerve. Attempt to create order by external military means: rise of gangster-dictators (Hitler, Mussolini) with active consent of the bourgeoisie and systematic terrorism by pretorian guards. Recrudescence of superstition and deliberate cult of savagery: barbarian invasions from within and without. Beginnings of megalopolitan exodus. Material deficiencies and lapses of cultural continuity: repression and censorship. Cessation of productive work in the arts and sciences.

Sixth and Final Stage: Nekropolis. War and famine and disease rack both city and countryside. The physical towns become mere shells. Those who remain in them are unable to carry on the old municipal services or maintain the old civic life: what remains of that life is at best a clumsy caricature. The names persist; the reality vanishes. The monuments and books no longer convey meaning; the old routine of life involves too much effort to carry on: the streets fall into disrepair and grass grows in the cracks of the pavement: the viaducts break down, the water mains become empty; the rich shops, once looted, remain empty of goods by reason of the failure of trade or production. Relapse into the more primitive rural occupations. The historic culture survives, if at all, in the provinces and the remote villages, which share the collapse but are not completely carried down by it or submerged in the debris. First the megalopolis becomes a lair: then its occupants are either hunted out by some warrior band, seeking the last remnants of conquest in gold or women or random luxuries, or they gradually fall away of their own accord. The living forms of the ancient city become a tomb for dying: sand sweeps over the ruins: so Babylon, Nineveh, Rome. In short, Nekropolis, the city of the dead: flesh turned to ashes: life turned into a meaningless pillar of salt.

16: Possibilities of Renewal

History is full of burying grounds: the dead forms and deserted shards of communities that had not learned the art of living in harmonious relations with nature and with other communities. The end stage, over which Spengler gloated, is an undeniable reality that has overtaken many civilizations: dead-food for the vulturelike imagination.

But one must not, like a Spengler or a Sorokin, make the mistake of identifying the *logical* stages of a process, as discovered and systematized by intellectual analysis, with the living reality. For in real life, in real cultures, history does not present a solid laminated block of uniform dimensions that one may break down into smaller blocks, each unified within itself to form part of a consistent whole. End-processes often occur in the middle of a culture; accidental mischances and injuries may bring to the middle-aged the normal deteriorations of senescence. Likewise early processes or rejuvenating reactions may be noted in the final phases of the most mechanized civilization. In short, time as experience and duration upsets this logical order, which is based chiefly on time as an attribute of spatial movement. Mutations arise in human communities from unexpected sources: the social heritage makes society much less of a unity than we are compelled to conceive it, by the nature of language, when we interrupt the complex stream of actual life in order to take account of it in thought. Out of these mutations, a new social dominant may arrive: veritably a saving remnant.

To take the simplest point of all: the final stage in civilization is often reached at an intermediate point in urban development. Witness fourteenth century Rome. It exhibited most of the characteristics of a Nekropolis, including a loss, not alone of the single title to papal supremacy, but of a good part of its population. Yet, after that nadir had been reached, a renewal took place: two centuries later its ruins stimulate Brunelleschi and its new buildings offer a challenge to the genius of Michelangelo. The other point to remember is that civilization is not, even in its utmost megalopolitan phase, confined to the world-cities alone. Though they cast their shadows over the farthest territories, neither their governments nor their armies nor their culture institutes can embrace with any degree of thoroughness the provinces they lay claim to: part of their dominion is mere bluff and pretense, unchallengeable until actually challenged.

Even in the ultimate stage of Tyrannopolis, the tyranny is only partly effective: Krilov contrives to tell his satirical fables and Epictetus, the slave, thinks his own thoughts and preserves autonomy within his soul. At this stage there still remain regions and cities and villages with other memories, other backgrounds, other hopes: though in shackles to the external dictatorship, they remain essentially withdrawn. In the heyday of the megalopolitan economy, such regional centers remain partly outside the cycle: some failure of enterprise, some lack of opportunity, or some sturdier sense of life-values keeps them from sharing the delusive growth and splendor of the metropolis.

When, through the processes of decay and destruction hastened by Tyrannopolis, the great cities sink into ruin, these other centers, though they may stagger from the blow, will nevertheless continue to live: indeed, they may live more intensely once the incubus of the

big city and its tyrannous system of political and financial administration is removed. Marseilles and some of the other towns of Provence had such a function after the disintegration of the old Roman
civilization in Italy: this fact, along with their closer contact with
Byzantium and the Arabic possessions, played a significant part,
no doubt, in that brilliant outburst of Provençal culture in the early
Middle Ages. On the other hand, to face the blacker side of the picture, the reverse process may happen: a process that doubly demands
our watchful care today: that is, a deteriorative phase of culture
may prolong its existence by capturing the fresh energies of a
younger growth. In this fashion, Byzantium reached up to paralyze
the "young" culture of sixteenth century Russia; and in similar
fashion, again, the Tyrannopolis of the Czars in Russia, which exhibited many of the symptoms of the end-process by the close of the
nineteenth century, has left its cruel mark on the fresh beginnings
made by the Soviet regime: furthering that aimless centralization
and that rigid bureaucratism and that habit of systematic repression
of valid differences which leaves no place for young initiative, or for
those forms of co-operation which, to be wholehearted, must be
voluntary.

In other words, the life course of cities is essentially different
from that of most higher organisms. Cities exhibit the phenomena of
broken growth, of partial death, of self-regeneration. Cities and city
cultures may have sudden beginnings from remote gestations; and
they are capable of prolongations as *physical organizations* through
the life-spans of more than one culture: witness Damascus, most
ancient of surviving towns, already venerable in St. Paul's day. It is
only as parable rather than as scientific statement that one may talk
of the spring or winter of a civilization as if the cycle had a climatic
inevitability, or of the birth and death of a culture-phase, as if any
contemporary observer could confidently recognize either the birth-
cry or the death-rattle.

Cities can take on new life by a transplantion of tissues from
healthy communities in other regions or civilizations: a few hundred
people, like the Huguenots in Scotland or Germany, or the Jews in
almost every civilization, may have a profoundly stimulating effect.
Today, the dispersal of the élite from Germany and Italy and in some

degree from Russia may be one of the elements that will compensate for the growing elements of barbarism within those countries. And these transplanted tissues need not even be in the form of living people: the collective organs of culture, signs, symbols, forms, the abstract and etherealized essences, may likewise exercise a decisive effect: witness the powerful influence of Roman monuments and Greek literature in temporarily supplementing the spent energies of the Middle Ages. All that is necessary is that the organism which receives these new tissues shall be in a state of readiness.

In short: the roots of a culture are deep. If the crown is blighted by disease, it may still put forth new shoots at the base; and in time these shoots may flourish and provide a new trunk and crown. All these are of course figures of speech: but they are means of counteracting and truing up analogies that are even more abstract, figures that are even more fanciful: the curve of a cycle, the succession of the seasons. Social life has its own laws and rhythms: much remains hidden or irrational: much escapes empiric observation and still more escapes statistical analysis. All one can say with any surety is this: when a city has reached the megalopolitan stage, it is plainly on the downward path: it needs a terrific exertion of social force to overcome the inertia, to alter the direction of movement, to resist the immanent processes of disintegration. But while there is life, there is the possibility of counter-movement, fresh growth. Only when the big city has finally become wasteland must the locus of life be elsewhere.

17: Signs of Salvage

The boast of the metropolis is that it is a world city, and the boast is not altogether a vain one. Thirty centers of world-contact, temporary concentration points for travelers and observers, for administrators and motivators, for students and scholars and technicians, would not be too many to serve a culture as complicated and many-sided as that which we now possess. Most of the existing world cities have become over-congested because they did have real advantages in international communication: they were the meeting-points of transcontinental and trans-oceanic highways: often they possessed a superior inheritance of culture institutes, reaching back into a unique historic past. These advantages would remain even if the present mass-agglomerations of people were reduced to a cluster of inter-related cities, no one of which would have over fifty thousand people, nor the cluster have more than a million: What was once present only in an urban *point*, is now available throughout a whole region.

But the world city in order to function as such requires a world order. A world in disorder can find no use for such a city, except to make it a center of political aggression and financial aggrandizement, incapable of performing the essential functions of a city even for its own teeming population. Any effective effort to reconstitute the metropolis demands something more than local traffic plans or local building regulations: as Benton MacKaye has said, to diminish the congestion of traffic at Times Square it may be necessary to re-route the export of wheat from the hinterland; and what is true for traffic holds for the other functions of the city. Most metropolitan planning has involved the use of seven local maids with seven mops to hold back the sea.

Any effort to reconstitute the metropolis, in other words, must go *against* the basic pattern of the metropolitan economy. It must work against population increase, against multiplying the mechanical facilities for congestion, against the expansion of the continuous urban area, against unmanageable bigness and irrational "great-ness." The proof that this alone provides a suitable occasion for the relief of metropolitan difficulties lies in the experience of the last twenty-five years.

Almost all the decisive improvements that have taken place in Wien, London, Berlin, and New York have been put through during the periods when the metropolitan financial system was in a state of collapse. It was in the midst of the dreadful period of inflation that Berlin captured a sufficient amount of outlying land to build great parks and housing communities and control the development of private land areas. Not till the collapse came could Berlin afford to take the steps that a small regional city like Ulm had been able to take a generation before. So, too, it was in the period of most dire need that Wien gathered in local taxes the funds necessary to float the great housing developments that were done under the socialist government of the municipality after the war: more improvement in a dozen years than capitalism and "prosperity" had achieved in a dozen decades. And it was in the midst of the great depression that began in 1930 that the city of New York, *through the utter bankruptcy of numerous landholders,* obtained a sufficient number of small plots to serve as local playgrounds: it was similarly as a by-product of the effort to increase employment through Public Works that the city obtained sufficient funds from the National Government to build two great colleges and to carry through a comprehensive program of park rehabilitation. Life-values came back to the city only after financial values had been deflated. From the standpoint of decent metropolitan living one might well speak of the "menace of prosperity."

In laying down the foundations for a new regional order, based on the culture of life, the metropolis nevertheless has a proud part to play. At present the world cities, through the very fact of monopoly, contain many of the best elements in man's heritage. Here the keenest criticism of the metropolitan regime has come forth; and it is here that the need for decentralization has been felt and intelligent plans for it worked out. Given the concentration of power and activity in the big city, the courage to attack large tasks, the ability to assemble, transport, and organize vast quantities of men and materials have grown up, too. Energy that has so far been mobilized here to produce congestion can also be utilized toward the rebuilding of the metropolis and the founding of a biotechnic regime. The biological renewal of modern life, through the cult of hygiene and the systematic pursuit of games and sports, is a product of the metropolis: so, too, the first redefinition of the social nucleus of the modern city, in the embryonic form of the Settlement House, the People's Palace, and the Community Center.

The settlement house, in fact, was the first effective effort, not merely to overcome the barbarism of the submerged areas of the metropolis, but to establish in its random neighborhoods an appropriate social nucleus which could serve as a meeting-point for its social and educational activities. Young clergymen and earnest young women, a Canon Barnett, a Jane Addams, instead of traveling to remote parts of the world to carry the gospel, began in the eighties to settle in the slums: they found people as benighted as the Fiji cannibals, and in many ways just as innocent of contemporary Western culture. These denizens of Whitechapel and the South Side were outcasts: without hope, without pride: victims not merely of exploitation but of what William Morris called the damned wantlessness of the poor.

The colonization of the slums by means of the Settlement House was an important event: not merely did it give the slum dweller himself his first glimpse of art, literature, drama, music, play: not merely did it provide a place for clubs and social groups to meet. Something else happened. The success of the Settlement House called attention to the fact that more prosperous neighborhoods were in fact equally devoid of the elementary organs of association: civically speaking, every middle-class neighborhood was a nonentity, too. It was, then, precisely out of the most degrading poverty and the most disorganized environment that the new conception of an organized urban neighborhood, with a central building adapted to a varied round of communal activities, took shape. This conception is fundamental to the best housing and community building that have been done during the past generation: it will probably remain, even though the name disappear and the institution be modified, the most fundamental cultural contribution of the metropolis to the new order.

To cast off the dead form of the metropolitan order, and to concentrate its surviving energies upon the social utilization of its real goods, within the greater regional framework, is perhaps the most pressing task of our civilization: the issues of war and peace, socialization or disorganization, culture or barbarism, rest in good part on our success in handling this problem. Already, the *symbols* of the new order have appeared. In new buildings, new schools, a new program of living, fresh mutations, have disclosed themselves: in the biological and the sociological sciences, the positive foundations for this order have been laid: an order more comprehensive than Marx conceived, and more profound in its demands and readjustments than a merely economic revolution. The next step lies in contriving the political organization appropriate to this new task, and in working out, in concrete detail, the effective economic means.

Before either of these steps can be taken, however, we must have a clearer visual picture of the actual changes that have occurred and of the new possibilities that have emerged. The dynamics of social change require an actual situation in time: a series of processes that can be hastened or retarded, energized or depleted: groups of people interacting with their place and their form of work, with other groups, with their social heritage: and a collective framework of interests and goals which, while slowly changing themselves, serve to concentrate and direct the intermediate social process. When all the other elements in social change are duly taken into account, the definition of the new framework itself becomes, not a piece of uto-pian wishfulness, but a decisive element in the whole process.

Periods of rapid social crystallization—as in Rome at the time of St. Augustine, or England in the time of Bentham—are periods when the community acquires, through critical inquiry and self-conscious re-orientation, a firm collective insight into its own pur-poses and a passionate faith in the possibility of a new attitude and a profound societal change: further command of the social processes follows. While the rational definition of the ideal framework does not alone effect the necessary transition, it is an important element in changing the direction of the blind process, and in hastening the necessary social adaptations. The strongest social organizations and social pressures, without such well-defined goals, dissipate their energies in uneasy random efforts occasioned by passing opportuni-ties. No goal, then no direction: no underlying plan, no consensus, then no effective practical action. If society is paralyzed today, it is not for lack of means but for lack of purpose.

CHAPTER V. THE REGIONAL FRAMEWORK
OF CIVILIZATION

1: New Patterns of Life and Thought

What has been called the triumph of urbanization has been very largely the systematic frustration of those social and co-operative endeavors which modern collective thought has made possible. Metropolitan civilization, with its resourceful technical ingenuity, its delicately articulated physical organization, has failed through its very structure to distribute the benefits that it potentially commands. *Starvation in the midst of plenty* applies to its social life no less than to its inequitable system of distribution.

But the human failure of metropolitan civilization has awakened compensatory reactions; and profound changes have been going on in life and thought which will alter the idolum out of which this civilization has grown. Society as a whole, fortunately, tends to act more wisely than its individual members. It retains areas of experience and reserves of force that the narrower vision of a single party, group, or generation does not encompass.

The orientation of thought toward the realities of organic life, something that in the eighteenth century went no further than the intuitions of the poet or the naturalist, had by the end of the nineteenth century become so pervasive that it entered even into the hitherto lifeless realm of mechanics: the telephone, the phonograph, the motion picture, the airplane, sprang out of an interest in the functions of organisms and could not have developed without a scientific knowledge of their processes. Steadily, for the past generation, a transformation has been going on in every department of thought: a re-location of interest from mechanism to organism, a change from a world in which material bodies and mechanical motion alone were real to a world in which invisible rays and emanations, in which human projections and dreams, are as real as any immediately visible or external phenomenon—as real and on occasion more important.

Nineteenth century industry had been mainly concerned, in its paleotechnic phase, with the inorganic processes of factory, steel mill, and mine. The first significant revelation of experimental biological knowledge to industry came through Pasteur's researches on the diseases of silkworms, and the rôle of ferments in wines. That knowledge, which was to lay the foundation for modern hygiene and medicine, did not go into circulation until the eighteen-seventies. It needed the triumphant demonstrations of medicine in the ensuing decades to give authority to a new world-view, which accords to the organism and the world of life the priority that had been accorded, from the seventeenth century on, to the machine and to a universe whose cold mechanical perfection was described by physics and astronomy.

The leading ideas of this organic order may be briefly summed up.

First: the primacy of life, and of autonomous but perpetually inter-related organisms as vehicles of life. Each organism has its own line of growth, that of its species, its own curve of development, its own span of variations, its own pattern of existence. To maintain its life-shape the organism must constantly alter it and renew itself by entering into active relations with the rest of the environment. Even the most sessile and sleepy forms of life must seize energy in order to maintain their equilibrium: thus the organism changes, by no matter what infinitesimal amounts, the balance of the environment; and the failure to act and re-act means either the temporary suspension of life or its final end. Not merely is the organism implicated in its environment in space: it is also implicated in time, through the biological phenomena of inheritance and memory; and in human societies it is even more consciously implicated through the necessity of assimilating a complicated social heritage which forms, as it were, a second environment.

Human beings and groups are the outcomes of an historic complex, their inheritance, and they move toward a conditioned but uncertain destination, their future. The assimilation of the past and the making of the future are the two ever-present poles of existence in a human community. In so far as Aristotle appreciated the future, as potentiality and possibility, he was more truly a sociologist than those thinkers of the past century whose minds, even when dealing with society, have stopped short with time-categories that completely suffice only for elementary mechanics.

The autonomy of the organism, so characteristic of its growth, renewal, and repair, does not lead to isolation in either time or space. On the contrary, every living creature is part of the general web of life: only as life exists in all its processes and realities, from the action of the bacteria upward, can any particular unit of it continue to exist. As our knowledge of the organism has grown, the importance of the environment as a co-operative factor in its development has become clearer; and its bearing upon the development of human societies has become plainer, too. If there are favorable habitats and favorable forms of association for animals and plants, as ecology demonstrates, why not for men? If each particular natural environment has its own balance, is there not perhaps an equivalent of this in culture? Organisms, their functions, their environments: people, their occupations, their workplaces and living-places, form inter-related and definable wholes.

Such questions as yet can evoke only tentative answers; but they provide a new starting point for investigation. And from the negative processes, the destruction and deterioration of the environment through man's misuse, much has already been learned: Marsh's classic treatise on the Earth and Man was followed by the highly intelligent surveys of natural resources, in terms of potential human use, by Major Powell and Raphael Pumpelly, and the later conservationists, from Van Hise to MacKaye. Beginning with Kropotkin's Mutual Aid the study of human ecology has taken a more positive turn: witness Huntington's studies of civilization and climate, the urban investigations of the Chicago school of sociologists, and above all, Patrick Geddes's lifelong effort to develop a sociology on the basis of biology, and a social art on the positive foundation of our biological, psychological and sociological knowledge. In the doctrines of emergents, organisms, and wholes, particularly as set forth in Lloyd Morgan and Whitehead, lie the outline of an appropriate metaphysics.

In emphasizing the importance of this new orientation toward the living and the organic, I expressly rule out false biological analogies between societies and organisms: Herbert Spencer and others pushed these to the point of absurdity. Such analogies sometimes provide useful suggestions, suggestions no less practical than those derived— with equally little realism—from the machine. But the point is that our knowledge directs attention to parallel processes, parallel conditions and reactions; and it gives rise to related pictures of the natural and the cultural environments, considered as wholes, within which man finds his life and being and drama.

So long as the machine was uppermost, people thought quantitatively in terms of expansion, extension, progress, mechanical multiplication, power. With the organism uppermost we begin to think qualitatively in terms of growth, norms, shapes, inter-relationships, implications, associations, and societies. We realize that the aim of the social process is not to make men more powerful, but to make them more completely developed, more human, more capable of carrying on the specifically human attributes of culture—neither snarling carnivores nor insensate robots. Once established, the vital and social order must subsume the mechanical one, and dominate it: in practice as well as in thought. In social terms, this means a re-orientation not only from mechanism to organism, but from despotism to symbiotic association, from capitalism and fascism to co-operation and basic communism.

There is one further important consequence of this recognition of the organic: that is, the disappearance of the boundary walls between the inner and the outer, the conscious and the unconscious, the external and the internal environment. With man there is no outer environment available except through the medium of society—that medium which supplies nourishment to the growing baby, equips it with the signs of language and the symbols of association, prepares it by cultural habituation to eat this food and reject that poison, to believe this truth and turn aside from that error. In order for the outer environment to function effectively, man must face it, seize it,

assimilate it: and when that is done, it is no longer an *outer* environment.

Within its figure on the web of life, each organism is by nature
selective: it extracts from the total environment, its potential field of
action, just those elements that can be taken in and that promote
growth or security. When it makes bad selections its life is impaired;
and when it goes on making them, it ultimately dies. As man's scale
of cultural development rises, nature becomes a more active element
in his culture, and his culture, in turn, becomes second nature. Thus
an ever greater part is played by deliberate selection, and by the
collective reconstruction of the environment in terms of man's needs,
desires, and purposes. The house, for example, has its origin in the
nest and the cave; but in what animal exigencies is there anything
to be compared to the burial tomb or the monument? Just as man
himself is the most triumphant example of man's domestication of
animals, so society is the result of man's long experiment in refining
the processes of animal association. One might almost define the city
as the structure through which domestication and association were
purposively united.

The time has come to express more fully this re-orientation toward
life and organism. In the present chapter I shall attempt to outline
the broader requirements of a life-conditioned environment: first,
in the barest terms of "air, water, and places"; and then in terms of
the economic and political pattern that is already present, like the
buds of spring, in the wintry thicket of metropolitan civilization.
Within this emerging regional framework, we shall more easily
find the place and form of the new urban community that has also
begun to emerge.

2: The Regional Outlook

Man's conscious relation to the earth underwent a profound change
in Western Europe in the fifteenth century. The desire to conquer
space and explore the unknown upset his more sedentary habits and
gave him fresh excuses for motion which undermined his close vege-
tative relationship to his native soil. But collectively, the great era of
exploration and colonization, which opened in the sixteenth century,
introduced a period of terrestrial neglect. In the act of seizing all

the habitable parts of the earth, the colonists of Africa and the Americas systematically misused and neglected their possession: first, perhaps, out of ignorance, but no less because, even when better knowledge existed, an imperious government, a rapacious economic corporation or individual, would set no bounds to greed or to momentary needs. Where industries developed, where towns spread, land values rose—and the land lost most of its value.

Today the period of exploration has come to an end, and our attitude toward the earth is undergoing another profound change: a by-product of our increased knowledge of the sources of life, and our critical examination of human history. We can no longer leave soils and landscapes and agricultural possibilities out of our calculations in considering the future of either industries or cities. For the era of the callous pioneer, who laid waste to a particular area, looted its natural resources, and moved on, is over: there is no place left to move. We have reached the end of our journey, and in the main, we must retrace our steps, and, region by region, learn to do intelligently and co-operatively what we hitherto did in such disregard of the elementary decencies of life. The grasp of the region as a dynamic social reality is a first step toward a constructive policy of planning, housing, and urban renewal.

In different countries, this consciousness of the underlying geographic conditions and earth-relations has taken different forms. In France, the home of regionalism as a deliberate movement, regionalism has meant first of all a protest against the excessive centralization that took place in politics and culture: it has led to the reconstitution of the provincial universities and to the active development of regions such as the French Alps, around Grenoble. In Denmark, regionalism meant the recapture of the native heritage of the ballads and the folk-literature, the founding of Folk High Schools in the countryside, and the growth of the co-operative movement—and scientific agronomy and breeding—in agriculture; in Czecho-Slovakia, it has meant the founding of an independent political state.

These movements are not unrelated; behind them are certain common ideas. At a period when the uniformities of the machine civilization were being overstressed, regionalism served to emphasize compensatory organic elements: above all, those differences that arise out of geographic, historic, and cultural peculiarities. In its recognition of the region as a basic configuration in human life; in its acceptance of natural diversities as well as natural associations and uniformities; in its recognition of the region as a permanent sphere of cultural influences and as a center of economic activities, as well as an implicit geographic fact—here lies the vital common element in the regionalist movement. So far from being archaic and reactionary, regionalism belongs to the future.

3: The Region as a Geographic Unit

Walking through the countryside in the United States, one may find in the midst of an open field or at the corner of a woodlot a granite post, with the name of one state on one side of it, and that of the adjoining state on the other side. Similar monuments exist at every national frontier, although the population in the transitional zone may be almost as similar to the casual eye as the inhabitants of New York and Connecticut.

Political boundaries of the "imaginary" kind have a hard-and-fast character: that is their convenience. They define the limits of certain man-made conventions and obligations, like constitutions and codes of law. The creation of such boundaries is part of man's efforts to create a more orderly social world: a world of uniform and predictable events. Indeed, the notion of giving some sort of spatial continuity to behavior patterns, instead of permitting them to change in form from one local district to another, with endless quirks and confusing variations, is one of the great political changes that separates the modern world of states from the spatially inconsecutive and muddled allegiances of the feudal world.

Underlying all our political conventions, however, is the basic fact of the earth itself; and the question is how far these political unifications correspond effectively to those provided by nature and other aspects of human culture. The formal partition of the landscape antedated, for the most part, modern geographic knowledge: it was the empirical work of statesmen and lawgivers who believed, for the most part, that differences between peoples or regions were man-made, and could be wiped out by an act of the legislature. Even the

New York State, while not a complete region, needs only to be rounded out by the inclusion of Northern New Jersey, and that part of Connecticut which swings over from a point opposite the central part of Long Island. Otherwise it has the major requirements for a human region: individuality and coherence, the possibilities of a balanced and partly self-sustaining agricultural and economic life, a diversity of resources and a variety of habitats from the partly primeval Adirondack mountains down to the coves, sand-dunes, and beaches of Long Island, with its mild climate, its early growing season, its duck-ponds, and its rich aquatic life. The original national traditions, those of the Dutch, the English, and the French Huguenots, have been variegated with later cultural strains; but from the beginning the international importance of the port of New York, to say nothing of the place occupied by Buffalo in grain shipments, has given New York a cosmopolitan standard: its typical sons, like Washington Irving, James Fenimore Cooper, Samuel Morse, and Herman Melville, were as much at home in Europe as in their own country, while its Whitman uttered his salute to the world and received the world's response before his fellow-countryman had measured his grand dimensions. The geological surveys instituted by the University of the State of New York in the forties were not merely a milestone in science: they were, in specialized form, a fragment of those publicly aided regional surveys whose making is the effective prelude to rational programs and plans. Its agricultural wealth lies not merely in its dairy regions, with their large surpluses of milk and cheese, but in the grape culture of the Mohawk Valley, where some of the finest American wines are made, and in apple orchards whose excellent apples have ironically often been pushed out of the metropolitan market in favor of insipid varieties that have traveled many thousand miles: another example of the metropolitan habit of carrying coals to Newcastle. In its power policies, its conservation policies, its setting aside of large areas for state parks and its buying-up of sub-marginal lands, New York State has demonstrated that steady movement toward rational socialization which a democratic political life makes possible: a movement that will be accelerated when the schools and universities of the state accept even more fully than now their responsibility for working out policies, laying down programs, and projecting plans. Through its initiatives in housing and regional planning, beginning with the setting up of the New York State Housing and Regional Planning Commission in 1923, with Clarence S. Stein as Chairman, New York laid the foundations for much of the work that has been done during the present decade throughout the country: both in public housing and in regional development.

[TOP] Three important phases in the development of the State of New York, as outlined by Henry Wright in the report of the first Housing and Regional Planning Commission (1926). The first period reached its fruition between 1840 and 1880. Mainly an eotechnic economy, based upon the use of local forests, local water mills for sawing wood and grinding grain and running machinery, with small factories situated in mainly agricultural villages and country towns. The second period was one of industrial and financial concentration; it probably reached its apex between 1910 and 1920, although the inordinate growth of Buffalo and still more New York continued by inertia, even after the main supply of immigrants from Europe had been cut off. In the third phase a new pattern of population distribution emerges, based upon new technical facilities and revised social aims: if its promise is seized, it means the substitution of a biotechnic for a pecuniary economy. Neither the congestion of the paleotechnic period nor the undiscriminating diffusion of the eotechnic period with its exploratory colonization: instead, the broadening out of the valley belts, as locus for settlement, rather than congesting already crowded centers along the railroad *line,* the utilization of a hitherto neglected area by Lake Ontario is pointed to by scientific study of climatic and soil maps; similar studies suggest the zoning of the state as a whole into major utilization areas. The planning of electric power and motor highways and housing developments so as to further a new type of balanced development is here plainly indicated. The partial socialization of hydro-electric power and the reservation of great parks have already taken place. The period of re-settlement and community building now opens before us. Instead of encouraging the further building up of metropolitan areas, already overburdened, a rational policy demands a systematic urban re-settlement in Greenbelt Towns, with a minimum expenditure on the elaborate mechanical means of congestion, and a sane provision of opportunities for *living.*

[BOTTOM LEFT] Regionalism as conceived by the administrator. The division is based upon considerations that are now superior to the old-fashioned divisions between the states; but the respect for the underlying geographic and cultural realities is subordinated to the administrator's convenience, and many of these proposed regional divisions are as arbitrary as the older historic lines. A first essay in a complex re-ordering of political realities that will require at least a generation of re-statement and criticism before the inevitable order will emerge.

[BOTTOM RIGHT] While the metropolitan area is not a region, since it is, by its nature, in a state of permanent unbalance, no region can be defined as a geographic, economic, and cultural complex without respect to the essential relationships between city and country. Since in most cases the metropolis has achieved the maximum growth because it possesses a maximum number of advantages, and so is a natural meeting point, the outline of a region is partly determined by the range of influence exerted by its natural capital. McKenzie's use of the sphere of newspaper circulation as a criterion of this influence is arbitrary; its convenience for measurement cannot make up for the absence of other data and criteria; but the resulting outline of regional units is closer to geographic and sociological realities than the administrative areas shown above.

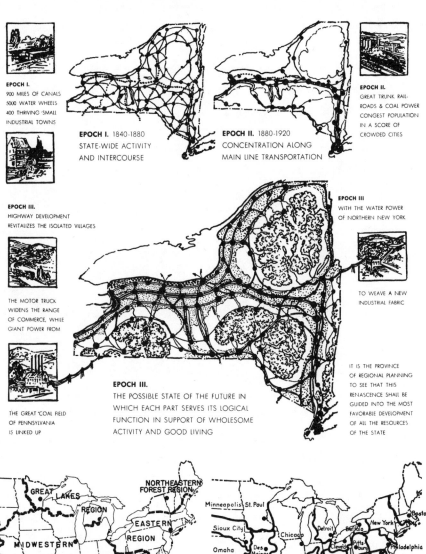

EPOCH I.
900 MILES OF CANALS
5000 WATER WHEELS
400 THRIVING SMALL
INDUSTRIAL TOWNS

EPOCH I. 1840-1880
STATE-WIDE ACTIVITY
AND INTERCOURSE

EPOCH II. 1880-1920
CONCENTRATION ALONG
MAIN LINE TRANSPORTATION

EPOCH II.
GREAT TRUNK RAIL-
ROADS & COAL POWER
CONGEST POPULATION
IN A SCORE OF
CROWDED CITIES

EPOCH III.
HIGHWAY DEVELOPMENT
REVITALIZES THE ISOLATED VILLAGES

EPOCH III
WITH THE WATER POWER
OF NORTHERN NEW YORK

THE MOTOR TRUCK
WIDENS THE RANGE
OF COMMERCE, WHILE
GIANT POWER FROM

TO WEAVE A NEW
INDUSTRIAL FABRIC

THE GREAT "COAL FIELD
OF PENNSYLVANIA
IS LINKED UP

EPOCH III.
THE POSSIBLE STATE OF THE FUTURE IN
WHICH EACH PART SERVES ITS LOGICAL
FUNCTION IN SUPPORT OF WHOLESOME
ACTIVITY AND GOOD LIVING

IT IS THE PROVINCE
OF REGIONAL PLANNING
TO SEE THAT THIS
RENASCENCE SHALL BE
GUIDED INTO THE MOST
FAVORABLE DEVELOPMENT
OF ALL THE RESOURCES
OF THE STATE

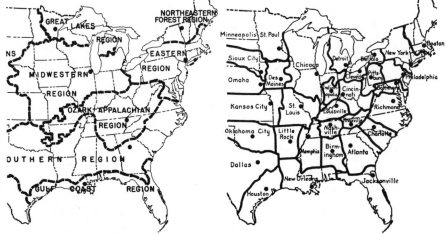

new democratic states, in defining the limits of territorial sovereignty, followed the arbitrary patterns of the absolute rulers and princelings of the baroque period. As in the delimitation of the political departments of France during the French Revolution, administrators usually chose to ignore natural regions, with their historic complexes and their customary privileges. They could not dissociate the older organic pattern from the feudal and ecclesiastical order that had grown up with it: antagonistic to the privileges of the latter, they sought to displace the reality of the first.

In general, during the nineteenth century, functional geographic associations and functional boundaries were disregarded. States were set up, municipalities were created, administrative districts bounded, new areas of authority outlined, with little concern for the geographic constants and for the underlying community relations founded upon them. Rivers, which are channels of unification for the communities on both sides, were even favored as boundary lines: what was solely a military obstacle was treated as an actual division. Little effort was made to create harmonious regional units that would give equal expression to the needs of the countryside and the needs of cities.

Up to a point, these arbitrary units of administration worked better than the facts warranted. The reason should be plain. In many cases any sort of boundary, defining the limits of obligation and interest, is better than no boundary at all: even an artificial association is more efficient than aimless, unorganized juxtaposition. But these new political units forced many institutions into molds that did not fit them, and they ceased to exercise effective control over organizations—like the great industrial corporations—that were set up on a continental or a worldwide basis; while the growth of the metropolis under the financial and imperial regime made it often form a homogeneous urban unit over areas under diverse and conflicting administrative authorities. After much strain and frustration, the weaknesses of these abstract divisions at last became apparent: meanwhile, the human geographer and the sociologist have opened our eyes to the fundamental geographic facts; and we can now define the regional complex, not in terms solely of men's wishes, but in terms woven into objective reality.

In what sense does the region exist as a geographic unit; and what conditions does it lay down for human occupation?

One may define a region by working upward from the smallest unit of human habitation, in terms of functions, activities, and interests; or by working downward, mainly in terms of land mass, climate, and physical interactions. The geographer divides the world into five great habitable land-masses. But one has only to examine these masses closely to see that while the differences between them are many, they are no greater than the differences that exist within them, among their subordinate areas. Each mass divides into provinces, regions, and sub-regions: these units form complexes that are more or less differentiated in pattern. Their geologic structure, soil, situation, climate, vegetation, and animal life differentiate them from other complexes.

As soon as one adds man to the picture the difference between areas becomes multifarious and subtle: for laws, manners, customs, the patterns of communal living, the forms of architecture, the village types and city types, the transformation of the original landscape into the humanly modified landscape of agriculture, with its orderly patterns and deliberate culture—all these are fresh factors of differentiation, marking off one region from another. In regions of long settlement indeed the aboriginal characteristics of the environment have been profoundly modified by man's occupation: many of the most valuable food-plants used in Western agriculture, for example, are exotics. As social conditions vie with natural conditions in establishing the regional character it becomes easier to define even the boundaries of the region in terms of the spheres of attraction, the dominant cities, rather than in terms of purely physical barriers, like the swamps and forests that originally bounded the counties of South England.

Now, the more thoroughly one is acquainted with the social and geographic facts in any area, the more keenly one becomes aware that unity and differentiation go hand in hand. When one searches for unity, the human race is obviously one. When one looks for differences one discovers not only national types and regional types, one discovers likewise important differences between a Florentine and a Neapolitan, between a Glasgow man and an Edinburgh man, even differences in language, accent, gesture, feeling between villages that are but a day's walk apart. Finally, one reaches the primordial unit of individuality and realizes that no two identical finger prints of different persons have yet been discovered. Unity does not annul difference; and difference does not undermine a dynamic unity.

There are accordingly two kinds of unity which one must clearly distinguish: unity by suppression, in which a single pattern of life is universalized, and that of unity by inclusion, in which a multitude of different patterns either find their common elements, or become elements in a more complex configuration that includes them. Unity by suppression is achieved by de-building organic relations and by the reduction of the complicated facts of life to a simpler system: such method is ingrained in all the generalizing processes of thought, and when such procrustean likeness and uniformity and unison is sought by the political administrator, the violence that he does to reality is not perhaps sufficiently noticed for the reason that the method itself grows out of one of the inherent limitations of thought—a limitation that sacrifices accuracy and comprehensiveness to the practical needs of the moment. Although one may treat a human being as an arbitrary numerical unit, one of a thousand that is born on a given day, one of ten thousand taxpayers in a certain income bracket, one does not eliminate him as a complex social reality. This is likewise true of regional units. De-building, in order to widen the scheme of life invoked by the metropolis and the governing state, ends in impoverishment: like a financial system in which the currency and the credit no longer summon up, on demand, the food and machinery and services which alone can give reality to the counters by which they are manipulated.

In general, one may say that geographic differences are primordial, while social differentiations, including those derived from urban association, are emergent: one is foundation, the other pinnacle. Merely by examining the geographic base one cannot tell what the social emergent will be; for, precisely because it *is* an emergent, precisely because it necessarily contains elements from other geographic regions and other cultures and other layers of historic experience, it is a new configuration, not given in the geographic complex itself. But geographic conditions nevertheless place the possibilities of cultural development within certain limits: the skills of the Eskimo are of no use in the tropical jungle.

Each regional complex then is marked by three special qualities. The first is its specific geographic character: certain common properties of soil, climate, vegetation, agriculture and technical exploitation.

Take the State of Ohio. The greater part of the state is glaciated; the land is fertile; and a network of small communities distributes the population fairly evenly over the whole area, with here and there a further concentration in cities like Toledo and Cleveland in the north and Cincinnati in the south. With its fertile fields, its vast nursery gardens of peonies, its tree-lined villages, the northern parts of Ohio present a physiognomy that curiously combines that of New England with that of Holland. On the surface, it is like a handsome Dutch landscape with all its dimensions magnified: the brick highways even underline the likeness. At the same time the villages themselves, often founded by New Englanders, have a closer relation to the agricultural type of settlement in New England than to the close urban pattern of the Netherlands, where land was more precious. But the formal political boundary does not define this regional complex: it is an historic emergent that now calls for understanding and further political and cultural expression. One of the main tasks of regionalism is to see and develop further the geographic and social realities that underlie a multitude of more or less empty formal differentiations. Often the latter are based on traditions, political interests, or institutions that no longer prevail.

Next, a region is characterized by the existence of a balance, a state of dynamic equilibrium, between its various parts: when any large alteration is made in one section of the environment, corresponding or compensating changes must be made, as a rule, in every other part. When man upsets the natural balance by introducing a new creature, as the jack rabbit was introduced into Australia, when he plows up the grassland in semi-arid areas in order to make an evanescent profit out of farming wheat, or when he removes the forest cover wholesale—he sets up a whole train of consequences that disrupt the complicated fabric upon which permanent human settlement is based: soil erosion, floods, insect pests, blights of various kinds, may follow such upsets.

One creature indeed man cannot help introducing—himself. And perhaps the chief problem of human settlement has been to adapt the planet to man's many new needs without completely disrupting the balance of nature. Favorable adaptations of the environment, like the systematic adaptation of the Nile floodlands to permanent agriculture, are the foundations for a great release in energy and a durable human culture. Each region has its own configuration: its own special partnerships and associations, its own favored resources, and its own equally characteristic dearths or impoverishments. These resources vary with the culture of the community itself. As the cultural heritage increases, a larger part of the environment becomes useful and meaningful: *the natural conditions of a region, so far from being nullified by the increase of culture and technical skill, are actually magnified.* The hunter knows the forest only as a home for game; but for modern man the forest is also a source of lumber, a protection against soil erosion, a recreation area, and a field for scientific observation.

Hence the popular notion that modern technology has lessened the importance of the natural habitat is precisely the opposite of the truth: likewise the notion that "regional differences fade out as isolation disappears." On a sandy spit like Cape Cod, for instance, there will be, originally only fishermen and primitive agriculturists: growers of corn, diggers of clams, pickers of cranberries in the bogs. Later, the same area, because of the availability of wood and sand, may nourish a glass industry, such as the ancient one at Sandwich; and at still a further stage, it may support an institute of scientific research at one end of the peninsula and a colony of artists at the other: each group revealing new resources in the environment. Meanwhile, a fresh succession of newcomers deposited on the original Indian layer—English, Portuguese, French-Canadian, Negro—increases the specific individuality of this particular regional complex. So far from disappearing with isolation, regional differences become more marked, as each new occupation, each new social interest, brings out a hitherto undiscovered color that modifies the common pattern. *Primitive* regional differences may diminish with intercultural contact: but *emergent* differences become more profound, unless the region itself is disabled by the metropolitan effort to wipe out every other mode of life except that which reflects its own image. This is a sociological fact of universal bearing.

From the human standpoint, the essential point about balance is that it involves the utilization of a variety of ecological groupings and a variety of human responses: balance and variety are the two concepts, in fact, which help one to define a region of cultural settlement. Likeness of interest and singleness of response are only one side of the regional pattern: used as a basis for communal organization such criteria would create one-sided, specialized regions in a state of imbalance and cultural impoverishment. What is no less important than the feeling of identity is the fact of variety: the meeting and mingling of diverse types, the "etherealization" and interchange of diverse environments, is essential to a sound regional life.

In conceiving a region, then, it is necessary to take an area large enough to embrace a sufficient range of interests, and small enough to keep these interests in focus and to make them a subject of direct collective concern. In older regions of settlement, the interplay of geography and history has produced such human areas: even if they have lost some of their attributes, the essential shell remains: a memory if not a fact. In newer parts of the earth it is important to understand, by intensive investigation, all the factors that lend themselves to scientific description, in order finally to build the complex earth-form, not discoverable in nature: the balanced human region. Take away the notions of variety and balance, however, and the very notion of the region becomes a mere spatial expression—applicable to any of the 108 different administrative divisions of the United States, for example, as made by this or that government department in Washington. Our task is to replace the primeval balance that exists in a region with organisms in a state of nature, by a richer environment, a more subtle and many-weighted balance, of human groups and communities in a state of high culture. The sort of regional planning that seeks some simple arbitrary pattern, more closely fitted to the convenience of the political or industrial administrator is regional in name only. Unfortunately the tendency to call any large-scale administrative unit a region—now a fashionable name—is one from which even the admirable Report on Regional Factors in National Planning is not free.

Finally, one comes to a third characteristic of natural regions. Unlike the old-fashioned political areas they have not—except in the case of isolated islands, oases, or high mountain areas—any definite physical boundaries. The region may be defined and delimited in thought; but this is largely a practical convenience: even the purely physical characteristics often grade into each other, with intermediate zones that belong partly to one, partly to the other area. As soon as the human communities are considered, the region becomes even more plainly a system of inter-relationships that overflow and become shadowy at the margins.

This means that all boundaries in black and white are, in one degree or another, arbitrary. Reality implies a certain looseness and vagueness, a certain failure of definition. To define human areas, one must seek, not the periphery alone but the center. Fawcett wisely took the regional capital as a means of defining his sub-regions in England; and in human culture generally, the urban spheres of attraction become geographic facts of utmost importance: for the urban center tends to focus the flow of energies, men, and goods that passes through a region, concentrating them, dispersing them, diverting them, re-routing them, in short, exerting a close and controlling influence over the development of region as a dynamic reality. Indeed, the bare physiographic area itself receives some of its contour through the operation of human needs and human processes: wherever man found even the primeval wilderness, up to the days of the airplane, his own footprints accompanied him, and participated in the definition. Nature provides the materials. Conceptually and concretely, man designs the structure. The region, no less than the city, is a collective work of art. That is why it requires the actions of men, as well as the specialized knowledge of geographer and sociologist, to define it.

4: The City as a Geographic Fact

Consider the city itself as an expression of regional individuality. Even in its most highly developed stages, the city is, among other things, an earth form. It is put together out of wood, stone, clay, asphaltum, glass. Its shape is conditioned by topography and the nature of the land; and the special requisites of the site alter with the needs of defense and industry and transportation. The numerical size of an urban settlement, before routes of trade have been secured, depends directly upon the agricultural capacities of the surrounding soils, combined with the yield of the nearest fisheries. And the possibility of reaching out into other regions for sustenance depends upon its situation. The most obdurate form of local control is that of the drinking water supply: one cannot even pitch camp conveniently for a night without water.

In the river, the region provides the first natural routes of transportation, which man later modifies into irrigation systems for his crops and transportation canals for his commerce. As the river is the easiest route to travel over, it has remained in existence longest as a utility: even the new railroad usually clung to its banks. Small wonder that the Nile and the Euphrates and the Hoang-Ho and the Donau and the Rhine were the roadbeds of their civilization. The river is a unifying agent, drawing together in its stream of transportation materials gathered from each side of its course, depositing its burden of goods and culture at the terminal cities, as the river itself deposits its silt at the delta. Ocean transportation on the land-locked seas was long a secondary form of transport; and it is only by degrees that cities have established themselves—though rarely without the aid of an oasis spring—on land routes and have planted themselves with success in unwatered parts of the hinterland.

Few cultures, unless isolated by insuperable barriers and numbed into submission by exceptional rigors of climate, have ever practiced anything like complete self-subsistence, or autarchy. Inter-regional transport is one of the pillars of urban life: it multiplies contacts, social relations, products; and by the very diversity of the resources it brings together contributes to the specific pattern of the city's life. The clogging of the main routes of transportation, such as the stop-

page of oriental trade through the Bosporus after the Turkish conquest of Byzantium may vitiate the life of a city which, like Venice,
lies at the other end of the route. On the other hand, the multiplication of trade routes may pour into a single center a larger population than it can handle competently: witness the uneasy sprawl of
Hamburg and London.

No less important is climate. The climatic belt in which cities have
flourished is a broad one: it is roughly coincident with the distribution of the hard grains, whose suitability for permanent storage probably contributed greatly to that stability and continuity out of which
city life could grow. One may speak of rye cities, wheat cities, maize
cities, rice cities. The city is, in effect, a means of overcoming partly
the effect of climatic conditioning and direct topographic control:
hence their wide range in temperature and height from Angkor to
Helsinki, from Rotterdam to Mexico City or Lassa. City life takes
one form in the Mediterranean area, where the mild climate de-
creases the need for protective shelter and increases the opportunity
for public life in the open. It takes another form in the North, where
the words "chimney" or "roof" are sufficient to indicate a dwelling
house. Climate does not so much limit the existence of cities as indi-
vidualize the type of urban adaptation. Each city has its characteristic play of weather, set off against its special landscape: the fog of
London, the stinging wind of Edinburgh, the luxuriant warmth of
palm-lined Los Angeles, the dramatic patches of sunlight in the
gloomy skies of Berlin, set in the midst of its pine-barrens.

One further influence of climate: its effects upon habits of eating
and drinking. Perhaps cities first developed in the warm valleys of
Asia Minor and Northern Africa not merely because the food supply
had increased but because a larger population could subsist on a
sparser diet than was necessary in the North. As one goes north-
ward, both the production of food and the eating of it become a
more engrossing daily occupation; and whereas the temperate
Greek regarded the habit of drinking undiluted wine as a barbarism,
the northern city dweller, battling with the dank winds, chilled by
the sloshy underfooting, depressed by the eternal dullness of the sky,
drinks much and often: not content with wine neat, he spices it, dis-
tills it, turns it into firewater.

Food and drink, no less than climate, add to the individuality of a city; and they affect the port and gesture and manners and alertness of the inhabitants. The bouillabaisse of Marseilles, the fried cakes of Amsterdam, the baked beans of Boston and the hot puddings of London, the cheeses of Rouen and the spaghetti of Naples—on all these climate, vegetation, regional occupations and regional needs, have left their mark. The quickening of European intellectual life in the urban coffee houses of the seventeenth century, and the befuddlement of the proletariat through cheap gin and brandy in the nineteenth, are capital events in the human culture of cities.

Diet, too, plays a part in differentiating castes in a city: not alone the lean diet of holiness and the fat diet of assertive sensuality, but the meatless diet of the peasant, as contrasted with the epicurean carnivorousness of the stout bourgeois, whose refined path of conduct never leads him, if he can help it, to the door of the slaughterhouse. Diet and drink, moreover, play a real if little examined rôle in the erotic ritual, particularly in the manner and duration of sexual intercourse: there is even evidence at hand now to indicate its effect upon procreation. The tendency of an urban diet to be mixed, *inter*-regional in origin, not limited to traditional materials or recipes, is of course characteristic of most other cultural aspects of city life. And like them, it serves to unite the citizens in a common cult: in no profane allusion one may say that every urban table is a communion table.

Because of its close, if not abject, dependence upon local building materials and local qualities of site, the city epitomizes the surrounding country and gives a special character to the natural setting. At no moment in its existence is the divorce between the man-made environment and the earth complete. The red sandstone of Strasbourg, the yellow clay of London, the red brick of Bremen, the gray limestone of post-medieval Paris, the brown sandstone of old Frankfort-am-Main—the very bricks and stones symbolize that underlying partnership between man and nature which is accepted and furthered, even while it is transformed, in the structure of the city.

The immediate geological foundations remain an important attribute of urban individuality; they seep into the consciousness in all sorts of indirect ways. The very infant at play, digging in the earth of his dooryard, is conscious of the ubiquitous sand if he lives in Rotterdam, of the oily shale if in Pittsburgh, or of the tantalizing gleam of mica in the schist of Manhattan. And as cities develop, external conditions become internal influences, while internal impulses work themselves out in new forms and patterns born of the playful necessities or earnest choices of the human imagination. Just as the climate and food give a peculiar gleam or sallowness to the skin, so the "internal" influences of a region—a religion, a scientific technique, an educational doctrine—will eventually alter the shape and distribution of its buildings.

If the earth acts upon the city in such immediate ways, the indirect processes are even more numerous and potent. Above all, each trade and industry tends, as nothing else in the city's life does, to maximize the environment: to concentrate within a limited area, the widest sweep of resources, products, processes, and modes of life. This phenomenon is so constant and so universal that it tends to escape notice; yet it is one of the most essential features of urban existence. A handful of people, settled in a village, with a personal range of movement limited to a day's walk, can, even in a state of intense awareness, embrace only a limited environment: their knowledge of life, however intense, will be confined to what their meadows and forests and immediate neighbors disclose to them.

The city, on the other hand, may cover a visible terrain more cramped than that of the village and its fields. But its invisible regional base, embraced through the raw materials that reach it, the technical methods that are acclimatized in its workshops, the personal and regional idiosyncrasies that are poured into it through its immigrants—its regional base is much broader. Because it extracts only the essence of the surrounding regions, because so much of life comes to it in physically dismembered or sublimated (symbolic) forms, the city embodies the region, and indeed the whole outside world, more fully than any other single fragment of landscape could do.

In the city, the environment takes on a more social form: indeed, through the media of the vocations, groups, and personalities so closely mobilized here, one part of the environment can react upon another part of the environment to produce results that would be impossible through direct intercourse and interaction. Once this

transmutation has taken place within the city, the abstract or symbolic products, no less than the concrete ones, can be transported
back to other parts of the earth.

Trade and industry have, therefore, a social significance within the
city that they do not possess in more primitive and one-sided environments: the richer the urban pattern, the more significant, in general, become the subordinate processes: and the greater the possibility for socially valuable mutations and inventions of more universal application. While over-devotion to the subsidiary economic
processes and their pecuniary evaluations may produce an insensate
culture, devoid of further significance, one cannot doubt the enliven-
ing effects of the more complicated processes of production, creation, and interchange: it distinguishes urban culture from village
culture.

In the very act of lending to economic aims the full cultural equipment of the city, the city also gives the stimulus of wider economic
and regional experiences to its specific cultural processes. By maxi-
mizing, by intensifying, the environment, the city vastly increases the
possibilities of fruitful inter-regional intercourse. It is for this reason
that the complete disappearance of the city is unthinkable, so long
as civilization remains intact—although the fundamental forms of
the city are all subject to radical alteration. Disurbanization and general dispersal would ruin the countryside no less than the urban
centers.

The complex effect of the region upon the city, and of the city in
turn upon the groups and individuals within it, has been very sensitively interpreted by Marcel Proust in the second volume of the
Remembrance of Times Past. Let me quote the passage:

"Last of all, and even more general than the family heritage, was
the rich layer imposed by the native province from which they derived their voices, and of which indeed their intonations smacked.
Between that province and the temperament of the little girl who dictated these inflections, I caught a charming dialogue. A dialogue, not
in any sense a discord. It would not have been possible to separate
the girl herself and her native place. She was herself; she was it
also. Moreover, this reaction of locally procured materials on the
genius who utilizes them and to whose work their reaction imparts

an added freshness, does not make the work any less individual, and whether it be that of an architect, a cabinet maker, or a composer, it reflects no less minutely the most subtle shades of the artist's personality, because he has been compelled to work in the millstone of Senlis or the red sandstone of Strasbourg, has respected the knots peculiar to the ash-tree, has borne in mind, when writing his score, the resources, the limitations, the volume of sound, the possibilities of flute or alto voice."

Note that this play of the local, individualized environment upon the community does not counteract the more universal forces that are also at work. For the very existence of universal forms and ideas within the city indicates, not merely the valiant effort of the human mind to create a viable abstract order, good for all times and places, but it also indicates the human desire to share experience; since the higher the degree of uniqueness, the smaller are the possibilities of finding a similar response in the bosom of one's neighbor. The local and the intense must be balanced off against the universal and the wide-spreading: the first must become more broadly *intelligible,* the second must become more narrowly *applicable.* Universals that cannot take root are of the same order as roots from whose stems no flower issues and no seeds disseminate themselves.

No region can ignore universal forces: the city, above all, is an instrument for capturing them and transmitting them more effectively. The spread of a universal religion, such as Buddhism or Christianity or Communism, or the conquest of a universal system of technics, like that now based on Western science, depends not merely upon the original power of the transformer but upon the delicacy and fine tuning of the regional receptors: both must be adequate. One has only to compare the original production per man hour in a British cotton factory with that in a Russian or Indian one or an English bricklayer's production with that of an American, to see how local habits of life modify the universal pattern and produce different quantitative as well as different qualitative results.

Only the careless eye will fail to detect deep cultural modifications from region to region, from city to city: quite as marked as the differences in the appearance of the common sparrow of Texas compared with the same species in New England. Beneath the Catholicism of Naples still lurk the forms of Venus and Diana: beneath the Protestantism of Germany, the violent gods and heroes of the Nibelungen tales still assert themselves. The region, then, is the warp upon which the fabric of communal life is woven. Even when the coarse geographic threads are unnoticed, their quality and number and closeness will affect the weaving of the ultimate cloth. The variety of these natural influences, the complexity and individuality of their assembled character in the city, are in fact a perpetual guarantee against man's inveterate tendency toward over-simplification: by this means he escapes that mechanization and falsification of the living reality which Bergson has correctly interpreted as a constant vice of human thought. Communities may wisely strive for uniformity, for certainty and fixity, for universality of pattern: indeed, unless they strove for these things the most precious human achievements would not be possible. But only upon this condition: that they shall never finally succeed.

5: The Earth as Home

Civilizations have risen and fallen without apparently perceiving the full import of their relations with the earth. For soil exhaustion and mineral exhaustion have been felt locally in other periods of history without stirring the rulers of the threatened communities to take effective measures against these dangers.

From the standpoint of earth-culture, modern civilization achieved its highest form, perhaps, in the Dutch communities of the eotechnic period, when the usual habits of wastage and degradation were reversed. Though Holland set an example to the rest of the world in the resourceful exploitation of her terrain, the example was largely ignored. The rapid spread of mankind to new countries, where the resources seemed boundless, encouraged a more primitive type of farming: lands were planted for a single crop, like cotton; and the farmers moved on to new areas when the older territories gave signs of exhaustion. Nomadic agriculture and nomadic forestry literally cut the ground from under the feet of countries like the United States. By the middle of the nineteenth century the process had gone so far in the Appalachian area that it awakened the consciousness of keen observers, like G. P. Marsh, to the universal aspects of the situation.

Viewing the result of this destruction from the standpoint of human habitability, Henry Thoreau suggested that every community in America should have, as part of its permanent domain, a portion of the wilderness, kept free for the citizens from all the encroachments of civilization, like the Royal Hunting Parks in England. A short while after this a movement was started to reserve through the Federal Government certain areas whose striking natural beauty should remain unscarred by permanent human settlement. The founding of the Yellowstone National Park in 1872, the first of a series of such reservations in the United States, was a capital event in regional culture. It was the first public recognition of the need for the primeval wilderness as a background for a civilized life, and of the value of the natural environment for other purposes than reckless financial exploitation. Utilitarian needs, such as the planting of the forests of England under Sir John Evelyn, in order to ensure a supply of timber for the British Navy, had hitherto governed the reservation of wild areas; and the state forests of Europe are one of the oldest forms of socialized ownership and activity. But although the forestry movement was, happily, to produce similar reservations in America, the United States National Parks were the first recognition of landscape as a communal resource.

Marsh and Thoreau were primarily concerned with the threatened extinction of the primeval wilderness and the impoverishments and dangers that might arise from the destruction of the forest cover. But other observers in the nineteenth century noted evils equally threatening in other provinces: Stanley Jevons pointed out that at the rate the coal beds were being exploited in the paleotechnic period, the supply of coal would give out within a century or two unless new resources were discovered or more thrifty ways introduced. While new deposits were in fact discovered and improved methods of coalburning reduced the actual consumption per horsepower, the prediction held true in general: for mineral resources, especially energy resources like coal and petroleum and lignite are irreplaceable once consumed. This is almost equally true of the more precious metals

[23] AGENTS OF REGIONAL DEVELOPMENT

The Tennessee Valley project, with its fundamental policy of public conservation of power resources, land, forest, soil and stream, in the public interest, is an indication of a new approach to the problems of regional development: an advance in certain ways over those already initiated in New York and Wisconsin. The river valley has the advantage of bringing into a common regional frame a diversified unit: this is essential to an effective civic and social life, and has been overlooked in many schemes of regional development that are erected on the basis of purely homogeneous resources or interests. Regional unity is partly an emergent: a cultural product: a result of co-operative political and economic action. Upland areas, from the Alps to Norway, from the Cascade Range to the Appalachians, are scenes for neotechnic planning with electric power and decentralized industry. In the Tennessee Valley and kindred areas, like the Upper Connecticut Valley, a basis can be laid, not merely for a more efficient industrial order, but for a new social order and a new type of urban environment, provided the requisite political courage and social imagination are collectively brought to bear.

[UPPER LEFT] High tension standards, marching across a rough terrain: expressive of the freedom of location that electric power, in contrast to old-fashioned uses of coal and water, carries with it. (*Photograph: Ewing Galloway*)

[UPPER RIGHT] Dam and spillway at Norris, Tennessee: power house below: the order and beauty of modern geotechnics. White coal: smokeless cities. (*Photograph: Tennessee Valley Authority*)

[MIDDLE] Upland area in Tennessee: potentially the scene of a more intensive settlement that will conserve rather than blot out the natural foundations for a good and durable social life. Sun, wind, cloud, earth, grass, forest, farm, garden—these are constants in human life that only shriveled imaginations would displace by mechanical substitutes: but the finer utilizations of these gifts of nature are themselves a product of a higher type of scientific and technical organization. Airplanes and electric lights are but beginnings: the sun-accumulator and the solar engine are already in embryonic existence: we await, among other things, an efficient electric accumulator, light and powerful, to displace the gasoline-driven engine, and a localized domestic method of sewage disposal which will convert sewage into fertilizer. Domestic hothouses capable of supplying fresh vegetables and fruits throughout the year should soon be available where power and fuel are cheap: these things promise a diminishment of wheeled transportation except for travel and association. (*Photograph: Tennessee Valley Authority*)

[BOTTOM] Top of the Norris Dam, facing the wild park area that has been set aside for recreation. (*Photograph: Tennessee Valley Authority*)

[TOP] Handsome interior of co-operative store in the new town of Norris, Tenn.: the unification of the modern retail market, partly expressed in metropolitan-financial terms in the chain store, is brought to its culmination in the co-operative store: elimination of wasteful duplications, ruinous competitive salesmanship, ballyhoo, and profit for absentee investors: such co-operatives are characteristic of the new housing throughout Europe: expressions of the same order. As goods become standardized and stabilized, in terms of biological need and tested performance and fair price, there will be a general curtailment of competitive retail selling. More products of the bulkier and more expensive sort will be available for critical inspection and buying by sample or by catalog in the special regional centers: more products, too, will be bought on the basis of tested knowledge, such as is now offered by the Consumers' Union. The big department stores and the big mail order houses have already been reorganizing their services on a regional basis, with warehouses and salesrooms in outlying areas. (*Photograph: Tennessee Valley Authority*)

[SECOND LEFT] Spillway of the Norris Dam: the reinforced concrete of Monnier's original bird-baths here utilized to harness a mighty current of water: a superb form, expressing the highest energy of the technical imagination: a form that recalls in its austere beauty Worringer's comparison of Egypt and America. (*Photograph: Tennessee Valley Authority*)

[SECOND RIGHT] Roadway atop Norris Dam: the use of elemental geometric forms, the slim metal column and the glass lighting globe reflects the spirit of the rest of the construction: no false monumentalism, no spurious allusions to other esthetic orders or other cultures. (*Photograph: Tennessee Valley Authority*)

[THIRD] Individual dwelling houses at Norris. A let-down: little of the order and imagination expressed in the Tennessee Valley Project itself or in the dams, reservoirs, construction works, and power plants, has been embodied in either the plan of the town or the architectural elements—with the exception of the interior of the co-operative store. These houses affect the weakly traditional—and in fact betray the living tradition. (*Photograph: Tennessee Valley Authority*)

[BOTTOM] Row of small houses at Neubühl, a co-operatively built community near Zürich. Example of modern design entirely in harmony with the order expressed in the Norris hydro-electric works, and more fully adapted to current habits of living than the sentimental fakes beloved of the suburban realty speculator and his imitators. Wide windows like these encourage the constant use of growing plants throughout the year as interior ornament: sunbaths for infants are possible behind them. The spontaneous building of sunrooms in rural America, in opposition to reactionary architectural precedent, is a sign that only a few American architects have as yet adequately interpreted the essential needs of their countrymen.

and rare-earths upon which so much of modern technology now depends: nickel, vanadium, tungsten, tantalum, manganese.

None of the original warnings about the need for dealing thriftily with natural resources was without point. The recovery of scrap metals has become an important business today; and the supply of metals has now become a sort of revolving capital fund, from which only a small part need be lost, from generation to generation, through wastage and wear. Like the general culture of the environment, this new trend must have important effects: for it *diminishes the rôle of the mine* and reduces the importance of the extractive occupations in the general economy. As the population of a country tends toward stability, the capital fund of minerals—unless drawn upon by outside areas or upset by some sudden shift in demand— will reach a point where it no longer needs to be augmented by mining, except for a small annual deficit. This day is being hastened by the more refined metallurgy and machine technics of the neotechnic regime, with its finer calculations, its dislike of superfluous bulk, and its use of other sources of power than coal.

Mark the result. Under paleotechnic methods of industry, the opening up of new mines and the settlement of the mining areas were characteristic marks of progress. Under the neotechnic complex just the opposite holds: the closing up of the mines and the diminishment of the mining process are the signs of technical advance.

What is happening to the coal industry and the railroad through the competition of petroleum will happen in the petroleum industry, too, as soon as new kinetic sources of power, such as the solar engine, supplement the present water-power resources. This further advance needs chiefly the perfection of an economic utility for the storage of electric energy. All these improvements indicate a revolutionary displacement. They are part of that change from the inorganic to the organic, from the destructive to the conservative utilization of land and energy that marks the transition from the paleotechnic to the neotechnic period, and will further mark the change from a purely mechanical ideology and method to a biotechnic one: technics based on the culture of life. Special energy crops, grown under the new scientific agronomy, may eventually further this transformation. And the psychological effect of this change must not be underestimated: the closing up of the mining industries, with their speculative animus, their gambling, their recklessness of human life, their indifference to beauty and order will produce results not confined to the mining areas alone.

The conservation movement, as it has been called in America, has perhaps been most beneficial in promoting a more economic use of raw materials. It has been less effective in creating an appropriate use of the region as a whole as a habitat for human living. For while it is to the interest of an industry to save raw materials instead of losing them to the dump pile, befouling rivers with them, or puffing them into the air, the pattern of outright individual land ownership makes it difficult to zone land areas for permanent uses that will best accord with the solid needs and interests of the community. But if the conservation of a single resource is important, the conservation of the region, as an economic and social whole, is even more important. If individual land ownership works against the best utilization of the land as a human resource, it is not the environment that must be sacrificed but the principle of unrestricted individual ownership.

Now land, like the people who live on it, is "given." It is only in a capitalistic civilization that people have come lightly to believe that land may be bought and sold, divided up, monopolized, and speculated in like any other commodity. Feudal land ownership knew no such levity: the feudal lord was a steward of the land: his rents and fees were fixed by custom: the meanest serf had a right to certain portions of the land, and if he could not leave it, neither could the land leave him. What is important in a sound scheme of land-utilization is not individual ownership but security of tenure: this is what makes possible continuity of use, encourages permanent improvements, permits long range investment of effort. The public control of land for the benefit of the region and the city as a whole is the outstanding problem for modern statesmanship: a problem toward whose solution even the legal nationalization of the land would be only a subordinate step.

The history of the division of the public lands originally possessed by the Federal Government of the United States shows that putative individual ownership and permanent tenure are contradictions. Ownership, where capital is needed to work the land, and where, in a bad season the farmer or owner comes under the sway of the money-lender, results in excessive *in*security. Even the temporary absence of a mortgage does not throw off this menace; and the increase of tenant farming in the United States, par excellence the home of the independent individual farmer, is a sure sign of social and economic insecurity, leading eventually to unthrifty forms of use.

Today, despite a constitutional propensity to guard the "rights of property," the community is the residuary legatee of the land in a very peculiar manner: it may take possession of real property without further ado as compensation for the non-payment of taxes over a certain period. In this passive sense, the communal interest in land is recognized. But to have permanent tenure in land under modern conditions and to ensure a measure of security to the individual worker or occupant, the community must be prepared to assume the active responsibilities of ownership: increasingly the land must be owned by the community, and placed in the trusteeship of appropriate municipal and regional authorities.

By owning the land, the community will dispense with the economically inert (that is, privileged or piratical) rôle of the private landlord: it will then be able to collect in the form of rent all those values that derive directly from social organization. Since regional communities are more permanent bodies than individual families or business organizations, they can undertake improvements of the land that the individual cannot wait for or hope to profit by. When population and industrial uses are stable, this system secures stability for the user: when the population is shifting, and new uses of the land are introduced, the divorce of public ownership from occupancy permits the most flexible type of adjustment, whilst it avoids the grave evil of absentee ownership and administration. As long as individual ownership is regarded as sacred, the most important needs of the community may be balked, and its most vital plans may be mangled: nothing can be done, even under the law of eminent domain, without more or less paying the landlord's price. By means of communal ownership, the land can be functionally apportioned with respect to the needs of communal life: planning may thus deal, not with the whims of individual owners, but with the stable needs of the community.

Regional planning is essentially the effort to apply scientific knowledge and stable standards of judgment, justified by rational human values, to the exploitation of the earth. Such knowledge was deliberately flouted in the opening up of the dry lands which have become the dust-bowl of America, and the commonwealth has paid dearly for that sacrifice to the demands of the individual farmer and speculator. No community can afford such luxuries of ignorance: the function of science is to reduce the area of such costly mistakes and finally wipe them out. Without the decisive control that rests with collective ownership, in the hands of responsible public administrators, working for the common good, regional planning is an all but impossible task: at best it must confine itself to weak admonitions, partial prohibitions, various forms of negative action: at most it can say what shall not be done, but it has little power to command the forces of positive action.

The common ownership of land would put the division and supervision of the land in the hands of the appropriate local and regional authorities, who would map out areas of cultivation, areas of mining, areas of urban settlement, as they now map out areas for public parks. On this basis, a stable social adjustment could be worked out for every part of the region, and for every type of resource and activity. This common ownership is not an objective in itself: it is merely a means toward creating a system of dressing and keeping the land as it must be dressed and kept for an advanced civilization. Something can indeed be done by education and public regulation where the obsolete system of private ownership and control is preserved; but infinitely more can and must be done by active authorities, capable not merely of suggestion but decisive action, capable of looking ahead over half a century or more, and borrowing funds on the basis of such long term action. A useful step toward this system of common ownership consists in a broadly applied scheme of land zoning: such as that provided in the current English law which "sterilizes" against change of use without public permission all existing rural areas, or like that worked out, again, under the ample administrative authority of Dr. Schmidt, with a special planning body, in the Ruhr district before 1933. A partial step in the same direction—restricting marginal lands against inappropriate uses—has been made in Wisconsin. But these are only preliminary steps. No intelligent community can avoid the further socialization of land once it discards the policy of furthering individual ownership for the sake of pecuniary gain.

One must not evade the fundamental issue. Modern civilization will not be able to use its collective energies and collective wisdom for the benefit of its members until the land goes back to the community from which it was originally derived and becomes part of the common stock. This should be particularly easy in the United States; for here there are no immemorial privileges of ownership and residence, no ancient titles that run back before the memory or written record of man; and here the greater part of the continent was still *public land* up to a century ago. Had there been sufficient wisdom and foresight, and had not the *mores* of capitalism and the shortsighted urge of the land-hungry worked against it, all this land might have remained in the hands of the Federal Government, as a permanent possession of the country as a whole.

What one proposes now is that a bad land policy, which confused stable occupation and security of tenure with the irrelevant concept of individual ownership, should be obliterated. In its stead, one proposes a sound land policy which shall vest ownership in the community, and guarantee tenure, for definitely assigned periods, to those who work the land thriftily and pay their communal taxes. This policy can be put into effect piecemeal, by permitting cities to buy up land necessary for their development and to hold it permanently: an indispensable aid in four-dimensional planning. It can be furthered by the state's buying up marginal agricultural lands, as in New York State, in order to turn them back into forest—or by the setting of great recreation areas, such as the Adirondack State Park in New York. But for regional planning on a grand scale to begin, the policy must apply to the holding of all land; and until this is effected planning can achieve only part of its potential results.

The difficulties in the method of piecemeal purchase should be plain. As one passes from waste areas and sub-agricultural lands to areas where land values have been steadily boosted as the result of intensive settlement and extensive improvements the possibility of purchase on a sufficient scale diminishes. No community is rich enough to redeem its own land as a whole at the prices asked by the present owners. Hence, except in Soviet Russia, where a revolutionary change in ownership took place, the most important steps in making the earth a permanent and satisfactory human home are halted by a small privileged class, upheld in turn by a much larger group who mistakenly hold exclusive land-ownership to be a symbol of power and independence. *But regional planning cannot be confined merely to backward areas;* hence the problem must be eventually faced and a new social policy of leasehold possession worked out, under forms which will combine individual security and collective interests. The alternative consists in public regulations so broad and drastic as to turn the individual proprietor into a mere trustee or steward. An ownership so limited—though perhaps useful in effecting a transition—is bound, however, to awaken the owner's resentful protest scarcely less than a scheme for outright expropriation with drastically limited compensation. The latter, in the form of pensions, seems to me preferable—though in the United States it would demand a social interpretation of the words "due process."

6: The Landscape: A Cultural Resource

Originating in the spectacle of waste and defilement, the conservation movement has tended to have a negative influence: it has sought to isolate wilderness areas from encroachment and it has endeavored to diminish waste and prevent damage. The present task of regional planning is a more positive one: it seeks to bring the earth as a whole up to the highest pitch of perfection and appropriate use—not merely preserving the primeval, but extending the range of the garden, and introducing the deliberate culture of the landscape into every part of the open country. Olmsted began his career as a park planner by giving advice to his farmer-neighbors on the layout of their house and grounds: it is time that park planning went back into the open country, from which, in the eighteenth century, it originated. The parking and landscaping of highways, such as the remarkable system in Westchester County, New York, is a first step toward these more universal forms of collective gardening and cultivation. The rapid extension of such arteries and recreation grounds around the great metropolises in America is an earnest of a deeper transformation.

Our planners in the past have had a tendency to single out the more striking forms of landscape. This was an inevitable heritage from the romantic movement, which attached itself to the "picturesque" and loathed more orderly and cultivated forms of beauty. There has been no comparable movement to cultivate other types of landscape and bring them up to a high pitch of esthetic delight. So it happens that in most parts of America the early canal systems have been permitted to lapse: the waterways have either been turned into open sewers or have been allowed to fall into a state of ragged disrepair, only finally to be covered up, as in New Jersey, by express highways. And the fault is not solely an American one. There have been similar sacrifices in Holland, due to the systematically insensate education of the old type of civil engineer. Have there not even been proposals to fill up the canals of Amsterdam in order to make them swift motor highways? A proposal to sacrifice for the sake of speed and noise, one of the most beautiful urban environments created by man.

If the culture of the environment had yet entered deeply into our consciousness, our esthetic appreciations would not stop short with stupendous geological formations like the Grand Canyon of Arizona: we should have an equal regard for every nook and corner of the earth, and we should not be indifferent to the fate of less romantic areas. Though the old canals no longer serve industrial uses in most parts of America, they have grand possibilities for recreation: they should, in fact, become the backbone of a regional park system, for swimming, boating, ice-skating, and ice-boat racing, to say nought of being specially stocked for fishing. So much so, that where these canals have not been left over from the eotechnic economy, they should be deliberately built, as is now being done along the Delaware River in Pennsylvania. Especially in the flatter regions of the Middle West, bereft of natural recreation areas, a system of lordly water courses, banked with grass, lined with trees, dotted with groves for picnicking and camping, should be built for the whole region, supplementing and rounding out the natural water drainage: no longer the mere half-mile water courses of the baroque park.

The reservation of coastal areas as wildernesses is equally important. For though we owe much to the romantic love of high mountains and mysterious forests, modern man finds other parts of nature
equally attractive: the pine barren, the savannah, the rocky coast, the
moorland, the sandy spit, no less than the more overwhelming species
of scenery: the bayberry, the sweetfern, the shrub-oak, and the low
blueberry can touch his spirit as they outline the contours of a headland no less than the mightiest pines. As for the ocean itself, it is the
least spoiled of all primeval wildernesses, except where it is tainted
by the adjoining land and the offal of its population. The recapture
of the coastal wilderness has become an important element in every
sound scheme of regional planning: South England feels the need
as well as Long Island. The reservation of the Everglades in Florida,
and of forest and heath in Marthas Vineyard, are welcome signs.
Similarly, the creation of a "Cape Hatteras National Seashore" by
Congress in 1937 sets an important precedent within the national
domain.

Each type of environment, then, has its special interest for man,
its special economic capacities—above all, its special uses as a social
habitat. The cultivated landscape of the plain with its soft meadows,
its human definitions and landmarks, its meandering rivers and its
quiet pauses of lake and marsh, is no less capable of enriching the
spirit than the hanging valleys of the Tyrol, where the sun does not
rise over the ice peaks until eleven o'clock in the morning. In the
second milieu man's principal care must be to step lightly and leave
as small an account of himself as possible: part of the value of the
primeval environment lies in maintaining an extreme contrast with
the region of close settlement. In the high forests he may erect a
chain of cabins and a trail: but he will not, if his sense of place-
possibility is disciplined and acute, provide for hotels, motor cara-
vans, main highways, or the other impedimenta of civilization. If our
modern culture, with all its resources and wealth, cannot afford the
final luxury of such unused spots, it is poor indeed.

While during the eighteenth century the Western European sharp-
ened his sense of place-possibility and discovered some of the joys
that the cultivated Chinese had so long known, there was a violent
movement in the other direction: in the act of pioneering, the Euro-

pean peasant and townsmen often lost some of that intuitive feeling for the environment that they had preserved by inertia in their original habitat. Instead of co-operating with nature in the new lands, they raped nature, eager for quick returns; and in the very act of violating her, rejected her best gifts and rejected the possibility of having permanent intercourse with her. Therein lies the vast irony of man's proud "Conquest of Nature" during the nineteenth century.

This rape took many forms: with respect to the landscape among the earliest was the building of funicular railways to the top of inaccessible Alpine spots, whose very glory demanded for full appreciation a pitting of man's energies against the difficulties of the ascent. One of the latest violations takes the form, in the United States, of motor roads that lead into the heart of a wilderness and concentrate urban populations in big recreation halls, playgrounds, and hotels that might better have been placed at the very doors of the metropolis. In the eastern part of the United States, the so-called skyline drives along the crest of the lonely Appalachians combine extravagant expenditure with a complete debauchery of the specific character and use of the mountain wilderness.

This form of desecration, in the act of making nature accessible, removes all that is valuable from the enjoyment of those who seek solitude and a renewed sense of the primeval. Both these spiritual needs increase in importance as man rises in the scale of civilization and is no longer harried by the crude enmities of nature: they are indispensable correctives to the mechanical rigors and the compulsive collective disciplines and the omnipresent crowds of modern life. Man must not merely have the privilege of selecting a type of environment in contrast to that which embraces his daily routine: each environment should exercise its own type of selective control: choosing its men.

The principle of democracy does not mean that every type of environment should be equally available to every type of person; and that every part of the natural scene should be as open to dense occupation as the concert hall of a great metropolis. This vulgarization of activities that are by their essential nature restricted and isolated would blot out the natural varieties of the habitat and make the whole world over into a single metropolitan image. In the end, it would mean that one must be content with only one type of life, and to accept only one type of environment: that of the metropolis—a degradation in both the geological and the human sense.

Such perversions of the cult of nature and the principles of democracy as are marked by the skyline drive and similar types of metropolitan invasion are carried to the final level of complete caricature in the exploitation of the great caves of Virginia. To increase accessibility, these caves are reached by elevators: they are lighted theatrically with different colors that play over the stalactites and the stalagmites as they might play over the body of a dancer in a cabaret. This series of mechanical "improvements" transforms a precious experience of darkness and mystery and danger, never to be forgotten by anyone who has explored a natural cave, into something that is on the exact level of a spectacle at Coney Island: indeed, the urban type of spectacle has the advantage of being less of a fake and more easy to reach.

A culture so innocent of genuine human and esthetic values as to encourage such exploitation will obviously stop at nothing. Hence it is under the seal of a non-metropolitan culture, still only in its embryonic phase, that genuine regional planning works: some of its worst enemies will long be those who espouse "nature" for purely metropolitan ends: profitable jobs, publicity, lavish expenditure for engineering and public works.

In sum, man cannot achieve a high level of economic life or culture in an environment whose resources he has plundered and defaced. And if even an economic system demands a balance between energy income and outgo, human culture demands a still greater degree of discrimination and care in the use of the environment: a more active sense of place-possibility, a more delicately poised equilibrium between the landscape and the modes of human occupation. To turn a forest into a metropolitan slum is an even more serious barbarism than would be the turning of a metropolitan area back into its primeval field or forest. Each type of landscape has its special meaning to civilized man. Astronomy, geology, biology, landscape painting, poetry, send man out to face nature in another mood from that of his ancestors. And it is precisely because our culture has reached a higher stage of development that we can no longer be satisfied with the impoverished conceptions of the environment that have hitherto satisfied the urban ego. We respect, as never before, the infinite variety of nature, and wish for the sake of both wealth and health to preserve it to the utmost degree. The greater number of natural resources man makes use of, the finer are the distinctions he makes between one part and another of his habitat.

The task of regional planning, as concerns both the earth and cities, is to make the region ready to sustain the richest types of human culture and the fullest span of human life, offering a home to every type of character and disposition and human mood: creating and preserving objective fields of response to man's deeper subjective needs. It is precisely those of us who recognize the value of mechanization and standardization and universalization who must be most alert to the need for providing an equal place for the complementary set of activities—the wild, the various, the spontaneous, the natural as opposed to the human, the lonely as opposed to the collective. A habitat planned so as to form a continuous background to a delicately graded scale of human feelings and values is the prime requisite of a cultivated life. Where that is lacking, men will fumble uneasily with substitutes, or starve.

7: The Economic Region

There are, as Benton MacKaye has noted, three types of economic region. The first is mainly self-sufficing and therefore in economic balance. Few regions today exhibit such a balance in its original simplicity: our wants and our technics have brought into existence a whole series of complicating factors.

The second type is the wholly specialized region: a part of the earth that, no matter what its potential variety, has devoted itself to the production of a limited series of commodities. Mining regions, particularly in the areas developed during the eighteenth and nineteenth centuries, are examples of such one-sided economic units. To create any sort of human equilibrium in such regions, the exports of the special products must be balanced by a great diversity of imports. This will partly counteract the environmental impoverishment: but only partly. Those activities and skills and experiences that arise out of the more varied use of the region will still be lacking. Under capitalist economics there is still a further weakness: only a fraction of the population in such an area will receive an income sufficient to import the ingredients necessary to a more rounded culture. And when an industry "gives out"—as certain textile plants gave out in New England, as coal mines gave out in Durham and Wales in England, the population is stranded.

The third type of economic region is that which has usually characterized advanced cultures: it is partly self-sufficing and partly specialized. It contains within its area a varied and representative range of resources; and out of its specialized products and individualized skills it obtains from other regions the elements that are needed for a many-sided human culture. Agricultural areas tend to the first type of balance: they limit their requirements and learn to do without many exotic products. Specialized industries tend to the second type: their achievement corresponds to that of the one-sided specialist, who eventually loses command of his own subject by the poverty of his life and thought outside the province of his specialization. Culture regions need the third type of economic base.

During the nineteenth century the tendency toward economic balance and variety within a given region was disparaged by the popular schools of economics. It was assumed, on the basis of England's exploitation of paleotechnic industry, that balance was to be achieved only on a planetary basis, through an international division of labor: such a scheme would have made permanent England's supremacy in utilizing coal and steam power for the mass production of textiles, cutlery, pottery, and other machine-made goods. The rest of the world was supposed to be content with the modest task of supplying some of the raw materials and consuming the products in return for their agricultural surplus. The region considered as a theater for human activity occupied no place in this scheme. Only its lop-sided potentialities for specialized production mattered.

One need not here go into the defects of this one-sided regime. Sufficient to say that it treated the region as a whole as a mine from which certain special materials were to be extracted, and it produced a one-sided, monotonous, socially crude life in its main industrial centers and factory villages. With the export of machines and technical knowledge to other countries, it was only a matter of time be-

fore each province, each region, would take over for itself the special processes of machine industry. The very fact that industrialism
became worldwide in its applications has kept it from developing
along the lines expected by the Manchester economists: that of international specialization for a single world market. Regions once
treated as mere sources have become manufacturing centers in their
own right. In America the Southern states not merely produce cotton
but weave it; while the shoe industry, once centralized in Brockton
and Lynn, has now created independent centers in the Middle West,
nearer to both the sources of supply and the local markets. As this
diffusion continues to take place, the balance of population must
likewise alter: internally, by fostering a variety of occupations
within any given region, and in hitherto predominantly agricultural
regions it will give mechanical industries and urban communities a
parity in the regional economy.

Metropolitan finance with its attempt to put over national labels
and trademarks, and to limit consumption to nationally advertised
products, dominated largely by metropolitan bankers and investors,
naturally opposes this tendency toward regional decentralization. To
this end it buys up local plants and welds them into single financial
organizations governed by a centralized bureaucracy. But in the very
act of establishing such wide controls it finally awakens counter-
forces. The protest of the local merchant against the chain-store has
already been recorded in the United States in State legislation: however ill-advised the restriction, the need for a different pattern of
control and operation is a genuine one.

Moreover, the increasing concentration of metropolitan finance
makes it necessary to invent a technique for decentralized management: this shifts responsibility for daily decisions to the point where
production takes place, and therefore allows a place for the development of greater autonomy. And the further specialization of production tends in the same direction: the building of a whole plant in
order to produce a single unit like a carburetor, a storage battery or
a bearing has done away with the need for heaping subordinate
plants in a single narrow district. Finally, the closer accountancy of
costs by metropolitan finance has revealed the necessity for reducing
the overhead expenses: not merely administrative costs, but rent,

taxes, transportation charges. All this works against the one-sided concentration of industry into a few limited industrial areas: it favors regional decentralization and regional diversity of occupation.

Up to the present generation, financial canons have worked against the more rational exploitation of resources and the more regional layout of industries and cities. In an effort to force a "national" market, against the natural regional affiliations and standards, an enormous amount of energy has been thrown into sales organizations, into advertising, into fashion-publicity, which might have been better used to raise the purchasing power of labor and to assist in a reorganization on regional lines of the essential means of produc tion. All these wastes are paid for, not merely in money, but in con fusion of mind and social deterioration. The questions what is "economic" and what is "profitable" belong to two different orders of thought: so far the latter, with its indifference to social values and consumptive needs, has been the almost exclusive determinant of the economic pattern of the region.

Professor J. Russell Smith, the economic geographer, has discussed the matter in the following words: "Perhaps this regional specialization of manufacture, like the regional specialization of agriculture, has gone too far. There are signs that it has. We may yet have a renewal of manufacture for local needs as we are already having of agriculture for local needs. Two comparatively new industrial factors make this possible. One is the widespread distribution of electric power in town, village, and home. . . . The second factor is standardization. These two factors make it possible to manufacture many small things in small villages, possibly even in the farm-home. It may become easier to transport the man's raw materials and his produce than his food. This may shift some of the manufacturing from Boston, Worcester, Detroit or Chicago to farms and villages in food-producing sections of New York State, Michigan, Manitoba, Saskatchewan, or the Rocky Mountain valleys. . . . It is possible that we are at the beginning of an era of the partial redistribution of manufacturing over the land where food production and climate and commercial access are good."

Kropotkin made similar observations and drew the same deductions a generation ago. What was bold prophecy when he first published Fields, Factories, and Workshops has now become a definite movement, as the technical means of economic regionalism and the social impulses that gave it direction have converged. For the other side of the industrialization of agriculture, which has been so rapidly going on alike under capitalism, co-operation, and socialism, is the ruralization of industry.

The possibility of creating economically balanced regions rests upon permanent geographic factors. These constants have in turn been reinforced by new inventions and fresh acquisitions of scientific knowledge which abet, rather than oppose, the tendency toward regional integration. Most of these favorable factors derive from what I described in Technics and Civilization as the neotechnic complex: a system of industry based upon the mobility of power, the use of electricity and a diversity of prime movers, upon the employment of light metals and precious elements, upon the maximum application of systematic scientific knowledge in the exploitation of resources and the organization of work: finally, upon the growing importance of the biological and social sciences even within realms hitherto occupied almost exclusively by the physical sciences and the purely mechanical arts.

Not the least effect of the neotechnic regime is the transformation of agriculture from a backward industry into an advanced one. Whereas the first technical improvements in agriculture were derived from the paleotechnic interest in machines considered as devices for labor saving and mass production, a good part of the recent improvements have been based upon chemical and biological knowledge: they have increased the absolute yields per acre. Among the earliest of these advances was the discovery of the rôle of fertilizers and crop rotation in maintaining the nutritional qualities of the soil: hence a tendency to displace single-crop farming, which characterized so much pioneer agriculture during the nineteenth century, by mixed crops. This means not only more conservative use of the soil: it means a more varied local food supply.

During the last generation the whole field of improvement has widened: soil regeneration through the use of nitrogen-producing crops has come: likewise the improvement of plant and animal strains, selective breeding toward potency of growth; the utilization of chemical wastes for soil enrichment; finally the intensification of crop yield, both as to time and space, through the cultivation of plants in specially prepared tanks, with scientific mixture of plant food, complete control of light and heat, and elimination of insect pests and blights. All these advances have, in one way or another, equalized agricultural advantages over greater areas and removed the incentives toward one-sided specialization.

Modern agronomy preaches the wisdom of reducing the area of soil cultivated and intensifying the method of cultivation. Even if every crop does not lend itself economically to artificial cultivation, the area needed for active farming is diminishing, and the area opened up to permanent tree culture and to purely spectacular horticulture is potentially increasing. So the pattern of agriculture originally set by the Dutch in the seventeenth century will come back again in new forms, just as the seventeenth century Dutch urban pattern is coming back again with appropriate modifications: that early mutation will probably become the new dominant.

Our modern knowledge of diet, with its stress upon the importance of fresh foods and the succulent leafy vegetables, reinforces this agricultural tendency. Already it has vastly lowered in the United States the per capita acreage devoted to wheat and corn. A *local* supply of fresh vegetables and fruits in every season will presently become the mark of biotechnic agriculture: for with the spread of electrical energy and the contraction of the agricultural acreage there is no reason why the major part of the supply should not come from the local region. Most of the machines and utilities needed by modern agriculture are collective in character and they employ electric power in increasing amounts. Moreover, for their effective use they need adequate technical training and constant revision in the light of fresh scientific knowledge: all this implies the effective inter-relation of agriculture with the city. Hence the need, even purely from the standpoint of agriculture itself, for a closer pattern of settlement within rural areas, and for a regional distribution of all the modern instruments of culture and co-operation.

To speak of agricultural areas, industrial areas, urban areas, will be to refer to an increasingly moribund division of labor. Rural regions will attract industry, foster a co-operative way of life, promote biotechnic urbanism; while industry must, for the sake of life-efficiency, seek a wider rural basis. Each village nucleus will thus be the embryo of a modern city, not the discouraged, depauperate fragment of an indifferent metropolis.

8: Power as Region-Builder

The same tendencies against overspecialization and overconcentration are at work in industry. Specialization within the industrial plant, with a vast capital outlay for machines designed for a single purpose, followed the fashionable pattern of the successful textile industries of the early nineteenth century: the formula at first seemed applicable to every part of the industrial process. But both experience and analysis have shown, during the last generation, that such specialization may be a serious liability: for one product whose outlines remain as firmly fixed as woven cloth, there are a score of others that have been subject to radical alterations; and it is necessary to keep the industrial plant flexible and adaptable. Small units, capable of diversified production and quick adaptation, are more economic than large units: they frequently justify themselves, likewise, by superior management, since the larger the organization the greater the amount of effort that must go into its supervision—and the supervision of the supervisor. The costly transformation of the Ford plant when it abandoned its early model and started to turn out a new type of car was a significant turning point: its moral has not been lost.

Up to the present, at least in the United States, this topographic decentralization of industry has been promoted chiefly for reasons of financial economy: often on dubious or anti-social grounds, as in the effort of the silk industry to escape unionization, or in the attempt to make profit out of a low standard of living among the workers, as in the cotton mills of the South.

Plainly, however, the new agents of power, communication, and transportation work to like effect in both industry and agriculture: they give equal service to city and country: a critical distinction between the neotechnic and the paleotechnic regime. Under modern conditions, an electric power plant may perhaps be gigantic in order to increase the operating efficiency or take advantage of a big head of water: but by means of long distance interconnecting transmission systems or grids, the power itself may be produced in many centers and made available over a wide area, with a balanced load and little idle plant. No longer is the river, the coal bed, or the railroad line the sole effective power area. In other words, power production no longer demands local concentration, either within the plant or within the manufacturing area. And the unity that was once achieved by the centralization of production in a single plant can now be achieved by plan, time-schedules, and other forms of administrative and technical co-ordination. Indeed, as the timing of the productive process becomes finer, the size of the efficient plant tends to diminish; since part of this size is due to the stoppages which tend to pile up material at various points.

But it is not power alone that has brought with it the possibility of a new industrial, and therefore an essentially different urban, structure. The same holds for systems of transportation and communication. The motor car has decentralized transportation as radically as the transformer and the motor have decentralized the applications of electric energy. Instead of the *train*, which increases in economy up to a point with the number of cars attached, we have begun to employ, since 1910, the motor car, the motor bus, the motor truck: a more flexibly used individual unit, which can start or stop, take the highroad or the branch road, at its own convenience, without waiting for other cars. And instead of the railroad *line*, which tended to centralize transportation along the main arteries, and which was more or less confined to the water level routes, at grades of two per cent or less, the motor car has brought into existence the new highway *network*. Thus the motor car can penetrate the hinterland in a more effective and economic fashion than the railroad could: for economy in railroading depends upon loading the tracks to maximum capacity and confining transportation, as much as possible, to the main routes. Moreover, the motor car can climb steep grades and penetrate hilly country with a freedom unknown to the railroad; and it makes an effective connecting link with the airplane field and the airplane, the latest means of fast cross-country transportation. The usefulness of the airplane has up to now been greatly lessened in congested metropolitan centers through the fact that it

takes as much time to journey five or ten miles from the airport on
the outskirts of the city as it does to cover fifty or a hundred miles
in the air.

The motor car has potentially opened up new frontiers of human
settlement, even as the airplane has extended the outposts of civilization to the very poles. For the uplands, which motors reach so easily,
are the seat of the fast-running young rivers and waterfalls, the
new sources of power; and by means of motor car and hydro-electric
plants areas that have hitherto been remote and uncultivated can now
support well-balanced industrial communities. The salubrious climate
of these uplands, with their varied sports of field and forest and
stream, make them, in many parts of the world, ideal centers for all-
year living. In the nineteenth century many of these regions were
the recreation grounds of the bourgeoisie: tomorrow they may become the favored seats of living for an enfranchised working class.
Norway, the French and the Swiss Alps, the Tennessee Valley, the
Columbia Valley, all begin to show the energizing and civilizing
results of these new forms of industrial energy, and the new types
of human equipment that may be installed for living and working.
Here again, to achieve the characteristic benefits of the new systems
of transportation, an open pattern of settlement must be maintained:
the greater the congestion, the lower the working efficiency of the
new transportation system.

With these new means of transportation and power-generation, special local advantages, once concentrated in a circumscribed center,
a mere point, can be distributed throughout a whole region. Even
under the metropolitan regime itself the unit is no longer the central district but an area with a radius of from ten to sixty miles of
the center. To complete this, the telegraph, the telephone, the radio,
the teletypewriter, and television apparatus have likewise arisen out
of the neotechnic complex. The effect of all these instruments is to
*enlarge the sphere of activity at the same time that they diminish
the need for physical movement and close settlement.* Plants or offices
that are two hundred miles apart today may be in closer effective
communication than when they were two miles apart a hundred years
ago. Yet most of the concentration of administrative units and industrial units assumes that obsolete century-old conditions still pre-

vail. The important thing that has happened is that the geographic region has become potentially the unit that the metropolis was under the past economic regime: it needs to be linked up, interlaced, and settled with a view to the new opportunities and the new conditions of life. With a fuller exploitation of the region as an economic unit, the need for costly cross-haulage and duplex movements of like commodities will be lessened.

Now that advanced technical processes lend themselves to the decentralization of production, the means of living can be once more produced in an environment fit for living: an environment that lends itself not only to production, but to a higher standard of consumption and more vivid creative activities. Under a regime of economic regionalism, industries would be varied and balanced locally in order to secure a varied and balanced life: likewise the multiform, many-threaded cultural heritage that goes with such a life. Extra-regional production and consumption, instead of stopping at national frontiers, would move, as they increasingly did during the nineteenth century, in worldwide channels of trade. Such a regime might require, for effective control, two systems of currency: a regional system and a foreign exchange system, in order to establish some sort of parity between disparate areas during the long, difficult period of transition. The experience of various European countries since the war, particularly that of Soviet Russia and Nazi Germany, show that the administrative obstacles, while serious, are not overwhelming.

Economic regionalism, I emphasize, cannot aim at either economic or cultural self-sufficiency: no region is rich enough or varied enough to supply all the ingredients of our present civilization: the dream of autarchy is merely a military dodge for putting a population in a state of mind appropriate to war. What regionalism does aim at is a more even development of local resources: a development that does not gauge success purely by the limited financial profits obtained through a one-sided specialization.

Neither does economic regionalism mean bare industrial decentralization. Such a tendency has been latent from the beginning of the paleotechnic revolution, with manufacturers seeking to utilize the cheap sites and cheap labor of the open country; and it is still taking place in patches for this same reason. The point is that centralization and decentralization are qualitatively empty terms: merely directions of movement. The question for regionalism is what sort of life, at any particular point in a region, such movements produce. A scattered development of subsistence farms, economically connected with a sweated industry, is no less undesirable a growth than the utmost congestion of a megalopolitan proletariat.

Under the new pattern, it is necessary not only to break up old centers of congestion but to create new centers of industrial and civic life, and to re-invigorate, with new plans and activities, such older towns and villages as are favorably situated and lend themselves to such renewal. But in so far as the new unit of economic and cultural life is the balanced region, rather than the vast amorphous metropolitan district, the needed movement, at the moment, is that which will result in a further emptying out of the central district, and a courageous re-building of life in what used to be, from the standpoint of the metropolis, merely the hinterland. Any point in the new region may be the locus of its maximum culture.

Economic balance is not a speculative concept. In the more simple eotechnic phase of industry it actually existed. The very difficulties of inter-regional transport made it necessary for the local community to rely chiefly upon its immediate resources, and to restrict haulage to exotic commodities of relatively limited bulk, unless they could travel by water.

During the first two hundred years of the seaboard settlement in America, the economic resources were used for the most part with thrift and intelligence, and industries and communities were in a state of balance. Out of this even-handed exploitation of regional possibilities an integrated regional life arose which came to its consummation, economically speaking, around 1850 in New York and slightly earlier, perhaps, in New England. Local mines, quarries, waterfalls, forests, fields, orchards, were woven together by a ramifying system of canals and highroads: this formed the basis of a multitude of settlements, no one of which, outside New York, achieved a disproportionate size. Small colleges and universities, together with lecture lyceums, were widely distributed: they served as nodes of cultural growth. A similar state had existed during the earlier part of the eotechnic period in Europe: the basis of its great cultural efflorescence: and in many regions it continued right down to the nineteenth century.

The problem for the regional planner and administrator is to effect a similar type of economic balance in terms of the more complicated modern industries, more lengthy production-chains, and more varied consumptive needs of today; for the self-sufficient life of a cruder agricultural regime is no longer possible, except in terms of gross cultural indigence. Certain Southern agrarians may fondly dream of such a life; but the more honest of them will also arbitrarily limit culture to the purely literary interests and language-skills of the ante-bellum regime: a pious renunciation of the modern heritage. In other words, they accept cultural impoverishment.

But in order to make economic planning possible, the field of planning cannot be confined to industries and services alone. No survey, however exact in all its preliminary methods, can arrive at sound results so long as the most important variables lie outside the province of the particular industry for which a production plan is made. Energy flow, production flow, goods flow must be directed finally into channels of human use. This means that at some point there must be a means of determining, for a given region and period, the norm of consumption in terms of food, clothing, shelter, recreation, education, and culture. The standards set for production must not only include private consumption but public works—houses and highways, parks and gardens, cities and civic institutes and all the interconnecting tissue that finally compose an organic region. Only when the whole has been plotted out can the individual function be directed with efficiency. Lacking such plans, there is a constant hiatus between productive energies and human fulfillments: the wheel turns rapidly, but the squirrel remains within his cage.

CHAPTER VI

1: Regionalism and Politics

The re-animation and re-building of regions, as deliberate works of collective art, is the grand task of politics for the opening genera· tion. It raises anew, in a form that now has fuller human significance, the fundamental questions of human inter-relationship across the ethnic, ideological, and cultural boundaries that have been carried over from the past. And as the new tasks of region-building imply shifts in the population, migration into more favored areas, and the building up or reconstruction of a multitude of new urban complexes, the politics of regional development become of critical importance. Not merely must we define and express the region: we must work out, by deliberate experiment, the areas for inter-regional co-operation and for super-regional authority. In displacing the functions of the power-state by those of the service-state we must also transform the structure of the existing organizations. The task calls for imaginative audacity and moral vision: how much so, one may discover by con-sidering the methods of political co-ordination that grew up in our recent past.

The process of political unification has taken place, throughout the world, in fairly generous disregard of geographic and economic realities. And the result is that political areas, economic areas, and cultural areas do not exist in concentric relationship: overlappings, duplications, conflicts, and blank spaces characterize our territorial relationships. Though the sovereignty of the state is supposed to polarize all these relationships it actually adds to the confusion, since it often attempts to displace in the interests of "unity" more natural allegiances. In general, political unification has meant de-regionalization: this is equally true in federal states, like the United States, and in unitary states like France. As the powers of the central government have waxed and its territory increased, the powers of the local regions and cities have waned: earliest perhaps in France, latest in Germany. Finally, each state has tended to reach the pathological condition wittily described by the French critic: apoplexy at the center and paralysis at the extremities.

In creating the semblance of political unity between diverse regions and communities, the idea of the nation has been an important one: a term inherently so vague and so contradictory that it must always be taken in a mystic sense, as meaning whatever the ruling classes hold it convenient to mean at the moment. Sometimes language is the key to nationhood: sometimes a common political territory: sometimes common institutions: sometimes all of these together. But a common language does not make the English and the Americans a single nation, and a common territory does not make the Germans and the Czechs in Czecho-Slovakia a single nation: so in any scientific sense the concept is worthless. Viewed realistically, however, "nationalism" is an attempt to make the laws and customs and beliefs of a single region or city do duty for the varied expressions of a multitude of other regions. To the extent that such a unity does not grow out of spontaneous allegiances and natural affiliations it must constantly be held together by deliberate effort: indoctrination in the school, propaganda in the press, restrictive laws, extirpation of rival dialects and languages, either by mockery or mandate, suppression of the customs and privileges of minorities.

The national state, fortunately, never achieves anything like the omnicompetence and omnipotence it aspires to. Only in times of war, when frontiers are closed, when the movement of men and goods and ideas across "national" boundaries can be blocked, when a pervading sense of fear sanctions the extirpation of differences, does the national state conform to its ideal pattern. All the great national states, and the empires formed around a national core, are at bottom war-states: their politics is war-politics; and the all-absorbing preoccupation of its governing classes lies in collective preparation for armed assault. The final caricature of this tendency is National Socialist Germany today, with its fatuous racial mythology (taken over from the descendants of Abraham), its operatic religion, and its cult of brutality: all focused on war.

In the so-called national state there is only an accidental correspondence between the outlines of the state and the departments of state administration on one hand, and the nature of the component regions on the other. Rival forces, rival authorities, rival centers of culture are suppressed under a centralized system of government: witness the fate of the provincial centers of France between 1600 and 1900, and observe what is happening in Germany, the ancient home of municipal freedom, today. The suppression of regional characteristics, in the interests of national unity, is systematically carried on by the modern state; and in this effort the political agents are powerfully abetted by the financial forces of the metropolis, seeking to impose uniform standards in order to guarantee their own control of the "national market."

But at the very moment, in the middle of the nineteenth century, when the repressive forces of nationalism seemed about to achieve an unqualified victory, they met a fresh challenge. It was in 1854 that the Félibrigistes first met in order to restore the language and the autonomous cultural life of Provence: that marked the conscious beginning of a regionalist movement that has grown slowly but steadily ever since. The Bretons and Provençals in France, the Czechs and Slovaks in the old Austro-Hungarian Empire, the Irish, Welsh, and Scotch in Great Britain, the Basques and Catalans in Spain, the Flemings and Walloons in Belgium—these and similar groups have asserted their claims to an autonomous regional life. If the movement took no hold on Germany during this period, it was only because that country, before the advent of the Nazis, was the outstanding example of an historic federalism which roughly satisfied the needs of regional and cultural autonomy: it needed only a political re-definition of the constituent regions, including a division of Prussia, to make Germany a world example of economic and cultural regionalism.

The rise of regional groups raised the specter of national disunity: a fatal image to states immersed in war or preparation for war. National systems of education have therefore attempted to break down whatever regional consciousness has survived: history is national history, and the focus of events is always the national capital, not the local city. Even more, metropolitan fashions and metropolitan propaganda, spread through magazines and newspapers, have sought to make the whole movement for regional autonomy seem, if not actually traitorous, a little ridiculous. Since the rulers of the state have refused to give regionalism a status in the existing structure of the political community, they have to some extent forced the movement toward autonomy to assume a recalcitrant and back-ward-looking air. Regionalism has been identified with sectionalism or separatism; and even the regionalists themselves have often laid too great stress upon the formation of fractional sovereign states, as if the evils of over-centralization and the superstitions of Austinian sovereignty were to be diminished by multiplying the opportunities for petty despotism.

At the very beginning of the regionalist movement, intelligent observers like Auguste Comte and still later, Le Play, not merely observed that it was bound to take place, because it satisfied the ultimate conditions of political existence: but Comte indeed predicted that within a century or so there would be a hundred and sixty such regional entities in Europe. Though that prediction has not been completely fulfilled, the fact is that there are now a greater number of states than there were in the middle of the nineteenth century; and what is more important, perhaps, a greater number of national languages are now in existence than were on the tongues of men a century ago. Political consolidation, in indifference to regional real-ities, has met with unexpected obstacles: under the even whitewash of "national unity" the colors of the underlying geographic, eco-nomic, and cultural realities are beginning to show through. Not the least important sign of this new regime is the recognition ac-corded under Lenin in Soviet Russia to the principle of cultural autonomy.

The fact is that real communities and real regions do not fit into the frontiers and the ideological pattern of the national state. The state is usually too big to define a single region, with its political, economic, and social elements in symmetrical relationships, and it is too small to include a whole society, like that of Western Europe or the North American Continent, which must ultimately become the sphere of a larger system of co-operative administration. The limits of functional authority, such as is involved in the organization of a continental railroad system or the steel industry, cannot rest effectively within the fortuitous boundaries of the state: the larger relationships need a larger framework of authority, and the more intimate relationships require a narrower field of effort. This is no less true of art and science and religion, which are by nature part of the common stock, not of a region, a province, or a state, but of a whole society. There is no way short of tyrannical repression in which the interests of a scholar, a man of letters, or a member of the Catholic Church can be kept within the boundaries of the national state. Real interests, real functions, real intercourse flow across such frontiers: while the effective organs of concentration are not the national states (which means in practice the exclusive pre-eminence of the national capital) but the regional city and the region. The local polarization of loyalties, for all sane political uses, does not involve the building of cultural Maginot lines.

"One of the main reasons for getting rid of power politics," an eminent political theorist of Oxford has said, "is to enable the world to get back to natural political groupings; and natural groupings mean smaller areas and smaller groups." Branford and Geddes, in Our Social Inheritance, have summarized the situation with equal perspicuity: "Does it not rather seem," they say, "as if something were wrong with this whole theory and practice of modern organization into great centralized states with their megalopolitan rivalry? Must we not seek some better mode of adjusting our human lives, if we would plough in peace and reap in safety? If uni-centralization be obviously intolerable, and septem-centralization [in the seven great national capitals] be so unstable and thus unpractical, must we not look . . . to the decentralization of these, as the true road to European peace and re-unity?"

At no point have the realities of social existence coincided with the claims, the demands, and the pretenses of the power-state: its politics can be successfully driven home, momentarily, only at the point of a bayonet. If this fact was true at the beginning of the baroque attempt to centralize power, it is even more massively true today, when worldwide transportation, travel, and communication, a worldwide system of intercourse through printed books and phono-graph records and moving pictures, have given to the most impor-tant activities of society a frame of reference that no longer can be restricted to the so-called national territories.

On one hand the state, as at present organized, tends to obliterate the intimacy of primary communities, organized on a basis of active daily association and face-to-face intercourse. And on the other hand, it often viciously obstructs the organization and control of activities on a continental and finally a worldwide scale. This applies to the allocation of limited resources, the passage of goods and people, the migration of individuals and families, and the exploitation of un-settled or extra-national territories. Power politics, as practiced in the past by Great Britain, France, Russia and the United States, and as threatened even more menacingly today by Italy, Germany, and Japan, works merely to add to the area of un-building and de-civilization.

Yet our inability to devise at once the appropriate structure for our civilization should be no cause for permanent discouragement. Most of the forces that work benignly toward the co-operation and communion of peoples are young: most of the forces that work against such intercourse are old, and are deeply ingrained in insti-tutional habits and in organizations. Our failure even to contrive a breathing space in bellicose effort—if one makes the very partial and dubious exception of the nineteenth century—is partly due to the inertia of historic burdens.

Too hastily we have attempted to achieve a more beneficent align-ment in culture, while retaining those power states whose existence perpetuates the habits of territorial conquest and class exploitation. One might as well turn over to a band of inveterate thieves the un-supervised guardianship of a public fund. The territorial extent of control, as implied in the original outline of the Society of Nations, could not counterbalance the inherent antagonism, on the part of its member-states, to any form of co-operation that implied a diminu-tion of their prestige and power. Such an attempt was plainly fore-doomed to failure; and as long ago as 1919 intelligent observers pointed out these grounds for believing that failure must ensue. What has taken place since has merely confirmed the realism of that elementary analysis.

But in the reorganization of the political community, as in the remoralization of modern society, which must go along with it, a generation is a small span of time: too short to hope for effective changes. Our present discouragement at the results of the last generation's effort is premature by at least a century or two. In the meanwhile, it is highly important to recognize the basic regional and economic realities that have been ignored by the mythology of the national state, with its egoistic schemes of conquest, dominion, and belligerent assertion.

No effort to improve the structure of communities and cities will be effective without re-defining the areas of territorial association in consonance with the objective geographic, economic, and social facts. And meanwhile, too, no effective change can be worked in the regional unit on the basis of past historic situations: what one seeks is not the ancient structure, but the emerging one: a structure that will include not only the geographic constants but the social variables, as these are redefined and projected from generation to generation. What we have to conceive and work out is a federal system of government which shall be based upon a progressive integration of region with region, of province with province, of continent with continent: each part loose enough and flexible enough to adjust to the continuing changes in local and transregional life. Once such a structure has been outlined, it will tend to make effective that concentric regrouping of political, economic, and cultural functions, whose absence is today a severe handicap to co-operative effort.

For the false stability of the national state, purchased by tyranny and suppression or sheer obliviousness to local characteristics, we must substitute the dynamic stability of a body politic in a state of tension and readjustment, in which no issues need ever pile up to the point where they will cause a morbid mobilization of violence and ill-will. Such a federal system must be conceived in the spirit of Blake's great dictum: One law for the lion and the ox is oppression.

Still another important principle must be embodied in the reconstitution of regions: that of social relativity. Here politics has still to recognize and express the deep change that has taken place in our entire world picture. In the Middle Ages, man naïvely regarded himself as the center of the universe; and Europeans regarded themselves as occupying a conspicuously central and favored position among the civilizations of the world—of which they were pathetically ignorant. This general view expressed itself politically in the hierarchical organization of society: a social pyramid of classes, whose apex was the pope or king: later a pyramid of communities whose apex and central point was the capital city. The baroque sense of time and space altered this picture in certain details; but it carried out completely, within the boundaries of the rising states, the hierarchic organization of medieval theory. And by turns one state or another succeeded to a central position within the European polity: while within that state the capital city concentrated the power and culture of the whole country.

In the light of our new world picture, these views are obsolete and the maintenance of such a system of relationships is absurd. From the standpoint of relativity, no one state can claim pre-eminence, and no one position within the community is central. Every unit and every activity, no matter how small, no matter how apparently insignificant, has a fundamental importance for itself, and ultimately for the whole body politic. Thanks to our system of instantaneous communication, any center may become, for a particular purpose or function, the center of the region: any particular region may become the center of the world. For certain types of surgical operation one must go, not to great New York, but to little Rochester, Minnesota; just as for a certain quality of intellectual culture one must still go to the universities of Oxford or Poitiers, not London or Paris.

Authority under the emerging regime of political relativity is a matter of functional competence, not a matter of mere bulk or spatial advantage: neither size, position, nor physical power—nor a monopoly of all these qualities—by itself determines the importance of a city or a community. For cultural individualities are incommensurable: proportionately, the smaller countries, like Belgium, Holland, Denmark, Sweden, and Norway, have contributed far more to the development of modern life than colossi like England and

[TOP] Suburban house by Frank Lloyd Wright. Following the handsome indigenous adaptations in wooden cottage architecture introduced in New England by H. H. Richardson, Wright began in the nineties on a fresh foundation.
Here a whole century of suburban experiment culminated in an organic union
of garden and house. In re-discovering the long strip window, in throwing aside
obsolete forms, in adapting the form of the house freely to the new requirements
of living, in embodying the middle western sense of hospitality and public
friendliness, Wright likewise dramatized the new sense of space, breaking down
the wall between the inner and outer environment and achieving freedom without sacrifice of order. Wright's work was the first symbol of the new order.

[SECOND ROW] Elements in the Japanese house. The Japanese capacity for elimination, their sense of exquisite purity and esthetic rigor embodied in the tea
room and the tea ceremony, their ingenious wood and paper technics, have been
at work on the western mind since the middle of the nineteenth century: first by
way of the Japanese print. Their use of sliding wall and sliding window, their
control of both exterior and interior space by these means, and their utilization
of the wall itself—rather than the cubby-hole closet—for storage and utility
offer pregnant suggestions which the western architect has still to translate
effectively into modern technical forms. This is civilization's partial compensation for the humorless barbarism of Japan's military caste.

[THIRD] Design for an Institute of Heliotherapy by Tony Garnier: an advanced
project for the treatment of tuberculosis whose excellent form antedates Le
Corbusier and the Cubists by half a generation. The indebtedness of modern
architecture to the hospital has been insufficiently recognized: unbroken walls,
doors without moldings, spotless interiors, partly derive from the post-Listerian
hospital. These advantages are now often counterbalanced in the institutions
themselves by a false idea of "hominess" which does not place sufficient trust
in the healing qualities of light, color, order, visual repose.

[BOTTOM LEFT] Modern American kitchen: a well-organized laboratory for the
preparation of food: compact, efficient, it ceases in itself to be a living room
but encourages the use of adjoining space as a dining area, since the forms
used are congruent with good modern furnishings. Modern form, indeed, begins to flow back from the kitchen and the bathroom, the two great biotechnic
utilities of the modern dwelling—which completely distinguish it from other
cultures—into the remaining rooms of the house. (*Photograph: Ewing Galloway*)

[BOTTOM RIGHT] Cage and exhibition house for primates in a modern zoo:
Regent's Park, London. The circular wall opens to the sunlight in fine weather
but can be closed completely: it thus adapts itself to the season and to the life
needs of the inmates. (*Photograph: Museum of Modern Art*)

[TOP LEFT] New York Public Library. Actual working facilities as a storage place for books and manuscripts and as a workplace for scholars and writers and readers seriously marred by the sacrifice of space, convenience, and efficiency to solidity and monumentality. Overcrowded within a decade of its opening. Light, air, space, and silence—the Benedictine luxuries, according to Dom Butler—were all forfeited in this inept design. (*Photograph: Ewing Galloway*)

[TOP RIGHT] London Underground Station: the excellent achievement of an administration whose posters have done more for public art than many more pretentious efforts at mural design. (*Photograph: Museum of Modern Art*)

[MIDDLE LEFT] New offices for the bureaucracy at Washington: a monument of irregional and irrational planning. Closed courts that trap the summer sun without taking advantage of summer breezes, window area sacrificed to classic massiveness, grotesque waste of money on tedious stone columns that further diminish light and air. Nowhere a clear indication of the purpose of the building or the location of departments. This unified building project might have set a masterly precedent for rational business building in every city: unfortunately, it was organized esthetically for an obsolete baroque street picture, characteristic of a despotic order. (*Photograph: Ewing Galloway*)

[MIDDLE RIGHT] Court at Sunnyside Gardens, Long Island, with common green in the center (F. L. Ackerman, Architect). Comprehensive and orderly design of a new order: the open court at right angles to the street or road is characteristic of *Zeilenbau* block organization. Sunnyside Gardens, in its combination of technical and social initiative, continued the work of the housing experiments begun in the Federal war housing projects: its demonstration of rational neighborhood planning and community development paved the way for the large-scale public housing movement that was taken up in Washington in 1932. The disintegration of the Sunnyside community during the economic crisis was a mark, not of any essential mistakes in design, but of the inevitable *insecurity of all individual home ownership*, even the non-speculative type fostered by co-operatives or limited dividend corporations, under our present financial structure. Only publicly owned housing can remedy this. (*Photograph: B. J. Lubschez*)

[BOTTOM LEFT] Palace of the Soviets in Moscow: a project whose archaic grandiosity recalls the Russia of Peter the Great rather than Lenin's comradely republic of free workers: the same kind of thinking shown here that characterizes the swaggering skyscraper blunders of American businessmen. But see Plate 27 for a different picture of the USSR. (*Photograph: Sovfoto*)

[BOTTOM RIGHT] Philadelphia Hosiery Workers' Union Apartments: not merely a symbol of the new order of planning and living, but likewise a token of the importance of the trade union movement and the co-operatives in focusing the *demand* for housing.

Germany. This fact was recognized, very wisely, in the original constitution of the United States, which allotted as many senators to tiny Rhode Island as to the vast state of Pennsylvania; and it is capable of further application. In the days of Goethe, Weimar exercised more cultural authority than centralized Berlin; and with the redistribution of physical energy, political power, and cultural interest that is now incipient, the principle of social relativity will be incorporated in both the regional and the urban pattern. No longer will a single center monopolize advantage, or substitute its activities for those of the whole.

2: The Process of Regionalization

Neither the regional nor the cosmopolitan organization of society is so remote or so chimerical as the exponents of financial and political centralization persuade themselves. For so ingrained are international processes in modern society that it is only by deliberate efforts that they can be starved or rooted out. Without constant interference on the part of the existing states, the industrial and scientific organizations of the modern world would, like the Rockefeller, Guggenheim, and Carnegie Foundations, overpass local lines.

Indeed, until the World War awakened reversionary tendencies, these new forms of organization had already gone far. The world before 1914 was a place in which men traveled in civilized countries without passports or special permission: where within the world capitals the broader allegiances of European society were replacing the more parochial limitations of nationalism. Similarly, the regional pattern of life was breaking through, once more, the imposed or self-imposed national uniformities. So far from going against the grain of modern culture, both regionalism and internationalism were working with the grain: it was the more traditional forms of bellicose etatism that worked against it; for even finance, if irregular, was nevertheless cosmopolitan.

The great opposition to a regional and cosmopolitan organization of political society comes from the psychological complexes that have been deliberately built up around the ideas of national sovereignty and centralized government. A large, so far unbreakable chunk of irrationality serves not merely as a handicap to co-operation, but as a justification of national antagonisms. Men have been encouraged to project upon their nation or the state godlike attributes of wisdom and power they would never claim in their right minds for themselves as identifiable individuals. Symbols like Fatherland, King, Il Duce, the Old Flag, serve to unite in compulsive automatic behavior people who might, in relation to the everyday realities of the common life, exercise rational judgment and good sense.

To nullify these atavistic emotional clusters and break up these formidable reflexes, a more humanized system of allegiances must be built up.

Here the historic development of the regionalist movement itself provides a helpful example: it reminds us that the course of development is not directly from scientific truth and rational judgment to social application and acceptance: the process begins rather with a dynamic emotional urge, springing out of a sense of frustration on one hand and a renewed vision of life on the other. Only at a later stage does the movement achieve a rationale: a systematic scientific and economic basis. Regionalism, as one of the French observers of the movement has pointed out, tends to pass through a regular cycle. It begins with a revival of poetry and language: it ends with plans for the economic invigoration of regional agriculture and industry, with proposals for a more autonomous political life, with an effort to build up local centers of learning and culture. This cycle of development seems to be so common that one might examine it in India as well as in Catalonia; but in the spirit of the regionalist, I prefer to draw my illustrations from an example closer at hand: the United States.

If France is the oldest exponent of conscious cultural regionalism, one might take the United States as an example of the latent, unconscious cultural processes, working out to much the same end. Before the Civil War there had come forth in the United States a number of culturally differentiated sections. Each had its characteristic polity and art and way of life. New England, Tidewater and Piedmont Virginia, South Carolina, Kentucky, Louisiana, had distinct and special traditions, even though the state boundaries did not always coincide with the regional complex. In New England and New York the poetic cycle of regionalism had begun, not a little aided by the original federal constitution of the states. Hawthorne, Emer-son, Thoreau, were New Englanders first, and "Americans" only for the sake of that wider unity—so necessary to a flourishing local life—that might equally have been worldwide as American. Al-though Whitman and Melville, in distinction to the New Englanders, tended to emphasize their identity with "These States" taken as a whole, one may see in that very concern the influence of the brisk cosmopolitan port of New York, the Empire City, already bidding for the financial leadership of the continent.

The cycle of prose and the cycle of practical action were disturbed by the Civil War, by the Western migration of farmers that followed the generous public distribution of land under the Homestead Act, and by the great influx of non-English-speaking immigrants. In this babble of tongues, in this flux of industrial enterprise, in this drift and shift of population, regional affiliations were lost: the new trusts, the oil trust, the steel trust, and the packing trust, utilized the older division of states merely in order to protect their enterprises from national regulation. But in the writings of Liberty Hyde Bailey in the East, and of Frederick Jackson Turner in the Middle West, the cycle of prose was not altogether neglected: indeed, Bailey was one of the great leaders in that revitalizing, and, as it were, re-ruralizing of thought that took place under the surface of the mechanical ex-ploitation of the nineteenth century. The work of the state colleges, with their rising schools of agriculture, carried on in detailed sur-veys and in practical experiments tasks that were being undertaken on a wider scale by the United States Department of Agriculture. Indeed, the county soil surveys of the latter department, though highly specialized reports on geological data, had in them also the germs of those broader land utilization surveys which are one of the characteristic instruments of regional planning. The unit-area was an arbitrary one; but the method itself was capable of being pushed further.

During the last decade or so the regional pattern, broken by the Civil War with its excessive emphasis upon the unifying and cen-tralizing tendencies of the power state, has been pieced together again. During the last generation, there has been opportunity for the newer groups to make permanent homes for themselves and to be assimilated into the landscape. To some extent this latter tendency has followed the original pattern of their homeland: California has selectively attracted Italians to its fruit-growing regions, while the hard winters of Minnesota have beckoned to the already acclimated Swedes and Norwegians.

These mingled strands of linguistic and cultural inheritance from the older countries lend their colors to the newer regional patterns that are emerging. So it happens that the cycle of poetry and the cycle of prose have revived: not least in the South, where the negative notion of sectionalism, a term of reproach invented by Northerners, has given way to the more positive interpretations of regionalism: some of the clearest and most enlightened expressions of the regional political philosophy are those that have issued from Professor Howard Odum and his colleagues at Chapel Hill, N. C.

The poetic consciousness of the regional setting and its cultural implications has come in the emergence of a group of poets and painters with distinct regional characteristics: artists conscious of their local identity and their local idiom even when their themes are not of a local nature. Carl Sandburg, Vachel Lindsay, Sherwood Anderson, Theodore Dreiser, Sinclair Lewis and Willa Cather in the Middle West have been followed by painters like Thomas Benton from Missouri and a rising school in Illinois. Ellen Glasgow, Julia Peterkin, and John Gould Fletcher in the South, together with later writers like John Crowe Ransom, are forerunners of that recasting of the cultural consciousness of the region which, at third and fourth remove, often plays such an active part in the political and economic movements of a later generation. Similar developments have taken place in many other places: notably Oklahoma, Nebraska, Montana, and New Mexico.

The same tendencies have appeared in other areas: the intuitions of the poets have been abetted by a fresh group of historians, anthropologists, economists, and geographers who have begun to delve more deeply into the materials of their local regions. Much that has been glozed over or neglected in our concern for superficially national interests and national attitudes, is in the act of being recovered and re-valued. Instead of unification by suppression of diversities we are now approaching a time when we may have a more effective unity through their representation and integration.

As for New England, it has never entirely lost its consciousness of being a regional entity. Even when the agricultural life was ebbing from it, during the period after the Civil War, some of its old vitality and individuality was embodied in the literary school of Sarah Orne Jewett and her successors. Winslow Homer and Albert Pinkham Ryder, to say nothing of George Fuller, perpetuated its heroic images of life in noble paintings, perhaps the finest that any artist has yet achieved in America, while at still a later stage, Robert Frost and E. A. Robinson preserved, in their several individualities, the essence of the old New England culture. New England, too, either fostered or harbored a new group of scientists and planners who were to embody the new interests of geotechnics, or earth-molding: G. P. Marsh, first of the conservationists, Shaler, the geologist, Charles Eliot, II, who carried Olmsted's conception of the landscape park into the wilder parts of the landscape, and Benton MacKaye, the founder of the Appalachian Trail, who has been one of the foremost philosophers and theoretic exponents of regional planning in our generation.

During the last fifteen years practical activity on regional lines has widened. The landmarks are many: the launching of the conservation movement by President Theodore Roosevelt in 1908, the masterly outline regional plan for the State of New York, published in 1926, the power and conservation projects undertaken on a great scale by President F. D. Roosevelt, in an effort to stay soil wastage and to achieve flood control. The interest in regions as foci of human activity has been growing. All these are important developments. The initiative taken in the Tennessee Valley, which treats as a unified area for power development a whole series of disunited county and state authorities, offers a strong precedent for kindred projects in other great units, such as the Columbia River Valley and the Connecticut Valley. These initiatives have not yet altered the focus of political life: indeed many of them are handicapped by the fact that they continue to operate through a tangle of irrelevant boundaries and jurisdictions: but at least they have made a departure. They should be pushed further, in sub-regional as well as interregional areas.

No less significant of the same general tendency to recognize the underlying geographic and economic realities are the new units of administration that have appeared. The division of the country as a whole into broad inter-regional provinces, for Federal Farm Loan Banks, for the Federal Reserve Banks, and for the administration of a unified railroad system during the war, indicated the first faint emergence of a new type of federal system. Within single local areas under conflicting political jurisdiction the organization of the Palisades Interstate Park Commission for New York and New Jersey, and the New York-New Jersey Port of New York Authority point equally to a more realistic and rational mode of administration.

If these new super-regional authorities and divisions are not to turn into another crazy-quilt of overlapping or inconsecutive areas, they should be based upon the geographic and cultural constants of the constituent regions. Plainly, there are provinces, that is, inter-regional areas, where the administrative authority must transcend the boundaries of the national state: the Great Lakes-St. Lawrence waterway is one. (In Europe, incidentally, the electrification project of the upper Rhine Valley is another, while, under any rational system of government, the coal-and-iron areas of Lorraine and the Saar Basin would be a third.)

While regions should become the basic units of political and economic life, the inter-relation of regions within the province, of provinces within the "country," is no less important: for both conflicts and co-operations must take place over these wider areas. But the reconstitution of regions will not automatically solve a community's problems: on the contrary, it will raise new problems; for, as A. E. once remarked, no country can marry any particular solution and live happily ever afterwards. The advantage of creating a sound basis for economic and social activities, is that the new problems will have greater significance; they will embody more important issues and lead to more fruitful results. Ideally, these inter-regional areas of jurisdiction and control and taxation—functions implied in the political definition of sovereignty—should be worked out by collective experiment. Such a method, however, is limited by various irrational factors. These form an obstacle even in countries like the United States and Canada, which have no military frontiers and no belligerent ambitions: hence temporarily the unit of *inter*-regional control must remain the existing political state.

Here, however, a distinction must be drawn between the dual functions of the state, as they have defined themselves during the last century, and even more during the last two generations. On one hand is the power state, that creation of the baroque imagination: a territorial unit, based on military force, devoted mainly to the protection of the powers, properties, and privileges of the ruling classes. Even in its earliest developments such a state performed certain important service functions: it maintained internal peace and order, protected the traveler on the king's highway, dispensed justice between individuals and corporate groups. One may say, however, that the power state supplied services for the common weal chiefly for the sake of enhancing its own power: the welfare of communities and regions was a secondary matter.

Out of this power state a different type of organization has grown up: a service state: the outcome of the effort, through democratic pressure, to reapportion the existing balance of power within the "nation," to equalize the privileges of different regions and groups, and to distribute the benefits of human culture. This type of activity derived originally from the necessity to regulate the hours of labor and the conditions of employment, first of all in England, in order to do away with the most hideous forms of exploitation: its activities extended to the regulation of housing and the provision of funds for the local improvement of housing: and even earlier, beginning in Prussia, it had taken over the function of education. In the United States, the activities of the Department of the Interior and the Department of Agriculture and the Department of Commerce, the Forest Service, the Parks Service, the Children's Bureau, are examples of the service state.

Though these two aspects of super-regional organization operate within the same general framework, they perform different functions and work to different ends. Perhaps the most critical problem for human society today is that of diminishing the rôle of the power state and undermining both its pretenses and its ultimately militaristic forms of authority. At the same time, we must look to a steady enlargement of the rôle of the service state, for, in contrast to the earlier form of the state, this emerging type expands its power for the sake of increasing its services, and these inter-regional and super-regional services are the essential complements of every form of local and regional activity. Our main problem is to constitute the service state so that it can operate, not as the arbitrary ruler and dictator of regional life, but as the willing agent of that life in all those functions which transcend the immediate limits of local control and regulation. Eventually one may look forward to the time when co-operation between service states, without regard to so-called national boundaries, will take place within an even larger framework: a step that is dimly foreshadowed in the Labor and Health Offices established by the League of Nations at Geneva.

While the power state, on its own premises, is jealous and intolerant of any subordinate groups or corporations or regional associations that claim autonomous functions, the service state, to perform its services effectually, must accept these realities of communal life at full value. Its own functions, indeed, are seriously handicapped if the regional units of initiative, administration, and control are paralyzed, or have failed, through some original deficiency, to develop. Professor Burgess, as far back as 1886, foresaw that the arbitrary constitution of the separate states in the United States would have a diminishing validity; he looked forward to an enlargement of national functions and the increase of independent "municipal" activity. If today one substitutes the term region for municipality, as being an exact equivalent under modern technological conditions, one may well accept the prophecy of this acute political scientist.

Plainly, therefore, the change from the power state to the service state cannot be effectually accomplished within the existing structure of the "nation" or "empire": there must be a drastic revision of the method as well as the area of control. But on the other hand mere inertia, mere legalistic bickering over state's rights or local privileges, mere attempts to substitute a more parochial past for the claims of a wider future will not succeed in restoring the political authority or the cultural life of a region or a group of regions. The right to challenge the power state can come only to those who are ready to utilize fully the equally wide sovereignty of the service state

in order to build up a more humanly satisfactory type of organization.

Regionalism must not make the mistake of the medieval municipalities: it must not fancy that it can control within its local area
alone economic and political forces that lie outside the scope of
any single area. As a positive political and cultural doctrine, regionalism implies an inter-regional framework: ultimately a world culture on every plane. Regionalism belongs, therefore, not to a sentimental past but to a more realistic future: a future that will diminish the sphere of the irrational in public life, and rise above the
obsessive mythologies and the life-defeating mechanisms of the
power state.

3: The Postulates of Regionalism

One can scarcely over-rate the significance of a sound political
pattern; or do justice to the mischief that has been caused by arbitrary systems of control and fictitious centers of allegiance. Part of
the difficulty that confronts the world today is due to the fact that
our political behavior has been conditioned by crazy dreams and
baseless beliefs that have no relation to reality: beliefs in the supremacy of the Anglo-Saxon race or the Nordic lineage, carried to
its last grotesque folly in the belief in a wholly imaginary "Aryan"
race: the desire to assume the White Man's Burden (now also the
Yellow Man's Burden), to paint the map red, to find a place in the
sun, to fill out the national boundaries, to establish a "safe" frontier.

All these attitudes and shibboleths place political behavior outside the realm of rational thought. They are the symptoms of a
power politics that has taken on a definitely pathological character.
In opposition to this wanton mythology, the regionalist points to
the following facts:

First: During the last three hundred years the populations of the
earth have, willy-nilly, become inter-related and unified: warfare,
famine, disease, the negative unifiers, have their repercussions in
the daily existence of even remote communities, while the organizing
forces of science and technics and instantaneous communication have
given a common ideological background to culturally and geograph-

ically sundered areas. Isolation is a delusion, and willful isolation is a morbid intensification of this condition.

Second: Rationally defined, the locus of human communities is the region. The region is the unit-area formed by common aboriginal conditions of geologic structure, soil, surface relief, drainage, climate, vegetation and animal life: reformed and partly re-defined through the settlement of man, the domestication and acclimatization of new species, the nucleation of communities in villages and cities, the re-working of the landscape, and the control over land, power, climate, and movement provided by the state of technics.

In other words, the region, as a unit of geographic individuation, is given: as a unit of cultural individuation it is partly the deliberate expression of human will and purpose. The poles of these two aspects of regional life are the raw physiographic region and the city: they express the extremes of natural and human control. The human region, in brief, is a complex of geographic, economic, and cultural elements. Not found as a finished product in nature, not solely the creation of human will and fantasy, the region, like its corresponding artifact, the city, is a collective work of art. One must not confuse the region, which is a highly complex human fact, with arbitrary areas carved out to serve some single interest, such as government or economic exploitation. The country within fifty miles of a metropolitan center is not a region just because it is a convenience for a metropolitan advertising agency or newspaper or planning board to call it so. The discovery of the rough outlines and elementary components of the region is a task for the sciences: the utilization of the region in all its varied potentialities as a theater of collective action is a task for democratic politics. The new regional disciplines complicate the task of finding and expressing political form; for they weaken faith in arbitrary simplifications: but in recompense, they promise a more durable pattern.

Third: The boundaries between regions are not sharp but graded: even when nature sets up relatively sharp frontiers, like seacoasts, the facts of human intercourse ordinarily break down these supposedly hard-and-fast boundaries, reducing or entirely overcoming physical obstacles. At the present stage in civilization man tends more and more to inter-regional and worldwide intercourse and association. To oppose this tendency, in the interests of military security, is to further barbarism. The facts of regional integration and inter-regional intercourse must be expressed through the technique of modern political administration, as well as through rational under-standing: communities must consciously educate themselves up to these conditions and needs. The parochial mind, stultifying in the village, has become a menace through carrying its suspicions and fears and naïve hatreds into the governance of the power state.

Fourth: Human institutions and relationships change in the course of relatively brief years or generations, whereas the basic geographic realities alter only over centuries or aeons. Hence it is important to keep the political and cultural pattern in a state of effective re-adjustment, within the more fixed lines laid down by the primordial region. But it is no less important to recognize, with Professor Roland Dixon, that "there is some reason . . . to believe that very often the strength of a culture, its virility and energy, and even its vitality, depends in no small measure on the tenacity of its environmental fibre, as does its richness and brilliance on the number and variety of exotic traits it contains." A rational system of political govern-ment must give a place to these two complementary conditions of culture. *A migration of the élite, from region to region, is a neces-sary stimulus to regional culture:* the higher cultural equivalent to that one-sided attraction toward the megalopolis which so fatally de-pleted the regions of their most precious human elements.

Fifth: No existing state or administrative lines are sacred or un-alterable. The political map of the world has always been in a state of constant flux; and it would be absurd to imagine that the tempo-rary forms achieved during an era of extreme instability and rapid transition were permanent ones. Many of the existing boundary lines, whether within or around a country, are but a few generations old; at most only a few centuries; and what has been created by man in the past can be re-defined and re-created in the interests of a more effective communal life.

Hence local administrative boundaries or national boundaries that interrupt the more fundamental configurations of regions, or the grouping of regions into inter-regional areas or provinces, must be progressively diminished: eventually wiped out. This means the devolution of political power and the building up of local centers of initiative and control: but it also means the closer interlinkage of regions through the service state, and the building up of areas of co-operation far beyond the frontiers of the national state.

Now, in most countries, with the exception of those smaller states which embrace only one or two regions, neither the state boundaries nor the local administrative units are based upon the fundamental economic and cultural facts. Result: a failure of focus within the local area: a distraction of interests and a confusion of effort. These conditions lead ultimately to a lapse or deterioration in the common life. The effective re-definition of regional areas—a scientific re-mapping of these areas and a political and cultural *re-willing* of them—is one of the essential preliminary tasks toward building up a co-operative and serviceable civilization. For as a man can have no fruitful traffic with the world around him, until he has a firm core of personality, so the region cannot engage in the necessary inter-changes and intercourse with other regions until it possesses an integrated life, on its own solid foundations.

This means that the cultural reconstitution of the region is an es-sential part of the political and administrative task. Our most rational plans await the emotive pressure of human purposes, human desires, human urges: the most admirable mechanism is inert until its engines are fueled by these means. And it is because regionalism actually has its basis in spontaneous human motivations, that one may look for-ward, confidently, to its wider conquests of rationality. In that great federation of regions and peoples which compose the Soviet Repub-lics of Russia, the first step toward this regional redefinition has al-ready been taken; and projects for similar readjustments have been current in France, Spain, and Great Britain for more than a genera-tion, while a similar rebirth of regional consciousness will, in all probability, be one of the stimulating reactions to the National So-cialist scheme of compulsive unification in Germany. Finally, in the United States, the work of the National Resources Committee and various State Planning Boards has opened the way toward a broad reconsideration of the essential problems in community building, regional design, and government.

Fortunately, the notion of the inviolable frontier is now dead even in a military sense: the airplane has robbed it of actuality. Railroads can be halted at frontiers; ships are confined to landing in ports and can be halted at ports; but man's latest invention, the airplane, laughs at these restrictions. For the first time in history every region, every city, is open to attack—open and relatively helpless. The longer the frontier, the greater the opening; the bigger the national capital, the more exposed to assault. *The task of modern civilization is to live in a wall-less world.* At present the nations are like people fleeing from a rainstorm who take refuge behind the walls of a ruin, forgetting that the roof itself has fallen down, and no matter how close they huddle to the wall, they will be drenched from overhead. There is no alternative: no system of bombproof shelters, no generosity in supplying gas masks, no mobilization of fire-fighting apparatus, will avail as defense: the only possible answer is the certainty of equal aggression *by the same means.* In cold realistic terms this implies that if we cannot create a wall-less world our civilization will die: it will die by inanition, through the terrified expenditure upon "protection," or it will die by common extermination, aggravated by neurotic fury, the first time an autarchic state attempts to overcome its self-imposed sense of enclosure by committing an aggression upon an equal.

The fact is that planning and co-operative enterprise must take the place occupied by political boundaries and purely legal codes in creating an orderly polity and an ordered economic life. Our present tariff barriers, which may be called supplementary military walls, in so far as they are not thievish efforts to enrich a special group of manufacturers at the expense of the whole community, are efforts to achieve, by altogether inadequate means, the effects of a planned system of production and distribution. Now the great worldwide commodities, such as wheat, cotton, and rubber, commodities which are necessarily grown for an inter-regional market, must be planned and rationed eventually by a world authority. The fact that attempts to do this have again and again broken down during the present state of economic anarchy, does not lessen the necessity nor should it blind us to the need for trying again under better auspices. Once a basic production was established; once the surplus was rationed, the social effects of a tariff would be created without walling off intercourse and without arbitrarily raising prices. Our walls are feeble, indeed disastrous, military measures to evade the necessity for altering an economic system based upon priority of property rights and profit-opportunities: while imperialism is the bastard effort to create an international framework for modern production on the basis of conquest, robbery, and class exploitation. Both these efforts are inimical to civilization.

We have still to create the adequate political framework for Western Civilization: a political framework which will recognize both the universalizing forces and the differentiating forces that are at work.

At the same time, we must create a groundwork, in city, in region, in province, for the differentiating forces that are so necessary to such a worldwide system: a foundation which will accept the differentiation of local tongues and dialects, which will foster, instead of trying to extirpate or standardize, the living speech, with its slang, its colloquialisms, its local variants, its color both in form and in pronunciation: local literatures, local forms of art and culture, from cooking to painting, from the platting and carving of the landscape to the variants on universal forms in engineering and architecture.

Originating in this or that region, a local force will rise to universality: co-operation will spread throughout the world from the little town of Rochdale, or the technique of psychoanalysis will penetrate every culture, once it has taken shape in Zürich and in Wien. Such inter-regional influence and intercourse must be made possible on a far greater scale than during the liberal era of the nineteenth century. Old persecution complexes and old fears of being poisoned by cultural food offered by a strange hand must be completely expunged. For make no mistake: the creation of a more orderly world, more susceptible to reason, more adequately founded on reality, awaits a re-orientation of the human ego: it demands a more effective psychological insight and a broader collective discipline.

4: Regional Planning: A New Task

The orderly development of the region and its finer articulation with other regions is the task of regional planning.

Planning involves the co-ordination of human activities in time

[FIRST LEFT] Factory for light industry in Detroit, Mich. Type of industrial unit that need not be placed in a separate zone, but which may often, was with the Spirella corset factory at Letchworth, be integrated in a predominantly residential development. Old-fashioned stereotyped zoning plans, still popular in America, would not permit such organic planning, any more than they would permit apartment houses in one-family blocks: so much the worse for this system of zoning.

[FIRST RIGHT] Apostolic Church designed by Oud for the Kiefhoek development at Rotterdam: a masterpiece of great esthetic purity and delight: a monument of the non-monumental.

[SECOND LEFT] Public Garden in Essen. Spacious formal order that owes none of its charm to mere holdovers of renascence gardening. The intelligent indigenous landscaping of Jones Beach, L. I., would serve equally well as an example of the new design if only the architecture belonged to the same order.

[SECOND RIGHT] Department store in Prague: latest product of a long development that began in Paris, was carried on in the Art Nouveau buildings of Paris and San Francisco, and further developed by Mendelsohn in Chemnitz and Dudok in Rotterdam.

[THIRD LEFT] Three-story apartment building in Warsaw: fine example of the spacious new vernacular that does not have to climb thirty stories into the air to be assured of its modernism.

[THIRD RIGHT] Part of the Town Hall at Hilversum, near Amsterdam: a handsome public building effectively designed as part of a living landscape, without invoking the now incongruous formalities of the baroque planners. No building or community development can be considered a satisfactory example of biotechnic design unless it includes open spaces and gardens as an integral part of its plan: this applies to every part of the urban environment.

[FOURTH LEFT] Modern school by Richard Neutra in California. Note removable outside wall: the easy transition of the class from indoor to outdoor activities: the opportunity to study and play in the open air. Note, too, that the amount of sun indoors can likewise be controlled, since too much may be as undesirable in the tropical climate of the south as too little. Schools of this type are common in Switzerland: Zürich has made notable public provision for small nursery units in its new housing developments.

[FOURTH RIGHT] South Russia: modern street with dwellings at right angles to the line of traffic: spacious, verdure-lined, composed: visually at least one of the better examples of modern housing in Russia, where imitations of American congestion, as in certain quarters in Moscow, too often compete with a disagreeably arid and over-systematized type of German rationalism. (*Sovfoto*)

PRAHA - Václavské nám.

Government aid in housing, first through restrictive legislation, then through slum improvement programs, then through loans at low interest rates and finally through actual supervision and building, has grown steadily for almost a century. Beginning in England in the 1850's the housing movement reached the United States in the form of philanthropic organizations for model housing, and not till 1917 did the government take more positive measures. War-housing, such as in Bridgeport (Black Rock) and in Yorkship Village, set a new standard in community development; but this precedent was neglected both during the period of housing shortage, 1918-1924, and during the miserable speculative boom that followed. Government housing received a new impetus in 1932, after President Hoover's Housing Conference, in the offer of Federal funds for limited dividend housing projects. In 1933 the aid to housing under the Public Works Administration was greatly extended: not sufficiently to meet the actual need for slum clearance and the re-building of blighted areas, but at least enough to make an admirable beginning. The triumph of the Public Works Administration has been to demonstrate superior methods of comprehensive planning and design, to show the advantage of large-scale operations and unified technical direction, to prove the desirability of planned housing, not for individuals, but for communities, with communal facilities provided as part of the original design. No urban community can afford the costly luxury of unco-ordinated and insecure private enterprise: for economy in the long run, it must plan and build its own housing as it now plans and builds its own waterworks and parks.

[TOP] Harlem Houses, New York. Handsomely designed apartments for Negroes, overlooking the Harlem River. Note approach through triangular park, right, the playground on the river front, the spacious open courts with ample light and air. Contrast with the legally permissible congestion and darkness of the "improved" new law tenements of 1901 in the background. In essentials of plan and arrangement, these quarters are superior to any comparable area of residential apartments in the city. (*Photograph: Public Works Administration*)

[MIDDLE] Ten Eyck Houses, Williamsburg district, Brooklyn. A blighted area, partly cleared and redeemed. The school in the center, though admirably placed and new, is an old-fashioned type that contrasts unfavorably with the apartments. Note the closing up of wasteful streets in the replanning of this area into superblocks: also the orientation of the houses for maximum sunlight, a typical modern innovation here somewhat marred by the introduction of wings at right angles to the main exposure. (*Photograph: Public Works Administration*)

[BOTTOM] Lakeview Terrace, Cleveland. Good plan, well-adapted to site, with combination of apartment house and smaller dwellings. Note the placement of the dwellings at right angles to the roads, the skillful use of contours on the left, the abandonment of useless and costly streets, the ample interior playground. (*Photograph: Public Works Administration*) and space, on the basis of known facts about place, work, and people. It involves the modification and re-location of various elements in the total environment for the purpose of increasing their service to the community; and it calls for the building of appropriate structures—dwellings, industrial plants, markets, water works, dams, bridges, villages, cities—to house the activities of a community and to assist the performance of all its needful functions in a timely and orderly fashion.

Regional planning is the conscious direction and collective integration of all those activities which rest upon the use of the earth as site, as resource, as structure, as theater. To the extent that such activities are focused within definite regions, consciously delimited and utilized, the opportunities for effective co-ordination are increased. Hence regional planning is a further stage in the more specialized or isolated processes of agriculture planning, industry planning, or city planning.

In every society there is some sort of spontaneous co-ordination of functions based upon tradition. But this sort of empirical "planning," though not altogether ineffective in a stable society working under long-tried conditions with well-established conventions and duties, was cancelled out by the changes that took place during the last three centuries. The growth of population, the multiplication of inventions, the rise of hitherto unknown needs and the employment of uncertain techniques, the acceleration of change itself—all these conditions turned empirical and spontaneous co-ordination into helpless mockeries. For lack of conscious plan, the empire of muddle arose: a maximum opportunity for social conflict and cross-purposes and duplication of effort, and a minimum means of achieving collective order. Planful order came only in patches through the work of the military strategist, the geographer, the architect, the engineer, and the competent industrial organizer. The chief opportunities to plan fell only to organizations that had the advantage of size and monopoly: the Bell Telephone System, for example, in the United States.

Each industry, each institution, each area, each civic entity, has need under modern conditions for a plan of activity and for a procedure in development. The more effective such an organization, the more certainly does plan play such a part in directing its internal activities. But all these separate instances of planning suffer from two things: a lack of understanding of the social meaning of the plan, and a failure to achieve co-ordination with other organizations, by dove-tailing, under a common authority, into a broader scheme for regional and inter-regional planning. Even organizations that attempt a maximum of scientific planning within their own walls tend to resist the need for this wider kind of co-ordination. Behind this skepticism and this hostility to plan lie certain presuppositions and prejudices that need to be thoroughly aired.

What is a plan? To the Oblomovs of the world a plan is a dodge for evading the realities of life and for avoiding the responsibilities of action. To them a plan is a purely fictitious contrivance, a series of propositions drawn up in graphic form on paper, which serve as a surrogate for reality. Such two-dimensional plans were the bane of architecture, when they became separated from the processes of building, and were elaborated by learned esthetes who had little direct knowledge of the technical processes of construction. Often, in the act of making such a plan, the object is forgotten: the paper design, elegant, symmetrical, unspotted by sordid considerations of cost, availability of materials, suitability to purpose, ignores important environmental facts. The paper landscape gardener forgets the drainage of the land and the adaptation of his flora to the climate: the paper architect plays with elegant decoration and achieves a formal balance on the façade and forgets to put the dining room near enough to the kitchen to keep the food from getting cold in service; the paper engineer—this is an actual case—designs an irrigation project with admirable skill in hydraulics, only to discover, after the water works have been built, that the soil is unfit for cultivation.

All such "plans" are inefficient and embarrassing when they are carried out: they are at their best when they are still on the drafting board. Too often, as in so many beautiful city planning and zoning schemes in the United States, they are piously docketed in the appropriate file, and something radically different is done from day to day by the powers that be. Planning, in the sense of making idle pictures and diagrams, of covering all the tough knots of reality with coats of esthetic paint, of making the wish a substitute for the thought, has justly earned the derision of hard-headed, intelligent people. Similarly, attempts to impose a limited order of reality upon the future actions of men—as in grandiose mappings of the New York of the future, a century in advance by the "practical" city plan commissioners of 1811—are often more mischievous in their fake order than the purely empirical provision for the day's needs would be.

In contrast, genuine planning is an attempt, not arbitrarily to displace reality, but to clarify it and to grasp firmly all the elements necessary to bring the geographic and economic facts in harmony with human purposes. Regional planning involves four stages. The first stage is that of survey. This means disclosing, by first-hand visual exploration and by systematic fact-gathering, all the relevant data on the regional complex. Since even the geographic constants have been altered in one degree or another by time-processes, the historic side of the survey is as necessary as the elementary topographic mapping.

The orderly arrangement and graphic presentation of these data, through maps, statistical charts, and photographs, are important aids in clearing the mind of confusion, partial observation, and misleading generalizations formed on the basis of insufficient evidence. Charles Booth and his associates in London, Patrick Geddes and his colleagues in Edinburgh, were perhaps the first to undertake a thoroughgoing civic survey as a preliminary to town planning and municipal action. Booth was the more exhaustive in his detailed, house-to-house canvass of living conditions in London: Geddes was the more broad-visioned, in that he included, as matters of first importance, the geographic setting, the climatic and meteorological facts, the economic processes, the historic heritage. Between them, long before industrial analysis had reached this systematic stage, they created a pattern for orderly diagnosis and treatment of civic conditions. As an ecological sociologist, Geddes made the necessary passage from the civic survey to the regional survey; and at various removes his example has been widely followed: note the surveys of various industrial areas, by Abercrombie and others in England.

The second stage in planning is the critical outline of needs and activities in terms of social ideals and purposes. Unfortunately, this is the element of planning that has been least developed. Within the still dominant economic system, the main purpose of plan would be to increase the pecuniary rewards to the owners of industry and in some faint degree perhaps to the workers therein. These pecuniary canons have tended to remain, under slight disguise, the accepted warrant of planning: hence the usual emphasis upon the means of transportation, the provision of fresh commercial opportunities, and the desirability of national self-sufficiency in times of war. Under such canons of planning, housing and community building would enter belatedly, if at all.

Planning, however, is a selective process: it demands evaluation and choice. Though the values that are to issue from effective regional planning must ultimately harmonize with actuality, they do not automatically derive from the immediate situation: they may, on the contrary, deliberately work against it. It is naïve to think that geographers, sociologists, or engineers can by themselves formulate the social needs and purposes that underlie a good regional plan: the work of the philosopher, the educator, the artist, the common man, is no less essential; and unless they are actively brought into the process of planning, as both critics and creators, the values that will be imported into the plan, when it is finally made, will be merely those that have been carried over from past situations and past needs, without critical revision: old dominants, not fresh emergents.

Planning will take one form in a country where the desire for bellicose achievement and conquest is uppermost: it will take still another where education and the nurture of life is the main aim of collective endeavor. Whether the resources of a region are utilized to build military airplane bases, strategic mobilization highways, and ammunition dumps, or to build schools, playgrounds, and parks is something that is not answered purely by geographic or technical data.

Not merely does planning, then, require a visualization of resources and activities and processes, by means of the regional survey: it demands a critical formulation—and revision—of current values.

One of the main difficulties in the way of applying the advanced collective technical processes and instrumentalities of thought to the

creation of a better commonwealth has been due to the dissipation
of values that has taken place during the last century. Though the
common instruments of production have increased the human basis
for association, the breakup of coherent value-systems has undermined the possibilities for unified action. And in addition, the values
of Orthodox Christianity, of Protestantism, of individualistic humanism, of capitalism, of humanitarianism and libertarianism, have
been weakened, not merely through conflict, but through internal
erosion. One may confidently prophesy the emergence of a new system of values, which will displace the debris of these dying systems:
a system shared, if not yet successfully formulated, by most men of
good-will today. But until this system has been defined, it will be
easier to expand or diminish the amount of social energy than to
alter its direction. In detail, however, a process of revaluation has
been going on generally for over a century: its most profound outcome has been the belief that the opportunities for the fullest manifestation of life belong, not to an exclusive minority, but to every
citizen, up to the limits of his capacities. What Christianity expressed
in terms of Heaven, a humanistic socialism expressed in terms of
daily living.

The third stage in planning is that of imaginative reconstruction
and projection. On the basis of known facts, observed trends, estimated needs, critically formulated purposes, a new picture of regional
life is now developed. In this picture a host of dispersed projects—
the dredging of a river here, the extension of a library service, the
shifting of an industry to a better location—are for the first time set
down in a fashion that discloses their essential spatial and temporal
inter-relationships. On this plan, blank spots, weaknesses, unused resources, disclose themselves and new means of repairing such handicaps perhaps suggest themselves: similarly, new opportunities, hitherto overlooked, become visible. No better picture of the integrating effect of plan can be offered than that made by Henry Wright's
sketch plan for New York: it is all the more significant because he
did not overlook the historic succession.

Here plan finally appears in the accepted sense of the word. For
a good part of these projects can be graphically drawn up. Such
plans, however, are instrumental, not final: what is planned is not

simply a location or an area: what is planned is an activity-in-an-area, or an area-through-an-activity. Such planning draws attention to the fact that the old question as to whether society is to be organized on territorial lines or on an economic and functional basis is almost meaningless. For a territorial society, such as a city or a regional authority, is not describable merely in terms of the area it governs; and similarly, a steel industry, owning or operating a multitude of mines, furnaces, sheds, railroads, cannot be described purely in terms of its corporate organization or the legal-political relations of workers, managers, stockholders, and consumers. The fact is that all associations and organizations are carried on through physical structures that exist in space, and that are geographically conditioned: only imaginary societies can do without a parcel of earth for site and the physical means of coming together. Regional planning is industrial planning in its place aspect: industrial planning is regional planning in its resource-activity-product aspect. This would be a truism were it not for the fact that the very word "plan" connotes in many minds merely the more static aspects of regional development: the mapping of the terrain and the disposition of forces, but not the movements of the troops or the issue of the battle.

At this stage of planning, the disciplined play of the creative imagination is extremely important; but unfortunately civilization has as yet presented little scope for the collective planner. In small compass, nevertheless, one may observe a parallel process at work: landscape architects like Olmsted and Eliot in America, architects like H. H. Richardson and Louis Sullivan, thrust deep roots into their civilization and had, in an extraordinary degree, the capacity to understand and express its new wants. In this stage of planning new combinations of old elements, and fresh additions from new sources, make their appearance. The re-modeling of the earth and its cities is still only at a germinal stage: only in isolated works of technics, like a power dam or a great highway, does one begin to feel the thrust and sweep of the new creative imagination: but plainly, the day of passive acquiescence to the given environment, the day of sleepy oblivion to this source of life and culture, is drawing to an end. Here lies a new field for intense creative activity.

Now these three main aspects of planning—survey, evaluation, and the plan proper—are only preliminary: a final stage must follow, which involves the intelligent absorption of the plan by the community and its translation into action through the appropriate political and economic agencies.

In this stage, the plan undergoes a readaptation as it encounters the traditions, the conventions, the resistances, and sometimes the unexpected opportunities of actual life. No plan can automatically foresee all contingencies: moreover, it loses some of its efficacy as plan if it sacrifices, at the beginning, the clarity of the ideal by timidly anticipating all the qualifications and reductions that ideals are subject to in the course of their translation. Nor can a plan, as such, provide for its own fulfillment: to emerge as a reorganizing agent, it must help conjure up and re-educate the very groups and personalities that will bring it to fruition. Weak plans, which hesitate to leave solid ground at all, are often far less effective than overbold ones that awaken the popular imagination: such success as totalitarian states have shown in their collective planning has perhaps been due to their willingness to cleave at a blow the Gordian knot of historic resistances.

No architect or engineer is skilled enough to be able to detail, with specific instructions, every act in such a simple job as that of building a house or installing a machine: on the contrary, he must rely upon the autonomous skill and comprehension of even the unskilled laborer. Plan, then, is not a substitute for intelligent choice, decision, or invention on the part of those who must execute it in detail: it rather assumes the existence of these qualities and organizes the milieu in which they can most effectively work. What is true in individual constructions is even more true in the complicated co-ordinations of society. Regional plans are instruments of communal education; and without that education, they can look forward only to partial achievement. Failing intelligent participation and understanding, at every stage in the process, from the smallest unit up, regional plans must remain inert. Hence the need for positive organs of assimilation. Regional plans must provide in their very constitution the means of future adjustments. The plan that does not leave the way open to change is scarcely less disorderly than the aimless empiricism that rejects plan. Renewal: flexibility: adjustment: these are essential attributes of all organic plans.

If the problem of planning is more complex today than ever before the means, too, have become more adequate. A community that is technically capable of inventing calculating machines for the solution of abstruse mathematical problems, and that can send talking images through space, cannot plead lack of ability when it comes to applying a more complex technique of thought and administrative procedure to its social needs. Part of the dislocation from which economic life suffers is due to the fact that our mechanical equipment has been more quickly invented and improved and scrapped than our means of social control. Except in a few matters like bookkeeping and the permanent record and limited liability organization, our vast industrial mechanisms have been built up empirically without sufficient attention to the psychology of human organization. We have isolated mechanical factors and learned to deal with them in a fruitful systematic manner; but we have still to invent that wider system of order which will assist in the transformation of our social relations: one of its symbols is the regional plan itself.

5: Survey and Plan as Communal Education

The party politics of the nineteenth century was as remote from the thick tissue of actual life as were its pecuniary canons of success. A voter might loyally cast his vote every election without touching on a single issue that concerned his immediate life, without an intimate knowledge of a single phase of political administration, from taxes to the school system, and without affecting for the better a single aspect of his working life or his daily environment. The system "worked" in an atmosphere of windy ignorance.

The new totalitarian states profess to regard the liberal politics of the nineteenth century with scorn; but in fact they carry on the same traditions in an even more costly way, with the further disadvantage that their political wind must be kept at high pressure in order to divert attention from the human sterility of the power state's achievements. The fascists go through the forms of voting without having the privilege of even casting a negative vote; they go through the forms of sounding out public opinion without daring to hear more than one side: even more than the most imperialist states of the nine-teenth century they endeavor to wipe out local differences, local pref-erences, local pressures. The totalitarian state has but two important functions: to prepare for war and to keep power in the hands of the governing party. This is not in the least a new form of politics: it is merely the old form, shamelessly reduced to its naked reality.

The fascist state may be defined as the war dictatorship of the power state frozen into a permanent form: opinion governed by war censorship, action governed by military coercion, all law converted, openly or implicitly, into martial law. In a sense, any fool can govern such a community; but only a fool would mistake such a process for government.

None of the attributes of an advanced civilization can be main-tained in a permanently cowed and servile population: the delicate initiatives, the fine co-operations, the deeper loyalties toward truth and rational judgment upon which our civilization depends cannot be preserved in governments that know no law, even in the spiritual life, except the whim of the dictator or the command of the party. If the totalitarian state still shows the surface characteristics, here and there, of our common civilization it is only because it still lives on the going energies of the more civilized generation that preceded it; so far as fascism succeeds, these energies will wane, and barbarism will progressively rise to the surface, whether hastened by war or not. Such peoples will sink to the level of ancient Sparta—at whose very "bravery" the ancient world sometimes smiled. Toynbee's inter-pretation of this possibility in the third volume of A Study of His-tory is extremely suggestive.

The real alternative to the empty political patterns of the nine-teenth century lies, not in totalitarianism, but in just the opposite of this: the restoration of the human scale in government, the multipli-cation of the units of autonomous service, the widening of the co-operative processes of government, the general reduction of the area of arbitrary compulsion, the restoration of the processes of persua-sion and rational agreement. Political life, instead of being the monopoly of remote specialists, must become as constant a process in daily living as the housewife's visit to the grocer or the butcher, and more frequent than the man's visit to the barber. If the leisure that man has been promised by the machine counts for anything, it must count for the extension of the privilege of being an active political animal. For every phase of group activity, industrial, professional, educational, has its political aspect: each activity raises special problems of power, organization, control, and discipline—problems that cry for intelligent and orderly solutions.

The opposite of tyrannical compulsion is not unconditional "freedom" but the systematic practice of rational discipline through education and co-operative service: through education the curve of the individual career may be ultimately harmonized with that of the community, not by a mere restriction of response to that desired by a governing despot, but by a widening of personal scope and opportunity, in those spheres of rational understanding and administrative action which are properly the concern of the citizen and the polity. That human conduct is full of irrational residues does not lessen this need: for what is true of human beings in the mass is equally true of self-elected rulers and leaders: in any case, the problem is to increase the area of rational judgments and rational political activity, and to divert or sublimate those forces which are inimical to co-operation. To the extent that political power becomes rationally conditioned and successfully diffused by education, the individual citizen will be reluctant to sacrifice his own initiatives and his own judgments to the terroristic monopoly of dictatorship. The impotence of the many is the power of the few—and vice-versa.

Where shall this return to political realities begin? Where better than in the region? All rational politics must begin with the concrete facts of regional life, not as they appear to the specialist, but as they appear first of all to those who live within the region. Our educational systems are only beginning to make use of the local community and the region as a locus of exploratory activities: but before the resources and activities of a region are treated as abstract subjects they should be understood and felt and lived through as concrete experiences. Beginning with the crawling of an infant in his home, the systematic contact with the environment should broaden out until it includes the furthest horizon of mountain top and sea: in a bout of sailing, fishing, hunting, quarrying or mining every child should have a firsthand acquaintance with the primitive substratum of economic life: the geography and geology of the textbook should be annota‑ tions to these experiences, not substitutes. So, too, with work in the garden, the vegetable patch, the hayfield and the grain field: here is the very substance of regional life, and no system of education, no urban environment, can be considered even remotely satisfactory that does not include these experiences as a vital element. Child labor, as Karl Marx pointed out, will be an essential part in all edu‑ cation once the element of exploitation is removed from it.

The next step toward a rational political life—note how different this process is from the military automatisms of the fascist—is the hitching of these concrete experiences to local surveys, more system‑ atically undertaken. The soil survey, the climatic survey, the geo‑ logical survey, the industrial survey, the historic survey, on the basis of the immediate local environment, are the next important instru‑ ments of education: this is a process of grasping in detail and as a whole what has hitherto been taken in through passive observation in city and countryside. All these local surveys, taken together, become the focus for a more general regional survey. Already such surveys have come to play an important part in English education: indeed the land utilization survey, completed recently in England, was carried out through the co-operation of the school children in every locality.

Such surveys, if made by specialist investigators alone, would be politically inert: made through the active participation of school chil‑ dren, at an appropriate point in adolescent development, they be‑ come a central core in a functional education for political life. It is in the local community and the immediate region, small enough to be grasped from a tower, a hilltop, or an airplane, to be explored in every part before youth has arrived at the period of political respon‑ sibility, that a beginning can be made toward the detailed resorption of government—an alternative to that half-world of vague wishes, idle dreams, empty slogans, pretentious mythologies in which the power politics of the past has flourished. The scientific approach, the method of intellectual co-operation, embodied in the regional survey, are moralizing forces, and it is only when science becomes an integral part of daily experience, not a mere coating of superficial habit over a deep layer of uncriticized authority, that the foundations for a common collective discipline can be laid.

Most of our educational routine, as built up during the past century, has reflected the dominant political and economic institutions: it has substituted mere paper counters for reality. The elimination of concrete views and concrete experiences has reduced rather than widened the sphere of effective education: finally, we arrived at the age of extreme specialization, the present age, when the amount of specialized knowledge, often accurate, often extremely refined, has far outstripped our capacity to make use of it as part of a consistent whole. The remedy for this is not to be found in any mechanical combination of specialisms: we might digest the contents of an encyclopedia without achieving anything more in the nature of unity than a headache. The cure lies rather in starting from the common whole—a region, its activities, its people, its configuration, its total life—and relating each further achievement in specialized knowledge to this cluster of images and experiences.

Here and there this organic approach to knowledge, as one with life, and to life as a constant function of knowledge, has been made in education: beginning at the lowest stage in the new nursery school. But the fact is that education, instead of rising above this unifying attitude, must keep it at every later stage, along with the element of deliberate play and art.

What is needed for political life is not mere factual knowledge: for this by itself is inert: what is needed are those esthetic and mythic impulses which open up new activities and carve out new forms for construction and contemplation. When the landscape as a whole comes to mean to the community and the individual citizen what the single garden does to the individual lover of flowers, the regional survey will not merely be a mode of assimilating scientific knowledge: it will be a dynamic preparation for further activity. The Boston Metropolitan Park System of Boston, one of the most varied and comprehensive in the world, owes its existence to just such regional surveys as practiced by Charles Eliot in his schoolboy rambles about the region. The Appalachian trail, again, owes not a little to the extra-curricular activities of Benton MacKaye, making as a mere youngster a systematic exploration of the environment of Shirley Center.

Once this more realistic type of education becomes universal, instead of being pieced into the more conventional system, we will create a whole generation that will look upon every aspect of the region, the community, and their personal lives as subject to the same processes: exploration, scientific observation, imaginative reconstruction, and finally, transformation by art, by technical improvement, and by personal discipline. Instead of an external doctrinal unity, imposed by propaganda or authoritarian prescription, such a community will have a unity of background and a unity of approach that will not need external threats in order to preserve the necessary state of inner cohesion. Science has given us the building stones of an orderly world. We need the further utilization of science, through the regional survey, regional exploration, and regional reconstruction if we are to increase the area of political rationality and human control. Visual synthesis provides a foundation for unified creative activity.

Once the human scale is overpassed, once the concrete fact disappears from view, knowledge becomes remote, abstract, and overwhelming: a lifetime's effort will not provide sufficient grasp of the environment. The more people who are thrust together in a limited area, without organic relationships, without a means of achieving an autonomous education or preserving autonomous political activities in their working and living relations, the more must they become subject to external routine and manipulation. The resorption of scientific knowledge and the resorption of government must go hand in hand. We must create in every region people who will be accustomed, from school onward, to humanist attitudes, co-operative methods, rational controls. These people will know in detail where they live and how they live: they will be united by a common feeling for their landscape, their literature and language, their local ways, and out of their own self-respect they will have a sympathetic understanding with other regions and different local peculiarities. They will be actively interested in the form and culture of their locality, which means their community and their own personalities. Such people will contribute to our land-planning, our industry planning, and our community planning the authority of their own understanding, and the pressure of their own desires. Without them, planning is a barren externalism.

At present, we have inferior forms of life because our metro-politanized populations throughout the world are both witless and wantless: true cannon-fodder, potential serfs for a new totalitarian feudalism, people whose imaginative lives are satiated by shadows, people whose voices are dimmed by loud-speakers, people whose will is capable of response only under mass stimuli and mass pressures, people whose personalities, instead of being represented by an in-teger, can be represented as but a fraction—one one-millionth of a voting crowd, a war-crowd, a drill-crowd.

The task of regional survey, then, is to educate citizens: to give them the tools of action, to make ready a background for action, and to suggest socially significant tasks to serve as goals for action. Ulti-mately, this becomes the essential duty of every vital school, every responsible university. In this concrete sense—and not in any vague hope—education is the alternative to irrational and arbitrary com-pulsion. The opposite of this is the reduction of education to drill and cram, and the reduction of the body politic to a corpse that is galvanically brought to some semblance of life by the application of external stimuli from the center. Such a state may create "heroes": it can never create a wide society of true personalities, men and women who have learned the arts of personal and communal living, who neither renounce the will-to-order nor seek to create it on a single monotonous pattern. Without such a broader cultural founda-tion, regional planning can have but a minor political significance. Once the cultural base is achieved, however, regional planning be-comes one of the essential attributes of a progressive civilization; and every effective economy it introduces tends to further the ca-pacity for association and to widen the field of significant action.

6: Conditions of Urban Re-building

Many things that were done hastily in the nineteenth century, be-cause there was in a sense no time to think, now have to be done over again. The division of the exploitable areas of the world between the existing powers of Europe, on a basis that lacked reason and justice, has become an intolerable anachronism: the empires that were founded on the notion that such a division was permanent must be dissolved, unless civilization itself is to be dissolved. On the way to that end the belligerent outlines and routines of the national state itself must be softened by systematic inter-regional co-operation: if neither of these things can be done so long as screaming tyrannies of the totalitarian states threaten more democratic and civilized modes of life, it will come after they have been liquidated: the men of good will outnumber the homicidal barbarians, and one day, it has been promised, peace will come to all men of good will.

One of the major tasks of the twentieth century is the re-settlement of the planet. The past three centuries have been centuries of random exploration. The pressure of population, rising first in Europe, and then in the Orient through forces originating in Europe, has pumped into the areas of low population-pressure millions of immigrants: to find a parallel for this movement one would perhaps have to go back to the desiccation of the grasslands of Central Asia, which thrust the Hun into the heart of Europe. Here again, unfortunately, the flow of population was spontaneous and unguided by sufficient knowledge; and much of the work of settlement must be done over again.

In North America, this need has already been recognized: farm lands that should have been left in forest are returning to forest; grassland that should have been left to the grazing of cattle, instead of being plowed for wheat, will return to grass again; grazing land in the West has been put back, through the Taylor Act, under close Federal control. Population that spread with no more social direction than the surface tension which gives definition to an ink blot, must be re-grouped and nucleated in a fashion that will make possible a co-operative civilized life. Industries that flowed into the centers of congestion in order to take advantage of cheap labor, must now flow out into new centers, where a better life is possible for the workers: conscious scientific intelligence must determine the new loci of industrial advantage, and organize industries and communities in such a fashion that neither the labor supply itself, nor the organized protection of the workers against exploitation, will rest on the mere congestion of population in crowded cities. Industries that during the nineteenth century naturally gravitated to the coal mine, the railroad line, or the cluttered seaport, must now be put in more advantageous areas, where the new sources of power and new modes of transport may be used to fuller advantage.

But although the decadent metropolitan form cannot long remain a dominant, the sources of urbanization nevertheless persist. The chief source is the increasing efficiency of agriculture. With mechanization of the main processes of plowing, harrowing, reaping, binding, threshing, milking, sorting, an even smaller number of people is capable of doing the original work; and with improvements in agronomy, through seed-selection, new stocks, and increased knowledge of the biochemistry of plant growth, both the number of people and the area engaged in agricultural production will be smaller: this will release a larger number of men and women for non-agricultural work. Hence the need for building urban communities remains, even though the population of a country as a whole approaches stability.

The danger is that this process of re-settlement and continued urbanization will continue, through inertia, in the forms that prevailed in the past. Most of our plans for urban development have been static: they have taken past habits, past technical methods, past legal codes, past financial opportunities, and past social attitudes as the sole elements that will condition future development. On this basis, it is easy to prove that, if the metropolis has increased in population in the past, it will continue to in future. Those who hold these views regard any other possibility as unthinkable—by which they mean, in reality, that they are incapable of further thought.

But apart from the fact that history is full of reverses in existing trends—above all in such tricky matters as urban increases in population—such plans for the future leave out of account all those elements that exist in the present only as imagination, desire, dream, and project: the latent social forces which materialize in each generation in unexpected forms. The incalculable element in every scheme for urban and regional planning is not what men have and are accustomed to: but what they want, and are ready, when the want has been organized and dramatized, to reach for. Without taking advantage of the directive force of the imagination, releasing elements not given, or not dominant, in a present situation, planning must remain a belated mopping up after the forces of life have spilled over:

never catching up with its opportunities, committed to drifting with the current, never tacking to catch a breeze.

Plans that do not rise out of real situations, plans that ignore existing institutions, are of course futile: mere utopias of escape. But plans that neglect to formulate the potential creative forces, even though they are perhaps feeble at the moment of formulation, are equally futile, no matter how copiously they are ballasted with statistics and quasi-scientific demonstration: they lend all their authority to an order that is already, by definition, past.

The difference between these two types of planning was well-exemplified in the difference between Henry Wright's Report on Regional Planning for New York State, in 1926, and the voluminous report on the Metropolitan District of New York by Thomas Adams and his associates during the same decade. Wright's report dealt not only with past facts but with new social and economic emergents: as a result the work of Wright and his associates laid a foundation for the regional planning movement throughout the United States. The Russell Sage report, on the other hand, was obsolete even at the moment of its original formulation, to say nothing of its final summary: a compendious handbook on how not to approach the future, and of what not to do. Adams's report committed the city to a continuance of its past mistakes: Henry Wright's report showed, in the existing situation, the latent possibilities for a new order: not a passive continuation but a re-integration.

Do not ignore the difference between these two orders of thinking: it underlies the approach to the whole problem of urban re-settlement and re-building that now confronts the Western World.

This problem has two sides to it: one is the building up of new centers on lines that embody current improvements in architecture, planning, and social insight; the other side is the re-building of existing centers, great and small, cutting out morbid tissue, restoring functional relationships that have lapsed, giving them, in the process of renewal, a parity with the newer communities. If the planning bodies accept the existing structures of finance and administration as sound, indeed as indispensable—because they have been bequeathed by the past—no important changes can be made in any part of the urban environment: planning will be little better than the application of plasters to the sore spots of civic life, or of beauty patches upon its diseased complexion.

The real opportunity for urban and regional development lies in the fact that the existing pattern of economic life cannot remain stable. The accretion of the debt structure in the great metropolises, the toppling pyramid of land values, make economic life precarious and effective social planning an impossibility. Hence the real need is to deflate this burdensome structure as a deliberate public policy and to set up a responsible public body capable of directing the flow of investment into social channels and to liquidate with the least possible hiatus the present speculative structure. Only with this radical alteration in objectives and methods will it be possible to build up through public aid and initiative alternative centers which will attract industry and population, on the basis of their own essential superiority of life. As the drift out of the overgrown cities begins, the opportunity for their re-planning will come. Need I recall again that the vast increase of the number of playgrounds in Manhattan was not a result of financial prosperity: it was the outcome of deflation, failure to pay taxes, bankruptcy, and loss of population.

Existing cities must eventually participate in the re-urbanization of the modern environment: but before they can become regional cities, capable of sustaining a well-balanced environment for their now miserably housed masses, the metropolitan regime as a whole must be progressively liquidated. In the process of urban development, social values and financial values are in decisive conflict: pecuniary canons of success have produced an environment destructive to life, and similarly, biotechnic standards of achievement must produce a system of values destructive to metropolitan finance. Our whole program of re-urbanization and housing demands a definite choice. That choice may not be revolutionary in the sense of implying a complete break and an overpowering catastrophe: but it is revolutionary in the sense that when, by steady pressure and day-to-day movement, it has achieved its end, the metropolis and the insidious pecuniary values of metropolitan life will be obliterated, and a new set of working institutions, more consonant with a humane scheme of values, will have taken its place. Planners who are not aware of these implications are sociologically too unsophisticated to be trusted with important functions: instead of helping to define an adequate public policy, they can only obfuscate the issues and sabotage a sound social program.

7: The New Method of City Development—Garden Cities

The above issues were first defined during the nineteenth century. Three groups of men had an influence upon our later conception of population grouping and civic design; and a fourth group has still to achieve widespread acceptance.

The earliest contributor to the housing movement was Robert Owen: an original if somewhat fanatical mind, the first manufacturer who, out of his own success as an enterpriser, deliberately set his face against the barbarizing social results of the new machine industry: a process he had observed at firsthand as an agent of a well-meaning owner, and as a working industrialist himself. Owen proposed, in order to enable the new industrial workers to rise out of the squalid state in which they lived under the new factory system, to build small balanced communities in the open country. The educational and social facilities needed by these new settlements, as well as adequate houses, would be a charge on production, no less than the wages of the workers.

In the orderly community for which Owen furnished plans, one finds the first attempt, apart from the literature of utopias, to define the nucleus, or basic cell, of city growth in relation to the new form of industrial organization that had grown up in the mechanized and power-driven factory. Owen's design was not merely radically better than any other urban pattern in the early nineteenth century: it had the advantage over the new upper class squares of Edinburgh or London in that it provided, as part of the plan itself, some of the essential features of social life. On the whole Owen's original essay even compares favorably with the better work done in the twentieth century, after more than a generation of intensive experiment: for one thing, his designs were not marred by a weak feeling for the quaint and the picturesque, and for another he was not afraid to give the community the convenience and compactness of a city.

Owen's combination of vision and practical experience gave a special influence to his doctrine: his hopes and feelings were a yeasty ferment that continued to work through the nineteenth century. He had his coadjutors and successors: Fourier's idea of a harmonic society had a richer psychological basis than Owen's somewhat arid rationalism, and Fourier's scheme for phalansteries—though sometimes fantastic and irrelevant—nevertheless contributed imaginative details to the conception of a rational civic economy. The phalanstery built by Godin, the steel manufacturer, at Guise in France was a direct outcome of Fourier's ideas: one of the first efforts at collective workers' housing *and* community building. Sheer necessity often caused the industrialist to build houses for his workers, when his plant was situated in the open country: this gave an opportunity for fresh initiative, and the work of Sir Titus Salt at Saltaire, in the eighteen-fifties, paved the way for later settlements such as those of Krupp at Essen, Cadbury at Bourneville, and Lever at Port Sunlight. In terms of open suburban living, the last two initiatives had an important immediate effect upon the design of middle class suburbs with generous allotments of open spaces: but the improvements they instituted, their good planning and their low density, kept them from having any decisive influence upon low cost workers' housing done by the speculator and the jerrybuilder.

In one important way these new communities differed from middle class suburban settlements: they were directly related to industry; they made provision for the social life of the workers; they tended to form a small civic whole. The weaknesses of such beneficent effort was that they existed mainly, if not entirely, at the initiative of the "enlightened employer," and they were sometimes tyrannical in the underlying financial and administrative arrangements—so much so that in the case of Pullman, Illinois, the irate beneficiaries rebelled. Despite weaknesses in social organization the new industrial garden villages were, on the whole, the best working class quarters that had been built since the charitable foundations of the sixteenth century—if one excepts, perhaps, the small towns and villages set up in New England, Pennsylvania, and parts of Ohio before the middle of the nineteenth century. If they did nothing else, they dissociated the processes of industry from the idea of human degradation in a filthy environment: a useful dissociation.

Meanwhile, the spectacle of colonization and city building was not lost on the more acute observers of the nineteenth century—however foreign the idea of the city was to its scheme of abstract thought. An English observer, Wakefield, published a book in which he advocated a more systematic application of the art of colonization in new lands; and another Englishman, James Silk Buckingham, exercised his imagination in the construction of an ideal city, Victoria, which had the distinction of being limited in population, and of accepting the social services that had sprung up through voluntary associations in the new industrial towns as essential elements in the new order of urban existence. Finally, Henry George, viewing the process of settlement in the Far West, observed how the congestion of population automatically raised land values: thus, so long as land remained in private hands, it imposed a tax upon all those who either directly or derivatively were forced to use expensive land. The more advanced the machine industry, the more complicated the transportation net, the more dense the population, the higher the private tax in the form of rent.

By the end of the nineteenth century, all these plans, dreams, and initiatives were still in circulation: their actual effect upon society, however, was practically nil. At this point a benign Englishman, unfettered by those forms of specialized competence that paralyze creative thought, published a book called To-morrow, re-issued in later editions as The Garden City. In this book the views of Thomas Spence and Henry George, those of Owen and Fourier and Wakefield and Buckingham, were fused into a new and by now thoroughly original conception: that of the garden city, or the balanced urban environment.

Howard started from the basic fact in nineteenth century urbanization: population was increasing, and it was being drawn toward the existing centers of industry, particularly to the already overcrowded metropolises. New quarters had to be provided every year for factories and for factory workers. Why should this colonization go on automatically in centers that were so dismally congested, already clotted with foul slums? Why should there not be a deliberate attempt to create new cities out of the surplus? Every new increment of population was, in effect, a fresh opportunity to reverse those tendencies which were making life in cities more prohibitive in cost and more unsatisfactory in the social result.

Here Howard seized on a point where the individual industrialist, with his philanthropic plans for decentralized industrial villages, or model towns, was weak, and where the more vulpine industrialist, who sometimes escaped to little centers in order to enjoy the benefits of sweated labor, was positively anti-social. Howard recognized the human limitations of what is called in America the Company Town —the town organized and controlled, if not entirely owned, by a single industry. Such a method of "decentralization" left everyone but the industrialist himself poorer; it removed the possibility of alternative industries or modes of living from the workers; and it naturally aroused the opposition of organized labor in the better-graded industries. The problem of organizing good industrial cities was something more, for Howard, than the problem of selecting good industrial sites or finding cheap land.

But Howard showed his keen social imagination in still another way: his vision was bi-focal: he saw the countryside as well as the city, and he observed that the rural areas were fast becoming depopulated because they had ceased, from the standpoint of economic and social opportunity, to be attractive. The young, the adventurous, the intelligent were drawn off to the big cities because, in so far as there was any life in this new civilization, it was focused in these centers. The depopulation of the country and the overpopulation of the city were aspects of a single set of facts: the problem of bettering life at both poles was a single one. Hitherto the movement into the cities had aimlessly piled up great dormitory areas, remote from the essential social institutions of the city, and no less remote from the recreational advantages of the country: pools of urban and suburban squalor. As for industry, it generally followed the lines of least resistance: even when it wished better quarters for its workers it usually lacked the resources to build them: a large, easily accessible labor market was essential. So the country became poorer in human resources; and the cities did not show any commensurate gains in civic improvement.

Howard proposed to rectify this condition: if colonization could be more wisely directed in foreign areas, as Wakefield taught, and as the settlement of New Zealand and Utah had demonstrated, why should not the internal colonization of a country be equally deliberate? Why leave to chance something that was by nature subject to social control, since, once the elementary urban services were introduced in the nineteenth century, nothing could be effectively done except with direct municipal aid? What was wrong was not that the late nineteenth century city was unplanned: but that it was belatedly and badly planned, and the control of its existence was too largely in the hands of private land speculators and private transportation companies, seeking their own profits, not the common good. New industrial sites were to be spotted and allocated to their appropriate use; new housing quarters were to be built: why should these functions not be undertaken in the name of civilization and civic life?

If new cities were deliberately founded, as reservoirs are formed in flood areas, the uncontrolled flood of population which plunged so devastatingly into the metropolis would be abated: there would be a chance to build a new type of civilization. The new type of regional center would combine the hygienic advantages of the open suburbs with the social advantages of the big city, would give an equal place in its scheme to the urban and the rural possibilities of modern life: in short, it would be a balanced environment. To this new urban nucleus—new, that is, to the nineteenth century—Howard gave the title of the Garden City. "Town and country," said Howard, "must be married, and out of this union will spring a new hope, a new life, a new civilization." Without using the concept of the region, Howard's contribution was to see the problem of city building and housing as a regional one.

The name "garden city" was quickly appropriated by groups and interests that had no conception of Howard's statesmanlike proposals: it has even in our day been treated by Thomas Sharp as a scapegoat for the open type of planning characteristic of suburbs since the Middle Ages. So it is important that we recognize what was essential and original in Howard's new concept. The first point to be noted is that the land in the garden city is not parceled out into individual ownership: it must be held by the common authority under which it is developed: such increments as may arise through the growth of the garden city must be reserved for the community.

Not merely did Howard seek to eliminate the private landlord: he eliminated the temptation to increase density in order to raise land values. He likewise did away with instability through irrational or speculative changes in land use.

The second important characteristic is controlled growth and limited population. The outward limit of urban development was set by Howard's proposal to surround every garden city by a permanent reserve of open country: to be used either for agriculture or recreation. This agricultural belt was not merely to serve as a green wall against the encroachment of other communities: it was to provide opportunity for local production of food, with a good market close at hand. Once the area and plan and density of such a plan were determined, its upward limit of growth was set. Howard put this figure at about thirty thousand; but that was a shot in the dark: the main point was the notion that a modern city, no less than a medieval town, must be planned to the human scale and must have a definite size, form, boundary. It was no longer to be a mere sprawl of houses along an indeterminate avenue that moved toward infinity and ended suddenly in a swamp. Howard conceived the notion of promoting urban growth up to the point of maximum service to the social and economic life of the center: further growth could take place, not by overcrowding or spreading, as in existing cities, but in the foundation of a new garden city on the same lines.

The third notion that Howard introduced as an important attribute of the garden city, no less important than its human scale, was that of functional balance. In its regional relations, there was to be a balance between town and country; in its internal development, there was to be a balance between home, industry, and market, between political, social, and recreational functions. By providing in his scheme for a balanced environment, with a full equipment of social services, Howard offset the disadvantages of one-sided schemes of decentralization.

Howard, in other words, not merely avoided the weaknesses of the specialized dormitory suburb and the specialized company town: he also eliminated the possibility of deterioration through success—unlimited agglomeration. Howard may be said to be the first modern thinker about cities who had a sound sociological conception of the dynamics of rational urban growth.

In his plans for relieving metropolitan congestion, for limiting peripheral expansion, and for creating new urban nuclei, Howard had been anticipated centuries before by Leonardo da Vinci: on what remote sands can that bold pioneer's footprints not be found? Leonardo had proposed to the Duke of Milan that he be permitted to build ten cities of thirty thousand inhabitants each in order to "separate this great congregation of people who herd together like goats on top of another, filling every place with foul odor and sowing seeds of pestilence and death." It is interesting to note that Leonardo's proposal for garden cities came to fruition in the same decade as his experiments with mechanical flight: he had in fact projected two of the main inventions of the new economy. But Howard's garden city was as great an advance over Leonardo's dreams as Wright's airplane was over his Great Bird; for one thing, the social milieu was ready, and for another, the new invention worked.

Howard's scheme was first broached in 1898. Letchworth, the first fully equipped garden city to be built after Howard's outline, was founded in 1904 by a specially organized public utility association. Both events occurred, if not before the main neotechnic inventions were made, at all events before they had gone fully into circulation: when Howard proposed this civic method of decentralization no one could yet estimate the concrete support that was to be offered to his general scheme by the development of the electric transmission grid, the motor car and the motor road and the use of motor vehicles for transporting goods, to say nothing of the universal reception of the telephone and radio and phonograph and motion picture. Only a few original minds of the period, notably Peter Kropotkin and Patrick Geddes, had seized upon the implications of all these inventions for our civilization as a whole.

Howard's outline for a garden city, which was a rational suggestion in 1898, nevertheless was compelled to encounter the blind counterdrift of paleotechnic industry, still empirical in organization, still indifferent to plan, still even more indifferent to the effects of a congested environment on health and working capacity. A generation ago, the garden cities movement was an uphill movement be-

cause the concentration of industries was still economically profitable: hence the garden city encountered technical as well as financial resistance from industries that were still mainly equipped to use
steam power. After 1910, however, the currents of industry and administration both reversed their direction. For one thing, the decentralization of power and transportation became technically as feasible
as it had been in the days of the windmill, the water mill, and the
canal; and the decentralization of administration likewise became
possible through the wide use of the telephone, and more refined
mechanical means of audit and control. Urban development continued on the old mass pattern, no longer because of objective mechanical or economic advantages, but because the financial order had
crystallized its pecuniary structure in obsolete buildings, obsolete
equipment, and obsolete, technically over-developed cities.

Letchworth, the first garden city, was a demonstration project undertaken by a private association. Its supporters were drawn from
those bourgeois groups that were well disposed to social experiment,
that were content to receive a limited return on their investment, and
that for a long time even forewent the payment of interest on their
debt. Because of the need for attracting industries to the new center,
it grew slowly: but the growth was healthy and solid; and it was
achieved without an essential sacrifice of the original principles.
While other settlements, namely Hampstead Garden Suburb, had
physical qualities of plan that equaled, perhaps surpassed, Letchworth, they were purely middle class developments: because of its
success in incorporating industries and in building workers' houses,
the garden city became a focal point in the mind of social-minded
planners and administrators throughout the world.

After 1920, however, the conditions for the success of the garden
city became more favorable: for now the garden city was no longer
an isolated biological sport: it was the concrete embodiment of neotechnic processes, as applied to city development. Wherever enlightened control made possible the building of large scale developments,
Howard's conception became a potent influence: Hilversum in Holland, the new satellite communities built under Ernst May in Frankfurt-am-Main, the new town of Radburn in New Jersey, embodied to
a greater or lesser degree Howard's principles.

The public policy that Howard advocated, however, long awaited
the support that can come only through a broad policy of regional
development. Hence the industrial re-settlement of England after
1925, which resulted in the industrial building up of the southern
counties around London, was a wantonly lost opportunity: a deplorable failure in civic statesmanship. Though thousands of working
class houses were built in this district for the accommodation of the
new workers, the work was done under the direction of existing
boroughs and counties, and the opportunity for laying out new cities,
as wholes, was neglected: Becontree, the most vast of the new working class suburbs, was even deprived of the possibility of taking advantage of the new Ford Motor works nearby, because those who
settled there were by legal and administrative mandate exiles from
the London slums, not new workers.

Accordingly an important step was taken in the United States
when the Suburban Resettlement Bureau was called into existence
in 1934 for the purpose of setting up a number of demonstration
garden sites, appropriately called greenbelt towns, throughout the
country. Like so many other good policies pursued under the administration of President Franklin D. Roosevelt, it lacked the advantage
of consistent executive support and it failed to gather to itself
the co-operation of the local communities affected: eventually the
bureau itself was dismantled at the very moment when, through trial
and error, it had begun to promise effective action. But the scope
and intention of these projects, as demonstrated by those that were
actually built, gave them a significance that mere housing estates,
planned in already built-up areas, often on inadequate or mangled
sites, did not possess. Perhaps the most critical failure of all, characteristic of the stultifying division that exists in practice between
regional planning, housing, and city building, lies in the fact that
no attempt was made to plan greenbelt towns for the area in which
a great project in socialized planning was being carried out: namely,
the Tennessee Valley.

Similar opportunities for co-ordinated large scale-planning have
presented themselves in the new industrial development of Soviet
Russia; but here the pattern has been defeated, in part, through
haste, and through a tendency toward giantism left over as a burden-

some heritage from the time of Peter the Great. Perhaps the closest approach to civic and industrial and agricultural planning, on a human scale, is that which the Dutch have embodied in their reclamation of land from the Zuyder Zee; but although Holland is pre-eminent in urban culture, the Dutch have not yet given the Zuyder Zee development the stamp of the best modern communities around Amsterdam or The Hague.

The slowness of the garden city in taking root is due to the fact that it is, so to speak, the native form only for a co-operative and socially planned society: one in which agriculture is on a parity with industry, and in which the necessary social basis in land ownership and land control is lodged in the community. To be built successfully, the garden city should be the product of a regional authority, with a wider scope of action than the municipality, and with greater local concentration than a centralized bureau operating from Washington, London, or Paris. The garden city can take form, in other words, only when our political and economic institutions are directed toward regional rehabilitation. What is important to recognize is that these new principles of urban development, as demonstrated by Sir Ebenezer Howard and his associates, are universal ones: they point toward balanced urban communities within balanced regions: on one hand, a wider diffusion of the instruments and processes of a high human culture, and on the other the infusion into the city of the life-sustaining environment and life-directed interests of the countryside.

CHAPTER VII.

SOCIAL BASIS OF THE
NEW URBAN ORDER

1: Architecture as Symbol

"The problems of bettering life and its environment are not separate ones, as political and other mechanically educated minds constantly think, and as religious ones have also too much come to believe. Nor is it, as politicians especially think—now with mistaken hope, or again with unnecessary discouragement—a matter of moving great numbers and masses before anything can be done. It is not a matter of area and wealth. It is at bottom an experimental problem, that of starting a re-adaptation." These words of Geddes and Branford have been verified during the last twenty years. In the housing of families and the building of communities a re-adaptation has started; and against the very grain of capitalist finance, over active protest and passive sabotage and dull indifference, the housing movement has continued to grow.

The symbol of this new adaptation is a common architectural form, and new types of communal layout. So far these growths have been sporadic: they have taken place, for the most part, on the outskirts of great cities, London, Amsterdam, Paris, Berlin, Wien; and they still bear some of the defects of their origin. But the movement toward better housing, not for isolated fortunate individuals, but for a whole community, is one that has been going on for a century; and it has now reached a point where the positive results have awakened desire and emulation. In this approaching transformation of our cities lies the justification of Patrick Geddes's prophetic words, in 1905, in describing the transition from the paleotechnic to the neotechnic phase of modern industry: "As the former period may be characterized by the predominance of the relatively unskilled workman and the skilled, so this next incipient age by the development of the chief workman proper, the literal *architektos* or architect; and by his companion, the rustic improver, gardener, and forester, farmer, irrigator, and their correspondingly evolved types of civil engineer."

In the transformation of the environment, architecture has a peculiar part to play. This arises not merely because buildings constitute such a large part of man's daily surroundings; but because architecture reflects and focuses such a wide variety of social facts: the character and resources of the natural environment, the state of the industrial arts and the empirical tradition and experimental knowledge that go into their application, the processes of social organization and association, and the beliefs and world-outlooks of a whole society. In an age of social disintegration and unrelated specialism, like the passing one, architecture loses most of its essential character: in an age of synthesis and construction, it steps forward once more as the essential commanding art.

And precisely because architectural form crystallizes, becomes visible, is subject to the test of constant use, it endows with special significance the impulses and ideas that shape it: it externalizes the living beliefs, and in doing so, reveals latent relationships. With the help of his orderly accurate plans, the architect brings together a multitude of crafts, skills, and arts, creating in the act of building that species of intelligent co-operation which we seek on a wider scale in society: the very notion of planning owes more to this art than to any other, except perhaps the co-ordinate art of the engineer.

The architect confronts human needs and desires with the obdurate facts of site, materials, space, costs: in turn, he molds the environment closer to the human dream. And in a social sense, architecture is more advanced than any purely mechanical technique because good building has always embodied, as an essential element in both design and operation, the understanding and expression of organic human purposes. In the state of building at any period one may discover, in legible script, the complicated processes and changes that are taking place within civilization itself. In a period of integration, such as we are now again on the brink of, architecture becomes a guide to order in every other department of activity.

Architecturally speaking, the nineteenth century was a period of disintegration. Buildings outwardly without roots in their landscape or affiliations with their society appeared in the midst of the growing cities. Such buildings were the work of individual architects, responsible only for their individual building: producing work that was bound to be swallowed up in the disorderly urban mass produced by the speculative builder, the ground landlord, and the industrial corporation, operating solely under the principles of laissez-faire. This original architectural Babel became more confused as foreign travel and wide archaeological research combined with a lack of creative impulse to encourage either dead imitation or a feeble eclecticism.

Originally the architects of the Renascence had turned to the dead for inspiration: as if the breath of life could come from the tomb. No one could doubt the improvements in farming that followed when Columella's treatise on farming began to influence progressive agricultural practice. No one could doubt the stimulus to mechanical invention that arose from the reprinting of Hero of Alexandria's experiments with the steam engine. But there was a vast difference between such experimental selection and lifeless imitation; in architecture, after Brunelleschi, what was taken over was not the process, capable of modification and complete alteration as new needs arose, but the external form: the dead stereotype of another culture. Note how post-sixteenth century architecture, instead of organizing the banked window further as a constructional form, relapsed into the more primitive system of the hole left gaping in the solid masonry wall: a loss both in terms of technical facility and livability; for the overhead glare of the tall rectangular window in turn resulted in a need for curtains to cut off some of the irritating light, while that entering in the lower part of the window was optically useless.

This period from the sixteenth century to the twentieth witnesses the fatal lack of connection between architecture and the dominant social sources of order. The proof that architecture in the social sense was dead lies in the series of dusty revivals that took place. People sought, in Roman forms, Greek forms, neo-gothic forms, finally in Romanesque and even Byzantine forms, some quick and easy route to a real society and a living culture: lacking the soil and the plants that could produce a beautiful efflorescence, they fashioned for themselves paper flowers. As drawn on paper, or photographed, who could tell the difference between the living and the dead? Unconsciously seeking the bread of social life, the architect offered decorated stones: empty symbols of a non-existent society. Meanwhile, the germs of a living order existed alike in building, in technics, and in the culture of the landscape; but the confused minds and irresolute purposes of the directing classes did not find it easy to accept these beginnings. The common Victorian justification for the new industrial buildings was not that they were good art, but that a progressive industrial civilization had no need for art.

Viewed on the surface, the battle of the styles that was carried on between the early baroque architects and the traditional medieval builder, or between the neo-classicists of the nineteenth century and the neo-medievalists, was trivial; for both schools were united in this respect: they had lost their connections with a common social milieu. Meanwhile society itself was losing all sense of a common order: its forms were capricious because its values were uncertain and it had yielded to a belief in purely quantitative achievement: fine architecture had become a matter of size and expense, while common building, divorced from human standards, became cheap, niggardly, cramped.

As if to add an ironic touch to this social disorganization, the field was marked out roughly between the two great schools. After the opening of the nineteenth century, the classic style claimed the government offices, the courts of justice, the police stations, the banks, the art museums; while the gothic style claimed the school, the university, the town hall, the church, the natural history museum. There would, of course, be occasional compromises and modifications in this program. Survivals that stubbornly refused to acknowledge their death, mistaking mumification for vitality, combined with mutations that shrank from the struggles of birth—such was architecture during most of the nineteenth century in those reaches of the community where it still had any significance. Even the most penetrating of critics was confused: Ruskin had the courage to admire the Ashmolean Museum at Oxford.

Yet, from the beginning of the nineteenth century on, a succession of thinkers and planners appeared who knew that a more fundamental attack must be made on the whole problem of form. With those who went into form from the standpoint of community planning, beginning with Robert Owen, I have dealt in another section. Here we are concerned with the architects who realized that society itself was the main source of architectural form, and that only in terms of living functions could living form be created. There were many forerunners in this movement: but perhaps the most important figure of all was William Morris; for Morris, with Philip Webb, created the famous Red House in 1851, where Morris was to spend the early part of his married life. Here an attempt was made to discard ornamental tags and go back to essentials: honest materials, well-wrought: plain brick walls: a roof of heavy slates: every detail as straightforward and sensible as in a seventeenth century English farmhouse.

Heretofore architectural monuments had alone been the center of appreciation and the accepted source of style: the Pantheon, the Maison Carrée, the palace of Diocletian at Spalato, the Cathedral of Strasbourg, St. Mark's in Venice. These monumental buildings, crystallizations of a whole social order, were mistakenly seized as starting points for architectural design. In the middle of the nineteenth century this error had been carried so far that little cottages cowered behind massive Greek pediments, and the student of architecture began his apprenticeship with a study of the decorative elements in classic monumental forms; while he had so little training in matter-of-fact design that he would leave his atelier, proud of his skill in handling pencil or brush, and ignorant of the first motions in handling a trowel or a plumb-line; capable of designing a Hall of Justice but without the capacity to design an honest dog-kennel, to say nothing of a human dwelling.

By making the dwelling house a *point of departure* for the new movement in architecture, William Morris symbolically achieved a genuine revolution. The doctrines he laid down with respect to its design were fundamental ones: implicit in them, as he himself realized in his development as a revolutionary socialist, was the conception of a new social order, oriented not toward mechanization and profits, but toward humanization, welfare, and service. Little though Morris liked the machine—little though he had *reason* to like it in its defective early manifestations—he had achieved an attitude toward form and society that was capable of utilizing and directing the real advances that were being made in the organization of men and materials and the impersonal forces of nature. If the factory was the nucleus of the paleotechnic community, the house was to become the nucleus of the biotechnic age: his instincts here served him well.

"Believe me," William Morris wrote, "if we want art to begin at home, as it must, we must clear our houses of troublesome superfluities that are forever in our way; conventional comforts that are no real comforts, and do but make work for servants and doctors; if you want the golden rule that will fit everybody, this is it: have nothing in your house that you do not know to be useful or believe to be beautiful." This clearing away of the historic debris, this stripping to the skin, was the first essential mark of the new architecture, as it was, in effect, for the new view of life and cosmic relations that was introduced by the systematic sciences. In building: the open window, the blank wall, the unlittered floor: nothing for show and nothing that cannot be shown.

The next great impulse toward coherent form came from the American master builder, H. H. Richardson. Starting work after the American Civil War, Richardson at first used the current eclectic symbols, and finally established a reputation for himself by his bold handling of monumental forms: so far, an obstacle to genuine achievement. But as Richardson entered more deeply into the problems of his age, and became familiar with its social and economic forces, he turned to the design of an office building, a warehouse, a railroad station, a public library: he found himself on new ground. Richardson discarded, step by step, the archaic touches and the hampering symbols: he worked with the fundamental forms of masonry, organizing the elements solely with a view to the practical and visual expression of the function to be encompassed: he carried the lesson Webb and Morris had worked out in the dwelling house into every aspect of building. Though it was only in his latest buildings that Richardson finally came face to face with the possibility of new form, organically based on the technical resources and social principles of the new society, he achieved a sort of preliminary integration in terms of masonry. He proved that the ugliness of utilitarian forms had not been due to their origins nor their uses but to the inferior quality of mind applied to their development. Organically conceived, a railroad station had no less capacity for beauty than a medieval fortress or a bridge; and a dwelling house in wood might be better related to human needs than a costly palace.

Richardson's work was confirmed at a later period in Europe by the advances of kindred architects: Berlage's handsome bourse in Amsterdam is a parallel example of great force and merit; and Richardson laid the foundation for the work of another group of architects, Adler and Sullivan, and Frank Lloyd Wright in Chicago, who carried the theme farther. Sullivan's task was to formulate, in social terms, the order that was implicit in Richardson's last work: he took up, perhaps unconsciously, perhaps quite independently, the rule laid down by the American sculptor, Horatio Greenough—form follows function. And Sullivan sought, on this basis, to create an architecture in which the fundamental principles formulated for one type of building would hold for other types—a rule so broad that it would admit of no exceptions. Such a rule must have its foundations, not only in the architect's mind, but in the political institutions, the working order, the social attitudes of his community. To formulate it in fact, and to translate it from fantasy to concrete reality, the architect needs the active co-operation of his contemporaries; and no one had better reason than Sullivan to appreciate the failure of energies and the paralysis of imagination that follows when the architect is either at odds with his community, or is forced to degrade his best energies in order to conform to the limitations of his clients. Taken together, Sullivan's buildings do not have that unity his doctrine demands.

It remained for Frank Lloyd Wright, working again in the same medium as Morris, the dwelling house, to effect a synthesis of nature, the machine, and human activities and purposes. Wright increased the size of the window opening and restored the horizontal window bank, which had been lost, except for a sporadic revival or two, since the seventeenth century. By altering the layout of the house and keeping it low, and close to the soil of the prairie, he made a fundamental change in the relation of the house and the land, and introduced the garden almost into the heart of the living room. Outside and inside became aspects of a single unity, as in the human organism: the house-in-nature, nature-in-the-house. Although Wright showed special gifts in using natural materials and in adapting his designs to the local landscape, he used, likewise with masterly facility, the modern constructional methods and the new utilities provided by the machine: he treated the machine as a collaborating agent of human purpose, not merely as the cheapener of costs and the purveyor of spurious imitations that it had been during the formative period of Morris's thought.

In his respect for the soil, the site, the climate, the environing region, Wright was in advance, not merely of his eclectic contemporaries, but of those metropolitanized interpreters of the "modern" who followed almost a generation later: his "prairie architecture," like his later "desert architecture" was true regional form. Wright, indeed, depolarized regionalism from its connection with the historic and the archaic: he oriented it toward the living present, which contains both the past and the future; and he brought together in his new building forms the special and the universal, the local and the world-wide. It is not by accident that Wright's prairie architecture took deepest hold in Holland, a country not without geographic parallels to the prairie and Great Lakes areas, though built to a different scale. He created, not a mechanical form to be copied, as the clichés of the classicist were copied in the eighteenth century, and those of Le Corbusier during the last decade: he created an organic form, to be adapted and modified, precisely because the principles upon which it was based were universal.

Wright's architecture was therefore, to an unusual degree, a prophetic synthesis: a microcosm of the new biotechnic economy. This synthesis antedated in its individual forms the best work done on similar lines in Europe: antedated it by a generation. Unfortunately, Wright's early work had the weakness of being conceived in response to demand within the communal pattern of the romantic suburb: an individual free-standing house for the well-to-do bourgeois family. Except for one abortive, over-ingenious effort at group housing, which accepted far too high a level of density, Wright did not pass on to the more fundamental problem of communal integration until he developed, during the present decade, the plans and models and projects of Broadacre City. That failure to incorporate the com-munal into the personal was perhaps responsible for the small extent of his influence in the actual housing movement, even after 1920.

All these architects were, in effect, the representatives of a society that had not yet appeared. Their contributions were like delicate seedlings, carefully nurtured, and well-grown in March, before the blanket of snow has lifted from the garden where they are to be transplanted: often they died before the weather had taken a favor-able change or the season had advanced sufficiently. The best of their buildings even when they were brought into the open were lost in weedy patches of speculative enterprise and industrial disorder: de-prived even of their main esthetic effect through the lack of a back-ground built on the same principles. Thus Wright's magnificent Larkin Administration Building rises like some enigmatic temple in the midst of a black industrial desert—contradicting but not sup-pressing the ugliness and disorder around it.

These architects, then, share a place with the romantic poets, like Blake and Whitman, who wrote for a non-existent democracy, and with romantic individualists in all the other arts who were attempt-ing to embody in their own personalities and in their own work some-thing that could not be brought into secure existence without the po-litical and social co-operation of a sympathetic community. In the main, these romantics were prophets of life: but of a life and order to come. What the artist created was but a sample, a small working model, which must be thrown as it were into mass production before the existence of the new pattern could be guaranteed and its full meaning for society realized.

In almost every country, similar innovators appeared and the first essays toward new form were made. Voysey, Mackintosh, Baillie-Scott, Lutyens, Unwin, and Parker in England: Van de Velde in Bel-gium: Wagner, Hoffmann, and Loos in Austria: Behrens, Poelzig, Schumacher in Germany, Berlage in Holland, Tony Garnier and the Perrets in France. And in each country, with the possible excep-tion of America, the new movement in life first registered itself in the arts and crafts, in printing, in textiles, in pottery, in furniture, before it became generalized and socialized as architectural and communal form. Being more closely connected with machine technics than the inherited handicrafts of building, it was perhaps natural that these subordinate departments of design should be influenced first. Perhaps another reason lies in the fact that the most fundamental change involved at first was a change in attitude and interest: a re-focusing of the social objectives. The desire for sunlight and open air appeared symbolically in the painting of the impressionists more than a generation before it became widespread in the community: almost two generations before it was embodied formally in architecture. Does not the mind tend to project in a more facile medium, that which responds quickest to the artist's impression, what can be embodied only through long painful processes of trial and error, and co-operative discipline, in the structure of the community? One has reason to respect such symbols—except when they are treated as fetiches and accepted as substitutes for the life which they postulate.

From the eighties onward there was no lack of vigorous and intelligently conceived individual buildings; but at first the esthetic conception prevailed over the more comprehensive social conception, which includes the esthetic as but one of its ingredients. One sees the danger of a purely esthetic formulation of the problem in the rise of the new style toward the end of the nineteenth century: the style called Art Nouveau in France and Jugendstil in Germany. The two main technical examples of this form were embodied in printing and in jewelry; and in the latter department, indeed, one is conscious of the benign influence of woman, never wholly at ease in the power-world of the machine, turning instinctively to the symbols of life: flowers and fruit and her own naked body. L'Art Nouveau was an early attempt to incorporate biological symbolism in the arts. In architecture, it disdained straight lines and rigid geometric surfaces: it cultivated wavy lines, lines of growth and free movement: the designer turned electroliers into sprays of metallic flowers, and a simple balustrade railing into a descending foam of metallic waves. The first marks of this type of floral ornament were to be found in the old iron bridges, and before its expression in the furniture of Bing at the Paris Fair of 1900 it had left its marks on the base of the Eiffel Tower.

In the actual handling of its materials, chiefly metal and glass, L'Art Nouveau showed many examples of brilliant architectural design, some of which was more decisively functional than that of later schools which paid greater verbal respect to the principle of function. What was weak in l'Art Nouveau was in fact not its constructive execution but its formal symbolism: its reliance upon extraneous ornament for an expression of its purposes. It was indeed high time that the living was expressed in architecture: this precisely was a necessary mark of the new biotechnic age that was dawning, an age effectively distinguished by the radical contributions of scientists like Pasteur in bio-chemistry, Geddes in bio-sociology, and artists like Rodin—if one may conclude the verbal parallel—in bio-sculpture.

But "living" in architecture means in adequate relation to life. It does not mean an imitation in stone or metal of the external appearance of organic form: houses with mushroom roofs or rooms shaped like the corolla of a flower. It was not flowered wallpaper that was needed in the modern house, but space and sunlight and temperature conditions under which living plants could grow: not pliant and moving lines in the furniture, but furniture that responded adequately to the anatomical form and physiological needs of the body: chairs that furthered good posture and gave repose, beds that favored sexual intercourse and permitted deep slumber. In short: a physical environment that responded sensitively to the vital and personal needs of the occupants.

Symbolically, the Art Nouveau architects were right in exhibiting and glorifying life: practically, they were mistaken, because in their art they exerted most of their zeal to provide only a formal counterfeit: mere ornamental forms. The problem for the new age was to create a new type of living environment: to enable people to live in cities without losing the fellowship of nature, and to group together for the sake of specialized social activities without losing the means of good health and the decent nurture of children. None of these needs could be satisfied by mere ornament, no matter how whimsically imaginative, or how vitally fluent that ornament might be. Architecture required structural forms which were organically at one with life: flexible, adaptable, renewable.

For this reason the reaction against l'Art Nouveau in Europe, which took shape in the cubist movement in painting, and in the constructivist movement in architecture, pointed form once more in the right direction. (The movement had never really taken hold in America, and Wright's early work needed no such admonition.) Contrary to l'Art Nouveau, the symbolism of cubism was mistaken: it glorified the machine as an unmitigated benefactor of mankind, in strange innocence of all the social horrors that had accompanied capitalist exploitation; it placed an excessive emphasis upon formal geometrical shapes, particularly the rectangle and the cube which do not characterize real machines; and it proposed to turn the dwelling house into a machine, without explaining why mechanism should exercise such a one-sided control over life. But cubism was the necessary corrective of the dogma of the wavy line which, in pursuing the external forms of life, forgot the objective conditions: the form of a bowl, as conditioned by the potter's wheel: the form of a room, as conditioned by the economic placement of beams, posts, windows.

Instead of disguising the forms of modern construction under a load of decoration, the cubists sought to dramatize them. The cubists went out of their way to use concrete, to exhibit cantilever construction, to raise the house above the ground on steel columns. And instead of seeking to display the egoistic touch of the individual architect, they sought after an anonymous method of design and a collective formula. Structurally speaking cubism performed an important work of purification: it divorced itself from capitalist canons of reputability and expense, and it cleared the ground for a fresh start. In its keen appreciation of the products of the machine (led by artists like Marcel Duchamp), it pointed toward more conspicuous efforts to achieve clean forms within other branches of industry than architecture.

Although cubism had at the beginning a certain bias against living forms, the fact is that the machine itself is a product and an instrument of life: the more perfect it becomes, the more it simulates the automatisms and self-regulating devices of real organisms and the more finely it mimics the eye, the ear, the voice, the memory. In the attempt to use the machine adequately and create a more universal order, the collective interests of cubism inevitably led toward the formulation, in modern terms, of a theory of the city.

Under the leadership of Le Corbusier the cubists ceased to concern themselves alone with the isolated architectural product: they passed on to the urban environment as a whole, and sought to place the entire process of building and re-building on a fresh foundation.

Le Corbusier himself began with the stale nineteenth century notion of the city so often explored in the time-romances of Mr. H. G. Wells: *la ville mécanique.* His early schemes explore a series of blind alleys: the skyscraper city, the traffic city, finally the grotesque combination of the two in a curving viaduct whose supports were to be filled with apartment houses. But by a steady process of re-formulation he has drawn closer to the biotechnic notion of *la ville radieuse:* a marked ideological improvement, and his plan for Nemours is one of the best rational layouts that has yet appeared. Thus life re-enters the picture, not in the form of extraneous ornament, but in the demand for air, sunlight, gardens, parks, playgrounds, recreation fields, and all the various forms of social equipment that are necessary for the stimulating life of the city: informal places of meeting and relaxation, like the café, and formal places of purposive education, like the museum and the university. In the orientation of architecture toward life and the processes of life the architect began with the decoration of the house: he ends with the city.

In their attempt actively to incorporate the machine into architecture the cubists were sometimes misled by a static and external conception of the machine; but unconsciously they were recognizing the direct tribute that the mechanical arts owed to improvements that were first made in the culture of living things, particularly in horticulture. The first evolved pattern of the new architecture appeared in the glass hothouse: the Crystal Palace in London was but the monumental embodiment of this mutation. Just as the Crystal Palace was the work of an engineer in the service of horticulture, so, by reverse process, the new system of ferro-concrete construction was the invention of the gardener, Monnier, seeking to build more efficient bird baths and fountain basins for his gardens.

The new improvements in domestic heating, too, were originally the conception of gardeners. One of the first persons to suggest steam heating was Sir Hugh Platt, who had the notion of conveying heat from a steam boiler on a kitchen stove through pipes to growing plants in order to keep them at a temperate heat, no matter what the conditions of the weather outside. In 1745 Platt's suggestion was improved by Sir William Cook, who published a diagram for heating all the rooms in the house from the kitchen fire. The full importance of these inventions was grasped for the first time by Paxton himself. In a letter to the Illustrated London News (July 5, 1851) he sketched out the design of a Crystal Sanitorium: not merely to give patients the benefit of extra oxygen from the growing plants, but for the sake of sunlight and room wherein to exercise in all weather. To make this possible, he suggested the installation of apparatus to provide filtered and heated air: the first proposal for complete air-conditioning—not as a mere remedy against baneful gases, as in mines or in the British House of Parliament, but as a positive aid to health.

Thus the new methods of construction, the new materials, and the new means of regulating the air of a building in order to adapt it more perfectly to the needs of living occupants *came directly from the biotechnics of gardening.* These changes were to prove more important to human welfare than the symbolic incorporation of floral shapes by means of carved ornaments and curved trusses.

Taken together, modern form, modern architecture, modern communities are prophetic emergents of a biotechnic society: a society whose productive system and consumptive demands will be directed toward the maximum possible nurture, under ever more adequate material conditions, of the human group, and the maximum possible culture of the human personality. What has so far been accomplished is but a taste of the more thoroughgoing order that is to come. So far, architecture and community planning have aided experimentally in the clarification of this order: but further re-valuations of doctrine and belief, further accretions of positive knowledge, will in turn alter profoundly the new communities we are in process of building. Throughout the world, a consensus is gradually being established among men of good will and effective competence. Let us then attempt to seek further the social basis of modern form, and to establish even more definitively its underlying principles.

2: Principles of Modern Form—Economy

Perhaps the main guiding principle of modern architecture is economy: economy of material, economy of means, economy of expression. And the reason why economy occupies the very center of our thought is that it is a sign of orderly understanding and perfect control—like the cut of a diver's body through the air, hitting the water without a splash.

Let us begin with the most elementary statement of economy: modern means of construction. Under past systems of architecture the actual strength and mass of a structure was determined by empiric practice: if a tower fell down, its foundations were too feeble or its top too heavy: a bad guess. Not merely is there a considerable range of difference between the strength of various natural materials; but there existed no reliable means for working out the tensile and compression strengths of various types of members: indeed, in some of their temples the Greeks, eager to reinforce their stones, carved channels for iron rods that actually weakened the structure.

During the last half century the creation of new manufactured building materials, like steel and reinforced concrete, with determinable strengths, determinable coefficients of expansion, radically altered the problem of building: it decreased the need for large solid members that built up into great sculptural masses. To use the least possible amount of material compatible with safety has become a mark of fine calculation and intelligent architectural insight: to be oversized, or overweight, is a sign of technical uncouthness, even if not immediately apparent to the eye. Building codes, framed according to the canons of guesswork, with an absurd margin of over-safety, do not generally recognize this change: but building codes, throughout the world, are overdue for revision.

The very interest in economy has given a special sanction to the lighter materials, which are easier to transport and usually easier to erect: the metal framework, the glass or composite surface to serve as sheath for the inner space, the flexible partition, have taken the place of clumsier and more static members. The esthetic attitude that goes with these new materials was very well put by J. J. P. Oud, the Dutch architect, one of the most able exponents of the new form:

"In place of the natural charm of walls and roofs of rough materials, unstable in their plasticity and uncertainly patined; in place of windows cut into small panes, nebulously glazed and irregularly colored; a new architecture will offer us the definite values of artificial materials, surfaces polished and finished, the scintillation of steel and the brilliance of paint, the transparent openness of large windows of plate glass. . . . Architectural evolution will lead us toward a style that will appear liberated from matter, although it is joined to it more completely than ever."

The entire functional development of architecture from the fifteenth century on, as Meyer remarked, is a response to the demand: "More light!" This development has thrown the structural emphasis from the supporting wall or column to the interior skeleton, from the enclosing *mass* to the bounding surface, from architectural form as the sculpture of solids to architectural form as the definition and articulation of voids. The age of crustacean building has given way to the age of vertebrates, and the wall, no longer a protective shell, has become a skin. Other organic changes within buildings have necessarily followed this development: a specialization of parts, a finer articulation of the various members, a system for maintaining a standard interior temperature and for renovating the air, which may be compared, roughly, with the action of heart and lungs in the body—while similarly the organization of the functions of ingestion (light, air, water, coal, gas, electricity) and that of excretion (inorganic and organic waste) has modified the nature of practically every structure.

The building is no longer a passive shell: it is a functioning organization in which the primitive aspect of shelter, as embodied in the original cave, and of symbol, as embodied in the monument, have become secondary attributes of more complicated processes. Some of these functions have indeed been provided for in other systems of architecture: they reached a high point in the eotechnic wood-and-water culture of the Japanese. But now their range has been extended through new forms of industrial fabrication, and their integration and expression, in fresh form, had become imperative.

To resist the use of these new materials and forms of construction is to resist the possibilities of order today. Not merely must one reject the decadent style-mongering of the suburban bourgeoisie, not merely must one throw over the obsolete grandiosities of height or expanse beloved by the conceited dictators of finance or government: one must reject, as still fundamentally inadequate, those more sensible stereotypes of traditional architecture embodied in the otherwise sound and generously planned cottages built by governmental agents, for example, in numerous English housing estates. Modern life has more to offer than these sober compromises and collective timidities would indicate. We do not glue feathers on the wings of airplanes because men have always associated flight with the forms of birds; and there is no reason why, to pay respect to traditional notions of domesticity, we should resort to similar practices in the building of houses—as if what architecture had now to offer the housewife were not something infinitely more attractive to her than slate roofs and roughly smeared stucco walls. The eighteenth century American farmhouse was a gracious traditional form: its fine lines and just proportions, which owed none of their charm to ornamental superfluity, derived from the same technics and culture that built its water mills and its wooden ships. Such harmony between the various parts of the environment is what architecture today requires, worked out in terms of contemporary order.

Even when, for the sake of harmony with the natural surroundings, natural materials may be appropriately used, the modern principle of economy will dictate that they be used in their modern technical form, not in more traditional shapes inherited from an incongruent past: not heavy half-timbers and ponderous oak paneling, for example, but sawed beams and light plywood paneling.

What is true of materials and construction is naturally also true of plan. Here, too, economy must prevail. A modern plan is successful only when it embraces every human need appropriate to the structure without waste of space, duplication, clumsy and inefficient means of circulation. This principle of economy is socially the opposite of the ancient canon of conspicuous waste. For the latter principle, in the interest of pecuniary and caste distinctions, emphasized the rôle of superfluity: rooms were scaled, not to their specific human uses, but solely for the purpose of impressing the spectator, no matter how difficult they might be to heat, or how oppressive they might feel to the individual occupant. Rooms were often duplicated on the plan, too, on either side of an axis, merely for the sake of achieving a formal balance for the eye of the observer outside. So, too, decoration would overlay the structural form: the product of the woodturner was marked with bulges, beads, indentations, which collected dust: the oak paneling was carved in floral or heraldic designs, and the ceiling was plastered with complicated geometric figures. Wherever a clear space remained, it was filled with some product of handicraft or *virtu,* partly because the craftsman himself delighted in such fantasies, even more because the patron took pleasure in sheer excess. Beauty? Perhaps. Show? Decidedly. A barn, a kitchen, a fortress might be built according to the canons of economy; but not works that symbolized social station or social function.

If economy today derives partly from the finer scientific calculations and the complicated inventions that enter into modern building —*inventions whose cost must be offset in other departments*—it has a social and esthetic basis as well. The social principle underlying the canon of economy rests on the fact that there is no modern utility or machine that we do not conceive as universal in its application. We do not have one type of electric light for the rich and another for the poor; we do not have one type of telephone, carved out of some ornate and precious material for the rich, and another type made of inferior materials, for peasants and clerks. All these instruments have an objective standard of performance, determinable by experiment: they are the products of a collective economy and are meant to fit into a collective whole. One's economic position may entitle one to a greater or smaller quantity, but the quality is fixed.

With respect to the fundamental goods of modern life, a basic equality has been partly established, and more and more goods and services are coming into line: this principle has even made its way into realms like clothes where class differences were once duly established by law, and where conspicuous differential waste for long went unchallenged. Such equalization rests in good part on the economies of mass production or on the no less important economies, as in municipal utilities, of collective distribution based on a social monopoly. Mass production itself demands, esthetically, an emphasis upon the generic, the standardized: upon forms freed from irregularity, superfluity, and imaginative caprice. *In order to make collective production and distribution possible on a scale that will embrace a whole society, economy must be a regulating principle in all design: for it is only by saving on the means and instrumentalities of life that a community can command the necessary abundance at the higher levels of art, science, education, and expression.* Economy, which in an earlier culture signified niggardliness, now provides the means for collective largesse. Holding to this principle means having enough to go round.

There is, however, an additional esthetic basis for economy in modern architecture. It lies in the fact that we live in a far more complicated world than that of the primitive craftsman and peasant: even the most limited person today in our urban communities is played upon by forces and stimuli so numerous, so insistent, so diverting, that he can achieve internal peace only by stripping to the essentials the visual environment. When there were no textbooks of natural history, no museums, no scientific abstracts, no illustrated papers and magazines, it might be amusing and instructive to have the animals in Noah's ark carved on a cathedral: then, truly, in Hugo's phrase, the cathedral was the stone book of mankind. But such decoration today is for the most part a distraction, at best a stale repetition of something that exists in more adequate form in treatises on biology and in museums of science. We demand that our modern environment become more legible, and above all, more serene. The clean surface, the candid revelation of function, the plain conspicuous lettering or symbolism of a sign or a building— these are the conditions that redefine our sense of beauty in urban structures.

To appreciate art and sculpture, as emotional experiences, we must detach them from the function of building: their permanent, non-detachable place has disappeared with the stone forms and the solid walls and stable relations which gave them their functional setting in other cultures. Much of the current demand for murals today is esthetically and socially atavistic: the mural that goes with the modern building is the poster: a form that can be duplicated, broadcast, and frequently renewed. The London Underground has been a more intelligent patron of modern art than more pompous public bodies—such as the United States Post Office—that choose to work in terms of an obsolete social situation.

The true symbol of the modern age in architecture is the *absence* of visible symbols: we no longer seek on the surface that which we can obtain effectively only through penetration and participation in the function of a structure. As our sense of the invisible forces at work in the actual environment increases—not merely our sense of physical processes below the threshold of common observation, but psychological and social processes too—as this sense increases we will tend to ask architecture itself to assume a lower degree of visibility: spectator's architecture, show architecture, will give way to a more thoroughgoing sense of form, not so conspicuous perhaps on the surface, but capable of giving intellectual and emotional stimulus at every step in its revelation.

Carried out imaginatively, the principle of economy becomes a positive pleasure in building: a sign of right relationship with life. Ships show this sense of economy, from modern sailing craft to the ocean liner: so do a great variety of machines; so, for the greater part, do dams and power-stations and factories. Perhaps one of the finest examples, not merely of utilitarian accomplishment but of positive esthetic impulse, is the modern American kitchen, even in houses that frequently contradict all its good features in every other room. Such economy is the moral flower of that long discipline of the spirit which Western man has undertaken during the last millennium under the forms of monasticism, capitalism, militarism, and mechanism: forms in which life was denied, rather than enhanced, for the ulterior purpose of holiness or power. Today, as we slough off the skin of old social habits, economy is at last ready to flow out of these life-constraining departments into a more balanced, a less sterile, human habitat.

3: The Rôle of Hygiene

Hygiene and sanitation were not unknown in other civilizations: what community could have survived the ordeal of close permanent quarters without a certain respect for their laws? But in our new biotechnic economy hygiene occupies a commanding place: not merely does it mean public defenses against disease: it means taking positive steps to make the whole environment favorable to health, animal joy, and length of days.

As long as the body was dualistically separated from mind, its systematic care might be slighted. But the new scientific conception of the organism that grew up in the nineteenth century reunited the physiological and the psychological processes: thus the care of the body became once more a moral and an esthetic discipline. By his researches in bacteriology Pasteur altered the conception of both the external and the internal environment of organisms; and with the progress of medicine, physicians turned attention from the noting of symptoms to the analysis of causes, from a one-sided readjustment of the organism through medication or surgery, to a many-sided readjustment that includes diet, habitation, regimen, social and psychological relations.

Partly, the nineteenth century interest in hygiene and sanitation was an automatic reaction: compensation against the miserably insanitary conditions, the devitalized diet, the constant state of ill-health and enfeeblement, in which the denizens of the nineteenth century towns lived. Advances in the biological sciences, in turn, threw into relief the misdemeanors of the new environment: its lack of sunlight and ultra-violet rays, its frequently infected public water supply, its wholesale materialization of conditions favorable to organic dissipation, physiological maladjustment, and disease.

Modern hygiene has established the fact that most of our cities, not least those big ones built mainly during the last fifty years, are biologically speaking life-inimical or life-destructive environments. When their crude rates for death and disease, of which boast is so often made, are subjected to critical analysis and correction for age-distribution, statistics prove that at almost every stage in life, the rural area with poor medical facilities and a crude system of sanitation is nevertheless decisively superior as an environment of life to the urban area, though the latter be equipped with all the latest services in medicine and sanitation. Moreover, there is an equally significant correlation between size and health: in general the bigger the city the poorer its showing. And there is an equally important correlation between biological fertility and the urban environment: not merely does the city reproduce at a lower rate than the country, but the bigger the city the lower the rate of reproduction. The highest expectations of life go with a country environment and the less industrialized occupations. (See Warren Thompson and the Report of the National Resources Committee on Cities.)

The effect of this biological knowledge, and the fresh interests that have developed with it, is further to shift the center of gravity from the world of the mine and the factory, to the world of the farmstead and the garden. The drift to the suburbs, which has been one of the most conspicuous features of the growth of cities during the past half century, was one response to the more constant concern with health and education that has characterized the life of the middle classes. The cult of cleanliness, upon which modern hygiene fundamentally depends, had its origins, as I have already pointed out, before the nineteenth century: it owes much to the Dutch cities of the seventeenth century, with their plentiful water supplies, their large house windows showing relentlessly every particle of dust in the interior, their tiled floors: the scrubbing and scouring and shining of the Dutch housewife became proverbial. But cleanliness got new reinforcements from medicine after 1870: instead of being a delicate upper class taste, scarcely popular even in aristocratic circles in the eighteenth century, it became a universal necessity. As a result, the farmer milking a cow today takes sanitary precautions which a London surgeon did not trouble to take before performing a major operation, until Lister taught him better. Hygiene magnified the importance of the water supply: not merely demanding purity, but increasing steadily the quantity necessary, as the habits of bathing and washing spread in widening circles from one economic group to another.

At last the paleotechnic indifference to darkness and dirt was exposed as a monstrous barbarism. Frequent hand washing and body washing, to say nothing of clothes washing, made the provision of running water an imperative element in house-planning or community-building. Whereas bathrooms were frequently not provided even for the finest houses early in the nineteenth century, by the end of the century the standard of a separate bathtub for every family—and if possible a separate bathroom—became a minimum ideal, if not an actual achievement, in every rational housing program. In lieu of this, large public bath-houses and public wash-houses were provided for the neighborhood.

With increasing rigor and effectiveness these hygienic requirements extended to the disposal of human excrement, garbage, and waste. The water-closet, invented by Sir John Harrington in 1596, was not perfected until 1778 when the inventive Bramah took a hand in its design. In the course of a century the installation of water-closets in urban houses rose rapidly: by the end of the nineteenth century the standard of one water-closet for every family became the most imperative sanitary precaution for close-built communities throughout the Western World. These individual improvements in the hygienic equipment of dwellings made a radical alteration in costs: together with instruments for lighting and heating the dwelling, refrigerating its food, and bringing it into contact with the outside world through telephone and radio, the new mechanical inventions accounted for an increasing proportion of the cost and upkeep of the structure: the shell cost relatively less, but the "internal organs" multiplied and the costs rose with them.

All these individual changes, moreover, had important collective consequences: they introduced the habit of municipal socialization as a normal accompaniment to improved mechanical service. The rationale of this development should be plain. The collective utilities necessary for the functioning of buildings and cities are in the main natural monopolies. Water had become too much a matter of public concern in big cities to be left to the supply of individual water companies, selling their product only to those who could afford to pay for the services, and continuing in business only so long as the company could show a profit. It became important to distribute pure water, for the sake of health, whether or not a particular family wanted it or could afford it. Such matters could no longer be left to whim. These facts held equally true of the systems for disposing of garbage, waste, and sewage.

In smaller centers private companies might be left with the privilege of maintaining these services, or they might even be left to the individual until some notorious outbreak of disease occurred through carelessness: but in the bigger cities, socialization was the price of safety; and so, despite the theoretic claims of laissez-faire, the nineteenth century became, as the Webbs properly pointed out, the century of municipal socialism. Each individual improvement within the building demanded its collectively owned and operated utility: water mains, water reservoirs, pumping stations: garbage wagons and rubbish wagons, incinerators and dumps: sewage mains, sewage reduction plants, sewage farms. Through this effective and widespread socialization, the general death rate and infant mortality tended to fall, after the eighteen-seventies: and the social investment of municipal capital in these utilities enormously rose.

And incidentally, the nature of the city itself changed, under pressure of these new utilities, just as radically as the nature of the new building: a greater share of its essential services was organized in underground systems: no less important than the visible structures and streets. As with the dwelling house, the potential improvements were partly frustrated through imaginative failure in revising the plan, layout, and structural requirements of the city. Even the theoretic formulation of the needs and opportunities of this more complex urban structure seriously lagged until 1920: in the minds of planners pictorial compositions were uppermost: only to be displaced, in the interests of the "practical," by equally half-baked avenue extensions and traffic plans and multiple streets.

From the establishment of personal cleanliness, new standards of hygiene spread to the dwelling house itself, and eventually to other parts of the environment. In 1877 Downes and Blunt established the bactericidal properties of light: the popularization of the camera, during the ensuing decades, likewise tended to make people photosensitive: but although architects like Richardson, Mackintosh and Wright sensitively recorded this change, the constant importance of natural light as an accompaniment and accessory of all living functions except sleep was slow to be recognized. Here again pathological conditions called attention to the more normal human uses: the importance of sunlight and fresh air in treating tuberculosis played a strong part, and the discovery of the rôle of ultra-violet rays in promoting growth was scarcely less critical. An interior accessible to light and air, above all in winter days in the upper latitudes, became a new requirement of good building design: this means shallow rooms, shallow buildings, careful orientation with respect to sunlight and prevailing winds.

Further scientific inquiry into the process of ventilation disclosed other facts of hygienic importance: the need for regulating temperature, humidity, and circulation of air toward appropriate optimums in both summer and winter. The New York State Commission on Ventilation discovered, for example, that the output of work fell 15 per cent when the temperature of the workroom was raised from 68 to 75 degrees, and that it was reduced by 37 per cent when the temperature was raised to 85 degrees. Similarly, the likelihood of incubating colds seems to be increased in temperatures above 68 degrees. The factors are so complicated that only in a rough way can ideal conditions as yet be laid down; but the possibility of discovering optimum conditions, adjusted to regional peculiarities of weather and climate, lies in no very remote future.

These things, at all events, are plain: air must stir, sunlight must penetrate, dirt must be eliminated, waste must be removed. From the furnishing of the room to the layout of the neighborhood, these requirements must be reflected in every detail. The closed court, the symbol of medieval protection, is not a modern form: the glass window that cannot be thrown wide to the sun is not a modern form, even though it be hung in a steel frame and opened automatically: floor coverings and window coverings that cannot be freely washed and sunned are not hygienically acceptable.

Only to a small degree are these various hygienic requirements met in the great bulk of urban buildings; and structures built after the eighteenth century are frequently much worse offenders against the decencies of hygiene than those erected before. Even many buildings of superficially modern design, with wide window openings or air-conditioning equipment, are in their plan and spacing far inferior to earlier examples. To achieve sunlight, air, health, in close urban quarters is usually beyond the skill of any individual architect: it involves a considerable knowledge of physiography, climatology, and astronomy, ordinarily not within the conventional province of the architect or the municipal engineer: good form is a collective product and requires collective collaboration in its production. No continuing cleanliness is possible in a city that harbors paleotechnic industries whose smoke and chemical effluvia have not been eliminated. Merely in order to provide daily sunbaths for growing infants, it is imperative to move the black industries outside a town and erect a permanent barrier of green open space between them and the rest of the community.

The point to be noted is that if the principles of hygiene are valid and important, they must be applied, not alone in the hospital or the home, but also in every other part of the environment. The factories and offices and stores in which the greater part of every urban population spends half its waking hours must be planned for a maximum living and working efficiency. Who can pretend that with all our advances in purely constructional technique any corresponding advances have been made here over a wide area? Individual factories on the outskirts of cities have sometimes achieved good form: say the Van Nelle Factory near Rotterdam. But the overbuilding and overcrowding of land, which has marked the development of office buildings in almost every city has added to the lethal qualities of bureaucratic routine: the dead airless space in these buildings is serious handicap to the work of the staff.

Here the need is obvious: the minimum standards for light and air and density that have been worked out for schools should apply equally to any and all business structures. If this does not fit in with the existing scheme of financial values, these values must be deflated. Instead of regarding the purely monumental swaggering of the skyscraper as the emblem of modern construction, every new office quarter must be planned with shallow buildings, duly oriented for light, spaced in such a fashion that the height shall never be greater than the space between the buildings to the front and the rear. Zoning ordinances that were constructed with due regard for positive scientific knowledge would establish these standards; whereas the metetricious height and setback regulations first introduced into the United States by the municipality of New York had no relation to these standards: their sole use was to establish the legal principle of control. On the principle here outlined, skyscrapers might still be built; but never without a sufficient area of open land to remove the possibility of congestion and blight—and incidentally the possibility of profit from congestion.

Hygiene demands, finally, that the quality of air, even when freed from noxious fumes and smoke, must be improved by the simplest means of renovation: open spaces filled with verdure and shrubbery, which not merely tend to equalize the temperature and freshen the air, but which provide the necessary relaxation for body and mind. Gardens are for delight, and delight by itself is an important factor in the maintenance of health. The dull and the dejected are more susceptible to infection than those who are in tone; and the worst months for health in the temperate zones are the shrouded months of winter, the indoor months, when only the more adventurous of city folk seek the open field and the waterside.

From the standpoint of hygiene, parks and gardens are not luxuries for the fortunate minority: they are essential if the city is to become a permanent habitat for man. The city that adequately commands the resources of modern civilization is not the city of stretched wharves and ships bringing goods from the ends of the earth: it is not the city of skyscraping towers that darken and congest the streets: it is not the city of the widest concrete roadways, the longest double-decked automobile drives, and the most overcrowded subways—it is the city in which every quarter is ribboned with gardens and parks. The Schrebergärten movement, which has been such a sanative influence in the congested German metropolises, giving the tenement dweller a small cultivation patch on the unused land of the outskirts, is but a first step toward ruralizing the urban environment. What the baroque planner gave to the palace and the upper class residential quarter alone, we now conceive as essential for every part of the city.

4: The Prolongation of Youth

England's early pre-eminence in the Black Industries has sometimes concealed the fact that she also led the revolt against this foul regime. This was not merely true of the English cult of nature, so pervasive, so devoted: but in the fact that games and sports, from the early nineteenth century on, came to occupy a greater share of everyone's leisure. Whether Waterloo was won on the playing fields of Eton is doubtful; most of her soldiers on that field had never gone to Eton: but the discipline of sport has not merely taught lessons in government and co-operative give-and-take that have been useful for political life: the relaxation of sport has contributed to that prolongation of youth which is perhaps the most significant biological trait of modern civilization. Is it not perhaps one of the reasons, along with a fuller dietary, a more careful sanitation, a more prudent physical regimen, for the astounding prolongation of life during the last century? Retarding maturity, we have increased the span of senescence.

By keeping girls and boys in a state of healthy distraction, by spreading more widely the preparation for professional service, modern society, particularly among the higher economic classes, has postponed the period of family responsibility. By making contraceptives available, it has helped put off childbearing to the desirable period of maturity. Whereas the women of many savage tribes or primitive agricultural regimes are old at twenty-five, through early responsibility and premature child-bearing, a well-bred modern woman remains active and wide-awake and sexually attractive well into her very belated senescence. Though this effect is slightly less noticeable among males, it nevertheless is equally real: look at the bearded sombre faces of the typical Victorian youths, and compare them with the fresh, biologically youthful faces of much older men today. Sport, play, and diminished sexual anxiety probably make the difference.

The cult of sport and the more suave care of the physical body proceeded from the country house and the English public school, set near a playing field. Only belatedly did they make their way into the heart of the city. In America, the first public playgrounds date back to 1871. No less significant than the provision of special urban places for children's play is the provision of special recreation grounds serving equally the adult: the public tennis court, the golf course, to say nothing of the general dedication of beaches to the more ancient pastime of bathing.

Our whole conception of a well-balanced environment has been altered by this cult of the body. In its specialized metropolitan forms, with its vast gladiatorial arenas for the professional exhibition of wrestlers and prize fighters, it has inevitably taken a degraded form; and the multiplication of such great stadia with their mass spectacles is not necessarily desirable. But special provision for the play of children must be made in each housing quarter, and in each neighborhood, if it is to fulfill its function as a biotechnic environ· ment: a provision in which relatively few cities have as yet caught up with needs, and in which many otherwise well-meaning efforts at better housing have likewise fallen short.

While the passing age prided itself upon its vast congeries of hospitals, from that at Edinburgh in the nineteenth century to such overpowering structures as the new Medical Centers, in New York, the mark of the biotechnic period will be the number of playgrounds, swimming pools, and beaches a city can afford. Here, admittedly, the great metropolises have taken the leadership in creating collective facilities for sport and play: the great stadium at Frankfurt-am-Main is an example. Such recreation and exercise was the privilege of the aristocratic minority in Athens: today these opportunities are open to every well-administered community: promising that physical dilation and pride which will increase the joy, the confidence, and the self-respect of the participants. Whereas in the tawdry commercial "playland" of an Indiana industrial town one might read over its portals the dismaying puritanic injunction—"Play Hard so that you may Work Hard"—over the playgrounds of the new age one may write with better sense, remembering the close association be-tween the Athenian palestra and the academy, the motto of another Indiana town—"Work, Study, Play." Youth takes sport seriously and achieves discipline; maturity takes sport playfully, and achieves youth.

5: Bi-polar Domesticity

The reduction of the household to a biological unit has been one of the most consequential steps in the whole process of urbanization. It is closely tied to two conditions which distinguish a biotechnic culture from cultures in which the nurture of life was an incidental by-product of existence. The first of these is the growing care of the child: an appreciation of childhood as a valuable phase of life in itself, not as an ordeal that is hastily to be passed through in order to attain the more blissful state of adult responsibility and autonomy. In modern times, the cult of the child began with Rousseau: out of his own sinister guilts and conflicts with respect to procreation he achieved a fresh view of the relationship: in its essentials, his views were fundamentally sound, from his preachment to mothers—Nurse your infants!—on to his conception that a life of activity in a simple natural environment was the best accompaniment to a child's normal growth. Up to this point, children had been little men and little women. Slowly, they came to achieve a life of their own in an environment that was—in families where choice was economically permitted—more and more molded to their activities.

This growing intensity of interest in the life of children was increased, no doubt, by the practice of birth control, which reduced the possibility of replacement, and made the individual child more precious to the parent, as well as the object of more concentrated attention and tender care. Birth control, indeed, has had a dual effect upon the family relation: it has introduced an element of deliberate choice in a situation where a capricious Providence had hitherto prevailed, it has given childbearing itself the special moral value which only objects of free choice have, and it has introduced the possibility of a more rational ordering of the individual phases of life—lengthening the period of erotic experiment and permitting parenthood to take place at the period of fullest physiological capacity.

At the same time, of course, contraception has vastly increased the erotic possibilities of marriage itself, as well as opening a door to bi-lateral erotic relationships outside marriage: there is no comparison whatever between a married pair of the sixteenth century, whose sexual life would normally be interrupted by a series of pregnancies right up to the menopause, and a married pair in the twentieth century: the difference is as great as that between the blessed Thomas More's conception of the sexual act, which he compared to the voiding of urine, and that of Havelock Ellis. Erotic courtship and the fullness of erotic expression are no longer wholly accidental and uncertain delights: still less are they confined to lubricious specialists in sex: they occupy an ever more abundant part of the daily life of healthy men and women. Despite its bludgeoning absolutisms, its vicious wars, the twentieth century may yet be known as the age of sexual efflorescence. In paradoxical fashion, domesticity and eroticism, once enemies as far apart as Antony's Octavia and his Cleopatra, have now advanced together.

These facts have an important bearing upon the place of the dwelling in the urban economy, and upon the internal design of the structure itself. For one thing, the child is no less entitled to space than the adult: he must have shelves and cupboards for his toys, room for play and movement, a place for quiet retreat and study, other than his bed. No housing standard is adequate that provides only cubicles or dressing rooms for the child, or forces him into the constant company of adults. The dwelling must be so arranged, so spaced, that the routine of physical care and the overseeing of activities shall demand the least wasteful sacrifice on the part of the mother: architects, even the best of them, still have much to learn in the proper arrangement of kitchen, living room, playroom, and garden.

At the same time, every part of the dwelling must be arranged equally with an eye to sexual privacy and untrammeled courtship. Private bedrooms alone are not enough: soundproof partitions are equally important, and in communal units soundproof floors. One of the reasons that the poor are so inept at using contraceptives is that the sanest and simplest devices a woman may use still require, if sexual joy is not to be changed into a sordid mockery, such facilities as go only with a well-equipped bathroom. Sexual intercourse must not forever be doomed, except for the luxuriously rich, to take place only, like burglary, under cover of darkness, in that part of the day when the energies are fast ebbing away: but before it can occur at any other times many weaknesses in house design will have to be rectified. Even at some little extra cost in corridor space the architect must eventually learn in house and in apartment design to separate the children's wing from the adult's wing.

And this restriction works both ways: for as children draw on toward maturity, they need, no less than their parents, inviolate apartments in which their hot discussions, their high confidences, their first essays in courtship, may take place. For lack of such space in America, a whole generation of girls and boys has grown up, cramped in the vulgar promiscuities of the automobile, from which they are too often graduated proudly into the no less shabby intimacies of the roadhouse or the overnight cabin: carrying into their erotic life the taint of something that is harried, esthetically embar-rassing and emotionally disintegrating. The home, the garden, the park, must be planned for lovers and for love-making: that is an essential aspect of an environment designed for human growth. Love-making and home-making, eroticism and domesticity, sexual delight and the assiduous nurture of children—these are among the highest human goals of genuine biotechnic planning. Everything from the distribution of open spaces to the heights of windows is affected by this program; and the sooner the architect and planner faces these facts of contemporary life and evaluates them intelli-gently, the quicker will he throw off the clichés of old-fashioned design, and the sooner will he realize that a great many of the economies in plan that have recently been effected have been pur-chased at too high a price. Good design means going back to funda-mentals: a child at work in a stable and reassuring world: a pair of lovers at play in a room where the scent of lilacs may creep through the window, or the shrill piping of crickets be heard in the garden below.

6: The Death of the Monument

One of the most important attributes of a vital urban environ-ment is one that has rarely been achieved in past civilizations: the capacity for renewal. Against the fixed shell and the static monu-ment, the new architecture places its faith in the powers of social adaptation and reproduction. The sign of the older order of archi-tecture, in almost every culture, was the House of the Dead: in mod-ern culture, it is the dwelling house, or House of the Living, renew-able generation by generation.

The human impulse to create everlasting monuments springs per-haps out of the desire of the living to perpetuate themselves: to over-come the flux and evanescence of all living forms. To achieve this in terms of biology only one means is possible: organic reproduction. All the classic civilizations, above all that of the Chinese, have re-garded the begetting of children as a sacred duty. Renewal through reproduction is the vulgar means of ensuring continuity: this and the transmission of the social heritage through memory, imitation and the written record. But there is still another means, springing not out of life and its renewing impulses, but out of death: a desire to wall out life, to exclude the action of time, to remove the taint of biological processes, to exclude the active care of other generations by a process of architectural mummification. The primitive burial mounds, the big stones of the Salisbury Plains or Brittany, the Pyramids and Sphinxes of Egypt, the grandiose gestures of a Sargon or an Ozymandias, of a Louis XIV or a Peter the Great: these represent that respect for death which is essentially a fear of life.

Ordinary men and women must be content to fix their image in their children. But the eminent and the powerful do not have sufficient faith in these powers of renewal: in their vanity, they seek a petrified immortality: they write their boasts upon tombstones; they incorporate their deeds in obelisks; they place their hopes of remembrance in solid stones joined to other solid stones, dedicated to their subjects or their heirs forever, forgetful of the fact that stones that are deserted by the living are even more helpless than life that remains unprotected and unpreserved by stones.

More or less, the ancient examples of these priestly and kingly cults have been taken over by civic communities: they, too, tended to sacrifice life to the monument. In general, one may say that the classic civilizations of the world, up to our own, have been oriented toward death and fixity: the immobilization of life. A Heraclitus might observe that all things flow, a Lucretius might see that man is a part of the eternally changing cycle of nature, but the aim of civilization was permanence: its highest achievement in cities was the static grandeur of a Pantheon or a Temple. The more shaky the institution, the more solid the monument: repeatedly civilization has exemplified Patrick Geddes's dictum, that the perfection of the architectural form does not come till the institution sheltered by it is on the point of passing away.

Thanks to this cult, permanence comes in the structures of the city: but death comes with it: the burial ground encroaches on the city and the city, with its mass of dead buildings, duly armored in stone, becomes a burial ground. The temple prepares for death, the monument consecrates it, the sacrificial altar sanctifies it, the learn-

ing of the schools rehearses it, the burial vault or the cemetery com-
pletes it. These beliefs and habits become pervasive: they eat into
urban routine. Records of state, the tables of the law, the correspondence of political functionaries, the decisions of the courts—
over all these activities a dead hand, a petrified hand, rules. The
very permanence of stone and brick, which enable them to defy
time, cause them also ultimately to defy life. Stone gives a false
sense of continuity, and a deceptive assurance of life: the shell seems
to pledge continuity by the fact that it continues to exist, outwardly
unaffected by the passage of events. But the fact is that exterior form
can only confirm an inner life: it is not a substitute. All living beliefs, all living desires and ideas, must be perpetually renewed,
from generation to generation: re-thought, re-considered, re-willed,
re-built, if they are to endure. The blight of ancient Rome upon the
imagination of Italy in the ensuing ages bears witness to the congeal-
ing strength of the monument: each generation mounts guard on a
cemetery, and repeats the password of its dusty challenge.

So long as men where wholly oriented toward death and the time-
less, the monument had a meaning: no sacrifice was too great to
produce it. Just as a poor Christian family today will spend half a
year's income to celebrate fitly the death of one of its members,
money that it would find impossible to spare for the birth or education of a child, so the civilizations of the past have sacrificed a good
part of their life, their income, their ideologic energy to the monument. For us today, beholding the world with eyes awakened by a
Buffon, a Goethe, a Darwin, a profound change has come about in
our biological conception of death and immortality: a change that
robs monumentalism of its main meaning. Biologically speaking,
death is an episode in life's renewal: the terminus of a radical
maladaptation. A theoretic immortality may exist for lower forms
of life, like the amoeba: it is absent in the higher organisms. Continuity for us exists, not in the individual soul as such, but in the
germ plasm and the social heritage, through which we are united to
all mankind and to all nature. Renewal comes through the sacrifice
of the parent to the child, of the having-lived to the living and the
yet-to-live.

Instead of being oriented, then, toward death and fixity, we are

By decree of the Consiglio Maggiore of Venice, in 1291, the glass furnaces at Castello were removed to Murano in order to free the city of industries that were either a nuisance or unhealthy: the pattern formed by the separate island, like this zoning ordinance itself, curiously anticipates the open order of modern urban planning. But modern zoning schemes, not least in America, are chiefly attempts to standardize and stabilize pecuniary values. City development, however, cannot forever be left to individual enterprise: it must be placed, as in Holland, under competent regional and local authorities, who are empowered to purchase land, to design and build and operate new communities—or who may delegate these functions to organizations that will work under their direction. *Functional zoning means a federal organization of a city's internal functions as well as a federal organization of cities within the region.*

[UPPER LEFT] Modern port facilities: Bremerhaven. Adequate arrangement of railroad yards, warehouses, docks, and means of access by water. (*Photograph: Ewing Galloway*)

[UPPER RIGHT] Modern industrial plant: lifted out of the entangling street pattern, surrounded by open land: a well-defined zone appropriately designed for its special needs. Discontinuous zoning of quarters, rather than continuous aggregation along corridor avenues, is characteristic of the new urban plan: each function placed in a specially designed environment and deliberately separated from the flow of traffic except for access. The creation of such zones is impossible in piecemeal planning by unco-ordinated individuals: it demands community planning and building. (*Photograph: Ewing Galloway*)

[MIDDLE] Modern English steelworks with housing for workers in the foreground. Contrast with the paleotechnic developments shown on Plate 11. This new type of plan made possible by the change from the competitive muddle of Victorian enterprise to the orderly public housing program, with state aid and state supervision of standards, put through by public authorities. In this change, England has, especially since 1920, led the world: thus turning the disorderly Black Country with its dark satanic mills into a Green Country. The plan itself, like many similar English examples, is unfortunately mediocre: local streets are too wide, orientation for sunlight is disregarded, the corridor avenue is retained; but the separation of the industrial zone, the agricultural zone, and the domestic zone is admirably clarified. (*Photograph: Aerofilms, Ewing Galloway*)

[BOTTOM] Public Works Administration Housing in Chicago. A sample of biotechnic order in the midst of metropolitan congestion and blight: when trees have grown, this new section will have the comeliness of one of the big quadrangles at Welwyn (see Plate 30). Developments like these will counteract the costly drift to the suburbs and will restore life to many old centers. (*Photograph: U. S. Public Works Administration*)

[TOP] Model of Broadacre City, designed by Frank Lloyd Wright. Extreme of decentralized planning: each family has a minimum of one acre of land: the scale of the whole city implies the universal pursuit of agriculture and the universal ownership and use of the motor car. Rectangular section as a design unit is characteristically regional in both historic and topographic sense. Underlying scheme a logical deduction from the premise that the technical means of occasional mobilization now takes the place for special purposes of mobilization by contiguity. Apart from the burden of providing such scattered housing units with necessary collective utilities, this plan makes no provision for the spontaneous association in primary groups—a handicap to mothers and children— nor does it sufficiently allow for close daily contacts as an indispensable element in group life. Broadacre City, then, is partly an overcompensated protest against the reckless and indiscriminate congestion of the metropolis. But its skeletal assumptions are sound. See Wright: The Disappearing City.

[MIDDLE LEFT] Welwyn, England: the second garden city, founded by Ebenezer Howard after the success of Letchworth (1904) was assured. It profited not merely by the government-aided provision of workers' houses but also by the southward migration of industry after 1925: a fact which permitted it in short order to become a balanced town with a strong industrial section: a mixed community. The use of cul-de-sacs and quadrangles is typically English: but the corridor avenue is not consistently abandoned, and the design lacks clarity. Housing through garden cities has now been undertaken by the municipality of Manchester in Wythenshawe, a new town designed by Barry Parker for 100,000 inhabitants, with a permanent agricultural belt of 1,000 acres, and one acre of open space to 50 people. Shopping districts in Wythenshawe are placed at the juncture of four neighborhood units. (*Photograph: Aerofilms*)

[MIDDLE RIGHT] While Le Corbusier's earlier mechanocentric plans for monumental skyscraper cities, with multiple streets, were essentially backward-looking, and his vermicular viaduct roadtown project was the aberration of an overingenious mind, his latest plan (with H. Breuillot) for the little town of Nemours in North Africa, shows that combination of social concentration and openness which is one of the marks of the new urban order.

[BOTTOM] Radburn, N. J. (H. Wright and C. S. Stein, town planners). Here was the first town built anywhere that consistently abandoned the corridor avenue lined with houses, that divorced the functions of domestic living from the noise and traffic of the street, and that provided a continuous belt of park space within the residential super-blocks, instead of placing the park on the outskirts. Each superblock was planned in relation to a school, a playground, and a swimming pool: open spaces were treated as part of the original cost of the development. By means of footpaths with underpasses and bridges one can walk from one part of the community to another without encountering a motor car.

oriented to the cycle of life, with its never-ending process of birth and growth and renewal and death: a process we can neither halt nor limit by ideological fixations or cunning inventions. The very stones of the ancient tombs are no longer for us true symbols of eternity: we know their secret processes and detect their faltering character: we see their civilizations, too, through the perspective of time, perspectives that reveal the feebleness of their boasted power and the frailty of their monuments. The forms that past cultures have chosen for immortality seem to us as essentially childish as the rag doll to which the infant playfully attributes life. Time is a bomb that splits the most august temple open, if indeed the wanton savagery of men does not anticipate death's weapon.

Now, the forms and patterns of past ages die slowly: the idea of fixity has itself been slow to resist change. The architectural embodiment of older notions of survival has persisted, despite the challenge of the modern world picture. The truth is, however, that the notion of material survival by means of the monument no longer represents the impulses of our civilization, and in fact it defies our closest convictions. These Valhallas and Lincoln Memorials, these Victor Emmanuel Monuments and Vimy Ridge Memorials, these "Eternal Lights" that go out when the electric power station breaks down or the bulb blows out—how many buildings of the last century, that pretend to be august and monumental, have a touch of the modern spirit in them? They are all the hollow echoes of an expiring breath, rattling ironically in the busy streets of our cities, heaps of stone, which either curb and confine the work of the living, like the New York Public Library, or are completely irrelevant to our beliefs and demands. The notion of a modern monument is veritably a contradiction in terms: if it is a monument it is not modern, and if it is modern, it cannot be a monument.

This is not to say that a hospital or a power station or an air beacon may not be treated as a memorial to a person or an event; nor is it to deny that a contemporary structure might not easily last two hundred years, or even two thousand: that is not the point. What will make the hospital or the air beacon a good memorial is the fact that it has been well designed for the succor of those who are ill, or for the guidance of men piloting airplanes: not the fact that it has taken form out of a metaphysical belief in fixity and immortality and the positive celebration of death. The gulf between these world views is immense. He who lives sincerely in one world cannot honestly encompass the other.

In most past civilizations the activities of the living were not real until they could be transposed into terms of death. In our emerging civilization death is meaningless until it can be transposed into terms of the living. In the recent Christian culture life was a probational period of preparation for death and the far more significant and important state of after-life: for us, death is a making way for life, and all the fixed and memorial processes, the written record, the painting, the sculptured stone, the photograph, the recorded voice, are offerings to the living—to be accepted, not out of duty to the dead, but out of loyalty to other remoter generations who will also be capable of deriving life from these symbols.

The death of the monument was intuitively forecast by more than one spirit during the last century. For the fact is that this architectural change has implications that go far beyond the conception of individual tombs, memorials, or public buildings: it affects the character of our culture as a whole and the very texture of urban life. Why, for example, should each generation go on living in the quarters that were built by its ancestors? These quarters, even if not soiled and battered, were planned for other uses, other habits, other modes of living: often they were mere makeshifts for the very purpose they were supposed to serve in their own day: the best under existing limitations that now no longer hold.

It was Nathaniel Hawthorne who asked this question: he put it into the mouth of the young photographer in The House of the Seven Gables and repeated it elsewhere. It is only now, perhaps, that we can plumb its full significance. The pastoral nomad spared himself the sacrifice of the living to the dead monument until he copied the ways of men in cities: he traveled light. Civilization today, for different reasons, with different ends in view, must follow this example of the nomad: it must not merely travel light but settle light: it must be ready, not for merely physical movement in space, but for adaptation to new conditions of life, new industrial processes, new cultural advantages. Our cities must not be monuments, but self-renewing organisms: the dominating image should not be the cemetery, where the dead must not be disturbed, but the field, meadow, and park-land, with its durable cover of trees, its light boundary lines, its changing crops for which the fields are plowed every year.

7: Flexibility and Renewal

Today, our distrust of the monument cannot end with the purely symbolic structures of religion and government; for the machines and utilities that have helped foster the dense occupancy of cities often take on a monumental character. Indeed, the Roman roads and aqueducts and sewers have survived at least as well as the Tomb of Hadrian and the Arch of Constantine, and the modern metropolis builds subways and new traffic arteries with something of the sublime collective indifference to earthly realities with which the burghers of the Middle Ages built cathedrals.

The more the energies of a community become immobilized in ponderous material structures, the less ready is it to adjust itself to new emergencies and to take advantage of new possibilities. A two-story building with shallow foundations may be easily torn down, if a different type of structure is needed. But a twenty story building has a deep foundation, elaborate mechanical equipment, an expensive superstructure: it is not easily demolished as a physical structure, still less easily as a credit structure, no matter how short its period of amortization. If such a building should be replaced by a smaller building, or by no building at all, the original capital investment will stand in the way of such rational adaptation.

Every part of the community's shell and equipment presents the same dilemma. The wholesale investment in electric street railways in the eighteen-nineties certainly retarded the development of automobile transportation a generation later: the over-investment in subways in big cities has made a stubborn enforcement of the pattern of congestion almost a condition of municipal solvency. And it is very easily possible that our present gigantic investments in sewage disposal systems, including special treatment stations and sewage farms, may retard the introduction of more simple apparatus that will liquefy and transform sewage close to the point of origin: one of those inventions long overdue.

It follows that every proposal to elaborate the physical shell of the community should be critically examined, and social alternatives to the mechanical means proposed should be canvassed, or the possibility of simpler and lighter mechanical equipment—decentralized rather than centralized, small rather than big—should be examined. Very often there is a live choice between mechanization and socialization: a choice that capitalism naturally prefers to be oblivious to, since its profits spring out of the production and sale of mechanical utilities: the more gigantic, the more numerous, the more profitable. So deeply ingrained is the pecuniary order that even a socialized republic like the USSR more than once has adopted capitalist methods, even superstitions, under socialist slogans.

Our older cities, planned as monuments, with heavy capital investments duly incorporated under capitalism in the toppling structure of mortgages and land values, are incapable of adjustment to fresh needs and fresh demands. Their assets are, as the saying is, frozen: from the standpoint of life they are preposterous and paralyzing deficits: obstacles to a flexible method of meeting new situations by means of appropriate structures. One of the most impressive advantages the small city has over the overgrown metropolis consists in the fact that it does not stagger under such a burden of capital outlays in non-productive utilities. The economy of settling light does not merely consist in a lower scale of investment and lower overhead: its value derives from the greater readiness to take advantage of fresh improvements. Small cities, where people continued to cycle or walk to work, were better prepared to take advantage of motor transportation than cities that had invested heavily in trolley cars, elevateds, and subways. Under a biotechnic regime we shall attempt to get by socialized planning what we have hitherto sought to achieve exclusively by means of costly mechanical equipment. Toynbee calls the process of culture, as a community assumes command over the environment and the physical means of life, "etherealization." In the development of a new type of living environment one may put this concept in a negative mode: de-materialization: a reduction of physical structures to their absolute functional minimum.

The deflation of our mechanical monuments, then, is no less imperative than the deflation of our symbolic monuments. For the biotechnic age will be progressively marked by a simplification of mechanical equipment. Our present overload of mechanical utilities in the dwelling house, the skyscraper, and the city, particularly marked in American cities, is a symptom of our inability to think and plan and act in terms of the total situation: we shrink back into the narrow utilitarian ideology of the machine. The fact is that the so-called Machine Age has treated machines as ornaments: it has invented the vacuum cleaner when it should have done away with the rug: it has retained the steam-heater to produce sub-tropical heat at great expense, when it should have invented better forms of permanent insulation, to do away with the extravagant heating of cold walls and windows: it has retained the private garage as an ornament to the free-standing house, when it should have used the art of community planning to group houses and garages into a more livable environment. Similarly, the advantage of new utilities such as the private automatic refrigerator and the private oil-burning automatic furnace are only half-used because they demand, for complete economy, a more economical pattern of streets, which will dispense with the old need for public access to private dwellings on the road.

If the machine were not in effect a monument, if it were not a symbol of our mechanocentric religion, such irrational expenditures could not be explained. It remains only to note that mechanolatry is a bastard religion: half its glories mock the very mechanical and scientific principles it superficially seeks to enthrone. As a monument the machine is subject to the same ironic deflation that applies to all other attempts to wall out life. In the past, what have been called the triumphs of civilization have often turned out to be studious collections of encumbrances, which finally stifle the possibilities of movement and resilient reaction, and lead ultimately to urban downfall.

Here again one meets the lesson already noted in the section on Economy. We have created for the communities of the past cumbrous physical shells: what we need in future is not so much a shell as a living environment, an organic body capable of circulation and repair and renewal in every organ, member, and tissue. The protective function of the city, which is the utilitarian side of these metaphysical concepts of fixity and permanence, has been overdone. For living creatures, the only real protection comes through growth and renewal and reproduction: processes that are precisely the opposite of petrification. The real offense in the doing over of Regent Street, London, for example, was not the wiping away of Nash's serene façades, but their replacement with flatulent buildings that are hideous to the modern eye, and far less in keeping with modern needs than Nash's buildings. An American traveler has explained the rich architectural tradition of the contemporary inhabitants of Bali as due in part to the fact that they build their buildings with an exceedingly impermanent volcanic stone, which lasts only about fifteen years: hence they have to renew their structures frequently and recarve the stone. This continued demand for art keeps alive a fine tradition in the decorative arts. In modern life glass and synthetic materials, now coming into fuller use in the work of the new pioneers, are valid symbols of this more vital and more enlightened social sense.

Unfortunately, the real promise of this development has been frustrated from two directions. The older schools of architecture have clung to obsolete monumental forms, and manufacturers seeking to exploit fresh materials have been tempted, again and again, to give them the superficial earmarks of earlier technical processes. From the standpoint of capitalist enterprise, on the other hand, there has been a systematic misdirection of effort during the last decade in the effort to contrive free-standing, individual, manufactured houses, which could be put on the market in the same fashion as the automobile. By concentrating on the purely technical element of improved pre-fabrication, the manufacturers of these individual structures have overlooked the critical fact that modern communal services and collective utilities have made the cost of free-standing houses prohibitive, except in the isolation of the open country: they have sought economy in the shell alone, without availing themselves of further economies that rest upon community planning and community building.

When one stresses the factor of *renewability* one does not overlook the fact that effective design involves the discovery of architectural constants that do not have to be renewed from generation to generation: to discover and establish these constants is one of the main tasks of the modern planner. In every art there are forms so implicit in the process, so harmonious with the function, that they are, for practical purposes, "eternal": the safety pin has changed little in form since the later bronze age: the number of silhouettes possible for a bowl or a pitcher that will pour effectively is limited —and so on. Renewability in architecture does not mean designing buildings that must collapse in fifteen years: still less does it mean making pre-fabricated houses whose superficial shape will undergo as many ephemeral and foolish style-changes as the motor car, merely in order to quicken the pace of style-obsolescence and keep the industry profitably occupied. Renewability means the design of buildings in such materials, and by such technical methods, that they may be easily made over, section by section, structure by structure, even neighborhood by neighborhood.

Is this not the great justification of the steel-framed building? For the internal skeleton can be fixed, in terms of sunlight and open spaces and density, while the internal and external partitions, which determine the character of exposure, the size of the rooms, the diverse functional requirements, can all be freely recast, as need requires. Mies van der Rohe made an important essay in this type of construction in one of his Berlin apartment houses, built in such a way that the number and size of the rooms could be changed at will: the late Raymond Hood, in much more conventional fashion, drew the plans for a similar type of building; and although the architectural constants usually have no scientific validity, the precedent for this type of planning was of course set long before in the American office building. Mr. Clarence Stein has shown the application of the same principle to the design of a modern art museum with a thoroughly flexible interior. Essentially, these methods are capable of extension to almost every type of structure, except those specialized for industrial purposes; and even here, in the light industries, with their relatively mobile equipment, the same set of constants— and a wide range of variables—can be worked out.

Does this mean that the modern city is to be renewed every generation? Does this mean that it will "grow" indefinitely and spread indefinitely? Does this mean that the processes of demolition and destruction, so violent in the nineteenth century, will continue on their way, destroying every vestige of the past? Yes to the first question: no to the second and third.

The extent of renewal will depend upon the proportion of variables to constants. Most of the urban quarters built during the last hundred years must undergo profound reconstruction: this is a work which, if systematically carried on, might well occupy a good part of the energies of the next two generations: a work of undoing and redoing. But the outburst of mechanical invention during the nineteenth century, with the rapid alteration of old methods of work and old ways of life and the great shift of population, undoubtedly has made the present generation exaggerate the number of social variables and to forget the constants. Purposive change tends to crystallize once it has achieved its goal: once instantaneous communication at a distance has been achieved, for example, no *faster* mode of communication can be established.

One of the great advantages of mechanical standardization is to increase the number of constants in the environment; and this is equally true of the advance of scientific knowledge. It is extremely unlikely that medical science will suddenly discover that dark and airless buildings are preferable to light and airy ones, or that a cultivated landscape is more inimical to life than a crowded, dusty street. Once we establish constants in our urban planning, a certain kind of variation and change that was common during the last century—changes toward higher densities and overbuilding—will no longer take place.

Some of these constants were achieved by other periods, and were permitted to lapse, through a failure to maintain real standards of life. Quarters built with even an approximation to the standards that are already visible in terms of modern science, quarters like the Place Vendôme in Paris or the Fuggerei in Augsburg, or Gray's Inn in London, have a far greater degree of permanence than the great mass of recent building. As we design our cities for permanent living, not for impermanent financial exploitation, we shall discover, no doubt, a whole series of biological and social constants that will vary little from generation to generation; or at all events, such variation as is necessary will take place within, not in opposition to, the permanent form.

8: The Mission of the Museum

All this is another way of saying that the city itself, as a living environment, must not be condemned to serve the specialized purposes of the museum. If the city is to escape being a confused rubbish heap, the function of preservation and storage must be taken over by the museum. The very meaning of the museum of art and social history is that it is able to detach the memorials of life from the culture that originally supported them. By confining the function of preservation to the museum, we thus release space in the rest of the city for the fresh uses of the living. Where the fragments of a local culture are to be preserved, one of the best means of effecting this is perhaps by the use of an historic building, such as the Taft Museum in Cincinnati, the Behnhaus and the St. Annen Kloster in Lübeck, the Musée de Cluny in Paris, and the historical museums of Edinburgh and London.

The museum gives us a means of coping with the past, of having significant intercourse with other periods and other modes of life, without confining our own activities to the molds created by the past. Starting as a chance accumulation of relics and "valuables," half safety-deposit vault, half show-room, the art museum has in the course of its development gradually discovered its special function: that of selectively preserving the memorials of culture. Here at last is a genuine means of escaping the monument. What cannot be kept in existence in material form, we may now measure, photograph in still and moving pictures, record in sound, and summarize in books and papers. We may—and should—do all these things while the life is still present, so that we shall have, filed away for future reference, not merely a fragment of the original shell, but a working knowledge of the physiology of the building or work of art.

As far as works of pure art go, this detachment may become complete. What makes a work of art eternal in the human sense is not the details it carries over from the dead past, but what it signifies against the background of our own experience. It follows that while the social history museum necessarily seeks to preserve and enshrine the background, the museum of art, properly speaking, should forego any such attempt. One does not need a medieval house to appreciate a picture by Roger van der Weyden or Breughel, because, even if we had the house, we could not see either the environment or the picture through medieval eyes. On the contrary: the more complete the detachment and the more effectively we can screen a symbol from what it meant to another generation, the more swift and final is our own response.

Not unfortunately it is in a sense by our misinterpretations of the past that the past lives again: true understanding would leave the past precisely where it originally was: it is by its "otherness" that the past enriches the present with hints, suggestions, meanings that had no existence in its own day. For a work of art is not a monument: if it has a life at all, it exists as a contemporary fact: a fact of esthetics, a fact of religion, a fact of philosophy. A museum that is properly designed, with ample facilities for storage and preservation as well as for show, serves to enlarge the circle of contemporary experience. But our intercourse with the past is selective: it cannot be otherwise. The encyclopedic culture of the metropolis attempts to preserve everything and show everything; it mistakes acquisition for appreciation, a knowledge of names and incidents for esthetic intuition, and mechanical imitation for cultural intercourse.

Such a culture turns the museum into a second metropolis: like the big city, it aims merely at bigness, and results in purposeless congestion and intellectual bewilderment. On the mere laws of chance something of value must accumulate in the debris, by reason of its extent. But in museums that grew out of a balanced regional culture, not out of an acquisitive pattern of life, each generation would have the opportunity to be in selective control of the past. Each city would have its special museum of civic history: each community within the larger urban cluster would have its type museum of natural history and human culture, portraying in compact and coherent form the actual environment: from the infinitely remote stars to the infinitesimal particles of protoplasm or energy: the place: the work: the people in all their ecological relations. Under such a mode of distribution, a great part of the collections might be centrally stored, so that there would be a wider and more systematic circulation of objects: but the outlet and place of exhibition would not be a confused, overgrown building. Even in the clumsy organization of the big capitals today there is a tendency in this direction: but any thorough-going application of these principles awaits the co-ordinate develop-ment of integrated neighborhood communities and integrated cities.

9: The Undifferentiated Background

Another significant social change has come about during the last three centuries; but it has only been partly consummated, and its expression in architecture has not been fully appraised. This is the transference of interest from caste to personality: the lifting of the naïve moral mask, and its replacement by a more complex tissue of individuality. The death of the monument has its counterpart in the disappearance of the uniform.

Although the English and French revolutions left a mark on every Western community, they were only partly able to remove the older foundations of caste and status. The process of social de-stratification took place most thoroughly in the countries of the New World, particularly in the United States, where under the pressure of con-quering the wilderness and seizing a vast territory, the old habits of life, the old gradations, the old subserviences were replaced by a more fluid sense of the personality. Not "Where have you come from?" but "What can you do?" was the question asked: not "What is your social *position?*" but "What is your business [function]?"

Under this new freedom, a virile type of personality emerged within a few generations, a type understood and celebrated by Emerson, Thoreau, Hawthorne, and Whitman. In the new lands, men were socially equal, politically equal: this meant that dif-ferences were no longer merely historic congealments but psycho-logical facts.

Backward and barbarous though this pioneer culture was in many ways, it achieved a practical revaluation of the personality which carried into daily living an animus that only the deepest psy-chologists, such as Shakespeare, had succeeded in achieving in a caste society. The naked man, the individuated man, divorced from his background of caste, *taken on his merits,* rose up from the hitherto stratified mass: his character, his conditions, his feelings were no longer conditioned by his economic class: a shiftless farmer, brought up in this new social environment, became a great military leader;

a rail-splitter became a statesman; a sailor became a profound tragic writer; a pencil maker became a philosopher. In contrast to the inhabitants of the more established European societies, the typical pioneer American was a mere jack-of-all-trades: but another way of expressing it is that he was no longer a caste-limited man. If the doctrines of the class struggle were slow to make headway in America, it was because to the average American of the old stock classes were no longer social realities. Equal opportunity to have access to the soil meant unlimited differentiation: it was only with the closing of the frontier and the hemming in of opportunity that social stratification fully set in.

The expansion of educational opportunity during the last century and the collective promise of leisure offered by the machine has reopened, on a higher level, the crude opportunities for social equality that the frontier environment provided. For the modern man, caste is not a permanent attribute of personality: and the personality itself, instead of being a static unit, with a single fatal shape which it bears till eternity, is a function of its habits and responses; a complex if coherent resultant of its manifold associations and linkages. Occupation and regional background may tinge the personality with certain unmistakable colors: but the generic and human, with their vast range of opportunity and choice, provide endless shades and combinations.

Wherever a modern sense of the human personality has penetrated, the external uniform disappears, except as a functional accommodation to climate or work: the internal uniform disappears at the same moment. One cannot automatically derive the conduct of the individual from the pattern of his caste, nor does the individual feel himself fully represented within the area of his purely occupational interests: he preserves, as it were, the standing of the amateur. This attitude springs not only out of a new social milieu but out of a profounder understanding of human aptitude and motive; since however the psychological evaluation and control of conduct is still in its infancy, the modern sense of the personality is still unexpressed—except perhaps in America, where it exists as a holdover of the pioneer experience.

Indeed, part of the world at this moment is in a regressive state:

the automatic compulsions of war-discipline have, in fascist states, re-created the image of the caste-ridden, uniformed individual, with no center of his own, and no life except that prescribed by the rulers of the state. A world of heroes and villains: a world of black shirts and brown shirts and blue shirts: a world in which personality ceases to have existence or value save in the anarchic despotism of the leaders—little men, magnified by martial law and public bullying into the external dimensions of greatness.

The uniform, in both its physical and metaphoric senses, is nevertheless an atavism: a degrading effort to ignore our deeper knowledge of the personality and to limit the effects of science upon human behavior. So long as a man could be fully characterized by his rank or station: so long as he was, in a complete and unified sense, a knight or a burgher or a serf, a pagan or a Christian, a Protestant or a Catholic, so long as these distinctions were primary and clean-cut, the character of his background played an important part in defining his position in society. His costume, often limited by sumptuary laws, was a kind of background: his background in turn was a kind of costume. In the parlor, in the dining room, in the garden, he attempted to impose his personality through his background: deliberately or unconsciously he would display how rich he was, how ancient his family lineage was, how mighty his caste was in the community: these things seemed important.

In such a society, the key to architecture was the class-differentiated decoration: the human personality was, so to say, a mere figure on the carpet. The presence and quality of curtains, say, in a middle class household established its claim to respectability: the quantity of bric-a-brac or linen had a similar effect: and to live in certain American towns on the wrong side of the railroad track was to suffer social ostracism from those on the right side. The one unforgivable sin from the standpoint of caste was the bare room—that is, the room that did not at once establish the owner's place in society; and as costume, through the vulgarization of textiles and furs, defied sumptuary laws and blurred the lines of class cleavage a little, the domestic background became even more important. Without a duly established background, the class-limited personality felt insecure: the quality of his character rested then upon mere performance, not upon the visible tokens of landed property, stocks, bonds, mortgages, upon emblems of acquisitive taste and acquisitive interest.

All these habits linger; but a fresh sense of the personality, in all its immense and fascinating complexity, has been awakened by modern psychology. Much as our modern attitude toward time and death differs from that which prevailed in the past, the modern attitude toward background and foreground differs even more; and the essential innovation of modern architecture is, in effect, to abolish the background and to concentrate attention on the foreground. Gone are the visible signs of riches, travel, and "cultural appreciation": the patterned wallpaper, the curious designs on rugs and carpets, the involved shapes of vases, bowls, tables, each object calling attention to itself, crying to be singled out, competing for attention with the occupants of the room.

Good design today follows the fashion first set in theater decorations by Appia: it concentrates attention upon the *action* and *function* in the foreground, and it does not permit attention to be diverted from the actors to the scenic background. It is the face, the voice, the gesture, the thought, that shall tell the story about the owner's personality: not what he has acquired by way of material goods: not by this fashion and that fancy applied to his material equipment. The more generic the background, the less obtrusive its effect, the more subtly will it tell its story—and the more effectively the actual human presence will count in the picture.

Not merely does the modern sense of the personality demand that the foreground should be focused sharply, and the background retreat: if the background is emphasized, one suspects weakness. The desire for external grandeur, the desire for meretricious luxury or display—what do these things point to except a sense of psychological inferiority or insecurity: a failure to express adequate social relationships. As a sexually unattractive man may attempt to salvage his failure as a lover by showering his wife or his mistress with gifts, so the socially inept personality must attempt to take refuge in the material background, to bolster up his sense of insecurity by taste for antiques or an eager adaptation of the latest trick of fashion.

Whether in doing so he identifies himself with his traditional caste, like a merchant of the seventeenth century, or attempts to "express

In plan the most important new element in the garden city is the lateral wall of agricultural or park land that surrounds and defines the community. Following the private initiative of Radburn, the U. S. Resettlement Administration, formed by the Federal Government in 1934, sought to combine housing with the building up of complete communities in areas favorable to sustained industrial and commercial employment. These projects were a step beyond Public Works housing: they recognized the possibility of creating an entirely superior type of urban organization by making a fresh start, instead of being confined to areas from which slums had been razed, already equipped with superfluous streets and utilities, as well as burdened by high land values. Numerous projects were planned; but only three were in process of building when this excellent initiative was capriciously discarded. Greenbelt, Maryland, here shown was the first to reach partial completion: Greendale, near Milwaukee, and Greenhills near Cincinnati exhibit similar principles with different types of plan. Great Britain and other countries had made the mistake, after 1919, of promoting housing without using the opportunity to re-centralize industry and population in complete and well-balanced garden cities. In the Greenbelt towns the United States seemed about to overcome this critical defect in its new governmentally financed housing. This enlightened policy should be resumed.

[TOP] General Layout of Greenbelt, Md. The plan was conditioned by a horse-shoe-shaped plateau. Full advantage was taken of wooded areas and existing trees. While not oriented consistently for maximum sunlight, the rows are rationally ordered within superblocks: a major economy. Note the by-passing of major highways, another characteristic of advanced planning. (*Photograph: Resettlement Administration*)

[MIDDLE] Type of house at Greenbelt. Straightforward design, with concrete blocks and bricks: open outlook and ample garden space. The schools and the community stores are carried through in the same manner: a vast advance over the second-hand picturesqueness of the better American suburb. Urbanity and openness—rather than the bogus rustic and the pseudo-historical—are the key to the new order of design. (*Photograph: Resettlement Administration*)

[BOTTOM] Airplane view of section of Greenbelt, while still under construction. Much more compact than the scatter-building (Streubau) of the nineteenth century suburb; much more open than the traditional types of city design. Shows the great benefits obtainable only through comprehensive design, large scale planning, scientific appraisal of needs, and unified land-ownership and large-scale building operations. Communities of this order were first projected by Robert Owen: they have now become a universal indication of biotechnic city design. (*Photograph: Resettlement Administration*)

[32] FRANKFURT-RÖMERSTADT: BIOTECHNIC ORDER

One of the earliest applications, beginning 1926, of modern methods of planning and building communities: so far probably the best. Parallel rows of houses in long blocks unbroken by traffic streets: narrow roads bordered with verdure for local service: large open spaces, with ample lawns, flower beds, and dining terraces behind the houses. The curving unit in the middle of the air-view is a four story high apartment block and retail business center, equally accessible from both ends of the community: the utilization of low and high units in this scheme gave opportunities for strong rhythms and accents, as in the two apartment units that stand out by the curving ramparts in the top picture. The varying orientation of houses was determined, not by sunlight exposure alone, but by other equally important elements—the lay of the land and the grand view across the Nidda Valley, permanently zoned for agricultural uses. If this development does not show the rigorous economies and stereotyped formulae of some later German schemes, it shows the artists' freedom of design which will be more and more possible in future as our communities turn their economic production to social ends: to plan economically for the future means, not cramping the work to the niggardly possibilities of today, but anticipating the higher standard of living well within our collective grasp—with its call for space and beauty rather than mere economy. To plan on low levels, on the basis of standardized and universally accepted poverty, is to plan for defeat: high standards of space are the best safeguard against obsolescence. The low-lying land beneath the parapet (*top photograph*) shows the individual cultivation gardens with their trim, collectively built, tool sheds: part of the green belt that sets off this community on two sides. The urbanity of the street picture, full of color and subtle variation, is far more stimulating than the mediocre suburbanism of more conventional contemporary schemes.

Here is an urban nucleus that meets the need for concentration (social advantage), for openness (hygienic and biological advantage), and for collective order and beauty: an environment in which the varied needs of the individual and the common life are effectively reconciled. But Römerstadt is only a sample: the widespread building of such units requires equally positive changes in industry, in economic standards, in political organization, and in culture: changes for which the older political parties and programs have only confused, partial, and contradictory formulations. The building of new communities, on a scale commensurate with social need, awaits the wider foundation, in every department, of a biotechnic culture. These new forms are prophetic of a new civilization: a civilization now in the same embryonic state that capitalism and mechanism were in the seventeenth century. Our generation faces the alternative of courageously going forward toward this civilization—or of relapsing into barbarism, marked by the muddled timidities of a disintegrating capitalism, and that neurotic substitute for an integrated order, fascism. . . . Forward!

his personality" in the romantic assumption of some form of architectural fancy dress, dissociated from his real environment, the
effort remains massively inept. The background is a mask, and we
see behind the mask—even as we see behind the puerile uniforms
and decorations and struttings of the totalitarian dictatorships—a
large confession of weakness and impotence in respect to the realities
of social life. We mark the subterfuges, the distortions, the evasions of
reality. The cult of the antique in furniture and decoration, the cult
of the exotic, the attempt to take over the time-bound vestiges of
other periods—what were these fading efforts but concrete utopias
of escape: the desire to establish little dream islands in the steely
sea of reality.

Today the seat of human individuality has altered. The garden, the
flower, the sculpture, the painting, the beautiful costume, the human
body and the human face, belong to the foreground: direct servants
of the personality, not badges of class and pecuniary position. *And
as the background becomes more standardized,* so that it no longer
applies to a single caste but a whole community, no longer to a
single community but a whole civilization, *so will the foreground
become more individuated.* Here we have in architectural taste that
necessity for combining the intimate and the individualized, which
we find in the region, with the generic and universalized, which we
shall find only in the widening of the processes of culture to our
whole planet. The common ground will thus become broader. But
immediate taste and psychological appraisal will become more refined, as the foreground becomes the main center of interest: a psychological foreground, freed from the factitious standardizations
of class, money, social rank. On this basis, within this setting, real
groups and real personalities will have the freedom to emerge, to
coalesce, to function, and to dissolve again.

10: Individuation and Socialization

What we have been discussing, in this new conception of architectural form, is in fact the concrete examples of sociality and individuality: both modes are undergoing radical changes. In the past,
each of these attitudes stood for a whole theory of society: they
came before us as social and political philosophies, clustered around

the dogmas of private property and individual liberty that had taken shape in the eighteenth century. They were looked upon as alternatives. Individualism was a theory that believed in the existence of atomic individuals as a primary fact. It held that these individuals had an inherent right to possess property and enjoy personal protection under the laws; and that no laws abrogating that species of personal freedom founded upon private property were valid. Socialism, in all its diverse manifestations, regarded the community as a primary fact, and it treated the welfare of the community as more important than the claims of any atomic individual to special protection or sustenance.

In actual practice, both these doctrines, during the last century, presented a sinister aspect. Masquerading under the noble slogans of the rights of man, pretending to continue its old war on despotic power, individualism established itself as the claim of small groups of privileged people to exploit the work of other men on the basis of a monopoly, partial or complete, of land, capital, credit, and the machinery of production. For the single despotism of the king, it substituted a multitude of petty, and not so petty, despots: industrialists, financiers, robber barons. "Socialism," on the other hand, has meant in practice the unlimited capacity of the government and the armed forces of the state to impose obedience and co-operation upon its subjects in times of war: pushed to its extreme, it becomes the state-deification of fascism and the unity of war-dictatorship. "Individualism" rested on the doctrine of the "free market" in which price exercises the functions of an almighty Providence: "socialism" rested on the doctrine of the closed frontier, in which every human activity within, thought itself, is subjected to state monopoly. The inequalities of the first and the uniformities of the second were equally oppressive to a good society.

In the senses in which individualism and socialism have gained currency, both are mythological distortions of the underlying facts of community life: the processes of individuation and socialization. In actuality, these terms are alternatives only in the sense that north and south are alternatives. They indicate directions of motion, without giving any descriptive reference to the goal to be reached. No

human society is conceivable in which, to some degree, both tendencies did not play an active part.

As concerns origins, the social theory is largely correct: society
exists as a fact in nature, and without an underlying symbiosis no
single member could survive. The more primitive the state of existence, the greater the influence of brute compulsion and irrational but
coercive tabu. The separation of the individual from the generic is
a social fact that occurs only in those socialized animals that have
some extra-organic means of inheritance; otherwise individuality is
a matter of accident and latent tendency. Only through a specific
social heritage, beginning with the art of language, can individuation
arise. The individual, left to himself, is not a source. Left to himself,
indeed, he would starve, go mad.

As concerns emergents, however, the theory of individuation is a
fact. When the apparatus of socialization becomes more adequate,
through language, through the written word, through the division of
labor, through the development of cities, special forms arise in the
hitherto less differentiated mass. Each group, each community, each
vocation, each habitat creates new patterns of individuality: by their
interaction in the close medium of the city, they provide endless per-
mutations and combinations in all its members. The common environment provides an underlying unity: the city itself may become the
cohesive symbol of that unity: but within that common environment
all the differentiations of a true culture arise with a wealth of example hitherto unexplored. Through intermixture of stocks and races
in the city, the biological inheritance, in turn, combines with the
equally complicated facts of social inheritance: these facts are individuated from moment to moment as personal experience. For practical purposes one often forgets the fact of individuation; but by intercourse with a de-individuated person, whose full human inheritance has been ideologically castrated, one realizes the difference between the deadened oneness of totalitarian doctrine and the vital
and many faceted product of a genuine community, in which social
conflicts and cultural intermixtures play an active part.

Both individuation and socialization must be respected in the design of cities and their separate structures. Unfortunately, working
under the false mythology of individualism, our modern capitalist

societies have in the past assigned values to "individual effort" in precisely those departments where standardized practices and social-ized controls are necessary. The right of an individual property owner to obtain by purchase or inheritance a parcel of land, and to use it entirely at his own pleasure under minor legal regulation, has been treated as sacrosanct; and the gains that have followed the collective procedures of science, the collective discoveries of technics, have been permitted to go, like ground rents, to lucky or rapacious individuals, when they should in fact have been kept in trust for the community. In a similar way, laissez-faire principles encouraged the individual prospecting for industrial sites, the individual parceling of ground, the individual owning and building of houses: although all of these are in essence collective functions which are preparatory to true individuation. Indeed, individuation cannot enter in a cul-tural sense until a good part of our activities are reduced to a mechanized or socialized routine: only by multiplying the functions of the spinal cord, making them automatic, can the higher functions of the brain be released. This is the essential truth underlying Aris-totle's otherwise barbarous remark that a good polity must rest on slavery.

Under an equally mythological sort of socialization, whether un-dertaken in the interest of a ruling financial class or the power state, the reverse of this tendency has been practiced. The state attempts to impose uniformity and "socialization" in matters of education, intellectual culture, and political judgment where, within the common pattern of the civilization (which "enforces" itself) a wide span of individuations should be encouraged. Contrary to the prevail-ing doctrine, no special measures should be taken, other than the common processes of discovering and systematizing truth, to extir-pate obsolete religions, discarded scientific doctrines, idiosyncrasies and aberrant beliefs: since it is sometimes by unexpected combina-tions in our social inheritance, or unorthodox re-interpretations of past beliefs, that important mutations are made. The tendencies mak-ing for human uniformity are indeed so deep, so abiding, that it is only by providing for free play in individuation that we can avoid the sessile habits, the dangerous encystments, of past civilizations.

Every community must attempt in its structure to reconcile stability and adaptation, standardization and flexibility, socialization and individuation. None of these qualities is a terminal point or objective: they are directions of movement and change. Good planning is an attempt to keep the whole environment in a state of dynamic equilibrium, in which freedom does not mean empty chaos, and in which discipline does not mean an even more vacuous death.

The great aristocracies of the past knew that the labor of a thousand serfs, the accumulations of vast congeries of buildings, with all the necessary land for their support, might not be too extravagant a price to pay for the culture of a truly enlightened and disciplined individual: in the long run, the millions would profit. But because of the social inequality and the bitter injustice of these arrangements, such aristocracies but rarely produced a Plato. Today, with our vast accession of energies, with our abundant collective resources, we have the opportunity of upholding these principles, not for the sake of an oligarchy, but for the welfare of every member of the community. The base must be generic, equalized, standardized, communal: the emergent must be specific, unstandardized, individual, aristocratic: differentiated groups, differentiated individuals, differentiated regional and civic communities.

11: From a Money-Economy to Life-Economy

In the pecuniary economy that developed during the last five hundred years, there was only one criterion of effort: profit. If more profit could be obtained by baking stones than by baking bread, stones would be baked, even though in fact people were starving. Scarcity and surplus, demand and supply, had reality not in relation to men's actual wants, but in relation to the market. Wants that could not be expressed in terms of the market remained unfulfilled, unless they were satisfied through an institutional life brought over from another period. Money was the symbol of power, and power was the chief end of man.

Under a pecuniary economy wants that can be expressed in terms of a demand in the market kept on expanding: this was marked first by an increase in the variety of goods offered, and second by an increase in the amount created through mechanized production. In order to make the highly specialized division of labor possible, in an anonymous and undirected production for a world market, it was necessary that wants should keep on increasing: likewise that the rate of consumption should be hastened: by this means alone could production be geared higher and profits increased, or at least kept secure. Saturation of the market, with new production limited to legitimate replacements, would decrease the opportunities for profit and undermine the existence of the over-expanded plant: stability meant, in terms of profit, frustration: contraction meant bankruptcy.

Under this pecuniary economy, the civic and domestic needs of the greater part of the population have never been satisfied through the ordinary processes of the market. Calicoes, knives, and watches might be cheaper, as they entered the channels of international trade and displaced increasingly the local products, by a price competition which often concealed the eventual inferiority of the goods: but the low wage levels which entered into the production of these cheapened goods made it impossible for any large mass of workers to make an adequate demand for dwellings and for the community equipment that goes with urban living.

This held true in the eighteenth and nineteenth centuries, with results that I have described in detail in earlier chapters: but the point is that it holds equally true today. *Without doubt the prime obstacle to urban decentralization is that a unit that consists of workers, without the middle class and rich groups that exist in a big city, is unable to support even the elementary civic equipment,* of roads, sewers, fire department, police service, and schools. At present it is only by remaining in metropolitan areas, where the taxes derived from the well-to-do districts can be partly applied to the working class quarters, that the worker can obtain even a modicum of the facilities for a good life.

This fact was discovered by the planners of Radburn, N. J., in attempting a rational organization of its municipal life and it was further demonstrated by Mr. Clarence Stein in a study made for the Resettlement Administration. It has been amply substantiated by the London County Council's efforts at municipal decentralization: Becontree, for example.

What effect did machine production, corporate economy, special‑

ized division of labor, and concentration of output on a blind market of buyers have upon the provision of dwelling houses? Here again
the total inadequacy of a pecuniary economy to satisfy the essential
biological and social needs of a community has been completely
demonstrated. As the standards of housing have risen, the opportunities for profit through their sale or rent have dropped. In a capitalist economy, this means that production has gone into other
channels. Result: a quantitative shortage in dwelling space has been
chronic in highly industrialized countries like England ever since
the beginning of the nineteenth century, and in the more overcrowded
industrial centers, like London, since the sixteenth century.

In order to make it possible for capital to enter this field at all, the
qualitative standards have kept consistently below the level of decency available under the existing technology. The dwelling house,
far more than the farm, has been the backward point of modern
technics. Wage levels and incomes have borne simply no relation
to the requirements for a decent dwelling. The failure of the pecuniary economy in this department is abysmal: all the more because
rent is the largest single item in a family budget: rising from ten or
fifteen per cent among the working classes of Holland to between
twenty and thirty per cent for those in other countries. Rents that
occupy more than twenty per cent of the total, especially on the lower
income levels, mean a sharp curtailment of vital necessities at other
points in the budget.

The failure of decent housing to obtain capital through competition in the market has led to widespread attempts to foster home-
ownership among the workers: under the guise of offering security,
those who have fostered this movement, including government
agencies, have sought to burden the worker with the risks: risks
whose returns are not sufficient to attract the necessary capital from
the more wary. This diversion of the worker's meager budget to housing not merely undermines his standard of life: it lessens his freedom of movement and, during a financial crisis or a local shutdown
often results in the complete loss of his entire investment—and the
roof over his head as well.

Needless to say, this is no solution of the housing problem: even
apart from the fact that the building of individual houses is techni-

cally an extremely wasteful process. Except for the income groups well on the comfort level, the building of houses for profit has been carried on throughout the Western World only by debasements of design: systematic overcrowding of the land, and overpopulation of the interior quarters on the part of those who must eventually rent them. And so long as pecuniary canons remain uppermost, there is no prospect for a change.

What do all these facts signify? They signify that some of the most essential items in the construction and equipment of cities can not be produced, on any terms, under a pecuniary economy; and that houses in particular can be built only by ignoring the positive standards, based on scientific data, that are appropriate in an advanced civilization. This discovery has been slowly sinking into the minds of thoughtful people for the last century; and in the realm of both city development and housing it has resulted in a series of measures that cannot be sanctioned in terms of private gain and pecuniary aggrandizement.

Housing, in fact, is the focal point in that change from a pecuniary to a biotechnic economy which has been slowly developing throughout the Western World, and which received a great impetus in the decade that followed the first World War. The older type of industrialism chose to meet the inadequacy of income to a genuine standard of life by maintaining low wage levels as long as possible and ignoring the possible existence of a positive standard of life. Whatever the worker could get along on, whatever a landlord could demand, in the main determined the rental levels and the standard of accommodation: even during periods of relative prosperity for the worker, housing remained a third choice in his expenditures. In Middletown the Lynds discovered workers who owned automobiles of the latest model, whilst they bred their families in houses that lacked even bare sanitary conveniences. Even the worker, guided by advertising, sales talk, and emulation, followed fashions.

Under the biotechnic economy, these conditions are reversed. Instead of wages and income directing market demand, vital demand determines the level of income and directs production into socially useful channels. First we must erect a standard of living. In terms of housing, the minimum standards are set by objective criteria of air, water, sunlight, heat, privacy, and so forth, and further modified by those social provisions which tradition and current investigation prove to be necessary for the nurture of children and the education of responsible citizens. At any given period, in any given region, these standards should set a minimum level for wages: industries that cannot meet such a level must be looked upon as economically inefficient and socially defective: to be abolished or taken over by the community.

Where such standards have been set to a greater or less degree in publicly aided housing one of two things must happen: either incomes in industry will rise to the necessary level, or the state will tax the larger incomes and make the re-apportionment directly in the form of subsidies to the housing: money lent at low interest rates, subsidies to rents to make up the difference between the cost of the house and the worker's ability to pay, or outright grants. In the governmental housing that has been undertaken so widely through Europe, beginning with the first efforts in England and Belgium after the middle of the nineteenth century, one or all of these methods have been used. Inevitably. Had the capitalist discovered for himself a way to supply decent housing to a depauperate or indigent population at a profit to himself he would have followed it.

Now, in a pecuniary economy, production for sale and profit dominates: the surplus over current need goes back, apart from minimum expenditures for private display and public services, into further mechanical production. In a biotechnic economy, on the other hand, consumption and service must take precedence. Production must be directed, in greater amounts, into channels where a surplus of energy is made available, either for direct use in life, as house, as city, as regional habitat, or for storage against future vital uses. The benefits of automatic machinery, the economies of finely organized production, the displacement of labor, the surplusage of modern agriculture all mean—if they mean any human benefit—this release of energy for the direct service of life. Whereas under a pecuniary economy profit came through the expanded rôle of the machine, the biotechnic economy will be marked by a general contraction of the machine and, with balanced regional economies, a diminution of the importance of the world market: now to be reserved for surpluses and specialties.

But consumption itself, under a biotechnic economy, is not consumption anyhow, in any quantities, toward any purposes. Capitalism had no need to inquire into the quality or end of consumption: indeed its most ardent advocates during the period of intellectual formulation even defended the adulteration of foods and drugs in the competitive market, on the ground that to erect a standard of purity would be to do away with free competition. Under a biotechnic economy consumption is directed toward the conservation and enhancement of life: a matter where qualitative standards are imperative. One uses the word life in no vague sense: one means the birth and nurture of children, the preservation of human health and well-being, the culture of the human personality, and the perfection of the natural and civic environment as the theater of all these activities. Here are substantial goals for consumption not envisaged in the abstract doctrine of increasing wants operating within an ever-expanding circle of new inventions and multiplying productive mechanisms.

Against the wasteful duplication of mechanical equipment, the aimless productivity, the random expansiveness of production under pecuniary canons of success, a biotechnic economy erects rational goals: the best possible environment for human nurture and culture: the primacy of consumptive and creative activities over the instrumental processes: the denial of "success" embodied in the destructive facilities of war and the mounting certificates of debt which mark the prevalence of a pecuniary economy. But to normalize consumption is to erect a standard that *no single class,* whatever its expenditures, *possesses today.* That standard cannot be set down in terms of any arbitrary sum of money, like the five thousand dollars a year suggested by Bellamy: for it involves the use of a complicated civic equipment whose individual appropriation is beyond the scope of even wealthy individuals. And indeed, the higher the vital standard, the less can it be expressed adequately in terms of money, and the more remote it is from the operations of the market. Vital standards must be expressed in terms of leisure and health and biological activity and esthetic pleasure and social opportunity: that is, in terms of goods and environmental improvements in which machine production and all the devious and indirect processes that subserve such production have but a subordinate part.

In putting a vital standard first, we thereby make the dwelling house, the school, and the city the concrete, all-engrossing end of industrial and agricultural production. *The aim is not more goods for more people to buy, but more opportunities for them to live: hence only such increases in goods as are instrumental to "the best life possible."* Under such an economic order, communal choices become more important than individual choices, and more and more of the activities of the citizen's life are released from pecuniary constraint.

Until such standards are erected, planned production is merely a wishful abstraction, and none of the preparatory incidents of current production, however resourceful in a technical sense, can contribute more than a modicum of their possible benefits to the community. Fortunately, our civilization as a whole is now at a point technically where it is feasible to give the population as a whole that basis in good breeding and good nurture which has hitherto been the exclusive possession of aristocracies.

This, then, is the meaning of the change that has been slowly taking place in our civilization since the third quarter of the nineteenth century. The increase of collectivism, the rising of municipal and governmental housing, the expansion of co-operative consumers' and producers' associations, the destruction of slums and the building of superior types of community for the workers—all these are signs of the new biotechnic orientation. This change is so deep, so pervasive, that it can be witnessed even in places where the profit system, which is its antithesis, has reached a pinnacle. One can behold it, for example, in the budget of a great municipality like New York, which annually spends more on education than even on transportation or street cleaning; one may watch it at work in a country like England, which has been tearing down slums and planting new communities whose tiled roofs are deeply embedded in green trees and greensward. One saw it on a grand scale in Germany when, in five quick years after 1925, before the suicidal impulses of Nazism got the upper hand, one beheld in every department of life the outlines of a new human culture: a complete conception of the good life which put pre-Nazi Germany at the very forefront of modern civilization.

Whereas the pecuniary economy expanded the rôle of the machine, the biotechnic economy enlarges the rôle of the professional services: a greater proportion of the income and free energy go into the support of the artist, the scientist, the architect and technician, the teacher and physician, the singer, the musician, the actor. This shift has been going on steadily during the last generation: the tendency is statistically demonstrable. But its significance has not been generally grasped: for its result must be the transfer of interest from the subordinate mechanical arts to the direct arts of life. And it brings with it another possibility, indeed another necessity: the universal rebuilding of cities for the sake not merely of better conditions of living, but of a more purposive creation and utilization of the social heritage: such a life as men have occasionally had a glimpse of in Jerusalem, Athens, Florence, or Concord.

12: Modern Housing by Communities

As I have already pointed out, the dwelling house occupies a peculiarly central place in the biotechnic economy. About ninety per cent of the structures in any urban community are houses; so, from the standpoint of practice, an adequate insight into the task of housing today is essential to the development of cities. The socialized provision of housing, in integrated neighborhood units, is the economic foundation for the biotechnic city.

Today, even the finest urban dwellings of the last century are, for the greater part, obsolete. They were conceived in terms of a limited and now outworn mode of living; few of them, even by drastic renovation, can encompass our modern demands. As mere shelters they are sometimes sufficient; but as a frame for living, they are absurd. All our new needs—our desire to avoid unnecessary menial labor, our more conscientious and efficient child care, our recognition of play as an essential part of life from childhood onward, our acceptance of the need for quiet and privacy—all these create a demand for a different type of dwelling and a different communal form. In many ways, we have already crossed the threshold of a new age; but our housing remains behind, clinging to dreams that no longer satisfy, making a parade of sickly archaic tastes, attempting to meet conditions that no longer exist and failing to take advantage of conditions that do exist and promise far more by way of human reward. Even much of the new housing done by both public bodies and private builders exhibits only a stuccoed modernity over an obsolete form.

The new approach to housing is distinguished by the fact that it no longer looks for a satisfactory dwelling house in terms of a single factor—good planning, an isolated advance in technical design, a more socialized system of exploiting the land. For the dwelling is in reality a very complex adaptation to an exceedingly complicated set of requirements; and it is quite unlikely that any simplified solution, expressible in purely mechanical terms, will satisfy all the necessary conditions. What is important is to treat the geographic, economic, social, technical, and personal requirements on a single plane. Twentieth century technics cannot be fitted into laissez-faire economics and seventeenth century taste. Improvements must be made co-ordinately all along the line, and the most spectacular advance is no advance at all until it is integrated. To conceive of a pre-fabricated house designed in a civic and environmental vacuum is to conceive of something that is, by definition, half-baked, scamped, and inadequate.

What is a modern dwelling? The new home is primarily a biological institution; and the house is a specialized structure devoted to the functions of reproduction, nutrition, and nurture. To expand the definition a little, the dwelling house is a building arranged in such a fashion that meals may be easily prepared and served, that the processes of hygiene and sanitation may be facilitated, that rest and sleep may be enjoyed without disturbance from the outside world, that sexual intercourse may take place with privacy and a minimum of distraction at all times in the year, and that the care of the young may be carried on under favorable conditions of companionship and supervision.

None of these functions, needless to say, is restricted to the dwelling house. But the house, with its special utilities, is peculiarly adapted to perform all of them in unison with the necessary co-operative help of the members of the household. Add to these primarily physiological requirements the provision of space for social intercourse and play and study, and the definition of the modern dwelling is complete. Certain functions, domestic in origin, require more ample space or special facilities; these should be taken out of the house even further than they are today: childbirth and infectious illnesses, weddings and funerals, need their communal buildings.

What remains is an irreducible minimum. With the return of entertainment to the house, through the phonograph, the radio and the motion picture—with the near-prospect of television—*the modern house has gained in recreational facilities what it lost through the disappearance of many of the earlier household industries.* The radio and the telephone, moreover, have made the house no less a center of communication than was the old market-place. So if certain functions have diminished, others have gained; while our growing concentration upon biological functions in general has increased the importance of this institution in relation to all competitive activities.

As a well-distributed leisure takes the place of hopeless unemployment, it is probable that more time will be spent within the environs of the house in future than during the passing transition from the mixed household to the single family group. Now more than ever, the intelligent design of the domestic environment has become a matter of critical importance: it demands a sensitive, well-balanced judgment, capable of distinguishing between primary and accessory needs.

Now, in order to provide for the essential biological functions of the dwelling house, we must ruthlessly cut down on many conventional requirements. We must abandon, not merely the old-fashioned desire for "ornament" and conspicuous waste; but we must also shave down the modern desire for ornament in the form of wasteful mechanical gadgets. As Henry Wright, again, was the first to demonstrate clearly, the simple walls and roof and foundations of a century ago has long ceased to constitute the structural reality of the modern house. Most of what was added to the structure, before 1750, was by way of ornament. After this time a succession of mechanical utilities pushed into the house: the heating stove, running water, the bathroom, the kitchen range and the gas lamp, the water closet, the central heating plant and the icebox, electric light, gas and electric ranges, automatic systems of refrigeration and heating, aerials for radios, garages for motor cars; finally, in the present decade, Palladio's original suggestions for air conditioning have been converted into a costly mechanical fact.

These new utilities and machines changed the nature of the dwelling house in two important ways. They broke down its self-sufficient isolation and linked it up, with specially built roads, water mains, sewer pipes, gas pipes, electric wires, telephone lines with other parts of the urban environment: the house functioned as an element in a collective unit, and the efficiency of the individual cell was now conditioned on the efficiency and economy of the whole. Well-equipped houses, without appropriately modified community plans, could achieve only a small part of their mechanical promise.

All these improvements, furthermore, added to the total cost of the house; for whereas the bare structure constituted originally about ninety per cent of the cost, today this structure constitutes but twenty per cent; and even the total cost of the fully equipped dwelling, with all machines and utilities installed, represents from forty-five to sixty-five per cent of the final cost of the dwelling. A reduction of the interest rate by two per cent gives a far more decisive saving than either cheese-paring or pre-fabrication can promise.

If one assumes a stationary family budget it would follow that for each economic group a far greater proportion would have to be spent on housing in 1940 than in 1740. Or if one assumes that the proportional relationship between housing, clothes, food, and other necessaries of life remains fixed, then the total income of the family would have to expand greatly in order to cover the rise in the expenditure. The alternative is deficient accommodations: lack of space, lack of equipment. Up to the present, for the greater part of the population, modern communities have contented themselves with deficient accommodations.

One must grant that many mechanical improvements have still to be made: in general, the internal equipment of the dwelling has not yet been scientifically reorganized. The co-ordination of all the mechanical utilities in a central stack, as proposed by Buckminster Fuller, has now been adopted by various manufacturers of pre-fabricated units in America; and it is no doubt capable of being pushed further: an advance in economy as well as in mechanical efficiency. But though every such gain must be avidly seized, the act of rationalization does not solve the problem of cost that results from the multiplication of utilities and services: nor will it be solved by the further pre-fabrication of floors, roofs, and walls, although each and all of these steps may be decisive improvements. The reason is plain: the external shell of the house is by now the least important part of its total cost: and one might cut the cost of the shell radically without reducing the total cost of land, equipment, improvements, finance, *and* structure by more than a relatively small per cent. The real justification for advances in pre-fabrication is that the eventual product will be a better one than the old clumsy masonry shells: it will be capable of expansion and renewal and adaptation in a fashion that more antique forms are not.

In the modernization of the dwelling during the last century most of our mechanical improvements have remained half-baked. Hence what has been gained in internal convenience—warm rooms in winter, running water, diminished demand for domestic service—has so far been partly forfeited through decrease of spaciousness. Every solution of the housing problem that does not confront the facts I have just spread out is meretricious. The modern house, because of its nature, cannot be a low-cost house: the analogy with the economies of the automobile through mass production is extremely deceptive, and the building of trailer-dwellings, recently started in the United States, has fully demonstrated this fact. It is a false solution to build a dwelling so small that the psychological harmony of family life is sacrificed to economy of space. It is a false solution to economize by doing without a cellar, since either an underground storeroom, or an overground storeroom that will cost approximately as much, is a necessary convenience of family life: storage has a part in every economic process. It is no solution to cover so much of the land, because it is high in price, that neither the open spaces nor the sunlight are sufficient. It is as much a false solution to provide all the mechanical utilities that modern life demands and to fail to supply usable space of good quality as it would be to produce a bare eighteenth century shell and not to equip it with any of these mechanical aids: the latter house would be cheap—but it could not satisfy modern requirements for urban living.

Finally, it is a false solution to suggest, as Fuller and others have done, that a more mobile type of dwelling will solve our difficulties. This proposal assumes that it is possible to escape permanently the cost of social services, schools, hospitals, libraries, government, roads, by moving outside areas where these services are supplied, or by moving away when asked to pay one's share toward their upkeep. As a means of recreation, a way of returning to an irresponsible gypsy life, camping here, moving there, the mobile house or trailer may be as delightful to those who have the proper temperament as life in a houseboat, the aquatic form of the mobile house. But such a house is either temporarily parasitic upon the nearest permanent community, or it must lack those necessary social and cultural attachments without which one sinks to the level of a bargeman: the proposal otherwise idiotically assumes that a "self-sufficient" structure is capable of supplying a self-sufficient life. This does not actually hold even for sanitation.

Such a "solution" is doubly regressive because it attempts to de-communalize the house and break down every last vestige of associative and corporative life: whereas the deepest need of modern life is to re-integrate the organs of association by forming new civic wholes. In short, this mechanical escapism, as embodied in the trailer and the trailer camp, is one of those ludicrous examples of ideological mis-cegenation of which the modern world is full: the neurotic offspring of romanticism and mechanism: the housing problem solved by re-ducing it to the provision of bare shelter and doing away with those communal relations which spring up only through close association and permanent settlement.

The reason for the widespread backwardness of housing through-out our civilization is that no fundamental change is possible except by means of a communal redistribution of income. The slum is the outward expression of physical impoverishment: slum demolition is poverty demolition, or it is nothing. And by the same token, the building of houses fit for the nurture of human beings is dependent upon making production and distribution directly subservient to bio-technic standards of consumption, available for the whole community. Any real effort to provide housing must attack this central economic problem.

Hence the importance for community housing of an active trade-union and co-operative movement: the first to push wages upward, claim a larger share of the total product, and create an effective political demand for government-aided housing: the second to organize and administer the units built, focusing and interpreting the consumer's demand, acting as mediator between the official agencies and professional services and the eventual occupants: in some cases, as in pre-Nazi Frankfurt, administering the housing itself. The *educational* services of these organizations are no less important than their political functions.

13: The School as Community Nucleus

The most important fact about group life today is not the pervasiveness of the machine through our mechanical devices for manifolding, recording, and transmitting its signs and symbols: the significant point is that the heritage so transmitted becomes progressively functionless and meaningless, unless it is accompanied by a reawakening of purposive group life. For a city, in order to act the part of a city, is a field for the interaction of "temporal and spiritual powers," as Comte would have said: it is a concentrated socialized environment, where administrators and energizers, assimilators and creators, may react upon each other in a common sphere. A community that does not plan and build the necessary structures for the common life will remain under a perpetual weight and handicap: its buildings may tower against the skies, but its actual social stature may be smaller measured by effective accomplishment than a decent country town.

The church was the essential social nucleus of the medieval city. All its adjacent institutions were dominated by the church: at no point in one's daily routine could one forget its purposes or escape its ministrations. In the baroque city the palace was a similar nucleus: theater and concert hall and art gallery were part of its show: shopping parade and military parade were subservient to its mode of existence: industry itself was dependent upon the palace for privilege as well as patronage. In the paleotechnic economy, the same part was played by the factory; while in the metropolis the market in all its various forms, from the ribbon of stores on the traffic arteries to the banks and stock exchanges and brokers' offices, played a controlling part in the city's design, or designlessness. Each new dominant re-crystallized, in a new pattern, with different tensions, different ponderables, every other institution in the city.

What are the new dominants in the opening biotechnic economy? They are not far to seek: the dwelling house and the school, with all their specialized communal aids, constitute the essential nucleus of the new community. And as the new region is the city writ large—a statement that is not to be taken as mere metaphor—we shall find in every well-organized and well-developed region the corresponding institutions, no longer serving a class, a minority group, but acting as organs of the whole community.

In older cities, the domestic neighborhood, even when formed on the basis of some original village, had no physical identity: it is only verbally that it detached itself from the larger urban area with which it coalesced. Suburbs, indeed, usually began their existence with visible marks of unity and isolation; but except in the case of remote and fortunate ones, they would eventually be swallowed up in the spreading mass of the city. In the new city, a neighborhood has visible definition. Its size is determined by the convenient walking distance for children between the farthest house and the school and playground in which a major part of their activities are focused. Its pattern is determined by the need of isolating school and home from the noise of traffic and its dangers: so main traffic arteries of any sort must never run through a neighborhood: they may exist at its boundaries, separated for both safety and amenity by a broad parkway: whatever traffic filters into the neighborhood must be that which directly subserves it, moving at a pace that respects the rights of the footwalker. Even country villages today often lack this element of safety and freedom from anxiety.

While the school has become a universal institution, and the main symbol of the educational process, the instruments of modern education are continuous with life itself: no mere building can fully house them, and the notion of making education "economical" or "comprehensive" by creating megalopolitan buildings holding from 1500 to 3000 pupils, and then expanding the scale of the neighborhood so that it can bestow a sufficient number of children on these buildings may be dismissed as a typical megalopolitan perversion. A neighborhood should be an area within the scope and interest of a pre-adolescent child: such that daily life can have unity and significance for him, as a representation of the larger social whole: and accordingly a special effort should be made in the design of neighborhoods to incorporate in them those light industries which directly subserve neighborhood life. There should be a compact, orderly industrial zone containing not only a garage and filling station, but likewise a laundry and a bakery: perhaps even a small electrically powered plant such as a wood-working shop or a garment factory: examples of the industrial process which the child at school may not merely inspect and understand, but also, perhaps, take part in as an educational experience. The direct observance of all kinds of industrial processes in the open workshops of Athens no doubt gave to Plato and his fellow citizens that visual acuteness and that intelligent grasp of the processes of existence which accounts for the extraordinary production of able minds in a town that certainly never harbored more than three hundred thousand people. If in addition a neighborhood could provide a place for other types of activity—such as a plant nursery or a painter's studio—the educational value of the equipment would be highly increased.

The class education of the past and the narrow vocational education of the passing order are both antagonistic to the biotechnic concept of education as the extension and refinement and integration of human experience in all its manifold aspects. The cultivation of the senses, by visual and tactile explorations of the environment, the intensification and communal refinement of feelings in the group activities of sport, in the theater, where the spectator and actor may interchange parts, in the civic festival and religious ritual, above all in the relations of friends, lovers, mates—this is the essential *business* of life, and all other business is trivial except as a preparation and an underpinning to these experiences. The active routine and the orderly duties of workshop, factory, farm, and office are likewise essential contributions to this education: but so far from education's being ordered merely to prepare the pupil for assuming the economic responsibilities of maturity, it is no less important to order industry so that it will contribute to the maturing educational needs of its members. The real question at every step is not simply what one does, but what one makes of it. The workaday economic relations become significant only as they contribute to the better ordering of life itself; and as we pass from the regime of specialization to the balanced industrial and personal economy, more effort must be made to develop the flexible and many-sided personality of the amateur, rather than the vocationally narrowed capacities of the specialist.

In America, partly by shaking off the caste system, partly by accepting the challenge of the frontier, we achieved this type of living education before the full onset of the machine: we have now to recover it in a world that has need both for the machine and for the high discipline of science. But such a new integration cannot be worked out merely with the aid of a specialized institutional routine: the best of schools must remain poor in certain essentials even in relation to the poorest of cities. *Under the new biotechnic economy, the city becomes again, as it has often been in the past, the chief instrument of education:* the wider school of the young and the university of the adult; whilst the factory, the meeting hall, the political committee, the scientific society become, as it were, *auxiliaries* of the school. And under such conditions an important result must follow: the processes and activities of the school will tend to set a mold for the social process as a whole.

The training of the young is a major preoccupation of all societies; and the school was one of the earliest differentiated institutions in the city: but in earlier cultures, the fixed pattern and limited possibilities of adulthood were usually taken as given, and the process of education was essentially one of pouring life into a predetermined mold. Since the eighteenth century, however, the molds have been broken: the period of education and the period of experiment, instead of being limited to youth, must now range over every phase of life: only the grave brings the process to an end. Under the impulse of psychological thought and revolutionary political hopes, directed toward the rational improvement of society, the school has, from the eighteenth century onward, tended to assume a more critical place in the whole political order: from Rousseau and Fichte to Dewey and Croce, pedagogy and politics have gone hand in hand, and the main interest of public education has been to effectuate, through collective means and processes, a better political society.

With the growth of specialized machine industry, the educational opportunities of the extra-school environment, in the confused, amorphous cities that this regime has produced, have become more limited. And the systematic technics of the modern factory or office, while it promotes a rationalization of the process itself, de-rationalizes—that is, makes automatic and non-reflective—the conduct of those in charge of the operation. What happens in the economic world happens also in the play-world: the listener to the radio, the spectator at the motion picture, tends to be passive and machine-conditioned. The results have become familiar: a growth of irrational conduct in the very midst of a meticulous mechanized order and a decrease of what Mannheim distinguishes as *substantial rationality*.

In order to prevent this hiatus from becoming greater, the humanizing and rationalizing elements in human conduct must be more fully incorporated in the organization of both school and city; while the automatic and compulsive processes, already as pronounced in the factory and the bureau as on the military drill ground, must be reduced and narrowed. This means, among other things, the introduction of small units, scaled to direct activity and participation, in every phase of organization: giantism must be challenged and made to prove itself not merely as mechanically adequate but as *humanly assimilable*.

We need, in every part of the city, units in which intelligent and co-operative behavior can take the place of mass regulations, mass decisions, mass actions, imposed by ever remoter leaders and administrators. Small groups: small classes: small communities: institutions framed to the human scale, are essential to purposive behavior in modern society. Very stupidly we have overlooked the way in which large units limit opportunity all along the line: not merely by physical friction of space, or the burden of a vast mechanical and administrative overhead, but also by diminishing opportunities for people with special capacities. Thus Sir Raymond Unwin has pointed out that twenty communities with a population of fifty thousand people would not merely be more adequately governed, probably, than one city that contained a million: it would, for example, give an opportunity for twenty mayors or city managers against one in the big center. This rule holds true in every other part of society. We demand the impossible in the way of direction and specialized service from a few people, and we fail to demand the possible from those who are better equipped to handle adequately a smaller job. With our overgrown institutions, overgrown colleges, overgrown corporations, overgrown cities, is it any wonder that we easily become the victims of propaganda machines, routineers, and dictators?

From the nineteenth century on the criteria of life began to pene-trate the school, and the school became the essential instrument in effective orientation of society toward whatever ends its members and its ruling classes conceived. The most progressive school of the early nineteenth century was called a children's garden; and that of the twentieth century is called a nursery school: both of them are far removed from the older way of treating children as little adults. The school, indeed, in the modern sense, may be defined as an environment modified for biological and social development: an environment especially concerned with growth, which no longer treats the processes of growth as accidental intrusions on an ideal pattern.

Under the paleotechnic and metropolitan regime, the school had the duty of making the population responsive to print, skilled in arithmetic, and docile to external stimuli. Today the school has another task: that of making the community as a whole capable of controlling its destinies: capable of disciplining and making over every aspect of its activities, the practical and the instrumental, the personal and the communal. A large order: it puts the school in the central position occupied by the Church in medieval Christendom.

From the drill school to the organic school: from the child school to the child-adult school: from a desiccated environment to a living environment: from closed issues and mechanical indoctrination to open inquiry and co-operative discipline as a normal process of living: that is one series of steps. From the part-time school, confined to a *building*, to the full-time school taking stock of and taking part in the whole life of the neighborhood, the city, the region: from an education whose truths and values are in good part denied by the actual environment and the social practice of the community to an education that is integral with the demands and possibilities of life and that shirks no needed effort to make over reality in conformity with purpose and ideal: here is another series of steps that mark the path of modern education.

A great distance as yet separates the new from the old: no community has as yet fully traversed it; for it is not merely a matter of a new program, a new kind of building, a new attitude on the part of student and teacher and parent: it is a matter of re-harmonizing the practical and the educational needs of the community through a drastic re-building of the entire structure. If the new school is the essential social nucleus, which bears the social heritage, the surrounding cell itself, its shape, its size, its structure, its special components, are no less essential to the process of development.

The institutions that are accessory, as it were, to the school are the public library and reading room, public workshops, studios, and laboratories, and public dance-halls and little theaters. In America both the settlement house and the school itself have demonstrated how these various activities may be effectively grouped, often in a single building, for service to the whole population at every age level. Here again, *what distinguishes the biotechnic community is not the introduction of any essentially new institutions so much as their adequate organization and incorporation as an elemental, indispensable part of the whole.* Most neighborhoods, even where public housing has been achieved, lack more than the most rudimentary physical facilities for a good social life.

It is no criticism of these proposals to urge that they are beyond the financial resources of our existing communities, on anything like the scale contemplated. That is equally true of good housing: both points may be freely granted. In an industrial system devoted solely to producing saleable goods for the market, we have not produced anything like the surplus necessary for well-balanced consumptive and creative activities. That is an elemental truth of the present economic regime. Neglect, disease, crime, illth are in one way or another signs of this environmental deficiency and economic anemia.

So far I have been talking about the essential civic nucleus of the neighborhood. These institutions must be enlarged in order to embrace a city; and there must be further buildings and organizations on a regional scale. But although the ascent to the region implies differences in scale, size, specialization, and opportunity, the fact is that all the facilities that are needed within the larger frame must exist, as active ingredients, in the life of the smallest and simplest unit. The great university, museum, laboratory, serving an élite drawn from every part of the world, will have its counterpart in the local community. And at the same time, the breaking up of overgrown megalopolitan institutions through the multiplication of local units—as in the Metropolitan Museum and the Colleges of the City of New York—is a needful step toward urban integration.

The important thing is to recognize the nature of the civic nucleus, and the necessity of a civic economy. Industry must be planned to put domestic and civic needs first, and industrial enterprise directed into such channels as will produce that surplus of energies out of which will come the equipment and structures, efficient equipment, handsome structures, needful to urban existence. A well-directed economy will reduce the number of manual workers and robots, will lessen the enterprise directed toward competitive salesmanship and advertising, will eliminate wanton wastes and stoppages: and it will multiply by manyfold the present supply of doctors, teachers, administrators, artists, scientists, and scholars.

A biotechnic economy demands that those interests and activities that directly subserve life shall come first; and that those which are instrumental to life, the extraction of raw materials, the preparation and processing of foods, the transformation of raw materials into all their thousand useful forms, shall be put second. The quantity, the direction, and the flow of the latter are to be determined, not by the standards of the market, but by the higher needs of man, as confirmed from year to year, from generation to generation by the desires of the many and the wisdom of the competent. "Recreation, education, welfare, and health are the most rapidly growing urban public services," observed the National Resources Committee in its report on cities (1937). As our cities become the object of broader planning and design, these activities will occupy a growing share in the total budget of every community; and their effective embodiment will be the first task of architect and community planner and administrator.

14: The Social Concept of the City

Much recent housing and city planning has been handicapped because those who have undertaken the work have had no clear notion of the social functions of the city. They sought to derive these functions from a cursory survey of the activities and interests of the contemporary urban scene. And they did not, apparently, suspect that there might be gross deficiencies, misdirected efforts, mistaken expenditures, here that would not be set straight by merely building sanitary tenements or widening narrow streets.

The city as a purely physical fact has been subject to numerous investigations. But what is the city as a social institution? The earlier answers to these questions, in Aristotle, Plato, and the Utopian writers from Sir Thomas More to Robert Owen, have been on the whole more satisfactory than those of the more systematic sociologists: most contemporary treatises on "urban sociology" in America throw no important light upon the problem.

One of the soundest definitions of the city was that framed by John Stow, an honest observer of Elizabethan London, who said: "Men are congregated into cities and commonwealths for honesty and utility's sake, these shortly be the commodities that do come by cities, commonalties, and corporations. First, men by this nearness of conversation are withdrawn from barbarous feritie and force, to certain mildness of manners, and to humanity and justice, whereby they are contented to give and take right, to and from their equals and inferiors, and to hear and obey their heads and superiors. Also the doctrine of God is more fitly delivered, and the discipline thereof more aptly to be executed, in peopled towns than abroad, by reason of the facility of common and often assembling; and consequently such inhabitants be better managed in order, and better instructed in wisdom. . . . Good behavior is yet called *urbanitas* because it is rather found in cities than elsewhere. In sum, by often hearing, men be better persuaded in religion, and for that they live in the eyes of others, they be by example the more easily trained to justice, and by shame-fastness restrained from injury.

"And whereas commonwealths and kingdoms cannot have, next after God, any surer foundation than the love and good will of one man towards another, that also is closely bred and maintained in cities, where men by mutual society and companying together, do grow to alliances, commonalties, and corporations."

It is with no hope of adding much to the essential insight of this description of the urban process that I would sum up the sociological concept of the city in the following terms:

The city is a related collection of primary groups and purposive associations: the first, like family and neighborhood, are common to all communities, while the second are especially characteristic of city life. These varied groups support themselves through economic organizations that are likewise of a more or less corporate, or at least publicly regulated, character; and they are all housed in permanent structures, within a relatively limited area. The essential physical means of a city's existence are the fixed site, the durable shelter, the permanent facilities for assembly, interchange, and storage; the essential social means are the social division of labor, which serves not merely the economic life but the cultural processes.

The city in its complete sense, then, is a geographic plexus, an economic organization, an institutional process, a theater of social action, and an esthetic symbol of collective unity. On one hand it is a physical frame for the commonplace domestic and economic activities; on the other, it is a consciously dramatic setting for the more significant actions and the more sublimated urges of a human culture. The city fosters art and *is* art; the city creates the theater and *is* the theater. It is in the city, the city as theater, that man's more purposive activities are formulated and worked out, through conflicting and cooperating personalities, events, groups, into more significant culminations.

Without the social drama that comes into existence through the focusing and intensification of group activity there is not a single function performed in the city that could not be performed—and has not in fact been performed—in the open country. The physical organization of the city may deflate this drama or make it frustrate; or it may, through the deliberate efforts of art, politics, and education, make the drama more richly significant, as a stage-set, well-designed, intensifies and underlines the gestures of the actors and the action of the play. It is not for nothing that men have dwelt so often on the beauty or the ugliness of cities: these attributes condition men's social activities. And if there is a deep reluctance, on the part of the true city dweller, to leave his cramped quarters for the physically more benign environment of a suburb—even a model garden suburb!—his instincts are partly justified: in its various and many-sided life, in its very opportunities for social disharmony and conflict, the city creates drama; the suburb lacks it.

One may describe the city, in its social aspect, as a special framework directed toward the creation of differentiated opportunities for a common life and a significant collective drama. As indirect forms of association, with the aid of signs and symbols and specialized organizations, supplement direct face-to-face intercourse, the personalities of the citizens themselves become many-faceted: they reflect their specialized interests, their more intensively trained aptitudes, their finer discriminations and selections: the personality no longer presents a more or less unbroken traditional face to reality as a whole. Here lies the possibility of personal disintegration; and here lies the need for re-integration through wider participation in a concrete and visible collective whole. What men cannot imagine as a vague formless society, they can live through and experience as citizens in a city. Their unified plans and buildings become a symbol of their social relatedness; and when the physical environment itself becomes disordered and incoherent, the social functions that it harbors become more difficult to express.

Before man can become fully humanized, the social man must break up into a thousand parts: so that each grain of aptitude, each streak of intelligence, each fiber of special interest, may take a deeper color by mingling with other grains, streaks, and fibers of the same nature. The undifferentiated common bond of primary association is weakened by these specialized associations; but the cable of civilization itself becomes stronger through such multiform twisting into a more complex and many-colored strand. From simple con-

sciousness of kind in the tribe or family to the developed consciousness of kind that goes with special associations and differentiated
groups: from habit to choice: from a fixed mold to a dynamic equilibrium of forces, from taking life as it comes to comprehending it
and redesigning it—that is the path of both human and civic development. This transfer of emphasis from the uniformities and common acceptances of the primary group to the critical choices, the purposive associations, and the rational ends of the secondary group is
one of the main functions of the city. The city is in fact the physical
form of the highest and most complex types of associative life.

One further conclusion follows from this concept of the city:
social facts are primary, and the physical organization of a city, its
industries and its markets, its lines of communication and traffic,
must be subservient to its social needs. Whereas in the development
of the city during the last century we expanded the physical plant
recklessly and treated the essential social nucleus, the organs of
government and education and social service, as mere afterthoughts,
today we must treat the social nucleus as the essential element in
every valid city plan: the spotting and inter-relationship of schools,
libraries, theaters, community centers, is the first task in defining the
urban neighborhood and laying down the outlines of an integrated
city.

If this is the correct interpretation of the nature of the city, a good
part of the work that has been done under the name of city planning
must be discounted and discredited: it has no more to do with the
essential functions of living in cities than the work of the scene shifter
and property man have to do with the development of Hamlet. This
is not to deny its use: for scene shifters have their use: but it is to
cast a doubt upon its sufficiency. The planning of cities by those who
have hitherto called themselves city planners is like having the play
itself written by the property man, or mistaking the stage directions
for the lines of the actors.

Though our conception of the physical structure of cities during
the last century has been inadequate even in purely physical terms,
like the movement of people and the service of industries, people
have been even more wantonly inept in their conception of the social
structure and the social activities of cities. With their eyes on the

purely material changes that are so necessary, even those who have striven most earnestly for improvement have been content to build mere buildings. But buildings do not make a city; and the adequate planning of buildings is only a part of the necessary social schema.

From the standpoint of city design, the sociological theory of groups has a direct bearing upon plan. One of the difficulties in the way of political association is that we have not provided it with the necessary physical organs of existence: we have failed to provide the necessary sites, the necessary buildings, the necessary halls, rooms, meeting places: hence in big cities the saloon and the shabby district headquarters, open only to the more sedulous party members, have served. As for industries, the political opportunities for association have been even scantier: in how many factory districts are there well-equipped halls of sufficient size in which the workers can meet?

On this point one may well quote the Webbs. "We do not think it is usually understood," they observe, "how greatly the efficiency of trade unionism may be increased, and its very character raised to the height of a service of public utility, merely by the provision of structural accommodation equal in dignity to that of a government department, in which all the several unions in each locality may be worthily housed together."

The town meeting of the New England political system had reality because it had dimensions and members: the citizens met face to face in a special building, the town hall: they saw and heard their fellow citizens, and they discussed problems relating to a unit immediately within their grasp and vision. But the peoples of the Western World have sought to live under an abstract and disembodied political democracy without giving its local units any other official organ than the polling booth. We have hitherto lacked the energy or the insight to provide the necessary meeting halls, committee rooms, permanent offices. We have still to organize neighborhoods and corporate organizations as if the political functions of the community were important ones. In the conglomerate masses we have called cities, it is no wonder that political life, as a concrete exercise of duties and functions, has given way to various subtle parasitisms and diversions. And contrariwise, in new communities that have been planned as social units, with visible coherence in the architecture, with a sufficient number of local meeting rooms for group activities, as in Sunnyside Gardens, L. I., a robust political life, with effective collective action and a sense of renewed public responsibility, has swiftly grown up.

The moral should be plain: we must design whole social units: we must design *cities:* and in the order of design the arrangement of the essential social institutes, their adequate provision and servicing, is a key to the rest of the structure. It is on the purely instrumental physical services that we must practice the most stringent economy, even parsimony; it is on the political and educational services that we must spend with a lavish hand. This means a new order of design and a different type of designer: it means that that emphasis will shift progressively from the stage-set to the drama, and that the handling of the social activities and relationships will engage the fuller attention of the planner. In time, this will have the effect of reducing the instrumental arts of town planning to fairly stable routine, while a greater amount of energy and economic support will be set free for the expressive arts: painting and sculpture, drama and music, will again have greater importance than sanitation and sewage and the studious habits of antisepsis.

The elemental unit of planning, then, is no longer the house or the houseblock: the elemental unit is the city, because it is only in terms of this more complex social formation that any particular type of activity or building has significance. And the aim of such planning is not the efficiency of industry by itself, or the diminution of disease by itself, or the spreading of culture by itself: the aim is the adequate dramatization of communal life: the widening of the domain of human significance so that, ultimately, no act, no routine, no gesture will be devoid of human value, or will fail to contribute to the reciprocal support of citizen and community. When this drama is sharply focused and adequately staged, every part of life feels an uprush of social energy: eating, working, mating, sleeping are not less than they were before, but far more: life has, despite its broken moments, the poise and unity of a collective work of art. To create that background, to achieve that insight, to enliven each individual capacity through articulation in an intelligible and esthetically stimulating whole, is the essence of the art of building cities. And less than that is not enough.

15: Contrapuntal Organization

One more point about the social nature of cities. Reformers and renovators, whose work usually is prompted by some raucous failure in the social machinery, are tempted to oversimplify in the opposite direction: they seek a harmony too absolute, an order whose translation into actual life would stultify the very purpose it seeks to achieve. The student of utopias knows the weakness that lies in perfectionism: for that weakness has now been made manifest in the new totalitarian states, where the dreams of a Plato, a Cabet, a Bellamy have at many removes taken shape. What is lacking in such dreams is not a sense of the practical: what is lacking is a realization of the essential human need for disharmony and conflict, elements whose acceptance and resolution are indispensable to psychological growth.

When we seek a more co-operative order in the design of cities, therefore, we are seeking an order in which more significant kinds of conflict, more complex and intellectually stimulating kinds of disharmony, may take place: in short, we seek a contrapuntal order. Hence the need for plans and buildings that shall not remain frozen against the assault of change, the rivalry of new ideas. One can easily imagine, for instance, a new cult of family life, growing up in the face of some decimating catastrophe, which would necessitate a swift revision in plans for housing and city development: a generous urge toward procreation might clash in policy with the view of the prudent, bent on preserving a barely achieved equilibrium. Such conflicts may occur on every level; and the struggle they provoke is no less essential to the good life than the most affable co-operation. Hence the positive need for variety in urban life: varied groups: varied personalities: varied activities.

Communities that are so small that the essential differences between people and groups must be prudently glozed over, or so large that they cannot intermingle and clash without violent disorder, fail to provide the best environment for the development of human character. Fellowship is a good; and the Lynds do well to recognize it as an attribute of Middletown: a representative attribute, character-istic of other parts of the world than the small towns of the American midland. But good-fellowship is not the whole duty of social man; and some of the highest products of the spirit have been achieved, not out of small contentments, but out of great frustration, antago-nism, disappointment, bitterness: Koheleth and Isaiah, Euripides and Shakespeare, Dante and Machiavelli, offer testimony to the higher disharmonies possible in Jerusalem and Athens and Florence and London. Psychological growth is more important than somatic sat-isfaction; and in designing cities we must provide an environment broad enough and rich enough never to degenerate into a "model community."

It was perhaps his understanding of this vitalizing challenge of dissonance that caused Patrick Geddes to be more interested in the renewal of historic cities than in the fresh building of model garden communities; and despite the difficulties of overcoming the vested interests that oppose urban renovation in existing centers, it is pre-cisely here, perhaps, that we shall find the necessary stimulus to create the best type of community design: witness Amsterdam, wit-ness the magnificent achievements in Frankfurt and Berlin before Nazism came in. Enough, then, to show that the city, if it is to func-tion effectively, cannot be a segregated environment: the city with a single class, with a single social stratum, with a single type of industrial activity, offers fewer possibilities for the higher forms of human achievement than a many-sided urban environment. (As else-where, this holds equally true for the region.) If metropolitan dis-tricts have grown at the expense of smaller towns during the last generation it is partly because, *under a metropolitan economy,* this dramatically viable many-sidedness is to be found only in metro-politan areas.

16: Principles of Urban Order

In giving this sociological answer to the question: What is a city? one has likewise provided the clue to a number of important other questions. Above all, one has the criterion for a clear decision as to what is the desirable size of a city—or may a city perhaps continue to grow until a single continuous urban area might cover half the

American continent, with the rest of the world tributary to this mass? From the standpoint of the purely physical organization of urban utilities—which is almost the only matter upon which metropolitan planners in the past have concentrated—this latter process might indeed go on indefinitely. But if the city is a theater of social activity, and if its needs are defined by the opportunities it offers to differentiated social groups, acting through a specific nucleus of civic institutes and associations, definite limitations on size follow from this fact. Without such limitations the community lacks social focus.

Plato defined the desirable size of a city as 5000: this was the number of people who could hear the voice of a single orator and so participate in the active political life of his day. In our time, new technical facilities have altered many social functions: but the principle of limitation is still imperative. In one of Le Corbusier's early schemes for an ideal city, he chose three million as the number to be accommodated: the number was roughly the size of the urban aggregate of Paris, but that hardly explains why it should have been taken as a norm for a more rational type of city development. If the size of an urban unit, however, is a function of its productive organization and its opportunities for active social intercourse and culture, certain definite facts emerge as to adequate ratio of population to the process to be served. Thus, at the present level of culture in America, a million people are needed to support a university. Many factors may enter which will change the size of both the university and the population base; nevertheless one can say provisionally that if a million people are needed to provide a sufficient number of students for a university, then two million people should have two universities. One can also say that, other things being equal, five million people will not provide a more effective university than one million people would. The alternative to recognizing these ratios is to keep on overcrowding and overbuilding a few existing institutions, thereby limiting, rather than expanding, their genuine educational facilities.

What is important is not an absolute figure as to population or area: although in certain aspects of life, such as the size of city that is capable of reproducing itself through natural fertility, one can already lay down such limits. What is more important is to *express size always as a function of the social relationships to be served.* There is an optimum numerical size, beyond which each further increment of inhabitants creates difficulties out of all proportion to the benefits. There is also an optimum area of expansion, beyond which further urban growth tends to paralyze rather than to further important social relationships. Rapid means of transportation have given a regional area, with a radius of from forty to a hundred miles, the unity that London and Hampstead had before the coming of the underground railroad. But the activities of small children are still bounded by a walking distance of about a quarter of a mile; and for men to congregate freely and frequently in neighborhoods the maximum distance means nothing, although it may properly define the area served for a selective minority by a university, a central reference library, or a completely equipped hospital.

The area of potential urban settlement has been vastly increased by the motor car and the airplane; but the necessity for solid contiguous growth, for the purposes of intercourse, has in turn been lessened by the telephone and the radio. In the Middle Ages a distance of less than half a mile from the city's center usually defined its utmost limits. The block-by-block accretion of the big city, along its corridor avenues, is in all important respects a denial of the vastly improved type of urban grouping that our fresh inventions have brought in. For all occasional types of intercourse, the region is the unit of social life: but the region cannot function effectively, as a well-knit unit, if the entire area is densely filled with people—since their very presence will clog its arteries of traffic and congest its social facilities.

Limitations on size, density, and area are absolutely necessary to effective social intercourse; and they are therefore the most important instruments of rational economic and civic planning. The unwillingness in the past to establish such limits has been due mainly to two facts: the assumption that all upward changes in magnitude were signs of progress and automatically "good for business," and the belief that such limitations were essentially arbitrary, in that they proposed to "decrease economic opportunity"—that is, opportunity for profiting by congestion—and to halt the inevitable course of change. Both these objections are superstitious.

Limitations on height are now common in American cities; drastic limitations on density are the rule in all municipal housing estates in England: that which could not be done has *been* done. Such limitations do not obviously limit the population itself: they merely give the planner and administrator the opportunity to multiply the number of centers in which the population is housed, instead of permitting a few existing centers to aggrandize themselves on a monopolistic pattern.

These limitations are necessary to break up the functionless, overgrown urban masses of the past. Under this mode of design, the planner proposes to replace the "mono-nucleated city," as Professor Warren Thompson has called it, with a new type of "polynucleated city," in which a cluster of communities, adequately spaced and bounded, shall do duty for the badly organized mass city. Twenty such cities, in a region whose environment and whose resources were adequately planned, would have all the benefits of a metropolis that held a million people, without its ponderous disabilities: its capital frozen into unprofitable utilities, and its land values congealed at levels that stand in the way of effective adaptation to new needs.

Mark the change already in process today. The neotechnic sources of power, transport, and communication do not follow the old highway network at all. Giant power strides over the hills, ignoring the limitations of wheeled vehicles; the airplane, even more liberated, flies over swamps and mountains, and terminates its journey, not on an avenue, but in a field. Even the highway for fast motor transportation abandons the pattern of the horse-and-buggy era. The new highways, like those of New Jersey and Westchester, to mention only examples drawn locally, are based more or less on a system definitively formulated by Benton MacKaye in his various papers on the Townless Highway. The most complete plans form an independent highway network, isolated both from the adjacent countryside and the towns that they bypass: as free from communal encroachments as the railroad system. In such a network no single center will, like the metropolis of old, become the focal point of all regional advantages: on the contrary, *the whole region becomes open for settle-ment.*

Even without intelligent public control, the likelihood is that within the next generation this diffusion and decentralization of urban facilities will go even farther. The Townless Highway begets the Highwayless Town in which the needs of close and continuous human association on all levels will be uppermost. This is just the opposite of the earlier mechanocentric scheme of Roadtown, as pictured by Edgar Chambless and the Spanish projectors of the Linear City. For the highwayless town is based upon the notion of effective zoning of functions through initial public design, rather than by blind legal ordinances. It is a town in which the various functional parts of the structure are isolated topographically as urban zones, appropriately designed for their specific use: with no attempt to provide a uniform plan of the same general pattern for the industrial, the commercial, the domestic, and the civic parts.

The first systematic sketch of this type of town was made by Messrs. Wright and Stein in their design for Radburn in 1929; a new type of plan that was repeated on a limited scale—and apparently in complete independence—by planners in Köln and Hamburg at about the same time. Because of restrictions on design that favored a conventional type of suburban house and stale architectural forms, the implications of this new type of planning were not carried very far in Radburn. But in outline the main relationships are clear: the differentiation of foot traffic from wheeled traffic in independent systems, the insulation of residence quarters from through roads; the discontinuous street pattern; the polarization of social life in specially grouped civic nuclei, beginning in the neighborhood with the school and the playground and the swimming pool.

Through these convergent efforts, the principles of the polynucleated city have been well established. Such plans must result in a fuller opportunity for the primary group, with all its habits of frequent direct meeting and face-to-face intercourse: they must also result in a more complicated pattern and a more comprehensive life for the region, for this geographic area can only now, for the first time, be treated as an instantaneous whole for all the functions of social existence. Instead of trusting to the mere massing of population to produce the necessary social concentration and social drama, we must now seek these results through deliberate community planning and closer regional linkages. The words are jargon; but the importance of their meaning should not be missed.

One might call this new method of designing city and region in working partnership the principle of unity by apportioned distribution rather than unity by centralization: the latter means physical spreading and control from a dominant center, whereas the first means functional *spotting*. Any one part of such a complex may become, for a special purpose, the center of the region. But instead of existing merely as a specialized unit, it is part of both a smaller unit, the local community or "city" in the old-fashioned connotation, and of a larger unit, the region—and finally of even greater groupings with wider ramifications: provinces and inter-regional areas.

The working library in any neighborhood should be, for whoever is capable of using it, the sum of all the separate libraries: this principle has already been wisely incorporated in the development of the branch library system in America, and, even more, in the relation of the greater libraries that serve the scholarly community to the Library of Congress. So, too, with every other item of equipment: every service grades upward in functional and topographic specialization, from the smallest residential quarter to the planet considered as man's home.

What is important in this emerging conception is not expressed in the notion of satellite cities—not even of satellite garden cities. For, as the very word indicates, it assumes that one particular city will retain planetary proportions; whereas, from the standpoint of social relativity and social integration, one must conceive that each unit, though ranging in size from five thousand to fifty thousand, will have equal "valence" in the regional scheme. Before the metropolis can achieve a healthy, orderly life, it must boldly re-build its own internal structure as well as its outlying areas on similar lines. And for any particular function, the largest city in the group will often be subordinate to a smaller unit: what is significant is not the quantity of inhabitants but the quality of service.

These new possibilities in city life come to us not merely through better technical organization but through acuter sociological understanding. To embody them in plans and programs and to dramatize the activities themselves in appropriate individual and urban structures, form the task of the coming generation.

To describe the modern community one would have to explore in detail the potentialities of life for modern man. In brief, the care of those whose labors and plans create the solid structure of the community's life must be to unite culture in all its forms: culture as the care of the earth: culture as the disciplined seizure and use of energy toward the economic satisfaction of man's wants: culture as the nurture of the body, as the begetting and bearing of children, as the cultivation of each human being's fullest capacities as a sentient, feeling, thinking, acting personality: culture as the transformation of power into polity, of experience into science and philosophy, of life into the unity and significance of art: of the whole into that tissue of values that men are willing to die for rather than forswear—religion. The culture of cities is ultimately the culture of life in its higher social manifestations. Plainly, to carry this study farther, to follow through its implications for the personality and the community, demands another book. But the outlines, I trust, are by now evident and easy to trace out.

The cycle of the machine is now coming to an end. Mankind has learned much in the hard discipline and the shrewd, unflinching grasp of practical possibilities that the machine has provided during the last three centuries: but we can no more continue to live in the world of the machine than we could live successfully on the barren surface of the moon. Man is at last in a position to transcend the machine, and to create a new biological and social environment, in which the highest possibilities of human existence will be realized, not for the strong and the lucky alone, but for all co-operating and understanding groups, associations, and communities.

"Men come together in cities," said Aristotle, "in order to live: they remain together in order to live the good life." Only fragments of this purpose are fulfilled in the modern world; but a new pattern of the good life is emerging, partly by pressure from within, partly by reaction against the disordered environment, the wry, dehumanized purposes, the ugly barbarisms that still prevail in the world at large.

Already, in the architecture and layout of the new community, one sees the knowledge and discipline that the machine has provided turned to more vital conquests, more human consummations. Already, in imagination and plan, we have transcended the sinister limitations of the existing metropolitan environment. We have much to unbuild, and much more to build: but the foundations are ready: the machines are set in place and the tools are bright and keen: the architects, the engineers, and the workmen are assembled. None of us may live to see the complete building, and perhaps in the nature of things the building can never be completed: but some of us will see the flag or the fir tree that the workers will plant aloft in ancient ritual when they cap the topmost story.

GLOSSARY

Certain terms, originally coined by Patrick Geddes a generation ago, have been freely used in The Culture of Cities. For the convenience of those who have not read Technics and Civilization, in which they are more fully defined, the following definitions are provided.

EOTECHNIC. Refers to the dawn age of modern technics: an economy based upon the use of wind, water and wood as power, with wood as the principal material for construction. Dominant in Western Europe from the tenth to the eighteenth century. Marked by improvements in navigation, glass-making, and the textile industries, from the thirteenth century on: by widespread canal-building and increased utilization of power and power-machines in the later phase.

PALEOTECHNIC. Refers to the coal and iron economy, which existed as a mutation in the eotechnic period (blast furnace and primitive railway) but began in the eighteenth century to displace the eotechnic complex, and became a dominant between 1850 and 1890. Key inventions: steam engine, railroad, steamship, Bessemer converter, various automatic devices in spinning and weaving. Up to the last quarter of the nineteenth century the eotechnic economy remained as a recessive.

NEOTECHNIC. Refers to the new economy, which began to emerge in the eighties, based on the use of electricity, the lighter metals, like aluminum and copper, and rare metals and earths, like tungsten, platinum, thorium, et al. Vast improvements in utilization of power, reaching its highest point in the water-turbine. Destructive distillation of coal: complete utilization of scrap and by-products. Growing perfection and automatism in all machinery. Key inventions: electric transformer, electric motor, electric light, and electric communication by telegraph, telephone, and radio: likewise vulcanized rubber and internal combustion engine. At the present time, the eotechnic complex is a survival, the paleotechnic is recessive, and the neotechnic is a dominant.

BIOTECHNIC. Refers to an emergent economy, already separating out more clearly from the neotechnic (purely mechanical) complex, and pointing to a civilization in which the biological sciences will be freely applied to technology, and in which technology itself will be oriented toward the culture of life. The key inventions, on the mechanical side, are the airplane, the phonograph, the motion picture, and modern contraceptives, all derived directly, in part, from a study of living organisms. The application of bacteriology to medicine and sanitation, and of physiology to nutrition and daily regimen, are further marks of this order: parallel applications in psychology for the discipline of human behavior in every department are plainly indicated. In the biotechnic order the biological and social arts become dominant: agriculture, medicine, and education take precedence over engineering. Improvements, instead of depending solely upon mechanical manipulations of matter and energy will rest upon a more organic utilization of the entire environment, in response to the needs of organisms and groups considered in their multifold relations: physical, biological, social; economic, esthetic, psychological.

BIBLIOGRAPHY

1: Introduction

This bibliography contains mainly two types of book: the kind that will enable the reader to deepen and widen his knowledge of the subject, and that which, though not covering specifically the field of the present volume, has been drawn upon for special documentation.

Most of the primary sources come under the second head; but, while utilizing and including these texts, I do not depart from the conviction that a work of synthesis must rest mainly upon facts already gathered and critically digested by the relevant specialists: in other words, upon what, from the standpoint of scholarship, must be classed as secondary sources. Those who are suspicious of this foundation show a distaste for the function of interpretation rather than a rationally grounded distrust of the method. All general views are of course open to corrections, both as to fact and as to interpretation; and I cordially welcome such aid.

The main weakness, perhaps, with respect to material in a work like the present one is not its partial reliance upon secondary sources, but the unfortunate absence of monographs on many important subjects. This lack shows a failure of spontaneous interest or systematic direction in many of the fields covered by this book. There is, for example, no good comparative history of municipal government and administration, so far as I am aware; nor has it occurred to anyone, apparently, to write a history of municipal institutions which would trace the function and organization of each separate element in the civic heritage. Such a book indeed perhaps awaits the writing of preliminary monographs upon the historic development of the town council, the water supply, sanitation, public assemblies, and civic institutes, and so forth, on a scale comparable to the existing study of, say, the Museum. The lack of detailed knowledge on the place and duties and earliest appearances of the City Architect points to but one of many fields that needs to be turned over. The absence of detailed critical analyses of even the bare statistics of health, disease, and mortality in city and country is scandalous: meaningless non-comparable units, like nations, are utilized for such statistics, thus avoiding a concrete approach to important facts about the environment. Sociological studies, corresponding to biological ones, on the embryology, morphology, and physiology of cities await a new corps of investigators: present historic and geographic surveys are still largely in the fact-finding stage: deficient in analytic grasp. A series of interpretative studies of important cities, pushing even more systematically along the lines laid down in Poëte's monumental study of Paris, is badly needed. Most histories, even of cities, are pre-civic and pre-sociological.

Fortunately, the most important original sources for the student of cities are not written or printed documents: they are the cities themselves, and the chief use of a literature, perhaps, is to provide clues and answers for the problems raised by a field study of the urban environment. There is no way of abbreviating this first-hand exploration of the environment and the first-hand experience that comes from living and working in cities: indeed, it is partly for lack of it that so many sociological analyses of the city have been so far from satisfactory.

While the study of particular cities, through books and documents as well as personal survey, is indispensable to the serious student, I have found it impossible within the limits of this bibliography to include more than a few outstanding books: notably Davidsohn's Florence and Poëte's Paris. The fact is that the list of books dealing with even a minor town would often prove larger than the present bibliography. Each student should compile his own bibliography for the city where he lives, or for the place that most keenly attracts his interest.

2: Civic and Regional Background

Up to now there have been few general treatises on cities in any language: indeed the lack of important historic and sociological investigations on cities as such is equaled only by a similar neglect in the field of agriculture and the cultivation of the landscape. These areas have lain outside the major spheres of scholarly and practical interest during the last few centuries, during which scholarship often exhausted itself upon trivial pursuits, more easily pursued in the seclusion of the study or the vault of archives.

Because of a persistent civic tradition brought down fairly intact from the Middle Ages, these weaknesses have not been as marked in the literature of Germany as in that of other countries. From Nitsch and Wilda, Maurer, and Riehl, through Below and Bücher, down to the writers of the last two decades, there has been a fairly exhaustive geographical, historical, and even sociological interpretation of the *German* city: a study marked by a concentration which, though admirable, has the defect of its qualities—provincialism.

While the more recent sociological interpretation of Sombart, Weber, and Tönnies has not been wholly adequate on the civic side, they have at least kept the concept of the city alive: even during that process of centralization and de-regionalizing that followed the Franco-Prussian war and the complete ascendancy of Berlin: indeed, German civic tradition will possibly survive the drastic unifications and docile automatisms of the National Socialists. The civic initiatives of the great burgomasters of Ulm and Frankfurt during the latter part of the nineteenth century, as well as the revival of architecture, probably gave an extra stimulus to the scholarly interest in the past, as well as direct aid to the work of urban reconstruction. Though German cities show some of the worst examples of capitalistic land exploitation, the basis for the great urban renewal that took place under the Republic between 1924 and 1932 was firmly laid.

If Germany is perhaps foremost in urban historic scholarship, France has to its credit the best work on the geographic foundations of cities. Though Le Play, with his rural and primitive preoccupations, did not push his analysis as far as the city—resting content with the family as the fundamental social unit—the work of Comte and Reclus and Le Play, as well as a later school of geographers headed by Vidal de la Blache and Brunhes, supplied the scientific foundations of the regionalist movement—and contributed to the recognition of the individuality of cities and regions. The monumental works of Lavedan and Poëte are of first importance: no serious student of the subject can do without them.

3: British Initiatives

In the English literature of cities, one finds a gap of a century between Adam Smith, perhaps the last of the classic economists who understood the social function of the city and the economic rôle of the political functions and first of a new order of economists, represented by Ashley. Except as a mere political area, the city had no place in the utilitarian tradition; and the first great revival of interest in the city came from another quarter: that of art. Unlike the German Romanticists, the English school had been mainly hostile to cities, or at least indifferent to them, though one of Wordsworth's noblest sonnets was inspired by the view from Westminster Bridge. But the love for Gothic architecture finally spread to its urban surroundings; and in the writings of Ruskin, particularly in the Stones of Venice, the city as a social organism received its first analysis, retrospective but realistic. The treatment was minute and fragmentary: the focus of architectural analysis was the stones, rather than the pattern of the whole. But Ruskin, so often treated contemptuously as a superficial esthete, was one of the first to preach a return to fundamentals in the design of cities: mark his demand in Munera Pulveris and elsewhere for fresh air and clean water as elemental pre-requisites for urban art.

In the eighties Charles Booth, following Mayhew's journalistic studies, began his monumental survey of London: during the same decade Patrick

Geddes, starting as a biologist, began to bring together the diverse sociological traditions of Comte and Le Play: the work of these two men was decisive in supplying both a mode of investigation and a comprehensive diagnostic toward planning and development. Geddes brought together the geographic and the historic sides of the survey: more than that, he united the hitherto quite separate interests of the scholarly investigators of the actual urban environment and the practical aims of the sanitarian, the housing reformer, the municipal engineer, and the town planner, who had sought to make piecemeal changes in that environment without often understanding it as either a social or a structural whole. Geddes's interest in the city as a biologist, a sociologist, and a philosopher, and his practical example as an organizer of civic pageants and cities exhibitions, no less than as planner, was undoubtedly the greatest single factor in the civic and regional revival that has taken place in the British Commonwealth, touching places as distant as India where Geddes, between 1914 and 1924, planned some fifty cities. One must not however forget the initiatives of great English industrialists like Salt, Cadbury, Lever, and Rowntree, the pioneer work of important architects like Webb, Baillie-Scott, Mackintosh, Parker, and Unwin, the statesmanlike leadership of John Burns, nor yet the decisive contribution of Ebenezer Howard.

None of Geddes's thinking about cities was ever adequately embodied in a monograph or a book. His Cities in Evolution is his most viable work on the subject, while his Report on Indore, in two volumes, is the fullest published embodiment of his method, his point of view, and his sociological insight. Some of his cities lectures were taken down stenographically, and typescript copies, made and preserved through the fine initiative of his colleague, Mr. John Ross, are preserved in the Outlook Tower in Edinburgh. The work of Geddes, and that of his brilliant colleague, Victor Branford, if it has lacked a sufficient number of continuators, has nevertheless had a wide influence: Herbertson's work on regional geography was a direct result: so too the numerous admirable regional surveys from that of Doncaster onwards.

4: The American School: Sociological Approach

In America, there is a long interval between Henry Carey and the Chicago school of urban sociologists, which begins properly with Charles Zueblin, who in turn had been deeply stimulated by the work of Geddes at the Outlook Tower in Edinburgh. The intermediate link is perhaps Charles Horton Cooley, on the theoretic analysis of groups and communities, and the influence of Olmsted and Charles Mulford Robinson on the practical side, particularly in the Middle West, where so much of their work was done. During the last decade there has been a considerable ripening of this fruit. The tying up of urban sociology with the preliminary biological discipline of ecology has been a helpful one: note also the contributing influence of Wheeler's bio-sociological studies. American sociologists as a whole, however, have too often left the city, and likewise the village, out of account: even the ethnologists, so given to field studies, have ignored the specific pattern of the habitat: dealing with material objects like canoes or weapons or methods of making fire, but not with the camp or village as another type of collective artifact.

One of the great sins of urban sociology in America, apart from the injudicious use of irrelevant statistics, has been a failure to utilize the geographic disciplines: most conspicuous perhaps in the Lynds' otherwise admirable study of Middletown: least so in Carpenter's The Sociology of City Life. Another great lack has been an absence of comparative knowledge of cities both in time and in space: hence a tendency to limit urban studies to the American city, to the *contemporary* American city, and—final provincialism—to the contemporary *metropolitan* form, as if it were in a sociological sense a final one. Hence a failure to enrich the background of the administrator and the planner. Another weakness American sociologists share pretty generally with their colleagues in other countries: an almost chronic inability to grasp the elementary Aristotelian distinction between the conditions of city life and its purposes and emergents: which results, unfortunately, in a further inability to ask interesting questions about the specifically human and cultural attributes of cities. Hence a tendency to concentrate upon population statistics, police regulations, and methods of sewage disposal: hence a serious failure to deal competently or exhaustively with institutions, social complexes, and social-esthetic structures as such, in terms of their function and meaning as integral parts of the urban habitat.

Much valuable work has been done by Park, Burgess, Wirth, Ogburn, and others: but it is doubtful if urban sociology will be able to proceed much farther without making fundamental alterations in its frame of reference. Cultural ecology must not merely adopt the methods of plant or animal ecology: it must advance further by studying that involved interplay between the physical environment and the conditioned functions of life on one hand, and the social milieu and the released functions—in which choice, desire, fantasy, and purpose play a part—on the other.

5: The Eutopians

Some of the most important works on cities lie outside the period treated in this book, or are radically different in method and scope from the more systematic treatises that have so far been considered. In Western literature, Plato and Aristotle, as one might expect, said not only the first word on the subject but often the last; for one may look in vain for a better mythological

account of the rôle of the division of labor in human society—and its mis-
application as well—than in the opening dialogue of Plato's Republic. Aristotle's Politics is likewise still serviceable: all the more because his concept
of the future as potentiality is more valid for organisms and groups than
the more external statistical conception of future events that now is fashionable: hence the special province of eutopias in his political philosophy.

This great tradition was re-opened by the utopian writers, beginning with
Thomas More; and in a sense all the utopians, from More and Andreae
down to Fourier, Bellamy, and Herzl, have been better sociologists than
more influential abstract thinkers like Machiavelli and Spencer, just because the utopians had a place in their scheme for the city, as the concrete
embodiment of community. Among pre-sociological writers one must say a
special word for Raleigh, Botero, and above all, Stow.

6: Imaginative Literature

One whole class of books, and not the least important, is almost unrepre-
sented in the following list: that is, works of the imagination. Unlike the old-
fashioned historian, I have not left out these works of fiction because of the
curious illusion that they are not documents or do not refer to facts: for the
facts of the imagination belong to the real world no less than sticks and
stones do. There is, indeed, no better clue to what people see and feel and do
than what finds its way into contemporary poems, plays and stories: they
have a sort of veracity which court records, account books, and newspaper
clippings do not possess: for they contain, in an excellent state of preservation, the living man and so much of his environment as he could respond
to and express.

No: the fact is that here, as in the graphic and plastic arts, one is merely
embarrassed by the wealth of documentation. If the reader has not at least
read his Boccaccio and Chaucer, he does not know the medieval city; if he
does not know Mann's Buddenbrooks or Proust's Combray, he will not
appreciate how much of that city survived into the nineteenth century.
For a documentation of the paleotechnic town Nicholas Nickleby and
Hard Times are as important as Engels and Chadwick: at a later stage,
Zola and Arnold Bennett are no less significant; and for extensive grasp
as well as detailed insight into the modern city Balzac is incomparable.

To neglect this vast wealth of sources under the impression that one was
being rigorous or scientific would merely betray the fact that one's science
and metaphysics still belonged to the seventeenth century. I will go farther:
no one knows the life of cities as a social fact who has not drawn upon the
plays and novels produced by men who have lived in cities and described
the existence of their inhabitants: and this is particularly true since the seventeenth century, when the social novel itself came into existence as the sub-

jective precursor of a systematic objective sociology. The London of Defoe, Fielding, Thackeray, Dickens, Meredith and Wells (particularly Tono-Bungay and the New Machiavelli), the cathedral towns of Anthony Trollope, the St. Petersburg and Moscow of Tolstoi, the French cities of Stendhal, Balzac, Hugo, the Chicago of Dreiser and the Midland cities of Sinclair Lewis, to say nothing of the Boston and New York of William Dean Howells —all such imaginative works are important enrichments of the experience of the student of cities. And if I may single out a contemporary work of fiction for its deliberate and extraordinary grasp of every phase of the urban scene, I would specially commend M. Jules Romains' great panorama: Men of Good Will.

7: Cultural Interpretation

Among the cultural interpreters who have dealt with cities, there are two whose work stands out particularly in relation to the present book. For direct example and influence, the most important is W. H. Riehl, whose classic Natural History of the German People, published in the middle of the nineteenth century—and unfashionable because at once belated and too "advanced"—has been strangely neglected, even in Germany. My debt to Riehl, which I acknowledged in Sticks and Stones in 1924, is one that I wish more people shared. The other writer is Oswald Spengler, whose Decline of the West, that strange rubbish heap of atavistic notions and arresting insights, sentimental perversities and intuitive profundities, was one of the first historical interpretations to put the city in the center of the stage once more.

8: Theory and Practice of Regionalism

On the subject of regionalism and regional development, including conservation, there is a succession of classic studies whose influence, though immediately negligible, has had a cumulative importance: among them note G. P. Marsh's Man and Nature, N. S. Shaler's Man and the Earth, Van Hise's The Conservation of Natural Resources and Benton and MacKaye's The New Exploration.

One of the most brilliant expositions of potential changes in man's relation to agriculture and industry was Kropotkin's Fields, Factories, and Workshops: the work of a scientist who continues to grow in importance as a penetrating thinker no less than a humane personality. While Marx's ideology was mainly a paleotechnic one, Kropotkin had by the end of the nineteenth century emerged from that narrow mold to the conception of a neotechnic life-economy: his anarchist communism, which is now indigenous only in Spain, may prove to be the necessary corrective of the sterile bureaucratization to which Marxism has so easily lent its doctrines, both in its Stalinist and Trotskyist forms.

In developing the concept of regionalism itself, the reader will find many useful suggestions in Geddes and Branford; but apart from the French school already mentioned, the most significant work so far is embodied in two public documents: Henry Wright's Report on a Plan for the State of New York, published in 1926 under the Housing and Regional Planning Commission, with Clarence S. Stein as Chairman; and the report of Professor John Gaus and his associates for the National Resources Board on Regional Factors in National Planning. Both reports are approaches to the problem of delimiting and developing the human habitat: reconnaissance of fresh territory. Not closed solutions but new openings. In spirit and outlook, The National Being, by George Russell (A.E.) is closer to the central doctrines of regionalism than many treatises which make free use of the name.

The new school of American regionalists that has taken root especially in the South—I would call attention particularly to the work of Odum, Moore, and Vance—has transformed Turner's descriptive interpretation of sectionalism in American life into a dynamic doctrine of social development. Odum and Moore's new book on American Regionalism, which I have had the privilege of reading in manuscript, is an outstanding effort to unify a diversity of regional approaches.

9: Planning and Development

So far I have been dealing mainly with the historical and sociological literature. It remains to say a word about the field of planning in its many aspects. The literature of city development is an ancient one that goes back to Hippodamus, who according to Aristotle also projected a utopia: indeed, there has been a steady connection between the practical city of everyday life and the projection of utopias: from Alberti to Robert Owen, and from Owen to Howard and Le Corbusier, the ideal plans of one generation have become the practical realizations of the next.

On the actual planning of cities, the esthetic emphasis has long been over-stressed: within this field the best books are those of Sitte, Brinckmann and Zucker. Lavedan's Histoire de l'Urbanisme and Poëte's excellent Introduction à l'Urbanisme are outstanding works. The best comparative introduction is Werner Hegemann's two volume summary of the International Cities Exhibitions in Berlin and Düsseldorf, 1910-1912. A more recent survey of similar territory, that of Bruno Schwan, is useful but indifferently done. In English, Unwin's Town Planning in Practice was of first importance at the time of its original publication; but its re-edition in 1932, without sufficient attempt to deal with later developments and theories of planning, relegates it to a somewhat historical position. Schultze-Naumburg's study of landscape and cities and architectural forms in his monumental work, Kultur-arbeiten, is more or less oriented to the past: otherwise it is a model of the sort of work that should be undertaken in every region. For further visual background see Creutzburg's superb album of illustrations: Kulturland-schaften der Erde.

Many technical advances have been made in city planning during the last generation. One of the most important was embodied in a little pamphlet, Unwin's Nothing Gained by Overcrowding, which demonstrated the extravagance of past attempts at congestion, which wasted in expensive streets what was saved on building land. I am familiar with no work which has made an effective critical analysis of all these changes and improvements: on matters like orientation, Zeilenbau, cul-de-sacs, high and low buildings, dogmatic positions have been taken, or attacked, with little real critical insight: the nearest approach is the somewhat tangential one of Henry Wright's Re-Housing Urban America. By far the most important book toward advancing the new concept of the city was undoubtedly Ebenezer Howard's The Garden City, first published in 1898 as Tomorrow. Le Corbusier's original contribution on The City of Tomorrow was almost as economically innocent and as mechanocentric as the puerile fulminations of New York's skyscraper architects during the nineteen-twenties: but his later book, La Ville Radieuse, indicates an advance. In formal opposition to Le Corbusier one must place Frank Lloyd Wright's The Disappearing City: it represents the extreme possibility of decentralization under modern technical conditions. Most of the current technical books on city planning are attempts to codify past practices or to make small adaptations to new exigencies: their prescriptions must be taken with reserve: "good for this day only."

10: Housing and Architecture

In the smaller unit, the housing estate and the neighborhood community, there has been greater opportunity for unified practice than in cities as a whole. See Catherine Bauer's admirable Modern Housing, which is particularly good in its esthetic analysis, and which shows many plans and photographs of actual developments. A careful perusal of Henry Wright's Re-Housing Urban America is perhaps the best possible introduction on the planning side. Since the notions of coherence and contemporaneity have, from the standpoint of the present book, a particular part to play in all contemporary design, let me call attention to two books which deal directly with the esthetic and social problem of form: H. R. Hitchcock's Modern Architecture and Walter Curt Behrendt's Modern Building. Monographs on F. L. Wright, Gropius, Oud, Le Corbusier, and others should of course be consulted.

11: Importance of Survey

The chief documents about cities are secondary to the city itself as document. That demonstration owes much to Ruskin, though in the meanwhile the archaeologists, from Schliemann on, have shown how much of the past may be recovered without benefit of the written record. Even the original landscape is often preserved in the stones, like the brooks of London, long covered up or filled, but still persisting in streets or in place names. A keen reader of cities is aware of geology and climate as soon as he enters the city: the site selected, the conformation of the streets, the area of window openings, the houses preserved, the ruins left behind, all tell their story: while the traffic in the streets, on the river, in the port, the movements and gestures of the inhabitants, add their tale to the public document of the city itself.

The first survey of a city should be cursory and random: taking in what one sees and what happens in no particular order, with no desire to anticipate or to take pre-determined routes or to make "short cuts" which in fact serve to cut short the possibilities of fresh experience. One should first float passively in a sea of impressions. When this first process of saturation has finished, one should take every opportunity to become part of the city, even in minor ways: purchases in shops and markets, visits to homes if introductions or chance acquaintances make them possible, above all, some definite work, if that presents itself. Only after a general immersion in the urban scene, should one attempt to explore it systematically from the center outward, and from its periphery in the open country back to the core. Here camera, sketch-pad, and notebook may be used with profit. At this point one may usefully bring in guides and local histories, not to carry in one's pocket, like a plan or a map, but to consult before and after the journey or ramble. But Wordsworth's injunction should be remembered, all the more because it goes against the grain of purposive intellectual activity and our usual pragmatic sense: "Think you, . . . that nothing of itself will come, but we must still be seeking?" A wise passiveness is an important counterpart to intense activity: and research can never dispense with the need for contemplation.

12: Museums and Guides

The detailed knowledge of at least one city is indispensable to the student of cities: detailed and many-sided, amplified and expanded over the course of the years. To concentrate one's studies, once they have the benefit of a grounding in visual survey and first-hand experience, the student should consult local museums. Those at London, Hamburg, Ulm, Augsburg, Edinburgh, and Paris I have found very rewarding; but they can be matched in many other cities: even in America cities like New York, Baltimore, Salem, have a rich quota of material. Most civic collections, unfortunately, are badly assorted and often meaningless from the standpoint of urbanism: overladen with curiosities and antiques. Even when they use models and maps, the exhibits are usually arranged by people in whom a purely antiquarian interest as to fact is superior to a social and cultural interest in the processes of urban life. Much must still be done in the re-assortment and re-selection of city museum collections: much will doubtless be done in future as people of less limited interests appear in the Board of Directors and among the museum curators: for a good city museum would be an indispensable part of an intelligent city planning department.

As to guides, the factual surveys of Baedeker, Muirhead, Grieben and others are of course indispensable: in America the new series of guides gotten out by the Federal Writers' Projects, under the Works Progress Administration, and handsomely illustrated, are superior to the older type of guide in the richness of their sociological and historical material, and in efforts at regional interpretation: this is particularly true of the New England Guides so far published. Their one weakness so far is in a lack of city plans and layouts. As for the latter, modern works, even European, leave much to be desired: city plans are usually so small that the plan is crowded, and except for the general layout and disposition of the most important buildings, they are not very helpful to the student. Every city should have available maps like those of the British Ordnance Survey on a scale of one foot equals a mile, so that the occupation of the land could be surveyed in detail, supplemented by airplane views. Airplane mapping itself will make this possible; and the decennial, or better lustral, record of changes in the city should be part of its orderly record. Where such maps are available, the student will do well to make use of them. Among the Encyclopedias both Brockhaus and Meyer have excellent small scale city maps.

13: Photographs and Motion Pictures

One further aid to the student should be noted: the motion picture. The newsreels often afford interesting, if all too brief, glimpses of cities in action in every part of the globe; and now and again in a dramatic picture, something of the flavor of a city is well projected. Thus La Kermesse Heroique has an exceptionally fine background, quite veraciously portrayed, of a late medieval city of the Lowlands: though the play is a farce, there is a heavy underpainting of reality which goes beyond the costumes. Pabst's Kameradschaft, a moving drama of the mine workers of Germany and France, has all the dimensions of the fierce paleotechnic environment; and no one will ever forget the harbor of Odessa who has seen the great Soviet film of the S.S. Potemkin, nor the heroic face of Madrid after a view of the areas the Fascists have devastated in Joris Iven's film. These are but samples: a more adult art of the motion picture would, without resorting to the perfunctory and dreary travelogue, doubtless have much richer offerings in this department.

For certain cities there are photographic collections, private and public.

of great interest. The documentations of Paris by Atget and of New York by Alfred Stieglitz are pre-eminent here; while the illustrated sections of the newspapers supplement them from day to day—often with striking prints. In America the Federal Arts Projects of the W.P.A. have contributed a treasury of important photographs. The collections of commercial photographers are likewise useful: particularly in the records of the present generation. For an earlier period the lithographs and etchings and engravings, upon which I have drawn freely for illustration, are rich in historic detail: some of the important books containing these prints are listed in the bibliography. So much for the highlights. The following list, though selective, pretty well covers the ground. Wherever possible, however, I have left out periodical publications: the student will find the necessary references in special bibliographies to which I call attention, and in, of course, the Index to Periodicals.

14: List of Books

Abercrombie, Patrick: *Town and Country Planning.* New York: 1933.
> Brief introductory sketch (Home University Series) dealing with the various historic and contemporary aspects of the subject. Limited appreciation of the real advances made during the last fifteen years.

Abercrombie, Patrick, and Brereton, B. F.: *Bristol and Bath Regional Planning Scheme.* Liverpool: 1930.
> One of a series of studies—see those of Sheffield, East Kent, Deeside, Oxfordshire—done by Abercrombie in collaboration with various other people. Intelligent, well-rounded, with an appreciation of the intimacies of regional planning, the beauty of landscape and the variety of local life, often lacking in similar American studies. Recommended.

Ackerman, Frederick L., and Ballard, W. F. D.: *A Note on Site and Unit Planning.* New York City Housing Authority: 1937.

Ackermann, Rudolph: *The Microcosm of London.* 3 vols. London: 1808.
Select Views of London. London: 1816.

Adams, Henry: *Mont-Saint-Michel and Chartres.* Boston: 1913.

Adams, Thomas: *Outline of Town and City Planning; A Review of Past Efforts and Modern Aims.* New York: 1935.
> Chiefly English examples and precedents.
Regional Plan of New York and Its Environs.
Vol. II: *The Building of the City.*
> See *Regional Survey of New York and Its Environs.*

Addams, Jane: *The Spirit of Youth in the City Streets.* New York: 1909.
Twenty Years at Hull House. New York: 1910.

Addison, Christopher: *The Betrayal of the Slums.* London: 1922.
> By the Minister of Health who helped initiate England's great post-war housing program.

Addy, Sidney Oldall: *The Evolution of the English House.* London: 1889.
(See Lloyd.)

Adshead, S. D.: *Town Planning and Town Development.* New York: un-
dated.

Aldridge, Henry R.: *The National Housing Manual.* London: 1923.

Allee, Warder Clyde: *Animal Aggregations: A Study in General Sociology.*
Chicago: 1931.
Animal Life and Social Growth. Baltimore: 1932.

Allen, George Cyril: *The Industrial Development of Birmingham and the
Black Country: 1860-1927.* Illustrated. London: 1929.
Valuable paleotechnic data.

Allen, John W.: *A History of Political Thought in the Sixteenth Century.*
London: 1928.

Alverdes, Friedrich: *Social Life in the Animal World.* New York: 1927.

American Society of Planning Officials: *Planning Bibliography,* April 1935.
(Strictly land-use planning.)

Anderson, Nels, and Lindeman, Eduard C.: *Urban Sociology; An Introduction to the Study of Urban Communities.* New York: 1928.
Study of the physical and psychological basis of the modern city. Main frame of
reference is a narrow one.

Anderson, William: *The Units of Government in the United States. Public
Administration Service, No. 42.* Chicago: 1934.

Andreae, Johann Valentin: *Christianopolis.* Trans. by F. E. Held. New York:
1916.
A late-medieval Utopia, particularly interesting for its sidelights on actual conditions.

Annals of the American Academy of Political and Social Science:
Housing and Town Planning: January 1914.
Current Developments in Housing: March 1937.

Aristotle: *Politics.*
The Politics still repays close reading: for methodology as well as civic insight.

Armstrong, P. C., and Robinson, F. E. M.: *City and Country; a Study in
Fundamental Economics.* Toronto: 1934.
Unimportant.

Aronovici, Carol: *Housing and the Housing Problem.* Chicago: 1920.

Aronovici, Carol (editor): *America Can't Have Housing.* New York: 1934.
Short contributions by various authorities.

Ashbee, C. R.: *Where the Great City Stands.* London: 1917.
By an architect who was one of the leaders of the post-Morris arts and crafts
movement.

Ashley, W. J.: *An Introduction to English Economic History and Theory.*
2 vols. Fourth Edition. London: 1913-14.

One of the earliest, and still one of the best summaries in English on medieval guilds and cities.

Ashley, W. J.: *Surveys; Historic and Economic*. London: 1900.
Discerning discussion of the medieval town and its institutions in reviews of Flach, von Below, Pirenne, Maitland, et al., by one of the best of the English economic historians.

Atterbury, Grosvenor: *The Economic Production of Workingmen's Houses*. New York: 1931. (In *Buildings; Their Uses and the Spaces About Them. Regional Survey of New York and Its Environs*, Vol. 6.)
Record of early twentieth-century attempts to simplify construction of the shell. See James Hole for Victorian precursors.

Avenel, Georges d': *L'Évolution des Moyens de Transport*. Paris: 1919.

Histoire Economique de la Propriété, des Salaires, des Denrées et de tous les Prix en Général Depuis l'An 1200 Jusqu'en l'An 1800. 7 vols. in 6. Paris: 1894-1926.
An incomparable work of exhaustive scholarship: indispensable. (See especially Vol. VI, Book V, Chapters 5 and 6.)

Histoire de la Fortune Française; la Fortune Privée à travers sept siècles. Paris: 1927.
(See Chapters 9 and 10 on Prix et Loyers des Maisons.)

Le Mécanisme de la Vie Moderne. 4 vols. Paris: 1900-03.
(See Vol. III: *La Maison Parisienne*.)

Richelieu et la Monarchie Absolue. 4 vols. 2nd ed. Paris: 1895.

Baer, C. H.: *Deutsche Wohn und Festräume aus sechs Jahrhunderten*. Stuttgart: 1912.

Bailey, Liberty Hyde: *The Holy Earth*. New York: 1915.

Universal Service. New York: 1918.
Background books on essential regionalism by a great agriculturist who was also a poet.

Balzac, Honoré de: *La Comédie Humaine*.

Le Père Goriot. Paris: 1835.

Le Cousin Pons. Paris: 1847.
Two fine examples from *Scènes de la Vie Parisienne*. It was not for nothing, as Brunetière pointed out, that Balzac was a contemporary of Auguste Comte.

Barde, Charles. See Rey, A. A.

Barker, Mabel: *Education for a State of Peacedom Through Regional Study*. In *A Conference on Regional Surveys*. London: 1915.

L'Utilisation du Milieu Géographique pour l'Education. Montpellier: 1926.
Valuable exposition of the applications of Regional Survey to education as first carried out under Geddes in Edinburgh. (See Geddes.)

Barker, Mabel (editor): *Exploration; Regional Survey*. London: 1938.
Pocket size notebook, interleaved for notes, with schedule of points and questions for regional surveyors. May be obtained from The Le Play Society, 1 Gordon Square, London, W.C. 1. (See also Fagg and Hutchins.)

Barnes, Harry: *The Slum; Its Story and Solution*. London: 1931.

Barnett, Mrs. Henrietta Octavia (Rowland): *Canon Barnett*. London: 1918.
First-hand account of the first Settlement House.

Bartels, Adolph: *Der Bauer in der Deutschen Vergangenheit*. Second Edition. Jena: 1924.
Historic illustrations.

Bartholomew, Harland: *Urban Land Uses; An Aid to Scientific Zoning Practice*. In *Harvard City Planning Studies*. IV. Cambridge: 1932.

Bassett, Edward M.: *Zoning . . . during the first twenty years*. New York: 1936.

Batsford, B. T.: *Amsterdam*. In Batsford's *Pictorial Guide Series*. London: 1936.

Bauer, Catherine: *Modern Housing*. New York: 1934.
By far the best recent survey: main stress on European example, particularly brilliant on the planning and architectural side. Good bibliography.

Bauer, Catherine, and Stein, Clarence S.: *Store Building and Neighborhood Shopping Centers*. In *The Architectural Record*: Feb. 1934.
Important: demonstrates vicious economic mischief of over-building and bad design.

Beaufoy, Samuel Leslie: *Six Aspects of Town Planning*. London: 1932.

Bechtel, Heinrich: *Wirtschaftsstil des Deutschen Spätmittelalters*. München: 1930.
Valuable.

Beeson, E. W.: *Port Sunlight; The Model Village of England*. New York: 1911.
Entirely photographs.

Behrendt, Walter Curt: *Die einheitliche Blockfront als Raumelement im Stadtbau; Ein Beitrag zur Stadtbaukunst der Gegenwart*. Illustrated. Berlin: 1911.

Die Holländische Stadt. Berlin: 1928.
Rich in insight and illustrations.

Der Kampf um den Stil im Kunstgewerbe und in der Architektur. Stuttgart: 1920.
Historical and critical interpretation of the modern attempt to achieve form in the industrial arts and architecture. Wide European and American reference, on the social as well as the esthetic foundations.

Der Sieg des Neuen Baustils. Stuttgart: 1927.

Modern Building; Its Nature, Problems and Forms. New York: 1937.
Excellent critical interpretation.

Bellamy, Edward: *Looking Backward: 2000-1887*. First Edition. Boston: 1888. New Edition. Boston: 1931.
Partial anticipations of neotechnic urban organization (mechanical).

Beloch, J.: *Antike und Moderne Groszstädte*. In *Zeitschrift für Sozialwissenschaften*. Breslau: 1898.

Below, Georg Anton Hugo von: *Das ältere Deutsche Städtewesen und Bürger-tum.* (In *Monographien zur Weltgeschichte,* Vol. VI.) Bielefeld: 1898.

Die Enstehung des modernen Kapitalismus und die Hauptstädte. In *Schmollers Jahrbuch.* Vol. 43, pt. 1. München: 1919.
Keen criticism of Sombart's position in his second edition.

Mittelalterliche Stadtwirtschaft und gegenwärtige Kriegswirtschaft. In *Kriegswirtschaftliche Zeitfragen.* Vol. 10. Tübingen: 1917.

Aus Sozial- und Wirtschaftsgeschichte; Gedächtnisschrift für Georg von Below. Stuttgart: 1928.
(See Essays by Häpke and Schneider.)

Territorium und Stadt. In *Historische Bibliothek.* Bd. 11. München: 1900.

Der Ursprung der deutschen Stadtverfassung. Düsseldorf: 1892.
Below's contributions to the legal and historic foundations of the modern city are important.

Bemis, A. F.: *The Evolving House.* 3 vols. Cambridge: 1933-36.

   Vol. I. *A History of the Home* (In Collaboration with John Burchard II).

   Vol. II. *The Economics of Shelter.*

   Vol. III. *Rational Design.*
The first work on this subject with any pretenses to completeness. Unfortunately, the treatment of the house as an isolated detachable unit, without reference to community, leads to emphasis on only one type, and to the ignoring of important historic material. Vol. II useful for its data on cost, but, like Vol. I, inadequate in its treatment of the communal complex. (See Wright, Henry: Re-Housing Urban America.)

Benians, Sylvia Mary: *From Renaissance to Revolution.* London: 1923.

Benson, Edwin: *Life in a Medieval City: Illustrated by York in the XV Century.* London: 1920.
Compact Summary. (See Green, A. S.)

Berlage, H. P.: *L'Art et la Société.* Brussels: 1914.

Bernan, Walter (pseudonym, see Robert Meikleham).

Berty, A., and Legrand, H.: *Topographie Historique de Vieux Paris.* 6 vols. 1866-97.

Besant, Walter: *Westminster.* London: 1895.
Short historic summary. See many other volumes by same author on various aspects of London.

Bird, Charles S., Jr., Chairman: *Town Planning for Small Communities.* Walpole Town Planning Committee, Walpole, Mass. (National Municipal League Series.) New York: 1917.

Black, Russell V., and Black, Mary Hedges: *Planning for the Small American City.* Chicago: 1933.

Blanchard, Raoul: *Une Methode de Géographie Urbaine.* In *La Vie Urbaine.* October 12, 1922.

Boardman, Philip L.: *Esquisse de l'Œuvre éducatrice de Patrick Geddes.* Montpellier: 1936.
Interesting doctor's thesis on Geddes's educational ideas. See Barker, Mabel.

Boissonnade, Prosper Marie: *Life and Work in Medieval Europe: Fifth to Fifteenth Centuries.* New York: 1927.

Bookwalter, John: *Rural Versus Urban; Their Conflict and Its Causes: a Study of the Conditions Affecting Their Natural and Artificial Relations.* New York: 1911.

Booth, Charles: *Life and Labor in London.* Seventeen vols. Begun 1889. London: 1902.
A monumental survey, exhaustive in details, but as difficult to grasp as a whole as the city it describes.

Botero, Giovanni: *A Treatise Concerning the Causes of the Magnificence and Greatness of Cities.* Trans. London: 1606.
Revealing.

Botkin, Benjamin Albert, editor: *Folk-Say; a Regional Miscellany.* Norman, Oklahoma: 1929-32.
Miscellany of contemporary material by and about the folk, by one of the leaders of the new cultural regionalism of the Middle West.

Brandt, Jürgen: *Landesplanung.* In *Deutscher Verein für Wohnungsreform: Schriften.* Berlin: 1929.

Branford, Benchara: *A New Chapter in the Science of Government.* London: 1919.

Branford, Victor. *The Drift to Revolution.* London: 1919.
One of the *Papers for the Present* that Branford edited. Brilliant.
Interpretations and Forecasts: A Study of Survivals and Tendencies in Contemporary Society. New York: 1914.
On the Calculation of National Resources. In *Journal of Royal Statistical Society.* Sept. 30, 1901.
Science and Sanctity. London: 1923.
Branford's most important book: uneven, but full of penetrating sociological insights.
Sociological View of Westminster. In *Sociological Review:* July 1930.

Branford, Victor (editor): *The Coal Crisis and the Future: A Study of Social Disorders and Their Treatment.* London: 1926.
Coal—Ways to Reconstruction. London: 1926.

Branford, Victor, and Geddes, Patrick: *The Coming Polity.* London: 1917.
Our Social Inheritance. London: 1919.
Branford's chapter on Westminster full of insight.

Bredius, Abraham, and others: *Amsterdam in de Zeventiende Eeuw.* 3 vols. 's Gravenhage: 1897-1904.

Breton, Nicholas: *The Court and the Country*. London: 1618 (see Hazlett, W. C.).

Briggs, Martin S.: *Rusticus; or the Future of the Countryside*. London: 1927.

Brinckmann, A. E.: *Deutsche Stadtbaukunst in der Vergangenheit*. Second revised edition. Frankfurt-am-Main: 1921.
Excellent discussion of esthetic elements of city building with many admirable German examples.

Plastik und Raum; als Grundformen künstlicher Gestaltung. München: 1922.

Platz und Monument. Berlin: 1908.

Stadtbaukunst des achtzehnten Jahrhunderts. Berlin: 1914.

Brooks, Evelyn C., and Brooks, L. M.: *A Decade of Planning Literature*. In *Social Forces:* Mar. 1934.

Brun, L. Charles: *Le Régionalisme*. Paris: 1911.
Good.

Brunhes, Jean: *Human Geography*. Trans. New York: 1920.
Excellent.

Bryan, P. W.: *Man's Adaptation of Nature*. New York: 1934.
Good summary. Unfortunately already out of print.

Bücher, Karl: *Die Bevölkerung von Frankfurt am Main in XIV. und XV. Jahrhundert*. Tübingen: 1886.
Occupational statistics, as well as general ones. Important as an introduction to early municipal statistics in general.

Die Entstehung der Wirtschaft. 2 vols. Tübingen: 1919-20.

Die Grosstadt; Vorträge und Aufsätze zur Städteausstellung. Dresden: 1903.

Buckingham, James Silk: *National Evils and Practical Remedies*. London: 1849.
Contains plans for a model town.

Buer, Mabel Craven: *Health, Wealth & Population in the Early Days of the Industrial Revolution*. London: 1926.
False picture of medieval sanitation, and misleading in interpretation of later paleotechnic industry, but useful on its own ground.

Burchard II, John: See Bemis and Burchard: *Evolving House*.

Burckhardt, Jacob: *The Civilization of the Renaissance in Italy*. Translated from Fifteenth Edition. New York: 1929.
Still suggestive, though no longer an adequate total view of the period.

Burgess, E. W. (editor) : *The Urban Community*. Chicago: 1926.
See also Park, Robert E.

Butler, Edward Cuthbert: *Benedictine Monachism*. London: 1919.

Cacheux, Emile: *Habitations Ouvrières*. Laval: 1882.

Cacheux, Emile: *Etat des Habitations Ouvrières à la Fin du XIXe Siècle.*
Paris: 1891.
Highly useful documentation of evils and remedies.

Cadoux, G.: *La Vie des Grandes Capitales; Études Comparatives sur Londres—Paris—Berlin—Vienne—Rome.* 2nd ed. Paris: 1913.
On water and transportation.

Campbell, Argyll, and Hill, Leonard: *Health and Environment.* London:
1925 (IV, V).
So far one of the best books on a subject still insufficiently explored, though Hippocrates was aware of its importance. See Sydenstricker.

Carden, Robert Walter: *The City of Genoa.* London: 1908.

Carne, Elizabeth T.: *Country Towns; and the Place They Fill in Modern
Civilization.* London: 1868.

Carpenter, Niles: *The Sociology of City Life.* New York: 1931.
A comprehensive text book of city life, limited historically by the fact that its main reference is to Rome. Also draws too heavily upon the limited area of contemporary American cities, while its few references to the medieval city are misleading. Nevertheless relatively satisfactory. See Anderson and Lindemann; also Gist and Halbert.

Carr-Saunders, A. M.: *The Population Problem; A Study in Human Evolution.* Oxford: 1922.

Carr-Saunders, A. M., and Jones, D. C.: *The Social Structure of England
and Wales.* London: 1927.

Castiglione, Baldessare: *The Book of the Courtier.* Venice: 1528. Trans.
New York: 1901.

Cerdá, Ildefonso: *Teoría General de la Urbanización.* Madrid: 1867.

Chadwick, Edwin: *Report on the Sanitary Condition of the Labouring Population of Great Britain.* London: 1842.
A classic summary of paleotechnic horrors.

Chadwick, Edwin (ed. Richardson, B. W.): *The Health of Nations.* 2 vols.
London: 1887.
Summaries and extracts of Chadwick's numerous papers.

Chambless, Edgar: *Roadtown.* New York: 1910.
An attempt "to lay the modern skyscraper on its side" and run the elevators and pipes in continuous line across country. What was valid in Chambless' proposal was later embodied in Zeilenbau schemes *divorced* from the corridor avenue. The scheme has been independently revived recently in England. A classic example of the non-sociological approach. See also Kern.

Chancellor, Edwin Beresford: *The Pleasure Haunts of London During Four
Centuries.* New York: 1925.
Full of valuable data.

Chapman, Harry: *Town and Regional Development: A Guide to the Town
and Country Planning Act, 1932.* London: 1933.

Chase, Stuart: *The Nemesis of American Business.* New York: 1931.
See chapter on The Future of the Great City.

Chase, Stuart: *Rich Land Poor Land; A Study of Waste in the Natural Re-sources of America.* New York: 1936.
Recommended. See also Sears.

Cheney, Sheldon: *New World Architecture.* New York: 1930.

Chroniken der deutschen Städte vom 14. bis ins 16. Jahrhundert. Lübeck.
5 vols. Transcription of Original Chronicles, edited by Historical Com-mission of Royal Academy of Science, München. Leipzig: 1884-1911.
There are equally voluminous chronicles for other cities.

Clapham, John Harold: *An Economic History of Modern Britain.* 2 vols.
Cambridge: 1930-32.
Comprehensive: with an underlying desire to offset the long tale of horrors that contemporary documents—and later interpreters like the Hammonds—reveal. Use-ful as a corrective to black one-sided accounts: but itself one-sided in its studious optimism.

Clark, Frederick P., and Woodruff, Joseph T.: *Progress Report to the Na-tional Resources Board on the Making of a Plan for New England.*
Boston: 1934.

Clark, Victor Selden: *History of Manufactures in the United States (1607-1928).* 3 vols. New York: 1929.

Clarke, Maude Violet: *The Medieval City State; An Essay on Tyranny and Federation in the Later Middle Ages.* London: 1926.
Useful study in a field that will repay further efforts in scholarly analysis.

Cleveland, Frederick A., and others: *Modern Scientific Knowledge of Na-ture, Man, and Society.* New York: 1929.
(See Chapter by L. L. Bernard.)

Cobden-Sanderson, T. J., and others: *Art and Life; and the Building and Decoration of Cities.* London: 1897.
Excellent expression of original Arts and Crafts movement, which had a strong influence on Unwin and the Garden City. See Lethaby.

Cohen-Portheim, Paul: *The Spirit of London.* London: 1935.
Admirably done portrait of contemporary London. See Rasmussen.

Commelin, Caparus: *Beschrijvinge van Amsterdam.* 2 vols. Amsterdam: 1693-94.

Committee on Community Planning of American Institute of Architects: *Reports.* New York: 1924, 5, 6, 7.
Attempts by group of leading American architects, including Stein, Wright, Acker-man, Bigger, to redefine the position of the architect in relation to community and city planning.

Considérant, Victor P.: *Description du Phalanstère et Considerations So-ciales sur l'Architectonique.* Paris: 1848.

Conway, William Martin: *Literary Remains of Albrecht Dürer.* Cambridge: 1889.

Cooley, C. H.: *Social Organization.* New York: 1909.

Cooley, C. H.: *Human Nature and the Social Order.* Revised Ed. New York: 1922.
Important books by perhaps the wisest of American Sociologists.

Corey, Lewis: *Land Speculation.* In *Encyclopedia of Social Sciences.*

Cornish, Vaughan: *The Great Capitals.* London: 1923.
Interesting essays in historical geography, with minor emphasis upon the physical shell.

National Parks, and the Heritage of Scenery. London: 1930.
Pleas for esthetic conservation of the landscape.

The Scenery of England; a Study of Harmonious Grouping in Town and Country. London: 1932.

Cosgrove, John Joseph: *History of Sanitation.* Pittsburgh: 1909.
Faute de mieux. The subject should long ago have been thoroughly canvassed by historians. See Feldhaus, Thorndyke, and Van der Bent.

Coulanges, Numa Denis Fustel de: *La Cité Antique.* 8 Ed. Paris: Trans. Boston: 1874.

Coulton, George Gordon: *Art and the Reformation.* New York: 1928.

The Medieval Village. Cambridge: 1925.
Does not deal with layout or physical character.

Cowper, Joseph M. (editor): *The Select Works of Robert Crowley.* London: 1872.

Creutzburg, Nikolaus: *Kultur im Spiegel der Landschaft; Das Bild der Erde in seiner Gestaltung durch den Menschen; Ein Bilderatlas.* Leipzig: 1930.
Magnificent picture book which should be part of every planner's background.

Crowley, Robert: See Cowper.

Crozet, R.: *Une Ville Neuve du XVIe Siècle; Vitry-le-François.* In *La Vie Urbaine.* August and October 1923.

Cunningham, William: *An Essay on Western Civilization in Its Economic Aspects.* 2 vols. New York: 1913.

Davidge, W. R., and Warren, Herbert (editors): *Decentralisation of Population and Industry; a New Principle in Town Planning.* London: 1930.
Excellent re-statement in terms of modern needs and opportunities of Howard's original garden city thesis, by various eminent British authorities.

The Growth of English Industry and Commerce During the Early and Middle Ages. 3 vols. First Ed. Cambridge: 1882.
Classic study with important references to village and town life.

Davidsohn, Robert: *Geschichte von Florenz.* 4 vols. in 8. Berlin: 1896-1927.
An exhaustive study.

Defoe, Daniel: *The Complete English Tradesman.* Fourth Ed. London: 1738.
Also 2 vols. London: 1726-32.
Invaluable. Sombart draws on it.

De Forest, Robert Weeks and Veiller, Lawrence: *The Tenement House Problem.* 2 vols. New York: 1903.

Study of the rise of the tenement in New York City and the movement for reform. For more comprehensive later study see Ford, James.

Defries, Amelia: *The Interpreter Geddes.* London: 1927.
Not a satisfactory exposition of the man and his thought; but with some recorded flashes.

Dehio, Georg Gottfried: *Geschichte der Deutschen Kunst.* 4 vols. of text and 4 vols. of plates. Leipzig: 1919-1934.
Deals thoroughly with individual works of art and architecture; but is now somewhat dated by the absence of reference to the social complex and the collective form that condition the individual structure.

Delano, Frederic A.: *A Proposed Housing Policy.* In *American City:* Jan. 1937.

Dickens, Charles: *Hard Times.* London: 1854.
Classic picture of the paleotechnic town, with archetypal characters of Gradgrind, Bounderby, and M'Choakumchild.

Sketches by Boz. London: 1836.
Here and in his later sketches Dickens left many invaluable impressions of London. See Mayhew.

Diedrichs, Eugen: *Deutsches Leben in der Vergangenheit in Bildern; Ein Atlas mit 1760 Nachbildungen.* 2 vols. Jena: 1908.
Graphic history of German social life: immensely rewarding to those who can read images as well as letters.

Dieffenbacher, J.: *Deutsches Leben im 12. und 13. Jahrhundert.* In *Sammlung Göschen.* Leipzig: 1907.

Dikansky, Mikhail: *La Ville Moderne.* Paris: 1927.
Considers the city solely from the standpoint of physical circulation.

Dixon, Roland B.: *The Building of Cultures.* New York: 1928.

Dodd, George: *Days at the Factories; or, the Manufacturing Industry of Great Britain Described; Series I: London.* London: 1843.

Dominian, Leon: *The Frontiers of Language and Nationality in Europe.* New York: 1917.

Dopsch, Alfons: *The Economic and Social Foundations of European Civilization.* Wien: 1923-4. Trans. New York: 1937.
Reinterpretation of so-called Dark Ages, emphasizing element of continuity.

Dorau, Herbert B., and Hinman, A. G.: *Urban Land Economics.* New York: 1928.
Comprehensive but conventional. See Hurd.

Douglass, Harlan Paul: *The Little Town; Especially in Its Rural Relationships.* New York: 1919.

The Suburban Trend. New York: 1925.

Dubash, Peshoton S. G.: *Hygiene of Town Planning and Vegetation.* London: 1919.

Dublin, Louis I.: *Health and Wealth.* New York: 1928.

Du Camp, Maxime: *Paris; ses Organes, ses Fonctions et sa Vie; Dans la Seconde Moitié du 19e Siècle.* Sixth Ed. 6 vols. Paris: 1875.
One of the few comprehensive but not exhaustive works on civic institutions—ecclesiastical institutions are for example omitted—made all the more valuable by excellent historic introductions.

Duffus, Robert: *Mastering a Metropolis; Planning the Future of the New York Region.* New York: 1930.
Summary, in the most favorable light possible, of the proposals made by the Regional Plan of New York group. See Mumford.

Dulac, Albert, and Renard, Georges: *L'Evolution Industrielle et Agricole depuis Cinquante Ans.* Paris: 1912.

Dürer, Albrecht: *Unterricht zur Befestigung der Städte, Schlösser und Flecken.* First Ed.: 1527. Also Berlin: 1840; Paris: 1870.

Dykstra, C. A., and others: See National Resources Board.

Eastlake, Charles Locke: *Hints on Household Taste.* London: 1869.
The lawgiver of taste in the mid-Victorian home, whose dreadful incised decoration left its scar on both wood and stone: all in an effort to practice "simplicity, honesty, and propriety."

Eberstadt, Rudolph: *Handbuch des Wohnungswesen und der Wohnungsfrage.* 2 Ed. Jena: 1910. 4 Ed. Jena: 1920.
A comprehensive digest.

Die Spekulation im neuzeitlichen Städtebau. Jena: 1907.
Reply to economists who justified the "free market" in land.

Neue Studien über Städtebau und Wohnungswesen.

Vol. I. *Städtebau und Wohnungswesen in Belgien. Wiener Wohnverhältnisse.* Jena: 1912.

Vol. II. *Städtebau und Wohnungswesen in Holland.* Jena: 1914.

Vol. III. *Die Kleinwohnungen und das Städtebauliche System in Brüssel und Antwerpen.* Jena: 1919.
Important discussion of old and new housing types, with valuable plans of late medieval housing foundations for the indigent.

Elton, Charles: *Animal Ecology.* New York: 1927.

Encyclopédie, ou Dictionnaire Raisonné des Sciences, des Arts et des Métiers. Recueil de planches. 33 vols. Paris: 1751-77.
The city as such is neglected: a significant omission. But the illustrations of urban life, particularly on the industrial side, are important.

Engels, Friedrich: *The Condition of the Working-Class in England in 1844.* Leipzig: 1845. Trans. London: 1887.
Terrible but incontrovertible picture. For more favorable side see Clapham.

Zur Wohnungsfrage. Three pamphlets in one. Leipzig: 1872. Trans. London: 1935.
A curious argument against housing reform, still occasionally repeated by loyal Marxians. Rests on unsound assumption that what the rich possess is good, and that there are enough quarters to go around if "shared."

Engerand, Fernand: *Les Amusements des Villes d'Eaux à Travers les Ages*. Paris: 1936.
Useful description of spas, baths, and watering resorts.

English Courtier, The, and the Countrey Gentleman: Of Civil and Uncivil Life. London: 1586.
In Inedited Tracts.

Enock, Charles Reginald: *Can We Set the World in Order? The Need for a Constructive World Culture; an Appeal for the Development and Practice of a Science of Corporate Life; a New Science of Geography and Industry Planning*. London: 1916.
A pioneering effort: note the date.

Espinas, Georges: *La Vie Urbaine de Douai au Moyen Age*. 4 vols. Paris: 1913.
The last two volumes present the historic evidence and documents.

Estienne, Charles, and Liébault, John: *Maison Rustique, or the Countrey Farme*. London: 1616.

Evans, Frederick Noble: *Town Improvement*. New York: 1919.

Evelyn, John: *Fumifugium; or the Inconvenience of the Aer and Smoake of London Dissipated*. London: 1661. Reprinted London: 1933.
Early zoning proposals: with a view to removing a nuisance that has persisted in London since the early Middle Ages.

Fagg, Christopher C., and Hutchins, C. E.: *Introduction to Regional Surveying*. Cambridge: 1930.
Particularly good on the side of natural science. Excellent illustration of Geddes's ideal type valley section. Recommended.

Falke, Jakob von: *Art in the House*. Trans. from third German Ed. Boston: 1879.

Falke, Otto von, and Schnitz, H. (editors): *Deutsche Möbel vom Mittelalter bis zum Anfang des 19 Jahrhunderts*. 3 vols. Stuttgart: 1923-4.

Farquharson, Alexander, and Branford, Sybella: *An Introduction to Regional Surveys*. London: 1924.

Fassett, Charles M.: *Assets of the Ideal City*. New York: 1922.
On the lines of Zueblin's American Municipal Progress.

Faure, Jean-Pierre: *Alger Capitale*. Paris: 1936.
Essay on the methods and tasks of modern townplanning with a bias in favor of vertical circulation.

Fawcett, Charles Bungay: *Provinces of England; a Study of Some Geographical Aspects of Devolution*. London: 1919.
In Geddes and Branford's Making of the Future Series.

Federal Writers' Projects: Massachusetts; a, Guide to Its Places and People. Boston: 1937.
Vermont; a Guide to the Green Mountain State. Boston: 1937.
Washington; City and Capitol. Washington: 1937.
Three of a series of guidebooks done under the Works Progress Administration which should do much to promote an adequate regional and historical conscious·

ness in the American citizen. Other volumes in this American Guide Series to follow.

Feldhaus, Franz Maria, and Siegfried, Karl: *Das blaue Badewannenbuch.* Schwarzenberg: 1932.
Origins of the bath-tub.

Feltham, John: *The Picture of London for 1803.* London: 1803.
The Picture of London for 1817. London: 1817.

Ferriss, Hugh: *The Metropolis of Tomorrow.* New York: 1929.
Actually the metropolis of yesterday: the infantile paper city erected by the megalopolitan business men and skyscraper architects of the nineteen twenties—a morbid dream enlarged and universalized by this able draughtsman.

Filene, Edward Albert: *The Way Out.* New York: 1924.
Plea for decentralization by a far-sighted merchant.

Fischer, Theodor: *Sechs Vorträge über Stadtbaukunst.* München: 1922.

Fisher, F. J.: *The Development of the London Food Market; 1540-1640.* In *Economic History Review:* April 1935.

Fletcher, Joseph S.: *Memorials of a Yorkshire Parish.* London: 1917.

Fleure, Herbert John: *Human Geography of Western Europe; a Study in Appreciation.* London: 1918.

Fleure, Herbert John, and Pelham, R. A. (editors): *Eastern Carpathian Studies; Roumania.* London: 1936.
Good example of regional reconnaissance survey, made by a Le Play Society group. See Barker.

Follett, Mary Parker: *Creative Experience.* New York: 1924.

Ford, James, and others: *Slums and Housing; with Special Reference to New York City; History; Conditions; Policy.* 2 vols. Cambridge, Mass.: 1936.
Does New York too much honor: what is needed is a more comprehensive history of the modern slum with international reference: small cities included.

Fourier, François Marie Charles: *Le Nouveau Monde Industriel et Sociétaire.* 1 vol. Paris: 1829. 2 vols. Paris: 1840.
A book whose wide influence has not yet been adequately estimated or understood.

Frank, Josef: *Architektur als Symbol.* Wien: 1931.

Frank, Waldo: *City Block.* Darien: 1922. Reprint. New York: 1932.
Novelist's fine interpretation of an urban milieu: New York.

Frankfurt, Das Neue; Internationale Monatsschrift für die Probleme kultureller Neugestaltung.
Supported by the city of Frankfurt during the period of its post-war renascence, this magazine did for city and regional planning what Die Form did for architecture and the industrial arts: expressions of a new creative spirit which made Germany, between 1925 and 1932, assume a world-leadership in the embodiment of the new culture.

Franklin, Alfred Louis Auguste: *La Vie Privée d'Autrefois; Arts et Métiers,*

Modes, Mœurs, Usages des Parisiens du XIIe au XVIIIe Siècle. 27 vols.
Paris: 1887-1902.
Highly useful.

Freeman, Edward Augustus: *Exeter.* In *Historic Towns Series.* London: 1886.
More history *in* a city than of a city.

Freeman, Edward, and Hunt, W., Editors: *Historic Towns Series.* 11 vols.
London: 1889-1893.
One of the early stirrings of the cities movement, with parallel manifestations in
Germany, Holland, and the United States.

Frey, Dagobert: *Architecture of the Renaissance from Brunelleschi to Michel
Angelo.* The Hague: 1925.

Gotik und Renaissance als Grundlagen der modernen Weltanschauung.
Augsburg: 1929.
Penetrating.

Friedell, Egon: *A Cultural History of the Modern Age.* 3 vols. München:
1927-31. New York: 1930-1932.

Galpin, Charles Josiah: *Social Anatomy of the Rural Community.* In *University of Wisconsin Bulletin No. 34.*

Rural Relations of the Villages and the Small City. In *University of Wisconsin Bulletin No. 411.*

Gantner, Joseph: *Die Schweizer Stadt.* München: 1925.

Grundformen der Europäischen Stadt. Wien: 1928.
Worthy, but somewhat formal, attempt to establish the historic filiation of modern
urban forms.

Ganzenmüller, Wilhelm: *Das Naturgefühl im Mittelalter.* Leipzig: 1914.

Garnier, Charles, and Ammann, A.: *L'Habitation Humaine.* Paris: 1892.
By a "historian who knew little architecture and an architect who knew little
history." (Preface.) Emphasis of course on isolated house; but a step beyond
Violette-le-Duc's *The Habitations of Man in All Ages.*

Gaus, John: See National Resources Board: *Regional Factors in National
Planning.*

Geddes, Patrick: *City Development; a Study of Parks, Gardens, and Culture
Institutes.* Edinburgh: 1904.
Report to the Carnegie Trustees on the development of Dunfermline.

City Deterioration and the Need of City Survey. In *Annals of the American Academy of Political and Social Science.* July 1909.

Cities; Being an Introduction to the Study of Civics. University of London
Extension Lectures Syllabus. London: 1907.

Cities in Evolution. London: 1915.
Most popular and available of Geddes's writings on cities; made up chiefly of
scattered papers, but with a unified point of view.

Country and Town in Development, Deterioration, and Renewal. University of London Extension Lectures Syllabus. London: copy without date.

Talks from My Outlook Tower. In *Survey Graphic:* Feb. 1, April 1, 1925.

Geddes, Patrick: *Town Planning in Patiala State and City.* Lucknow: 1922.

Town Planning Toward City Development; a Report to the Durbar of Indore. Two vols. Indore: 1918.
> Between 1914 and 1924 Geddes made or revised plans for some fifty cities in India and Palestine. The Report on Indore is the completest expression of his town-planning methods and his sociology and philosophy: Vol. II, which deals with the cultural foundations of the city, is particularly recommended.

The Civic Survey of Edinburgh. Edinburgh: 1911.
> From the nineties onward Geddes was a tireless advocate of city surveys as preliminary to intelligent town-planning and city design; and this little pamphlet indicates how much one who knows his subject can put in small compass.

Civics as Applied Sociology. In *Sociological Papers.* London: 1905.

A Suggested Plan for a Civic Museum. In *Sociological Papers.* London: 1906.

Geddes, Patrick, and Branford, Victor: Seen Branford.

Geddes, Patrick, and Mears, F. C.: *Cities and Town Planning Exhibition: Guidebook and Outline Catalog.* Belfast: 1911.
> Refers to Geddes's original and unique collection that was sunk during the first World War; his later collection, still probably intact, would serve as a foundation for a civic museum.

Geddes, Patrick, and Slater, Gilbert: *Ideas at War.* London: 1917.

Geddes, Patrick, and Thomson, J. A.: *Life; Outlines of General Biology.* 2 vols. New York: 1931.
> The chapters on the social applications of biology—along with his systematized charting of life and society—are by Geddes: the best summary of his thought available in print, though it does small justice to his demonic insight and his extraordinary intellectual reach.

Geisler, Walter: *Die Deutsche Stadt; Ein Beitrag zur Morphologie der Kulturlandschaft.* Stuttgart: 1924.

George, Henry: *Progress and Poverty.* New York: 1879.
> Economics of urban land increment and monopoly: weak in its positive proposals to remove monopoly without removing incentives to monopoly.

George, Mary Dorothy: *English Social Life in the 18th Century; illustrated from contemporary sources.* London: 1923.

London Life in the XVIIIth Century. New York: 1925. London: 1925.
> Good.

Gerard, P. (C. E.): *How to Build a City: Designed for the consideration of founders of towns, architects, civil engineers, sanitary organizations, municipal authorities, builders, and especially the managers of the various railroads to the Pacific.* Philadelphia: 1872.

Gerlach, Walther: *Die Entstehungszeit der Stadtbefestigungen in Deutschland; Ein Beitrag zur Mittelalterlichen Verfassungsgeschichte.* In *Leipziger Historische Abhandlungen.* Vol. XXXIV. Leipzig: 1913.
> Analysis of various concepts of city and village in German Middle Ages.

Gierke, Otto: *Natural Law and the Theory of Society; 1500 to 1800.* 2 vols. Trans. Cambridge: 1934.

Political Theories of the Middle Age. Trans. Cambridge: 1900.
From *Das Deutsche Genossenschaftsrecht:* one of the best early statements of the modern sociological theory of groups. See Cooley and MacIver.

Gilpin, William: *Forest Scenery.* First Edition, London: 1791; Second Edition (Revised): 1794.

Giry, A.: *Histoire de la Ville de Saint Omer.* Paris: 1877.
Important source of data on "advanced liberties" of medieval town.

Giry, A., and Réville, A.: *Emancipation of the Medieval Towns.* Trans. in *Historical Miscellany.* New York: 1907.

Gist, Noel Pitts, and Halbert, L. A.: *Urban Society.* New York: 1935.
Textbook.

Gleichen-Russwurm, Alexander von, Editor: *Kultur- und Sittengeschichte aller Zeiten und Völker.* 24 vols. in 12. Hamburg: 1929.
Valuable for its many illustrations.

Glotz, Gustave: *The Greek City; and Its Institutions.* Paris: 1928. Trans. New York: 1930.

Godfrey, Hollis: *The Health of the City.* Boston: 1910.
A fair early treatment of air, waste, noise and housing.

Goethe, Johann Wolfgang von: *Dichtung und Wahrheit.* Trans. London: 1848.
See the many admirable passages on medieval urban survivals.

Gomme, George Laurence: *The Village Community; with Special Reference to the Origin and Form of its Survivals in Britain.* New York: 1890.

Gooch, R. F.: *Regionalism in France.* New York: 1931.

Goodrich, Carter, and others: *Migration and Economic Opportunity; the Report of the Study of Population Distribution.* Philadelphia: 1936.
Careful study of the difficulties besetting decentralization of industry and population under the present capitalist regime. See Pratt.

Gotch, John Alfred: *Growth of the English House, 1100-1800.* London: 1909. Rev. Ed. London: 1928.

Gould, Elgin R. L.: *The Housing of the Working People; A Special Report of U. S. Committee of Labor.* Washington: 1895.

Gras, Norman S. B.: *History of Agriculture in Europe and America.* New York: 1925.
One of the few books available on a topic whose history has received even less attention than that of cities. A subject that awaits the new cultural historian. A coordinate history of the modification of landscape forms is also badly needed. See Meitzen and Prothero.

Industrial Evolution. Cambridge, Mass.: 1930.

An Introduction to Economic History. New York: 1922.
Follows the general line of Bücher; but leaves the impression that metropolitanism is a final stage.

Gras, Norman S. B.: *Regionalism and Nationalism*. In *Foreign Affairs*. April 1929.

Green, Alice Stopford: *Town Life in the Fifteenth Century*. 2 vols. London: 1894.
Classic.

Gregorovius, Ferdinand Adolf: *History of the City of Rome in the Middle Ages*. 8 vols. Stuttgart: 1859-1872. Trans. 13 vols. London: 1894-1902.

Grisebach, August: *Die alte deutsche Stadt in ihrer Stammeseigenart*. Berlin: 1930.
Richly illustrated; particularly with a varied lot of house-types.

Gropius, Walter: *The New Architecture and the Bauhaus*. London: 1935.

Gross, Charles: *The Gild Merchant; a Contribution to British Municipal History*. 2 vols. Oxford: 1890.
A fine work in which the conclusions in Vol. I are backed by a second volume of citations from original sources.

Grosstadt, Die. *Vorträge und Aufsätze zur Städteausstellung*. Dresden: 1903.
Includes essays by Bücher and Ratzel and Simmel—the latter on *The Big City and the Spiritual Life*.

Guicciardini, Francesco: *Counsels and Reflections*. London: 1890.
Classic contemporary revelation of Baroque wisdom on the plane of morals and politics.

Hamlin, Talbot Faulkner: *The American Spirit in Architecture*. New Haven: 1926.
Amply illustrated.

Hammarstrand, Nils: *Cities Old and New*. In *Journal of the American Institute of Architects*. New York: 1926.
Well-digested summary of early town planning from classic times onward.

Hammond, John Lawrence and Barbara: *The Skilled Labourer (1760-1832)*. London: 1917.
The Town Labourer (1760-1832). New York: 1919.
The Village Labourer (1760-1832). London: 1911.
Graphic and well-documented studies: indispensable for an understanding of the paleotechnic town.

Hardy, Charles Oscar: *The Housing Program of the City of Vienna*. Washington: 1934.

Hardy, Marcel E.: *The Geography of Plants*. Oxford: 1920.

Hassert, Kurt: *Die Städte; geographisch betrachtet*. In *Aus Natur und Geisteswelt*. Leipzig: 1907.
Small but masterly study.

Havemeyer, Loomis (editor): *Conservation of Our Natural Resources*. New York: 1930.

Haverfield, Francis J.: *Ancient Townplanning*. Oxford: 1913.
Limited notion of plan; now superseded by Poëte and others.

Hazlitt, William Carew, Editor: *Inedited Tracts; Illustrating the Manners,*

Opinions and Occupations of Englishmen during the Sixteenth and Seventeenth Centuries. Containing Civil and Uncivil Life; The Court and the Country; The Serving Man's Comfort. London: 1868.

Head, George: *A Home Tour through the Manufacturing Districts of England in the Summer of 1835.* London: 1836.

Heckscher, Eli F.: *Mercantilism.* 2 vols. London: 1935.

Hegel, Karl: *Die Entstehung des Deutschen Städtewesens.* Leipzig: 1898.
Origins of the city and city government in medieval Germany. See also Preuss.

Hegemann, Werner: *City Planning, Housing; Historical and Sociological.* 2 vols. New York: 1936-7.
Muddled.

Der Städtebau, Nach den Ergebnissen der Allgemeinen Städtebau-Ausstellung. 2 vols. Berlin: 1911-13.
Superb piece of documentation and systematic survey. Still valuable: far more so than any other work of the author.

Das steinerne Berlin: Geschichte der grössten Mietskasernenstadt in der Welt. Berlin: 1930.

Hegemann, Werner, and Peets, Elbert: *The American Vitruvius; Civic Art.* New York: 1922.
The title properly betrays the retrospective tendencies and the esthetic approach of this monumental compendium. Now badly dated.

Heilig, Wilhelm: *Stadt und Landbaukunde.* Berlin: 1935.
Illustrations of organic forms of older village and city growth. Like most such books now issuing from Nazi Germany, it is flagrantly unfair to the good work done before 1933.

Held, F. E.: See Andreae.

Helm, William Henry: *Homes of the Past; a Sketch of Domestic Buildings and Life in England from the Norman to the Georgian Age.* New York: 1921.

Herbertson, A. J. and F. D.: *Man and His Work; an Introduction to Human Geography.* London: 1917.
Herbertson's study of the major natural regions laid the foundation for later work by Fennemann and others.

Herzl, Theodor: *Altneuland.*
A modern utopia, too little known even to Zionists, which ranks almost with Howard's Tomorrow.

Heyne, Moritz: *Das Deutsche Wohnungswesen von den ältesten geschichtlichen Zeiten bis zum 16. Jahrhundert.* Vol. I in *Fünf Bücher Deutscher Hausaltertümer.* Leipzig: 1899.
Valuable.

Hilbersheimer, Ludwig: *Grosstadtarchitektur.* Stuttgart: 1927.
Analysis of the possibilities of more rational architectural order possible in the big city: particularly good in suggestions for office and business sections. Contrast to American skyscraper projects.

Hill, Leonard: See Campbell.

Hintze, Hedwig (Guggenheimer): *Regionalism.* In *Encyclopedia of the Social Sciences.* New York: 1930.
Perhaps the best brief summary in any language, except for the section on America, where the facts are scanty and the interpretation painfully inadequate.

Hirth, Georg: *Das Deutsche Zimmer.* 2 vols. München: 1899.

Kulturgeschichtliches Bilderbuch aus drei Jahrhunderten. 6 vols. 2 Ed. Leipzig: 1899-1901.
Pictorial documentation of modern cultural history mainly from prints. Indispensable.

Historic Towns Series: See Freeman, E. A.

Hitchcock, Henry-Russell: *The Architecture of H. H. Richardson and His Times.* New York: 1936.
Rounds out Mrs. van Rensselaer's original account of this great proto-modern who paved the way for Sullivan. For fine appreciation of Richardson see Sullivan's Kindergarten Chats: effectual refutation of the depreciation by Hegemann in City Planning, Housing.

Modern Architecture; Romanticism and Reintegration. New York: 1929.
Valuable pioneer study; mainly esthetic in focus. See also Behrendt and Pevsner.

Hitchcock, Henry-Russell, and Johnson, Phillip: *Modern Architecture.* New York: 1932.

Hobhouse, Christopher: *1851 and the Crystal Palace.* London: 1937.
Complete first-hand documentation is accessible to those who have access to files of *Illustrated London News.*

Hobson, John A.: *Wealth and Life; a Study in Values.* London: 1929.
Ruskin's essential economic doctrine, re-stated by an able modern economist.

Hodgson, Francis: *Venice in the Thirteenth and Fourteenth Centuries (1204-1400).* London: 1910.

Hoepfner, Karl A.: *Grundbegriffe des Städtebaues.* 2 vols. Berlin: 1921-28.
In part already dated by newer conceptions of open order.

Hoffbauer, Theodore J. H.: *Paris à Travers les Ages; Aspects successifs des monuments et quartiers historiques de Paris depuis le XIIIe siècle jusqu'à nos jours. Fidèlement restitués d'apres les documents authentiques.* 2 vols. Paris: 1875-1882.
Illustrations excellent. Contributions by authorities like LaCroix and Franklin. See Poëte.

Hole, James: *The Homes of the Working Classes; with Suggestions for Their Improvement.* London: 1866.
Good statement of the capitalist dilemma by an advocate of model housing who saw the difficulties. Contains important data on contemporary experiments.

Holland, William King: See Middle West Utilities.

Hoover, Herbert: See President's Research Committee and President's Conference.

Hough, Walter: *Fire as an Agent in Human Culture.* In *Smithsonian Institution Bulletin 139.* Washington: 1926.

Housing America. (By the Editors of *Fortune.*) New York: 1932.
America's lacks and deficiencies in Housing competently revealed: but anything like a positive program vitiated by the authors' naïve belief that the private manufacturer could solve the crucial economic difficulties by building individual prefabricated houses.

Housing Conference, President Hoover's: See President's Conference.

Howard, Ebenezer: *Garden Cities of Tomorrow.* London: 1902. (First edition published as *Tomorrow.* London: 1898.)
A close study of this classic is important for every serious student of housing, city planning, or regional development. Sir Ebenezer was originally a court stenographer: so much for specialization. His book has had consequences more far-reaching than the two English cities that have issued out of it.

Hubbard, Theodora, and Henry Vincent: *Our Cities Today and Tomorrow.* Cambridge, Mass.: 1929.

Hugenberg, Alfred: *Die neue Stadt.* Berlin: 1935.
Worthless.

Hughes, Thomas, and Lamborn, E. A. G.: *Towns and Town Planning, Ancient and Modern.* Oxford: 1923.
Useful short introduction.

Hughes, W. R.: *New Town; a Proposal in Agricultural, Industrial, Educational, Civic, and Social Reconstruction.* London: 1919.

Hugo, Victor: *Notre Dame de Paris.* Paris: 1831.
The sociological approach to the past owes more to the novelists like Scott and Hugo than to the professed historians and sociologists.

Huizinga, Johann: *The Waning of the Middle Ages.* Trans. New York: 1924.
Splended in its revelation of the complexities and contradictions of the medieval idolum.

Hunt, Wray: *The Growth and Development of the English Town.* London: 1931.
Elementary text in the *Simple Guide Series.*

Hunt, W.: See Freeman, E. A.

Huntington, Ellsworth: *The Human Habitat.* New York: 1927.
Perhaps the soundest if not the most original of the author's numerous studies.
Civilization and Climate. New Haven: 1915. Revised Edition: 1933.
An original thesis on the relation of climate and weather to human productivity: somewhat vitiated by parochial assumptions as to what constitutes civilization.

Hurd, Richard Melanchthon: *Principles of City Land Values.* First Ed. New York: 1903. Fourth Ed. New York: 1924.
Deservedly of high repute in a field where till recently it stood almost alone. Many illustrations of early stages of growth in American cities. By a business man who really understood his business.

Hürlimann, Martin: *Deutschland; Landschaft und Baukunst.* Berlin: 1931.
Berlin; Berichte und Bilder. Berlin: 1934.
Das Mittelmeer; Landschaft, Baukunst und Volksleben im Kreise des Mittelländischen Meeres. Berlin: 1937.

Hürlimann, Martin: *La France;* with an introduction by Paul Valéry. Paris: 1927.
Selection from a larger list of sumptuously designed and illustrated books on cities and landscapes, done by the same author. While the illustrations are mainly selected with an eye to beauty, rather than all-round truth, the books fill a serious gap.

Hussey, Christopher: *The Picturesque.* New York: 1927.

Hutchings, G. E.: See Fagg.

Hutton, William: *The History of Birmingham.* Fourth Ed. London: 1819.

A Journey from Birmingham to London. Birmingham: 1785.

International Housing Association: *Slum Clearance and Reconditioning of Insanitary Dwellings.* Two vols. in one. Stuttgart: 1935.
One of a series of volumes published by this association in German, French, and English, of importance to students of Housing.

James, Harlean: *Land Planning in the United States.* New York: 1926.

James, Herman G.: *Municipal Functions.* New York: 1917.

Janssen, Johannes: *History of the German People at the Close of the Middle Ages.* 8 vols. Freiburg: 1881-1894. Trans. 17 vols. London: 1895-1925.
Still useful.

Jean-Desthieux, François: *L'Evolution Régionaliste du Félibrige au Fedéralisme.* Paris: 1918.
Complete account of history of regionalist movement in France. See Gooch.

Jeanneret-Gris, Charles Edouard: See Le Corbusier.

Jennings, Hilda: *Bryn Mawr: A Study of a Distressed Area.* London: 1934.
Based on a social survey of an area in the South Wales coalfield.

Joerg, W. L. G.: *Geography and National Land Planning.* In *Geographical Review.* April 1935.

Joerg, W. L. G., and Mackintosh, W. A. (editors): *Canadian Frontiers of Settlement.* 9 vols. Toronto: 1934-36.

Jones, David Caradog (editor): *The Social Survey of Merseyside.* 2 vols. London: 1934.
Factual study; maps but no photographs.

Jones, Thomas Jesse: *The Sociology of a New York City Block.* New York: 1904.

Kampffmeyer, Hans: *Die Gartenstadtbewegung.* Leipzig: 1909.
By a gallant spirit who left his mark on the German housing movement, and who fortunately died in 1932 before the humiliating arrival of National Socialism.

Kehr, Cyrus: *A Nation Plan.* Washington: 1920.
A pioneering work in its field. Uncritical on certain matters like national unification, and limited by concentration on purely physical side of planning. See MacKaye, Benton.

Keir, Malcolm: *Economic Factors in the Location of Manufacturing Industries.* In *Annals of the American Academy of Political and Social Science.* Philadelphia: 1921.

Kellogg, Paul U. (editor): *The Pittsburgh Survey*. 6 vols. New York: 1909-1914.

Monumental survey of a representative industrial city: an overhauling not unlike the later Middletown, but with more emphasis on the social workers' point of view and specific.interests. Lacking on the civic and urban side, it is nevertheless one of the outstanding demonstrations of the survey method.

Kern, Robert: *The Supercity; a Planned Physical Equipment for City Life*. Washington: 1924.

A variant on Chambless's Roadtown: much better thought out; but with something of the same innocence as to the relation of physical utilities and social purposes.

King, W.: *Chronicles of Three Free Cities*. London: 1914.

Kohl, Johann Georg: *Der Verkehr und die Ansiedlungen der Menschen in Ihrer Abhängigkeit von der Gestaltung der Erdoberfläche*. 2 Ed. Leipzig: 1850.

Sombart pokes fun at this work; but its emphasis on transportation as one of the critical factors in city development is not unsound.

Kropotkin, Piotr: *Fields, Factories, and Workshops; or Industry Combined with Agriculture, and Brainwork with Manual Work*. First Ed. Boston: 1899. Revised Ed. London: 1919.

Sociological and economic intelligence of the first order, founded on Kropotkin's specialized competence as a geographer and his generous social passion as a leader in communist anarchism. Able analysis and penetrating interpretation.

Mutual Aid. London: 1904.

Pioneer work on symbiosis in sociology: one of the first attempts to redress the one-sided Darwinian emphasis upon the more predatory aspects of life. Note chapter on Mutual Aid in the Medieval City.

Kuczynski, Robert R.: *Population Movements*. Oxford: 1936.

Kulischer, A. M. and Y. M.: *Kriegs- und Wanderzüge; Weltgeschichte als Völkerbewegung*. Berlin: 1932.

Attempt to interpret world history in the light of migrations.

Kulischer, Josef M.: *Allgemeine Wirtschaftsgeschichte*. 2 vols. München: 1928-29.

Excellent bibliographies.

Lanciani, Rodolfo Amedeo: *Golden Days of Renaissance in Rome*. Boston: 1906.

Larwood, Jacob (pseudonym for H. D. J. van Schevichaven): *The Story of the London Parks*. London: 1881.

Laski, Harold Joseph: *The Problem of Administrative Areas*. In *Smith College Studies in History*. Northampton: 1918.

Laski, Harold Joseph (editor): *A Century of Municipal Progress; 1835-1935*. London: 1935.

Useful.

Lavedan, Pierre: *Qu'est-ce que l'Urbanisme? Introduction à l'Histoire de l'Urbanisme*. Paris: 1926.

An introduction to the documents, plans, and other sources for a history of urbanism, rather than to the subject itself. More for the specialist than the general student.

Lavedan, Pierre: *Histoire de l'Urbanisme.* Vol. I. Antiquité, Moyen Age. Paris: 1926.
First rate. Fully documented with plans and illustrations. Second volume on *l'Époque Classique* has long been promised.

Géographie des Villes. Paris: 1936.
Good beginning in comparative morphology, but with insufficient institutional reference.

Lavisse, Ernest: *Histoire de France Contemporaine depuis la Revolution jusqu'à la Paix de 1919.* 10 vols. Paris: 1920-22.
Exhaustive; illustrations good, too.

Le Corbusier: *Vers une Architecture nouvelle.* Paris: 1923. Trans. *Towards a New Architecture.* New York: 1930.
A book whose literary influence made the author the dominating architect of Europe. Essentially a combination of classic formalism and the machine, with an esthetic derived from cubist painting, Le Corbusier's thought produced a needed clarification: turning attention from problems of decoration to those of construction. At first puritanic in its austerity, the author's architecture became, in his more elaborate houses, a baroque played with machine forms. Unfortunately Le Corbusier's formulas have lent themselves to academic imitation: sometimes by himself.

Urbanisme. Paris: 1924. Trans. *The City of the Future.* New York: 1930.
Defense of standardization, mass-production, the machine. Suggestions for an elaborately mechanical metropolis, with widely spaced skyscrapers and multiple-decked traffic ways: closer to a genuine order than the gaudy projects of the New York skyscraper architects of the same period: but innocent of economic limitations, and superficial in its grasp of social factors.

Précisions. Paris: 1930.
The gist of Le Corbusier's South American lectures, with even more fanciful schemes for skyscraper roadtown.

La Ville Radieuse; Collection de l'Equipement de la Civilisation Machiniste. Boulogne: 1934.
Most mature of Le Corbusier's works; symptomatic of a transformation from purely mechanical ideology to the more biotechnic outlook. Recommended.

Legrand, Jacques G., and Landon, C. P.: *Description de Paris et de ses Edifices.* 2 vols. Paris: 1806-1809.

Leinert, Martin: *Die Sozialgeschichte der Grosstadt.* Hamburg: 1925.

Le Play, Frédéric: *Les Ouvriers Européens.* 6 vols. 2 Ed. Tours: 1877-79.
L'Esquisse d'une Division Provinciale de la France.
One of the early attempts to suggest reconstitution of the old regions of France.

Lethaby, William Richard: *Form in Civilization.* London: 1922.
Wise reflections on the social problem of modern form. See Behrendt and Ozenfant.

Levainville, J.: *Caen; Notes sur L'Evolution de la Fonction Urbaine.* In *La Vie Urbaine:* August, October 1923.

Lewis, Nelson P.: *The Planning of the Modern City.* New York: 1916.

Lewis, Sinclair: *Babbitt.* New York: 1922.
The novelist's complement of Middletown.

Lichtenberg, Reinhold, Freiherr von: *Haus, Dorf, Stadt; Eine Entwicklungs-geschichte des antiken Städtebildes.* Leipzig: 1909.

Lindeman, Eduard C.: See Anderson, Nels. *Wealth and Culture; A Study of One Hundred Foundations and Community Trusts and Their Operations.* New York: 1936.

Lippmann, Walter: *Public Opinion.* New York: 1922.

Lipson, Ephraim: *The Economic History of England.* 3 vols. New York: 1929-31.

Lloyd, Nathaniel: *A History of the English House; from Primitive Times to the Victorian Period.* London: 1931.
Excellent.

Lloyd, Thomas Alwyn: *Planning in Town and Country.* London: 1935.

Loftie, William J.: *A History of London.* 2 vols. London: 1883.

Lohmann, Karl B.: *Principles of City Planning.* New York: 1931.
Summary of current American practices rather than principles.
Regional Planning. Ann Arbor: 1936.
Synopsis of the subject.

London County Council: *Housing Estates; Statistics for the Year 1929-30.* London: 1930.
Housing of the Working Classes in London. London: 1913.
London Housing. London: 1937.
Records of a Herculean accomplishment in slum-razing and community housing.

London School of Economics and Social Science: *New Survey of London Life and Labor.* 9 vols. London: 1930-35.
A compendious survey that seeks in effect to bring Booth up to date.

London Society, The: *London of the Future.* Edited by Sir Aston Webb. New York: 1921.

Lynd, Robert S. and Helen M.: *Middletown.* New York: 1929.
An able survey, though weak on the geographic side and lacking in comparative cultural reference. See Kellogg, P. U.
Middletown in Transition; a Study in Cultural Conflicts. New York: 1937.
Less exhaustive but perhaps more penetrating than the first study.

Mächler, Martin: *Demodynamik.* Berlin: 1933.

MacIver, Robert M.: *Community.* London: 1917.
Society; Its Structure and Changes. New York: 1931.

MacKaye, Benton: *Employment and Natural Resources.* Washington: 1918.
The New Exploration; a Philosophy of Regional Planning. New York: 1928.

Important not merely for point of view but for suggestions of method. MacKaye, originally a forester, and the founder of the Appalachian Trail, is a regionalist in the great tradition of Thoreau, Marsh, and Shaler.

MacKaye, Benton, and Mumford, Lewis: *Townless Highways for the Motorist.* In *Harper's Magazine:* August 1931.

Regional Planning. In *Encyclopedia Britannica.* 14 Edition.

Mackenzie, Findlay, Editor: *Planned Society; Yesterday, Today and Tomorrow.* New York: 1937.
A symposium by thirty-five economists, sociologists, and statesmen. Many important papers and full bibliography.

Maclear, Anne Bush: *Early New England Towns.* In *Studies in History, Economics, and Public Law.* New York: 1908.

Maitland, Frederick William: *Township and Borough.* Cambridge: 1898.

Mann, Thomas: *Lübeck als geistige Lebensform.* Lübeck: 1926.
Summary of spiritual and cultural influence of a great city upon its greatest son.

Mannheim, Karl: *Ideology and Utopia.* Bonn: 1929. Trans. New York: 1936.

Marsh, George P.: *Man and Nature; or, Physical Geography as Modified by Human Action.* New York: 1864.
A masterpiece of geographic thought, at long last being re-discovered by the geographers. Laid the foundation for the conservation of natural resources, particularly forests.

Marshall, T. H.: *The Population of England and Wales from the Industrial Revolution to the World War.* In the *Economic History Review.* April 1935.
Judicious survey.

Martin, Alfred von: *Deutsches Badewesen in vergangenen Tagen.* Jena: 1906.
Soziologie der Renaissance. Stuttgart: 1932.

Matchoss, Conrad (editor): *Technik-Geschichte.* Volume on Roads and Roadmaking in *Beiträge zur Geschichte der Technik und Industrie.* Vol. 23. Berlin: 1934.

Maunier, René: *Essais sur les Groupements Sociaux.* Paris: 1929.
L'Origine et la Fonction Economique des Villes; Etude de Morphologie Sociale. Paris: 1910.
Important less for what it establishes than for what it attempts.

Mayhew, Henry: *London Labor and the London Poor.* 4 vols. London: 1861-62.
Journalistic but full of interesting material.

Mazel, Henri: *La Synergie Sociale.* Paris: 1896.

McKenzie, Roderick D.: *The Metropolitan Community.* New York: 1933.

McLachlan, Norman W.: *Noise.* London: 1935.

McNamara, Katherine: *Bibliography of Planning; 1928-1935.* Cambridge, Mass.: 1936.

Meakin, Budgett: *Model Factories and Villages.* London: 1905.

Meikleham, Robert: *On the History and Art of Warming and Ventilating Rooms and Buildings.* 2 vols. London: 1845.
Important: a rare book in a poorly explored field. Needs an even more exhaustive successor.

Mercier, Louis Sebastien: *The Picture of Paris; Before and After the Revolution.* Paris: 1781-88. Trans. London: 1929.
Memoirs of the Year 2500. Trans. Liverpool: 1802.
Utopia interesting for historic sidelights.

Merian, Matthaeus: *Topographia Bohemiae, Moraviae et Silesiae.* Frankfurt-am-Main: 1650.
Topographia Germaniae. Frankfurt-am-Main: 1642. Reprinted in small format. München: 1935.
Handsome woodcuts of cities, with curious and sometimes historically informative data. One of the great sources of knowledge as to the state of the late medieval town. Hill and church tower took the place of the airplane for the artist. See Blaeu, Munster.

Metz, Friedrich: *Die Hauptstaedte.* Berlin: 1930.

Meuriot, Paul: *Du Concept de Ville Autrefois et Aujourd'hui.* In *La Vie Urbaine.* Paris: 1919.
Des Aglomerations Urbaines dans l'Europe Contemporaraine; Essai sur les Causes, les Conditions, les Conséquences de leur Développement. Paris: 1898.
Statistical study of urban concentration in the nineteenth century with special reference to France.

Meyer, Alfred Gotthold: *Eisenbauten.* Esslingen: 1907.
Important study of development of use of iron in building: good historically and technically.

Middle West Utilities Company: *America's New Frontier.* Chicago: 1929.
Interesting study of possibilities of economic regionalism.

Migge, Leberecht: *Deutsche Binnenkolonisation; Sachgrundlagen des Siedlungswesens.* Berlin: 1926.
A rural approach to the problem of resettlement. Not to be confused with later experiments with low-grade "Randsiedlungen" in Germany.
Die wachsende Siedlung. Stuttgart: 1932.
Suggestions for biotechnic housing in rural environment, with a house designed for growth of the family, and the land adapted for cultivation.

Miller, Hugh: *First Impressions of England and Its People.* New York: 1875.

Mirabilia Romae; Indulgentie et Reliquie ad Urbis Rome in Latino. Rome: c. 1495.
First modern guide book.

Molmenti, Pompeo G.: *Venice, Its Individual Growth from the Earliest Beginning to the Fall of the Republic.* 6 vols. Trans. Chicago: 1906-8.

Montesquieu, Baron de (Charles de Secondat): *The Spirit of the Laws.* Two vols. Geneva: 1749. Translated. Rev. ed. New York: 1899.
One of the first modern attempts to link geography and politics.

Moore, Charles: *Daniel H. Burnham; Architect; Planner of Cities.* 2 vols. Boston: 1921.
Biography of one of the great exponents of imperialist city design.

Moore, Harry E.: *What is Regionalism.* In *Southern Policy Papers No. 10.* Chapel Hill, N. C.: 1937.
(See also Odum, Howard.)

Morris, William: *News from Nowhere.* London: 1891.
Though as dreamlike as Hudson's *A Crystal Age*, the theme of this utopia is like some fantastic arcadian prelude to our biotechnic economy: much closer to the new idolum than Bellamy or Wells, although Morris speaks with an accent more foreign to our thinking.

Architecture, Industry, and Wealth. London: 1902.

Hopes and Fears for Art. Boston: 1882.
Samples from one of the great critical and constructive minds of the nineteenth century, whose thoughts on architecture and social life are still important.

Mukerjee, Radhakamal: *Regional Sociology.* New York: 1926.
Good conspectus.

Ecological Contributions to Sociology. In *Sociological Review.* October 1930.

Müller, Emile: *Habitations Ouvrières et Agricoles.* Paris: 1856.

Müller, Emile, and Cacheux, Emile: *Les Habitations Ouvrières en Tous Pays.* First Ed. Paris: 1879. Second Ed. Paris: 1903.
Exhaustive survey of model housing schemes for the working classes; the second edition shows many plans exhibited at the Paris Exposition of 1900. See Hole, James.

Mumford, Lewis: *The Story of Utopias.* New York: 1922.

Sticks and Stones; a Study of American Architecture and Civilization. New York: 1924.
The first historic treatment of this subject in English; but the one-sided views of the influence of the machine expressed in the later chapters were modified in *The Brown Decades* and in *Technics and Civilization.*

The Brown Decades; a Study of the Arts in America; 1865-1895. New York: 1931.
Exasperatingly superficial.

American Dwelling House. In *American Mercury.* October 1929.

The City. In *Civilization in the United States, by Thirty Americans.* New York: 1922.
Better than its date might indicate.

The Intolerable City. In *Harper's Magazine.* February 1926.

Housing. In *Modern Architecture*, edited by Hitchcock, Henry-Russell and Johnson, Phillip. New York: 1932.

Machinery and the Modern Style. In *New Republic.* August 3, 1921.

Mumford, Lewis: *Mass Production and the Modern House*. In *Architectural Record*. January-February 1930.

The Metropolitan Milieu. In *America and Alfred Stieglitz*, edited by Norman, D., Frank, W., Rosenfeld, P., and Mumford, L. New York: 1934.
Study of interplay of geographic and cultural influences in a great city, focused through a single personality. Recommended.

Plan of New York. In *New Republic*. June 15 and 22, 1932.
Painstaking and detailed criticism of defects of The Regional Survey and Plan of New York (which see).

The Fourth Migration. In *Survey Graphic*. May 1925.

Technics and Civilization. New York: 1934.
Study of the machine in its social, cultural, and economic aspects. Complementary in scope and theme to the present volume.

Mumford, Lewis (editor): *Regional Planning Number, Survey Graphic:* May 1925.

Munro, William Bennett: *Municipal Administration*. New York: 1934.
American practice.

Municipal Government and Administration. New York: 1923.

The Government of American Cities. New York: 1913.

The Government of European Cities. New York: 1909. Revised. New York: 1927.

Munster, Sebastian: *Cosmographia*. Basel: 1552.
Valuable.

Murray, David: *Museums; Their History and Their Use*. 3 vols. Glasgow: 1904.
Definitive.

Museum of Modern Art, The, of New York: *Modern Architecture*. New York: 1932.

Nash, Elizabeth Gee: *The Hansa*. London: 1929.

National Association of Housing Officials: *A Housing Program for the United States*. Chicago: 1934.

National Planning Board (U. S.): *Final Report; 1933-4*. Section Two: *A Plan for Planning*. Washington: 1934.

National Resources Board (U. S.): *State Planning; a Review of Activities and Progress*. Washington: 1935.
Compact informative survey of state-planning activities in various states. But neglects to note the first systematic introduction of State Planning, that of the New York State Housing and Regional Planning Commission (which see).

Regional Factors in National Planning. Washington: 1936.
A public document of unusual excellence: the best discussion of the problems of administration and planning, with reference to regional realities, that has appeared. Occasionally confuses the concept of the specialized planning area with the reality of a regional complex, by using the adjective regional to cover both.

Regional Planning; New England. Washington: 1936.

Our Cities; Their Rôle in the National Economy. Washington: 1937.
Good study despite a weakness on the historic side and a tendency to overlook or

straddle economic and social questions closely bound up with the maintenance of dominant pecuniary economy.

Neutra, Richard J.: *Amerika.* In *Neues Bauen in der Welt* Series. Wien: 1930.

New Survey of London Life and London Labor. See London School of Economics.

New York State Housing and Regional Planning Commission: *Final Report.* Albany: 1926.
With Clarence S. Stein as Chairman, Henry Wright as Planning Adviser and George Gove as Director, the commission made a series of important investigations, culminating in the above report. Wright's contribution here was the regional parallel to Howard's Garden City; and the above report is a benchmark of regionalism in American politics. See also MacKaye, Wright, Stein.

New York State Planning Board: *A Graphic Compendium of Planning Studies.* Albany: 1935.
State Planning for New York. Albany: 1935.

Nolen, John: *City Planning.* New York: 1929.

New Towns for Old. Boston: 1927.
Nolen understood possibilities of the small town.

Oberhummer, Eugen: *Der Stadtplan; Seine Entwicklung und geographische Bedeutung.* Berlin: 1907.
Examples largely from older cities.

Obermeyer, Henry: *Stop That Smoke!* New York: 1933.
Popular study of the smoke nuisance and problem of its abatement.

Odum, Howard W.: *Southern Regions of the United States.* Chapel Hill, N. C.: 1936.
Able analysis of regions and regional problems by the leading sociologist of the New South.

Odum, Howard W., and Moore, Harry E.: *American Regionalism.* New York: 1938.
Effective outline of various approaches to contemporary regionalism in the United States. Critical and compendious.

Ogburn, William Fielding: *Social Characteristics of Cities.* Chicago: 1937.
Useful analysis of the census returns with cities grouped according to size.

Olmsted, Frederick Law: *Public Parks and the Enlargement of Towns.* Cambridge, Mass.: 1870.
One of the earliest and best expositions of comprehensive park planning.

Olmsted, Frederick Law, Jr., and Kimball, Theodora: *Frederick Law Olmsted, Landscape Architect; 1822-1903.* 2 vols. New York: 1928.
Professional papers and significant biographic data.

Oppenheimer, Franz: *Stadt und Bürgerschaft; Die Neuzeit.* In *Oppenheimers System der Soziologie,* vol. 4, part 3.

Ostwald, Hans: *Berlin und die Berlinerin: Eine Kultur- und Sittengeschichte* Berlin: 1911.
Well illustrated with contemporary prints.

Ottokar, Nicola: *The Medieval City-Communes.* Privately printed. Florence: 1933.

Owen, Robert: *A New View of Society.* London: 1813.

Ozenfant, Amédée: *Foundations of Modern Art.* Paris: 1928. Trans. New York: 1931.
Good: not least on architecture.

Palladio, Andrea: *The Architecture of Palladio in Four Books.* Venice: 1581. Trans. London: 1742.
Indispensable clues to the baroque plan.

Park, Robert E., Burgess, E. W., and McKenzie, R. D.: *The City;* with a Bibliography by Louis Wirth. Chicago: 1925.
Papers relating to the city as an ecological formation.

Pasquet, D.: *Londres et les Ouvriers de Londres.* Paris: 1914.
Good.

Paul-Boncour, Joseph: *Le Féderalisme Economique: Etude sur les Rapports de l'Individu et les Groupements Professionels.* Paris: 1900.
A discussion, historic, economic, political, on the growth of associations and their political rule.

Pearson, Sidney Vere: *The Growth and Distribution of Population.* London: 1935.
Discursive and unfortunately not adequate.

Peel, J.: *Topographia Galliae.* Amsterdam: 1660-1663.

Peets, Elbert: *Haussmann.* In *Town Planning Review.* June 1927.
Current Town Planning in Washington. In *Town Planning Review.* December 1931.
(See also Hegemann.)

Penstone, M. M.: *Town Study; Suggestions for a Course of Lessons Preliminary to the Study of Civics.* London: 1910.
For schools; English illustrations.

Perret, Jacques: *Des Fortifications et Artifices.* Frankfurt-am-Main: 1602.
Demonstrates how completely the town was sacrificed as an entity to artillery defense. City plans show possibilities of quadrangular and irregular semi-open plan.

Perry, Clarence: *The Neighborhood Unit.* In *Regional Survey of New York.* Vol. 7. *Neighborhood and Community Planning.* New York: 1929.

Person, Harlow Stafford: *On the Technique of Planning.* In *Bulletin of the Taylor Society.* November 1934.

Peterson, Arthur Everett, and Edwards, George W.: *New York as an Eighteenth Century Municipality.* 2 vols. New York: 1917.
Medieval survivals in the New World.

Petrie, William Flinders: *The Revolutions of Civilization.* London: 1911.

Pevsner, Nikolaus: *Pioneers of the Modern Movement; from William Morris to Walter Gropius.* London: 1936.

Well-illustrated and replete with useful historic data; not always satisfactory in interpretation. See Behrendt.

Pica, Agnoldomenico: *Nuova Architettura Italiana.* Milano: 1936.
Comprehensive and well-illustrated study of modern Italian architecture, with the text only in Italian. Architecture and engineering under Fascism, even more than under Nazism, is a proof of the unity of *organization* in Western culture, even though the gap has widened during the last fifteen years as to the means and ends of *association*. See Sartoris.

Pidoux, Joseph: See Rey, A. A.

Pinder, Wilhelm: *Deutscher Barock; die grossen Baumeister des 18. Jahrhunderts.* Leipzig: 1929.

Pirenne, Henri: *Medieval Cities; Their Origins and the Revival of Trade.* Princeton: 1925.
Historical and political account of the medieval city with special emphasis upon Flanders. Holds view of urban origins exactly opposite to Sombart's.

Plato: *The Republic*

Timaeus

Critias

The Laws
The *Republic* still has more effective sociology, albeit in mythic form, than most textbooks of sociology, allegedly scientific.

Platz, Gustav Adolf: *Die Baukunst der neuesten Zeit.* Berlin: 1927. Second Edition. Berlin: 1930.
Undue emphasis on European, especially German, architecture. See Sartoris.

Poëte, Marcel: *Comment s'est formé Paris.* Paris: 1925.
A tiny book full of a lifetime's knowledge. See below.

Introduction à l'Urbanisme; l'Evolution des Villes; la Leçon de l'Antiquité. Paris: 1929.
Admirable introduction. First third analyses the social, economic and geographic components of the city plan; the remaining part is a specific study of the city in ancient civilization, Egyptian, Mesopotamian, and Greco-Roman. The approach is organic and historical.

Une Vie de Cité; Paris de sa Naissance à nos Jours. 3 vols. text; 1 vol. illustrations. Paris: 1924-1931.
A monumental work of the first order.

Pound, Arthur: *The Golden Earth; the Story of Manhattan's Landed Wealth.* New York: 1935.

Powell, Lyman P. (editor): *Historic Towns of New England.* New York: 1898.

Historic Towns of the Middle States. New York: 1899.

Historic Towns of Southern States. New York: 1900.

Pratt, Edward Ewing: *Industrial Causes of Congestion of Population in New York City.* New York: 1911.
Good in its day; and still better than some later studies.

President's Conference on Home Building and Home Ownership. Washington, D. C.: 1931.
Important: paved the way for President Roosevelt's public housing policy.

President's Research Committee on Social Trends: *Recent Social Trends in the United States*. 2 vols. New York: 1933.
Useful data; some of it available in expanded monographs: see McKenzie.

Preuss, Hugo: *Die Entwicklung des Deutschen Städtewesens*. Vol. I. Leipzig: 1906.
Excellent.

Price, Uvedale: *Essays on the Picturesque as Compared with the Sublime and the Beautiful*. 3 vols. London: 1810.

Pückler-Muskau, Hermann L. H. von: *Tour in England, Ireland, and France; 1826-1829*. Philadelphia: 1833.

Purdom, Charles B.: *Building of Satellite Towns*. London: 1926.
Town Theory and Practice. London: 1921.
The Garden City. London: 1923.
Well-digested books by one who had participated in, as well as observed, the building of the English garden cities.

Quennell, Marjorie and C. H. G.: *History of Everyday Things in England*. 3 vols. London: 1930-34.
For children; but until a more adult work comes forth on the same topic it must serve all ages.

Raleigh, Walter: *Observations Concerning the Causes of the Magnificencie and Opulency of Cities*. In *Works*. Vol. II. London: 1751.
Not devoid of interest.

Rasmussen, Steen Eiler: *London: The Unique City*. New York: 1937.
Beautiful interpretation of the life and architectural forms of the most lovable of great capitals by an enthusiastic Dane who knows his subject well. Well-illustrated.

Ratzel, Friedrich: *Studies in Political Areas*. In *American Journal of Sociology*. November 1897.

Regional Survey of New York and Its Environs. 8 vols. New York: 1927-31.
Vol. 1. Haig, R. M., and McCrea, R. C.: *Major Economic Factors in Metropolitan Growth and Arrangement*. 1927.
Uses argument in favor of economic advantages of city as automatic justification of congested urban areas of metropolitan pattern.
Vol. 2. Adams, Thomas, and others: *Population, Land Values, and Government*.
Vol. 3. Lewis, H. M., and Goodrich, E. P.: *Highway Traffic*.
Vol. 4. Lewis, H. M.: *Transit and Transportation*.
Vol. 5. Hammer, L. F., and others: *Public Recreation*.
Sets extremely low standards.
Vol. 6. Bassett, E. M., and Williams, F. B.: *Buildings, Their Uses, and the Spaces About Them*.

Regional Survey of New York and Its Environs. Vol. 7. *Neighborhood and Community Planning.*

Vol. 8. Lewis, H. M.: *Physical Conditions and Public Services.*

Regional Plan. Vol. 1. *The Graphic Regional Plan;* Vol. 2. *The Building of the City.*

In all, a mass of exhaustive statistical data (much highly useful), well-meaning half-truths, and contradictory plans and prescriptions, dignified by almost ten years of labor, a million dollars in expenses, and ten monumental volumes. The premises upon which the survey was conducted were sociologically unsound: continued population growth up to 1965 was treated as axiomatic and the economic stability of the metropolitan regime was taken for granted. The real task of transforming the inner area of the metropolis was shirked and the duty to prepare to receive larger increments of population in the immediate outlying areas was not even subjected to skeptical inquiry. For exhaustive criticism see articles by Mumford in the New Republic, June 15 and 22, 1932.

Renard, Georges François: *Guilds in the Middle Ages.* Trans. London: 1919.

Renard, G. F., and Weulersse, G.: *Life and Work in Modern Europe; Fifteenth to Eighteenth Centuries.* London: 1926.
Valuable.

Rey, A. Augustin, Pidoux, J., and Barde, C.: *La Science des Plans des Villes.* Lausanne: 1928.
Pioneers on the subject of orientation for sunlight. Most of the dogmatic prescriptions on the subject current in advanced architectural circles in the nineteen-thirties ignored the facts of meteorology, on the naïve assumption that East-West exposures gave maximum sunlight. A subject upon which close regional study is highly necessary, since a solution must include not merely sunlight, but winds, seasonal exposure, physiological need, and working habits.

Richardson, Benjamin Ward: *Hygeia; A City of Health.* London: 1876.
Though in his program of hospitalization Richardson is still in advance of contemporary communities, some of his most advanced prescriptions are now below standard.

Riehl, Wilhelm Heinrich: *Die Naturgeschichte des Volkes als Grundlage einer deutschen Social-Politik.* Vol. I. *Land und Leute;* Vol. II. *Die bürgerliche Gesellschaft;* Vol. III. *Die Familie;* Vol. IV. *Wanderbuch* (als zweiter Theil zu *Land und Leute*). Sixth Ed. Stuttgart: 1866-82.
Important work by a great cultural historian of the same rank as De Sanctis in Italy: also neglected. See especially chapters on the city in Vols. I and IV, and on the house in Vol. III.

Culturstudien aus drei Jahrhunderten. Stuttgart: 1859.
See essays on Das landschaftliche Auge and the Augsburger Studien.

Robinson, Charles Mulford: *The Call of the City.* New York: 1908.

City Planning. New York: 1916.

The Improvement of Towns and Cities. New York: 1901.
Essays by a mid-American who did much to popularize the notion of civic beauty.

Rogers, J.-E. Thorold: *Six Centuries of Work and Wages.* New York: 1884. London: 1884.

Romains, Jules: *Men of Good-Will.* Paris: 1932-current. Trans. New York: 1933-current.

A masterpiece in urban description and interpretation: a series that caps a great tradition that stems back to Stendhal, Balzac, Hugo, and Zola.

Rostovtsev, Mikhail, and others: *Urban Land Economics.* Ann Arbor: 1922.
Note especially Rostovtsev on cities in the Ancient World and Dr. Mary Shine's *Urban Land in the Middle Ages.*

Rouse, Edward Clive: *The Old Towns of England.* New York: 1936.
A good book in the invaluable English Countryside Series.

Ruhr District Settlement Association: *Die Tätigkeit des Siedlungsverbandes Ruhrkohlenbezirk.* Essen: 1926.
Brief exposition of the scope of this great regional planning scheme as developed under Dr. Schmidt.

Ruskin, John: *Unto This Last.* London: 1862.
Munera Pulveris. London: 1872.
Ruskin was the first economist to express the realities of energy income and living standards in relation to production. His grasp of the consummatory and creative functions, neglected by the money economists, makes him—despite frequent solecisms—the fundamental economist of the biotechnic order.

The Stones of Venice. 2 vols. London: 1851.
Social interpretation of architecture and architectural interpretation of societies both have their essential beginnings here.

Russell, George William (A.E.) : *Cooperation and Nationality.* Dublin: 1912.
The National Being. Dublin: 1916.
Though not boasting the obvious clichés of regionalism this is a real contribution: an expression of that Ireland, now vanished, which was both regional and interregional in its culture, before relapsing into its present sterile parochialism.

Salaman, Malcolm C.: *London; Past and Present.* London: 1916.
A Studio book, well-illustrated.

Sand, René: *Health and Human Progress; An Essay in Sociological Medicine.* Trans. London: 1935.
Good bibliography. See also Campbell and Hill.

Sander, Paul: *Geschichte des Deutschen Städtewesens.* In *Bonner Wissenschaftliche Untersuchungen.* Heft 6. Bonn: 1922.

Sartoris, Alfredo: *Gli Elementi dell' Archittetura Funzionale.* Milano: 1935.

Schedel, Hartmann: *Das Buch der Chroniker.* Nürnberg: 1493.
Richly illustrated by woodcuts of cities done by Michael Wohlgemuth. The technique is rough and the factual accuracy dubious: one stock cut, for example, is used over and over again to represent various cities.

Scheffler, Karl: *Die Architektur der Grosstadt.* Berlin: 1913.
Good study.

Der Neue Mensch. Berlin: 1935.
Not without insight; but a little disappointing.

Holland. Leipzig: 1930.
Fine picture of the land, its cities, its art.

Schevill, Ferdinand: *History of Florence; from the Founding of the City through the Renaissance.* New York: 1936.

Excellent within its own particular frame; but somewhat lacking on the specifically civic side.

Schevill, Ferdinand: *Siena: The Story of a Medieval Commune.* New York: 1909.

Schlesinger, Arthur Meier: *The Rise of the City; 1878-1898.* New York: 1933.
American history with a view to various urban manifestations; but, as usual with historians of the passing generation, without grasp of the city as organic whole.

Schmidt, Friedrich Christian: *Der Bürgerliche Baumeister.* 4 vols. in 6. Gotha: 1790-99.
Historic interest alone.

Schmoller, G.: *Deutsches Städtewesen in Älterer Zeit.* In *Bonner Staatswissenschaftliche Untersuchungen.* Heft 5. Bonn: 1922.

Schott, Sigmund: *Die Grosstädtischen Agglomerationen des Deutschen Reichs; 1787-1910.* Breslau: 1912.
Statistical analyses.

Schultz, Alwin: *Das häusliche Leben der Europäischen Kulturvölker vom Mittelalter bis zur zweiten Hälfte des XVIII. Jahrhunderts.* München: 1903.

Schultze-Naumburg, Paul: *Kulturarbeiten.* München: 1916.
Vol. 1. *Hausbau.* Vol. 2. *Gärten.* Vol. 3. *Dörfer und Kolonien.* Vol. 4. *Städtebau.* Vol. 5. *Kleinbürgerhäuser.*
Die Gestaltung der Landschaft durch den Menschen: Vol. 7. Part I. *Wege und Strassen,* Part 2. *Die Pflanzenwelt und ihre Bedeutung im Landschaftsbilde;* Vol. 8. Part 3. *Der Geologische Aufbau der Landschaft und die Nutzbarmachung der Mineralien,* Part 4. *Die Wasserwirtschaft;* Vol. IX. Part 5. *Industrie,* Part 6. *Siedelungen.*
A work of fundamental importance upon the artful and orderly transformation of the environment by man. While the standpoint of the author is traditional and somewhat backward looking, this series of books is one of the great monuments of its generation: not less representative because the author was also an advocate of dress reform.
Die Kultur des weiblichen Körpers als Grundlage der Frauenkleidung. Jena: 1901.
One of the first books to use for other than "artistic" purposes photographs of naked girls: the comparison between the natural bodies and the monstrosities produced by fashionable deformation was a powerful element in dress reform. The relation between architectural style and costume is a theme that still awaits the right critic.

Schulze, Konrad Werner: *Stadt und Land als organischer Lebensraum.* Stuttgart: 1932.

Schumacher, Fritz: *Strömungen in deutscher Baukunst seit 1800.* Leipzig: 1935.
Valuable study of the various movements in modern architecture with particular reference to Germany, by an architect who left his mark on every phase of modern Hamburg before 1933.

Schumacher, Fritz: *Darstellungen des soziologischen Zustandes im Hamburgisch-Preussischen Landesplanungsgebiet.* Hamburg: 1931.

Wesen und Organisation der Landesplanung im Hamburgisch-Preussischen Planungsgebiet. Hamburg: 1932.
Two of a series of reports on land planning in the Hamburg area which shows how much can be done with a small personnel and modest means, provided the director has a consistent point of view and a firm grasp of social relationships. (Compare with Regional Survey of New York.)

Das Werden einer Wohnstadt; Bilder vom neuen Hamburg. Hamburg: 1932.

Schumacher, Fritz, and Arntz, W.: *Köln.* München: 1923.

Schwan, Bruno (editor): *Town Planning and Housing Throughout the World.* Berlin: 1935.
Essays by "leading authorities." Translations usually execrable. Not to be compared to Hegemann, but the best available reference work now.

Scott, Jesup W.: *Future Great City of the World in the Central Plain of North America.* Toledo: 1868.

Scott, Mackay Hugh Baillie-: *Houses and Gardens.* London: 1916.
Well-illustrated book which shows how high a level the best English architects had reached in their free interpretation of modern needs before the curiously hollow recession into Georgian good taste.

Sears, Paul Bigelow: *Deserts on the March.* Norman, Okla.: 1935.
Admirable presentation of the durable ecological relationships that govern man's exploitation of the earth.

Sennett, Alfred Richard: *Garden Cities in Theory and Practice.* 2 vols. London: 1905.
A history and criticism of the garden city, with some interesting early suggestions on the advantages of rationalization.

Shaler, Nathaniel Southgate: *Man and the Earth.* New York: 1905.
(See also Marsh, George Perkins.)

Sharp, Thomas: *Town and Countryside; Some Aspects of Urban and Rural Development.* New York: 1933.
Vigorous argumentative book on the principles of urban and rural planning, somewhat marred by a perverse animus against the garden city, as if open building and "Streubau" were one.

Sidgwick, Henry: *Development of European Polity.* London: 1903.
Early study of the rôle of the city in politics.

Simmel, Georg: *The Great City and Cultural Life.* In *Die Grosstadt.* Dresden: 1903.

Simon, John: *Reports Relating to the Sanitary Condition of the City of London.* London: 1854.
Important documentation.

English Sanitary Institutions; Reviewed in Their Course of Development and in Some of Their Political and Social Relations. London: 1890.
Exhaustive and excellent.

Sinclair, Robert: *Metropolitan Man; the Future of the English.* London: 1937.
Interpretive study, with ample factual and documentary substantiation of the glory and horror of big city life for John Citizen.

Sismondi, Jean Charles Leonard: *History of the Italian Republics in the Middle Ages.* Trans. and condensed. New York: 1895.
First published in 16 vols. in 1815.

Sitte, Camillo: *Der Städtebau nach seinen künstlerischen Grundsätzen.* Wien: 1899. Fifth Ed. 1922.
Keen analysis of city forms from the esthetic and social point of view: the first real understanding of the method of layout in the medieval city, particularly in the squares with their frequently asymmetrical arrangement. While Sitte's appreciation of the functional significance of irregular or adaptive planning led to caricatures by his followers, his own work was usually intelligent and sound.

Smith, Adam: *An Inquiry into the Nature and Causes of the Wealth of Nations.* 2 vols. London: 1776.
Chapters I and III in Book III show that Smith had a fundamental understanding of the political economy in its fullest sense, including the economy of cities and public works. The dropping out of this view from the later economists was symptomatic.

Stadt, Die Neue.
Continuation of *Das Neue Frankfurt* (which see).

Smith, Joseph Russell: *North America.* New York: 1925.
Fine example of contemporary regional geography.

Sölch, Johann: *Die Frage der zukünftigen Verteilung der Menschheit.* In *Geografiska Annaler:* 1929.

Sombart, Werner: *Krieg und Kapitalismus.* München: 1913.
Luxus und Kapitalismus. München: 1913.
Both these books throw much light on the baroque city.

Der Moderne Kapitalismus. Four vols. München: 1902-1927.
See vol. 2, Second Part, on Ursprung und Wesen der modernen Stadt, for his theory of the city: also Chapter 25, vol. 3 (first half) for relation of population movements and city building. Sombart, like Bücher, Schmoller, and Weber, has much to say about the city; and his notion of the city as primarily a group of consumers, though perhaps historically misleading in its overemphasis of the rôle of the clerical and landed classes, as if all cities were Residenzstädte, is logically correct—as opposed to the usual emphasis upon the market and the function of exchange as primary.

Der Begriff der Stadt und das Wesen der Städtebildung. In *Brauns Archiv.* Vol. 4. 1907.

Die Entstehung der Städte im Mittelalter. In *Rivista di Scienza.* Vol. 3. 1907.

Städtische Siedelung. In *Handwörterbuch der Soziologie.* Stuttgart: 1931.

Speckels, Daniel: *Architectura von Vestungen.* 1608.

Speed, John: *England, Wales, Scotland and Ireland.* London (?): 1627.

Spengler, Oswald: *Der Untergang des Abendlandes.* München: 1920. Trans 2 vols. New York: 1928.

Important because of emphasis upon the rôle of the city as a formative factor in culture. Has also occasional flashes of profound architectural insight, though usually not without some intermixture of those strange residual barbarisms which disgraced part of German thought even before they had been crystallized by the National Socialists into a system.

Starkey, Thomas: *England in the Reign of Henry VIII; a Dialogue between Cardinal Pole and Thomas Lupset.* Written between 1536-38. London: 1878.

Stein, Clarence S.: *An Outline for Community Housing Procedure.* In *The Architectural Forum.* 1932.

    Housing in the United States. Under *Social Architecture* in *Encyclopedia Britannica.* 14 Ed.

Stein, Clarence S., and Bauer, C. K.: *Store Building and Neighborhood Shopping Centers.* In *Architectural Record.* February 1934.

Stephenson, Carl: *Borough and Town; a Study of Urban Origins in England.* Cambridge, Mass.: 1933.
Important. Valuable summary of existing theories of medieval urban origins and well-directed employment of topographic evidence.

Stokes, I. N. P.: *Iconography of Manhattan.* 6 vols. New York: 1915-28.

Storer, John: *Our Cities; Their Present Position and Requirements.* London: 1870.

Stow, John: *A Survay of London; Conteyning the Originall, Antiquity, Increase, Modern Estate, and Description of that City, etc.* First Edition. London: 1598. 2 Edition: 1603. (Reprinted in Everyman Series.) 6 Ed. revised and edited by John Strype. 2 vols. London: 1754-5.
All in all, one of the great classics in urban historiography.

Strieder, Jakob: *Studien zur Geschichte kapitalistischer Organisationsformen; Monopole, Kartelle und Aktiengesellschaften im Mittelalter und zu Beginn der Neuzeit.* München: 1914. 2 Ed. enlarged: 1925.
See especially the chapter on church, state, and early capitalism.

Stuebben, Josef: *Der Städtebau.* Berlin: 1890.

Sullivan, Louis Henry: *Kindergarten Chats.* Washington: 1934.
Reflections on contemporary architecture and civilization by the great leader of the Chicago school.

Survey Graphic: *Regional Planning Number.* May 1925.
First general exposition in the United States of the aims of modern regionalism and regional planning. Contributions by members of the Regional Planning Association of America (not to be confused with that of New York), including Stein, Ackerman, Bing, MacKaye, Wright, and Chase.

Sydenstricker, Edgar: *Health and Environment.* New York: 1933.
Good.

Taine, Hippolyte Adolphe: *The Philosophy of Art in the Netherlands.* Paris: 1869. Trans. New York: 1873.

    The Ancient Regime. In *The Origins of Contemporary France.* New York: 1896.

Tait, James: *Mediaeval Manchester and the Beginnings of Lancashire*. Manchester: 1904.

Tappan, Henry P.: *The Growth of Cities*. New York: 1855.

Taut, Bruno: *Die Neue Wohnung*. Leipzig: 1924. Fourth Ed. enlarged: 1926.

Taylor, E. A.: *Paris; Past and Present*. London: 1915.
Studio book. Well-illustrated.

Taylor, Graham Romeyn: *Satellite Cities: a Study of Industrial Suburbs*. New York: 1915.
An early study of the internal decentralization of the metropolis through the building of an industrial rim for the heavy industries.

Taylor, Thomas Griffith: *Environment and Nation; Geographical Factors in the Cultural and Political History of Europe*. Chicago: 1936.

Taylor, William Cooke-: *Factories and the Factory System; from Parliamentary Documents and Personal Examination*. London: 1844.

Notes of a Tour in the Manufacturing Districts of Lancashire in a Series of Letters to His Grace the Archbishop of Dublin. London: 1842.

Tennessee Valley Authority; 1933-1937. Washington: 1937.
Well-organized presentation of aims and achievements.

Terpenning, Walter A.: *Village and Open Country Neighborhoods*. New York: 1931.
First-hand study of importance to planners.

Thackrah, Charles Turner: *The Effects of the Principal Arts, Trades, and Professions, and of Civic States and Habits of Living, on Health and Longevity with a Particular Reference to the Trades and Manufactures of Leeds*. London: 1831.

Thomas, James Henry: *Town Government in the Sixteenth Century*. London: 1933.
Recommended. Based on a study of a group of English towns.

Thompson, John Giffen: *Urbanization; Its Effects on Government and Society*. New York: 1927.
Unimportant.

Thompson, Tracy E.: *Location of Manufactures: 1899-1929; a Study of the Tendencies Toward Concentration and Toward Dispersion of Manufactures in the United States*. Bureau of Census. Washington: 1933.

Thompson, Warren S.: *Population Problems*. New York: 1930.
American sociological scholarship at its best. Wide in range, exhaustive, and intelligent. Ablest treatment of population, particularly in relation to city growth, to date.

Thomson, Robert Ellis: *The History of the Dwelling House and Its Future*. Philadelphia: 1914.
An early attempt based on insufficient data: the subject still waits its master.

Thoreau, Henry David: *Walden*. Boston: 1854.

Thoreau, Henry David: *Cape Cod*. Boston: 1865.
Fundamental classics in regionalism.

Thorndike, E. L., and Woodyard, Ella: *Individual Differences in American Cities*. In *American Journal of Sociology*. September 1937.
Attempt to apply general scheme worked out for individuals to differences between cities.

Thorndike, Lynn: *Sanitation, Baths, and Street-cleaning in the Middle Ages and Renaissance*. Reprinted from *Speculum*. Cambridge, Mass.: 1928.
Important judgment of an undisputed authority: should wipe away ignorance and misinterpretation in a field where popular American scholarship, even now, remains deficient.

Tout, Thomas Frederick: *The Collected Papers of Thomas F. Tout; with a Memoir and Bibliography*. Manchester: 1934.
See especially the chapters on Medieval Town Planning and on the origin of the English bureaucracy. While Tout's survey of the new towns and bastides opened new ground his contribution is weakened by the fact that he held a restricted notion as to what constitutes plan.

Town Planning Review, The. Liverpool: 1911- current.
Invaluable.

Toynbee, Arnold Joseph: *A Study of History*. 3 vols. London: 1934.
A monumental attempt to interpret the development of cultures. Very good in its analysis of the general environment; but so far inadequate because of failure to recognize the critical importance of the city and the cloister in the development of both institutional forms and personality.

Traill, Henry D.: *Social England*. 6 vols. London: 1909.

Turner, Frederick Jackson: *The Significance of Sections in the United States*. New York: 1932.
Turner, while retaining the concept of sectionalism, is in fact the first American historian to appreciate the underlying and perduring influences of regionalism in a country whose uniformities and likenesses have too often been taken for granted.

United States Housing Corporation: *War Emergency Construction; Housing War Workers*. Washington: 1920.
Report of one of the too easily forgotten government war-housing efforts during the first World War: a precedent and example for the work undertaken again fifteen years later.

Unwin, Raymond: *Nothing Gained by Overcrowding*. London: 1918.
First published in the early nineteen hundreds, this exposition of the economic futility of overcrowding has become a classic. Sir Raymond was the first person to demonstrate the relation between frontage and street-and-utilities costs: a discovery that led logically to the cul-de-sac building of England, the Zeilenbau developments of Germany, and the superblocks as developed under Henry Wright's analysis in America.

Town Planning in Practice; An Introduction to the Art of Designing Cities and Suburbs. First Edition. London: 1909.
Admirable introduction to the principles of the new town planning as developed up to 1910. Unfortunately the later 1932 edition makes no effort to digest recent revisions in both theory and practice.

Vance, Rupert B.: *Human Geography of the South; a Study in Regional Resources and Human Adequacy*. Chapel Hill, N. C.: 1935.

Important contribution to American regionalist thought. Fairly exhaustive bibliography.

Van der Bent, T. J.: *The Problem of Hygiene in Man's Dwellings*. New York: 1920.

Van Hise, Charles Richard: *Conservation of Natural Resources*. New York: 1910.
Classic.

Van Hise, Charles Richard, and Havemeyer, Loomis: *Conservation of Our Natural Resources*. New York: 1930.

Vaughan, Robert: *The Age of Great Cities*. London: 1842.

Vidal de la Blache, Paul Marie Joseph: *Principles of Human Geography*. Trans. New York: 1926.

Villes d'art Célèbres, Les. 76 vols. Paris: 1906-1936.
Mainly useful for pictorial documentation. See also Hürlimann.

Violet-le-Duc, Eugene Emmanuel: *Maisons*. In *Dictionnaire Raisonné de l'Architecture Française du XIe au XVIe Siècle*. Vol. 6. Paris: 1863.
Habitations of Man in All Ages. Trans. London: 1876.
Now sadly outmoded.

Vogel, F. R.: *Das Amerikanische Haus*. Berlin: 1910.

Voigt, A. H., and Goldner, P.: *Kleinhaus und Mietskaserne*. Berlin: 1905.
Defense of speculation in land and speculative building. Eberstadt called it a "catechism for speculatordom."

Vossler, Karl: *Medieval Culture*. Trans. 2 vols. New York: 1929.
Completest exposition of the medieval world picture: in relation to Dante, but all-inclusive.

Wagner, Otto: *Die Grosstadt: Eine Studie*. Wien: 1911.

Wakefield, Edward Gibbon: *A View of the Art of Colonization*. London: 1849. Reprinted. Oxford: 1914.
Influenced Howard.

Walker, Charles Rumford: *The American City*. New York: 1937.
The "biography" of an American city of the northwest, particularly as revealed in the crisis of the 1934 strike.

Wallace, Alfred Russel: *Social Environment and Moral Progress*. New York: 1913.

Ware, Caroline Farrar: *Greenwich Village, 1920-1930*. Boston: 1935.

Waugh, Frank Albert: *Country Planning*. New York: 1924.

Webb, Sidney and Beatrice: *English Local Government from the Revolution to the Municipal Corporation Act. The Story of the King's Highway*. New York: 1913.
The Manor and the Borough. Part 1 and 2. New York: 1908.
Soviet Communism; a New Civilisation? 2 vols. New York: 1936.

Webber, Adna Ferrin: *The Growth of Cities in the Nineteenth Century; a Study in Statistics.* New York: 1899.
Important: All the more so because it has not tempted emulation.

Weber, Adolf: *Die Grosstadt; und ihre sozialen Probleme.* Leipzig: 1908.

Weber, Alfred: *Theory of the Location of Industries.* Chicago: 1929.
Attempt to work out theoretical distribution in terms of costs of transportation and labor, working regionally, and agglomerative factors within industry.

Weber, Max: *Wirtschaft und Gesellschaft.* 2 vols. 2nd Ed. Tübingen: 1925. (*Grundriss der Sozialökonomie.* Abt. 3.)
Second part of Vol. I has chapter on the city.

Weeden, William B.: *Economic and Social History of New England, 1620-1789.* 2 vols. Boston: 1890.

Wells, Herbert George: *Anticipations.* London: 1902.
Tono Bungay. London: 1909.
New Machiavelli. London: 1911.
A Modern Utopia. London: 1905.

Wheeler, William Morton: *Emergent Evolution and the Development of Societies.* New York: 1928.
Brief but important discussion of the doctrine of emergence, as applied to societies.

Whitaker, Charles Harris. *The Joke About Housing.* Boston: 1920.
From Ramses to Rockefeller. New York: 1934.
A social interpretation of architecture by a distinguished critic whose work as editor of the Journal of the American Institute of Architects put the housing and community planning movement in the United States on new foundations.

Whitaker, Joe Russell, and Parkins, A. E.: *Our Natural Resources and Their Conservation.* New York: 1936.

Whitney, Milton: *Soil and Civilization; A Modern Concept of the Soil and the Historical Development of Agriculture.* New York: 1925.
Dynamic conception of rôle of soil: useful corrective of one-sided quantitative conception in Willcox's *Re-Shaping Agriculture.*

Wickham, Archdale Kenneth: *The Villages of England.* London: 1932.

Wiebeking, Karl Friederich: *Architecture Civile.* 7 vols. München: 1827-31.

Wiese, Leopold von: *Ländliche Siedlungen.* In *Handwörterbuch der Soziologie.* Stuttgart: 1931.

Wijdeveld, H. Th., Editor: *Wendingen; Frank Lloyd Wright.* Santpoort, Holland: 1925.
Completest monograph on Wright's work in English.

Willcox, Oswin William: *Re-Shaping Agriculture.* New York: 1934.
Agrobiologist's interpretation of modern possibilities of selective plant breeding and intensive cultivation. (See Kropotkin.)

Williams, Frank Backus: *The Law of City Planning and Zoning.* New York: 1922.

Williams-Ellis, Clough: *England and the Octopus.* London: 1928.

Winslow, E. A. and C.: *Factory Sanitation and Efficiency*. In *Smithsonian Institution Annual Report:* 1910-11.

Wirth, Louis: *Localism, Regionalism, and Centralization*. In *American Journal of Sociology*. January 1937.

Wolf, Paul: *Städtebau: Das Formproblem der Stadt in Vergangenheit und Zukunft*. Leipzig: 1919.

Wood, Edith Elmer: *The Housing of the Unskilled Wage Earner*. New York: 1919.

Housing Progress in Western Europe. New York: 1923.

Recent Trends in American Housing. New York: 1931.

Slums and Blighted Areas in the United States. In *Housing Division Bulletin No. 1*. Washington: 1935.
Careful studies by an able student and earnest advocate of good housing.

Woods, Robert Archey: *The Neighborhood in Nation-Building*. Boston: 1923.

Woolston, Howard: *The Urban Habit of Mind*. In *American Journal of Sociology*. March 1912.

World Economic Planning; the Necessity for Planned Adjustment of Productive Capacity and Standards of Living. The Hague: 1932.

Wright, Frank Lloyd: *Modern Architecture*. Princeton: 1931.
Brilliant exposition of the principles of organic form by the most original and resourceful living exponent in architecture. Wright, the arch-antagonist of Le Corbusier, expressed the nature of the new biotechnic form from his earliest work onward: using the machine but not dominated by it.

The Disappearing City. New York: 1932.
Brief exposition of a possible type of urban organization in which agriculture would be the fundamental occupation and an acre the minimum area occupied by a family. One of a number of possible lines of development on biotechnic lines: the extreme of decentralized living.

Wright, Frank Lloyd, and Brownell, Baker: *Architecture and Modern Life*. New York: 1932.
Discussion of this great architect's underlying ideas, motifs, purposes.

Wright, Henry: *Re-Housing Urban America*. New York: 1935.
Comprehensive survey by a gifted technician and planner: a fine humane intelligence who left a deep mark on the entire movement for housing and regional planning. See also New York State Housing and Regional Planning Commission's Final Report: mainly the work of Henry Wright.

Yearbook of Design and Industries Association: The Face of the Land. London: 1930.
Illustrations of good and bad culture of the landscape.

Young, George Malcolm, Editor: *Early Victorian England; 1830-1865*. 2 vols. New York: 1934.

Zeiller, Martin: *Topographia Franconiae*. Frankfurt-am-Main: 1648.

Topographia Helvetiae, Rhaetiae et Valesaiae. Frankfurt-am-Main: 1654.
Another great illustrated travel book, invaluable for its woodcuts of medieval survivals. See Merian.

Zimmerman, Erich W.: *World Resources and Industries; a Functional Appraisal of the Availability of Agricultural and Industrial Resources.* New York: 1933.
> Except for lack of material on the important precious metals, this work is thorough and well-conceived. Recommended.

Zimmern, Alfred E.: *The Greek Commonwealth.* Oxford: 1911. 5 Ed., revised. Oxford: 1931.
> A magnificent survey of the Greek polis.

Nationality and Government. London: 1918.

Zimmern, Helen: *The Hansa Towns.* New York: 1889.
> Good.

Zola, Emile: *Paris. Rome. Lourdes.* Trans. New York: 1898.
> Conceived as a trilogy in which the cities themselves are in effect characters. Zola bridges the gap between Balzac and Romains.

Zorbaugh, Harvey Warren: *Goldcoast and Slum.* Chicago: 1929.

Zucker, Paul: *Entwicklung des Stadtbildes; die Stadt als Form.* Wien: 1929.
> Valuable. Good bibliography of older literature and pictorial documentation.

Zueblin, Charles: *American Municipal Progress.* New York: 1916.

ACKNOWLEDGMENTS

Even more than in Technics and Civilization, my chief intellectual debt is to my master, Patrick Geddes.

To take over Geddes's contributions in block, however, would be to betray their organic nature. Not mimicry and automatic acceptance, but a vital assimilation, was what Geddes sought; for to him thinking was a function of living, not a sequestered sort of play. While I have sometimes utilized Geddes's bold summaries and short cuts, I have never felt bound to respect the mere letter of his teaching, nor to give its details the same emphasis that they had in his own schemata. Many disciples slay or betray their masters while they are still alive, perhaps *because* they are still alive. By waiting till Geddes's death before embarking on these systematic works I perhaps avoided that sad necessity.

But on the subject of cities there were few areas where Geddes was not master: he was not merely a profound sociological observer but a practicing townplanner. There were not many departments that Geddes did not at one time or another cover; little that he did not, if only by a passing flicker of epigram, illuminate. On the literature of cities I have had the advantage of perhaps assimilating a larger amount of material than was available to Geddes during the formative period of his thinking, before 1910; and I have had the good fortune, thanks to contemporary advances in architecture, community planning, and politics, to be able to trace out further certain lines of development about which he was necessarily a little vague, for lack of concrete example: for instance, the nature of biotechnic architecture. But my debt nevertheless remains a large and inclusive one.

Along with Geddes, I owe more than a passing tribute to his colleague, Victor Branford. Sharing quarters with Branford in Le Play House in 1920, walking and talking with him, in Westminster and Chelsea, in the New Forest and Glastonbury and Oxford and Hastings, gave me not a little of my civic education. If the illustrations in the present book have any special pith, they owe much to what I learned, against the very grain of my bookish education, directly from Branford's example.

To my colleagues in the Regional Planning Association of America I owe a debt I can scarcely describe in detail: I am consoled by the Greek proverb which Socrates dwells on in The Republic, that friends hold everything in common. But I cannot omit recording my original obligation to Charles Harris Whitaker, the brilliant editor of the Journal of the American Institute of Architects, who brought us all together; nor fail to express my grati‑ tude for the constant inspiration and example and help of Clarence S. Stein and Benton MacKaye. Not least, I must pay special tribute to the late Henry Wright, whose gallant spirit and unflinching sincerity left a deep mark upon all of us, for his adventurous mind touched nothing in the realm of his professional interests that it did not radioactively transform. To another member of this group, Catherine Bauer, the book owes its present form: her challenging criticisms of the original draft, finished in 1931, helped turn the work from a compact restatement of past views into what I trust has proved a more penetrating and wide-ranging study.

In many matters covered in The Culture of Cities the writer's voice (out‑ side his immediate circle) was a lone one between 1920 and 1930. The Regional Planning Number of the Survey Graphic was almost abandoned in 1924 because the editors, though sympathetic, were not convinced that the subject was in the realm of fact and possibility. If the world has caught up with—and perhaps gone beyond—our original formulation of the tasks of regional reconstruction and city-development, the fact itself is a welcome one. And since practical administrators have already moved far toward es‑ tablishing new regional and civic conceptions, I have sought, with a confi‑ dence borrowed from the events themselves, to map even more boldly the next moves.

For their critical suggestions on the manuscript, in one draft or another, I owe my hearty thanks to a group of self-sacrificing friends: Charles Ascher, Walter Curt Behrendt, Lee Simonson, and Clarence Stein. In a study trip in 1932, on a fellowship from the John Simon Guggenheim Memorial Founda‑ tion, I was the recipient of manifold courtesies from municipal officials all over Europe: my obligations here, as well as to friendly scholars and ad‑ ministrators in the various fields I have touched, are too numerous for men‑ tion without the possibility of invidious neglect. Finally, the ability to carry this book to completion, with further travel and pictorial illustration, above all time for research and meditation, was made possible by a grant from the Carnegie Corporation of New York; and I herewith place on record my warm thanks for their ready interest and aid.—L. M.

INDEX

NOTE: The numbers in brackets [ ] indicate illustrations as distinguished from the main body of text.